RITUAL, PLAY AND BELIEF, IN EVOLUTION AND EARLY HUMAN SOCIETIES

The origins of religion and ritual in humans have been the focus of centuries of thought in archaeology, anthropology, theology, evolutionary psychology and more. Play and ritual have many aspects in common, and ritual is a key component of the early cult practices that underlie the religious systems of societies in all parts of the world. This book examines the formative cults and the roots of religious practice from the earliest times until the development of early religion in the Near East, China, Peru, Mesoamerica and beyond. Here, leading prehistorians, biologists and other specialists bring a fresh approach to the early practices that underlie the faiths and religions of the world. They demonstrate the profound role of play in ritual and belief systems and offer powerful new insights into the emergence of early societies.

Colin Renfrew was formerly Disney Professor of Archaeology and Director of the McDonald Institute for Archaeological Research in the University of Cambridge, and Master of Jesus College Cambridge from 1986 to 1997. He is the author of many publications, including *Prehistory: The Making of the Human Mind* (2008). He is a Fellow of the British Academy and Foreign Associate of the National Academy of Sciences of the USA, and was the recipient of the Balzan Prize in 2004.

Iain Morley is Academic Coordinator of the School of Anthropology and Museum Ethnography at the University of Oxford. He has previously been Director of the degree in Cognitive and Evolutionary Anthropology and Lecturer in Palaeoanthropology at the University of Oxford, and was formerly a Fellow of the McDonald Institute for Archaeological Research in Cambridge. He has produced numerous articles and books, including *Becoming Human: Innovation in Prehistoric Material and Spiritual Culture* (2008), *Image and Imagination: A Global Prehistory of Figurative Representation* (2007) and *The Prehistory of Music: Human Evolution, Archaeology and the Origins of Musicality* (2013).

Michael Boyd is Senior Research Associate at the McDonald Institute for Archaeological Research at the University of Cambridge. He is co-director of the current Keros excavation project, assistant director of the Keros Island Survey, and co-editor of the Keros publications series. He has published a book on Mycenaean funerary practices, and has co-edited two volumes on funerary archaeology: one with a worldwide perspective, *Death Rituals, Social Order and the Archaeology of Immortality in the Ancient World: Death Shall Have No Dominion* (2016), and the other concerned with *Staging Death: Funerary Performance, Architecture and Landscape in the Aegean* (2016).

RITUAL, PLAY AND BELIEF, IN EVOLUTION AND EARLY HUMAN SOCIETIES

Edited by

COLIN RENFREW
University of Cambridge

IAIN MORLEY
University of Oxford

MICHAEL BOYD
University of Cambridge

CAMBRIDGE
UNIVERSITY PRESS

University Printing House, Cambridge CB2 8BS, United Kingdom

One Liberty Plaza, 20th Floor, New York, NY 10006, USA

477 Williamstown Road, Port Melbourne, VIC 3207, Australia

314–321, 3rd Floor, Plot 3, Splendor Forum, Jasola District Centre, New Delhi – 110025, India

79 Anson Road, #06-04/06, Singapore 079906

Cambridge University Press is part of the University of Cambridge.

It furthers the University's mission by disseminating knowledge in the pursuit of education, learning, and research at the highest international levels of excellence.

www.cambridge.org
Information on this title: www.cambridge.org/9781107143562
DOI: 10.1017/9781316534663

First published 2018

Printed in the United Kingdom by TJ International

A catalogue record for this publication is available from the British Library.

ISBN 978-1-107-14356-2 Hardback

This volume is dedicated to the memory of

Sir Patrick Bateson FRS (1938–2017)

CONTENTS

Notes on the Contributors   *page* xi
Acknowledgements   xiii

1   INTRODUCING *RITUAL, PLAY AND BELIEF, IN
    EVOLUTION AND EARLY HUMAN SOCIETIES*   1
    Iain Morley

2   INTRODUCTION: PLAY AS THE PRECURSOR OF
    RITUAL IN EARLY HUMAN SOCIETIES   9
    Colin Renfrew

PART I PLAY AND RITUAL: FORMS,
FOUNDATIONS AND EVOLUTION IN
ANIMALS AND HUMANS

3   THE ORIGINS, EVOLUTION AND
    INTERCONNECTIONS OF PLAY AND
    RITUAL: SETTING THE STAGE   23
    Gordon M. Burghardt

4   PLAY AND CREATIVITY   40
    Patrick Bateson

5   PRETEND AND SOCIO-DRAMATIC PLAY IN
    EVOLUTIONARY AND DEVELOPMENTAL PERSPECTIVE   53
    Peter K. Smith

6   PRETEND PLAY, COGNITION AND LIFE-HISTORY
    IN HUMAN EVOLUTION   66
    Iain Morley

7 FROM PLAY AND RITUALISATION TO
   RITUAL AND ITS ARTS: SOURCES OF UPPER
   PLEISTOCENE RITUAL PRACTICES IN LOWER
   MIDDLE PLEISTOCENE RITUALISED AND PLAY
   BEHAVIOURS IN ANCESTRAL HOMININS   87
   Ellen Dissanayake

PART II PLAYING WITH BELIEF AND
PERFORMANCE IN ANCIENT SOCIETIES

   8 MAYA SACRED PLAY: THE VIEW FROM EL
     PERÚ-WAKA'   101
     David Freidel and Michelle Rich

   9 COMMUNAL PERFORMANCE AND RITUAL
     PRACTICE IN THE ANCESTRAL PUEBLOAN ERA OF
     THE AMERICAN SOUTHWEST   116
     Claire Halley

   10 ARCHITECTURE AND IMAGERY IN THE EARLY
      NEOLITHIC OF SOUTH-WEST ASIA: FRAMING
      RITUALS, STABILISING MEANINGS   129
      Trevor Watkins

   11 DANCING WITH MASKS IN THE PROTO-HISTORIC
      NEAR EAST   143
      Yosef Garfinkel

   12 RITUAL, MIMESIS AND THE ANIMAL WORLD IN
      EARLY CHINA   170
      Roel Sterckx

   13 MANIPULATING THE BONES: EATING AND
      AUGURY IN THE MALTESE TEMPLES   187
      Caroline Malone

PART III THE RITUAL IN THE GAME, THE
GAME IN THE RITUAL

   14 PLAY, RITUAL AND TRANSFORMATION: SPORTS,
      ANIMALS AND MANHOOD IN EGYPTIAN AND
      AEGEAN ART   211
      Lyvia Morgan

15 BULL GAMES IN MINOAN CRETE: SOCIAL AND
   SYMBOLIC DIMENSIONS   237
   Nanno Marinatos

16 EPIC GAMES   250
   Nigel Spivey

17 THE BALLGAME, BOXING AND RITUAL BLOOD
   SPORT IN ANCIENT MESOAMERICA   264
   Karl Taube

18 RITUALS, GAMES AND LEARNING   302
   Evangelos Kyriakidis

PART IV FROM PLAY TO FAITH?
DISCUSSION

19 PLAY AND RITUAL: SOME THOUGHTS FROM A
   MATERIAL-CULTURE PERSPECTIVE   311
   Lambros Malafouris

20 BELIEVING IN PLAY AND RITUAL   316
   Robin Osborne

21 THE PENTAGRAM OF PERFORMANCE: RITUAL,
   PLAY AND SOCIAL TRANSFORMATION   321
   Iain Morley

Index   333

NOTES ON THE CONTRIBUTORS

Patrick Bateson was Emeritus Professor of Ethology at the University of Cambridge, UK.

Gordon M. Burghardt is a professor at the University of Tennessee's Department of Psychology and the Department of Ecology and Evolutionary Biology, USA. gburghar@utk.edu

Ellen Dissanayake is Affiliate Professor at the University of Washington's School of Music in Seattle, USA. ed3@u.washington.edu

David Freidel is Professor of Anthropology at Washington University in St. Louis, USA. dfreidel@wustl.edu

Yosef Garfinkel is Professor of Prehistoric Archaeology and of Archaeology of the Biblical Period at the Hebrew University of Jerusalem, Israel. garfinkel@mail.huji.ac.il

Claire Halley is a professional field archaeologist and independent scholar. clairehalley123@gmail.com

Evangelos Kyriakidis is Senior Lecturer in Aegean Prehistory and Leventis Senior Fellow in Heritage Management at the University of Kent, UK. E.Kyriakidis@kent.ac.uk

Lambros Malafouris is Johnson Research and Teaching Fellow in Creativity, Cognition and Material Culture at Keble College, Oxford, UK. lambros.malafouris@keble.ox.ac.uk

Caroline Malone is Professor of Prehistory at the Queen's University in Belfast, Ireland. c.malone@qub.ac.uk

Nanno Marinatos is Professor and Head of the Department of Classics and Mediterranean Studies at the University of Illinois, Chicago, USA. nannom@uic.edu

Lyvia Morgan is an Honorary Research Associate at the Institute of Archaeology, University College London, UK. lyviamorgan@aol.com

Iain Morley is Academic Coordinator of the School of Anthropology and Museum Ethnography at the University of Oxford, UK. iain.morley@anthro.ox.ac.uk

Robin Osborne is Professor of Ancient History, Faculty of Classics at the University of Cambridge, UK. ro225@cam.ac.uk

Colin Renfrew is Emeritus Disney Professor of Archaeology at the McDonald Institute for Archaeological Research, University of Cambridge, UK. acr10@cam.ac.uk

Michelle Rich is a Mellon Postdoctoral Curatorial Fellow in the Department of the Art of the Ancient Americas at the Los Angeles County Museum of Art, USA. michellerich0927@gmail.com

Peter K. Smith is Emeritus Professor of Psychology at the University of London's Unit for School and Family Studies, Goldsmith's College, London, UK. p.smith@gold.ac.uk

Nigel Spivey is Senior Lecturer at the University of Cambridge's Faculty of Classics, UK. njs11@cam.ac.uk

Roel Sterckx is Joseph Needham Professor of Chinese History, Science and Civilization at the University of Cambridge's Faculty of Asian and Middle Eastern Studies, UK. rs10009@cam.ac.uk

Karl Taube is Professor and Chair of the Department of Anthropology at the University of California in Riverside, USA. karl.taube@ucr.edu

Trevor Watkins is Emeritus Professor of Near Eastern Prehistory at University of Edinburgh's School of History, Classics and Archaeology, UK. master.watkins@gmail.com

ACKNOWLEDGEMENTS

The editors are very grateful to the following for their contributions to bringing this volume to fruition: The John Templeton Foundation for generously funding the symposium and the wider 'Becoming Human: The Emergence of Meaning' project; The McDonald Institute for Archaeological Research, Cambridge, for hosting the symposium and the research project; Nicholas Humphrey for valuable insight and commentary during the symposium; Mila Simões de Abreu, Pamela Jane Smith, Xinyi Liu, Patricia Duff, Ester Oras, Jen Moore and Lídia Colominas for indispensable help during the symposium; Beatrice Rehl, Asya Graf and Kaye Tengco Barbaro at Cambridge University Press for accepting the manuscript and patiently progressing its publication; three anonymous reviewers of the manuscript; and, most recently, Ramesh Karunakaran and Ami Naramor (Newgen Knowledge Works) for efficient production and excellent copy editing, respectively.

To Nick

With great appreciation,

Iain

INTRODUCING *RITUAL, PLAY AND BELIEF, IN EVOLUTION AND EARLY HUMAN SOCIETIES*

Iᴀɪɴ Mᴏʀʟᴇʏ

This volume has its genesis in a multidisciplinary symposium held in the McDonald Institute for Archaeological Research in Cambridge entitled *From Play to Faith: Play, Ritual and Belief, in Animals and Early Human Societies*. All of the authors represented here contributed papers to the symposium and participated in extended discussion over four days, in light of which the papers were developed for this book. The symposium formed part of the project *Becoming Human: The Emergence of Meaning*, generously funded by the John Templeton Foundation. This project, which has also produced the volume *Death Rituals, Social Order and the Archaeology of Immortality in the Ancient World: "Death Shall Have No Dominion"* (Renfrew et al. 2015), had as its focus the early evidence for human behaviours that relate to central concepts in ritual and religion, and followed directly from the similarly motivated project *The Roots of Spirituality*, also funded by the John Templeton Foundation at the McDonald Institute.

The theme of the present volume derives directly from long-standing interests on the part of the editors regarding ritual and religion in prehistoric human societies and, in particular, the development of approaches to understanding these behaviours derived from exploration of the cognitive foundations of human behaviour and experience (often termed 'Cognitive Archaeology').

Pursuit of the specific theme of relationships between ritual and play behaviours in animals and humans was catalysed by the attendance of the present writer at a talk given by Gordon Burghardt in

Cambridge following the publication of his own book *The Genesis of Animal Play: Testing the Limits* (Burghardt 2005). Several of the key characteristics of play in animals that he outlined there seemed to bear striking similarities with key aspects of ritual practice and, furthermore, could be closely interwoven with our existing interests in relationships between ritual, performance, embodied action, music, dance and cognitive evolution (e.g. Renfrew and Morley 2007, 2009; Renfrew et al. 2009; Morley, 2009, 2013; Malafouris and Renfrew, 2010; Morley and Renfrew, 2010). In light of this we invited the colleagues represented here to contribute to elucidating the extent to which these apparent parallels and relationships between ritual and play are genuine and what, if anything, they can tell us about the origins of ritual and the importance of play, in our species, *Homo sapiens*, and in human societies in the past.

This book begins from the observation that ritual activities and play behaviours, including structured games, have a number of significant traits in common. Furthermore, play and ritualised behaviours are widespread in the animal kingdom, and a sequence of increasingly complex play behaviours constitutes an important, perhaps essential, part of normal human cognitive development.

These traits suggest deep-rooted biological foundations to play behaviours and, potentially, to some of the fundamental aspects of ritual behaviours as well. This volume constitutes an exploration of these apparent continuities between play and ritual, plus their discontinuities, and their relationships with processes such as performance, transformation, mimesis and social learning in animals and humans. In a second strand of investigation, it specifically explores the relationships between rule-structured games, play and ritual in a cross-section of early human societies. It thus constitutes a contribution not just to the literature on the archaeology and prehistory of ritual, but to that concerned with the biological and cognitive foundations of ritual and religion.

We are not the first to propose such fundamental connections; Huizinga (1944/1955) coined the term *Homo ludens* in his seminal work (of the same name) to describe our species, seeing play, ritual and performance as fundamentally interrelated throughout our human activities. Others have since explored in detail the development and biological foundations of play behaviours in either animals or humans (several of whom contribute to this volume). Further researchers are especially concerned with the relationships between organised games and rituals (again, several feature within this volume). But, we believe, this volume represents the first attempt to explicitly explore the connections between play and ritual in prehistory by bringing together pre-eminent researchers in these fields.

The volume is organised around three major themes in the exploration of relationships between play and ritual.

The first section (Part I) examines play behaviours in animals and humans, their nature, roles, relationships with other abilities, including those that are important in ritual activities, and their possible roles and relationships in an evolutionary context.

The second section (Part II) looks at relationships between ritual behaviours, play and performance in a number of ancient societies from a selection of locations and periods, and the extent to which we can understand these relationships and their importance on the basis of archaeological and, where available, documentary evidence.

The third section (Part III) takes this theme a stage further by exploring the relationships between formal games, play and ritual, and their social and religious roles, in a further selection of ancient societies.

The volume concludes (Part IV) with chapters that take an overarching view of the topic, with discussion and analysis of the issues and conclusions that are – and are not – raised by the preceding chapters.

The first chapter, by Colin Renfrew, outlines and explores the core concepts and issues underlying exploration of relationships between ritual, play, games, performance and religion, and previous major contributions to investigating these critical human behaviours. This chapter elaborates and considerably expands our original manifesto and motivation for undertaking the present study, and contributes significantly to developing an understanding of the major themes upon which the following chapters focus.

PART I PLAY AND RITUAL: FORMS, FOUNDATIONS AND EVOLUTION IN ANIMALS AND HUMANS

Burghardt

Gordon Burghardt has carried out extensive research on play behaviours in a very wide range of animals, their forms, roles and relationships with other abilities. Here he reviews this evidence, along with his own explanatory framework, situating play behaviours in their ethological contexts and exploring parallels and differences between these and ritualised and ritual behaviours. He highlights that there has been a long history of the scholars studying play behaviours in animals and humans proposing that play behaviours may contribute importantly to cognitive development, behavioural innovation and creativity, and that they can form essential scaffolding for the development of social norms such as moral behaviour and concepts of fairness. All of these are important prerequisites for and components of religious thought and ritual behaviours. Meanwhile, amongst evolutionary psychologists considering evolutionary foundations for ritual and religion in human evolution, the roles of play in humans and in other animals that have implications for our longer evolutionary heritage have largely been neglected. By considering core definitional components of play and ritual behaviours in both animals and humans he goes on to examine how these behaviours may indeed share important commonalities of form and function.

Bateson

Patrick Bateson has worked extensively on play behaviours in non-human primates and other mammals. Here he elaborates upon the universality of play behaviours in mammals, and upon the principal criteria for identifying play behaviours, including the extent to which 'playfulness' need be evident. Bateson explores the circumstances in which play activities are carried out and the characteristics that they exhibit in a wide variety of animals, before discussing the question of what play is 'for' – what beneficial roles it may be said to fulfil in the ontogenic development of the animals, and in their evolutionary context. In particular, he then goes on to explore relationships between play behaviours and the development of creativity and problem-solving in different species, including in important examples of human innovations. Finally, he relates this creative aspect to the systematic alteration of states of consciousness by humans, which is so often a feature of ritual activities.

Smith

Peter Smith turns to detailed discussion of play behaviours in human children, to their parallels in the play behaviours of our nearest relatives, the higher primates, and to their differences, in the elaboration of forms of play that seem to be particular to humans. Smith has produced a large body of work studying the importance of play behaviours in human children and, recently, their place in evolution. In particular he focuses on *pretend play*, or *imaginative play*, as a form that is uniquely developed in humans, with potentially wide-ranging significance for cognitive development. This includes social pretend play, and socio-dramatic play, and has the potential to be viewed as part of a package of behaviours that rely on the development of symbolic capabilities, made possible by cognitive abilities such as self-awareness, theory of mind and language that, whilst having precursors in our closest relatives, are uniquely developed in humans. He looks at similarities and differences between play and games with rules, which have often been observed to have

similarities with ritual and, indeed, overlap in use (a theme explored further by contributors to the third section of this book). He then goes on to look in detail at the evolution of pretend play, evolutionary rationales for its function, and relationships between pretend play, imagination and creativity, traits that have important implications for religious and ritual thought, including testimony, pretence and belief in invisible agents.

Morley

The chapter by Morley situates these differences in the development of human play behaviours in the context of hominin evolution. The first part of the chapter explores the natures of different types of play behaviours in apes and humans and their relationship with the emergence of certain critical cognitive skills, including some of those required for ritual behaviours and supernatural beliefs. It examines the relationship between these play behaviours, especially *pretend play*, and life-history stages in ape and human development, in particular *infancy* and *early childhood*. Humans feature a uniquely extended *early childhood* stage of development, and it is during this stage that much of the development of *pretend play* occurs, including many of the elements of cognitive sophistication that have relevance for religion, performance and ritual behaviours. The second part of the chapter examines the palaeoanthropological evidence for the appearance in human ancestors of a modern human-like pattern of these life-history stages, and the implications that this may have for the emergence of *pretend play* and the abilities that underlie it in our immediate and more distant ancestors.

Dissanayake

Concluding this section, Ellen Dissanayake explicitly proposes that what is commonly recognised as ritual in humans has its origins in constituent elements of play and ritualised behaviours, as observed in many non-human mammals. She discusses how these elements also constitute antecedents and components of wider 'arts', which are also key ingredients of rituals, and factors in the efficacy of arts-based rituals in instilling belief and doctrine in participants. Dissanayake explores the ritualisation of behaviours in a variety of ethological and human contexts, especially parent–infant interactions, and the evolutionary development and role of meta-representation in play and ritual. This is followed by discussion of the participatory aspects of ritual in particular, and then the components that ritualised and play behaviours contribute to human ritual practices. In particular, Dissanayake elaborates the hypothesis that the specialised components of play and ritualised behaviours in animals provided the evolutionary foundations for religious ritual behaviours in human ancestors, in which context they serve to, amongst other things, coordinate and unify the group and alleviate anxiety.

PART II PLAYING WITH BELIEF AND PERFORMANCE IN ANCIENT SOCIETIES

Freidel and Rich

In David Freidel and Michelle Rich's exploration of sacred play among the Maya, they engage directly with overlaps that existed, and still exist, between toys, sacred items, performance and ritual. Their discussion of the "enduringly complex" relationship between play and ritual in the Maya world begins with the example of the 'bring Chahk' rain ceremonies in which boys perform roles with clear overlaps with *pretend/imaginative play* as outlined in the preceding section. This clearly also features elements that are far from playful, as did the Maya ballgames they discuss, which are also covered in detail by Taube in Part III. They examine a series of cases in which play behaviours and formal games carry great significance in Maya mythology and ritual practices. They go on to explore in particular the case of the Maya city of El Perú-Waka'. The material culture at the site shows clear overlaps between items used in chance games and musical performance with important ritual roles, linking play and ritual in the elite and common realms of experience. In addition, the monumental architecture and iconography reinforces connections between organised play and games, performance, play with identity, and ritual practice, including the

notions of solidarity and alliances and playing with risk in creating tension and cathartic resolution.

Halley

Moving to the North American Southwest, Claire Halley discusses the role of communal performance, especially dance, in the contemporary and prehistoric Puebloan populations of the region. Whilst these may be full of fun and laughter, the actions, paraphernalia and content are intimately tied to religious beliefs, worldview, values and identity. Play, including clowning and playing with (transformations of) normal conventions and accepted behaviours, is an integral part of religious practice and ritual performance. Meanings and roles are reversed, at once entertaining and playful, and serious in reinforcing conventions that exist under 'normal', non-ritual circumstances. Halley goes on to explore how ritual and symbolic meanings, identity and solidarity are created and reinforced in the context of these communal performances, especially dance, and the extent to which we can gain insight into the long history of these activities in the archaeological evidence of communal architecture and iconography generated by the occupants of this region.

Watkins

The chapter by Trevor Watkins further explores the preceding themes of the relationships between monumental architecture, performance space and activities, and the creation of ritual symbolism and communal identity, this time in the context of the emergence of Neolithic populations in South-West Asia. With particular reference to Göbekli Tepe in south-east Turkey, Watkins examines the archaeological evidence for a succession of large-scale, non-domestic constructions of late Epi-Palaeolithic and Neolithic date in South-West Asia, and their relationships with communal ritual practice and the creation of complex symbolic systems. He does so in the context of discussion of proposed limitations in cognitive evolution, which are argued to shape the necessity for the creation of communal activities for the maintenance of social bonds, and in the context of niche construction theory. Amongst the critical elements of human cultural niches created, it is argued, is the developmental environment within which children learn the complex body of cultural knowledge and beliefs that they then begin to practice. Relating communal performance to recent theories of the cognitive science of religion, Watkins argues that the built environment, in which ritual performance took place, physically manifested cultural information as part of the niche in which the development of ideas and beliefs occurred, including the otherwise 'make-believe' of super-human agents.

Garfinkel

Retaining the focus on the Near East (South-West Asia), and on performance, Yosef Garfinkel focuses in particular on the evidence for performative rituals that play with identity, in particular, the evidence for masked ritual in the Neolithic of the region. Beginning with discussion of the universal nature in humans of religion, and the role of ritual in publicly consolidating the abstract concepts within religion and cosmology, he goes on to look at the universal performance of dance and its effects and roles in ritual and religious contexts. The chapter then examines in particular masks as used in ritual and dance performance. Garfinkel assembles (for the first time) a rich record of archaeological evidence for the use of masks in the proto-historic Near East, including masks themselves and depictions of their use. He goes on to discuss the use of these in ritual and dance, interpreting them in the context of evidence for the use of masks in performance amongst traditional societies. Masks have the potential to transform identity and roles, through hiding identity, homogenising identity, imposing identity or exaggerating characteristics, and through marking a distinction between the performance context and 'normal' contexts, all common features of play behaviours.

Sterckx

Roel Sterckx discusses the relationships between ritual, play and perception of animal behaviour in pre-imperial and early imperial China. The behaviours of animals and humans were not only seen as parallel and contingent, but the behavioural (and anatomical) qualities of animals were described in terms of ritual requirements and human virtues, and "the origins of music, movement and dance were closely linked to animals". Formal, 'ritualised' performative behaviour was seen to apply to both humans and animals, but adherence to ritual etiquette or 'propriety', as opposed to instinctive interactions, was seen to distinguish human from animal nature. The chapter goes on to discuss examples where appropriate human behaviours were seen as derived from, or to have parallels in, the ritualised behaviour of various animals, as well as the case of ritual games derived as performative enactments of animal contests. Melody, rhythm and dance were in particular seen as derived from the discovery and observation of sound and movement in nature, in which they were embedded. But meanwhile a clear distinction was maintained between the moral propriety required to behave ritually (to whatever extent possessing parallels with animal behaviours), versus, in contrast, play and sports, seen as lacking such moral propriety, in spite of their other parallels.

Malone

Returning to the theme of performative play-acting in the ritual context, Caroline Malone examines the evidence for competitive feasting and ritual at the Neolithic prehistoric temples of Tarxien, Malta. Reconstructing the evidence from the original excavation diaries, this chapter explores the relationships between feasting, animal conceptualisations and cosmology, looking at the roles of animals and identity in the symbolic expression of ritual belief. Artefacts from the temple complexes include monstrous hybrid and semi-human forms, imagery modelled in clay, incised on pottery or carved on limestone, some of which cause Malone to question whether their use was serious or humorous, as well as the extent to which transformations of identity between animal and human in ritual contexts may have been significant.

Part III The Ritual in the Game, the Game in the Ritual

Morgan

Lyvia Morgan explores relationships between ritual, games, play, performance and transformation, focusing in particular on the representations of these activities in ancient Egyptian and Aegean imagery. She observes initially that play can be ritualised in its form and function, effecting transformations, such as from youth to maturity or maturity to regeneration. Furthermore, it has been argued that underlying all performance is the ritualisation of play (in its broad sense); performance includes public play, games, dance, music, ceremony and ritual, and boundaries between these categories are permeable, with each potentially encompassing aspects of the others, especially in the ancient world. Her chapter goes on to focus in particular on the imagery of games, sports and hunting in Egyptian and Aegean Bronze Age art, proposing that underlying these are concepts of ritualised transition through social performance. These include scenes of the play and games of children and young men in which the performative play implies bodily preparation for adulthood. Morgan goes on to discuss the performance of the – often agonistic – games and their ritual significances, proposing that many of the representations of play, games and performance reflect transformational ritual content. She also proposes that direct parallels may have been made between the agonistic play (play-fighting) of animals and those represented in the ritualised human games, including the adoption of animal-like properties as a consequence.

Marinatos

Focusing specifically on the Bull Games in Minoan Crete, Nanno Marinatos discusses the ritual and ideological dimensions of the games, and their relationships with particular Minoan deities. The games consist of both bull-leaping and bull-grappling, as two different activities carried out in different ways by different participants, and Marinatos interprets the evidence for each of these in the context of their representations as well as their comparative and cultic context in the wider geographical area. She suggests that the games were publicly performed for large audiences, fulfilling roles testing and reaffirming elite bravery and credibility, including their association with divine patronage and sanction.

Spivey

Drawing upon a range of evidence, from figured ceramics to military equipment, Nigel Spivey discusses the ideology behind the formal sporting contests of archaic and ancient Greece and the motivations for 'play' in the period. He explores the connections – and their limitations – of the organised games of sport and athletics with warfare. For example, certain sports are (relatively) 'safe' versions of behaviours that in their usual context (of conflict) would be dangerous or fatal. This shows a clear parallel with the 'play-fighting' of animals and children, and the wider common element of play and ritual of featuring behaviours that are transposed from their 'normal' context into a new one, where they have different rules and effects. Actual combat could also be performative, theatrical and rule-bound. He suggests that one reasonable conception of a game is "a voluntary attempt to overcome unnecessary obstacles", and that when physical exertion (often to exhaustion) is added, it becomes not just a 'game', but a 'sport'. Further, he posits, situating such activities in sanctuaries adds ingredients that make the activities ritual too. In the case of conceptions of 'game' and 'sport', it is notable that these definitions could be said to encompass various types of animal and child play, including rough-and-tumble and object play. Spivey goes on to look at what the games were *for* – what their perceived origin was, what were the motivations behind carrying them out, and how they related to the concept of worshipful, immortal heroism.

Taube

Continuing the theme of ritual games, but returning to Mesoamerica, Karl Taube analyses the evidence for ritual blood sports, including the Olmec and Maya ballgame and previously underexplored ritual boxing. Both were not only formalised sources of entertainment, but had intensely religious significance too. He discusses how the ballgame and its associated human sacrifice were related directly to ritual practices concerning rainfall, fertility and abundance and, similarly, how the ritual boxing (with stone gloves) was related to fertile rainfall and the god of rain. He discusses the iconographic and architectural evidence for both competitive 'sporting' elements to these activities and their important ritual components, highlighting how "public sport and sacred ritual overlap in profound ways". He discusses the representations and role of ritual boxing, as well as architectural features of the ballcourts designed to allow their ritual flooding, mixing the symbolically highly fertile blood that was the aftermath of the games with the water that was the blood of the Earth. In contemporary (and probably ancient) examples of ritual boxing, masked costumes provide transformations of identity, marking the activity as distinct from prosaic life, and incorporating "otherworldly fun" alongside excitement and fear.

Kyriakidis

Evangelos Kyriakidis begins his theoretical discussion of similarities and differences between games and rituals with the observation that the two can be very difficult to distinguish archaeologically. But whilst they have much in common with each other, he argues that they are distinct in a significant respect – that whilst participants in games are engaged actively throughout, those in rituals have a passive 'intention-in-action'. According to Kyriakidis, both rituals and games can be defined as institutionalised "set activities with a special (not-normal) intention-in-action, and which are specific to a group of people" (and this "special (not-normal) intention-in-action" is also a defining characteristic of play behaviours). Furthermore, he highlights some significant structural similarities between rituals and games: both feature rules that separate them from the 'normal', or quotidian world; the means by which their ends are achieved are often through following

non-contiguous processes within the framework of the specific rules that apply in their non-quotidian circumstances. However, he initially argues that they also differ in that the outcomes of rituals are fixed, while those of games are not, and that participants in rituals are followers of prescribed practice whilst those in games are agentive players. It becomes clear over the course of the discussion that this distinction applies to some rituals and not others. He goes on to discuss how in both rituals and games, their departure from the rules of the quotidian world leads to participants entering a 'new' world, undergoing new experiences and impacting learning as a consequence.

PART IV FROM PLAY TO FAITH? DISCUSSION

Malafouris

Bringing together themes developed in the preceding chapters, Lambros Malafouris discusses these relationships between ritual, play and games from the perspective of material culture. Each has to be enacted – performed – through the use of material things and/or bodies before they can be thought about or conceptualised. He discusses how play might be defined, in light of the preceding discussions, and the questions this raises about its recognition in past contexts, and goes on to posit that a powerful linking theme between play and ritual (and the realisation of belief through ritual) is *performance*. He discusses also how this manifests in the various archaeological evidence mentioned in the latter chapters, before turning to the cognitive and evolutionary implications of the approaches to the evidence taken in the earlier chapters. He concludes with discussion of the role of material culture in scaffolding the development of play and ritual.

Osborne

In reviewing the foregoing chapters, Robin Osborne asks to what extent the initial ideas that ritual and play are related have been confirmed or refuted.

Is ritual indeed involved in play and games? Can performative ('ritual') behaviours amongst animals serve a purpose without being meaningful? Is make-believe play related to the ability to create beliefs? He first of all highlights some distinctions between ritual and play that he sees as emergent from the preceding evidence. These include the extent to which they have fixed, or anticipated outcomes, the extent to which chance factors (including errors) are encouraged or minimised in the proceedings. But at the same time, both play and ritual define themselves in opposition to the 'normal', are purposive and social. In both ritual and play, performance of roles distinct from the 'normal' is important, and these take place in their own world where specific rules and consequences apply. Osborne goes on to propose that in the context of this 'difference from normality' shared by both play and ritual there is nevertheless a significant distinction: play signals that in its contrast to 'normal' events, less is happening than you might think, whereas ritual signals that in its contrast to 'normal' events, more is happening than you might think. They are similar, parallel, but pulling in different directions. He concludes that the experience of play was indeed crucial for preparing humans for not only ritual, but for engagement with the supernatural world of belief, effected through ritual.

Morley

The concluding chapter of this volume seeks to draw out core intellectual themes developed by the contributors, and in light of these proposes a framework for understanding the origins and effective structures of ritual – and other forms of performance – in the cognitive structures which make possible and are developed in the context of play behaviours.

REFERENCES

Burghardt, G. M. 2005. *The Genesis of Animal Play: Testing the Limits*. Cambridge, MA: MIT Press.

Huizinga, J. 1955. *Homo Ludens: A Study of the Play Element in Culture*. Boston, MA: Beacon.

Malafouris, L. & Renfrew, C. 2010. *The Cognitive Life of Things: Recasting the Boundaries of the Mind*. Cambridge: McDonald Institute Monographs.

Morley, I. 2013. *The Prehistory of Music: Human Evolution, Archaeology, and the Origins of Musicality*. Oxford: Oxford University Press.

Morley, I. 2009. Ritual and music – parallels and practice, and the Palaeolithic, in *Becoming Human: Innovation in Prehistoric Material and Spiritual Culture*, eds. C. Renfrew & I. Morley. Cambridge: Cambridge University Press, 159–75.

Morley, I. & Renfrew, C. 2010. *The Archaeology of Measurement: Comprehending Heaven, Earth and Time in Ancient Societies*. Cambridge: Cambridge University Press.

Renfrew, C., Boyd, M. & Morley, I. 2015. *Death Rituals, Social Order and the Archaeology of Immortality in the Ancient World: Death Shall Have No Dominion*. Cambridge: Cambridge University Press.

Renfrew, C., Frith, C. & Malafouris, L. 2009. *The Sapient Mind: Archaeology Meets Neuroscience*. Oxford: Oxford University Press.

Renfrew, C. & Morley, I. 2009. *Becoming Human: Innovation in Prehistoric Material and Spiritual Culture*. Cambridge: Cambridge University Press.

Renfrew, C. & Morley, I. 2007. *Image and Imagination: A Global Prehistory of Figurative Representation*. Cambridge: McDonald Institute Monographs.

2

INTRODUCTION: PLAY AS THE PRECURSOR OF RITUAL IN EARLY HUMAN SOCIETIES

COLIN RENFREW

The role of play as a precursor of ritual in human societies has been widely recognised. And in order to understand the possible relations between play and ritual it is necessary to have some understanding of what is meant by both terms. Each has been used in widely different ways. In defining play Pellegrini (2009), writing from the perspective of human child development, establishes four domains of play: social play (involving interaction with peers), locomotor play (sometimes involving exaggerated movement), object-directed play, and pretend play (or 'as-if' play). In his discussion of animal play, Burghardt (2005, 70–82) distinguishes five criteria, leading to a concise definition: 'Play is repeated, incompletely functional behaviour, differing from more serious versions structurally, contextually or ontogenetically, and initiated where the animal is in a relaxed or low-stress setting'. Ritual has been variously defined by several scholars. Bell (1997, 138–69) has six basic ritual attributes: 1) formalism; 2) traditionalism; 3) disciplined invariance; 4) rule governance; 5) sacral symbolism; and 6) performance. But her emphasis on sacred symbolism seems to contradict the existence of secular rituals, and Rappaport in his discussion (1999) does not use sacral symbolism as a defining feature of ritual. Aspects of play and ritual are compared, and consideration is then given to the problems of detecting or recognising each in the archaeological record. In practice both are most clearly recognised when places of congregation or of assembly can be identified, while

ritual may sometimes be recognised also in the accompanying paraphernalia of symbolic or ceremonial artefacts. The formal similarities between play and ritual are then briefly considered. One feature which emerges is that ritual behaviour among humans frequently involves the gathering of assemblies or congregations, while play among animals is more often dyadic (or solo) in character rather than collective. But perhaps this is partly a definitional feature, since gatherings in herds, flocks and shoals are often excluded from considerations of play on a priori grounds which may themselves merit further consideration.

"Ritual is the primordial form of serious play in human evolutionary history" (Bellah 2011, 92).

INTRODUCTION

The systematic study of early human societies and of their development has, in recent years, sometimes avoided the range of behaviours that might be described as 'non-functional'. So while studies of early subsistence and early technology have developed rapidly, it was an early criticism of processual archaeology (as the 'New Archaeology' of the 1960s and 1970s came to be called) that it often overlooked the ideational sphere, and that indications of early ritual or early religion were not as intensively studied as they had been a generation earlier.

Archaeologists have more recently turned to a systematic analysis of ritual and cult (Renfrew 1985; Barrowclough & Malone 2007; Kyriakidis 2007; Insoll 2011), but the subject of play has not been so systematically explored in the archaeological context. This is surprising, since that subject has been very coherently studied in the field of child development (Piaget 1962; Pellegrini 2009; Smith 2010). And animal play has been the subject of careful study for many years (Bateson 1956; Thorpe 1966; Burghardt 2005). A consideration of the role of play in the course of the early development of human societies may therefore now be timely.

The sometimes rather restrictive functionalism of early processual archaeology has now broadened in its scope and been followed, among other developments, by a cognitive archaeology (Preucel 2006) in which a systematic attempt can be made to study the ways of thought which were developed and followed in earlier times. Precisely because play is non-functional, and not purposefully directed towards a well-defined and practically attainable goal, it has a place beside ritual (and religion) among those human activities to which considerable resources of time and energy may be directed. This is not to say that ritual is non-purposive, but as with play, its rewards are not always immediate or direct. As Gordon Burghardt (2005, 3) indicated using as an epigraph the words of Johan Huizinga (1955, 5) from his pioneering work *Homo ludens*: "Now in myth and ritual the great instinctive forces of civilised life have their origin: law and order, commerce and profit, craft and art, poetry, wisdom and science. All are rooted in the primeval soil of play."

BACKGROUND

There is much to learn about human behaviour from some understanding of animal behaviour, of ethology. This is particularly so when one is thinking in an evolutionary sense about the early development of those aspects of human behaviour which were novel 5 to 10 or 12,000 years ago, although sometimes apparently prefigured in the behaviour of some other animal species. This may certainly be the case when we look at aspects of ritual, which in many

areas of the world can first be clearly documented in the archaeological record over about that time span. That is when the first enduring monuments were erected. Ritual behaviour is indeed documented earlier, in the Upper Palaeolithic period, and perhaps earlier still, but the evidence then for ritual practice, apart from the existence of human burials being performed in conventionalised ways, is sparse.

The material evidence for play is less abundant, since many kinds of play involve actions or activities that are less highly structured than are those of ritual. The formalism of ritual is often lacking: play is often characterised by "behavioural plasticity" (Pellegrini 2009, 47). The informality of play makes its documentation in the archaeological record less easy. Certainly the ballcourts of Mesoamerica, where the ballgame was performed, abundantly document the practice of the game. Yet if we take account of the various kinds of behaviour which may be described as 'performances', the scope for the material documentation of play becomes much wider. The theatres of ancient Greece are one well-known case where performances were organised. The 'plazas' in Mesoamerica and in pre-Columbian coastal Peru were undoubtedly used for processions and other performances, as were the central courts of the 'palaces' of Bronze Age Crete. Such ceremonies may fall into the rather ill-defined classificatory area lying somewhere between play and ritual, as arguably do many civic ceremonies the world over, including inaugurations, coronations and investitures. Most of the monuments in the world have, since the time of their inception, been used as the venue for public performative ceremonies. Some of these ceremonies, especially those instituted in a religious context, may have involved the fulfilment of supposed obligations, including the offering of sacrifice. But other monuments, such as the Coliseum of Rome or the Olympic stadia constructed in the world's great cities over the past century and more, have had the more secular purpose of entertainment.

In order to understand the possible relations between play and ritual in early societies, it is necessary to have some understanding of what is meant by both terms. Each has been used in widely different ways, and each has been defined in many different ways.

DEFINING PLAY

To give a satisfactory definition of play, as most commentators have indicated, is no easy task. When considering primarily play in humans, for Huizinga (1955), play was seen as voluntary, distinct from ordinary life, disinterested (not goal-directed) and dependent on some order or rules. But, as Burghardt (2005, 69) shows, this definition is hard to apply directly to animal play. It would be helpful to have some further definition which would make some of the distinctions clearer. The *Shorter Oxford English Dictionary* (Onions 1978, 1604) offers four principal meanings for the verb 'to play': to exercise oneself in the way of diversion or amusement; to engage in a game; to perform instrumental music; to perform dramatically. These certainly catch some of the distinctions made by Pellegrini (2009), writing from the perspective of human child development. He establishes four domains of play: social play (involving interaction with peers); locomotor play (involving exaggerated movement); object-directed play (e.g. playing with a ball, or with building-bricks or a top); and pretend play (or 'as-if' play). On reflection, however, three of his domains – social, object-directed and pretend – can be subsumed under the Oxford Dictionary's 'to engage in a game', which reveals itself as a catch-all category.

Pellegrini's four domains have relevance for animal play also. Burghardt (2005, 70–82) devotes three chapters of his *The Genesis of Animal Play* to problems of definition, distinguishing five criteria for recognising play:

1. That the performance of the behaviour is not fully functional in the form or context in which it is expressed;

2. That the behaviour is spontaneous, intentional, pleasurable, rewarding, reinforcing or autotelic ('done for its own sake');

3. That it differs from the 'serious' performance of ethotypic behaviour structurally in at least one respect: it is incomplete (generally through inhibited or dropped final elements), exaggerated, awkward or precocious;

4. That the behaviour is performed repeatedly in a similar, but not rigidly stereotyped form during at least a portion of the animal's ontogeny;

5. That the behaviour is initiated when an animal is adequately fed, healthy and free from stress or intense competing systems (e.g. feeding, mating, predator avoidance). In other words, the animal is in a 'relaxed field'.

These allow him to formulate a one-sentence definition: "Play is repeated, incompletely functional behaviour differing from more serious versions structurally, contextually or ontogenetically, and initiated where the animal is in a relaxed or low-stress setting."

It is easy to see that some forms of play among humans involve behaviours not encountered among animals. Among these are both the use of developed linguistic expression (e.g. words) and the use of various functionally specific artefacts (including musical instruments). Yet the careful discussion of animal play clarifies some aspects of human play also. Such consideration makes clear that play should be distinguished from exploration and curiosity. Also that repetitive stereotypical behaviour, as found among captive animals, should fall into a special category and be distinguished from play. Indeed the behaviour of 'head banging', seen in some cases of human imprisonment and obsessive-compulsive disorders, seems a closely comparable behaviour and should also be distinguished from play.

The four main categories of play among human as distinguished for instance by Pellegrini, (locomotor, social, object and pretend) are sometimes reduced to three when animal play is discussed. The fourth, pretend play (sometimes termed 'as-if' play), is often omitted, perhaps because it is felt to involve symbolic representation, since a capacity to use symbols is not generally accepted as a feature of non-human animals. Yet at times the definitional categories become strained. For instance, in social play, whether among animals or humans, when an 'attacker' and a 'defender' are engaged in a play fight, the two roles may be reversed, and the defender now takes the role of attacker. It is here that there seems little distinction to be made between social and pretend play, although the 'as-if' feature used as a defining criterion of pretend play implies a symbolic relationship. As Burghardt (2005, 105) remarks: "In animals with elaborate and prolonged play fighting bouts, there do seem to be rules (e.g. inhibitions) that must be honoured for play to continue." For animals to be able to switch between well-defined roles in this way must imply some capacity to recognise that there do exist alternative roles and when they are appropriate.

Another feature of interest is the practice of self-handicapping in the course of locomotor play, where the stronger animal may use less advantageous strategies to keep his 'opponent' as an active participant in the game. And the phenomenon of 'metacommunication', for instance the 'play bow' in dogs, a signal by which it is mutually understood that what follows is play, seems a notably sophisticated behaviour. Construction play is common enough among children, and may be compared with building behaviour among animals (including nest building) in those cases where there is not a clear functional outcome.

Ritual play is a much-discussed category which is clearly of interest in the present consideration, although different commentators use different implied definitions for both terms. Some rituals are considered play by Sutton-Smith (1997), including sporting events and festivals. And ritualised performances occurring on significant social occasions, such as Trooping the Colour (Renfrew 2007a) or Degree Day (Huizinga 1955; Dissanayake 1992), would seem to fall within the criteria for play discussed previously.

Whether one may appropriately speak of ritual behaviour among animals must partly be a matter of definition. So it is to the topic of ritual and its definition that we should now turn.

DEFINING RITUAL

Ritual in human societies has been variously defined (Verhoeven 2011). That it can be defined at all has been called into question (Humphrey & Laidlaw 1994, 70). Bell (1997, 138–69) in her monograph distinguished six basic attributes of ritual (see also Bell 2007) which can certainly further the discussion:

1. Formalism of expression and gesture,
2. Traditionalism, with conformity with earlier cultural practices,
3. Disciplined invariance, involving repetition and physical control,

4. Rule governance, restricting human action and interaction,
5. Sacral symbolism, with the use of sacred symbols,
6. Performance, involving actions undertaken in public.

But the emphasis here on sacral symbolism need not contradict the existence of secular rituals, for instance many of those performed on civic occasions which need not have a religious undertone. Indeed national symbols – the Union Jack, the American eagle – are often elevated almost to sacred status, and the blessing of the deity invoked upon them. Kyriakidis (2007, 294) escapes this pitfall with his definition: "Ritual is an etic category that refers to set activities with a special (not normal) intention-in-action, and which are specific to a group of people." Another recent definition (Renfrew 2007a, 109) makes a related point: "Ritual employs practices that are time-structured and involve performance, with the repetition of words and actions in formalised ways." Certainly Roy Rappaport in his influential discussion offers a concise definition which does not make explicit reference to sacral symbolism: "I take the term 'ritual' to denote *the performance of more or less invariant sequences of formal acts and utterances not entirely encoded by the performers*" (1999, 24).

He goes on to list several features or elements whose conjunction is unique to ritual, for no single feature of ritual is peculiar to it. These are:

1. Encoding by other than performer
2. Formality (as decorum)
3. Invariance (more or less)
4. Performance (although not all performances are rituals)
5. Formality (vs. physical or functional efficacy).

Rappaport's features equate to a considerable extent with the attributes identified by Bell, with the exclusion of sacral symbolism. But he assimilates rule governance to formalism and invariance, and introduces the notion of formality as contrasted with physical efficacy.

"That ritual is 'in earnest' does not mean that the formal action of ritual is instrumental in any ordinary sense. It is not" (Rappaport 1999, 46). It is notable that this feature of ritual equates precisely with Burghardt's first criterion for play. The observation that ritual should be 'in earnest' is, however, certainly not a conditional criterion for play.

Joyce Marcus (2007, 48) writing from an archaeological perspective and with reference to Mesoamerica, lists eight components of ritual:

1. One or more performers
2. An audience (humans, deities, ancestors)
3. A location (temple, field, patio, cave, top of an altar)
4. A purpose (to communicate with ancestors, to sanctify a new temple)
5. Meaning, subject matter and content
6. Temporal span (hour, day, week)
7. Actions (chanting, singing, playing music, dancing, wearing masks, and costumes, burning incense, bloodletting, sacrificing humans or animals, smoking, making pilgrimages to caves or mountain tops)
8. Food and paraphernalia (stingray spines, obsidian blades, cones and spheres of opal incense, balls of rubber, paper streamers, beverages, meats, tamales) used in the performance of rites.

Whether one may appropriately speak of ritual among non-human animals is no doubt partly a matter of definition. Certainly it is common to speak of rituals of courtship, for instance among birds and fish. The repetitious and formalised behaviours employed in courtship are sometimes referred to as play, but with the more rigorous definitions for play more recently employed, mating behaviours are likely to fall foul of Burghardt's first criterion (since they are functional, at least in their intention), and also his fifth criterion, since they are intensely competitive (see Burghardt 2005, 257). That they have a serious purpose may preclude courtship behaviours from being regarded as play, but that certainly does not exclude them from being regarded as rituals. That they have meaning may be thought obvious: in every case the active partner in the ritual is conveying the message: 'I want to mate with you.' Indeed they would seem to fulfil all of Bell's criteria (except the fifth, which we have already excluded in secular contexts), and most of those set out by Marcus.

In the light of these definitions, it is interesting to consider here to what extent ritual, as understood here, would fall within the category of play, or within the special subcategory of play termed 'games'. Conversely we should ask in what circumstances play, whether among animals or humans, may validly be described as ritual.

ASPECTS OF PLAY AND RITUAL

The performative behaviours involved both in play and in ritual may sometimes leave traces in the archaeological record. But both are notoriously difficult to identify, and for very much the same reason: neither is devoted to immediately functional purposes. This point emerges clearly from most definitions of play, but is notably lacking in some of the definitions of ritual discussed earlier, although clearly noted by Rappaport. Yet a clue is given in the emphasis in those definitions upon the element of *performance*. The actions of ritual are performative, which may imply that they are intended to be viewed by others: they are declarative and are usually expressive. What sometimes goes unsaid in those definitions is that the performative actions of ritual are usually not in themselves directly productive. That is not to deny that the performer or spectator may consider them appropriate or efficacious. But they rarely have an immediate end-product beyond the beliefs of those involved: as Rappaport observes (1999, 46), the formal action of ritual is not instrumental in any ordinary sense.

This gives the important clue about the undertakings which involve ritual or are accompanied by ritual: that they are not in themselves immediately and functionally productive in the material world. Many rituals are periodic, in that their timing is calendrically determined. The timing and occurrence of others is determined by social factors or by the realities of life. Many rituals accompany rites of passage, whether of private individuals or of rulers. Others are of an institutional nature. Indeed some of the most significant rituals among humans are used in the solemnification (and hence validation) of what may be called 'institutional facts' (Searle 1995; Renfrew 2007b, 102). These are facts, like the declaration of peace or war, or the solemnisation of marriage, which are based on the common understanding of the society that the proposition in question ('war is declared'; 'Smith is elected president') is valid. These are the powerful rituals which are in themselves transformative in social terms. They have a direct effect upon human relations, but not upon the material world.

It is here that the similarities between play and ritual are at their strongest. Play is not functionally productive: in the primary sense it is not functional. Ritual likewise does not directly transform the material world. Its transformative power lies in introducing humans to a new social reality: that A and B are married, that Parliament is dissolved. Note that we are speaking mainly of secular rituals. Religious rituals can rarely be expected to produce immediate and demonstrable material results. (The miracle of the loaves and fishes is not often repeated.)

Detecting Play and Ritual in the Archaeological Record

Precisely because many of the actions undertaken in play and in ritual are based on, or are modified versions of, actions undertaken in the course of everyday life, they are often difficult to isolate or identify in the archaeological record. In general there are three sets of circumstance which facilitate their observation. These are: the production of special artefacts used in play or ritual; the designation or construction of special places for the performance of play or ritual; and the depiction of such performances.

The formal similarities noted previously between the actions of play and of ritual also mean that the archaeological traces of the special behaviours involved are often not conclusive as to whether it is play or ritual that is involved. Indeed the ambiguities involved pose interesting questions as to whether play and ritual can always be distinguished. Like the paintings of Paula Rego (McEwen 1992), they may conjure up an ambiguous world where ritual and sometimes sexuality overlap play.

The artefacts of play and of ritual are often very similar. Toys often take human or animal form,

as do the effigies or idols of many rituals. The toy drum of the boy 'soldier' is but a miniature version of the drum used in more serious processions. The 'as-if' role of pretend play often requires that the toy resembles the object from real life that is simulated (the toy airplane for the airliner, the doll for the glamorous adult). The role of artefacts used in ritual has much the same symbolic relationship where X (the symbol) represents Y (the thing signified) in context C (the ritual).

Board games perhaps represent a special case. Early versions of chess and of snakes-and-ladders are known from the ancient world. And counters are found that were used in the course of board games. But counters were also used, with serious purpose, in keeping track of the ownership and management of livestock (Schmandt-Besserat 2010). In such a case the use of the counter is indeed symbolic, but its directly functional purpose disqualifies it from the realm of play.

The places where play occurs, when specific provision is made for it, often resemble places set aside for ritual. There must be space for action, whether in the stadium, the dance floor or the stage. The nature of the action determines the shape of the space. The race track, like the *spina* of the hippodrome, or the *cursus* of a Neolithic monument, is linear in form. The *theatron* (place for viewing) is semi-circular. The amphitheatre or *circus* for gladiatorial combat or for boxing is round. The stadium for football is oval.

The special places designated for play, like many of those prepared for ritual performance, make ample provision for spectators. In a ritual performance all those present are in a sense participants, not mere spectators, but it is often easy to identify the main protagonists in ritual, and distinguish them from more passive participants. When play is institutionalised, therefore, the place set aside for the *agones*, the games, may be obvious enough to the archaeologist. Such is the case for the stadia and theatres of ancient Greece and Rome. And so it is for the ballcourts of Mesoamerica. But while the requirements for spectators may dictate the form of places set aside for public play, the requirements for public ritual may be more demanding. Deities can be very demanding in their special requirements with respect to place.

Shrines and monuments are often located with more respect for the sacred landscape than for the public requirements of easy access.

The depiction of play and of ritual again often offers room for ambiguity. And it is not difficult to see why. Ritual is usually performative, and often playful. It is frequently accompanied with musical instruments, which are often used on joyful occasions. In the Western world, a brass band is used more often to accompany a celebration than a funeral. So when musical performances are depicted, they may be in a context of pleasure and play, or of ritual, or indeed of both. When games are depicted, they may be playful competition, or they may be depicted in a ritual context. The Mesoamerican ballgame was clearly a serious matter taking place in a ritual context and following carefully prescribed rules. Indeed the ballgame had a significant role within the Mesoamerican ritual economy (Wells & Davis-Salazar 2007, 13 and 271), accompanied by gambling on a considerable scale, which however confirms its status as a form of play, whose outcome could not be confidently predicted. The Panhellenic games of ancient Greece were played at the greatest sanctuaries of the gods: at Olympia and Nemea (sacred to Zeus), at Delphi (to Apollo), at Isthmia (to Poseidon). The ambiguity is particularly clear with the funeral games of ancient Greece, described by Homer, when games were held in honour of the deceased. The winner was awarded a valuable prize.

PLAY AND RITUAL AT PLACES OF CONGREGATION AND ASSEMBLY

The theme of assembly and congregation is an important one in the study of animal behaviour, and it may not be unconnected, in some cases, with the phenomenon of play (if not, perhaps, of ritual). Shoals of fish, schools of porpoises, herds of ungulate mammals and flocks of birds congregate together. Insects swarm. The formal properties of flocking and of swarming have been systematically studied. I am uncertain, however, whether it has been argued that the aesthetic qualities so obvious to the human observer in the behaviour of flocking among birds have been regarded as 'pleasurable' among the birds

themselves, in the way sometimes argued for play behaviour among animals. It may be that the leaping of porpoises can be described as locomotor play.

The related theme of collective play has perhaps been less systematically addressed: most examples of play among animals discussed in detail in the ethological literature seem to deal with dyadic relationships. Nor have I yet, in a rather brief survey of the relevant literature, found reference to the role of conspecific spectators in play behaviour.

This is puzzling, since among humans, although much play is dyadic (two-participant) in character, play is also quite frequently organised in collective groups. Many games are played by teams of participants. It is similarly the case that most human rituals have more than two participants, and many have also large numbers of observers. The role of the spectator is an important one. Many rituals are designed to be performed in public.

Certainly, if we turn again to the early archaeological record, it is the presence of spectators which sometimes makes the practice of play and ritual visible. Places of assembly are increasingly well documented in the early archaeological record. But their role in the early development of ritual and of religion has not yet been coherently assessed.

The evidence for a place of congregation or assembly may take several forms. In the first place, there may be provision for large numbers of people. Spectators are amply provided for in the theatres and stadia of ancient Greece, in the plazas of pre-Columbian Peru and Mesoamerica and in the great courts of the Minoan palaces. In some cases, for instance in Crete, wall paintings depict large numbers of people participating in assemblies at these locations.

A second useful indicator is the presence of a major monument. The paradigm case is the Neolithic monument of Stonehenge in south England, around 2500 BC, where the transportation and erection of the stones is thought to have required 30 million work-hours. Its circular form and conspicuous character certainly make it a viable focus as a place of assembly. It has been seen as the apex of a hierarchy of monuments in Neolithic south Britain used for the public practice of ritual (Renfrew 1973). The labour invested in the construction of a monument does not, however, guarantee that it was a place of regular assembly. It has sometimes, for instance, been argued that the ditch and bank which surrounds the circle of stones in a henge monument had the purpose of excluding those persons who were not entitled to enter. Yet the 'attractive' power of Stonehenge is attested by the frequent finds there and nearby of artefacts, notably stone axes, which can be shown to have been brought from afar.

The earliest major monument yet known, or rather ensemble of monuments, is at the site of Göbekli Tepe in eastern Turkey, dating to around 9000 BC (Schmidt 2006). There an impressive circle of large stone slabs or stelae, many of them carved in low relief with depictions of animals, encloses two larger slabs, three metres tall, in a configuration that seems to have been repeated several times on the site. The prodigious feat of quarrying, carving and erecting these stones, many of which still stand today, seems to have been undertaken by hunter-gatherers who did not yet live in permanent village settlements. Although there is little direct evidence for the ritual use of the 'temple' or 'sanctuary' at Göbekli Tepe, it is clear that large groups of hunter-gatherers from the area must have come together to create these monuments. This was, by definition, an assembly or congregation of people. These collective acts may themselves have led to the formation of social units which may not previously have existed, as has been argued for the megalithic burial monuments of Neolithic Britain (Renfrew 2001). It is from the collective engagement in creative work in this way that new social relationships are forged, and given symbolic expression in the monument which is created. The organisation needed to bring together the labour force needed to undertake such constructions will have involved many social occasions, with the provision of food and drink, used no doubt to consolidate the intention and willingness to complete the building work. Such occasions of socially determined eating and drinking are often termed *feasting*. They can involve a range of ritual behaviours (Dietler 2011).

The behaviour at such major places of congregation or assembly is of its nature periodic. The people participating can do so only on an occasional basis.

Even with the development of larger centres of population, for instance with the development of cities, great gatherings at monuments, or in plazas and places of assembly, are time-structured. They cannot be an everyday occurrence. Communal play and ritual are both time-structured, often in rather similar ways.

So it is that attendance on these periodic occasions involves travel by the participants, often over long distances. In a ritual context, the journey may be regarded as a pilgrimage and the travellers as pilgrims. There are some interesting points of similarity, in the field of animal behaviour, with the breeding migrations of a wide range of animal species. Of course that enterprise is too serious to be regarded as play and the notion of ritual can hardly apply. But in terms of congregation and dispersal, at well-determined periodic intervals (annual among most animal species), there are clearly formal similarities. Among humans pilgrimage, like childbirth, may usually have a less than annual frequency. But the prodigious distances travelled for a major pilgrimage such as the Haj seem less astonishing in the context of the distances of up to 10,000 miles covered annually by sea turtles between their foraging and breeding grounds.

FROM PLAY TO RITUAL

Play

There are many intriguing formal similarities among behaviours designated play among animals and humans, as the review of the definitions set out earlier will suggest. In particular many forms of animal play and play among human children (or between mother and child) are effectively isomorphic. Locomotor and social play are both closely comparable between animals and children. Object play, for instance with a ball, is comparable also. Even pretend play, although more developed among children, can be claimed in cases of role reversals among animals, as noted previously.

It is directly from these that many of the games played by human adults clearly develop. Many sports are simply systematised locomotor and social play (e.g. athletics) or object play (e.g. golf).

Much human play is more explicitly structured in a competitive or agonistic format, yet the roots of a 100-metre race are easy to discern in the animal world. Indeed racing uses animals effectively, albeit in more structured form, with greyhound racing or horse racing or indeed chariot racing, so popular in Byzantium. Boxing and wrestling clearly emerge from the 'rough-and-tumble' play of animals and children.

Team games involve a feature which may have no close parallel in the animal world: the within-group cooperation of two or more conspecific groups which are working competitively between groups. This is of course the configuration among humans in warfare, when the first principle of play (non-serious, not-for-real) is supressed. There may be parallels to this configuration (in a non-play context) among social animals which are organised in packs (e.g. wolves) or communities (e.g. chimpanzees), when two such packs or communities are in conflict.

Team games often fall also within the category of object play, since they frequently involve a ball and other equipment (goal, net, bat). All these games are forms of play which are governed by rules, but they can be described effectively without much emphasis upon their rules. In this they differ from games like chess, which are entirely established and constituted by the rules. This is perhaps true of most board games.

In reviewing play, mention should be made of three other categories. The first is musical performance, which can certainly be compared with song in birds, where the elaboration sometimes exceeds the requirements of functionality. The use of musical instruments is an elaboration seen already in the Palaeolithic period (see, for example, Morley 2013).

Dance also has early origins, perhaps in the Palaeolithic, although it is not well documented until the representational art of the Neolithic (Garfinkel 2003).

Theatrical performance is of course usually heavily dependent upon language, but it has its roots also in mime. And mimicry has its roots, or at least its antecedents, in the animal world. The aural and indeed verbal mimicry of the parrot is not always included in discussions of play, yet may well fall within the criteria listed earlier.

Ritual

The similarities between play and ritual in humans are evident, but they have not yet been systematically addressed. That may partly follow from the emphasis upon religious ritual which is a feature of so many discussions, including those of Bell and Marcus. Bell's fifth attribute of ritual is 'sacral symbolism', and in the discussion of Marcus' components, four and five refer to 'purpose' and 'meaning'. But recent discussions of ritual have emphasised the significant role of secular ritual (e.g. Kyriakidis 2007), so that even a Minoan 'peak sanctuary' can be viewed in terms of the institutionalised rituals performed there, which can be viewed in secular rather than religious terms (Kyriakidis 2005).

The important point that rituals have a well-defined meaning and purpose, as indicated by Marcus and implied by Bell, is called into question by the detailed study by Humphrey and Laidlaw (1994). There they consider the Jain rite of worship, in which the principal ceremony is the *puja* ritual. And they reach the conclusion that "anthropologists have been mistaken in thinking that the communication of meanings is distinctive or definitional of ritual" (2).

"As we have tried to show in some detail for the *puja*, elaborate models, coherent meanings, and consistent interpretations of the rite are things which people *may come to have*, through and as a reaction to, performing it. These models do not underlie it. … It is better to see the discursive models and meanings of rituals as one of the possible responses to ritual, rather than as underlying its constitution" (Humphrey & Laidlaw 1994, 265).

This is an important point in itself. And it has significant implications for the evolution of religious thought and practice. For in discussing the very early origins of some forms of ritual, it should no longer be assumed that the belief systems in more recent times which were associated with that ritual form were similarly associated in much earlier days.

The six basic attributes of ritual identified by Bell may perhaps be reduced to five (with the elimination of sacral symbols, seen as pertaining to religious but not to secular ritual). The distinction between play and very serious or even solemn activity is not always easy to maintain: several devotees of football have arranged that, following their demise, their cremated ashes be interred or scattered near the goalposts on the pitch of the football club of their allegiance. These attributes, of formalism, traditionalism, disciplined invariance, rule governance and performance, can certainly be applied to games among adult humans, and in many cases among children also. Many are also features of forms of play that are not usually described as 'games'. Rappaport (1999, 45), in his discussion of games, cites the interesting comments of Lévi-Strauss (1962, 31–2) on 'treating a game as a ritual'.

Interestingly, many of these features are also, at least to some extent, features of animal play, bearing in mind some of the distinctions that have been considered.

An Evolutionary View of Ritual and Congregation

The background of animal behaviour, primarily in the field of play, but also in that of collective behaviour and of migration, makes a promising introduction to a consideration of the origins of ritual and of religion. As many have noted, play among humans, especially children, shares many of its features with play among animals. And as we have seen, many of the features of ritual are prefigured in those of play. This is particularly the case when we include secular rituals in the discussion, and note the view of Humphrey and Laidlaw (1994, 2), contra Bell (1997) and Marcus (2007, 48), that the communication of meanings is not a defining feature of ritual.

To recognise that play among animals and humans has many features which are later seen in human rituals and religions does not however mean that an evolutionary path has been established. That traditionalism is a feature of ritual (Bell's first attribute) does not necessarily imply continuity with earlier human societies, let alone earlier animal species, in some long-term evolutionary pattern of descent. The thread of continuity is not often easy to discern.

It is important first to consider which of the perceived similarities between animal play and human rituals are simply homologous forms which have arisen independently. Humans, like most of the animals we are considering, each have two parents, and are separate beings reared by one or two of these parents, independent beings which move freely through the world. They lead social lives, as indeed they are constrained to do, among other things for the purposes of mating. Their social life can involve games and rituals. These are general features which they share with many other species. A number of structural analogies can arise simply from the general shared features.

Ritual behaviour among humans frequently involves assemblies and congregations, which can necessitate travel over great distances (e.g. pilgrimage). It is tempting here to make a comparison with the congregation of other species in large groups (e.g. herds, flocks, shoals), often involving migration over large distances. But before the analogy should become too tempting, note that play behaviour among animals is not usually invoked in discussions of flocking behaviour or of migrations. This is partly a feature of the definitional constraints imposed by ethologist students of play, but partly also because play behaviours are contrasted with those manifested in the more stressed conditions of mating or feeding. So it must be accepted that some of the similarities arise simply from the analogous conditions which pertain when independent individuals interact together socially in large numbers. Remember that most play among animals is dyadic in nature.

Nonetheless, enough similarities and suggestive indications remain to suggest that the study of the origins of religion and of ritual behaviour in early human societies may be enriched by the careful consideration of play among animals and humans. It is clear from the present discussion that the term *performance* is a key concept. It is a suitably ambiguous term on which to end. For many performances are solo performances. But, whether by accident or intention, they often have large audiences.

References

Barrowclough, D. & Malone, C., 2007. *Cult in Context: Reconsidering Ritual in Archaeology*. Oxford: Oxford University Press.

Bateson, G., 1956. The message 'this is play'. In B. Schiffer (ed.), *Group Processes*. New York: Josiah Macy Jr. Foundation, 145–242.

Bell, C., 1997. *Ritual: Perspectives and Dimensions*. Oxford: Oxford University Press.

Bell, C., 2007. Response: defining the need for a definition. In E. Kyriakidis (ed.), *The Archaeology of Ritual*. Los Angeles: Cotsen Institute of Archaeology, University of California, 276–88.

Bellah, R. N., 2011. *Religion in Human Evolution*. Cambridge, MA: Harvard University Press.

Burghardt, G. M., 2005. *The Genesis of Animal Play*. Cambridge, MA: MIT Press.

Dietler, M., 2011. Feasting and fasting. In T. Insoll (ed.), *The Oxford Handbook of the Archaeology of Ritual ad Religion*. Oxford: Oxford University Press, 179–94.

Dissanayake, E., 1992. *Homo aestheticus. Where Art Comes from and Why*. New York: Free Press.

Garfinkel, Y., 2003. *Dance at the Dawn of Agriculture*. Austin: University of Texas Press.

Huizinga, J., 1955. *Homo ludens. A Study of the Play Element in Culture*. Boston, MA: Bacon.

Humphrey, C. & Laidlaw, J., 1994. *The Archetypal Actions of Ritual*. Oxford: Clarendon Press.

Insoll, T. (ed.), 2011. *The Oxford Handbook of the Archaeology of Ritual and Religion*. Oxford: Oxford University Press.

Kertzer, M., 1988. *Ritual, Politics and Power*. New Haven, CT: Yale University Press.

Kyriakidis, E., 2005. *Ritual in the Bronze Age Aegean: the Minoan Peak Sanctuaries*. London: Duckworth.

Kyriakidis, E., (ed.), 2007. *The Archaeology of Ritual*. Los Angeles: Cotsen Institute of Archaeology, University of California.

Lévi-Strauss, C., 1962. *The Savage Mind*. London: Weidenfeld and Nicolson.

Marcus, J., 2007. Rethinking ritual. In E. Kyriakidis (ed.), *The Archaeology of Ritual*. Los Angeles: Cotsen Institute of Archaeology, University of California. 43–76.

McEwen, J., 1992. *Paula Rego*. Oxford: Phaidon.

Morley, I., 2013. *The Prehistory of Music: Human Evolution, Archaeology, and the Origins of Musicality*. Oxford: Oxford University Press.

Onions, C. T., 1978. *The Shorter Oxford Dictionary*. Oxford: Clarendon Press.

Pellegrini, A. D., 2009. *The Role of Play in Human Development*. Oxford: Oxford University Press.

Piaget, J., 1962. *Play, Dreams and Imitation in Childhood*. New York: W. W. Norton.

Preucel, R. W., 2006. *The Archaeology of Semiotics*. Oxford: Blackwell.

Rappaport, R. A., 1999. *Ritual and Religion in the Making of Humanity*. Cambridge: Cambridge University Press.

Renfrew, C., 1973. Monuments, mobilisation and social organisation in Neolithic Wessex. In C. Renfrew (ed.), *The Explanation of Culture Change, Models in Prehistory*. London: Duckworth, 539–58.

Renfrew, C., 1985. *The Archaeology of Cult: The Sanctuary at Phylakopi*. London: British School at Athens.

Renfrew, C., 2001. Commodification and institution in group-oriented and individualising societies. In G. Runciman (ed.), *The Origin of Human Social Institutions*. London: British Academy, 93–118.

Renfrew, C., 2007a. The archaeology of ritual, of cult, and of religion. In E. Kyriakidis (ed.), *The Archaeology of Ritual*. Los Angeles: Cotsen Institute of Archaeology, University of California, 109–22.

Renfrew, C., 2007b. *Prehistory: The Making of the Human Mind*. London: Weidenfeld & Nicolson.

Schmandt-Besserat, D., 2010. The token system of the ancient Near East: its role in counting, writing, the economy and cognition, in I. Morley & C. Renfrew (eds.), *The Archaeology of Measurement, Comprehending Heaven, Earth and Time in Ancient Societies*. Cambridge: Cambridge University Press, 27–34.

Schmidt, K., 2006. *Sie bauten de ersten Tempel*. Munich: C. H. Beck.

Searle, J., 1995. *The Construction of Social Reality*. Harmondsworth, Penguin.

Smith, P., 2010. *Children and Play*. Oxford: Wiley-Blackwell.

Sutton-Smith, B., 1997. *The Ambiguity of Play*. Cambridge, MA: Harvard University Press.

Thorpe, W. H. 1966. Ritualization in ontogeny: I. Animal play. *Philosophical Transactions of the Royal Society of London, Series B* 251, 311–19.

Verhoeven, M., 2011. The many dimensions of ritual. In T. Insoll (ed.), *The Oxford Handbook of the Archaeology of Ritual and Religion*. Oxford: Oxford University Press, 115–32.

Wells, E. C. & Davis-Salazar, K. (eds.), 2007. *Mesoamerican Ritual Economy*. Boulder: University Press of Colorado.

PART I

PLAY AND RITUAL: FORMS, FOUNDATIONS AND EVOLUTION IN ANIMALS AND HUMANS

3

THE ORIGINS, EVOLUTION AND INTERCONNECTIONS OF PLAY AND RITUAL: SETTING THE STAGE

GORDON M. BURGHARDT

Play and ritual, as usually defined, seem to be disparate phenomena, one focused on freedom and flexibility, the other on formality and rigidity. In actuality, they have many common elements, and these will be explored from a comparative perspective grounded in ethology, evolution and play theory. The description and recognition of play in diverse species and contexts, along with its origins and evolution, are discussed along with the origin of rituals in both everyday life and communal activities in human and non-human animals. The early history of linking ritualization as an important process of symbolic communication in animal courtship, dispute resolution and other ethotypic phenomena, with parallels in human cultural activities, can be traced back to the seminal papers by Oskar Heinroth and Julian Huxley in 1911 and 1914 respectively, which first described ethological ritualization. These early papers also drew many comparisons between avian and human displays and accompanying psychology, but these were lost as behaviourism flourished in comparative psychology and cultural anthropology became suspicious of evolutionary approaches to human cultural practices. In the interim, many compelling comparative data were acquired, some of which will be reviewed, along with preliminary modelling of evolutionary scenarios using comparative data. Both play and ritual are products of individual development and historical processes and a relatively recent Christian ritual with playful traits is given as an example. Today, with the development of dual inheritance theory, gene-culture co-evolution and the growing and rich biological, anthropological and archaeological data capable of being analyzed with modern behavioural, evolutionary and phylogenetic methods and theory, the intellectual landscape is rapidly changing. Thus, intriguing and important opportunities for collaboration, synthesis and extension across many areas of human life, including spirituality and religion, are now compelling.

INTRODUCTION

Play and ritual are universal in human behaviour and certainly both are common in non-human species as well. Play, however, is not expressed only through overt behaviour, but also takes place in our imagination, thinking and planning (Burghardt 2005). Is it reasonable to postulate that we can collect relevant data and develop models for the transition from behavioural play to mental or 'interior' play that then foster the distinctive human imagination and creative processes we find applied to both natural and supernatural phenomena? Do rituals, as does play, encapsulate and expand our mental lives? Can we ground human cultural and intellectual advance, including cultural rituals, not just in reason and rationalism, but in neurobiological phenomena originating in playfulness, evolutionary and ecological processes, recurring normative behavioural demands and accompanying emotions? More specifically, what is the possible role of play in the origins and history of ritual practices? Schechner (2013) has gathered together the ideas of many scholars on play and ritual, but systematic analysis is just beginning and some important theorists claim that ritual "is the form of action opposite to play" (Henricks 55). Thus these questions are only a précis of some topics to be explored here on play and ritual based on an ethological emphasis and ongoing current research, along with a brief introduction to animal play and ritualization.

The overarching question posed here is whether play can be viewed as a driver of both cultural rituals and the ritualization of 'instinctive' behaviours in animals that result in elaborate, complex and superficially useless behaviour that appear to characterize both play and rituals (e.g. courtship, territorial and dominance displays). If so, what are the similarities and differences in the processes involved? Can we observe in various playful or challenging contexts the development of behavioural rituals at the individual and social levels? Certainly, behavioural development is crucial for psychological growth of understanding causal relations (e.g. Theory of Mind) and emerging behavioural rituals.

Play is perhaps the most prominent feature in the development of many young animals, including, in spectacular fashion, non-human primates and especially human children (Pellegrini 2011; Bateson, Chapter 4, this volume; Smith, Chapter 5, this volume; Morley, Chapter 6, this volume; Dissanayake, Chapter 7, this volume). How does play and reaction to challenging physical and social stimuli affect and channel subsequent behavioural repertoires? Do the play and rituals of childhood impact and in some way drive adult and social rituals and games, or vice versa? While I cannot definitively answer these important questions, they are relevant to the topic of this volume.

PLAY AND RITUAL

I have studied play from a biological perspective for many years, resulting in a number of publications, including a book (Burghardt 2005), as well as other writings exploring recent research on play (Graham & Burghardt 2010), applications to human behaviour, including children (Burghardt 2010, 2011), and how play may be involved in major reorganizations of behaviour systems (Burghardt 1988). Play may not only be of great importance in normative social and cognitive development and behavioural innovation, but also critical to an understanding of belief systems, religion and spirituality. Although there has been considerable interest in such integration (cf. Rossano 2010; Bellah 2011), a comprehensive analysis is still lacking. Play is, however, considered by some leading play researchers as essential scaffolding for the development of moral behaviour and fairness/equity in animals as well as people (e.g. Bekoff & Pearce 2009), certainly a topic central to much discussion of religion. While recent books on play usually do not have entries for religion, ritual, spirituality or innovation in the index, there are plenty of entries on games (e.g. Pellegrini 2011). Games are, of course, often ritualistic, as has been often noted (e.g. Huizinga 1955), but the link with the concept of ethological ritualization has not been seriously evaluated as a source of religious practices. In fact, although beyond the scope of this chapter, many influential treatments of ritual practices and ritualization that attempt to accommodate biological findings and an evolutionary approach view ethological findings as actually largely irrelevant (e.g. Boyer & Liénard 2006; Liénard & Boyer 2006).

Additionally, evolutionary psychologists have, by and large, ignored play as an important topic in understanding human nature. Textbooks by leading evolutionary psychologists (e.g. Buss 2011) ignore play entirely, as well as religion (but see de Braak 2013). Indeed, much of the non-human animal literature, except for occasional references to apes, is also left out, as if our prehuman evolutionary history had few useful insights to contribute to understanding our present behaviour, culture and mental abilities (Burghardt 2013b). Current scholars on religion are innovatively addressing religion as a product of our evolutionary history, as documented and summarized in many recent monographs and edited volumes (e.g. Bulbia et al. 2008; Feierman 2009; Pyysiäinen 2009; Wade 2009; Rossano 2010;

McCauley 2011). However, play has been almost totally absent in these recent speculative, theoretical and empirical treatments as well. Rituals, especially religious rituals, on the other hand, have been studied for centuries, but findings from evolutionary comparative ethology and animal behaviour do not yet seem to have been effectively incorporated. The possible links among play, rituals, evolution, beliefs and religion may thus seem improbable, but I will try, albeit briefly, to substantiate the importance of exploring these connections, along with some of the hypotheses and predictions that can be tested. It is thus useful to clarify what is meant here by both play and ritual.

PLAY

Play in animals is diverse and generally divided into the categories of solitary locomotor/rotational play, object/predatory play and social play. The similarities of play in non-human animals with that in people are compelling. Human play categories such as construction play, parallel play, pretence, games and so on also have some rudimentary counterparts in other species (Burghardt 2005, 2011). Pellegrini (2009) and Smith (2009) provide updated and scientific reviews of play in children and, admirably, link the child-play literature with the often independently pursued study of play in non-human species (see also Pellegrini 2011, and Smith, Chapter 5, this volume). Today most students of animal behaviour agree that play originates in species' characteristic instinctive behaviour and basal brain mechanisms, which are also linked to learning, novelty and addictions in both humans and non-humans. Pellis and Pellis (2009) provide a current review of the neurobiology and functions of social play, including the role that cortical structures play in the modification and effective adjustments seen in play as it develops in individuals.

But what is play? This question has been debated for years, and is perhaps even more problematic than a definition of religion. If play is viewed as merely fun, non-serious, flexible, non-stereotyped and only a phenomenon of youth, and rituals as serious, solemn, rigid and formal, then a connection between them, especially an evolutionary one, seems suspect at the start. Defining play was a challenge, but also a necessity, if one wants to look at the phenomenon in a truly comparative framework and not arbitrarily limit the purview of play. Indeed, this issue was taken up in the second-longest chapter of my book on play. What I did was look at the many characteristics and terms used to define play, generally unsuccessfully, and group the major salient ones into five criteria, all of which need to be met before a phenomenon in humans or other animals can be confidently viewed as playful. None of the traits listed at the beginning of this paragraph is necessary. These criteria have subsequently been widely accepted (e.g. Pellegrini 2009; Pellis & Pellis 2009; Smith 2009) and were used as the opening definitional chapter in a handbook on play and development (Burghardt 2011; Pellegrini 2011).

Without going into the five criteria here in detail, a short résumé is this: play is not only highly diverse, but shares several basic universal properties resulting from ancient evolutionary processes we are only beginning to understand. Briefly, these criteria state: Play [1] is incompletely functional in the context in which it appears; [2] is spontaneous, pleasurable, rewarding or voluntary; [3] differs from other, more serious behaviours in form (e.g. exaggerated) or timing (e.g. occurring early in life before the more serious version is needed); [4] is repeated, but not in abnormal stereotypic form (e.g. distressed rocking, pacing); and [5] is initiated in the absence of acute or chronic stress, sometime referred to as a relaxed field. The criteria do not necessitate knowing the subjective or motivational state of the animal, which is often very difficult in many species. The criteria seem to cover accepted examples of all three kinds of play (locomotor/rotational, object/predatory and social) in animals as well as the additional types sometimes viewed as limited to humans (e.g. pretence, construction and verbal). The claim made here is that such a scheme is more useful than any available alternative, since if all five criteria are met, we can identify play in any species or context. Note that many games have rules and follow a set 'discourse' but are still playful. The use of this definitional approach has allowed for play being identified in many species in which it was previously ruled out as a possibility (reptiles, fishes, frogs, insects and even, recently, spiders (Pruitt, Riechert & Burghardt 2012). The evolutionary linkages and similar processes underlying play in humans and non-humans, especially rough-and-tumble play in children, is generally not contested. The same should be true for clearly culturally situated and influenced play and games. Consider criteria 2, 3 and 5. Compulsory 'play' or games may not be play as defined here, though the same actions involved may, in other contexts, be playful. Thus, settings and context are important, something also true for ritual performances. Ritual games leading to potentially deadly outcomes may be informative, merged phenomena related to risky, serious or deep play.

Four additional points need to be made. First, the functions and adaptive value of play are not at all clear to researchers on this topic and there is continuing controversy. In fact, studies of what seem to be common-sense views of play function ("practicing and honing technical skills that will later prove useful") are in fact unsupported by the majority of research studies (citations in Burghardt 2005; Pellis & Pellis 2009; Graham & Burghardt 2010; but see Bateson, Chapter 4, this volume), although play as a way of managing stress is a current proposal being explored (Burghardt 2014a). Studies of wild monkeys show that play facilitates peaceful interaction with strangers (Antonacci, Norscia & Palagi, 2010) and this could certainly apply to rituals as well.

To help show that play behaviour, even in the same species, may have different functions and derive from different sources, I developed a three-process model involving primary, secondary and tertiary play (Figure 3.1). This allows a more robust evolutionary trajectory for play, as well as for some play being a by-product, exaptation or directly adaptive. Second, play can be evaluated using comparative phylogenetic methods and studies show, for example, that sexual and non-sexual play in adult primates has evolved repeatedly in different social, ecological and evolutionary contexts (Pellis & Iwaniuk 2000). Third, the neural bases of play are being uncovered to a considerable extent (Panksepp 1998; Pellis & Pellis 2009; Panksepp & Biven 2012), and their links with brain regions and neurotransmitters underlying basic behavioural systems of feeding, drinking, mating, bonding, parental care, fighting, learning, emotions, addictions and

obsessive-compulsive behaviour documented. In relation to emotions, Panksepp and Biven (2012) propose that neuroscience research validates their view that seven primary emotion systems, one of which is play, are common to all mammals, and rooted in the ancient origins of the mammalian brain and perhaps earlier. These behavioural and emotional systems are all also found in rituals, as discussed later in this chapter. Fourth, social play in both human and non-human animals has some features generally not found in solitary play such as play signals that mark a behaviour as being play or inviting playful interactions, self-handicapping to maintain playful interactions and role reversals where animals take turns being the dominant or 'winner'. These features may be especially important in the kinds of play leading to social rituals as contrasted with solitary repetitive behaviour early writers termed *habits*.

THE ORIGINS AND EVOLUTION OF PLAY

There are a number of views on the evolution of play, mostly based on various theories I cannot discuss here (for recent treatments, see Graham & Burghardt 2010; Bateson 2011) but most are based on hypothesized adaptive functions at the tertiary level presented earlier and do not address origins. My view is that play, although originating out of primary processes such as those listed in Figure 3.1, became elaborated due to the operation of a variety of surpluses beyond what was needed for survival, including those of time, energy and capacity to engage in complex behaviour. This constellation I have termed *surplus resource theory* (SRT), and it seems promising in terms of hypothesis generation and testing. Detailed descriptions are available (Burghardt 1988, 2005). While simple in conception, the factors postulated as influencing play and its evolution are numerous and involve many aspects of behaviour, ecology, physiology and development, outlined in Figure 3.2.

One of the predictions of SRT about play that has been generally confirmed is that play and cultural innovation occur when a population has surplus resources and time to engage in behaviour beyond mere survival. Thus, play richness, frequency and

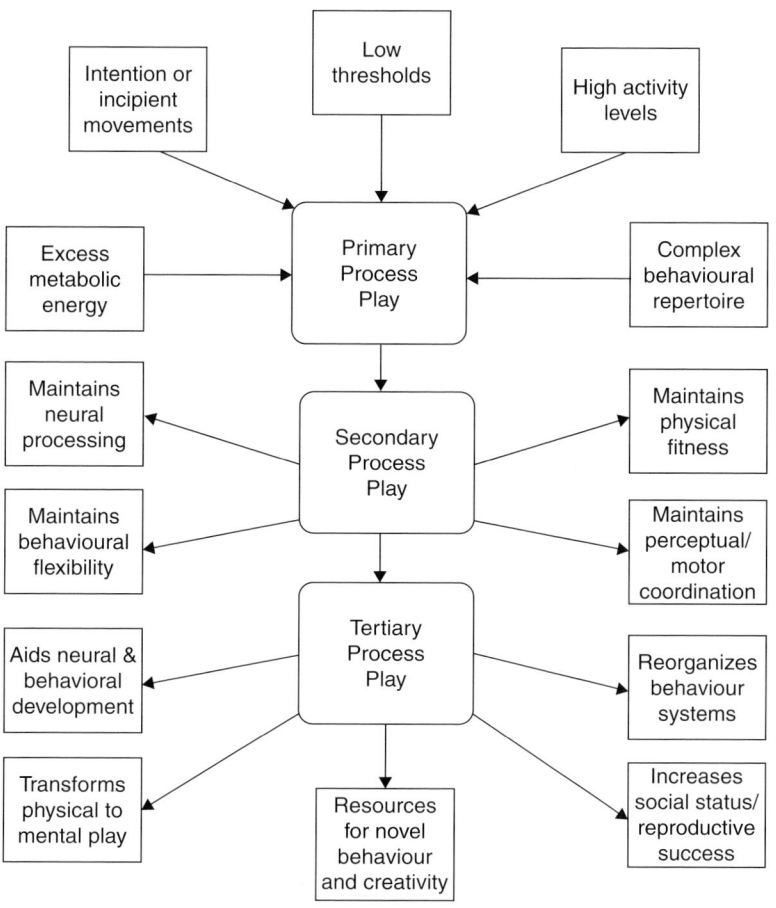

Figure 3.1 The three play processes (from Burghardt 2005).

complexity are predicted to occur more in such settings. For example, animals are predicted to engage more in play in environments with ample nutrition, eating a more energy-rich diet than a low-calorie one, being under little stress from predation and so on. Monkeys eating a frugivorous diet should, everything else being equal, play more than those eating a folivorous diet. After discussing ritual, I will present some data allowing testing of such predictions using comparative data. Eventually, we should be able to do this with human play data from various populations, ethnicities, ecologies and geographical locales.

Ritual

The concept of ritual can be introduced by looking at a common basic definition: this one is from Wikipedia: "A ritual is a set of actions, performed mainly for their symbolic value." Of course it has been defined in more complex ways by many scholars in different fields, as discussed later in this chapter

and elsewhere in this volume. Rituals in religion and many aspect of human life have been well noted. We have rituals in greeting friends and strangers, eating meals, courting and preparing for bed as well as in the 'high' rituals seen in religious, graduation, sports and political gatherings. In these latter settings, clothing, symbols and movements are often more stylized, rigid and formal, but, and this is important, these are relative. Still, the attention-getting nature of rituals is often pointed out as a salient feature. The definition of ritual above also certainly includes many rituals in the behaviour of other animals, including courtship, nest building, communication, territorial and mutual defence, competition for mates and resources, foraging methods and so on (Rogers & Kaplan 2002). Bluffs, vocalizations, colour changes and movements can all have symbolic significance in animal interactions even if not consciously performed or functionally understood. Indeed, many human rituals are rote or habitual, yet 'work' in bonding, courtship and social dominance. A behaviour pattern can convey a symbolic message of many kinds, and these are well

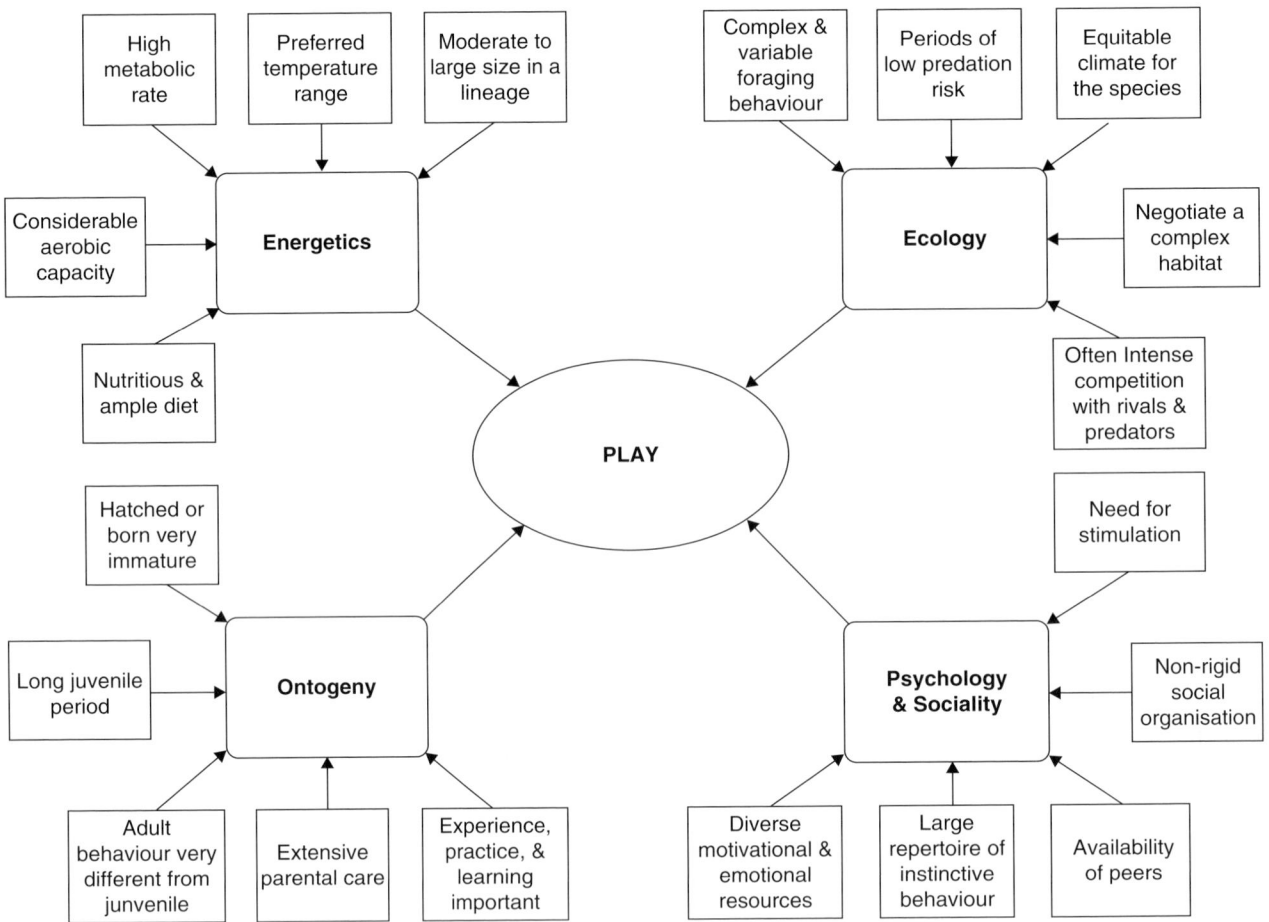

Figure 3.2 The four major sources of input moderating the expression and evolution of play (from Burghardt 2005).

documented in an extensive literature. The often elaborate courtship 'dances' and agonistic encounters among conspecific animals were well described by naturalists studying birds, insects and other animals. Sexual selection, as formulated by Darwin, seemed to be an important aspect of inter- and intra-specific interactions. The origin of these symbolic signals may involve cognitive aspects (Matthews 2011), but, as argued later in this chapter, the processes underlying rituals both 'instinctive' and 'cultural' may have more commonality than we think when not viewed through a limiting anthropocentric lens.

Rituals have been recorded across human cultures, especially in the realm of religion, in the many treatises that appeared after the age of exploration. Two notable early compilations are those of Ross (1675) and Hurd (1785). Both expressed some amazement at the diversity found, though they tied the various rituals to the specific religions more than to natural processes in their social and physical

environments that may have led to their creation. In the late nineteenth century, anthropologists began collecting and systematizing the available information in colourful and provocative ways (e.g. Frazer 1890; Lang 1899) and such reports then found their way into sociological (e.g. Durkheim) and psychological (e.g. Freudian) theorizing about religion. These writers, whose understanding of evolution was not very deep, really did not look to animal behaviour for insights into religion. An exception is the volume by Marshall (1898), who was very informed on evolution and animal behaviour, which looked at "the relation of instinct to reason, with special study of the nature of religion". Unfortunately, under the sway of behaviourism, the rich diversity of ritual behaviour was largely ignored in studies of both human and non-human psychology.

Catherine Bell (2009a, 2009b) was an influential recent contributor to the study of ritual. Among the many topics she discussed, the distinction between thoughts and action was prominent. If thoughts are religious beliefs, and actions are the ritual acting out of those beliefs, then rituals are outcomes of beliefs. But what about the reverse, ritual practices affecting beliefs? Her goal is ultimately to rethink ritual as practice, but finally backs away from any theory of ritual after evaluating the many perspectives available. Furthermore, she felt ritual would have to be distinguished from ceremony, magic and social etiquette, whereas many scholars would find such distinctions largely untenable. And, although Bell made passing mentions of ethological approaches, they were left undeveloped. In this she was similar to Boyer and Liénard (2006), who thought that the similarities between animal and human rituals were only analogical, not ones involving any shared evolutionary similarities – this in spite of their use of neurological data on compulsive disorders in the basal ganglia to support their theory that ritual practices were largely derived from evolved precaution systems dealing with external threats – clearly, for them, rituals were mostly negative and not joyful events. In fact, the linking of ritual with abnormal stereotypies and compulsive behaviour is common (e.g. Eilam et al. 2006) and leads to largely avoiding ritual practices of interest to the participants in this volume.

However, there are recent exceptions. An interdisciplinary anthropological/psychodynamic book (Seligman et al. 2008) postulates that rituals are "as if" and in essence pretend play. But ritual is contrasted with "sincerity" in what at one level makes sense to me and at another seems somewhat confused, perhaps because the four authors from different fields were, admittedly, of less than one mind. The controversial issue of the function of human rituals at a more sophisticated level than whether faith healing works is tackled from various perspectives in Sax, Quack and Weinhold (2010). That ritual performances are adaptive in animal societies, however, is shown whenever courtship leads to mating, begging leads to feeding and stylized fights solve disputes without injuries.

Bell reviews many definitions of ritual and ritualization and finds them wanting also, and settles on using "the term 'ritualization' to draw attention to the way in which certain social actions strategically distinguish themselves in relation to other actions"

(2009a, 74). As stated, this does not exclude non-human animals or privilege cultural over genetically evolved patterns of behaviour. Boyer and Liénard (2006) attempt a more formal criteria-based system in which they list five similarities across all rituals including: obsessive-compulsive disorders (e.g. handwashing), childhood rituals (e.g. bedtime) and cultural rituals (e.g. worship). These shared properties are: 1) Rituals are compulsory and failure to perform them will lead to anxiety etc. 2) Rituals are rigid and must adhere to a script. 3) Rituals involve goal-demotion, in which the ordinary performance goals of the behaviour from which the rituals are derived are unmet. 4) Rituals are repeated and redundant. 5) Rituals involve a restricted range of themes, particularly involving pollution and cleansing. Note that 3 and 4 are also characteristic of play and 5 also applies as animals and people play in often limited ways, allowing us to readily distinguish social play in cows and cats, and object play in wolves and seals, for example. In humans, most active games involve throwing, kicking, hitting, wrestling/tackling and so forth, actions that have been argued as being evolutionary-derived patterns from our hunting and tribal warfare past (Burghardt 2005). Similarity 1 is a clear separation from play, perhaps. Similarity 2 assumes that 'rigid' is akin to stereotypy in animals. This is something found often in captive animals as a pathology, but as 'habits' that work, relative stereotypy may be found in both play and rituals. In fact, play can become overly compulsive and addictive, as in gambling and marathon running (Burghardt 2005).

Rossano (2010), in a more ethologically sensitive discussion of religion, also lists several properties of rituals as formalized and rule-governed sequences of behaviour. 1) Rituals are widespread across the animal world and often involve communication. 2) Rituals are attention grabbing and promote prolonged social interaction. 3) Rituals "build trust, promote social harmony, and reinforce social relations" (p. 83), especially in non-human primates. 4) Some rituals seem essential for some categories of social interactions. 5) Use of rituals is influenced by social upbringing and socialization. 6) Ritual behaviour may be essential for acquiring other social and cognitive skills. While these six points do not hold for all rituals, and thus are similar to the early definitions of play, they subsume rituals into the natural life of animals more so than other recent treatments of ritual in discussions of religion.

The Origins and Evolution of Rituals

But how did rituals arise and evolve? Differences among closely related species in their display and other behaviour were apparent early on, of course, and Darwin in *On the Origin of Species* gave convincing evolutionary scenarios for the evolution of hive building in bees, slave making in ants and behavioural differences in varieties of domesticated animals such as dogs. It was more than 50 years before a major advance in the study of animal rituals in display occurred, around the same time, apparently independently, by two of the pioneers of ethology, Oskar Heinroth (1911) and Julian Huxley (1914). Both noted, through observation of birds, how complex courtship and other rituals were based on the incorporation of behavioural and stimulus elements from one behaviour system to another. In other words, the common notion that ritualization is merely making a behaviour pattern more stereotyped, and perhaps noticeable, was not really the key aspect of ritual formation at all. For example, head dipping in courtship could be seen as stylized, ritualized movements derived from drinking behaviour. There are now many examples of behaviour moving from one context to another, including nest-building movements in territorial disputes among male stickleback fish. These also often can involve both behavioural and morphological signals (e.g. egg spots on fins of some male cichlid fishes that serve to enhance fertilization of eggs in mouth-brooding species). The exploitation and exaggeration by animals of stimulus qualities that are 'supernormal' has been well documented in numerous species, including humans (Burghardt 1973). A compendium of examples is documented in Eibl-Eibesfeldt (1999), Foster (1995) and recent textbooks of animal behaviour. Social play may itself be ritualized from behaviour patterns in other contexts, and many examples have recently been brought together in a comparative review (Palagi et al. 2016).

An important literature on ritualization has been developed concerning humans by the pioneering human ethology studies of non-Western cultures by Eibl-Eibesfeldt and others. For example, the common human courtship and bonding ritual of kissing has been derived from parental mouth-to-mouth passing of food to infants prior to the commercial availability of baby food (see Eibl-Eibesfeldt 1999), and the often unconscious eyebrow flash can be seen in many contexts from surprise to flirting. Rossano (2010) also mentions numerous additional examples. Clearly, rituals and play both can be derived from evolutionary processes, a view echoed in the writings of Huizinga (1955, 5), who explicitly derived most human cultural practices from myth and ritual, which are themselves 'rooted in the primaeval soil of play'. More recently, in Sutton-Smith's (1997) magisterial discussion of the seven 'rhetorics' of play, festivals, rituals, social reversals (e.g. Mardi Gras) and other social scripts are incorporated into play, though with different 'players' than usually found in psychological discussions of play.

For my purposes, religion is characterized, in its behavioural manifestation, as a primarily ritual activity. Beliefs and theology are secondary, derived concerns. In fact, some recent scholarship has made the case that 'religion' as usually understood today, centring on faith and belief and separated from the other aspects of the social life of the tribe or culture, was primarily a product of early Protestant and Enlightenment writers (Batnitzky 2011). At the least, this suggests that religion may have originated as ritual activities that served to identify a tribe, population etc. as a unity, promote bonding among them and synchronize, motivate and heighten emotion-laden, group-level behaviour. Such roles of rituals have also been described in animals from parental care, to group defence (cf. meerkats being vigilant in synchrony), to bouts of shouting and screaming in chimpanzee troops. The latter often occur in the rain dance of chimpanzees.

> Rain-dance: At the start of heavy rain, several adult males perform vigorous charging displays. Displays tend to return the males to their starting position, to be coordinated or in parallel, may include slow charges as

well as rapid and may involve a variety of display patterns (e.g. ground slap, buttress-beat, branch drag, pant-hoots). (Whiten et al. 2001, 1492)

Roles of dance, singing and noise (music) in the origins of human religion are often proposed (e.g. Wade 2009; Bellah 2011). Interestingly, Whiten and colleagues (2001) document that not all chimpanzees engage in this behaviour, and when they do, there are 'cultural' differences among them.

Building on Huxley's pioneering insights, a Royal Society of London symposium was held on 'Ritualization of Behaviour in Animals and Man' in 1966. Full of details of animal rituals and insightful speculation on humans, this volume appeared before the rise of sociobiology and the focus on adaptation rather than process and mechanism, as well as prior to an evolutionary psychology that largely ignored comparative animal behaviour and phylogenetic patterns (Burghardt 2013b). A number of anthropologists were involved in this meeting, but until now serious applications of the ideas in this pioneering event have been largely lacking.

How did ritualization actually occur? One of the early ethological ideas found the origins of rituals and displays in motivational conflicts. These involved the arousal of two, often competing motivation systems such as approach/withdrawal, feeding, antipredator vigilance etc. There are four primary behavioural outcomes of such conflicts grouped into redirection, displacement, alternation and simultaneous ambivalent behaviour (Burghardt 1973). The latter, for example, has been used in the derivation of threat displays from attack and flight systems and their associated communicatory signals. But deriving elements incorporated into sequences of behaviour from seemingly disparate behaviour was not random or haphazard. Just as in human religious rituals, aspects of feeding, drinking, washing, hunting and so forth are brought into social contexts. However, the origins of such ritualization in play was not appreciated (with one exception noted later in this chapter), nor the linkages between the processes underlying 'instinctive' and cultural ritualization. Analogous perhaps, but the mechanisms were viewed as probably disparate, supporting the views of Boyer and Liénard. Even Konrad Lorenz (1974) in his Nobel lecture focused on organic and cultural evolution as largely separate and independent processes, though surprisingly analogous.

ONTOGENETIC RITUALIZATION

Recently a literature has developed on what has been termed *ontogenetic ritualization*. Studies on non-human primates document the development of novel communicative signals, both gestures and sounds, which are then incorporated into a population's behavioural repertoire. Too large to review here and somewhat controversial (see Palagi et al. 2016), some of the key papers are those on gestural communication in chimpanzees (Tomasello et al. 1997; Liebel & Call 2012) and on the development of an attention-getting sound in chimpanzees (Taglialatela et al. 2012). Tomasello and colleagues (1997) specifically mention play as a key source for the novel gestural signals. Perhaps the most remarkable, however, is the work on Japanese monkeys in a captive population that developed the habit of knocking stones together to make a sound, which spread throughout the population, is transmitted across generations, and is now a quite formalized and rigid occurrence (Huffman 1984). I saw this performed repeatedly by monkeys of all ages and sexes when I visited the Kyoto Primate Institute several years ago. Is this an instance of play becoming a ritual? In any event, this is the most thoroughly documented of any cultural transmission process in any non-human species (see Burghardt 2015 for additional details and references) and play was a key factor. Can more rudimentary steps be found in other settings?

Gene-culture co-evolution is a major area of active study in evolutionary psychology, ever since the publication of Boyd and Richerson (1985). Even before then, however, J. M. Baldwin (1896) posited a process he called 'organic selection', now typically termed the *Baldwin Effect*, whereby behaviours initially plastic or learned could become behaviourally stereotyped and genetically fixed.[1] For example, Baldwin noted that plastic, flexible behaviour is more adaptive in changing variable environments. When the environment once again becomes stable, such learned or plastic innovations become more fixed, stereotyped and universally interpreted. This was proposed as a means of bringing Lamarckian-like processes within the gambit of natural selection. For years this idea was either scorned or ignored by many (though not all) major evolutionary biologists. A major criticism was that it could not be tested. Today, however, its role in evolution is increasingly recognized. Lande (2009) has extended Baldwin's insight to include the evolution of variability itself. Furthermore, the involvement of developmental plasticity in evolutionary innovation is now a major area in evolutionary biology (e.g. Moczek et al. 2011). Such theory advances hypotheses that can be tested both empirically and through modelling of human rituals and religious practices. For example, did the social transitions and upheavals occurring in the 'Axial age', 800–200 BC, in Mediterranean and Asian civilizations (Bellah 2011) undergird the rapid development of religious innovations, which subsequently became fixed for long periods of time? Examining such phenomena in light of the work on biological and cultural evolutionary processes cited previously in this chapter could be useful. Is it a coincidence that perhaps the most ancient widespread religion, Hinduism, has benefitted from exceptionally long periods of relative social stability in India?

Interestingly, Baldwin actually developed his organic selection model to deal with what he called 'social heredity' and such prominent human traits as language and social life. He was also a pioneering developmental psychologist, a major influence on Piaget (Baldwin 1895), and was convinced that play was an important entré into social life, volition and imitation. So enamoured was he of play that his wife translated, and he wrote the foreword to, the first scholarly book published on animal play (Groos 1898). Many decades later, in the 1966 seminal symposium on ritualization organized by Julian Huxley, the eminent British ethologist, W. H. Thorpe wrote his chapter on ritualization, ontogeny and animal play. Some lines from his opening page are worthwhile quoting (Thorpe 1966, 39). After defining uses of ritual in both animal and human behaviour, emphasizing the symbolic aspect, he writes:

The ritual acts of religion are the ideal examples where every act of a complex rite symbolizes to the participant, some significant facet of doctrine or dogma. Through the ages the acts themselves have often become simplified and stereotyped, have been reduced to a minimum, so as to mime the original idea in the simplest possible manner, often with the utmost economy of gesture. … Today I am simply going to discuss very briefly the most clear-cut case of ritualization as it develops in the life of the individual animal – namely in 'animal play'.

The idea that play is at the source of many human cultural attainments and institutions is not new. As briefly mentioned earlier, perhaps the foremost early scholar who suggested that play is the basis of both the cultural attainments of humans and the rich rituals of human life was Huizinga in his seminal book, *Homo Ludens* (1955). He viewed play as an essential component of our instinctual nature: "Now in myth and ritual the great instinctive forces of civilized life have their origin: law and order, commerce and profit, craft and art, poetry, wisdom, and science. All are rooted in the primaeval soil of play" (5). Other writers on the human condition have also been enamoured of the role of play in rituals (e.g. Turner 1982) and religion and theology (e.g. Miller 1970). Miller, for example, has chapters titled "Play Is Religion" and "Religion Is Play". All these works and many others (e.g. Sax 1995) refer to play as essential to religion and spiritual experience. However, these writings have often different conceptions of play and almost universally do not take the findings on animal play into account. A major exception is the German theologian Walter Pannenberg, whose book on theological anthropology has extensive discussion of play, animals and ethology and who went so far as to claim that "representational play finds its perfect form in cult" (1985, 331).

Finally, play, ritual and religion in childhood have been addressed briefly by Rossano (2010), who began his discussion with a child's development and use of imagination. He pointed out that humans need to have mental representations not just of the immediate sensory events surrounding them at the moment, but also representing events that might or could happen. Pretend play, which is common at ages two and three, provides a vehicle for trying out, or imagining, various alternative scenarios. This role of play has been discussed previously (e.g. Burghardt 2005), but Rossano goes on to the ability to detect agency, also termed *Theory of Mind*, in conspecifics. Although hotly contested still, even apes seem to have this only to a limited degree. Rossano uses the example of a chimpanzee being able to understand that a person wanting an apple will shake a tree limb to obtain it, but not that the person is shaking the limb so vigorously in order to impress a pretty girl passing by. In a subsequent paper (Rossano 2012), he furthered the claim that the main role of rituals is to transmit and maintain social norms, which he claims are uniquely human.

A series of experimental papers (see Bering 2011) documents how children gain beliefs and then attribute them to others based on available information. It is from these experiences, presumably gained through pretence, imaginary friends and other near-universal developmental processes, that ideas of not only realistic, but also supernatural agents and agency develop. Similarly, play can lead to ritualistic patterns of behaviour. Rossano argues that adult supernaturalism evolved after social rituals of dancing, chanting and singing developed. Through their rhythmic nature, these activities can have hypnotic, pain-reducing and healing effects. Adding the supernatural imagination from childhood to adult social rituals made them even more dramatic and effective. Additionally, "If religion represents a supernaturalizing of social life, then we would expect that the gods we envision would reflect the social worlds we inhabit" (Rossano 2010, 123). In any event, developmental psychology cannot be omitted from understanding religion, ritual and ideas of gods, souls and other beliefs. Play may be the evolutionary phenomenon that jump-started the whole process.

CAN THE IDEAS BE TESTED?

One way to test evolutionary ideas about play and ritual is to review, comprehensively, the historical literature and available data on human and non-human play and rituals to evaluate the similarities and differences among them in their origins, development and function. This is a major undertaking, and while we have begun to develop such a comprehensive database, comparable to the Human Relations Area Files, with the help of Brian O'Meara and the National Institute for Mathematical Biological Synthesis at the University of Tennessee, real progress awaits adequate funding. Here is an outline of an approach we are exploring.

To investigate long-term evolutionary dynamics, phylogenetic computer methods are employed. These combine information about the relationships of living organisms and trait data with mathematical models for the evolution of traits. A phylogeny for nearly all mammals exists (Bininda-Emonds et al. 2007) and phylogenies for many other species, especially those with available ethological data, are either available or readily computable. There is a rich set of phylogenetic models available to apply to play and ritual phenomena. For character correlations of continuous characters, the method of independent contrasts (Felsenstein 1985) has a long history, though new methods allowing for intraspecific variation (Stone, Nee & Felsenstein 2011) are also available. For testing whether the presence of a particular discrete character increases the chance of evolving another character, such as whether having abundant surplus resources leads to increased incidences of play behaviour, the methods of Pagel (1994, 1997) prove useful. Models for investigating the effect of a discrete trait on a continuous trait mean (Butler and King 2004; Beaulieu et al. 2012) are also available. All these models have found widespread use in both biological and anthropological contexts. My colleague Brian O'Meara's research programme involves the development of new phylogenetic methods (e.g. O'Meara et al. 2006; Stack et al. 2011; Beaulieu et al. 2012). Our approach applies models chosen using the Akaike Information Criterion (Akaike 1973; Burnham & Anderson 2002) in order to balance model fit and complexity. In the following example, we use parameter estimates based on model averages using Akaike weights (Burnham & Anderson 2002).

As an example of the work that is possible, we have done preliminary analyses on adult primate non-sexual social play (O'Meara et al. 2015). Primate phylogenies are readily available (Arnold, Matthews & Nunn 2010). Data on play came from compilations

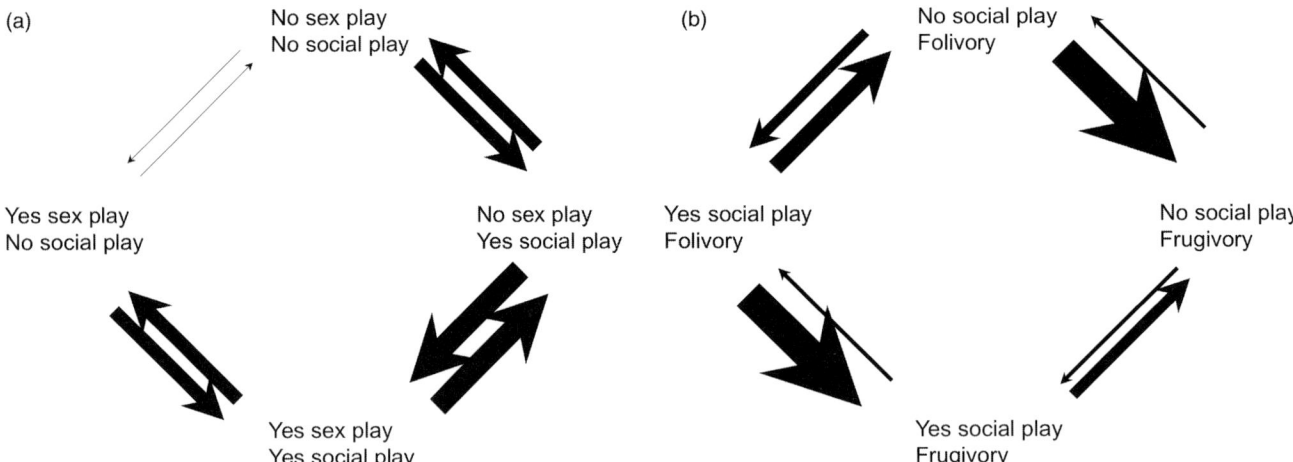

Figure 3.3 Evolution of adult play in primates, using data from more than 100 primate species. (a) When evolving from an ancestor without any play, social play evolves before sexual play, which helps explain its greater incidence in nature. (b) Role of frugivory (fruit eating) and folivory (leaf eating) and social play evolution. The loss rate is higher for primates eating leaves rather than fruits, consistent with the expectations of SRT, as frugivorous species should have more surplus resources to use in play. We also find that the rate of play evolution has dropped over time in primates to just 3% of its initial rate, suggesting that what once was labile has become relatively fixed in many species (Auerbach et al. 2015; O'Meara et al. 2015). Line widths are proportional to Akaike-weighted model averaged transition rates from a variety of models. Analyses performed using diversitree (FitzJohn, Maddison & Otto 2009) in R (R Development Core Team 2012) and GEIGER ((Harmon et al. 2008), a package in R).

from Burghardt (2005) based on Pellis and Iwaniuk (2000) with data on foraging traits, longevity, body size and other non-play traits coming from other available datasets (Ernest 2003; Nunn et al. 2004). The play data involved the occurrence, or not, of social play and/or sex play in adult primates, including humans, though the current analysis did not include sex play. Our initial dataset included a tree and data on up to 19 traits for 185 primate species, though not all traits were measured for all species. We wrote our own R (R Development Core Team 2012) scripts to process the data and automate the analyses. Our analyses (see Figure 3.3) suggest that, in primates, social play is lost at a higher rate than it is gained, which is expected for complex traits, though selection for social play should reduce this trend.

While data on traits such as body size and diet are becoming more widely available (Ernest 2003; Nunn et al. 2004), compilations of play data are still rare. To remedy this, we have begun taking entries in a play database (www.brianomeara.info/play). We have created a relatively user-friendly front end for this. Our intent is to make the data available to the research community as we publish articles using it. This will be accomplished using an interactive

website that will be created as well as permanent deposition of static files on datadryad.org, a public repository supported by the National Science Foundation and other granting agencies that has partnered with 21 biology journals as a repository.

This database will be expanded to include data on habitat, social organization, diet, body size, physiological, including brain metrics, and the nature and diversity of ritualized complexity in displays. We will specifically be looking at the relationships among different kinds of play and its complexity with display diversity in species including birds, non-human primates and rodents, as well as in different human communities. We will catalogue, from the literature, details of ritual displays in animals in different settings, and code, for example, the typical duration and complexity of courtship and territorial displays using standard ethological methods and stereotypy indices (Lehner 1996), as well as the descriptors used in phylogenetic behavioural models. Ours will have, however, more detail than typical ones involving play. These usually use a nominal score that merely classifies play into a single dimension using, for example, a scale from 1–5 or 1–3. These may not be sufficient, however, as our most critical analyses, testing SRT and other models, will incorporate detailed quantitative data on ecology, metabolic rate, social organization, developmental trajectories and so on. For example, does play diversity predict ritual and display diversity? Which types of behaviour (e.g. feeding, nest building, courtship, agonistic, parental care) are incorporated most readily into rituals in both human and non-human behaviour? Some species have much more elaborated rituals than others. Is such diversity more prone to evolve in species with more complex, intense and frequent play? Is age a factor in such linkages if they occur? Does ritual complexity and investment of time and energy in rituals in humans and non-humans have similar relationship as they do in play? Does play variability and resultant display complexity show relationships supporting the Lande (2009) extension of the Baldwin Effect? Can the rich diversification of religion and the entry of more ethical dimensions that took place during the axial age be related to social upheavals, the growth of cities and breakdown of tribal ties and other changes on a geographical scale? This could test the conditions that the Lande extension of Baldwin would predict.

FINAL THOUGHTS ON ANIMALS AND HUMAN RITUALS AND PLAY

Future goals include studies of the development of ritual-like behaviour in non-human primates through both playful or threatening encounters, and organizing anthropological and archaeological data on types of ritual and display to perform comparable analyses using the new and innovative phylogenetic methods. For example, from what we know about the early origins of religious phenomena, how have elements changed over time with major ecological and technological change? Surplus resource theory (SRT) posits that play can evolve repeatedly under a suite of ecological, physiological, life history and social conditions, and thus can provide tests of which aspects of religious phenomena change more quickly than others and in what ecological, social and technological settings. Using modern evolutionary models, we should also be able to incorporate syncretism (lateral change) in a way similar to recent findings in gene evolution and transmission.

Climate and climate change are pending issues which human civilization and their institutions need to confront. A recent challenging thesis argues that freedom of various kinds, including economic, political and fulfilling individual potential, are most prominent in countries with temperate challenging environments and economic wealth (Van de Vliert 2013). He even finds significant relationships within countries, such as China and the United States, where climate and economic well-being vary greatly. Playfulness can serve, I suggest, as a surrogate for 'freedom' in societies both human and non-human, and thus serve to test his thesis more generally and outside the anthropocentric box (Burghardt 2013a). Conversely, the prevalence of ritual and religiosity may vary with climate and social conditions in other ways. In any event, our unintended experiment in enduring worldwide climate change may lead to insights, gathered over decades, in how play and ritual change with environmental and economic shifts, if the right questions are posed.

Returning to the theme of this book in closing, many examples are discussed in the following chapters on elements of play in rituals, including dance, masks, singing, music, art and sports in early human (and also current) ritual and religious practices. Birds can dance and vocalize in most elaborate ways to music that moves humans to do the same. Interestingly, these birds are most often in the parrot family and such behaviour seems limited to those with vocal imitation abilities (Schachner et al. 2009). Facial and behavioural mimicry and mimesis occurs in play in non-human primates as well (Palagi et al. 2016). But beyond this, animals are often central in the origins of rituals, religious behaviour, mythology and thought. Interestingly, archaeological findings suggest that rituals of Neolithic people in the Near East were based on crane dances (Russell & McGowan 2002). These dramatic dances by cranes fit all the play criteria (Dinits 2013).

However, the most common animals across the world and diverse cultures involved in human religious symbolism and ritual are snakes. This is true even of Christianity, as shown in a masterful and exhaustive recent volume by Charlesworth (2010). Serpents are sources of fear, wonder, attraction and fascination for a variety of reasons (Burghardt et al. 2009), and the experiential aspects induced by them have been documented in many contexts. Furthermore, non-human primates respond to snakes with a diversity of curiosity and fear as seen in people. With Japanese colleagues I have gathered many hours of video of monkeys reacting to snakes that, along with other studies, show similar emotional reactions to them as with other fear-inducing stimuli, including those used to induce fear in some religious practices (Burghardt & Bowers 2017). On the other hand, Pentecostal churches in the south-east United States have incorporated handling venomous snakes into their church rituals (based on the five 'signs' in the last chapter of the Gospel of Mark). As this practice is only about 100 years old, is clearly costly and risky and has evolved somewhat independently in different churches etc., it is a prime candidate for testing ideas on the integration of experience and behaviour in religious practice. My observations establish that for many snake handlers, particularly younger ones, the behaviour is clearly playful, although risky, and satisfies all the play criteria (Burghardt 2014b). Extensive phenomenological interviews with snake handlers have been carried out (Hood & Williamson 2008). From these it is evident that handling of the snakes is only performed when the handlers feel utterly confident that the spirit (God) is moving them to do so. They have no fear and are in the ultimate relaxed field, something that the snakes also perceive, apparently, as the level of deadly bites is remarkably low. As one young male (and males handle far more often than females) mentioned on a recent radio interview in Knoxville, Tennessee, his relatives have commented that when he is handling snakes, he acts like a kid in a candy store! Meeting him later he readily confirmed this view. So, while the participants are serious and view their actions as deeply religious, following a ritual they derive from the Bible, the links with play, including deep and risky play similar to the games described elsewhere in this volume, may be more intimate than most of us would ever have thought, and bring this conceptual circle to at least a preliminary close.

ACKNOWLEDGEMENTS

Brian O'Meara contributed greatly to the analysis of transitions in play and prepared Figure 3.3. Sergio Pellis provided essential play data for this analysis. I want to thank the participants at the Cambridge symposium for comments and suggestions, especially Pat Bateson for providing background on the history of the "Baldwin Effect." Vladimir Dinets provided useful comments on an earlier draft and suggested the crane example. Chris Silver also provided useful comments. My ideas on this topic were enriched through discussions in the Play, Evolution, and Sociality working group at the National Institute of Mathematical and Biological Synthesis at the University of Tennessee, funded by the National Science Foundation, and while I was a fellow at the Center of Theological Inquiry in Princeton, NJ.

NOTE

1 Although two other scholars proposed a similar idea the same year, Douglass Spalding, an innovative experimental pioneer in the study of animal behaviour and instinct, anticipated the idea in a popular, though serious magazine in 1873 (Haldane 1954).

REFERENCES

Akaike, H., 1973. Information theory as an extension of the maximum likelihood principle, in *Second International Symposium on Information Theory*, eds. B. N. Petrov & F. Csaki. Budapest: Akademiai Kiado, 267–81.

Antonacci, D., L. Norscia & E. Palagi, 2010. Stranger to familiar: wild strepsirhines manage xenophobia by playing. *PLoS One* 5, http://dx.doi.org/10.1371/journal.pone.0013218.e13218.

Arnold, C., L. J. Matthews & C. L. Nunn, 2010. The 10k Trees website: a new online resource for primate phylogeny. *Evolutionary Anthropology* 19, 114–18.

Auerbach, J. D., A. Kanarek & G. M. Burghardt, 2015. To play or not to play? That's a resource abundance question. *Adaptive Behavior* 23, 354–61.

Baldwin, J. M., 1895. *Mental Development in the Child and the Race*. New York: Macmillan.

Baldwin, J. M., 1896. A new factor in evolution. *American Naturalist* 30, 441–51, 536–53.

Batnitzky, L., 2011. *How Judaism Became a Religion*. Princeton, NJ: Princeton University Press.

Bateson, P., 2011. Theories of play, in *The Oxford Handbook of the Development of Play*, ed. A. D. Pellegrini. New York: Oxford University Press, 41–7.

Beaulieu, J. M., D.-C. Jhwueng, C. Boettiger & B. C. O'Meara, 2012. Modeling stabilizing selection: expanding the Ornstein-Uhlenbeck model of adaptive evolution. *Evolution* 66, 2369–83.

Bell, C., 2009a, org. 1992. *Ritual Theory, Ritual Practice.* Oxford: Oxford University Press.

Bell, C. 2009b, org. 1997. *Ritual. Perspectives and Dimensions.* Oxford: Oxford University Press.

Bellah, R. N., 2011. *Religion in Human Evolution.* Cambridge, MA: Harvard University Press.

Bekoff, M. & J. Pierce, 2009. *Wild Justice: The Moral Lives of Animals.* Chicago, IL: University of Chicago Press.

Bering, J., 2011. *The Belief Instinct.* New York: W. W. Norton.

Bininda-Emonds, O. R. P., M. Cardillo, K. E. Jones, R. D. E. MacPhee, R. M. D. Beck, R. Grenyer, S. A. Price, R. A. Vos, J. L. Gittleman & A. Purvis, 2007. The delayed rise of present-day mammals. *Nature* 446, 507–12.

Boyd, R. & P. Richerson, 1985. *Culture and the Evolutionary Process.* Chicago, IL: University of Chicago Press.

Boyer, P. & P. Liénard, 2006. Why ritualized behavior? Precaution systems and action parsing in developmental, pathological, and cultural rituals. *Behavioral and Brain Sciences* 29, 1–56 (includes commentaries and responses).

Bulbia, J., R. Sosis, E. Harris, R. Genet, C. Genet & K. Wyman (eds.), 2008. *The Evolution of Religion: Studies, Theories, & Critiques.* Santa Margarita, CA: Collins Foundation Press.

Burghardt, G. M., 1973. Instinct and innate behavior: toward an ethological psychology, in *The Study of Behavior: Learning, Motivation, Emotion, and Instinct,* eds. J. A. Nevin & G. S. Reynolds. Glenview, IL: Scott, Foresman, 322–400.

Burghardt, G. M., 1988. Precocity, play, and the ectotherm-endotherm transition: profound reorganization or superficial adaptation, in *Handbook of Behavioral Neurobiology, Vol. 9, Developmental Psychobiology and Behavioral Ecology,* ed. E. M. Blass. New York: Plenum, 107–48.

Burghardt G. M., 2005. *The Genesis of Animal Play: Testing the Limits.* Cambridge, MA: MIT Press.

Burghardt, G. M., 2010. The comparative reach of play and brain: perspective, evidence, and implications. *American Journal of Play* 2, 338–56.

Burghardt, G. M., 2011. Defining and recognizing play, in *The Oxford Handbook of the Development of Play,* ed. A. D. Pellegrini. New York: Oxford University Press, 9–18.

Burghardt, G. M., 2013a. Play, animals, resources: the need for a rich (and challenging) comparative environment. *Behavioral and Brain Sciences* 36, 5, 20–1.

Burghardt, G. M., 2013b. The Janus faced nature of comparative psychology – strength or weakness? *Evolutionary Psychology* 11, 762–80.

Burghardt, G. M., 2014a. A brief glimpse at the long evolutionary history of play. *Animal Behavior and Cognition* 1, 90–8.

Burghardt G. M., 2014b Faith, play, and the death of Jamie Coots. www.psychologytoday.com/blog/we-question-therefore-we-live/201402/faith-play-and-the-death-jamie-coots

Burghardt, G. M., 2015. Creativity, play, and the pace of evolution, in *Animal Creativity and Innovation,* eds. A. B. Kaufman & J. C. Kaufman. Philadelphia, PA: Elsevier, 129–59.

Burghardt, G. M. & R. I. Bowers, 2017. From instinct to behavior systems: an integrated approach to ethological psychology, in *APA Handbook of Comparative Psychology: Vol 1. Basic Concepts, Methods, Neural Substrate, and Behavior,* eds. J. Call, G. M. Burghardt, I. M. Pepperberg, C. T. Snowdon, & T. Zentall. Washington, DC: American Psychological Association, 333–64.

Burghardt, G. M., J. B. Murphy, D. Chiszar & M. Hutchins, 2009. Combating ophiophobia: origins, treatment, education and conservation tools. In *Snakes: Ecology and Conservation,* eds. S. Mullin & R. Seigel. Ithaca, NY: Cornell University Press, 262–80.

Burnham, K. P. & D. R. Anderson, 2002. *Model Selection and Multimodel Inference: A Practical Information-Theoretic Approach.* Berlin: Springer Verlag.

Buss, D. M., 2011. *Evolutionary Psychology: The New Science of the Mind,* 4th ed. Boston, MA: Pearson, Allyn, and Bacon.

Butler M. A. & A. A. King, 2004. Phylogenetic comparative analysis: a modeling approach for adaptive evolution. *American Naturalist* 164, 683–95.

de Braak, H. van. 2013. *Evolutionary Psychology.* Harlow: Pearson.

Charlesworth, J. H., 2010. *The Good and Evil Serpent.* New Haven, CT: Yale University Press.

Dinets, V. 2013. Crane dances as play behavior. *Ibis* 155, 424–5.

Eibl-Eibesfeldt, I., 1999. *Grundiss der Vergleichennden Verhaltensforschung.* Munich: Piper.

Eilam, D., R. Zor, H. Szechtman & H. Hermesh, 2006. Rituals, stereotypy, and compulsive behavior in animals and humans. *Neuroscience and Biobehavioral Reviews* 30, 456–71.

Ernest, S. K. M., 2003. Life history characteristics of placental nonvolant mammals. *Ecology* 84, 3402.

Feierman, J. R. (ed.), 2009. *The Biology of Religious Behavior: The Evolutionary Origins of Faith and Religion.* Santa Barbara, CA: Praeger.

Felsenstein J., 1985. Phylogenies and the comparative method. *American Naturalist* 125, 1–15.

FitzJohn, R. G., W. P. Maddison & S. P. Otto, 2009. Estimating trait-dependent speciation and extinction rates from incompletely resolved phylogenies. *Systematic Biology* 58, 595–611.

Foster, S. A., 1995. Constraint, adaptation, and opportunism in the design of behavioral phenotypes. In *Perspectives in Ethology: Behavioral Design* (Volume 11, ed. N. S. Thompson). New York: Plenum Press, 61–81.

Frazer, J. G., 1890. *The Golden Bough: A Study in Comparative Religion*. 2 vol. New York: Macmillan.

Graham, K. L. & G. M. Burghardt, 2010. Current perspectives on the biological study of play: signs of progress. *Quarterly Review of Biology* 85, 393–418.

Groos, K., 1898. *The Play of Animals* (E. L. Baldwin, trans.). New York: Appleton.

Haldane, J. B. S., 1954. Introducing Douglas Spalding. *British Journal of Animal Behaviour* 2, 1–11.

Harmon, L. J., J. T. Weir, C. D. Brock, R. E. Glor & W. Challenger, 2008. GEIGER: investigating evolutionary radiations. *Bioinformatics* 24, 129–31.

Heinroth, O., 1911. Beiträge zur Biologie, namentlich Ethologie und Psychologie der Anatiden. *Deutsche Ornithologische Gesellschaft* 1910, 589–702.

Henricks, T. S. 2015. Play and the Human Condition. Urbana, IL: University of Illinois Press.

Hood, R. W., Jr. & W. P. Williamson, 2008. *Them that Believe: The Power and Meaning of the Christian Serpent-Handling Tradition*. Berkeley: University of California Press.

Huffman, M. A., 1984. Stone-play of *Macaca fuscata* in Arashiyama B troop: transmission of a non-adaptive behaviour. *Journal of Human Evolution* 13, 725–35.

Huizinga, J., 1955. *Homo Ludens: A Study of the Play Element in Culture*. Boston, MA: Beacon.

Hurd, W., 1785. *A New Universal History of the Religious Rites, Ceremonies, and Customs of the Whole World: Or, a Complete and Impartial View of all the Religions in the Various Nations of the Universe*. London: Alexander Hogg.

Huxley, J. S., 1914. The courtship habits of the Great Crested Grebe (*Podiceps cristatus*); with an addition to the theory of sexual selection. *Proceedings of the Zoological Society of London* 35, 491–562.

Lande, R., 2009. Adaptation to an extraordinary environment by evolution of phenotypic plasticity and genetic assimilation. *Journal of Evolutionary Biology* 22, 1435–46.

Lang, A., 1899. *Myth, Ritual and Religion*. 2 vol., new edition. London: Longmans, Green, and Co.

Lehner, P. N. 1996. *Handbook of Ethological Methods*, 2nd Ed. Cambridge: Cambridge University Press.

Liebel, K. & J. Call, 2012. The origins of non-human primates' manual gestures. *Philosophical Transactions of the Royal Society B* 367, 118–28.

Liénard, P. & P. Boyer, 2006. Whence collective rituals? A cultural selection model of ritualized behaviour. *American Anthropologist* 108, 814–27.

Lorenz, K., 1974. Analogy as a source of knowledge. *Science* 185, 229–34.

Marshall, H. R., 1898. *Instinct and Reason*. London: Macmillan Co.

Matthews, J., 2011. *Starting from Scratch: The Origin and Development of Expression, Representation and Symbolism in Human and Non-human Primates*. London: Psychology Press.

McCauley, R. N., 2011. *Why Religion Is Natural and Science Is Not*. Oxford: Oxford University Press.

Miller, D. L., 1970. *Gods and Games: Toward a Theology of Play*. New York: World Publishing.

Miller, J. H. & S. E. Page, 2007. *Complex Adaptive Systems: An Introduction to Computational Models of Social Life*. Princeton, NJ: Princeton University Press.

Moczek, A. P., S. Sultan, S. Foster, C. Ledón-Rettig, I. Dworkin, H. F. Nijhout, E. Abouheit & D. W. Pfennig, 2011. The role of developmental plasticity in evolutionary innovation. *Proceedings of the Royal Society B* 278 (1719), 2705–13.

Nunn, C. L., S. Altizer, W. Sechrest, K. E. Jones, R. A. Barton & J. L. Gittleman, 2004. Parasites and the evolutionary diversification of primate clades. *American Naturalist* 164, S90–S103.

O'Meara, B. C., C. Ane, M. J. Sanderson & P. C. Wainwright, 2006. Testing for different rates of continuous trait evolution using likelihood. *Evolution* 60, 922–33.

O'Meara, B. C., K. L. Graham, S. M. Pellis & G. M. Burghardt, 2015. Evolutionary models for the retention of adult–adult social play in primates: the roles of diet and other factors associated with resource acquisition. *Adaptive Behavior* 23, 381–91.

Pagel, M., 1994. Detecting correlated evolution on phylogenies – a general-method for the comparative-analysis of discrete characters. *Proceedings of the Royal Society of London Series B-Biological Sciences* 255, 37–45.

Pagel, M., 1997. Inferring evolutionary processes from phylogenies. *Zoologica Scripta* 26, 331–48.

Palagi, E., G. M. Burghardt, B. Smuts, G. Cordoni, S. Dall'Olio, H. N. Fouts, M. Reháková-Petr°u, S. M. Siviy & S. M. Pellis, 2016. Rough-and-tumble play as a window on animal communication. *Biological Reviews* 91, 111–27. doi: 10.1111/brv.12172.

Panksepp, J., 1998. *Affective Neuroscience*. Oxford: Oxford University Press.

Panksepp, J. & L. Biven, 2012. *The Archaeology of Mind: Neuroevolutionary Origins of Human Emotions*. Oxford: Oxford University Press.

Pannenberg, W., 1985. *Anthropology in Theological Perspective*. Philadelphia, PA: Westminster Press.

Pellegrini, A. D., 2009. *The Role of Play in Human Development*. New York: Oxford University Press.

Pellegrini, A. D. (ed.), 2011. *The Oxford Handbook of the Development of Play*. New York: Oxford University Press.

Pellis, S. M. & A. N. Iwaniuk, 2000. Adult–adult play in primates: comparative analyses of its origin, distribution and evolution. *Ethology* 106, 1083–104.

Pellis, S. M. & V. C. Pellis, 2009. *The Playful Brain. Venturing to the Limits of Neuroscience*. Oxford: Oneworld Press.

Pruitt, J. N., G. M Burghardt & S. E. Riechert, 2012. Nonconceptive sexual behaviour in spiders: a form of play associated with body condition, personality type, and male intrasexual selection. *Ethology* 118, 33–40.

Pyysiäinen, I., 2009. *Supernatural Agents. Why We Believe in Souls, Gods, and Buddhas*. Oxford: Oxford University Press.

R Development Core Team, 2012. *R: A Language and Environment for Statistical Computing*. Vienna, Austria: R Foundation for Statistical Computing.

Riis, O. & L. Woodhead, 2012. *A Sociology of Religious Emotion*. Oxford: Oxford University Press.

Rogers, L. J. & G. Kaplan, 2002. *Songs, Roars, and Rituals. Communication in Birds, Mammals, and Other Animals*. Cambridge, MA: Harvard University Press.

Ross, A., 1675. *Panzebia or a View of all the Religions in the World (5th ed.)*. London: John Williams.

Rossano, M. J., 2010. *Supernatural Selection. How Religion Evolved*. Oxford: Oxford University Press.

Rossano, M. J. 2012. The essential role of ritual in the transmission and reinforcement of social norms. *Psychological Bulletin* 138, 129–49.

Russell, N. & K. J. McGowan, 2002. Dances of the cranes: crane symbolism at Çatalhöyük and beyond. *Antiquities* 77 (297), 445–55.

Sax, W. S., 1995. *The Gods at Play. Līlā in South Asia*. Oxford: Oxford University Press.

Sax, W. S., J. Quack & J. Weinhold (eds.), 2010. *The Problem of Ritual Efficacy*. Oxford: Oxford University Press.

Schachner, A., T. F. Brady, I. M. Pepperberg & M. D. Hauser, 2009. Spontaneous motor entrainment to music in multiple vocal mimicking species. *Current Biology* 19, 831–6.

Schechner, R. 2013. *Performance Studies: An Introduction*. London: Routledge.

Seligman, A. B., R. P. Weller, M. J. Puett & B. Simon, 2008. *Ritual and its Consequences: An Essay on the Limits of Sincerity*. Oxford: Oxford University Press.

Smith, P. K., 2009. *Children and Play*. Oxford: Wiley-Blackwell.

Stack, J. C., L. J Harmon & B. C. O'Meara, 2011. RBrownie: an R package for testing hypotheses about rates of evolutionary change. *Methods in Ecology and Evolution* 2, 660–2.

Stone, G. N., S. Nee & J. N. Felsenstein, 2011. Controlling for non-independence in comparative analysis of patterns across populations within species. *Philosophical Transactions of the Royal Society, Series B – Biological Sciences* 366, 1410–24.

Sutton-Smith, B., 1997. *The Ambiguity of Play*. Cambridge, MA: Harvard University Press.

Taglialatela, J. P., L. Reamer, S. J. Schapiro & W. D. Hopkins, 2012. Social learning of a communicative signal in captive chimpanzees. *Biology Letters* 8, 498–501.

Thorpe, W. H., 1966. Ritualization in ontogeny: I. Animal play. *Philosophical Transactions of the Royal Society of London. Series B – Biological Sciences* 251 (772), 311–19.

Tomasello, M., J. Call, J. Warren, G. Y. Frost, M. Carpenter & K. Nagell, 1997. The ontogeny of chimpanzee gestural signals: a comparison across groups and generations. *Evolution of Communication* 1, 223–53.

Turner, V., 1982. *From Ritual to Theatre: The Human Seriousness of Play*. New York: PAJ Publications.

Van de Vliert, E., 2013. Climato-economic habitats support patterns of human needs, stresses, and freedoms. *Behavioral and Brain Sciences* 36 (5), 1–57.

Wade, N., 2009. *The Faith Instinct. How Religion Evolved and Why it Matters*. New York: Penguin Press.

Whiten, A., J. Goodall, W. C. McGrew, T. Nishida, V. Reynolds, Y. Sugiyama, E. G. Tutin, R. W. Wrangham & C. Boesch, 2001. Charting cultural variation in chimpanzees. *Behaviour* 138, 1481–516.

4

PLAY AND CREATIVITY

PATRICK BATESON

This chapter elaborates upon the universality of play behaviours in mammals, and upon the principal criteria for identifying play behaviours, before discussing the circumstances in which play activities are carried out and the characteristics that they exhibit in a wide variety of animals. Next the question of what play is 'for' is explored – what beneficial roles it may be said to fulfil in the ontogenic development of animals, and in their evolutionary context. Finally it goes on to explore relationships between play behaviours and the development of creativity and problem-solving in different species, including in important examples of human innovations.

Play and *ritual* are terms that are used with distinct meanings in different disciplines. In studies of animal behaviour, ritual refers to the stereotyped ways in which different individuals will interact with each other, particularly in courtship. This is a far cry from what anthropologists consider when dealing with human rituals. Play is used in an even greater number of ways. Brian Sutton-Smith's usage extends from the use of metaphors to beauty contests, playing the piano and playing cricket to doing risky things like bungee jumping (Sutton-Smith 1997). In contrast, most psychologists and biologists use play for non-serious activities which may have no immediate utility. For that reason, rule-governed competitive sports are 'played', but they are rarely if ever conducted playfully. Sports and many games are often treated as being deadly serious. Similarly, theatrical plays in which the actors are required to have learned their lines do not have associated with them much lightness of mood, except perhaps

in improvisation on the stage and ad libbing. I do not regard the lumping together of all the different meanings of play as helpful. It probably impedes any critical discussion of the origins of human ritual. Whether the use of play by those like me who work on play in animals can contribute to the study of ritual I doubt, but I shall describe what I know in this chapter. It is a condensed version of a book by myself and Paul Martin (Bateson & Martin 2013) and follows the same theme as in an article by myself (Bateson 2014).

DEFINING PLAY

Over the years a number of psychologists and biologists have attempted to bring order to the subject of play by listing the various criteria by which play behaviour might be recognised (Fagen 1981; Burghardt 2005). Five defining features of play, which have emerged from studies of play in many species, are:

1. The behaviour is spontaneous and rewarding to the individual; it is intrinsically motivated and its performance serves as a goal in itself. Play is 'fun'.
2. The player is to some extent protected from the normal consequences of serious behaviour. The behaviour appears to have no immediate practical goal or benefit. Social forms of the behaviour may be preceded or accompanied by specific signals or facial expressions indicating that the behaviour is not serious. Play is the antithesis of 'work' or 'serious' behaviour.

3. The behaviour consists of actions or, in the case of humans, thoughts, expressed in novel combinations. Social forms of the behaviour may be accompanied by temporary changes in social relationships, such as role reversals, in which a normally dominant individual may become temporarily subordinate while playing, and vice versa. Play is a generator of novelty.

4. Individual actions or thoughts are performed repeatedly (though they do not resemble stereotypes such as the circular pacing seen in animals kept in impoverished conditions); they may also be incomplete or exaggerated relative to non-playful behaviour in adults. Play looks different.

5. The behaviour is sensitive to prevailing conditions and occurs only when the player is free from illness or stress. Play is an indicator of well-being.

These criteria overlap extensively with those articulated by Gordon Burghardt, who devoted a substantial portion of his book to characterising the defining features of play and relating them to observational evidence from numerous species (Burghardt 2005). His analysis led him to suggest five criteria by which play can be recognised. They are broadly similar to the core features listed earlier. Neither set of criteria defines *playful* play. For play to be playful, a sixth feature must also be present:

6. Playful play (as distinct from the broader biological category of play) is accompanied by a particular positive mood state in which the individual is more inclined to behave (and, in the case of humans, think) in a spontaneous and flexible way.

Playfulness, the defining feature of playful play, is a positive mood state that is not always detectable in observable behaviour. The behaviour of a playful human is captured by numerous synonyms, including *cheerful, frisky, frolicsome, good-natured, joyous, merry, rollicking, spirited, sprightly* and *vivacious*. Some of these terms relate to human emotions that could not be readily identified in animals without much anthropomorphic projection. Some, though, are descriptive of visible behaviour and can be defined ostensively, such as when two kittens engage vigorously in social play. In animals, as in humans, playfulness may be inferred from the context in which it occurs. What the animals do may vary – from playing with objects at one moment to playing with another individual at the next – but the playful state underlying their behaviour is the same.

Play, as defined previously, can manifest itself in many different ways in humans. It may be solitary, social, pretend, imaginary, symbolic, verbal, sociodramatic, constructional, rough-and-tumble, manipulative and so forth (Power 2000; Pellegrini 2009). These forms of play differ in their structure, their underlying motivation and, quite probably, their biological functions. For example, the rough-and-tumble play of a four-year-old child wrestling with another four-year-old is visibly quite different from that of, say, a solitary 10-year-old staring into space, lost in a fantasy. The criteria for recognising play in animals work well when applied to the rough-and-tumble play of a child, but pretend play requires additional definition (Smith 2010). Applying non-literal meanings to actions and objects is a central feature of pretend play in humans. It involves imitative actions in a non-functional context, such as pressing a toy stethoscope against the chest of a doll.

Such instances of pretend play are easy to define ostensively by pointing to examples, and a case can be made for defining similar behaviour seen in the great apes. For example, young female chimpanzees behave maternally towards sticks, ceasing to do so when they have real offspring to care for (Kahlenberg & Wrangham 2010). This stick-carrying behaviour consists of holding or cradling sticks, pieces of bark, small logs or woody vines with the hand, mouth or underarm or, most commonly, tucked between the abdomen and thigh. Individuals carry sticks for periods ranging from a minute to more than four hours, during which time they rest, walk, climb, sleep and feed as usual. The occurrence of stick-carrying is greatest among juvenile females and resembles the pretend play of human children.

The pretend play of an older child, who can describe what he or she is thinking and doing, may be viewed as part of a package of characteristically human behaviour and cognition, much of which is internalised. This complex package includes the use of language, self-awareness and an understanding of how other humans think and are likely to behave

(Smith 2010). The definition used earlier would not readily apply to such examples, though many could be described as playful.

The criteria for recognising play would exclude behaviour in which the player is stressed or hurt by another. The unpleasant aspects of human 'play' can include teasing, bullying and shunning, as well as hurting and being hurt. The negative side of 'play' is also apparent in other animals. For example, researchers observed how male adult horses who were most likely to initiate what looked like play were also the ones who, according to other criteria, were the most chronically stressed. The stressed horses behaved as though the 'play' were an outlet for frustrated aggression (Hausberger et al. 2012). If so, it would not constitute play in the terms defined earlier, and it would certainly not be playful play. Similarly, I have noticed how tense kittens could be just before launching themselves at a sibling. They would arch and swish their tails (Bateson 2011). If grabbed from behind by a human at just that preparatory phase, they would scream, apparently in fright, and retreat from the other individual. They lacked the positive, relaxed mood associated with playfulness, but if they had not been disturbed, their mood would have relaxed and their behaviour would have satisfied our core features. Mood can also change in the opposite direction. Occasionally, social play degenerates into a spat and the behaviour becomes aggressive. For one of the participating individuals the encounter can become disagreeable and the playful mood rapidly evaporates. The change of mood means that the behaviour can no longer be regarded as playful, and if the individual becomes stressed, then it may no longer even constitute play.

Play behaviour has been recognised in a large number of mammal and bird species. As far as the behaviour of young mammals is concerned, it seems likely that few if any species will be found where play in one form or another is absent. In birds, play has been recorded in parrots, hornbills, babblers and members of the crow family. The existence or not of play in other vertebrate taxonomic groups is much more controversial (Manning & Dawkins 2012). Gordon Burghardt examined the possibility of play in taxonomic groups other than birds and mammals (Burghardt 2005). He identified instances of behaviour in fish and reptiles that look somewhat like object play in birds and mammals. According to Burghardt, some invertebrates such as octopi and even spiders might also exhibit play-like behaviour. For example, sexual acts between males and immature female spiders that do not result in the union of sperm and egg are found to decrease the subsequent latency to an act resulting in fertilisation and increase in maternal investment in the offspring (Pruitt, Burghardt & Riechert 2012). The authors argued that the non-conceptive behaviour had formal similarities with play in birds and mammals. The conclusion that spiders and other invertebrates engage in play may seem implausible, even if it does follow logically from a precise definition that works for birds and mammals. What this example does illustrate is the considerable difficulty of defining play.

As in humans, the play of other species can manifest itself in distinctly different forms. For example, when describing play in a mammal as generally playful as the domestic cat, it becomes clear that different components of its play behaviour are displayed in different situations. For instance, arching of the back, which is often seen in social play, does not appear in play with objects. Similarly, pouncing on objects, especially furry objects, is not seen in locomotor play. Moreover, the developmental trajectories of these different forms of play are not the same. In cats, social play starts well before weaning, whereas object play rises sharply in the seventh week after birth, several weeks after the kittens have started to take solid food. Different structural features are therefore required to characterise these different sub-categories of play.

Dolphins are magnificently playful animals and particularly good subjects for investigating the different manifestations of play. Captive dolphins play readily with balls and other toys. In the wild, they play with feathers, seaweed, sponges and other objects. They also play with bubble rings, which they create for themselves from their blowholes. Dolphins play with these items in a variety of ways, such as pushing them around, throwing them in the air or swimming through their bubble rings. They are also highly social, playing extensively with each other. Thirty-seven different types of play have been described in the young of the bottlenose dolphin (Kuczaj et al. 2006). Examples include holding a ball, swimming and tossing a ball simultaneously, using the mouth or chin to dribble a ball at the surface or under the water, pushing a ball with a body part, trapping a ball between a hard surface and part of the body, using a ball as a rubbing tool, and placing a ball into enclosed spaces and then releasing it. These and other categories of play are spontaneously produced by the dolphins and need no reinforcement by trainers with rewards of food or praise.

In some species, specific social signals are used to denote that what follows is play rather than serious behaviour. Dogs, for example, signal their readiness to play by dropping down on their forelegs and wagging their tails. In domestic cats, a bout of social play is often initiated by one kitten crouching with its head held low and paddling its back legs before pouncing on another kitten (West 1974). Chimpanzees have a special 'play face' – a distinctive facial expression that precedes and accompanies a bout of social play.

Social play is marked by a degree of cooperation between the players. Competition is limited and roles are often reversed. So individuals that are normally dominant in non-playful contexts may allow themselves to adopt a subordinate role during play and vice versa. A mother cat playing with her kitten will sometimes be the object of a playful attack and sometimes initiate it (Mendl 1988). This exchange of roles during play is particularly striking when members of different species are reared together, such as dogs and cats, cats and rats, dogs and deer, dolphins and whales and so on. The participants play avidly and they frequently exchange roles, as if they share the same set of basic rules for play.

When social play is in full swing, many patterns of 'serious' behaviour are apparent, but they are not exactly the same in form or motivation. Playing kittens may pounce on each other, as though fighting or attacking prey, but their biting is soft and when they wrestle their claws are retracted. (This seems to be an inhibition that emerges as animals get older, because earlier in development they can bite hard and scratch each other.) Similarly, playing monkeys may mount each other, as though sexually, but no actual penetration occurs.

While the occurrence of play tends to decline with the onset of adulthood, it may still be seen in later life. Play is obvious at times in adult domestic cats and dogs. Their behaviour is not just a consequence of domestication – play in adults has also been seen in many wild species including wolves, coyotes, Cape hunting dogs, gorillas and dolphins (Kuczaj et al. 2006).

And, of course, play is also seen in adult humans, when they have the time and inclination. Adult humans typically play less than children.

Another of the defining features of play listed earlier is its sensitivity to prevailing conditions. In general, play is an indicator of psychological and physical well-being (Held & Spinka 2011). It is usually the first activity to disappear if the individual is stressed, anxious, hungry or ill. Experimental evidence backs this up. In one study, for example, playing rats that were exposed to cat hair immediately stopped playing or soliciting play, and their play remained suppressed for several days after this mildly stressful experience (Panksepp 1998). A number of laboratory and field studies have suggested that young mammals that have been short of food play less compared with when they are better fed; examples include squirrel monkeys. For example, wild-living meerkats were found to play more when they were provisioned with extra food (Sharpe et al. 2002).

Shortage of food tends to suppress play in humans as well. In a comparison of under-nourished and well-nourished children aged 7–18 months in West Bengal, the under-nourished boys (for whom the sample size was adequate, unlike girls) showed less vigour in their play (Graves 1976). Similarly, a study of Kenyan toddlers found a correlation between the children's food intake and how much they played (Sigman et al. 1989). Many aspects of poverty, such as a requirement to work, can reduce a child's opportunity for play (Milteer & Ginsburg 2012). All are a cause for concern, but reduced motivation to play, caused by poor health and poor nutrition, will compound the other problems. As in other species, children's play happens only when basic short-term needs have been satisfied and the individual is free from stress.

The motivation to play has many of the same characteristics as the motivation for other activities such as eating. The more an individual has been deprived of play, the more it will play when given the opportunity, as though compensating for the previous shortfall (Jensen 1999). More saliently, an individual is prepared to work in order to be given the opportunity to engage in play. Opportunities to play are themselves rewarding, reinforcing the activity that provided the individual with the chance to play. In one experiment, for example, an opportunity to play worked effectively as a reward when rats made the correct choice in a maze (Humphreys & Einon 1981). Like food, the opportunity to play is a natural reinforcer of other behaviour.

An individual absorbed in playing seems not to require any external reward. Many experimental psychologists concerned with how behaviour is controlled have tended to focus on external rewards or punishments, which are more amenable to experimental manipulation. External rewards such as food are powerful ways of shaping behaviour. In the first half of the twentieth century, B. F. Skinner founded a whole school of research in which animals' responses to different schedules of reinforcement with food were automatically recorded. When the reinforcements occur in a particular context, that context can itself become rewarding. So a food reward delivered after the performance of a particular act may be given only when the trainer has, for example, triggered a device that emits a clicking sound. After a while, the sound alone can be used to reward another act. In the language of experimental analysis of behaviour, the sound is a secondary reinforcer whereas the food is the primary reinforcer.

Both primary and secondary reinforcers are external and, in the case described, depend on the trained individual being intrinsically motivated to take food. The motivation for learning the rewarded behaviour is said to be extrinsic. In the case of play, particularly when the individual is playing on its own, the motivation is intrinsic – that is, no external reward is needed. In social play the reactions of the play partner may provide additional reward, increasing the likelihood that the initiator will continue playing. If the partner does not respond playfully, the initiator will stop. Nevertheless, the initiator's behaviour starts spontaneously and may be marked by a characteristic play signal. The spontaneous character of the behaviour is obvious and highlights the distinction between extrinsic and intrinsic motivation.

The various forms of play within a species, and the different ways in which these change with age, suggest that different forms of play are controlled differently (Bateson 1981). Moreover, as play merges with adult behaviour, the motivational systems probably change with age. Aggressive acts can become incorporated into social play, and prey-catching in carnivores can become incorporated into object play.

FUNCTION

What play is for? This question is not directed at the individual's motivation. It is concerned with how the various aspects of play increase the individual's chances of survival and reproducing itself.

In the history of thinking about the function of play a very large number of hypotheses have been offered. When young animals playfully practise the stereotyped movements they will use in earnest later in life, they are often thought to improve the coordination and effectiveness of these behaviour patterns. The short dashes and jumps of a young gazelle when it is playing bring benefits that may be almost immediate, as it faces the threat of predation from cheetah or other carnivores intent on a quick meal, and needs considerable skill when escaping (Gomendio 1988). Even though the benefits may be immediate in such cases, they may also persist into adult life.

Most theories of the functions of play have continued to focus on its role in enabling the developing individual to acquire and practise complex physical skills and, by so doing, fine-tune neuromuscular systems. Others, observing how much young animals play with each other, have emphasised that the individual also develops social skills and cements its social relationships; play may also serve to improve its capacity to compete and cooperate with other members of its own species. Play can make an individual more resistant to stress, enlarge its repertoire. Play may enhance an individual's resourcefulness and flexibility and make it able to adjust to new conditions. Play may enhance its ability to cooperate with others and to coexist with older members of its own species. Play may increase its knowledge of its home range. Play, or at least some components of it, allows the young animal to simulate, in a relatively safe context, potentially dangerous situations that will arise in its adult life. It learns from its mistakes, but does so in relative safety. On this view, play exerts its most important developmental effects on risky adult behaviour such as fighting, mating in the face of serious competition, catching dangerous prey and avoiding becoming someone else's prey. Indeed, the behaviour patterns of fighting and prey-catching are especially obvious in the play of cats and other predators, whereas safe activities such as grooming, defecating and urinating have no playful counterparts. None of the suggestions about the function of play is mutually exclusive. Moreover, if play is heterogeneous, as I believe it is, then the plethora of explanations is hardly surprising.

When differences between the sexes arise in play, as they often do, these are reflected in differences between the sexes in the activities of adults (Meaney & Stewart 1985). For instance, young female chimpanzees seemed to behave maternally towards sticks, doing so much more than males and ceasing to do so when they have real offspring to care for (Kahlenberg & Wrangham 2010). Stick-carrying consisted of holding or cradling detached sticks, pieces of bark, small logs or woody vines, with their hand or mouth, underarm or, most commonly, tucked between the abdomen and thigh. Individuals carried sticks for periods of one minute to more than four hours during which they rested, walked, climbed, slept and fed as usual. The occurrence of stick-carrying peaked among juveniles and was higher in females than males. This sex difference could not be explained by a general propensity for females to play with objects more than males – several types of object such as weapons were played with more by males. Males in many species, including humans, do more rough-and-tumble play than females and engage in more agonistic behaviour when adults (Auger & Olesen 2009).

The ideas about play leading to the acquisition of knowledge and greater resilience with long-term benefits are distinct from the idea of play as a mechanism for generating novel solutions, which is the primary thrust of this chapter. Play has features that are likely to make it especially suitable for finding the best way forward in a world of conflicting demands. In acquiring cognitive skills, individuals are in danger of finding sub-optimal solutions to the many problems that confront them. In deliberately moving away from what might look like the final resting point, each individual may get somewhere that is better. Play may, therefore, fulfil an important probing role that enables the individual to escape from false end-points or 'local optima'. An analogy is a mountain surrounded by lesser peaks. A climber might get to the top of a lesser peak only to discover that she had to descend before scaling a higher one. When on a metaphorical lower peak, active ways of getting off it can be highly beneficial. In practice, this could mean that the activities involved in play discover possibilities that are better than those obtained without play.

Testing the Hypotheses about Function

The utility to an individual of having a characteristic that enhances its chances of surviving and reproducing is testable in principle but much less often so in practice. Evidence for the utility of play has not been readily forthcoming (Martin & Caro 1985). Nevertheless, play has real biological costs. Animals expend more energy and expose themselves to greater risks of injury and predation when they are playing than when they are resting. Play makes them more conspicuous and less vigilant. For example, young Southern fur seals are much more likely to be killed by sea lions when they are playing in the sea than at other times when they are in the sea (Harcourt 1991). The costs of play must presumably be outweighed by its benefits, otherwise animals that played would be at a disadvantage compared with those that did not. Among the suggested costs for human children are poor socialisation, physical fitness, mental health and creativity. If play is beneficial, then it follows that depriving the young animal of opportunities for play should have harmful effects on the outcome of its development other things being equal.

Play interactions by rats enhanced their subsequent behavioural plasticity and response to novel situations. Rats were reared from 20 to 50 days in one of three conditions: in pairs; or in isolation with or without one hour of daily play-fighting experience (Einon & Potegal 1991). They were rehoused in small groups at 50 days, when the frequency of play starts to wane, so that they were not isolated at the time of testing. They were tested for how they responded defensively at 80 to 100 days by being placed in the home cage of another adult for 10 minutes. Play-deprived animals spent significantly more time immobile after they had been attacked than did animals of the other two groups. The increased immobility associated with play fighting deprivation was not caused by baseline differences in emotionality such as those elicited by a novel environment, the presence of a strange animal, or non-social aversive stimuli. Furthermore, play-deprived rats were not more reactive when pinched with forceps to stimulate a bite delivered by a conspecific, whether or not another rat was present behind a divider.

The deprivation experiments suggest that previously isolated rats' greater reactivity is restricted to situations involving pain coupled with close proximity to and contact with another rat. Since no differences in defensive behaviour occur, the maladaptive effect of play deprivation would seem to be specific.

A different approach to understanding the functions of play relies on correlations between the behaviour of young animals and their subsequent lives. Play and survival were observed in the offspring of 11 families of individually identified, free-ranging brown bears in Alaska (Fagen & Fagen 2004). Cubs which played more during their first summer survived better from their first summer to the end of their second summer. This could have been for a variety of reasons. The Fagens examined statistically several potential confounding factors: cub condition, prenatal and first-year salmon availability (an important resource for bears) and maternal characteristics (Fagen & Fagen 2009). Controlling for these factors confirmed that the more the bears had played when they were cubs, the more likely they were to survive to their first year. The association between amount of play and survival persisted into subsequent years of the bears' lives when they reached independence. The amount of play accounted for 35% of the variance in the percentage that survived. Just how play benefited the bear cubs could not be determined, but the pre-adult mortality might result

from events occurring during the stressful environmental conditions of winter hibernation and early spring. Resistance to exposure and infectious disease might be involved. Possibly play produces a more resilient individual both behaviourally and immunologically. If so, it would be capable of withstanding stress in ways that physical condition alone would not predict. In other populations or species, these same factors could still be important, but in different ways – in mediating development and performance of behaviour patterns involving predator avoidance and defence, for example. Predator avoidance and defence necessarily involve cognition and emotion, whether the argument is made in physiological or behavioural terms.

In a study of feral horses, maternal condition influenced play behaviour only in males, with sons of mothers in good condition playing more (Cameron et al. 2008). When a son and a daughter of the same mother were compared, the daughter played more when its mother was in poor condition and the son played more when its mother was in good condition. Mothers of foals that played more lost more condition and weaned their foals earlier, indicating that play behaviour was affected by maternal investment. An important finding of the study was that those individuals that played more survived better and had better body condition as yearlings despite weaning earlier.

In both the studies of free-living bears and horses, it remains possible that an unmeasured third variable explained the results. The individuals that played less may have been less healthy from the outset. Nevertheless, the results are consistent with the hypothesis that playing when young reaps benefits later in life.

CREATIVE ANIMALS

In one of Aesop's fables, a crow, half-dead with thirst, came upon a pitcher but found very little water in it. He could not reach far enough down with his beak to get at the water. After many attempts, he took a pebble and dropped it into the pitcher. He went on dropping in pebbles, raising the water level a little at a time, until at last he was able to reach the water.

The fable has now become a reality, not with a crow, but with another member of the crow family, the rook (Bird & Emery 2009). In the rook's case, the prize was a mealworm lying on the surface of water in a transparent plastic tube. The rook could not reach the mealworm with her beak, but just as in Aesop's fable, when given a pile of pebbles, the bird dropped pebbles into the water one by one until she had raised the water level enough and she could reach the larva.

The experiment was extended with two Eurasian Jays, also members of the crow family (Cheke, Bird & Clayton 2011). The birds were given piles of two different types of object that could be dropped into the water. One was a pile of pebbles and one was a pile of pieces of cork of the same size as the pebbles. The Jays quickly discriminated between the pebbles that raised the water level and the corks that floated on top and did nothing to raise the level.

Many years before, similar examples of apparently immediate and insightful understanding of problems were found in chimpanzees (Köhler 1925). When a banana was suspended out of reach of the chimps, they piled wooden boxes on top of each other so that the banana was within reach when they climbed on top of the platform they had created for themselves. In another experiment, Köhler gave the chimps sticks which could be slotted together and used to reach bananas placed more than arm's length away outside their cage. The chimps seemed to have a clear idea of what to do in each case. In Köhler's phrase, they were "unwaveringly purposeful". No trial and error was required. They had insight into the problems Köhler had set for them. It was as though they said to themselves: "Aha, I know what to do."

Innovatory use of tools has been frequently observed in both birds and mammals. Among the birds, members of the crow and parrot families provide striking examples. In particular, the kea (Huber, Rechberger & Taborsky 2001) and the New Caledonian crow (Hunt 1996) are especially remarkable. The two species were compared using a box that could be accessed in different ways (Auersperg et al. 2011). Food could be extracted by four different techniques, two of them involving tools. If a stick tool was used, it had to be manipulated so that a food reward could be knocked off a pole and delivered to

a point where the bird could get it. If a marble ball was used as a tool, it had to be inserted into an opening, which connected to a tube directed at the central pole on which was placed a food reward. When inserted into the tube, the marble rolled down the tube and knocked the reward off the pole and the food was again delivered to a point where the bird could get it. The crows were more efficient in using the stick tool, the kea the ball tool. The differences reflected in part the ease with which the two species could handle the tools.

Dolphins and related sea mammals are extraordinarily creative. In captive conditions, rough-toothed dolphins were trained to produce novel behaviours on command, and were reinforced for doing so (Pryor, Haag & O'Reilly 1969). This procedure resulted in significant increases in novel behaviour, and demonstrated that the dolphins could remember behaviour patterns that they had already performed and could learn to produce novel patterns for which they had not previously been trained. In the wild, the generation of bubbles from their blowhole under water was used by a bottlenose dolphin to drive its fish prey to the surface, where it could readily catch them (Fertl & Wilson 1997).

A remarkable example of innovation is the cooperative foraging in small groups of humpbacked whales observed in south-east Alaska and the west coast of South America. Many species of marine mammals use bubbles to catch prey, but some humpbacked whales are unique in the elaborate way they use the bubbles to surround shoals of herrings. One whale blows a long, circular line of bubbles that rises to make a curtain. Other whales make calls that drive the herring towards the bubble wall. As the fish come close to the bubbles, the bubble-blowing whale encloses the wall of bubbles around them, creating a cylinder with the fish trapped inside. The other whales position themselves at the bottom of the cylinder and the herring flee upwards, driven by the whales' calls from beneath them. The whales move upwards together and as they approach the surface, each one opens its mouth wide and consumes the fish in a big gulp. With its buccal cavity full, the whale closes its mouth and forces all of the water out by straining it through the baleen that hangs down from the palate. This keeps all of the food inside while getting rid of the water. At this point, the whales can swallow their food (Wiley et al. 2011). This remarkable technique occurs in only a few populations of humpbacked whales, most notably those feeding in southern Alaska, suggesting that at one point it was an innovation.

These examples of innovative solutions to problems suggest remarkable cognitive abilities on the part of animals. But how did these abilities develop? One possibility is that they are expressed spontaneously, involving little or no dependence on relevant previous experience.

Another possibility often raised in discussions of innovation is that the individual generalised from experience obtained in other contexts (Shettleworth 2010). In the course of play earlier in their lives, individuals discovered properties of the environment that proved crucial when they were later faced with a new challenge. Young crows are extremely playful, actively manipulating objects in ways that could reveal much about what leads to what. They certainly pick up small stones and they may even drop them into puddles, raising the level of the water. Similarly, young chimps readily play with sticks, and if they had been given bamboo sticks they might have discovered that the smaller one could be threaded inside the hole of the larger one and so create a longer stick. This was supported by one small-scale experiment which indicated that a chimp with prior opportunity to play with sticks solved the problem, whereas individuals that had not had such an opportunity failed (Birch 1945). As for the whales, their much better-studied relatives, the dolphins, are renowned for their playfulness. Maybe the whales too had put together their remarkable hunting technique from playfully blowing bubbles and learning that fish would not swim through a bubble screen. Then they cooperated to create a cylindrical screen and drive the fish upwards to the surface, where they could be caught easily.

WHAT IS CREATIVITY?

A broad distinction may be drawn between creativity and innovation (Bateson & Martin 2013). In human behaviour, creativity refers to coming up with a new idea, whereas innovation refers to changing the way things are done. Although creativity and innovation are often treated as synonymous, the terms can be usefully distinguished. Measures of human creativity have been strongly influenced by the distinction between converging and diverging styles of thought (Guilford 1956). When asked about what can be done with, say, a brick, the converger says it is used for building a wall. The diverger suggests many different uses, such as a doorstop, a hammer, breaking windows, repelling an attacker, grinding up to make red paste and so forth. The differences are measured by what is called the 'Alternate Uses Task'.

Torrance identified three main components of creativity: fluency, flexibility and originality (Torrance 1972). Fluency refers to the number of unique ideas that are generated when a person is asked about uses for a particular object. Flexibility refers to the capacity to switch between approaches; someone who generates ideas within one category will be perceived as less flexible than someone who generates ideas from multiple categories. Originality refers to the novelty of an idea without relying on routine or habitual thought. It is possible for somebody to be fluent without being original or original without being fluent. A fluent person might come up with a long list of commonplace uses for a brick. An original person would suggest uses no one had thought of before.

Creativity is usually necessary for innovation, but it is not sufficient. Indeed, the most creative people are often not the best innovators. In the arts and sciences, the distinction may be blurred because creativity does not necessarily involve implementation of any kind. Creativity is regarded as innovative because judgement is involved and the outcome affects others. The distinction between creativity and innovation is not nearly so clear in many of the animal examples. Even so, considerable time can elapse between a creative act and a subsequent innovation. In humans, some individuals are better at being creative than they are at being innovative, and some innovators rely on the ideas of others. In animals, that difference is harder to observe and generally what is seen is the end product of what may be a long process. The exceptions are the novel behaviour patterns expressed by dolphins.

LINKS BETWEEN PLAYFULNESS AND CREATIVITY

Play involves breaking the rules. Playful play involves having fun while doing so. From the play may emerge a new perspective or a tool that might be used at a later date in combination with other tools to solve a new challenge. In their different ways, both of these aspects of play are creative.

Wolfgang Amadeus Mozart was well known, notorious even, for his playfulness. The high-spirited pranks and jokes were reflected in his music. For example, his three-voice canon (KV 559) consists of a nonsensical Latin text which when sung sounds like bawdy German. Pablo Picasso was once filmed painting onto glass. The onlooker saw the picture emerge, but viewed from the other side of the glass. Picasso started by quickly sketching a goat and then rapidly embellishing it. Other shapes appeared and disappeared; colours were mixed and transformed. By the end of the film, the goat had long since gone and it would have been hard to say what the picture was all about. Picasso had been playing – probably showing off – but clearly enjoying himself hugely.

M. C. Escher wrote about his art in the following way: "I can't keep from fooling around with our irrefutable certainties. It is, for example, a pleasure knowingly to mix up two- and three-dimensionalities, flat and spatial, and to make fun of gravity." Famous products of this approach were his impossible staircases.

The discoverer of the antibacterial properties of penicillin, Alexander Fleming, was famous for his playfulness. He was accused disapprovingly by his boss of treating research like a game, finding it all great fun. When asked what he did, he said: "I play with microbes" and went on "it is very pleasant to break the rules and to be able to find something that nobody had thought of". Another famously playful scientist and Nobel prize-winner was Richard Feynman. When he was getting bored with physics at an early stage in his career, he wrote: "Physics disgusts me a little bit now, but I used to enjoy doing physics. Why did I enjoy it? I used to play with it. I used to do whatever I felt like doing – it didn't have to do with whether it was important for the development of nuclear physics, but whether it was

interesting and amusing for me to play with." He decided that he would play with physics again irrespective of how important it might be. Then, while playing at work, everything flowed effortlessly and he made fundamental contributions to nuclear physics.

Social play is marked by the cooperation between the partners. It is non-competitive and roles may be reversed. So individuals that are dominant in non-playful contexts may allow themselves to adopt a subordinate role during play. Sometimes the playfulness is explicit. Jim Watson described the playful nature of scientific creativity when he and Francis Crick had set themselves the task of uncovering the structure of DNA (Watson 1968). Their main working tool had been a set of coloured balls superficially resembling the toys of preschool children. Watson wrote: "All we had to do was to construct a set of molecular models and begin to play – with luck, the structure would be a helix." It was indeed a helix and the paired structure of the helix provided the means for the molecule to replicate itself. Another example of the role of playfulness in cooperative scientific creativity is provided by Andre Geim and Konstantin Novoselov, who won the 2010 Nobel Prize for physics. The prize was awarded for their discovery of the wonder material graphene. Although I shall not develop the distinction here, generating novel ideas and implementing them seem to involve different cognitive styles. The people who are most creative are very often not those who test them and develop them into useful products.

The celebrated examples of playful people who are also enormously creative are striking, but they may be exceptional. Is this link between playfulness and creativity more general? To find out, people were asked in an online survey whether they viewed themselves as playful and creative (Bateson & Nettle 2014). The respondents were presented with a series of statements and asked to state whether each one was very characteristic of themselves and, if so, to score 1 or very uncharacteristic of themselves and, if so, to score 7. They could score anywhere between 1 and 7 depending on their sense of how the statement reflected their own behaviour. "Acting playfully" and "Coming up with new ideas" were the statements in which we were particularly interested. These statements were embedded in a number of other statements designed to assess different dimensions of personality (Nettle 2007). A total of 1,536 people responded to the survey. The individuals who reckoned that they were playful also reckoned that they were creative. The correlation between "Acting playfully" and "Coming up with new ideas" was massively significant. To validate this finding, the respondents were asked to offer ideas for the uses of two items, a jam jar and a paperclip. Those individuals who produce few answers are referred to as 'convergers' and those who produce many suggestions are known as 'divergers'. The typical response from a converger when asked for uses for a paper clip was "Clip paper together." The response from one diverger (presumably a woman) was: "Clip papers, unfold to clean fingernails, clip bra, general clothes fixing in an emergency, put on a magnet for a science experiment for children, make a mobile with lots of them, make a sculpture with one or more of them, earrings, pick a lock." The respondents who regarded themselves as playful and producers of new ideas were massively more likely to give lots of uses for a jam jar and a paper clip.

Creativity can be influenced by specific forms of education. Courses to enhance creativity in adults have been established and are sometimes successful. Practical measures can also help. Even so, a number of obstacles lie in the path of personal creativity (Csikszentmihalyi 1996). Exhaustion from too many demands, distractions that fragment thought, plain laziness, and lack of direction can all get in the way of being creative. Csikszentmihalyi argued that all of these can be overcome and offered advice on how to do it. The first step, he suggested, is to free up time from the pursuit of predictable goals in order to engage curiosity and look for surprises. With mental energy enhanced, Csikszentmihalyi recommended deliberately avoiding time-wasting distractions, such as aimlessly watching television, and making use of the natural rhythms of the body since most people are especially productive at certain times of the day. He also suggested finding particular spaces and places that enhance reflective thought and creativity.

Mood is crucial. Many authors have noted how a positive state of mind stimulates creativity (Lyubomirsky, King & Diener 2005). That positive state can be enhanced by humour. Humour and play have common features. They both involve social signals, are associated with a positive mood and are sensitive to prevailing conditions. They both tend to occur in protected environments, they are intrinsically motivated and they do not require additional external reward. Certain forms of humour, like play, rely on generating novel combinations of thoughts and the consequences can be highly creative. These links between playfulness and humour may be much more than mere analogies. Playfulness encourages humour and humour encourages playfulness and the result is greater creativity. Another way of enhancing creativity, though controversial, is through the use of drugs.

PSYCHOACTIVE DRUGS AND RITUALS

Numerous drugs besides alcohol have been used to create altered states of consciousness in many different cultures for thousands of years and are commonly used in present-day rituals. Opium from a poppy, cocaine from the leaves of the coca plant, mescalin from the Peyote cactus, ergot from the Claviceps fungi that infect grasses such as rye, psilocybin from 200 species of Basidiomycota mushrooms and many more examples all contain a psychoactive substance.

The psychological experience induced in humans under the influence of psychedelic drugs is multifarious and idiosyncratic, but nevertheless a broad range of common characteristics has been identified (Sessa 2008). These include alterations in the user's perceptions (in all the sensory modalities), changes in the emotions and expansion in an individual's thinking and identity. A particular feature of the experience encompassed by all these characteristics has special relevance to the creative process. The feature is a general increase in the ability to deal with complexity and an increase in openness, such that the usual restraints that encourage humans to accept preconceived ideas about themselves and the world around them are challenged. Another important feature is the tendency for users to assign unique and novel meanings to their experience. When drugs do have some effect, they vary enormously in how they act on the brain.

In the extensive research carried out on psychoactive drugs, the emphasis has been on experiences that enable people to perceive things in a different way or to connect previously unrelated bits of information. Here the link with play is analogous. Altered states of consciousness induced by some psychoactive drugs occur in protected contexts, for example. More importantly, when people are in such states, they combine thoughts in novel ways. These effects may be relevant to the conditions in which rituals are established.

CONCLUSIONS

The word *play* is used in many ways that have nothing to do with the activities in animals and human children described by biologists and psychologists. Playful behaviour in the sense I have used it in this chapter is defined by pointing to examples that people readily recognise once they have been shown them. It may involve novel combinations of actions. Some actions occur outside their usual context and may be exaggerated. In the social play of animals, roles may be reversed with the dominant individual handicapping itself. A core feature of play is its intrinsic motivation, which is powerful while it lasts. No additional external reward is required. Playful play is associated with a positive mood and when it occurs is taken as an indicator of well-being. The mood is typically suppressed by illness, anxiety or chronic stress and is highly sensitive to prevailing conditions.

Does any of what is known about play in the sense used by biologists and psychologists help in understanding the origins of ritual? At the outset of this chapter I expressed scepticism. Even so, the positive mood associated with play and the creativity associated with playfulness may provide some pointers to what happens when humans establish new rituals. So once the different use of terms are set on one side, the work on animals may have something to contribute after all.

REFERENCES

Auersperg, A. M. I., von Bayern, A. M. P., Gajdon, G. K., Huber, L. & Kacelnik, A. 2011. Flexibility in problem solving and tool use of kea and New Caledonian crows in a multi access box paradigm. *PLoSone* 6, e20231.

Auger, A. P. & Olesen, K. M. 2009. Brain sex differences and the organisation of juvenile social play behaviour. *Journal of Neuroendocrinology* 21, 519–25.

Bateson, P. 1981. Discontinuities in development and changes in the organization of play in cats, eds K. Immelmann, G. W. Barlow, L. Petrinovich & M. Main, *Behavioral Development*. Cambridge: Cambridge University Press, 281–95.

Bateson, P. 2011. Theories of play, ed. A. D. Pellegrini. *The Oxford Handbook of the Development of Play*. New York: Oxford University Press, 41–7.

Bateson, P. 2014. Play, playfulness, creativity and innovation. *Animal Behavior and Cognition* 1, 99–112.

Bateson, P. & Martin, P. 2013. *Play, Playfulness, Creativity and Innovation*. Cambridge: Cambridge University Press.

Bateson, P. & Nettle, D. 2014. Playfulness, ideas and creativity: a survey. *Creativity Research Journal* 26, 219–22.

Birch, H. G. 1945. The relation of previous experience to insightful problem-solving. *Journal of Comparative Psychology* 38, 367–83.

Bird, C. D. & Emery, N. J. 2009. Rooks use stones to raise the water level to reach a floating worm. *Current Biology* 19, 1410–14.

Burghardt, G. M. 2005. *The Genesis of Animal Play: Testing the Limits*. Cambridge, MA: MIT Press.

Cameron, E. Z., Linklater, W. L., Stafford, K. J. & Minot, E. O. 2008. Maternal investment results in better foal condition through increased play behaviour in horses. *Animal Behaviour* 76, 1511–18.

Cheke, L. D., Bird, C. D. & Clayton, N. S. 2011. Tool-use and instrumental learning in the Eurasian jay (Garrulus glandarius). *Animal Cognition* 14, 441–55.

Csikszentmihalyi, M. 1996. *Creativity: Flow and the Psychology of Discovery and Invention*. New York: HarperCollins.

Einon, D. & Potegal, M. 1991. Enhanced defense in adult-rats deprived of playfighting experience as juveniles. *Aggressive Behavior* 17, 27–40.

Fagen, R. 1981. *Animal Play Behavior*. New York: Oxford University Press.

Fagen, R. & Fagen, J. 2004. Juvenile survival and benefits of play behaviour in brown bears, *Ursus arctos*. *Evolutionary Ecology Research* 6, 89–102.

Fagen, R. & Fagen, J. 2009. Play behaviour and multi-year juvenile survival in free-ranging brown bears, *Ursus arctos*. *Evolutionary Ecology Research* 11, 1–15.

Fertl, D. & Wilson, B. 1997. Bubble use during prey capture by a lone bottlenose dolphin (*Tursiops truncatus*). *Aquatic Mammals* 23, 113–14.

Gomendio, M. 1988. The development of different types of play in gazelles: implications for the nature and functions of play. *Animal Behaviour* 36, 825–36.

Graves, P. L. 1976. Nutrition, infant behavior, and maternal characteristics: a pilot study in West Bengal, India. *American Journal of Clinical Nutrition* 29, 305–19.

Guilford, J. P. 1956. Structure of intellect. *Psychological Bulletin* 53, 267–93.

Harcourt, R. 1991. Survivorship costs of play in the South American fur seal. *Animal Behaviour* 42, 509–11.

Hausberger, M., Fureix, C., Bourjade, M., Wessel-Robert, S. & Richard-Yris, M.-A. 2012. On the significance of adult play: what does social play tell us about adult horse welfare? *Naturwissenschaften* 99, 291–302.

Held, S. D. E. & Spinka, M. 2011. Animal play and animal welfare. *Animal Behaviour* 81, 891–9.

Huber, L., Rechberger, S. & Taborsky, M. 2001. Social learning affects object exploration and manipulation in keas, *Nestor notabilis*. *Animal Behaviour* 62, 945–54.

Humphreys, A. P. & Einon, D. F. 1981. Play as a reinforcer for maze-learning in juvenile rats. *Animal Behaviour* 29, 259–70.

Hunt, G. R. 1996. Manufacture and use of hook-tools by New Caledonian crows. *Nature* 379, 249–51.

Jensen, M. B. 1999. Effects of confinement on rebounds of locomotor behaviour of calves and heifers, and the spatial preferences of calves. *Applied Animal Behaviour Science* 62, 43–56.

Kahlenberg, S. M. & Wrangham, R. W. 2010. Sex differences in chimpanzees' use of sticks as play objects resemble those of children. *Current Biology* 20, R1067–8.

Köhler, W. 1925. *The Mentality of Apes*. London: Paul, Trench & Trubner.

Kuczaj, S. A., Makecha, R., Trone, M., Paulos, R. D. & Ramos, J. A. A. 2006. Role of peers in cultural innovation and cultural transmission: evidence from the play of dolphin calves. *International Journal of Comparative Psychology* 19, 223–40.

Lyubomirsky, S., King, L. & Diener, E. 2005. The benefits of frequent positive affect: does happiness lead to success? *Psychological Bulletin* 131, 803–55.

Manning, A. & Dawkins, M. S. 2012. *An Introduction to Animal Behaviour*. 6th edition. Cambridge: Cambridge University Press.

Martin, P. & Caro, T. M. 1985. On the functions of play and its role in behavioral development. *Advances in the Study of Behavior* 15, 59–103.

Meaney, M. J. & Stewart, J. 1985. Sex differences in social play: the socialization of sex roles. *Advances in the Study of Behavior* 15, 1–58.

Mendl, M. 1988. The effects of litter-size variation on the development of play-behaviour in the domestic cat – litters of one and two. *Animal Behaviour* 36, 20–34.

Milteer, R. M. & Ginsburg, K. R. 2012. The importance of play in promoting healthy child development and maintaining strong parent–child bond: focus on children in poverty. *Pediatrics* 129, e204–13.

Nettle, D. 2007. *Personality: What Makes You the Way You Are*. Oxford: Oxford University Press.

Panksepp, J. 1998. *Affective Neuroscience*. New York: Oxford University Press.

Pellegrini, A. D. 2009. *The Role of Play in Human Development*. Oxford: Oxford University Press.

Power, T. G. 2000. *Play and Exploration in Children and Animals*. Mahwah, NJ: Erlbaum.

Pruitt, J. N., Burghardt, G. M. & Riechert, S. E. 2012. Non-conceptive sexual behavior in spiders: a form of play associated with body condition, personality type, and male intrasexual selection. *Ethology* 118, 33–40.

Pryor, K. W., Haag, R. & O'Reilly, J. 1969. The creative porpoise: training for novel behavior. *Journal of the Experimental Analysis of Behavior* 12, 653–81.

Sessa, B. 2008. Is it time to revisit the role of psychedelic drugs in enhancing human creativity? *Journal of Psychopharmacology* 22, 821–7.

Sharpe, L. L., Clutton-Brock, T. H., Brotherton, P. N. M., Cameron, E. Z. & Cherry, M. I. 2002. Experimental provisioning increases play in free-ranging meerkats. *Animal Behaviour* 64, 113–21.

Shettleworth, S. J. 2010. *Cognition, Evolution and Behavior* 2nd edition. New York: Oxford University Press.

Sigman, M., Neumann, C., Baksh, M., Bwibo, N. & McDonald, M. A. 1989. Relationship between nutrition and development in Kenyan toddlers. *Journal of Pediatrics* 115, 357–64.

Smith, P. K. 2010. *Children and Play*. Chichester: Wiley-Blackwell.

Sutton-Smith, B. 1997. *The Ambiguity of Play*. Cambridge, MA: Harvard University Press.

Torrance, E. P. 1972. Predictive validity of Torrance tests of creative thinking. *Journal of Creative Behavior* 6, 236–52.

Watson, J. 1968. *The Double Helix: A Personal Account of the Discovery of the Structure of DNA*. New York: Scribner.

West, M. 1974. Social play in the cat. *American Zoologist* 14, 427–36.

Wiley, D., Ware, C., Bocconcelli, A., Cholewiak, D., Friedlaender, A., Thompson, M. et al. 2011. Underwater components of humpback whale bubble-net feeding behaviour. *Behaviour* 148, 575–602.

5

PRETEND AND SOCIO-DRAMATIC PLAY IN EVOLUTIONARY AND DEVELOPMENTAL PERSPECTIVE

PETER K. SMITH

Helen, a four-year-old, is sitting in a playhouse, by a table with a plastic cup, saucer and teapot. She calls out, 'I'm just getting tea ready! Come on, it's dinner time now!' Charlotte, also four, answers 'Wait!'; she wraps up a teddy in a cloth in a pram, comes in and sits opposite Helen, who says, 'I made it on my own! I want a drink.' (She picks up the teapot.) 'There's only one cup – for me!' (pretends to pour tea into only one cup). Charlotte pretends to pour from the teapot into an imaginary cup, which she then pretends to drink from. Darren, a three-year-old, approaches. Charlotte goes and closes the door, shutting a pretend bolt and turning a pretend key; but Helen says, 'No, he's daddy; you're daddy aren't you?' (to Darren). Charlotte 'unbolts' and 'unlocks' the door, and Darren comes in (Author's observations in a playgroup).

Pretend or fantasy play is a fascinating aspect of the behaviour of children from around two to six years of age. Pretence and fantasy are generally taken to mean an 'as if …' orientation; actions, objects and verbalisations have non-literal meanings. A circular motion of hands represents turning a steering wheel; a wooden block represents a cake; a grunting noise represents a bear growling. Often, such play involves distinct pretend roles such as mummy, fireman, doctor, monster.

PRETEND OR FANTASY PLAY IN NON-HUMAN SPECIES

There are clear similarities in the kinds of rough-and-tumble play and sensorimotor object play seen in mammals, and especially the non-human primates, and in human children (Burghardt, Chapter 3, this volume; Bateson, Chapter 4, this volume). But in the case of pretend play, matters are different. At least by the common criteria we use for assessing pretend play in human children (that is, non-literal meaning of actions, objects and verbalisations), it would appear to be entirely lacking in most animal species.

A possible candidate for pretence in other species would be play signals such as the play face, or play bow, which signals playful rather than aggressive intent in mammals such as monkeys, canids, felids, ursids (Bekoff & Allen 1998); these might be argued to have an 'as if' meaning. Indeed play-fighting itself could be seen as non-literal in the sense that the apparently aggressive actions are not actually aggressive (Mitchell 2007). However, the usual argument against taking such behaviours as pretence is that these are simply pre-programmed signals or actions, seen only in play, which indicate playful intent by the actor (Gómez & Martín-Andrade 2005). There is no awareness of pretence or intention to pretend or deceive; "the simulation is in the eye of the observer, not the player" (Mitchell 2007, 64).

If we see awareness and intention as part of the definition of pretend, then we can view pretend play as part of a package of symbolic abilities, including self-awareness, Theory of Mind and language, which characterises humans and of which we see only simple precursors even in the cognitively most advanced non-human species. Any exceptions to the absence of pretend play in animals may be found with the great apes (Gómez & Martín-Andrade 2005).

There are some accounts of what might count as pretend play in the great apes. Hayes (1951) reared a young chimpanzee, Viki, and provided an account of how she apparently had an imaginary pull-toy. This was when she actually did drag real pull-toys behind her. Hayes observed Viki walking along making tugging motions with one hand behind her. She also placed one hand above the other as if raising the imaginary toy. These actions were seen several times with some variations. At a similar anecdotal level, Morris (1962) recounts how, after a visit to a vet for an injection, a chimpanzee gave itself pretend injections, making the appropriate hand movements.

Other examples in enculturated chimpanzees (those reared by humans in a largely human environment) include Washoe, the first sign-language-taught chimpanzee, washing a doll in water in a bathtub; and Austin, a chimpanzee trained to use lexigrams, who ate as if using an imaginary spoon from an imaginary plate and rolling it around his lips. Amongst bonobos, de Waal (1989) has described games of blind man's bluff, and Savage-Rumbaugh (1986) described how Kanzi, also taught lexigrams like Austin, would hide and eat imaginary food.

Matevia, Patteson and Hillix (2002) brought up a gorilla called Koko to learn sign language. Koko was reported to take part in a variety of pretend episodes. These included using signs, for example kissing a doll and signing 'good'; and pretending to drink from an empty cup and signing 'sip'. She also made loud slurping sounds while 'drinking' from an empty cup.

Documented cases of great ape pretend in the wild are rare, but Gómez and Martín-Andrade (2005) quote a few possible examples: an eight-year-old male chimpanzee carried around a log in various positions reminiscent of carrying a baby, and an eight-year-old female broke off a stick and carried it similarly, following her mother who was indeed carrying a baby. Gómez and Martín-Andrade consider that such symbolic play (usually, 'doll' or maternal play) is "not a characteristic pattern of wild chimpanzees, but a marginal, exceptional occurrence" (2005, 147). Nevertheless, some more examples have been collated by Kahlenberg and Wrangham (2010).

All these accounts are of quite simple types of pretend play, which scarcely develop to role playing or any extended narrative sequences. However, they may suggest some simple abilities for pretence in the great apes. In this sense, they parallel corresponding evidence for simple abilities in theory of mind, language and self-recognition. Mitchell (2007) also mentions possible pretend play in dolphins: after seeing a person exhaling cigarette smoke, a young dolphin suckled a mouthful of milk from her mother, returned to the window where she saw the person, and squirted out the milk 'as if' it were smoke.

Do such examples actually merit being called pretend play? Lillard (1994, 214), writing about human children, defined pretence as requiring six features: a *pretender*, a *reality*, and a *mental representation* that is *projected onto reality*, with *awareness* and *intention* on the part of that pretender. This is a 'tough' definition of pretence; it implies conscious intention, and an awareness of both the pretend reality and the actual reality, and thus some meta-representational ability. This would rule out most or all non-human pretence. It would also rule out much pretend play in infants (from 15 months to two years) (Jarrold et al. 1994). Generally, both non-human pretence, and that of young infants too, comprises simple, imitative actions done in a non-functional context ('feeding' or cuddling a 'baby', for example). We do not know to what extent the pretender is 'aware' of intentionally simulating reality. We only become confident of this when slightly older children use language to explicitly assign roles ('you be daddy') or negotiate or explain pretence ('it's not for real; we're only pretending').

Mitchell (2007, 53–4) provides a definition of pretence as: "Pretending is intentionally allowing an idea, at least part of which an agent knows to be inaccurate about or unrelated to current reality (i.e. fictional), to guide and constrain the agent's behaviors (including mental states)." This does not require the same level of conscious awareness as Lillard's. Mitchell suggests some simpler precursors to full-blown pretence: he describes 'schematic play' as "enactment of schemas based on relatively canalized processes for perceptual-motor integration that is not based on associative learning or imitation of another's actions" (2007, 64). This could apply to play fighting and use of play signals. He continues with the concept of 'pre-symbolic play' or functional symbolic play, as imitation; plus some ability in visual-kinaesthetic matching – the ability to recognise the spatial or bodily similarity between their visual experience of another and their own kinaesthetic experience, and make some matching action to that observed. Procedures visually observed in others ('feeding a baby') may be imitated through one's own body actions, as in the maternal or 'doll' play examples sometimes reported in great apes.

Verbal self-report is important in knowing whether play with objects involves pretence. Smilansky (1968) distinguished construction play from symbolic or pretend play, and a three- or four-year-old child assembling bricks or Lego might be classed as engaged in construction play. However, if you ask that child, 'tell me what you are doing?', they may reply 'making a spaceship' or 'making a cage to put monsters in' (Takhvar & Smith 1990). It is the verbal report that allows us to infer an awareness of intent to pursue a non-literal idea and to be confident of symbolic pretend play.

THE DEVELOPMENT OF PRETEND PLAY IN CHILDREN

The beginnings of pretend or fantasy play in children can be seen from about 12–15 months of age. Piaget (1951) described this in detail, recording the behaviour of his children. Many studies of pretend play around the 1970s were carried out by watching a child when he or she was put with some objects in a laboratory playroom. This had the advantage of a standardised procedure in documenting age trends. Such work (e.g. Fenson et al. 1972) identified three developmental trends, also obvious from observational studies such as Piaget's. These were *decentration*, *decontextualisation* and *integration*.

Decentration refers to incorporating others into pretend activities. Usually, young children do pretend actions first with themselves, then with another object or person. For example, Piaget's daughter Jacqueline started with pretending to sleep on a cloth herself, and later got her toy animals to do so. Another common action is to pretend to feed a doll with an empty cup. By around 24 months, the child

can get the doll itself to act as an agent, rather than have things done to it.

Early pretend play also depends heavily on realistic objects – dolls, and actual cups, combs, spoons, etc., or realistic substitutes. *Decontextualisation* refers to the ability to use less realistic substitute objects – for example, a wooden block as a 'cake', or a stick as a 'gun'. The more different the object from its referent, the more difficulty children have in using it in a pretend way; but adults can help the process by modelling or prompting the pretend use. Fein (1975) presented two-year-olds with either realistic objects (plastic cup; detailed horse model) or less realistic objects (clam shell; vaguely horsey shape). After modelling by an adult, 93% of two-year-olds would imitate making a detailed horse model 'drink' from a plastic cup; however, only 33% would imitate making a vaguely horsey shape 'drink' from a clam shell. The less realistic objects made the pretence more difficult, especially as two substitutions were needed (the horsey shape and the clam shell). If the horse or the cup alone were realistic, 79% and 61% of the children respectively could imitate successfully.

By three years of age, this kind of decontextualised pretence occurs much more spontaneously in children's play. They also begin to incorporate imaginary objects or actions, without any real or substitute object being present. While possible for three- and four-year-olds, this is easier still in middle childhood. Overton and Jackson (1973) asked children of different ages to pretend to brush their teeth or comb their hair. They found that three- and four-year-olds mostly used a substitute body part, such as a finger, as the brush or comb, whereas most six-to-eight-year-olds (and indeed, adults) imagined the brush or comb in their hand.

Integration refers to combining a number of pretend acts, and perhaps actors, into some kind of narrative sequence. For example, a child might put a teddy to bed, wake it up, wash it and feed it breakfast. Perhaps another teddy will be brought along to play with it.

Solitary and Social Pretend Play

The studies during the 1970s and 1980s were mostly based on observations in constrained laboratory situations, where infants were provided with particular toys. Basically, these were observations of solitary play. Limitations of this approach were highlighted by Haight and Miller (1993), based on video films of children playing at home. This was a naturalistic longitudinal study, from 12 months to 48 months. While a minority of the pretend play they observed was solitary, about 75% of pretend play was social – first with mothers or parents, later with friends (peers). Even early pretend play was mostly social in character.

Howes and Matheson (1992) described stages in the development of social pretence, based on both the observational and experimental literature. The mother (or older partner, perhaps a sibling) typically has a 'scaffolding' role – supporting the play a lot at first, by, for example, suggesting and demonstrating actions. For instance, the mother might 'give teddy a bath' and then hand teddy to the infant. Thus a lot of early pretend play by the child is imitative; it tends to follow well-established 'scripts' or story lines, such as 'feeding the baby' or 'nursing the patient'. Realistic props help to sustain pretend play, but as children get to three or four years, they are less reliant on older partners and realistic props. They take a more active role in initiating pretend play; they adapt less realistic objects or even just imagine the object completely; and they show an awareness of play conventions and negotiate roles within play sequences.

Socio-dramatic Play

From three years onwards, pretend play very commonly involves social role-playing skills with peers. The term *socio-dramatic play* was brought into prominence by Smilansky (1968). This refers to dramatic play (the child is clearly enacting a role) that is also social. Typically, two to six children may be involved at any one time: it is difficult, without the support of more publicly acknowledged rules, for young children to sustain larger numbers of participants over a period of time. Smilansky used other criteria for socio-dramatic play, such as a sustained narrative sequence lasting at least 10 minutes, but these further criteria were not widely used by others.

Smilansky argued that socio-dramatic play was very important in development, and this led her to develop 'play training' schemes. Providing suggestive props (dressing-up clothes, semi-realistic toys), and taking children on visits (e.g. to a zoo, a hospital) were helpful in facilitating socio-dramatic play, but these were much more effective if nursery staff themselves took a lead in initiating such play, suggesting themes and helping children sustain the narrative. In effect, nursery staff were providing the 'scaffolding' to get complex socio-dramatic play going, for children who (presumably) had lacked such scaffolding from parents previously. This technique has been used in supplementation studies of pretend and socio-dramatic play.

Language is often used playfully in socio-dramatic play episodes: 'Hello, my name is Mr Elephant!'; 'Hello, my name is Mr Donkey!' In school-age children, rhymes and wordplay are common. The repetition of well-known verses, with variations, has more in common with the rule-governed games common by the age of six or seven years.

Imaginary Companions

As pretend play becomes 'decontextualised' (freer from lifelike props such as dolls), many children not only make use of imaginary actions or objects, but actually develop an imaginary companion (IC). Young children talk to their ICs and engage in pretend activities with them, and complex narrative sequences and histories may be involved. The proportion of children having an IC varies from around 25% to 65% in different studies, and it is most frequent between three and eight years; they are mostly abandoned by 10 years (Taylor 1999).

Most evidence suggests that children with imaginary companions, while generally strong in pretend play orientation, are not confused about the status of their imaginary companions and are aware they are different from real friends. Taylor, Cartwright and Carlson (1993) compared 12 children with ICs to 15 who did not have ICs, at four years of age. Those with ICs provided stable descriptions of them over a seven-month period; they were more likely to engage in fantasy play in a free-play session; but did not differ from those without ICs in their ability to distinguish fantasy and reality.

Distinguishing Fantasy and Reality

When children are engaging in any pretend play, they do not usually confuse this with reality. This can happen sometimes: when an adult joins in with a one- or two-year-old's play, the child can be confused as to whether the adult is in 'pretend' or 'real' mode; for example, if a child knocks an empty cup over in play and mother says, 'you spilled your tea, better wipe it up,' the child may actually pick up a cloth to wipe it. However, more usually, and especially by three or four years, the pretence–reality distinction is a stable one. Suppose a child pretends a wooden block is a cake for a tea party; if she confused pretence and reality, she would actually try to eat the wooden block! This seldom happens! By three years, children often signal the pretend mode in their play, for example, 'let's pretend to be families. You be daddy.'

Direct interviews with three-year-olds also confirm that they can generally distinguish real from imaginary situations, and understand the use of the words 'real' and 'pretend'. Woolley and Wellman (1990) demonstrated that by three years, children use terms like 'real' and 'pretend' in sensible ways in actual play: 'you're not really dead, we're just playing.' They also do so in experimental tasks; for example, if the researcher pretends to brush her teeth, and asks, 'Am I really and truly brushing my teeth or am I pretending to brush my teeth?,' the great majority of three-year-olds answer correctly that this is pretence.

Gender Differences

There do not seem to be substantial differences in frequency of engaging in pretend play. Göncü, Patt and Kouba (2002) concluded that findings are inconsistent and dependent on the play environment, the toys available and the kinds of activities measured. However, there are sex differences in the themes of pretend play. While girls' pretend play often involves domestic themes, boys' pretend play is often more physically vigorous, rough-and-tumble type activity,

perhaps with superhero themes (Holland 2003). Girls seem to use their more mature language abilities in pretend play (Göncü et al. 2002). However, the rough-and-tumble type fantasy play more typical of boys generally involves more participants (Smith 2010).

Pretend Play and Friendship

Children's pretence is more sustained and complex when they are playing with friends, compared to acquaintances (Howes & Matteson 1992). The mutuality and emotional commitment of friends may motivate children to sustain cooperative interaction, plus they can predict better how a friend will respond to particular play suggestions.

Gottman (1983) examined the processes of developing and maintaining friendships in young children. He observed pairs of children (three to nine years) playing in their homes; in one study, the pairs were previously unacquainted, and Gottman observed them over three sessions. Often, children would establish a simple common-ground activity, such as colouring with crayons, that they could do side by side; they might 'escalate' this by 'information exchange' or 'self-disclosure', perhaps commenting on the other's activity, or saying something about what they liked or wished to do. If successful, the pair would move on to introducing a joint activity. Often, such a joint activity would involve pretend.

For example, Gottman (1983, 56–7) describes interactions between D (in his own house) and J (visiting), both young four-year olds. After some information exchange, J says, 'pretend like those little roll cookies too, OK?' and D replies, 'and make, um, make a, um, pancake, too'. Later D tries to introduce role play, and there is some negotiation: D: 'I'm the mummy.' J: 'Who am I?' D: 'Um, the baby.' J: 'Daddy.' D: 'Sister.' J: 'I wanna be the daddy.' D: 'You're the sister.' J: 'Daddy.' D: 'You're the big sister!' J: 'Don't play house. I don't want to play house.' Despite J offering progressively higher-status roles (but not equal to 'mummy'!), this negotiation ended in failure, and what Gottman calls a de-escalation. For a while they returned to pretend meal preparation.

Gottman describes the social skill of friendship formation as managing levels of closeness and conflict by escalating and when necessary deescalating levels of play. Colouring side by side has low risks and low benefits (in friendship terms). Simple pretend (e.g. pretending blocks are cookies) is a step up and role play a step further. Gottman argues that pretend play has a central role in the development of friendship.

Games with Rules

Games with rules are seen by developmental theorists, from Piaget onwards, as being a rather distinct category from play. The play of preschool children does often have some rule structure; for example, if someone is role playing 'doctor' to a 'patient', there are some constraints on what he or she is expected to do, exerted by the other participants. Nevertheless, any rules or constraints are largely private to that particular play episode, and can be changed at any time ('I'm not the doctor now, I'm a policeman'). By the time children are six or seven years old, rule-governed games like hopscotch, tag or football take up much more playground time. These are games with public rules, sometimes codified, with much less latitude for change. The transition from play to games is a gradual one; especially in younger children, game rules may be adapted to suit the circumstances and numbers of players available (Piaget 1951). Nevertheless, there are several distinctions between play and games, which are important as in some respects games may be more similar to rituals (Dissanayake, Chapter 7, this volume). Some differences between play and games are summarised in Table 5.1.

Pretend Play as a Universal Human Feature?

Fully developed pretend play, including role play and socio-dramatic play, seems universal in human societies, from anthropological accounts (Lancy 1996). There are variations in the amount and type of such play, and it is influenced by the extent to which play is culturally cultivated, accepted or curtailed (Gaskins 1999; see later in this chapter); but its presence appears ubiquitous.

Among hunter-gatherer peoples, Konner (1972) observed Kalahari San children using sticks and pebbles to represent village huts and herding cows. In the Hadza of Tanzania, children make dolls out of rags, and play at being predators (Blurton Jones 1993). Gosso and colleagues (2005, 233) not only describe pretend and fantasy play amongst South American Indian communities such as the Parakana, but state that "children of all forager groups studied exhibit fantasy play." Such play is generally tolerated by adults rather than encouraged and is generally imitative of adult roles in such societies. Gosso and colleagues (2005) argue that one of the functions of play is to keep children busy so that the adults can carry out their chores.

Amongst settled agricultural communities, again pretend play is generally present; but some reports suggest at low frequency. Gaskins (1999) observed children up to five years in a Mayan village community in the Yucatán, Mexico, and found that while pretend play happened, it was rare. Not only was it not encouraged by adults, but adults often placed early work demands on children. Even young children may be asked to help in looking after even younger siblings, running errands, scaring birds away from crops, preparing food, selling food etc.

Even when pretend play is not infrequent, it can often be rather formulaic in terms of what is enacted. Lancy (1996) described play in Kpelle children in Liberia. Pretend play was imitative of adult roles; for example, play at being a blacksmith involves the kinds of social roles (blacksmith, apprentice, client) and behavioural routines (fetching tools, lighting fire, hammering) that, in more complex forms, are seen in adult behaviour. Martini (1994) observed children in the Marquesas Islands, Polynesia; they generally played in groups, away from adult supervision. Fantasy play comprised about 12% of all play episodes observed. Of these, half consisted "of isolated episodes of using objects symbolically, such as making mud bananas", and about half involved scripts and roles, such as "ship" play, "fishing", "hunting" and "preparing feasts". According to Martini (1994, 84), "children … follow the same fantasy script from one performance to the next."

Table 5.1 Some comparative aspects of play and games in children

	Play	Games
Number of players	Seldom more than five or six	Can be much larger numbers in team games
Rule structure	If present, private to the players	Generally conform to more 'public' expectations
Constraints	Little constraint on course or ending of play	Constrained to follow certain procedure(s) and achieve certain outcome(s)
Audience	Usually no audience	Often an audience

Children with Autism

Children with disabilities may show some delay or difficulties in play. The syndrome that has attracted most research attention in relation to pretend play is autism. Many studies have shown that children with autism show less spontaneous pretend play than do control children matched for chronological or mental age, and what pretend play they do show tends to be repetitive and stereotyped (Jarrold 2003). This has been related to a meta-representational deficiency (i.e. a difficulty in mentally constructing representations of representations; for example, understanding that a block is not really a 'cake' but just a 'pretend cake') linking to their difficulties in theory of mind tasks. Other possibilities are that the difficulties are generative (following from a lack of flexibility or executive function), or that they result from a lack of motivation or incentive (Jarrold 2003; Kelly 2006).

Pretend Play as a Lifespan Activity

Although pretend play declines in frequency after middle childhood, it can be argued that it does not disappear. Göncü and Perone (2005) and Perone and Göncü (2014) consider that pretending forms a continuum from childhood to adulthood. In adulthood, people pretend in dramatic improvisations, poetry and dance; activities which enable ludic (playful or enjoyable) development of representations of experiences with affective significance. They argue that when Western adults pretend, for example in improvisational theatre, "they do it for the same reason as children, i.e. to relive and work through experiences of affective significance that they are not able to do in real life, except that adults' play consists of issues of

adult life and children's play consists of issues of their own kind" (Göncü and Perone 2005, 142).

PRETEND PLAY: THEORIES AND FUNCTIONS

Many theorists have suggested that pretend play has important functions in development. There are some good reasons to suppose that there are benefits to pretend play. These include the evolution of pretend play and its species-specific nature in humans, the cross-cultural universality, the deficits in pretend play in autism and some other conditions and the 'design features' of pretend play.

The Evolution of Pretend Play

The instances of pretend play in the great apes are relatively infrequent and quite simple. They do not take up any appreciable time or energy budget. There is no compelling argument for such play having a strong functional significance. Most likely, the episodes described are by-products of the evolution of symbolic intelligence, going along with abilities to imitate, visual-kinaesthetic matching, ability to recognise oneself in a mirror, proto-language abilities such as apes' signing and abilities to engage in tactical deception.

On this line of reasoning, the motivation for children to engage in pretend play and their facility in doing so would have evolved during hominid evolution, during the approximately 4 million years since the australopithecines branched off from other ape-like species. Harris (2000) and Carruthers (2002) place the origins of pretend play very recently in human evolution, with the advent of *homo sapiens* some 150,000 to 100,000 years ago. They cite the "sapient paradox" (Renfrew 2007); a postulated gap between the emergence of *homo sapiens* as a species, perhaps some 150,000 to 100,000 years ago, our dispersal from Africa some 70,000 to 50,000 years ago and the clear expression of many typically human behaviours not seen until the 'creative explosion' of the Upper Palaeolithic period about 40,000 years ago. This was manifested in new stone-tool industries, cave art, body ornaments, burial practices and a steady move towards engagement with the creative properties of stone, clay and metal from around 12,000 years ago. Harris (2000, x) sees this as evidence for "a new power of the imagination", the evolutionary emergence of which is related to the ontogenesis of pretend play in children. Carruthers (2002) suggests that during the 'gap', a childhood disposition for pretend play was selected for, over a period of perhaps 50,000–60,000 years. This selection would have been based on a pre-existing disposition to play (e.g. rough-and-tumble play).

Dating the emergence of pretend play so recently is interesting but very speculative. The existing evidence from the great apes suggests that the potential for pretend play may have been around at the time of the split, millions of years ago. If we assume that facility with pretend play would have depended on language ability, it is plausible that it evolved in parallel with the evolution of language. The timing of that is also a matter of great controversy, although advanced syntactical language may well date to the emergence of *homo sapiens* (MacWhinney 2005).

Cross-Cultural Universality of Pretend Play

Pretend play is more or less ubiquitous in human societies. It varies in frequency, depending a great deal on time, opportunity and attitudes of adults; but it happens, and in favourable circumstances it happens a lot. Slaughter and Dombrowski (1989, 290) wrote that in the light of the anthropological evidence, "children's social and pretend play appear to be biologically based, sustained as an evolutionary contribution to human psychological growth and development. Cultural factors regulate the amount and type of expression of these play forms." Reviewing anthropological studies, Gaskins, Haight

and Lancy (2007) describe three types of societies with differing attitudes to play: culturally curtailed play (adults restrict play, often because they want children to help in subsistence tasks even from a young age – typical of some agricultural societies); culturally accepted play (play is tolerated – typical of hunter-gatherer societies); and culturally cultivated play (play is actively encouraged and valued – typical of modern industrial societies).

Deficits in Pretend Play in Autism and Some Other Conditions

Pretend play is less frequent or absent in children with autism; it is also less frequent and complex in children suffering emotional trauma. Harris (2000, 2007) takes this as an indication that the presence of pretend play is associated with positive functioning (as opposed to psychopathology) and thus may be associated with progressive aspects of development.

The Design Features of Pretend Play

Pretend play follows a rather predictable time course. It is fully characteristic of both genders. Harris (1994, 256) argued that "The stable timing of its onset in different cultures strongly suggests a neuropsychological timetable and a biological basis." This would tie in with the universality arguments to suggest that pretend play has benefits, especially during the infant and preschool years when it is most frequent. At these ages, it is clear that in pretend play, and especially in socio-dramatic play, children are engaging in quite a lot of cognitive and social activities, compatible with it aiding various developmental competences in the preschool years.

Design features (the characteristics of pretend play) also provide a plausible argument that pretend and especially socio-dramatic play give practice in narrative skills. Early pretend play has a simple story line ('feeding baby'), but soon becomes more complex (i.e. a sequence of feeding and bathing baby and putting baby to bed). In socio-dramatic play, the narrative line being followed can be quite sustained and can be less dependent on routine scripts (i.e. more innovative elements such as putting out a fire, fighting monsters, travelling to a foreign country are incorporated).

THEORIES CONCERNING THE FUNCTION OF PRETEND PLAY

Smilansky (1968) suggested that socio-dramatic play was generally important for cognitive and language development, role-taking and creativity. Her work on play tutoring led to a raft of studies in the 1970s and 1980s that examined pretend and socio-dramatic play in relation to a wide range of cognitive and linguistic skills.

Alexander (1989) argued that social-intellectual play (or pretence) allows practice in "an expanding ability and tendency to elaborate and internalize social-intellectual-physical scenarios", using these to "anticipate and manipulate cause-effect relations in social cooperation and competition" (p. 480).

Mitchell (2007, 70) suggested that "pretending about others was adaptive because of the utility of imaginative planning or apprenticing (learning by matching one's own actions to another's) or both." Lancy (1996, 89) argued that "make-believe play can provide opportunities for children to acquire adult work habits and to rehearse social scenes"; this is a commonly held view in the anthropological literature.

Psychodynamic theorists have also argued for emotional benefits of pretend play, for example in coping with difficult emotional situations, and mastery of traumatic events (e.g. Peller 1954). This can be cited for the basis of play therapy (see Smith 2010, for a discussion of this).

Pretend Play, Imagination and Creativity

Harris (2000, 2007) hypothesised the role of pretend play in the development of the imagination generally. He cites how children use their imagination in a number of important cognitive processes. One is reasoning from unfamiliar premises. Suppose a child is told, 'All fishes live in trees. Tot is a fish. Does Tot live in the water?'. A successful answer to this hypothetical question requires a child to suspend belief in the real world and enter into an imagined one. A second process is judgements about obligation (for example, 'you should wear an apron when you paint'). A correct judgement about an unfamiliar obligation (such as 'you should wear a helmet when you paint') would require an ability to imagine a course of action not previously experienced in the real world. Harris also cited a third process, learning from testimony. Children can learn from what adults tell them ('testimony') concerning events, processes or entities that are difficult for them to observe first-hand – perhaps about other countries, other people or mythical or religious entities. This too requires an ability to transcend experience that is directly encountered. Harris argued that imagination is necessary for all of these, and that pretend play is the crucible of the imagination in this respect.

Taking an evolutionary perspective, Carruthers (2002) suggested that pretend play in childhood was selected for, because it enhanced creativity in adulthood. He argued that creativity in adulthood would have payoffs directly, in terms of e.g. better tools, therefore better hunting and foraging success; and, via sexual selection, as a way of becoming more attractive to the opposite sex and increasing reproductive success (by means of body ornaments, cave art or other creative displays). He thus argued that "the function of pretence should be to practice and enhance the kind of creativity which acquires so much significance in our adult lives."

His argument was in part based on the design features of pretend play. Creativity requires both the generation of a novel hypothesis or idea, and then the exploration of that idea, developing it and working out its consequences. In pretend play too there is first an initial supposition or imagined scenario, and then this is acted out or explored following familiar scripts and drawing inferences. (Although Carruthers does not make this additional point, *social* pretend play would be especially effective at developing a pretend supposition, because of the negotiations and sharing of meanings and knowledge that will take place.)

Carruthers (2002) also critiqued Harris' (2000) view that pretend play functions to provide practice in mental model building of the kind necessary for text and discourse comprehension, and understanding of testimony about the not-here-and-now. He asks why would pretend play be the best way to get such understanding – why do children have to suppose imaginary things, rather than just recollecting past events or speculating about distant ones?

Pretend Play, Narratives and Early Literacy

Socio-dramatic play and imaginary companions have a story line and thus provide natural opportunities for developing narrative competence in children. Nicolopoulou (2006, 249) argued that "we should approach children's play and narrative as closely intertwined, and often overlapping, forms of socially situated symbolic action." The integration of (pretend) play and of storytelling takes time. Socio-dramatic play is seen as highlighting identification with and understanding of roles, and developing rich and vivid characters, which are, however, of a generic type (doctor, monster etc.); whereas children's initial storytelling shows more concern with constructing and elaborating coherent plots. Through the pre-school years, these abilities become more integrated.

This approach suggests that as play and story-telling become more integrated, they reciprocally assist in the development of narrative skills, including comprehension of stories, but also more widely the construction of possible and imaginary worlds (Bruner 1986). Engel (2005) argued that the integration of play and story-telling skills allows children to engage in two types of narrative play, which she calls *what is* and *what if*. In *what is* play, children pretend the kinds of things they know of in their everyday world; in *what if* play, they go beyond this into more fantastic realms beyond their direct experience. A child using a banana as a pretend telephone, to pretend to talk to his or her dad, would be an example of *what is* play; whereas if the banana was used as a magic rocket to go to the moon, this would be *what if* play. Engel (2005, 524) writes that "The worlds of *what if* and *what is* comprise particularly important spheres for the young child, as they offer two different ways of exploring imagined experience. Both involve pretence, but one rests on plausible reconstructions of every day lived experience, while the other rests on

exploring implausible and often magical events and explanations."

A related argument is that socio-dramatic play links to early literacy development (Christie & Roskos 2006). Narratives in play provide opportunities for enhancing pre-reading or literacy skills by structuring such play in various ways, for example by providing print materials, introducing message sending into the story line etc. Christie and Roskos (2006) distinguish several relevant components of early literacy. One is oral language, and the evidence of sophisticated language use in socio-dramatic play. A second component is phonological awareness. The ability to talk about language is related specifically to children's phonemic awareness, or their awareness of the rule governing the sound system of English (or whichever language they are using). An important component in learning to read involves children learning letter-sound correspondence. This could be facilitated by the kind of rhyming and language games seen in toddlers. A third component is print awareness. Much socio-dramatic play can facilitate this, for example 'signing in' to a 'doctor's surgery'. In addition, general background knowledge and narrative integration are seen as helpful in school readiness skills.

Narrative skills probably have a long history in human evolution, and it is quite conceivable that the play-narrative link is important in considering why pretend play evolved. However, the kinds of pretend and socio-dramatic play seen in non-Western societies and described in the anthropological literature appear to be very predominantly *what is* play. The kinds of expanded or fantastical possibilities characteristic of *what if* play may be a relatively recent cultural development. Also literacy (unlike spoken language) is a relatively recent human invention, dating back a few thousand years. It is not plausible that pretend play was selected for such skills in our evolutionary history, although this does not preclude that it can have such benefits in modern societies.

Pretend Play and Theory of Mind

Some researchers have theorised that pretend play is causally related to acquiring a theory of mind – the understanding that another person may hold a false belief. Since knowledge and beliefs are 'representations' of reality, theory of mind involves a representation of a representation, a second-order or 'meta-representation'. Adapting objects for pretend purposes suggests some cognitive meta-representational skills (an object is represented as something else, in the mind).

Perner, Ruffman and Leekam (1994, 1236) stated that "pretend play is perhaps our best candidate for a cooperative activity which furthers the eventual understanding of false belief." The argument is consistent with an evolutionary perspective (both pretend play and theory of mind being abilities that are present at very simple levels in great apes, but much more evolved in humans); and with the simultaneous deficits of both pretend play and theory of mind in autism. The design features of pretend play also provide a plausible case. In social fantasy play, children typically talk about mental and cognitive states in the process of negotiating roles; e.g. 'doctors can't say that'.

Models of Benefits of Pretend Play

Smith (2010) suggested three models for examining the relationship between pretend play (or indeed, play generally) and developmental outcomes. Model [1] is that pretend play is a by-product of other aspect(s) of development, with no important developmental consequence(s) of its own. It is 'epiphenomenal'. Model [2] is that pretend play is a facilitator of developmental consequence(s); it can help bring about important developmental consequence(s), but it is not essential for this if other expected developmental pathways are present ('equifinality'). Model [3] is that pretend play is necessary or crucial for important developmental consequence(s); in the absence of pretend play, these developmental consequences will not occur or will at least be significantly held back. This is a 'play ethos' view (Smith 1988), that play is essential for development. Many play workers and theorists would assume this.

It is possible that through the course of human biocultural evolution there have been shifts from one model to another. We could envisage some shift from model [3] to model [2] if recent cultural changes now provide more pathways to development than was the case in earlier times. For example, creative thought or narrative competence might have been functions of pretend play in our hominid ancestors, but organised imaginative and creative activities in schools and kindergartens could now provide such benefits. Or, it is possible that model [1] shifted to model [2] or [3] if an existing ability was put to new uses; the Harris and Carruthers arguments about the selection for pretend play in *homo sapiens* would be such a case, if we assume that the prior ape-like abilities of simple pretence were non-functional 'spin-offs' (model [1]).

Main sources of evidence are cross-cultural comparisons, correlational studies and experimental studies. However, the evidence is certainly not conclusive. Smith (2010) concluded that model [2], or equifinality, is the most supported in terms of the evidence. Lillard and colleagues (2013) review three similar models for the importance of pretend play, in relation to a large number of developmental outcomes. They conclude that for the outcomes of language, narrative and emotion regulation, there is insufficient evidence; for executive function and social skills, there is evidence against pretend play being 'essential', so supporting 'equifinality' or 'epiphenomenal'; for reasoning, they argue 'equifinality' is supported; and for problem solving, creativity, intelligence, conservation and theory of mind, they argue that 'epiphenomenal' is supported. They conclude that "Despite over 40 years of research examining how pretend play might help development, there is little evidence that it has a crucial role; equifinality and epiphenomenalism have as much if not more support" (2013, 27).

SUMMARY

Pretend play may, according to one's definition, have some origins in advanced animal species such as the great apes; but more than other kinds of play, it is distinctly human. It can be taken as a cross-cultural universal, despite variations in amount and in adult support. There is a definite developmental sequence, with socio-dramatic play being characteristic of three- to six-year-olds. There are a number of theories about the developmental importance of pretend play, but as yet, the evidence that it has a crucial role in development is lacking.

Although primarily a childhood phenomenon, some characteristics of pretend play carry through to adult life. These include enjoyable and/or ritualised expression, often within a narrative structure. Other aspects such as large numbers of participants, public rules and an audience are more typical of games than play (Table 5.1). However, developmentally, play precedes games with rules, and aspects of play continue into games. With play we have rituals private to the players, albeit often stereotyped representations from adult life. In games we have rituals with more publicly agreed rules.

REFERENCES

Alexander, R. D. 1989. Evolution of the human psyche, in *The Human Revolution*, eds. P. Mellars & C. Stringer. Edinburgh: Edinburgh University Press, 455–513.

Bekoff, M. & Allen, C. 1998. Intentional communication and social play: how and why animals negotiate and agree to play, in *Animal Play: Evolutionary, Comparative, and Ecological Perspectives*, eds. M. Bekoff & J. A. Byers. Cambridge: Cambridge University Press, 97–114.

Blurton Jones, N. G. 1993. The lives of hunter-gatherer children: Effects of parental behavior and parental reproductive strategy, in *Juvenile Primates: Life History, Development, and Behavior*, eds. M. E. Pereira and L. A. Fairbanks. New York: Oxford University Press, 309–25.

Breuggeman, J. A. 1978. The function of adult play in free-ranging Macaca mulatto, in *Social Play in Primates*, ed. E. O. Smith. New York: Academic Press, 169–91.

Bruner, J. S. 1986. *Actual Minds, Possible Worlds*. Cambridge, MA: Harvard University Press.

Carruthers, P. 2002. Human creativity: its cognitive basis, its evolution, and its connection with childhood pretence. *British Journal of the Philosophy of Science*, 53, 225–49.

Christie, J. F. & Roskos, K. A. 2006. Standards, science, and the role of play in early literacy education, in *Play=Learning*, eds. D. Singer, R. Golinkoff & K. Hirsh-Pasek. Oxford: Oxford University Press, 57–73.

de Waal, F. B. M. 1989. *Peacemaking Among Primates*. Cambridge, MA: Harvard University Press.

Engel, S. 2005. The narrative worlds of *what is* and *what if*. *Cognitive Development*, 20, 514–25.

Fein, G. G. 1975. A transformational analysis of pretending. *Developmental Psychology*, 11, 291–6.

Fenson, L., Kagan, J., Kearsley, R. B. & Zelazo, P. 1972. The developmental progression of manipulative play in the first two years. *Child Development*, 47, 232–5.

Gaskins, S. 1999. Children's lives in a Mayan village: a case of culturally constructed roles and activities, in *Children's Engagement in the World: Sociocultural Perspectives*, ed. A. Göncü. New York: Cambridge University Press, 25–61.

Gaskins, S., Haight, W. & Lancy, D. F. 2007. The cultural construction of play, in *Play and Development: Evolutionary, Sociocultural and Functional Perspectives*, eds. A. Göncü & S. Gaskins. Hillsdale, NJ: Lawrence Erlbaum, 179–202.

Gómez, J. C. & Martín-Andrade, B. 2005. Fantasy play in apes, in *The Nature of Play: Great Apes and Humans*, eds. A. D. Pellegrini & P. K. Smith. New York: Guilford, 139–72.

Göncü, A., Patt, M. B. & Kouba, E. 2002. Understanding young children's pretend play in context, in *Blackwell Handbook of Childhood Social Development*, eds. P. K. Smith & C. H. Hart. Oxford: Blackwell, 418–37.

Göncü, A. & Perone, A. 2005. Pretend play as a life-span activity. *Topoi*, 24, 137–47.

Gosso, Y., Otta, E., Morais, M. L. S., Ribeiro, F. J. L. & Bussab, V. S. R. 2005. Play in hunter-gatherer society, in *The Nature of Play: Great Apes and Humans*, eds. A. D. Pellegrini & P. K. Smith. New York: Guilford, 213–53.

Gottman, J. M. 1983. How children become friends. *Monographs of the Society for Research in Child Development*, 48 no 3; serial no 201.

Haight, W. L. & Miller, P. J. 1993. *Pretending at Home: Early Development in a Sociocultural Context*. Albany: State University of New York Press.

Harris, P. L. 1994. Understanding pretense, in *Children's Early Understanding of Mind*, eds. C. Lewis & P. Mitchell. Hove: Lawrence Erlbaum, 235–9.

Harris, P. L. 2000. *The Work of the Imagination*. Oxford: Blackwell.

Harris, P. L. 2007. Hard work for the imagination, in *Play and Development: Evolutionary, Sociocultural and Functional Perspectives*, eds. A. Göncü & S. Gaskins. Hillsdale, NJ: Lawrence Erlbaum, 205–25.

Hayes, C. H. 1951. *The Ape in our House*. New York: Harper & Row.

Holland, P. 2003. *We Don't Play with Guns here*. Philadelphia. PA: Open University Press.

Howes, C. & Matheson, C. C. 1992. Sequences in the development of competent play with peers. Social and social pretend play. *Developmental Psychology*, 28, 961–74.

Jarrold, C. 2003. A review of research into pretend play in autism. *Autism*, 7, 379–90.

Jarrold, C., Carruthers, P., Smith, P. K. & Boucher, J. 1994. Pretend play: is it metarepresentational? *Mind and Language*, 9, 445–68.

Kanlenberg, S. M. & Wrangham, R. W. 2010. Sex differences in chimpanzees' use of sticks as play objects resemble those of children. *Current Biology*, 20, R1067–8.

Kelly, R. 2006. An Exploration of the Role of Executive Functions in the Symbolic Play of Children with High-Functioning Autism, Children with Asperger's Disorder, and Typically Developing Children. Unpublished doctoral thesis, LaTrobe University, Australia.

Konner, M. 1972. Aspects of the developmental ethology of a forging people, in *Ethological Studies of Child Behaviour*, ed. N. Blurton Jones. Cambridge: Cambridge University Press, 285–304.

Lancy, D. F. 1996. *Playing on the Mother Ground: Cultural Routines for Children's Development*. New York: Guilford Press.

Lillard, A. S. 1994. Making sense of pretence, in *Children's Early Understanding of Mind*, eds. C. Lewis & P. Mitchell. Hove: Lawrence Erlbaum, 211–34.

Lillard, A. S., Lerner, M. D., Hopkins, E. J., Dore, R. A., Smith, E. D. & Palmquist, C. M. 2013. The impact of pretend play on children's development: a review of the evidence. *Psychological Bulletin*, 139, 1–34.

MacWhinney, B. 2005. Language evolution and human development, in *Origins of the Social Mind*, eds. B. J. Ellis & D. F. Bjorklund. New York & London: Guilford Press, 383–410.

Martini, M. 1994. Peer interactions in Polynesia: a view from the Marquesas. In *Children's Play in Diverse Cultures*, eds. J. L. Roopnarine, J. E. Johnson & F. H. Hooper. Albany: State University of New York Press, 73–103.

Matevia, M. L., Patterson, F. & Hillix, W. A. 2002. Pretend play in a signing gorilla, in *Pretending and Imagination in Animals and Children*, ed. R. W. Mitchell. Cambridge: Cambridge University Press, 285–304.

Mitchell, R. 2007. Pretense in animals: the continuing relevance of children's pretense, in *Play and Development: Evolutionary, Sociocultural and Functional Perspectives*, eds. A. Göncü & S. Gaskins. Hillsdale, NJ: Lawrence Erlbaum, 51–75.

Morris, D. 1962. *The Biology of Art*. London: Methuen.

Nicolopoulou, A. 2006. The interplay of play and narrative in children's development: theoretical reflections and concrete examples, in *Play and Development: Evolutionary, Sociocultural and Functional Perspectives*, eds. A. Göncü & S. Gaskins. Hillsdale, NJ: Lawrence Erlbaum, 247–73.

Overton, W. F. & Jackson, J. P. 1973. The representation of imagines objects in action sequences: a developmental study. *Child Development*, 44, 309–14.

Peller, L. E. 1954. Libidinal phases, ego development and play. *Psychoanalytic Study of the Child*, 9, 178–98.

Perner, J., Ruffman, T. & Leekam, S. R. 1994. Theory of mind is contagious: you catch it from your sibs. *Child Development*, 65, 1228–38.

Perone, A. & Göncü, A. 2014. Life-span pretend play in two communities. *Mind, Culture and Activity*, 21(3), 200–20.

Piaget, J. 1951. *Play, Dreams, and Imitation in Childhood*. London: Routledge & Kegan Paul.

Renfrew, C. 2007. *Prehistory: The Making of the Human Mind*. London: Weidenfeld and Nicolson.

Savage-Rumbaugh, E. S. 1986. *Ape Language: From Conditioned Response to Symbol*. New York: Columbia University Press.

Slaughter, D. & Dombrowski, J. 1989. Cultural continuities and discontinuities: impact on social and pretend play, in *The Ecological Context of Children's Play*, eds. M. N. Bloch & A. D. Pellegrini. Norwood, NJ: Ablex, 282–310.

Smilansky, S. 1968. *The Effects of Sociodramatic Play on Disadvantaged Preschool Children*. New York: Wiley.

Smith, P. K. 1988. Children's play and its role in early development: a re-evaluation of the 'play ethos', in *Psychological Bases for Early Education*, ed. A. D. Pellegrini. Chichester & New York: Wiley, 207–26.

Smith, P. K. 2010. *Children and Play*. Chichester: Wiley-Blackwell.

Takhvar, M. & Smith, P. K. 1990. A review and critique of Smilansky's classification scheme and the 'nested hierarchy' of play categories. *Journal of Research in Early Childhood*, 4, 112–22.

Taylor, M. 1999. *Imaginary Companions and the Children Who Create Them*. New York: Oxford University Press.

Taylor, M., Cartwright, B. S. & Carlson, S. M. 1993. A developmental investigation of children's imaginary companions. *Developmental Psychology*, 29, 276–85.

Woolley, J. D. & Wellman, H. H. 1990. Young children's understanding of realities, nonrealities, and appearances. *Child Development*, 64, 1–17.

6

PRETEND PLAY, COGNITION AND LIFE-HISTORY IN HUMAN EVOLUTION

Iain Morley

INTRODUCTION

This chapter explores the relationships between different types of play behaviours in apes and humans and their relationship with the emergence of certain critical cognitive skills, including some of those required for ritual behaviours and supernatural beliefs. It examines the relationship between these play behaviours, especially *pretend play*, and life-history stages in ape and human development, in particular *infancy* and *early childhood*. It then goes on to discuss the palaeoanthropological evidence for the appearance in human evolution of a modern human-like pattern of these life-history stages, and the implications this may have for the emergence of *pretend play* and the abilities that underlie it, including imitation.

LIFE-HISTORY STAGES IN APES AND HUMANS

Before exploring the different types of play behaviours exhibited in apes and humans, it is necessary to outline the commonly recognised developmental stages undergone by immature apes and humans, as a clear conception of these periods is relevant to the discussion of the incidence of play behaviours.

Humans and apes show broadly very similar life-history trajectories, but with some important differences, to which have been attributed great significance in terms of the development of the

cognitive abilities characteristic of modern humans. The stages of development in apes and humans have been variously named and defined, but it will be necessary here to identify terms and characteristics that we can use with consistency. For example, Hochberg (2008) and Geary and Bjorklund (2000) use the terms *infancy*, *childhood*, *juvenility* and *adolescence*. Many researchers prefer to refer to childhood as *early childhood* and the following period as *middle childhood/juvenile* (e.g. Smith 2010; Thompson & Nelson 2011), and this is the convention followed here. These stages are characterised by the following features in apes and humans (see also Figure 6.1):

Infancy: The period in which offspring are breast-fed; in traditional (hunter-gatherer) human societies, this is typically until the age of around 3 years. In chimpanzees, weaning occurs around 4–5 years of age (Geary & Bjorklund 2000).

Early childhood: From weaning until the eruption of the first permanent molars (M1); in humans, this is typically from around 3 until around 6.2±0.8 years (Macchiarelli et al. 2006) of age. In chimpanzees, the eruption of M1 occurs at around the same time as weaning, 4–5 years of age (Ponce de León et al. 2008), resulting in the absence of an equivalent *early childhood* stage. The presence of this period in humans is considered highly significant by many (e.g. Bogin 2003; Thompson & Nelson 2011). In humans, *pretend play* comes to accompany other forms of play,

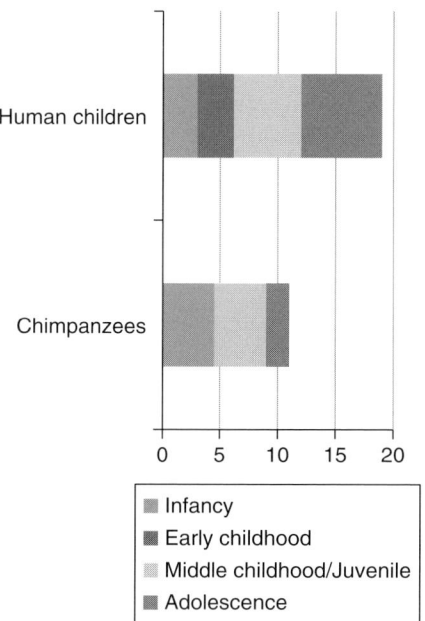

Figure 6.1 Developmental life-history stages in apes and humans, by age in years. Note that this represents a typical pattern; there is some small variation in onset times of each stage (Geary & Bjorklund 2000; Bogin, 2003; Macchiarelli et al. 2006; Hochberg 2008; Smith 2010; Thompson & Nelson 2011).

beginning at the start of this period and increasing dramatically in frequency (Haight & Miller 1993; Smith 2005 (in Pellegrini & Smith 2005)).

Middle childhood/juvenility: From eruption of first permanent molars until the onset of sexual maturity. In humans, this is from around 6.2±0.8 years of age until around 12. In chimpanzees, the *juvenile* period lasts from 4–5 until around 9 years of age (e.g. Thompson & Nelson 2011). This period is characterised by no longer being dependent on parental care, despite not yet having reached sexual maturity (Smith 2010). "As with other social mammals, this is often a time [in humans] of social and other forms of play, as well as a time during which parental dependency decreases and peer influence increases" (Geary & Bjorklund 2000, 58). In chimpanzees, the majority of growth to adult stature occurs during this period; in humans, much of this growth is deferred until adolescence.

Adolescence: In humans, this is a period from the onset of sexual maturity until full physical growth has been achieved (from around 12 years until

18–20 years), and is characterised by a prolonged period of physical development incorporating a growth spurt. In other higher primates, the majority of physical growth has been completed by the time of the onset of sexual maturity. Some authors (e.g. Hochberg 2008) do not attribute to other primates a clearly-identifiable adolescence, since they lack a clear growth spurt; others (e.g. Thompson & Nelson 2011) do identify an adolescent period in apes, since some growth does still occur between the ages around 9 (onset of sexual maturity) until around 11 (completion of growth). This stage features exploration of adult social and sexual roles, and the juvenile social behaviours become increasingly adult-like. This period is characterised by no longer being dependent on parental care for survival, although full adulthood has not yet been reached. In humans, some dependence on parents typically continues during this time, however, for somewhat longer in industrialised societies than in traditional societies (Geary & Bjorklund 2000).

In short, humans have a shortened *infancy* relative to chimpanzees and the eruption of the first permanent molars occurs later, which results in an *early childhood* phase prior to *middle childhood/juvenility*. *Middle childhood/juvenility* is slightly longer in humans than in chimpanzees, and is completed slightly earlier in chimpanzees; this is followed by an adolescent period which is greatly extended in humans relative to chimpanzees. For the purposes of this chapter, it is the development of the *early childhood* phase and the different character of the *middle childhood/juvenile* phase that are of particular relevance in relation to the manifestation and significance of play behaviours in human evolution.

TYPES OF PLAY IN APES AND HUMANS AND THEIR RELATIONS TO LIFE-HISTORY

Play behaviours of various kinds are nearly ubiquitous in mammals, and are especially prolific in primates, with all species of great apes spending significant proportions of their time on play behaviours (Lewis 2005). These include *social play* (such as play fighting), *locomotor play* (solitary physical activities such as jumping, and social activities such as chasing), *object play* (such as transforming, manipulating and ordering objects), and what may be a form of *imaginative play*, play-mothering, involving carrying and tending to an infant – though this could be viewed as a form of imitative object play (Smith 2010). Great apes' *social play* incorporates use of communicative facial expressions and gestures. Pellegrini and Smith (2005) divide play in humans and apes into three main types – *social play* (including physical rough-and-tumble (R&T) play), *object play* and *pretend play* (also known as *fantasy play* or *imaginative play*), and these terms will be followed here.

These behaviours allow engagement with the world, physical and social, in ways that allow exploration of new approaches and refinement of existing ones, in contexts that lack the normal negative consequences of failure (Bateson 2005). This clearly has the potential for considerable benefits, from the point of view of individual ontogeny, and thus, potentially, selective advantages through greater reproductive success of those individuals engaging in these beneficial activities. Bateson (2005) outlines several benefits that contribute specifically to the development of working knowledge of the environment, including recognition of objects, their affordances (potential uses) and what they may conceal and causal relationships between actions and events. These observations pertain to the physical environment, but have parallels too in the social environment. In addition, the stimulation and fine-tuning of muscular and neurological systems can clearly have immediate and longer-term benefits. So play behaviours may allow the acquisition and refinement of skills, physical, cognitive and social, and would be particularly advantageous when acquiring those skills in 'real' contexts would be either dangerous or ineffective (Smith 1982, 2010).

In chimpanzees, play behaviours increase rapidly in frequency up to the age of around 2 years (late *infancy*), and then start to tail off during the *juvenile* period; they tend to be replaced by social grooming interactions instead as individuals approach *adolescence* (sexual maturity) at around 9 years of age, but some play behaviours do persist into adulthood (Smith 2010).

In the case of humans, the length of time in which such activities can be carried out and developed is greatly increased relative to our nearest relatives, with the addition of the *early childhood* stage to the *juvenile* stage, as is the scope of the activities themselves. One view of the value of play activities in human children sees them "as part of a package of adaptations involving prolonged immaturity, opportunities for learning (in a broad sense), and parental investment in such learning" (Smith 2010, 78–9).

Play activities may provide excellent opportunities for experiences and 'training' that would be difficult or dangerous to replicate otherwise including, in the case of *pretend play*, development of social skills (Smith 2010). It is difficult, however, to demonstrate that the latter do so *more* effectively than other types of social activity. Smith (2007, 2010) sees them as more facilitative than uniquely driving of such developments and refinements:

> "[P]lay may have evolved as a general-purpose learning mechanism – for physical coordination and muscular strength, learning about making and using objects, finding out about peers and how they think and behave" (p. 216). It may not be essential for these things, but it is certainly useful. (Smith 2010)

Both humans and apes engage in all three types of play behaviours to some degree, and *social play* (including R&T) and *object play* have some particularly clear parallels between humans and apes (Smith & Pellegrini 2005). There are striking similarities between the 'rough-and-tumble' (R&T) form of social play in great apes and humans, and across human cultures, including wrestling, grappling, controlled punching and hitting, fleeing and pursuing, often accompanied by play faces, smiles, laughs and playful vocalisations (Fry 2005). It seems to be a human universal to engage in R&T play, with boys engaging in it somewhat more than girls, although there are cultural variations in terms of the themes (fantasy elements) of the play, as would be expected (Fry 2005).

Social organisation has a direct impact on play behaviours, in terms of the opportunities for and types of play exhibited. In chimpanzees, males and females form segregated same-sex groups within the wider community, and in this context learn social and technical skills related to sex-specific adult roles (Pellegrini & Smith 2005). In the case of males, these include roles related to predation and dominance, including coordinating skilled movements, and in the case of females, handling infants and forming alliances, for example. It has been argued (Alexander 1989) that play with conspecifics constitutes an important social context in which such skills have evolved and are refined, in particular during the *juvenile* and *adolescent* periods. Similar patterns appear to exist across human societies, especially in the case of polygynous groups that do not have highly stratified roles (Pellegrini & Smith 2005).

Pretend Play

Pretend play shows more discontinuity between apes and humans than other play types do, however. *Pretend play* appears to be ubiquitous in human societies, even if it shows some variation in quantity and form (Schwartzmann 1978; Slaughter & Dombrowski 1989; Gosso et al. 2005; Smith 2010). *Pretend (fantasy) play* is typically (and unsurprisingly) shaped by the nature of activities carried out in that society, generally being imitative of adult roles in both forager and settled agricultural communities (Smith 2010). Where *pretend play* is curtailed, this is often as a consequence of the children instead being required to actually take on adult tasks (Gaskins 1999) such as scaring birds away from crops, preparing food, selling produce and looking after younger siblings (Gaskins 1999; Smith 2010) (although the latter does not necessarily preclude play).

Note too that humans persist in pretend play into adulthood. Activities requiring many or all of the same skills as pretend play include dramatic performance, storytelling, poetry, dance and ritual. These activities are related on a continuum and have much in common with each other (see also McConachie 2011). As Smith (2010) points out, these are all "activities that enable development of representations of experiences with affective significance" (p. 169). These overlaps will be explored further.

Incidence of *pretend play* activities in human children increases dramatically with age during *infancy*, from around 0.1% of waking time at the age of 1 year, to around 5.5% at 2 years, to 21% at 4 years (Haight & Miller 1993). Pretend play is especially prevalent during the *early childhood* stage (between the ages of 3 and 6), and has a very stable onset time across cultures, suggesting a biological basis and, perhaps, a basis in selection (Smith 2005).

Interestingly, pretend play amongst the younger children (2–4 years) often involves pretending that objects represent other objects, but by the age of 6–8 years, children will often *imagine* the existence of an object without a real-life referent for the object itself other than the actions of using it. Unlike the children in *infancy*, these older children in *early childhood* are able to carry out imaginative acts that are *decontextualized* from a direct referent. This latter case must rely on meta-representation and cannot be attributed solely to imitation.

There is evidence for social pretend meta-representation emerging from ca. 2.5–3 years of age, and clear evidence of it from 3–4 years (onset of *early childhood*), with children of this age adopting and changing roles, and negotiating with others the progress of the 'script' of the play activity. This involves meta-representation of the play activity itself as a *topic* of interaction in its own right as well as being a form of interaction itself, and also relies on some engagement with the mental states of the conspecifics involved (Smith 2005).

From around 3 years old (around the onset of *early childhood*), many children also develop some form of imaginary companion; this mostly occurs between 3 and 8 years of age (during the *early childhood* stage), but most have abandoned such behaviours by the age of 10 years (towards the end of the *middle childhood/juvenile* stage and the onset of *adolescence*) (Smith 2005). Having an imaginary friend would appear to rely on the ability to represent to oneself a set of mental states of another individual, to some degree at least, a capacity which must similarly underlie the ability to conceive of a deity and its views.

Whilst some limited *pretend play* does occur in apes, it is infrequent and relatively simple (Smith 2010). Gómez and Martín-Andrade (2005) propose that the quantitative and qualitative differences between the *pretend play* of apes and humans are a consequence of the evolution in humans of developed symbolising, representational, communicative and imitative capacities, only some of which are present in apes. In particular, the forms of pretend play involving meta-representation, which appear in humans around the onset of *early childhood*, rely on the development of cognitive capacities in children, including symbolising and Theory of Mind (ToM), which apes only develop to a limited degree (Smith & Pellegrini 2005).

There is some commonality apparent, though, in earlier types of *pretend play*, which in apes and humans are predominantly imitative – in particular where *object* and *fantasy play* overlap, where object-based pretend play takes place which may merely involve imitation (e.g. pretending to eat, drink or carry a baby). This occurs in children from 15–24 months of age (during the *infancy* stage), and has been observed in apes (Smith & Pellegrini 2005, 295). It would seem, however, that the conditions created when chimpanzees are hand-reared (and in some cases linguistically trained) can sometimes lead to the presence of the types of cognitive interactions between individuals that have fostered imaginative and fantasy play in humans (Gómez & Martin-Andrade 2005).

Smith (2010) considers it most likely that rather than these episodes of pretend play having any functional significance in chimpanzees, they are more likely a by-product of the evolution of abilities such as imitation, visual-kinetic matching, self-recognition and tactical deception, and of the capacity for some symbolic intelligence and communicative abilities. The change in sophistication of *imaginative play* that humans exhibit around the onset of *early childhood* (at 3–4 years old), incorporating meta-representations of the world and others' mental states, appears to be something that apes do not replicate (Smith & Pellegrini 2005).

The evidence of some basic pretend play amongst great apes would suggest that the potential at least for some pretend play was present in our last common ancestor with chimpanzees (Smith 2010). Exactly what the relationship is between the development of the sophistication of pretend play and the complexity of other cognitive capacities on which it relies requires further investigation.

It is noteworthy that these abilities (imitation, visual-kinetic matching, self-recognition, tactical deception and the capacity for some symbolic intelligence and communicative abilities) are clearly critical in human pretend play too, and all of these abilities have developed in sophistication in humans relative to chimpanzees; they form core foundations of the complexity of social interaction and information transmission that is so characteristic of and uniquely developed in our species. One common factor in most if not all of these abilities is the ability to form clear conceptions of the mental states and intentions of others (ToM) – this underpins these capabilities, from imitation and emulation, to deception and communication. Indeed, pretend play behaviours significantly develop in complexity with the emergence of ToM abilities at the onset of *early childhood* (3–4 years of age). If the pretend play of apes is a by-product of the presence in them of their more limited versions of these abilities, the sophisticated and ubiquitous pretend play in humans could perhaps simply be a more complex by-product of our more complex versions of those underlying abilities. Alternatively, the emergence of and increased opportunity for pretend play in humans could actually have contributed to the continued development of these underlying capabilities – each feeding the evolutionary development of the other through a bootstrapping feedback.

Smith (2010) discusses how *pretend play* may be related in important ways to the acquisition of ToM abilities. Both of these abilities (*pretend play* and ToM) develop during the same period (*early childhood*), are universal in humans and absent in other animals (with the exception that apes show some limited amount of both), both are severely detrimentally affected in autism and, Smith observes, pretend play activities that involve interaction with others would seem to rely on the ability of a child to conceive of others' beliefs and understandings of the activity, as would the ability to represent an imaginary friend. There is clearly a strong link between the emergence of pretend play and the emergence of ToM abilities; it is not clear, however, whether there is any causal relationship between them, in one of them facilitating the emergence of the other.

It is interesting that the common inter-birth interval in humans (3–4 years) broadly coincides with the durations of the early stages of development (*infancy*, *early childhood* and *middle childhood/juvenility*). In most traditional societies, breastfeeding ceases at around 3 years, and the child is weaned. This constitutes one of the principal criteria for the end of *infancy* and the beginning of the *early childhood* phase. This process of cessation of breastfeeding has a direct impact on the inter-birth interval, since female fertility is suppressed during breastfeeding; this results in the typical inter-birth interval of 3–4 years. What this means is that (for all but the youngest child in a family) the arrival of a younger sibling coincides with the emergence of a variety of increasingly complex socio-cognitive skills, including ToM, associated with the onset of *early childhood*.

This presents opportunities for interactions between children of different ages that exercise abilities such as caring for others ('mothering' younger children), taking their perspective (for example by accommodating the limitations of younger children), at just the time that those abilities are emerging and can be refined. The fact that especially important socio-cognitive skills emerge at the (traditional) time of weaning may not be a coincidence, and interactions with other, younger siblings provide what may be an important forum for the refinement of those emerging abilities. Furthermore, with a typical inter-birth interval, a child making the transition from *infancy* to *early childhood*, who has an older sibling, will be making that transition at the time that the older sibling is making the transition from *early childhood* to the *middle childhood/juvenile* stage. This provides yet more scope for valuable interaction between both children at these transitional stages. These timings could thus have important impacts on social and especially family group organisation, with important benefits associated with defined family groups fostering sibling interaction.

Much has been written about the value of older adults surviving beyond reproductive age providing additional care for young children whilst the parents are engaged in other activities (see, for example, Hawkes et al. 1998; O'Connell et al. 1999; Marlowe 2000; Peccei 2001). It may be observed by a similar token that the extension of the *childhood* period in humans, once independence from parents is reached but before sexual maturity and the starting

of their own families, allows older children also to take an important role in childcare that would otherwise (with a short childhood period as in chimpanzees) not be possible. This interaction could be of significant benefit, in terms of the practice and development of emerging cognitive skills, to both the juvenile and the younger children (one of whom would be in *early childhood* and the other in *infancy*).

RATIONALES FOR THE IMPORTANCE OF *PRETEND PLAY* IN COGNITIVE EVOLUTION, AND ITS RELATION TO CAPACITIES FOR RITUAL AND BELIEF

Some recent syntheses have offered evolutionary explanations for relationships between *pretend play* in human children and the emergence of human-specific cultural phenomena including creativity and innovation (Carruthers 2002), performance and ritual (McConachie 2011) and culture itself, in the sense of cultural structures and transmission of cultural information and practice (Nielsen 2012). Other authors have discussed benefits at the individual developmental level; Perner, Ruffman and Leekam (1994) argue that *pretend play* from around 3–4 years could be the most effective cooperative activity for furthering understanding of false belief in others (i.e. development of ToM abilities). Mitchell (2007) suggests that *pretend play* was adaptively advantageous because of the opportunities that it provided for learning through imitative matching of actions, and imaginative planning of future scenarios. Another advantage suggested by Alexander (1989) is that *pretend play* provides opportunities to learn about the cause-and-effect relations in social interactions, and how to anticipate and manipulate these in cooperation and competition (Smith 2010).

Pretend Play, Creativity and Innovation

Carruthers (2002) argues that both childhood *pretend play* and adult creative thinking and problem-solving rely on the ability to generate and manipulate imagined possibilities (suppositions). On the basis that many of the physical play behaviours seen in other animals evidently fulfil roles of practising adult behaviours, Carruthers argues that, in an equivalent way, human *pretend play* likely provides practice for some equivalent adult behaviours – namely, imaginative and creative thinking. He goes on to propose that the emergence of greater creative thinking and problem-solving behaviour in the evolution of our species was a product of the opportunities provided by increased incidence of childhood *pretend play* for the refinement of this capacity to manipulate imagined possibilities.

Human creativity relies especially on two critical abilities: the first is a capacity to generate new ideas, for example, by spotting new analogies (Carruthers 2002), and the second the abilities to recognise and realise the potentials of these new ideas. The first stage, the generation of a novel hypothesis or concept, involves holding this idea in mind – *entertaining* the idea rather than necessarily believing or endorsing it (to use the terminology of Finke et al. 1992; Carruthers 2002) – in which case it can then be developed, explored, manipulated and, perhaps, then put into practice.

Carruthers points out that such a process is strongly analogous to the processes which must be undertaken in order to engage in pretend play. "An episode of pretence will begin with an initial supposition or imagined scenario. … The child then acts as if that supposition were true, following familiar scripts and/or drawing inferences appropriate to its truth in the light of their background knowledge. … Often, too, yet further suppositions will be introduced into the play episode, serving to elaborate and extend the pretence" (p. 230).

Given these similarities in the cognitive demands of these types of activities, Carruthers suggests that "it does seem plausible that the young of our species should engage in supposition-for-fun in childhood in order that they may be better able to suppose-for-real when they reach adulthood" (p. 230). He goes on to argue the stronger position that the apparent increase in innovative and creative behaviours seen in Upper Palaeolithic *Homo sapiens* is a consequence of an increase in the opportunity for pretend play in childhood, which provided the necessary practice for the development of adult creative thought, between the appearance of *Homo sapiens*

and the appearance of the conspicuously innovative and symbolic behaviours of the Upper Palaeolithic. According to this model, the *capacity* to engage in such thought processes accompanies the emergence of language capacities, present in early *Homo sapiens*, but they do not manifest in the form of creative and innovative adult behaviour until circumstances emerge in childhood that allow practice in the form of frequent pretend play.

These equivalences are certainly very interesting and it would indeed be odd if there was not some close relationship between these abilities in childhood and adulthood. The question is, of what that relationship could be, and whether it must follow that the childhood behaviour exists in order to provide practice aiding the development of the adult behaviour – and that the adult behaviour *depends on* such practice, both ontogenically (in development) and phylogenically (in evolution).

One possibility is that this phenomenon could represent the perpetuation into adulthood of the childhood capacity for imaginative play – a form of human behavioural neoteny – which is itself a by-product of other, related cognitive changes (such as outlined earlier in this chapter – imitation, visual-kinetic matching, self-recognition, tactical deception and the capacity for some symbolic intelligence and communicative abilities – as in apes; Smith 2010). This is not to diminish the importance of the benefits of the creative thought in adulthood, just to say that the connection between this and the childhood play need not be one with any direct role in the form of practice.

Alternatively, it may be that childhood pretend play and adult creative thought are similar by-products of a shared set of cognitive capacities (those outlined previously in this chapter) which themselves carry selective advantages. Neither, either or both of pretend play and creative thought may then confer selective advantages in their own right as exaptations (though *neither* seems unlikely). Indeed, Smith (2007, 2010) finds that the experimental evidence for *direct* benefits of participating in pretend play is distinctly equivocal; he argues that there is no clear evidence for a deleterious effect on adult behaviour of a lack of imaginative play in childhood – though more research is needed, and ontogenic exceptions don't necessarily undermine a phylogenic role for such connections. Pretend play may, according to Smith, however, be a *facilitator* of development of creative thinking in adulthood, having a shared cause and thus attributes, without being itself the progenitor of creative thought.

As discussed earlier in this chapter, apparently imaginative episodes of pretend play are witnessed in human children from the age of around 18 months, with objects seemingly being used to represent other objects and scenarios being enacted. An example frequently given is of young children using a banana (or other object) as a telephone receiver, in which it is argued that a *meta-representation* of an alternative reality, of the banana *as* a phone, must be utilised. Whilst later episodes of pretend play certainly require meta-representation – entertaining a supposition or imaginary scenario (as Carruthers 2002 proposes is analogous to the process involved in creative thought) – whether all examples of what we see as pretend play need do so requires further scrutiny.

In fact, rather than an imaginative *meta-representation*, the human propensity for *over-imitation* may be essential here. Chimpanzees learn actions by what has been termed *emulation* rather than *imitation* – they successfully identify the desired end-point of a sequence of actions that they are observing. Then, when they execute the task themselves, they frequently attempt to achieve the identified goal by somewhat varied means, for example by cutting superfluous actions from the action sequence. The learning of the sequence is ends-orientated rather than means-orientated. Human children, on the other hand, tend to *imitate*, that is, reproduce the action sequence observed as exactly as possible, to the extent that they actually *over-imitate* and reproduce extraneous actions that fulfil no direct purpose in achieving the desired end (Horner & Whiten 2005; Nielsen & Blank 2011; Nielsen 2012). In other words, action-sequence learning in humans is initially means-orientated rather than ends-orientated. This appears on first inspection to be less intellectually sophisticated than what is achieved by chimpanzees when learning new action sequences. Identifying the desired goal of a sequence and thus being able to modify your actions in order to achieve

that goal more efficiently according to the circumstances would appear on first inspection to be more sophisticated and more efficient (and more likely to lead to innovation) than pure *imitation* (which ironically we colloquially term *aping*). Indeed, we are often encouraged to think this way in adulthood ('thinking outside the box'). However, it has been argued that the human propensity for *over-imitation*, especially in children, whilst seemingly inefficient and thus disadvantageous, in fact has the potential to carry considerable benefits (Boyd & Richerson 1985; Tomasello 1999; Whiten 2005). It allows the rapid acquisition of valuable skill sets before even the cognitive capacity is present to understand how they achieve their outcome. In fact, it allows the acquisition of skills in both children and adults in this way. We can hold a desired *end* in mind, know which *means* are required to achieve it, and then execute those means without any clear understanding of how they achieve that end. It allows the high-fidelity transmission of practice between individuals and, critically for human culture, across generations. Because of the capacity for meta-representation, we have the capacity to revisit and modify these actions afterwards, and this is where innovation and creativity can be introduced (as Carruthers 2002 argues), but this is after the behaviour sets have been initially acquired by high-fidelity imitation. Great ape *emulation*, on the other hand, whilst potentially more efficient in the immediate term, does not carry the same potential for high-fidelity transmission of practice across generations – or, perhaps, such stable reproduction of actions within an individual's own lifetime (which themselves provide a model for the learning of others – and the more stable the better).

To return to the example of using a banana as a telephone receiver, the basic act of holding a banana (or other object that bears some resemblance to a phone) to the head and vocalising need only result from *over-imitation*, not *meta-representation*. In fact, it might be that without a propensity for *over-imitation* no animal will do this. Since the banana is incapable of fulfilling the *ends* of using a telephone, and can only fulfil, through some degree of physical resemblance, some aspects of the *means* associated with using a telephone, an animal that relies on *ends*-orientated learning would not make the connection between a banana and a telephone. Only an animal that learns action sequences by prioritising *means* would make the connection between a banana and a telephone – that is, that a banana has, by virtue of its physical form, the physical *affordance* to fulfil some of the *means* of using a telephone.

Note that a human infant needs to have no understanding whatever of what a phone is actually being used for (the true *ends*) when another individual is observed making a phone call in order to accurately reproduce the actions of holding a similar-shaped object to their ear and vocalising into it. In fact, it seems unlikely that an infant less than 18 months old has a clear understanding of what a phone actually does, and how – the concept that the phone allows them to speak to someone who is not present – so it is equally unlikely that they are carrying out a meta-representation that the banana that they are holding is allowing them to achieve the same *ends*. On the contrary, for the infant, the means *is* the end. The banana, by virtue of its resemblance to a phone, is being used in *exactly the same way* as the phone, as far as the infant is concerned. No meta-representation of *pretending* that the banana is a phone is required, because over-imitation emphasises the *means* of the action sequence, not the *end*, and thus emphasises the physical affordances of the banana, not its functional affordances (which bear no relation to those of a phone).

The earliest examples of 'pretending' in play, in children in mid-*infancy*, may rely only on over-imitation, not meta-representation, but the presence of this imitative play provides the foundations upon which true pretend play can be built, as the cognitive capacities for meta-representation emerge around the transition of the *infancy* and the *early childhood* phases – as understanding of categories of objects (and their limited genuine *affordances*) emerges, such play would rely on a capacity for meta-representation, in order to make such actions imaginative, via 'affordances of resemblance', a sort of *analogical thinking*. Without the propensity – drive, even – to over-imitate, these foundations for true pretend play might not exist at all, and nascent meta-representational abilities would have nothing on which to build in the early play context, to generate true pretend play.

Pretend Play Capacities, Ritual and Supernatural Belief

Bateson (2005) outlines some frequently occurring features of certain types of play behaviours in humans and other animals, some, but not all, of which seem to be in common with aspects of ritual practice. For example, playful behaviours often resemble behaviours carried out in 'normal' contexts, but without their immediate biological consequences. In social play, different social roles may be adopted, including reversal of roles normally held; in play involving physical activity, movements may be exaggerated in forms relative to their normal practice, and performed repeatedly. In some species, play activities are preceded by specific actions that indicate that what follows is of a different nature to 'normal' practice of those activities, marking a separation between the subsequent activity and 'real-life' practice of comparable actions. Play behaviours also frequently invoke genuine biological costs, including increased energy expenditure, conspicuousness to predators or adversaries and risk of injury (Bateson 2005). Each of these traits has parallels in certain ritual practices.

Many of the cognitive capabilities required for pretend play are also necessary for key features of ritual behaviours and supernatural belief. As Carruthers observes, "If pretence facilitates testimony about the not-here-and-now and religion involves beliefs about the not-here-and-now, then it is easy to see how such activities might in principle be dependent upon pretend play" (2002, 236, footnote 7). To which might be added the specific observation that a capacity for the conception of the not-here-and-now is essential for holding afterlife beliefs. In addition, the capacity to hold in mind possible future scenarios, in particular in the form of outcomes of actions, is essential for the conception of the functionality of rituals, whose presumed/intended outcome (*ends*) may be considerably deferred in time from the (*high-fidelity, over-imitated*) ritual actions (*means*) intended to bring them about.

Carruthers (2002) emphasises that creative thinking is not only useful in reasoning about the known world, but also in "enabling us to generate novel explanations and hypotheses, about the unseen causes of observed events, say". This, it may be noted, is also a central feature of many religious beliefs. This is also related to our understanding of causality, though, and we often explain this in terms of *agency* – and this relies on ToM as well as, perhaps, the mooted Hyperactive Agency Detection Device (HADD) (e.g. Barrett 2007; Guthrie 2007).

McConachie (2011) explores relationships between play, performance and ritual from an evolutionary point of view. McConachie points out that performance – of character roles, ritual roles, music, dance etc. – requires that kind of meta-representation seen in *early childhood* pretend play, and the ability to undertake the *conceptual integration* required to relate the two 'realities' to each other. Referring also to Donald's mimetic stage, and the performance of repeated actions through mimesis, he goes on to define performance as "an emergent activity of human evolution, performance is an intentional, emotionally expressive, event-centred phenomenon involving pattern and attention in social interaction – i.e., a type of play – that entails conceptual integration." (p. 43). To McConachie, then, performance is a type of play; in turn, he considers (after Boyd 2009) that "rituals tied to religious beliefs are the evolutionary offspring of play and performance" (p. 45), in that they rely on the presence of the capacities that already underpin play and performance.

In the end, he says, "Unlike play, our ancestors could not engage in religious rituals until they could manage double-scope blending; only the emergence of performance from play made ritual, along with theatre and games, possible" (p. 48). In fact, it could be argued that the emergence of performance from play in fact refers to the emergence of pretend play from the other types of play that we share with other animals – the type of capabilities for play that we see emerging and developing in sophistication during the period of *early childhood*.

THE EVOLUTION OF LIFE-HISTORY STAGES IN FOSSIL HOMININS

There are strong reasons to believe, then, that the development of the capacities that human children use in pretend play, which develop rapidly in form and frequency of use in the late *infancy* and *early*

childhood stages, but which are largely absent in apes along with the early childhood stage, are also critical foundations of other definitively human behaviours, including performance, ritual and cultural transmission. What can the palaeoanthropological and primatological record tell us about the emergence of the *infancy, early childhood* and *middle childhood/juvenile* stages of childhood in human evolution?

Higher primates, relative to other mammals, have a longer *juvenile* period (also known as *middle childhood* in humans). As has been discussed earlier in this chapter, humans, in turn, also feature an additional period prior to this, known as *early childhood*, and the period following the juvenile period, *adolescence*, is also considerably lengthened in humans relative to apes (Thompson & Nelson 2011). In sum, this results in humans having a developmental period that is almost twice the length of that of apes – for apes, growth and sexual maturity are reached by around the age of 11 years, whereas in humans, this is not fully achieved until around 18–20 years.

The development of the cognitive skills that are argued to underpin complex social relations, cultural transmission, innovation and creativity, and aspects of ritual and belief occurs during the stages of childhood, and these skills are prolifically manifested in the course of play activities, especially pretend play. These stages of childhood are uniquely lengthened in humans relative to our nearest relatives, the great apes, and it has been argued that the unique developmental sequence of humans has had a major impact on the emergence and development of these abilities (e.g. Thompson & Nelson 2011). Is it possible to identify when in the human evolutionary record these changes in ontogeny emerged? Is the human developmental sequence unique to *Homo sapiens*, or is there evidence of it in earlier ancestral hominins?

Identifying markers for onset and duration of the developmental periods in fossil species is complicated. This is in part because the developmental periods themselves are variously defined by researchers (in each of primate studies, human studies and hominin studies), and partly because the interpretation of the fossil evidence for them is itself complicated and can produce equivocal interpretations.

Attempts to develop life-history models for hominins from palaeoanthropological evidence have a long history, and as increasingly sophisticated analyses of the physical data have been developed there has been a burst of literature on the subject. Some authors have attempted to model the emergence of human life-history as a whole (e.g. Smith and Tompkins 1995; Key 2000; Leigh 2001; Robson & Wood 2008; Zollikofer & Ponce de León 2009) and others have explored in particular the significance of the *early childhood* (Thompson & Nelson 2011) and *juvenile* stages (e.g. Hochberg 2008; Thompson & Nelson 2011).

Markers for developmental stages include skeletal growth (e.g. Graves et al. 2010; Martín-González et al. 2012), cranial growth, as an indicator of brain development (e.g. Coqueugniot et al. 2004; Vinicius 2005; DeSilva and Lesnik 2006; Leigh 2006), and dental growth rates and eruption rates (e.g. Dean et al. 2001; Macchiarelli et al. 2006; Smith et al. 2007; Olejniczak et al. 2008; Ponce de León et al. 2008; Guatelli-Steinberg 2009; Bermúdez de Castro et al. 2010; Smith et al. 2010).

There is only space here to explore briefly the implications of these various sources of evidence. Physiological changes, such as the fusing of cranial bones, the fusing of the epiphyses of long bones, the development and eruption of teeth and the growth of the brain can all be used as accurate ways of determining the age of death of both chimpanzees and humans. The order and age of eruption of teeth, in particular, correlate very robustly in primates with life-history stages. However, while these processes occur at particular times in each genus, allowing aging of individuals *within* those genera, the age at which each of these physiological changes occurs varies between chimpanzees and humans. Their timing is thus likely to be different from both humans and chimpanzees in the case of fossil hominins, and the timing of these changes is one of the variables that we are seeking to understand in reconstructing hominin life-history. Thus our principal sources of evidence for aging hominin specimens are actually the variables we are seeking to understand. This complicates matters. It means that all of these changes need to be understood in relation to each other to be able to determine not just the relative chronology for each change, but an absolute chronology (duration). Fortunately,

progress in the understanding of dental formation processes has provided a valuable chronological framework on which to relate the other physiological changes. Teeth feature markings analogous to the growth rings of trees, called striae of Retzius and perikymata, which form at a constant rate as the teeth grow in the jaw. These form at somewhat different rates in humans and chimpanzees, but it has been possible to model the rates of this process in fossil hominins, aided by the fact that teeth very often preserve well in the fossil record when other skeletal evidence may be lost. However, the analysis of perikymata and the striae of Retzius that give rise to them is a developing science, and has produced results which in some cases remain equivocal (see, for example, Guatelli-Steinberg 2009).

Here we will look in particular at analyses related to brain growth rates and molar eruption in hominins, as being most significant to our principal interest in the emergence of the early stages of childhood and cognitive development at that time.

Dental Development

In apes and humans, significant life-history traits such as increase in brain size, age at first reproduction and overall lifespan correlate closely with identifiable stages of dental development, so analysis of the dentition of hominins has been used in attempts to identify the emergence of the human pattern of life-history. Two main dimensions have been examined: enamel growth rates, and the times of first permanent molar (M1) eruption (which, as noted previously, in modern higher primates and humans, indicates the beginning of the *middle childhood/juvenile* stage of development). The patterns of M1 eruption described here for chimpanzees, *Homo erectus*, *Homo neanderthalensis* and *Homo sapiens* are illustrated in Figure 6.2 for ease of comparison.

Chimpanzees and Australopithecines

Chimpanzees have an earlier age of eruption for M1 and shorter development times for anterior teeth than modern humans do, meaning

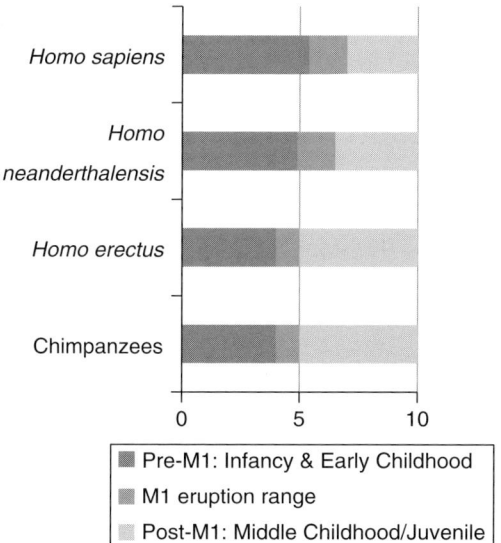

Figure 6.2 M1 eruption timing (relative to 95% brain size being reached at age 10) (Geary & Bjorklund 2000; Dean et al. 2001; Macchiarelli et al. 2006; T. Smith et al. 2007; Ponce de León et al. 2008; Guatelli-Steinberg 2009; T. Smith et al. 2010)

that both occur much more closely in time. Australopithecines had molar eruption times similar to those of chimpanzees as well as shorter incisor formation times than modern humans (Guatelli-Steinberg 2009).

Incisor formation times in humans can be quite plastic, and anterior teeth in primates are also potentially subject to variation on the basis of sexual selection and diet; for these reasons, Guatelli-Steinberg (2009) concludes that there are big question marks regarding whether *anterior* teeth formation times are of any clear relevance to life-history variables. Furthermore, given that enamel secretion rates are very constrained amongst apes and humans, we would expect that hominins with larger teeth would take longer to form them, so this might not be a good indicator of other life-history variables (Smith et al. 2007). The eruption of M1, however, is a much more robust indicator of life-history stages and, as outlined earlier, is a key marker of the timing of the start of the *juvenile* stage in apes and humans. The delayed eruption of M1 in humans is thus strongly correlated with the existence of the *early childhood* stage, which is unique to humans amongst the higher primates today – and not seen in australopithecines either.

Homo erectus

The enamel growth trajectory of australopithecines and the earliest *Homo* (*H. habilis* and *H. rudolfensis*) resembles that of modern and fossil African apes, rather than showing the slower trajectory of modern human enamel growth. In fact, the data considered for *Homo habilis* and *Homo rudolfensis* accord so closely with that of australopithecines that Dean and colleagues (2001) consider that this supports previous suggestions (on other criteria) that these species should be allocated to the genus *Australopithecus* rather than *Homo*.

The *sequence* of key events in tooth growth in *Homo erectus* – in the formation of the teeth and their order of emergence – has been shown to resemble the sequence in modern humans, but the rate of this process is unlikely to have been the same, since the enamel formation process is somewhat different (Dean et al. 2001). Specimens of *Homo erectus* from Nariokotome (Africa) (a.k.a. *Homo ergaster*) and Sangiran (Java) show shorter enamel formation times than in modern *Homo sapiens*. Dean and colleagues' (2001) analysis shows that the crown formation times for *anterior* teeth in Nariokotome are within the range of those of australopithecines, being more rapid than in *Homo sapiens*, and the Sangiran data show earlier estimates for *posterior* tooth eruption time too. Dean and colleagues (2001) estimate a first permanent molar (M1) emergence time of 4–4.5 years for *Homo ergaster/erectus*, interpreting this as having shifted somewhat, in line with changes in brain size, from that of African apes and australopithecines, but not yet deferred as much as in modern humans. Other authors, however (e.g. Ponce de León et al. 2008), give an M1 emergence time of 4–5 years for chimpanzees too, which suggests that little or no change from this timing is exhibited by early *Homo ergaster/erectus*.

Early *Homo* thus tend towards the human *pattern* of formation, but overlap with the range of African apes in dental formation *time*. The Neanderthal specimen Tabun C1, however, falls within the human time range (Dean et al. 2001). The data considered by Dean and colleagues (2001) suggest that the shift in enamel growth rates had occurred by the time of larger-brained Neanderthals (at least by 100 kyr ago) and modern humans, but had not done so at the time of early *Homo erectus*.

Further, Dean and colleagues (2001) suggest their data indicate that an extended developmental period like that of *Homo sapiens* arose *after* early *Homo erectus*, once brain and body size were within the range of modern humans (as is the case for Neanderthals and some (preceding) *Homo heidelbergensis*).

Homo antecessor

There are few analyses so far of the dental development of hominins on the lineage between *Homo erectus* and the appearance of Neanderthals and modern humans. Equivalent analyses of specimens of *Homo heidelbergensis* would be especially interesting in this regard. However, Bermúdez de Castro and colleagues (2010) analyse the dental development of two juvenile hominins from Atapuerca TD6 (Gran Dolina), dating to just under 1 million years ago (classed as *Homo antecessor* by these authors, descended from *Homo erectus* but earlier than *Homo heidelbergensis*). They conclude that this species showed a *sequence* of dental eruption the same as modern humans, as well as an extended period before the eruption of M1, as in modern humans, estimating age of emergence of M1 to be between 5.3 and 5.5 years (if enamel secretion rates were the same as in chimpanzees) or between 6.3 and 6.5 years (if enamel secretion rates were the same as in modern humans). Either range would place M1 eruption in *Homo antecessor* close to the range seen in modern humans (given by Smith et al. 2010 as 4.7–7.0 years, and by Macchiarelli et al. 2006 as 6.2±0.8 years). This finding accords well with the expectation that such extension of childhood prior to M1 emergence should correlate with increase in brain volume. In the case of *Homo antecessor*, as in late *Homo erectus*, brain size exceeds 1000cc in adulthood.

Homo neanderthalensis

Early studies suggested that Neanderthal dental development fell within the range known for modern humans, albeit with some aspects (or some specimens) being at the faster end of the human range. But more recent studies (see later in this chapter) have generated slightly different findings (Guatelli-Steinberg 2009).

Macchiarelli and colleagues (2006) found that there is some species-based difference in morphology and rate of Neanderthal molar teeth development, but the timing overlaps with the range seen in modern humans. They analysed not only crown formation, but also the development of internal molar structure. They show that whilst there are some species-specific traits in root formation duration in Neanderthals, according with some differences in tooth morphology, the timing of molar crown formation and root growth matches that of modern humans.

The perikymata patterns on the anterior teeth of Neanderthals show that the (relatively larger) incisors and canines of Neanderthals formed more rapidly than those of (some) modern humans. As noted, a better correlation with life-history variables and brain growth is provided by M1 emergence time, though, in all primates. Since in both great apes and humans, tooth height at eruption is made up of similar proportions of root to crown, Macchiarelli and colleagues' (2006) analysis of root formation in the immature La Chaise Neanderthal molar allowed them to predict that M1 emergence would have occurred at around 6.7 years of age, which is within the range of modern humans (6.2±0.8 years). Neanderthals also feature a similar position of the 'neonatal line', a marker on the tooth correlating with the time of birth. This suggests "similar timing of tooth initiation relative to birth in Neanderthals and modern humans, and a predictable extended period between birth and M1 emergence, by which time about 90% of brain volume would have been attained" (p. 750).

In contrast, Smith and colleagues (2007) found, on the basis of analysis of a different immature Neanderthal specimen from Scladina, that molar eruption time appeared to be earlier in this individual than in modern humans. By analysing periradicular band formation in the root and stress-event markers across the dentition, they estimated that the age of death of the Scladina juvenile was around 8 years, but the second molar (M2) had erupted (in modern humans, this usually occurs between 10 and 13 years on average, although note that there is much variation in this in *Homo sapiens*, and the eruption of the second and third molars is less robustly correlated with life-history events than is the eruption of M1 in apes and humans (Guatelli-Steinberg 2009)). While it was not possible to exactly identify the age of eruption of the M1, its root growth was complete and the tooth crown featured wear consistent with an estimated age of eruption of before 6 years (Smith et al. 2007).

Whilst earlier than the age calculated by Macchiarelli and colleagues (2006) for the La Chaise Neanderthal, the estimated age of M1 eruption of 6 years still falls within the range of modern humans of 6.2±0.8 years. As Guatelli-Steinberg (2009) points out, it may also be the case that differences between the La Chaise Neanderthal from France and the Scladina Neanderthal from Belgium simply reflect temporal and regional variation in Neanderthal populations. It may also be the case that the different age estimates generated for the two specimens by Macchiarelli and colleagues (2006) and Smith and colleagues (2007) are a product of the different root-formation analyses used.

More recent analysis of a much larger sample by Smith and colleagues (2010) concluded that most Neanderthal tooth crowns grew more rapidly than is the case in human teeth, leading to an overall more rapid process of dental maturation. However, this is still significantly extended over that of earlier *Homo* species – but the period of dental immaturity is especially prolonged in *Homo sapiens*, more so than in Neanderthals.

Smith and colleagues (2010) used a sample of 90 permanent teeth from 28 Neanderthal individuals, 39 permanent teeth from 9 fossil *Homo sapiens* individuals, and compared them with 464 permanent teeth from more than 300 recent human individuals. They found that, whilst the enamel cuspal secretion rates are virtually the same in Neanderthals and *Homo sapiens*, because the cuspal enamel of Neanderthals is thinner, it formed over a shorter time (Neanderthals have the same *volume* of enamel on their molars, but this is spread more thinly over a larger volume of coronal dentine (Olejniczak et al. 2008)). It is not possible to summarise here all of the different variables of their analysis, but they conclude that Neanderthal M1 crown formation was complete

around 6 months earlier than the average in humans, and that the eruption of M1 in Neanderthals likely occurred within the faster half of the modern human range (given here as 4.7–7.0 years).

They also again concluded that the M2 and M3 molar emergence times in Neanderthals appear more similar to those of *Homo erectus* identified by Dean and colleagues (2001) than to those of *Homo sapiens*, though this is very variable amongst modern humans.

Early *Homo sapiens*

Smith and colleagues (2007) analysed the dentition of the early *Homo sapiens* from Jebel Ihroud, Morocco, dated to around 160,000 years ago. This showed a dental development and molar emergence pattern within the range of modern humans, more similar to modern humans than to earlier *Homo*. Interestingly, the anterior teeth (incisor and canine) formation times were more similar to those of modern Europeans than to southern African populations of modern humans, and unlike the more rapid anterior tooth formation time of Neanderthals.

Smith and colleagues (2007) comment that the extended period of development before first molar emergence time in the Jebel Ihroud *Homo sapiens* "and by implication childhood, implies the advent of corresponding social, biological, and cultural changes necessary to support highly dependent children with prolonged opportunities for social learning in early childhood" (p. 6123). Note that the evidence of delayed M1 eruption times in *Homo antecessor* and Neanderthals, even if perhaps slightly earlier on average than in modern humans, should allow a similar observation to be made regarding their social, biological and cultural traits.

Brain Development

The pattern of brain growth in humans differs from that of chimpanzees, in that a much smaller percentage of adult brain development is present at birth in humans, meaning that much of the significant development of the brain and cognitive abilities occurs in the post-partum environment. The gross

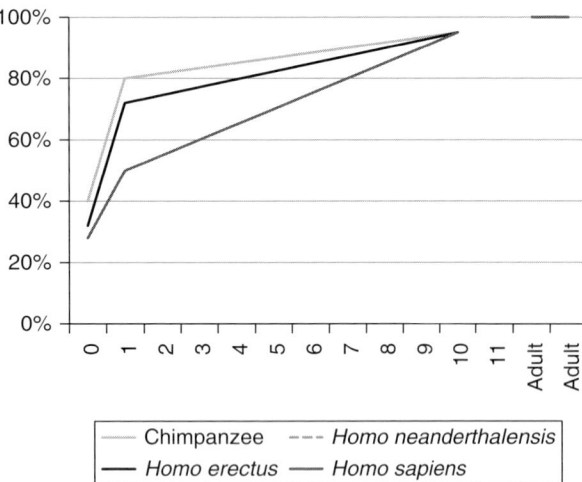

Figure 6.3 Rate of brain growth from birth to age 10 (95% of adult in all cases) in %. *Homo neanderthalensis* and *Homo sapiens* lines are coincident (Coqueugniot et al. 2004; Rightmire 2004; DeSilva and Lesnik 2006; Leigh 2006; Ponce de León et al. 2008).

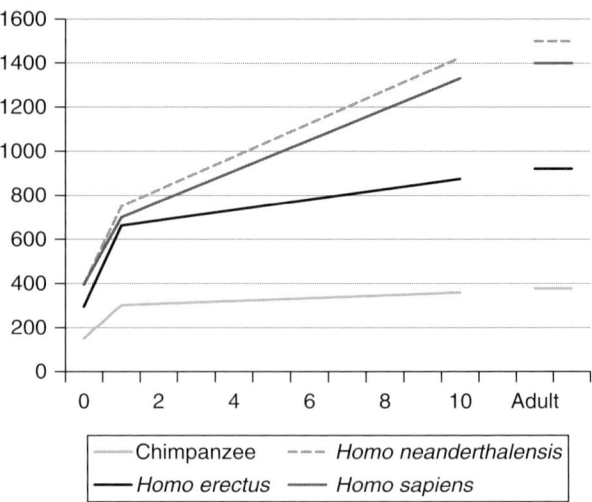

Figure 6.4 Rate of brain growth from birth to age 10 (95% of adult in all cases) in cc. Final adult size illustrated at right (Coqueugniot et al. 2004; Rightmire 2004; DeSilva and Lesnik 2006; Leigh 2006; Ponce de León et al. 2008).

volume that must be generated before maturity is also considerably greater, requiring substantial energetic investment. The patterns of brain growth (in chimpanzees, *Homo sapiens*, *Homo erectus* and *Homo neanderthalensis*) discussed in this section are represented graphically in Figure 6.3 (relative rate of brain growth in % of adult size) and Figure 6.4 (absolute rate of brain growth in cm³).

The human brain is about 27–29.5% of adult size at birth (ca. 380–415g), reaches 50% of adult size by 1 year of age (ca. 700g), and by 10 years of age, 95% of adult brain size is reached (Coqueugniot et al. 2004; DeSilva and Lesnik 2006).

Chimpanzees are born with an average brain mass of 150.9±17.0g, around 40% of adult brain size, which increases to 80% of adult size by the end of the first year (Coqueugniot et al. 2004; DeSilva and Lesnik 2006). The total duration of brain growth does not differ greatly between humans and chimpanzees, however (Leigh 2006).

Humans achieve their larger brain size than chimpanzees not through much-increased *duration* of growth, but through a much-increased *rate* of growth maintained throughout childhood (Ponce de León et al. 2008). In relative terms, then, the increase in brain size is similar in the first year of life of chimpanzees and humans (nearly doubling in volume), but the volume of brain matter that must

be generated is much greater in humans, and a much greater percentage of adult volume must be grown between 1 year old and maturity. This means that the majority of human brain growth occurs whilst the human infant is interacting with the rich post-partum environment (Coqueugniot et al. 2004), during the *early childhood* and *middle childhood* stages, when play behaviours are especially prominent and pretend play in particular, and the capacities underpinning it, undergo significant development.

It also means that humans have a much longer period of dependency on parental investment (secondary altriciality) before the onset of the *juvenile* stage, with all of the attendant energetic and social costs that must be met.

A major question for our investigation, then, concerns when this pattern of development emerged in human evolution. Is it unique to *Homo sapiens*, or do we see something of this pattern in earlier hominins?

Homo erectus

Coqueugniot and colleagues (2004) analyse the well-preserved calvaria of an immature *Homo erectus* from Mojokerto, Java, to attempt to identify the extent to which brain growth in this species resembled that of either chimpanzees or modern humans. On the basis of the maturity of cranial features (in comparison with chimpanzees and modern humans), they estimate the age of the individual to have been between 0.5 and 1.5 years. Its endocranial volume (the space housing the brain) was estimated using CT scanning to be 663cc. They then compared this volume with the average adult volume of *Homo erectus* brains to calculate the percentage of adult brain size that had been achieved in this individual. On this basis, they estimate that the Mojokerto child had achieved 84% of average adult *Homo erectus* brain size, matching more closely the chimpanzee brain development trajectory than that of modern humans.

However, the comparative sample used by Coqueugniot and colleagues (2004) to generate average adult *Homo erectus* brain size requires further scrutiny. This included a very divergent range of specimens, which varied widely in adult endocranial volume from 600–1059cc. For example, this included the early *Homo* specimens from Dmanisi, Georgia which have exceptionally low endocranial volumes of 600, 650 and 780cc, and which are classed by many as *Homo georgicus* rather than *Homo erectus* (or *ergaster*). In relation to these specimens, the Mojokerto child has clearly developed 100% of adult brain size at 0.5 to 1.5 years of age, which does not match any pattern in either apes or humans; this would suggest that the Dmanisi specimens are not good models for inclusion in *Homo erectus* brain size calculations. The sample also did not include other known specimens of *Homo erectus* with brain sizes of up to 1251cc, which would clearly have had an impact on the average brain size calculated for adult *Homo erectus*, and would have reduced the Mojokerto child's percentage of adult brain size achieved. Consequently the sample used by Coqueugniot and colleagues (2004) generates an adult brain size average of 878cc for *Homo erectus*, whereas other analyses give an average of 1008cc (Rightmire 2004) for this species (Leigh 2006).

Being conservative, if only the other known Indonesian specimens of *Homo erectus* are included in the calculations of average adult brain size, whose endocranial volumes range from 850–1059cc, this gives a value of 72% of adult brain size achieved by the Mojokerto child. This falls between that of humans (50%) and chimpanzees (80%) at 1 year of age. Instead using Rightmire's (2004) average of 1008cc for adults gives a value of 66% of adult volume for Mojokerto. Where the child fell on the estimated age range of 0.5–1.5 years clearly also would have a great influence on the extent to which this pattern of brain growth resembles either chimpanzees or humans. If the child is closer to 1 year of age, this would suggest that *Homo erectus* had already, at ca. 1.8 million years ago, developed a brain growth trajectory divergent from that of the African apes and australopithecines and closer to that of modern humans.

Leigh (2006), in response to Coqueugniot and colleagues' (2004) paper, emphasises the relevance of absolute brain growth as well as proportional brain growth (relative to adult volume). He points out that estimates of the neonatal brain size of *Homo erectus* infants, and the absolute brain size of the Mojokerto child, both fall within the range of *Homo sapiens* at those stages; the Mojokerto child's brain size is consistent with that of *Homo sapiens* children as young as 10 months old. This suggests, then, a pattern of brain growth in early ontogeny in *Homo erectus* that is very similar to that of modern humans, a pattern which is distinct from apes and australopithecines and may be a defining characteristic of the *Homo* genus (excluding 'transitional' *Homo/Australopithecus habilis* and *rudolfensis*). He concludes that "while both hominin species [*erectus* and *sapiens*] show comparable early growth rates, the obviously larger adult brain size of *H. sapiens* may arise from divergence in rates of later growth, differences in total duration of growth, or both" (p. 107). This means that secondary altriciality and its accompanying energetic, metabolic and social costs likely emerged early in the *Homo* genus, with *Homo erectus*. The later growth trajectory differs, however, in how a larger absolute adult brain size is achieved.

DeSilva and Lesnik (2006) carry out a comprehensive analysis of a large sample of chimpanzee and human neonates to reassess the brain size of these species, and its percentage of adult brain size; it had become clear that many earlier studies were quoting figures that were generated from very small samples and had not been reassessed. Their new figures are those quoted earlier in this chapter; they also explored the implications of these for hominin life-history, in reassessing the extent to which *Homo erectus'* probable brain size at birth resembled each of these figures for chimpanzees and modern humans.

According to DeSilva and Lesnik's (2006) analyses, applying a chimpanzee-like model of brain growth to *Homo erectus* would result in a *Homo erectus* neonate having a brain size of 394.5±87.8g. Applying a modern human-like model, on the other hand, would predict a *Homo erectus* brain size at birth of 295±68.4g. The latter is much closer to the figure that Walker and Ruff (1993) estimated (200–240g) would have been the maximum that could have been birthed by *Homo ergaster* (early *erectus*) on the basis of the pelvis of the Nariokotome individual (when corrected for age and sex). In fact, it may be added that the human pattern of 28% of adult brain size at birth would generate a neonatal brain size of 238g for that specimen, which has a projected adult volume of 850g – matching very well Walker and Ruff's (1993) estimated parturitional maximum.

This lower estimate for brain size at birth alters Leigh's (2006) finding slightly, in that it means that *Homo erectus'* brain size at birth was less than that of modern humans, but by 1 year of age it was within the range of humans in absolute size. This fits better with the implications of Coqueugniot and colleagues' (2004) analysis, of a somewhat increased *rate* in *Homo erectus* (see discussion earlier in this chapter).

It thus seems that *Homo ergaster/erectus* most likely showed a human-like pattern of prenatal brain growth (DeSilva & Lesnik 2006), and a pattern of brain growth in the first year of infancy that was slower than that of chimpanzees but still more rapid than that of modern *Homo sapiens* (Coqueugniot et al. 2004; Leigh 2006). This species thus shows a pattern of development that combines elements of the developmental patterns of both higher primates and modern humans in a unique way. This finding (illustrated in Figure 6.4) is also further supported by recent additional analyses of the Mojokerto child by O'Connell and DeSilva (2013).

Homo neanderthalensis

Ponce de León and colleagues (2008) modelled brain growth rates in Neanderthals and concluded that their brain size at birth was similar to that of *Homo*

sapiens. According to their analysis, Neanderthals featured more rapid brain growth in early infancy than modern humans do but the same total duration of development, which resulted in the overall larger absolute brain size possessed by Neanderthals. Large, rapidly growing brains require high energy investment and large, late-maturing mothers, leading Ponce de León and colleagues (2008) to conclude that Neanderthal life-history must have been at least as slow as that of modern humans.

They conclude that a neonatal brain size of ca. 400cc was likely to be a feature of the last common ancestor of both Neanderthals and *Homo sapiens*, and that this may be the maximum possible from an obstetric perspective, regardless of subsequent brain growth. This requires significant energetic investment on the part of the mother prior to birth, as well as after birth, when, in Neanderthals and *Homo sapiens* at least, very high rates of brain growth are sustained in infancy, with brain size nearly doubling in the first year of life. There must have been significant selective advantages to counteract these costs. One advantage of this pattern is that it could provide the necessary substrates for complex learning during early childhood (Leigh 2006). The evidence discussed previously regarding *Homo erectus* suggests that a similar pattern was in place already in that species, even if the absolute brain volumes were less.

Ponce de León and colleagues (2008) do caution, however, that increase in absolute brain size does not correlate strongly with brain *maturation* in modern humans, so does not necessarily indicate the development of cognitive skills.

Conclusions from Palaeoanthropological Evidence

Reconstruction of hominin life-history on the basis of analysis of palaeoanthropological remains can be complicated, but the techniques are undergoing a period of rapid refinement. The evidence discussed earlier, whilst in some ways equivocal, allows the following conclusions at this stage.

In terms of both brain growth patterns and dental development and emergence, australopithecines are widely agreed to closely resemble the African apes (gorillas and chimpanzees) of today. Similar observations would appear to pertain to the 'transitional' *Homo* species, *habilis* and *rudolfensis*. However, *Homo ergaster/erectus*, around 1.8 million years ago, does show some divergence from this pattern. As well as having a much larger adult brain size than earlier hominins (ca. 850–1150cc), and a body size within the range of *Homo sapiens*, this species most likely shows a modern human-like pattern of brain growth *in utero*, being born with a significantly underdeveloped brain relative to adult volume, contrasting with the pattern in chimpanzees. Their brain was probably rather smaller than a human or Neanderthal brain at birth, however, but by the age of 1 year was within the range of brain size of a modern human child of the same age. This represents a pattern that is different from either chimpanzees or humans today; *erectus*' early substantial brain growth took place in the rich post-partum social context entailing significant energetic investment, but appears to have retained a rate of growth to the (smaller than modern human) adult size that is more like that seen in chimpanzees. This matches the evidence from the dentition, which suggests that although a human-like order of emergence of dentition occurred, the M1 eruption occurred in this species at about the same time as it does in chimpanzees.

In sum, these data suggest that early *Homo erectus* did not experience the critical *early childhood stage*, but that the cognitive development occurring in *infancy* may have been enriched relative to that of chimpanzees. It may be that with *Homo erectus* we see an increase in the importance of the *infancy* stage relative to cognitive development, which lay the foundation in later species for the emergence of the *early childhood* stage. It is towards the end of the *infancy* stage in modern humans that we see the strong propensity for *over-imitation* come to the fore, which lays an important foundation for pretend play behaviours subsequently (see Section 2). It has been argued (e.g. Nielsen 2011) that in the rigorously replicated forms of Acheulian hand-axe technology produced by *Homo erectus* we see the manifestation of a similar propensity for over-imitation for the first time. It is also with *Homo erectus* that Donald (2001) sees the first evidence for the importance of mimesis.

Neanderthals seem to have shown a pattern of brain growth very similar to that of modern humans, being born with brains of about the same size, but growing them slightly faster in absolute terms to achieve an overall greater volume in adulthood. Thus it would seem that, as in modern humans, much of Neanderthal brain growth occurred in a rich post-partum social environment, and that they experienced clear secondary altriciality. Dental evidence from Neanderthals suggests a pattern somewhat different from modern humans (although significantly more modern human-like than ape-like), with more rapid formation of enamel and earlier eruption of M2 and M3 molars in the *juvenile* stage. However, by the most significant measure as regards life-history, the eruption of M1, Neanderthals fell within the range of modern humans. This clearly indicates the presence in Neanderthals of an *early childhood* stage. Future research may elaborate the extent of any difference in Neanderthals' *juvenile* stage, and its significance, but it would seem that they experienced an *infancy* and *early childhood* much like that of modern humans. Such a pattern is thus likely to date to our last common ancestor with Neanderthals (a *Homo heidelbergensis*-like hominin). Future analyses of *Homo heidelbergensis* specimens will hopefully shed further light on this. Initial analyses of the immature *Homo antecessor* specimens from Atapuerca Gran Dolina (ca. 1 million years old), which post-date the *Homo erectus* specimens analysed and probably predate our last common ancestor with Neanderthals, suggest that this pattern of *infancy* and *early childhood* may date at least to then, and coincide with the emergence of adult brain sizes in excess of 1000cc.

It would seem, in sum, that *Homo erectus* showed the first significant divergences from the great ape developmental trajectory, with a more modern human-like *infancy* stage, and that a modern-human-like pattern of *infancy* and *early childhood* emerged over the course of the development of *Homo erectus* into the last common ancestor of Neanderthals and modern humans. It is likely that aspects of later development (i.e. the *juvenile* and *adolescent* stages) continued to differ in these species. These differences are also likely to have been very significant in different ways, but require further investigation and are beyond the focus of this chapter.

CONCLUSIONS

There are strong parallels between the play behaviours of humans and other primates with respect to *social play* and *object play*, but a divergence when it comes to *pretend play*. The earliest examples of *pretend play* in humans, in late *infancy*, appear to have some parallels in chimpanzees, but these may rely largely on imitation rather than meta-representation. This may be greatly facilitated in its complexity in humans by the propensity in human children for *over-imitation*, providing a strong foundation for later *pretend play*. By the time humans are transitioning from *infancy* to the human-unique *early childhood* stage, other emerging cognitive capacities, including ToM, self-recognition, tactical deception, analogical thinking, symbolic intelligence and communicative abilities make meta-representation possible, and with it increasingly complex pretend play.

In *early childhood*, the complexity of *pretend play* develops, building upon these emerging cognitive abilities, and may also provide an excellent forum in which to develop, refine and relate these abilities. The *early childhood* stage is unique to humans amongst higher primates today and would appear to be essential for providing the opportunity for the development of these skills. These abilities also form core foundations for thought processes such as anthropomorphisation of objects, conceptions of absent beings and deferred consequences of actions, which also form foundations of aspects of spiritual beliefs and ritual behaviours. Indeed play behaviours more broadly contain structural elements that are shared with structural elements of ritual action, and could have formed a foundation for the emergence of such structures in the ritual context.

Palaeoanthropological evidence suggests that a pattern of brain growth diverging from that of apes emerged in early *Homo erectus* (or *Homo ergaster*), ca. 1.8 million years ago, with increased importance of brain growth in *infancy* due to the brain's relative immaturity at birth. This may have fostered the development of imitative capacities in this species, in particular *over-imitation*, which occurs in *infancy* in modern humans, and which is suggested by the archaeological evidence of Acheulian hand-axe tool production in some members of this species. There is no evidence, however, on the basis of first permanent molar (M1) emergence, of an *early childhood* stage in early *Homo erectus* analogous to that in modern humans, in which *pretend play* sees such significant development.

By the time of *Homo neanderthalensis* there is evidence of a brain growth trajectory very similar to that of modern humans over *infancy* and *childhood* (although slightly more rapid in overall terms due to the greater adult brain mass in Neanderthals). While there are species-specific differences in the rate of emergence of some aspects of the dentition, it appears that Neanderthal first molars emerged at a time within the range of modern humans, if at the more rapid end of that range, indicating the definite existence of an *early childhood* stage in Neanderthals. Since the presence of this pattern of *infancy* and *early childhood* is in common between Neanderthals and modern humans, it is likely that it was a feature of the last common ancestor of these species, 600–800,000 years ago, and that *early childhood* developed between early *Homo erectus* and this last common ancestor with Neanderthals. Neanderthals may still have shown some considerable differences from modern humans in terms of the duration of the *juvenile* and *adolescent* stages, however, and these would have implications of their own beyond those explored here for the earlier stages.

Since some aspects of *pretend play* are shared between chimpanzees and modern humans (and thus were likely exhibited by the last common ancestor of both, ca. 6 million years ago), it is likely that all subsequent hominins engaged to some degree in *pretend play*. The human and chimpanzee patterns of *pretend play*, in terms of their complexity and importance for developing later cognitive skills, diverge at the end of the *infancy* stage and are greatly developed in the *early childhood* stage in humans. If a similar pattern pertained in fossil hominins, this would lead to the conclusion that the proposed increasingly imitative (rather than emulative) *pretend play* of early *Homo erectus* was subsequently built upon during an increasingly lengthening *early childhood* stage in the last common ancestor of Neanderthals and modern humans. It would seem likely that these latter species had similar opportunities for pretend play, though these may have differed in their manifestation (as a consequence of cultural and cognitive differences) and subsequent development in *juvenility* and *adolescence*.

REFERENCES

Alexander, R. (1989) Evolution of the human psyche. In P. Mellars & C. Stringer (eds.) *The Human Revolution: Behavioural and Biological Perspectives on the Origins of Modern Humans*. Princeton, NJ: Princeton University Press, 455–513.

Barrett, J. (2007) Gods. In H. Whitehouse & J. Laidlaw (eds.) *Religion, Anthropology and Cognitive Science*. Durham, NC: Carolina Academic Press, 105–32.

Bateson, P. (2005) The role of play in the evolution of great apes and humans. In A. Pellegrini & P. Smith (eds.) *The Nature of Play: Great Apes and Humans*. London: Guilford Press, 13–24.

Bermúdez de Castro, J., Martinón-Torres, M., Prado, L., Gómez-Robles, A., Rosell, J., López-Polin, L., Arsuaga, J. & Carbonell, E. (2010) New immature hominin fossil from European Lower Pleistocene shows the earliest evidence of a modern human dental development pattern. *Proceedings of the National Academy of the Sciences of the USA* 107, 11739–44.

Bogin, B. (2003) The human pattern of growth and development in palaeontological perspective. In J. Thompson, G. Krovitz & A. Nelson (eds.) *Patterns of Growth and Development in the Genus Homo*. Cambridge: Cambridge University Press, 15–44.

Boyd, B. (2009) *On the Origin of Stories: Evolution, Cognition and Fiction*. Cambridge, MA: Belknap Press.

Boyd, R. & Richerson, P. (1985) *Culture and the Evolutionary Process*. Chicago: University of Chicago Press.

Carruthers, P. (2002) Human creativity: its cognitive basis, its evolution, and its connections with childhood pretence. *British Journal of the Philosophy of Science* 53, 225–49.

Coqueugniot, H., Hublin, J.-J., Veillon, F., Houët, F. & Jacob, T. (2004) Early brain growth in *Homo erectus* and implications for cognitive ability. *Nature* 431, 299–302.

Davis, P., Zhang, S., Winkworth, A. & Bandler, R. (1996) Neural control of vocalisation: respiratory and emotional influences. *Journal of Voice* 10, 23–38.

Dean, C., Leakey, M., Reid, D., Schrenk, F., Schwartz, G., Stringer, C. & Walker, A. (2001) Growth processes in teeth distinguish modern humans from *Homo erectus* and earlier hominins. *Nature* 414, 628–31.

DeSilva, J. & Lesnik, J. (2006) Chimpanzee neonatal brain size: implications for brain growth in *Homo erectus*. *Journal of Human Evolution* 51, 207–12.

Donald, M. (1991) *Origins of the Modern Mind: Three Stages in the Evolution of Culture and Cognition*. Cambridge, MA: Harvard University Press.

Donald, M. (2001) *A Mind So Rare: The Evolution of Human Consciousness*. London: Norton.

Finke, R., Ward, T. & Smith, S. (1992) *Creative Cognition*. Boston: MIT Press.

Fry, D. (2005) Rough and tumble social play in humans. In A. Pellegrini & P. Smith (eds.) *The Nature of Play: Great Apes and Humans*. London: Guilford Press, 54–85.

Gaskins, S. (1999) Children's lives in a Mayan village: a case of culturally constructed roles and activities. In A. Gönkü (ed.) *Children's Engagement in the World: Sociocultural Perspectives*. Cambridge: Cambridge University Press, 25–61.

Geary, D. & Bjorklund, D. (2000) Evolutionary developmental psychology. *Child Development* 71, 57–65.

Gómez, J.-C. & Martin-Andrade, B. (2005) Fantasy play in apes. In A. Pellegrini & P. Smith (eds.) *The Nature of Play: Great Apes and Humans*. London: Guilford Press, 139–72.

Gosso, Y., Otta, E., Morais, M., Ribeiro, F. & Bussab, V. (2005) Play in hunter-gatherer society. In A. Pellegrini & P. Smith (eds.) *The Nature of Play: Great Apes and Humans*. London: Guilford Press, 213–53.

Graves, R., Lupo, A., McCarthy, R., Wescott, D. & Cunningham, D. (2010) Just how strapping was KNM-WT 15000? *Journal of Human Evolution* 59, 542–4.

Guatelli-Steinberg, D. (2009) Recent studies of dental development in Neanderthals: implications for Neanderthal life histories. *Evolutionary Anthropology* 18, 9–20.

Guthrie, S. (2007) Anthropology and anthropomorphism in religion. In H. Whitehouse & J. Laidlaw (eds.) *Religion, Anthropology and Cognitive Science*. Durham, NC: Carolina Academic Press, 37–62.

Haight, W. & Miller, P. (1993) *Pretending at Home: Early Development in a Sociocultural Perspective*. Albany: State University of New York Press.

Hawkes, K., O'Connell, J. F., Jones, N. B., Alvarez, H. & Charnov, E. L. (1998) Grandmothering, menopause, and the evolution of human life histories. *Proceedings of the National Academy of Sciences* 95, 1336–9.

Hochberg, Z. (2008) Juvenility in the context of life history theory. *Archives of Disease in Childhood* 93, 534–9.

Horner, V. & Whiten, A. (2005) Causal knowledge and imitation/emulation switching in chimpanzees (Pan troglodytes) and children (Homo sapiens). *Animal Cognition* 8, 164–81.

Jürgens, U. (1992) On the neurobiology of vocal communication. In H. Papousek, U. Jürgens & M. Papousek (eds.) *Nonverbal Vocal Communication*. Cambridge: Cambridge University Press, 31–42.

Key, C. (2000) The evolution of human life history. *World Archaeology* 31, 329–50.

Leigh, S. (2001) Evolution of human growth. *Evolutionary Anthropology* 10, 223–36.

Leigh, S. (2006) Brain ontogeny and life history in *Homo erectus*. *Journal of Human Evolution* 50, 104–8.

Lewis, K. (2005) Social play in the great apes. In A. Pellegrini & P. Smith (eds.) *The Nature of Play: Great Apes and Humans*. London: Guilford Press, 27–53.

Macchiarelli, R., Bondioli, L., Debénath, A., Mazurier, A., Tournepiche, J.-F., Birch, W. & Dean, C. (2006) How Neanderthal molar teeth grew. *Nature* 444, 748–51.

Marlowe, F. (2000) The patriarch hypothesis. *Human Nature* 11, 27–42.

Martín-González, J., Mateos, A., Goikoetxea, I., Leonard, W. & Rodríguez, J. (2012) Differences between Neanderthal and modern human infant and child growth models. *Journal of Human Evolution* 63, 140–9.

McConachie, B. (2011) An evolutionary perspective on play, performance and ritual. *TDR: The Drama Review* 55, 33–50.

Mitchell, R. (2007) Pretense in animals: the continuing relevance of children's pretense. In A. Gönkü & S. Gaskins (eds.) *Play and Development: Evolutionary, Sociocultural and Functional Perspectives*. London: Psychology Press, 51–75.

Nielsen, M. (2012) Imitation, pretend play, and childhood: essential elements in the evolution of human culture? *Journal of Comparative Psychology* 126, 170–81.

Nielsen, M. & Blank, C. (2011) Imitation in children: when who gets copied is more important that what gets copied. *Developmental Psychology* 47, 1050–3.

O'Connell, C. & DeSilva, J. (2013) Mojokerto revisited: evidence for an intermediate pattern of brain growth in *Homo erectus. Journal of Human Evolution* 65, 156–61.

O'Connell, J. F., Hawkes, K. & Jones, N. B. (1999) Grandmothering and the evolution of *Homo erectus. Journal of Human Evolution* 36, 461–85.

Olejniczak, A., Smith, T., Feeney, R., Macchiarelli, R., Mazurier, A., Bondioli, L., Rosas, A., Fortea, J., de la Rasilla, M., Garcia-Tabernero, A., Radovčić, J., Skinner, M., Toussaint, M. & Hublin, J.-J. (2008) Dental tissue proportions and enamel thickness in Neanderthal and modern human molars. *Journal of Human Evolution* 55, 12–23.

Peccei, J. S. (2001) A critique of the grandmother hypotheses: old and new. *American Journal of Human Biology* 13, 434–52.

Pellegrini, A. & Smith, P. (2005) Play in great apes and humans. In A. Pellegrini & P. Smith (eds.) *The Nature of Play: Great Apes and Humans*. London: Guilford Press, 3–12.

Pellegrini, A. & Smith, P. (2005) *The Nature of Play: Great Apes and Humans*. London: Guilford Press.

Perner, J., Ruffman, T. & Leekam, S. (1994) Theory of mind is contagious: you catch it from your sibs. *Child Development* 65, 1228–38.

Ponce de León, M., Golovanova, L., Doronichev, V., Romanova, G., Akazawa, T., Kondo, O., Ishida, H. & Zollikofer, C. (2008) Neanderthal brain size at birth provides insights into the evolution of human life history. *Proceedings of the National Academy of Sciences of the USA* 105, 13764–8.

Rightmire, G. (2004) Brain size and encephalization in early to mid-Pleistocene *Homo. American Journal of Physical Anthropology* 124, 109–23.

Robson, S. & Wood, B. (2008) Hominin life history: reconstruction and evolution. *Journal of Anatomy* 212, 394–425.

Schwartzmann, H. (1978). *Transformations: The Anthropology of Children's Play*. New York: Plenum.

Slaughter, D. & Dombrowski, J. (1989). Cultural continuities and discontinuities: impact on social and pretend play. In M. Bloch & A. Pellegrini (eds.) *The Ecological Context of Children's Play*. Nowood: Ablex, 282–310.

Smith, B. & Tompkins, R. (1995) Towards a life history of the hominidae. *Annual Review of Anthropology* 24, 257–79.

Smith, P. (1982) Does play matter? Functional and evolutionary aspects of animal and human play. *Behavioural and Brain Sciences* 5, 139–84.

Smith, P. (2005) Social and pretend play in children. In A. Pellegrini & P. Smith (eds.) *The Nature of Play: Great Apes and Humans*. London: Guilford Press, 173–209.

Smith, P. (2007) Evolutionary foundations and functions of play: an overview. In A. Gönkü & S. Gaskins (eds.) *Play and Development: Evolutionary, Sociocultural and Functional Perspectives*. London: Psychology Press, 21–49.

Smith, P. (2010) *Children and Play*. Oxford: Wiley-Blackwell.

Smith, P. & Pellegrini, A. (2005) Play in great apes and humans: reflections on continuities and discontinuities. In A. Pellegrini & P. Smith (eds.) *The Nature of Play: Great Apes and Humans*. London: Guilford Press, 285–98.

Smith, T., Tafforeau, P., Reid, D., Grün, R., Eggins, S., Boutakiout, M. & Hublin, J.-J. (2007) Earliest evidence of modern human life history in North African early *Homo sapiens. Proceedings of the National Academy of Sciences of the USA* 104, 6128–33.

Smith, T., Tafforeau, P., Reid, D., Pouech, J., Lazzari, V., Zermeno, J., Guatelli-Stainberg, D., Olejniczak, A., Hoffman, A., Radovčić, J., Makaremi, M., Toussaint, M., Stringer, C. & Hublin, J.-J. (2010) Dental evidence for ontogenetic differences between modern humans and Neanderthals. *Proceedings of the National Academy of Sciences of the USA* 107, 20923–8.

Thompson, J. & Nelson, A. (2011) Middle childhood and modern human origins. *Human Nature* 22, 249–80.

Tomasello, M. (1999) *The Cultural Origins of Human Cognition*. Cambridge, MA: Harvard University Press.

Vinicius, L. (2005) Human encephalization and developmental timing. *Journal of Human Evolution* 49, 762–76.

Walker, A. & Ruff, C. (1993) The reconstruction of the pelvis. In A. Walker & R. Leakey (eds.) *The Nariokotome Homo erectus Skeleton*. Cambridge, MA: Harvard University Press.

Whiten, A. (2005) The second inheritance system of chimpanzees and humans. *Nature* 437, 52–5.

Zollikofer, C. & Ponce de León, M. (2009) The evolution of hominin ontogenies. *Seminars in Cell & Developmental Biology* 21, 441–52.

7

FROM PLAY AND RITUALISATION TO RITUAL AND ITS ARTS: SOURCES OF UPPER PLEISTOCENE RITUAL PRACTICES IN LOWER MIDDLE PLEISTOCENE RITUALISED AND PLAY BEHAVIOURS IN ANCESTRAL HOMININS

Ellen Dissanayake

A contemporary discussion of play or ritual in animals and early humans will do well to begin with an appreciation of these classic concepts as formulated by the founders and pioneers of ethology (see also Renfrew, Chapter 2, this volume). As an academic field, ethology – the naturalistic study of behaviour from an evolutionary perspective (Burghardt 2005, 10) – had only a half-century lifespan (roughly from the 1930s to the 1980s) before being incorporated into the newer fields of evolutionary psychology, behavioural ecology and cognitive psychology. Yet the close observations and descriptions of play and ritualised behaviours in animals by early ethologists have informed interesting and stimulating recent theory in a variety of subjects in humans (e.g. Rappaport 1999; Watanabe & Smuts 1999; Bjorklund and Pellegrini 2002; Schechner 2002; Burghardt 2005; Feierman 2009) and are, I believe, relevant to archaeological understanding of ritual and the formation of religious belief. Studies in affective neuropsychology and neuropsychiatry (e.g. Panksepp 1988; Panksepp & Biven 2012) make clear that there is a continuity of animal and human minds and behaviour.

In this chapter, I propose that what anthropologists call 'ritual' originated in several constituent elements of play and ritualised behaviours – to be described later. These can be observed in many non-human animals and are assumed to have developed further during the evolution of brain and behaviour of Lower Middle Pleistocene hominins. I further suggest that these elements, gradually elaborated in ritual contexts, are antecedents and components of what are called 'arts'. I maintain that it is primarily through participation in 'arts'-filled rituals that (religious) belief and doctrine are instilled and reinforced (see Burghardt, Chapter 3, this volume, who also considers belief and doctrine 'secondary' concerns; see also Garfinkel, Chapter 11; Renfrew, Chapter 2; Watkins, Chapter 10, this volume).

Ritualisation

One of the most interesting and original observations ethologists describe is *ritualisation* of behaviour. It is important to emphasise that the term, although derived semantically from a seeming correspondence with human rites or rituals, nevertheless has a precise ethological meaning that is to be distinguished from other uses that are not specifically ethological.

In 1914, while studying the courtship behaviour of the great crested grebe (a bird), Julian Huxley proposed that highly stereotyped communicative signals in animals had evolved by natural selection in the same way as more instrumental behaviours (see also Watanabe & Smuts 1999). He coined the term *ritualisation* to refer to this process. In the 1950s, ethologists (e.g. Tinbergen 1952, 1959; Eibl-Eibesfeldt 1971, 1989; Hinde 1982; Lorenz 1982) expanded Huxley's insight and described how the process occurs.

In ritualisation, components of a behaviour that occurs as part of normal, everyday, instrumental activity – such as preening, nest-building, preparing to fly or caring for young – are, as it were, 'selected' or taken out of context, 'ritualised', and used to signal an entirely different motivation – usually an attitude or intention that might then influence (affect or manipulate) the behaviour of another animal. For example, the head movements gulls use to pluck grass for building a nest may be co-opted and ritualised to signal aggression (thus driving another gull away), or behaviours derived from feeding young may become ritualised and used for courtship (i.e. touching bills, offering a token with the bill or coughing as if regurgitating, in order to attract and seduce a mate).

The process of ritualisation refers to particular changes or 'operations' that make the new activity prominent, distinctive and unambiguous (Smith 1977, 328; Eibl-Eibesfeldt 1989, 439–40). Unlike the original instrumental or 'ordinary' precursor behaviour, ritualised movements or sounds become 'extraordinary' and thus attract attention. They typically become (a) *simplified* or stereotyped (formalised), and (b) *repeated* rhythmically, often with a 'typical' intensity (Morris 1957) – that is, with a characteristic regularity of pace. The signals are frequently (c) *exaggerated* in time and space, and (d) further emphasised or *elaborated* by the development of special colours or anatomical features. The peacock's display is a canonical example of a ritualised behaviour that originated in such simple precursors as pecking the ground for food and lifting, spreading and fanning the tail feathers for thermoregulation (see Eibl-Eibesfeldt 1971, 44–7).

Another alteration of ordinary behaviour can be seen in the 'displacement activities' of animals when they are in uncertain or conflicted circumstances. As in ritualised behaviours, body movements used in everyday contexts such as grooming (scratching, preening) or locomotion are transformed, becoming *stereotyped* – that is, *exaggerated*, patterned in space and time and regularised (*repeated*). Such movements

reduce tension in the displaying animal at the same time as they signal its mood and intentions to conspecifics (Lorenz 1982, 249–53).

Although ethologists suggested that there were parallels or analogies between ritualised behaviours in non-human animals and particular kinds of behaviour in humans (e.g. greetings and partings, smiling in submission), to my knowledge none identified an actual human ritualised behaviour. However, in several articles (e.g. Dissanayake 2000, 2001) I have argued that apparently universal, cross-culturally observed interactions between mothers and small infants possess many noteworthy characteristics of a biologically ritualised behaviour. That is, visual, vocal and gestural expressions drawn from common adult contexts of affinity and intimacy (Look at, Smile, Open Eyes, Open Mouth, Mutual Gaze, Eyebrow Flash, Head Bob Backwards, Head Nod, Head and Body Lean Forward, Soft but High-Pitched and Undulant Sounds, Reassuring and Sympathetic Touching, Pats, Hugs and Kisses) are simplified or stereotyped, repeated or sustained, exaggerated and elaborated – all serving to temporally coordinate and emotionally unite the mother–infant pair. Some of these behaviours can be seen in affiliative contexts in higher primates (King 2004), suggesting that they probably occurred in early hominins.

Psychologists have described a number of important adaptive psychological and cognitive benefits of these interactions to babies. These include assisting emotional equilibrium, self- and interactive regulation, socialisation, language-learning, cognitive development and acquisition of the parental culture (see list in Dissanayake 2008, 254). Importantly, neurochemicals secreted in the mother's brain when she intensifies these affinitive behaviours inadvertently create tender and loving feelings towards her infant, assuring more attentive care (Carter 1998; Nelson & Panksepp 1998; Carter, Lederhandler & Kirkpatrick 1999; Panksepp, Nelson & Bekkedal 1999).

Infants are born ready to respond to and coordinate their own behaviour with these extraordinary affinitive signals. In fact, by their responses, infants 'teach' their caretakers to speak and act this way: they 'reward' extraordinary signals with smiles, wriggles and coos, but are unresponsive to adult-style discourse directed to them. The mother–infant interaction can be viewed as a co-created evolved adaptive behaviour with benefits to both infant (survival) and mother (reproductive success).

Play

Mother–infant interaction is often described, thought of and experienced as playful or a kind of play (e.g. Stern 1977). It is spontaneous, improvised and self-rewarding; both partners show that they are enjoying themselves. Between three and four months of age, infants become bored with the soothing predictable interaction described previously. Instead, they desire suspense and surprise, which mothers provide in action games and songs such as Peek-A-Boo, This Little Piggy or Round and Round the Garden. Manipulation of expectation rests, I suggest, on Desmond Morris's ethological notion of 'typical intensity', described when he noted that the iteration of a ritualised movement or sound has a typical rhythmic regularity and intensity in time (1957). If humans (including four-month-old infants) were not aware of typical intensity of a repeated, regular stimulus, they would not be susceptible to its manipulation. Recent studies of the nature and evolution of a capacity for temporal and affective entrainment (a shared sense of rhythmic timing and affective state) suggest that some of the abilities for cross-modal integration of timing and 'beat' information in music begin to emerge early in infancy in interactions with parents (Phillips-Silver, Aktipis & Bryant 2010; Phillips-Silver and Keller 2012).

As described by early ethologists (e.g. Meyer-Holzapfel 1956), play – though difficult to define – is common to all social animals and is often based in recognising and creating an 'as if' or 'other' world, or a 'meta-reality'. Because play occurs in all higher mammals, we can reasonably assume that young hominins, like other primates, played. Although it is not known when fantasy play (pretence) began in our remote ancestors – evidence for its occurrence in great apes is controversial (Pellegrini & Bjorklund 2004; Smith, Chapter 5, this volume) – it is universal in human children, where it frequently occurs in a social context (see also Smith, Chapter 5, this volume, and Morley, Chapter 6, this volume). Interestingly,

pretend play requires the player to take a stance that is different from reality (Lillard 1993): something (say, a stick) is substituted for something else (a doll to hold or a horse to ride). When playing, human children, like other social animals, alter their ordinary behaviour using devices like the operations of ritualisation described in the previous section. For example, 'frame markers' such as exaggerated voice or movement signal to others that 'this is play' (Leslie 1987; Pellegrini & Bjorklund 2004, 31). Actions of play also may be stereotyped, use rhythmic and other kinds of repetition and be elaborated (Meyer-Holzapfel 1956). The predisposition to adorn the self or to present a 'different' self with costume, easily observed in the play of children as well as more seriously in adults, also creates a state of being that is recognisably extraordinary.

Using the hands for play should also be mentioned. As toolmakers and users, it is not surprising that members of our species evolved to find satisfaction and even pleasure in using their flexible and dexterous hands. This is evident even in babies who from their first months are preoccupied with their hands. First they reach out, then grasp and manipulate anything within reach, and finally develop a precision grip. Usually in about the third year, when given a drawing or marking implement, children will spontaneously use it on a suitable surface. The marks at first look like locomotor and exploratory play, with energetic large, often circular arm movements. As motor skill improves, children learn to draw with "orderly growing complexity" from "an inner imperative" (Fein 1993, xiii) – that is, the process is self-taught (Burrill 2010). They spontaneously 'play with form' (Alland 1983), as they make scribbles with meandering lines or dots and flecks, then geometric shapes – circles, arcs, more deliberately drawn and intersecting lines, spirals – which are frequently repeated, exaggerated and elaborated (Kellogg 1970; Fein 1993).

Meta-representation

During the evolution of humans, as during child development, brain growth and reorganisation eventually enabled what has been called 'meta-representation' or 'decoupling' – the ability to pretend and to understand pretence in others (Leslie 1987; Cosmides & Tooby 2000) and to appreciate fiction as distinct from reality (Tooby & Cosmides 2001). A related capacity is 'mental time travel', the ability to recall the past in order to imagine the future (Suddendorf & Corballis 1997). Other investigators speak of the development of explicit or working memory that permits one to juggle the past and present, aiming for future goals (Kavanagh, Andrade & May 2005). Although implicit memory presumably exists to varying degrees in all species with a nervous system, allowing for simple conditioning, explicit memory seems to be unique to humans and probably developed in stages, which Bjorklund and Pellegrini (2002, 122–4) have assigned to Merlin Donald's four stages of hominin cognitive evolution (Donald 1991). I use their scheme heuristically, appreciating of course that the particular characteristics are matters of degree and that they occur on a continuum (see also Renfrew, Chapter 2, this volume, and Morley, Chapter 6, this volume). The stages can be very minimally described as follows.

The first cognitive stage, 'Episodic Culture', characterises Australopithecines (as well as primates and even other animals). Individuals live in what can be called a 'continuous present', reacting to occurrences as they appear in their environment by general instinctive programmes such as approach, avoid, fight, flee or freeze. Memory is of specific events in the past that have rich perceptual content, different from (and additional to) procedural memory (of how to do things).

The second cognitive stage, 'Mimetic Culture', characterised *H. erectus*, whose tool manufacture required inventing and remembering a variety of complex procedures as well as maintaining and transmitting them to others. Mimesis involves the ability to produce conscious, self-initiated, representational acts that are intentional yet not symbolic. Donald cites trades and crafts, games, athletics, 'a significant percentage of art forms', various aspects of theatre, including pantomime, and most social ritual as being within the capabilities of mimetic cultures. He reminds us that mimesis can incorporate a wide variety of actions and modalities, such as tones of voice, facial expressions, eye movements, manual signs and gestures, postural attitudes, patterned whole-body

movements of various sorts and long sequences of these elements (1991, 167, 169).

Although Donald dissociates mimetic skill from the symbolic and semiotic devices on which modern human cultures depend, he proposes that it has many of the properties of language, which developed during a long transitional period to the third cognitive stage, 'Mythic Culture', in which humans had speech and highly developed semiotic skill – the ability to invent and use signs to communicate thought. Donald considers Mimetic Culture to have continued after the reign of *H. erectus* (from upwards of 1.5 million to about 300,000 years ago) in a transitional phase to Mythic Culture, which is characteristic of modern humans (from about 50,000 years ago, though more recent finds may revise this age upwards considerably: see Henshilwood et al. 2002; Vanhaeren et al. 2006; Bouzouggar et al. 2007; d'Errico et al. 2009). He emphasises the monumental effects of speech on human cognition – on what could be thought once there were words to think with. The fourth cognitive stage, 'Theoretic Culture', emerges from the ability to store symbols externally in books, film, recordings and now electronic forms.

Among the properties of language that Donald describes in Mimetic Culture (intentional communication, recursion and differentiation of reference), he does not include the prosodic (emotional, expressive) half of language, which I suggest would have been used and developed by ancestral mothers interacting with infants. Researchers have posited 'intense maternal care' or 'intensive parenting' as early as 1.8 million years ago (Rosenberg 1992; Leakey 1994; Falk 2004, 2009; Flinn & Ward 2005, 31), permitting the interactive mother–infant ritualised behaviour described earlier to evolve and contributing to the invention of pre-symbolic ritual in Mimetic Culture (see next section).

Whether or not one accepts Donald's scheme in all details (an analytic and critical task that is not necessary for my purposes here), I suggest that it would have been possible for meta-representational ability to develop in early hominins during the long pre-symbolic and pre-linguistic stage of Mimetic Culture. Evidence of foresight and sophisticated tools in pre-sapiens humans can be found as early as 400,000 years ago with the discovery of wooden spears, six to seven feet long, with more than 10,000 animal bones near Schöningen in Germany (Thieme 1997) and between 110,000 and 80,000 years ago in beautifully carved bone harpoons from Katanda in Zaire (Yellen et al. 1995).

Rather than simply reacting in the moment to hunger or danger and following the promptings of instinct, ancestral humans with a developing explicit memory were able to remember past events that were desirable or undesirable and then attempt to forestall unpleasant experiences and ensure satisfying ones. (With this statement, I do not mean to discount that squirrels cache nuts for the winter, some chimpanzees have been observed putting aside a stick for future use, and similar examples. Birds such as the Western scrub-jay and other corvids show remarkable abilities to remember the past and plan ahead [Clayton, Bussey & Dickinson 2003; Raby et al. 2007].)

I suggest that the human cultural invention of ritual behaviour and religion was grounded in the ancestral capacity for meta-representation, which not only is related to explicit memory and foresight, but, I submit, includes expansion of the recognition of the extraordinary that is implicit in ritualised behaviours and play. I further claim that although it has not been sufficiently recognised and described by other scholars, a predisposition to *deliberately create the extraordinary*, especially in response to matters of biological importance with high affective valence, is inherent in human nature as it evolved during the transition from Mimetic to Mythic Culture as just described and as further elucidated in the next section.

The Invention of Religion

Awareness of Ordinary and Extraordinary

The behaviours of play and ritual have many similarities, but one seems particularly relevant to the subjects of this volume: the capacity to discriminate between an ordinary or mundane order, realm, mood or state of being and another that is unusual, extraordinary or supernatural. These are imprecise terms and may be considered scientifically or philosophically

inadequate, although other contributors to this volume have used similar terminology (e.g. Renfrew, 'as if' as a meta-category, 'special' artefacts, 'special' places; Kyriakidis, the coming together in games and rituals is "not every day", "[b]oth ritual and games are special actions, in that they are separated from the mundane world"; Garfinkel, "dance is ... not associated with any everyday functional activity"; Halley, Puebloan dances are "removed from everyday life"; Osborne, "both ritual and play define themselves by opposition to the 'normal'").

The distinction seems apt to account for evidence that as early as 250,000 years ago ancestral hominins noticed stones with unusual patterns or markings and carried them to their dwelling sites (Oakley 1971; Dissanayake 1988) or hammered cupules on stone surfaces (Bednarik 2008), thereby making 'ordinary' rock 'extraordinary'. I am aware that anthropologists sometimes describe the worldviews of traditional peoples as making no distinction between natural and supernatural realms, considering themselves and non-human entities and forces all equally real inhabitants of their cosmic order (e.g. Tonkinson 1978, on the Mardudjara in Australia). However, actions in rituals demonstrate that holders of these worldviews nevertheless make their bodies, surroundings, movements and utterances different from their ordinary state, showing that they make deliberate distinction between imbibing a ritual drink and quenching one's thirst or giving thanks to the forest with a dance and casually moving around in the forest. It is this distinction that I am concerned with here.

As described earlier, ethological observations show that infants with caretakers, young children and many other animals also recognise and even create non-ordinary 'realities' in ritualised behaviours and play (Burghardt, Chapter 3, this volume). If birds and babies can do it, one should not be surprised that this capacity could exist in ancestral humans.

Ritual as Participation

Psychologists confirm that humans are fundamentally motivated to achieve some level of control over events, resources and relationships that are significant in their lives and become distressed when this control is lacking (Geary 2005). Individually, we appraise the circumstances of our lives in terms of elements such as pleasantness, certainty, anticipated effort, control, legitimacy or perceived obstacle (Ellsworth 1991). Perceived uncertainty may produce fear and anxiety (Keltner, Ellsworth & Edwards 1993), with the release of stress hormones such as cortisol, which can have a number of deleterious physiological consequences (e.g. Flinn et al. 1996, 127). The pernicious effects of stress are reduced when individuals have a sense of control over uncertain circumstances (Whybrow 1984; Sapolsky 1992; Huether et al. 1996), and people generally have a strong desire to *do something* to affect circumstances for which a good outcome is desired but not assured (Malinowski 1948, 60; Lopreato 1984; Rappaport 1999). For humans, acting together as a group is more reassuring than doing nothing or acting alone (Taylor 1992).

Humans use memory and foresight for practical ends: they make tools for procuring food and weapons for predation or defence; they concoct remedies for wounds and illness. However, in most if not all small-scale societies that anthropologists have described (e.g. Guss 1998), practical preparation is usually considered insufficient. In the case of biologically important concerns, people do something *more* to try to influence or ensure the outcome they desire. They make things associated with these matters special – extraordinary – even to the point of creating complex physical and mental constructions or ways of doing things that are not obviously relevant to the vital matter at hand. These complex 'constructions' or 'ways' are called rituals or ceremonies. They are a primary feature of social life in small-scale groups, surrounding people from birth and throughout their lives (Tambiah 1979; Rappaport 1999). The often excessive amounts of time, energy and material resources devoted to preparing for and participating in ritual practices indicates how important they are to individuals and societies (see Watkins, Chapter 10, this volume).

I suggest that existential uncertainty – leading to emotional investment or 'caring about' – was the original motivating impetus for the invention of ritual in humans. One can observe in every society that rituals are meant to affect biologically important states of affairs whose attainment is

uncertain – assuring food (see Malone, Chapter 13, and Taube, Chapter 17, this volume), safety, health, fertility, prosperity and successful transitions through important life stages. It is an anthropological axiom that rituals occur at times of transition and uncertainty (van Gennep 1960/1909; Turner 1969), and it is worth mentioning that ritualised behaviours in animals also occur when the situation is 'ambivalent' (Hinde 1982, 126).

Although they occur in every society, human ritual practices are not instinctive; indeed, they are culturally highly varied and complex. Yet if examined closely, their individual components can be regarded as extensions or elaborations of the innate operations of ritualised and play behaviours: faces, bodies, body movements, vocalisations, surroundings and materials (such as pigment, shells, stones or feathers) are transformed from their ordinary state to an extraordinary one by means of one or more of the operations that comprise ritualised behaviours and play (Simplification, Repetition, Exaggeration, Elaboration and Manipulation of Expectation, as described earlier).

Such behaviour could occur spontaneously. Margaret Mead (1976) described the Manus engaging in monotonous chanting when chilled and miserable or frightened at night – much like the Trobrianders who chanted charms in a singsong voice during a terrifying storm (Malinowski 1922). In such a manner, I suggest that as they engaged in the operations of ritualisation (already part of a 'behavioural reservoir' that existed in mother–infant interactions and children's play), ancestral hominins in Donald's Mimetic Culture were psychologically comforted and felt relieved of tension – particularly if the operations were performed in a coordinated fashion with others. Already in infancy, the operations assist bio-behavioural self-regulation and infant homeostasis (Hofer 1987; Gianino & Tronick 1988). Simplification and repetition of movements relieve tension in stressed animals (Charmove & Anderson 1989). Adult humans show similar behaviour, sometimes called 'comfort' movements, when they repeatedly tap a foot, wiggle a knee or wind a strand of hair around a finger. It has been reported that doing a repetitive task such as tapping a key, compared to verbally describing what one experiences while watching a traumatic film, reduces subsequent painful, uncontrollable flashbacks like those that affect sufferers of post-traumatic stress disorder (Holmes, Brewin & Hennessy 2004).

Humans, like all primates, come together when under threat or other stress (Caporael 1997; Taylor et al. 2007), and the behavioural phenomenon of individuals engaging in highly coordinated actions is widespread in pairs and groups of humans and other animals. Even without deliberate orchestration, individuals tend to 'behaviourally' match the actions or postures of others (Bernieri & Rosenthal 1991; Dugatkin 1997; Chartrand & Bargh 1999).

It is perhaps not surprising that humans should behave in ritualised ways when stressed. Examples of 'superstition' ('a wrong idea about external reality') are reported in laboratory pigeons who, when given food at random and thus unpredictable time intervals, began to perform stereotyped and elaborated movements, as if their behaviour might have an effect on the food-releasing mechanism in their cage (Beck & Forstmeier 2007). Examples cited include turning around counter-clockwise in the cage, thrusting the head into one of the upper corners of the cage and 'tossing' the head as if placing it beneath an invisible bar and lifting it repeatedly.

Although to my knowledge neuroscientific studies have not been conducted specifically on participants in rituals, conclusions from other research can be cited to support a hypothesis that engaging in the operations of ritualised behaviours has adaptive effects. Several studies of participants in musical activities such as singing, dancing and drumming (which by their nature require coordinating regularised behaviour with other individuals) revealed that subjects had a higher pain threshold, lower levels of depression, anxiety and fatigue and an increase in vigour after the session, compared to a control group (Koelsch, Offermanns and Franzke 2010; Dunbar et al. 2012). These effects are attributed to the release of 'endorphins' or 'endogenous opioids' and oxytocin, often referred to as 'bonding hormones'. Panksepp and Biven (2012, 307) describe further beneficial effects of these neurohormones, such as behavioural indications of individual confidence and social comfort.

Affinitive behaviours and emotions, such as those created and reinforced by the operations of mother–infant interaction (in humans and other mammals) and participation in temporally coordinated and integrated multimodal (facial, vocal, gestural) behaviours (see Garfinkel, Chapter 11, and Halley, Chapter 9, this volume), activate the orbitofrontal cortex (OFC) and other reward centres of the brain, such as periaqueductal gray (PAG) (Carter et al. 1999; Miller & Rodgers 2001; Bartels & Zeki 2004). Brown and Dissanayake (2009) speculate that the functional properties of OFC provide important insight into the multimodal processing so central to the components of ritualised behaviours, whether in mother–infant interactions or participation in group-wide rituals. In both contexts one finds entrainment, joint action, emergent coordination, planned coordination, chorusing, turn-taking, imitation, complementary joint action, motor resonance, action simulation and mimesis (Phillips-Silver & Keller 2012, 3) as described for the Hopi circle dance by Halley, Chapter 9, this volume.

Even though oxytocin's primary function in all mammals seems to be its contribution to maternal nurturing, its contribution (along with other endorphins) to the reduction of the stress hormone cortisol (Uvnäs-Moberg 1999; Heinrichs et al. 2003; Taylor et al. 2008) supports an argument that participation with others in coordinated music-making, as in the songs and dances of ritual practice, relieves individual anxiety and emotional tensions (Koelsch et al. 2010; Dunbar et al. 2012). Among individuals who coordinate their behaviour in time, oxytocin additionally promotes cooperation, trust and bonding – all obvious adaptive benefits of the ritualised and ritual behaviours that foster and sustain these outcomes (Shaver, Hazan & Bradshaw 1988; Hazan & Zeifman 1999).

Play, Ritual, Arts and Belief

The previous sections support my hypothesis that the evolutionary beginnings of religious rituals can be traced to the specialised components of play and ritualised behaviours that I have repeatedly described here – visual, vocal and gestural signals that attract attention and indicate to other participants, animal or human, that 'this is not ordinary or everyday'.

Again, these components (which I will now refer to as *aesthetic* devices or operations) are Simplification (Stereotypy), Repetition, Exaggeration, Elaboration and Manipulation of Expectation, all of which are amodal or polymodal in that they can occur visually, vocally or gesturally in both space and time.

Discussions by archaeologists of Pleistocene hominins do not usually mention evolved behavioural predispositions as described by ethologists such as play between mothers and infants or play in children. Yet it is universally observable that children precociously and pleasurably not only respond to but use aesthetic operations in art-like behaviour. For example, before their first year babies spontaneously vocalise with and move to music. When a little older, they sing with others or alone, dance, mime, make believe, play with sounds and words, decorate themselves and their possessions and make marks – recognising that these are non-ordinary.

These predispositions are raw material for adult rituals, a society's major occasions for making ordinary reality extraordinary. Visually arresting costumes, masks and other body ornamentation, altered and embellished artefacts and surroundings, chanting, dancing, singing, drumming, versifying and performing – all transform ordinary bodies, objects, environments, movements and utterances (see Renfrew, Chapter 2, this volume). We can call these extraordinary behaviours 'arts', and most rituals, whatever else they may be, can be considered as 'collections of arts', since without these transformations, it is hard to imagine what a ceremony would consist of.

Moreover, I think it is now clear that not only creators of rituals, but practitioners of the arts in all times and places, including the present day, also use the same aesthetic devices (on their behaviours in visual, vocal and gestural modalities and on various materials) in order to attract the attention of others, sustain their interest and evoke and shape their emotions.

One might consider the aesthetic devices to be *aesthetic 'primitives'*, immediately attracting attention in any sensory modality (as lines, contours, edges, colours and other 'visual primitives' stimulate the visual cortex before being analysed in higher cortical centres) because they are recognised instantly – perceptually, cognitively and emotionally – as being

unlike ordinary or familiar stimuli (Dissanayake, 2016). Depending on what follows, their effect can be momentary or sustained, of mild interest or overpowering affect. Perceptions that startle or dazzle manipulate expectation and provide emotions of surprise, wonder, fear and awe. They seem to occupy another order of experience or state of being that is often interpreted as 'spiritual'.

Although art-filled ritual practices themselves may or may not resolve the immediate vital problems that are their proximate motivation, they inadvertently address and satisfy evolved needs of human psychology. Through their characteristic aesthetic operations, ritual practices create and reinforce emotionally satisfying, reassuring and psychologically necessary feelings of *mutuality* or intimate relationship with another person (Hinde 1975) and *belonging to a group* (Hinde 1975; Baumeister & Leary 1995; Dissanayake 2000). They *coordinate and unify* group members in a feeling of 'oneheartedness' (see Garfinkel, Chapter 11, and Halley, Chapter 9, this volume) as they *relieve individual and group anxiety* by instilling confidence and fostering a sense of control of disturbing circumstances. Further, they provide to individuals a sense of *meaningfulness* or cognitive order (belief) and individual *competence* insofar as they give emotional force to explanations of how the world came to be as it is and what is required to maintain it. These basic needs resemble the seven social functions of musical participation ('Seven Cs') described by Koelsch and colleagues (2010, 308–10): contact, social cognition, co-pathy, communication, coordination, cooperation and cohesion.

When anthropologists conceptualise a society's 'rituals' as part of its symbolic cognitive belief system, they may overlook the fact that regardless of the doctrine or meanings conveyed, rituals are constituted of art-like behaviours *and would not exist without them*. Because of the inseparability of religious practice and art-like behaviour, it is plausible to suggest that the arts arose in human evolution as components of ceremonial behaviour rather than as independently evolved activities. In any case, an ethological approach entails that one distinguish between religious belief and religious behaviour (Feierman 2009). Such a distinction revives the emphasis on the behavioural and emotional means of instilling and reinforcing a society's beliefs that was described by early twentieth-century anthropologists such as Bronislaw Malinowski (1948) and A. R. Radcliffe-Brown (1952, 155), who proposed that religion in small-scale societies was less a matter of beliefs than of rites, indeed that belief was an *effect* of rites (see also Garfinkel, Chapter 11; Renfrew, Chapter 2; Watkins, Chapter 10, this volume).

Belief in religious dogma may or may not have been biologically adaptive, but the behavioural vehicles (arts participation) that installed and reinforced religious beliefs could inadvertently become adaptive. For example, formal organisation and articulation behaviourally instil a psychological sense of control over disorderly or disturbing content, thereby allaying anxiety. Or if further anxiety is created, as in some rituals, by being shaped and shared, it becomes a means to a further end of coping. Through a ceremony's arts, its messages or meanings are reinforced and the practitioners convinced that they are addressing and affecting the matter at hand. When used in culturally created ritual performances that transmit beliefs, aesthetic primitives bring emotional force to the messages, reinforcing their effect on participants.

Contemporary neuroscience reveals that belief, like other higher cognitive functions, rests on emotion (Damasio 1994; see also Kyriakidis, Chapter 18, this volume). Although literate people can read doctrinal texts and be persuaded to hold certain beliefs, for most of human history, belief was instilled nonverbally in individuals as they participated in song, dance and other vehicles of entrainment by means of neurohormonal effects of the aesthetic devices that were used in these activities.

As a final addendum to the views presented here, I propose that although the residue of specific beliefs may be difficult to find in the archaeological record, wherever one finds any or all of the aesthetic devices manifested in material form (as structure or decor), one can infer that their makers were likely to have been motivated by emotionally valenced beliefs.

References

Alland, A., Jr. 1983. *Playing With Form*. New York: Columbia University Press.

Bartels, A. & S. Zeki, 2004. The neural correlates of maternal and romantic love. *Neuroimage* 21(3), 1155–66.

Baumeister, R. F. & M. R. Leary, 1995. The need to belong: desire for interpersonal attachments as a fundamental human motivation. *Psychological Bulletin* 117(3), 497–529.

Beck, J. & W. Forstmeier, 2007. Superstition and belief as inevitable by-products of an adaptive learning strategy. *Human Nature* 18(1), 35–46.

Bednarik, R., 2008. Cupules. *Rock Art Research* 25, 61–100.

Bernieri, F. J. & R. Rosenthal, 1991. Interpersonal coordination: behaviour matching and interactional synchrony, in *Fundamentals of Nonverbal Behaviour*, eds. R. S. Feldman & B. Rimé. Cambridge: Cambridge University Press, 401–32.

Bjorklund, D. F. & A. D. Pellegrini, 2002. *The Origins of Human Nature: Evolutionary Developmental Psychology*. Washington, DC: American Psychological Association.

Bouzouggar, A., N. Barton, M. Vanhaeren, F. d'Errico, S. Collcutt, T. Higham et al. 2007. 82,000-year-old shell beads from North Africa and implications for the origins of modern human behavior. *Proceedings of the National Academy of Sciences* 104(24), 9964–9.

Brown, S. & E. Dissanayake, 2009. The arts are more than aesthetics: neuroaesthetics as narrow aesthetics, in *Neuroaesthetics*, eds. M. Skov & O. Vartanian. Amityville, NY: Baywood, 43–57.

Burghardt, G. M., 2005. *The Genesis of Animal Play: Testing the Limits*. Cambridge, MA: MIT Press.

Burrill, R., 2010. The primacy of movement in art making. *Teaching Artist Journal* 8, 216–228.

Caporael, L. R., 1997. The evolution of truly social cognition: the core configuration model. *Personality and Social Psychology Review* 1, 276–98.

Carter, C. S., 1998. Neuroendocrine perspectives on social attachment and love. *Psychoneuroendocrinology* 23, 779–818.

Carter, C. & M. Altemus, 1999. Integrative functions of lactational hormones in social behaviour and stress management, in *The Integrative Neurobiology of Affiliation*, eds. C. Carter, I. Lederhendler & B. Kirkpatrick. Cambridge, MA: MIT Press, 361–71.

Carter, C., I. Lederhendler & B. Kirkpatrick, (eds.), 1999. *The Integrative Neurobiology of Affiliation*. Cambridge, MA: MIT Press.

Charmove, A. S. & J. R. Anderson, 1989. Examining environmental enrichment, in *Housing, Care and Psychological Well Being of Captive and Laboratory Animals*, ed. E. F. Segal. Park Ridge, NJ: Noyes Publications, 183–202.

Chartrand, T. L. & J. A. Bargh, 1999. The chameleon effect: the perception-behaviour link and social interaction. *Journal of Personality and Social Psychology* 76, 893–910.

Clayton, N. S., T. J. Bussey & A. Dickinson, 2003. Can animals recall the past and plan for the future? *Nature Reviews Neuroscience* 4, 685–91.

Cosmides, L. & J. Tooby, 2000. Consider the source: the evolution of adaptations for decoupling and metarepresentation, in *Metarepresentations*, ed. D. Sperber. Oxford and New York: Oxford University Press, 53–115.

Damasio, A., 1994. *Descartes' Error: Emotion, Reason, and the Human Brain*. New York: Grosset Putnam.

d'Errico, F., M. Verhaeren, N. Barton, A. Bouzouggar, H. Mienis, D. Richter et al. 2009. Additional evidence on the use of personal ornaments in the Middle Paleolithic of North Africa. *Proceedings of the National Academy of Sciences* 106(38), 16051–6.

Dissanayake, E., 1979. An ethological view of ritual and art in human evolutionary history. *Leonardo* 12(1), 27–31.

Dissanayake, E., 1988. *What Is Art For?* Seattle: University of Washington Press.

Dissanayake, E., 1999. Antecedents of the temporal arts in early mother–infant interaction, in *The Origins of Music*, eds. N. L. Wallin, B. Merker & S. Brown. Cambridge, MA: MIT Press, 389–410.

Dissanayake, E., 2000. *Art and Intimacy: How the Arts Began*. Seattle: University of Washington Press.

Dissanayake, E., 2001. Becoming *Homo aestheticus*: sources of aesthetic imagination in mother–infant interactions. *SubStance* 30(1,2), 85–103.

Dissanayake, E., 2006. Ritual and ritualization: musical means of conveying and shaping emotion in humans and other animals, in *Music and Manipulation: On the Social Uses and Social Control of Music*, eds. S. Brown & U. Volgsten. Oxford: Berghahn, 31–57.

Dissanayake, E., 2008. The arts after Darwin: does art have an origin and adaptive function?, in *World Art Studies: Exploring Concepts and Approaches*, eds. K. Zijlmans & W. van Damme. Amsterdam: Valiz, 241–63.

Dissanayake, E. (2016). Mark-making as a human behavior, in *Darwin's Bridge: Uniting the Humanities and Social Sciences*, eds. J. Carroll, D. P. McAdams, & E. O. Wilson. New York: Oxford University Press, 101–30.

Donald, M., 1991. *Origins of the Modern Mind: Three Stages in the Evolution of Cognition and Culture*. Cambridge, MA: Harvard University Press.

Dugatkin, L. A., 1997. *Cooperation Among Animals: An Evolutionary Perspective*. Oxford: Oxford University Press.

Dunbar, R. I. M., K. Kaskatis, I. MacDonald & V. Barra, 2012. Performance of music elevates pain threshold and positive affect: implications for the evolutionary function of music. *Evolutionary Psychology* 10(4): 688–702.

Eibl-Eibesfeldt, I. 1971. *Love and Hate: The Natural History of Behaviour Patterns*, translated by Geoffrey Strachan. New York: Holt, Rinehart and Winston.

Eibl-Eibesfeldt, I. 1989. *Human Ethology*, translated by Pauline Wiessner-Larsen and Anette Heunemann. New York: Aldine de Gruyter.

Ellsworth, P., 1991. Some implications of cognitive appraisal theories of emotion, in *International Review of Studies of Emotion*, vol. 1, ed. K. Strongman. New York: Wiley, 143–61.

Falk, D., 2004. Prelinguistic evolution in early hominins: whence motherese? *Behavioural and Brain Sciences* 27(4), 491–503.

Falk, D., 2009. *Finding Our Tongues: Mothers, Infants & The Origin of Language*. New York: Basic Books.

Feierman, J. R. (ed.), 2009. *The Biology of Religious Behaviour: The Evolutionary Origins of Faith and Religion*. Santa Barbara, CA: Praeger.

Fein, S., 1993. *First Drawings: Genesis of Visual Thinking*. Pleasant Hill, CA: Exelrod Press.

Flinn, M. V., R. J. Quinlan, S. A. Decker, M. T. Turner & B. G. England, 1996. Male-female differences in effects of parental absence on glucocorticoid stress response. *Human Nature* 7(2), 125–62.

Flinn, M. V. & C. V. Ward, 2005. Evolution of the social child, in *Origins of the Social Mind: Evolutionary Psychology and Child Development*, eds. B. Ellis & D. Bjorklund. London: Guilford Press, 19–44.

Geary, D. C., 2005. Folk knowledge and academic learning, in *Origins of the Social Mind: Evolutionary Psychology and Child Development*, eds. B. J. Ellis & D. F. Bjorklund. New York: Guilford, 493–519.

Gianino, A. & E. Z. Tronick, 1988. The mutual regulation model: the infant's self and interactive regulation and coping and defensive capacities, in *Stress and Coping*, eds. T. Field, P. M. McCabe & N. Schneiderman. Hillsdale, NJ: Erlbaum, 47–68.

Guss, D. M., 1998. *To Weave and Sing: Art, Symbol, and Narrative in the South American Rain Forest*. Berkeley & Los Angeles: University of California Press.

Harris, J. R., 1995. Where is the child's environment? A group socialization theory of development. *Psychological Review* 102, 458–89.

Hazan, C. & D. Zeifman, 1999. Pair bonds as attachments: evaluating the evidence, in *Handbook of Attachment: Theory, Research, and Clinical Applications*, eds. J. Cassidy & P. R. Shaver. New York: Guilford, 336–54.

Heinrichs, M., T. Baumgartner, C. Kirschbaum & U. Ehlert, 2003. Social support and oxytocin interact to suppress cortisol and subjective responses to psychosocial stress. *Biological Psychiatry* 54, 1389–98.

Henshilwood, C. S., F. d'Errico, R. Yates, Z. Jacobs, C. Tribolo, G. A. Duller, et al. 2002. Emergence of modern human behavior: Middle Stone Age engravings from South Africa. *Science* 295(5558), 1278–80.

Hinde, R., 1975. *Biological Bases of Human Social Relationships*. New York: McGraw Hill.

Hinde, R., 1982. *Ethology: Its Nature and Relations With Other Sciences*. New York and Oxford: Oxford University Press.

Hofer, M. A., 1987. Early social relationships: a psychobiologist's view. *Child Development* 58, 633–47.

Holmes, E. A., C. R. Brewin & R. G. Hennessy, 2004. Trauma films, information processing, and intrusive memory development. *Journal of Experimental Psychology: General* 133(1), 3–22.

Huether, G., S. Doering, U. Rueger & E. Ruether, 1996. Psychic stress and neuronal plasticity: an expanded model of the stress reaction processes as basis for the understanding of adaptive processes in the central nervous system. *Zeitschrift für Psychosomatische Medizin und Psychoanalyse* 42, 107–27.

Huxley, J., 1914. The courtship habits of the great crested grebe (*Podiceps cristatus*) together with a discussion of the evolution of courtship in birds. *Journal of the Linnean Society of London: Zoology* 53, 253–92.

Huxley, J., 1966. Introduction, in *A Discussion on Ritualisation of Behaviour in Animals and Man*, organized by Sir Julian Huxley. Philosophical Transactions of the Royal Society of London, Series B. Biological Sciences 772, 249–71.

Kaptchuk T. J., C. E. Kerr & A. Zanger, 2009. Placebo controls, exorcisms, and the devil. *Lancet* 374 (9697), 1234–5. (10 Oct.).

Kavanagh, D. J., J. Andrade & J. May, 2005. Imaginary relish and exquisite torture: the elaborated intrusion theory of desire. *Psychological Review* 112(2), 446–67.

Kellogg, R., 1970. *Analyzing Children's Art*. Palo Alto, CA: Mayfield.

Keltner, D., P. Ellsworth & K. Edwards, 1993. Beyond simple pessimism. *Journal of Personality and Social Psychology* 64, 740–52.

King, B. J., 2004. *The Dynamic Dance: Nonvocal Communication in African Great Apes*. Cambridge, MA: Harvard University Press.

Koelsch, S., K. Offermanns & P. Franzke, 2010. Music in the treatment of affective disorders: an exploratory investigation of a new method for music-therapeutic research. *Music Perception* 27(4), 307–16.

Leakey, R., 1994. *The Origin of Humankind*. New York: Basic Books

Leslie, A. M., 1987. Pretense and representation: origins of 'theory of mind'. *Psychological Review* 94, 412–26.

Lillard, A. S., 1993. Pretend play skills and the child's theory of mind. *Child Development* 64(2), 348–71.

Lopreato, J., 1984. *Human Nature and Biocultural Evolution*. Boston, MA: Allen and Unwin.

Lorenz, K. Z., 1982. *The Foundations of Ethology: The Principal Ideas and Discoveries in Animal Behaviour*, translated by K. Z. Lorenz and R. W. Kickert. (Original German publication 1981). New York: Simon and Schuster.

Malinowski, B., 1922. *Argonauts of the Western Pacific*. London: Routledge and Kegan Paul.

Malinowski, B., 1927. The life of culture, in *Culture: The Diffusion Controversy*, eds. G. E. Smith, B. Malinowski, H. J. Spinden & A. Goldenweiser New York: Norton, 26–46.

Malinowski, B., 1948. *Magic, Science, and Religion*. Boston, MA: Beacon Press. Original publication 1925.

Mead, M. 1976. *Growing Up in New Guinea*. New York: Morrow. Original publication 1930.

Meyer-Holzapfel, M., 1956. Das Spiel bei Säugetieren. *Handbuch der Zoologie* 8, 1–26.

Miller, W. B. & J. L. Rodgers, 2001. *The Ontogeny of Human Bonding Systems: Evolutionary Origins, Neural Bases, and Psychological Manifestations*. Boston, MA and Dordrecht: Kluwer Academic Publishers.

Mithen, S., 2005. *The Singing Neanderthals: The Origins of Music, Language, Mind and Body*. London: Weidenfeld and Nicolson.

Morris, D., 1957. 'Typical intensity' and its relation to the problem of ritualisation, *Behaviour* 11, 1–2.

Nelson, E. E. & J. Panksepp, 1998. Brain substrates of infant–mother attachment: contributions of opioids, oxytocin, and norepinephrine. *Neuroscience and Biobehavioural Reviews* 22, 437–52.

Oakley, K. P., 1971. Fossil shell observed by Acheulian Man. *Antiquity* 47, 59–60.

Panksepp, J., 1998. *Affective Neuroscience: The Foundation of Animal and Human Emotions*. Oxford: Oxford University Press.

Panksepp, J. & L. Biven, 2012. *The Archaeology of Mind: Neuroevolutionary Origins of Human Emotions*. New York: Norton.

Panksepp, J., E. Nelson & M. Bekkedal, 1999. Brain systems for the mediation of social separation-distress and social-reward: evolutionary antecedents and neuropeptide intermediaries, in *The Neurobiology of Affiliation*, eds. C. S. Carter, I. Lederhendler & B. Kirkpatrick. Cambridge, MA: MIT Press, 222–41.

Pellegrini, A. D. & D. F. Bjorklund, 2004. The ontogeny and phylogeny of children's object and fantasy play. *Human Nature* 15(1), 23–43.

Phillips-Silver, J., C. A. Aktipis & G. A. Bryant, 2010. The ecology of entrainment: foundations of coordinated rhythmic movement. *Music Perception* 28(1), 3–14.

Phillips-Silver, J. & P. E. Keller. 2012. Searching for roots of entrainment and joint action in early musical interactions. *Frontiers in Human Neuroscience* 6(26), 1–11.

Raby, C. R., D. M. Alexis, A. Dickinson & N. S. Clayton, 2007. Planning for the future by Western scrub-jays. *Nature* 445, 919–21.

Radcliffe-Brown, A. R., 1952. Religion and society, in *Structure and Function in Primitive Society*. Glencoe, IL: Free Press, 153–77. Original publication in *Journal of the Royal Anthropological Institute* (1945) 75(1–2), 33–43.

Rappaport, R. A., 1999. *Ritual and Religion in the Making of Humanity*. Cambridge and New York: Cambridge University Press.

Rosenberg, K. R., 1992. The evolution of modern human childbirth. *Yearbook of Physical Anthropology* 35, 89–134.

Sapolsky, R. M., 1992. Neuroendocrinology of the stress response, in *Behavioural Endocrinology*, eds. J. R. Becker,

S. M. Breedlove & D. Crews. Cambridge, MA: MIT Press, 287–324.

Schechner, R., 2002. *Performance Studies: An Introduction*. New York: Routledge.

Schiefenhövel, W., 2009. Explaining the inexplicable: traditional and syncretistic religiosity in Melanesia, in *The Biological Evolution of Religious Mind and Behaviour*, eds. E. Voland & W. Schiefenhövel. Berlin: Springer, 143–64.

Shaver, P. R., C. Hazan & D. Bradshaw, 1988. Love as attachment: the integration of three behavioral systems, in *The Anatomy of Love*, eds. R. J. Sternberg & M. Barnes. New Haven, CT: Yale University Press.

Smith, W., 1977. *The Behavior of Communicating: An Evolutionary Approach*. Cambridge, MA: Harvard University Press.

Stern, D. 1977. *The First Relationship*. Cambridge, MA: Harvard University Press.

Suddendorf, T. & M.C. Corballis, 1997. Mental time travel and the evolution of the human mind. *Genetic, Social, and General Psychology Monographs* 123, 133–67.

Tambiah, S. J., 1979. A performative approach to ritual. *Proceedings of the British Academy, London* LXV, 113–69. Oxford: Oxford University Press.

Taylor, S., 1992. *The Tending Instinct: How Nurturing Is Essential to Who We Are and How We Live*. New York: Henry Holt.

Taylor, S. E., 2007. Social support, in *Foundations of Health Psychology*, eds. H. S. Friedman & R. C. Silver. New York: Oxford University Press, 145–71.

Taylor, S. E., L. J. Burklund, N. I. Eisenberger, B. J. Lehman, C. J. Hilmeet & M. D. Lieberman, 2008. Neural bases of moderation of cortisol stress responses by psychosocial resources. *Journal of Personality and Social Psychology* 95(1), 197–211.

Thieme, H., 1997. Lower Paleolithic hunting spears from Germany. *Nature* 385, 807–10.

Tinbergen, N., 1952. 'Derived' activities: their causation, biological significance, origin and emancipation during evolution. *Quarterly Review of Biology* 17, 1–32.

Tinbergen, N., 1959. Comparative studies of the behaviour of gulls (*Laridae*): a progress report. *Behaviour* 15, 1–70.

Tonkinson, R., 1978. *The Mardudjara Aborigines: Living the Dream in Australia's Desert*. New York: Holt, Rinehart and Winston.

Tooby, J. & L. Cosmides, 2001. Does beauty build adapted minds? Toward an evolutionary theory of aesthetics, fiction, and the arts. *SubStance* 30(1,2), 6–27.

Turner, V., 1969. *The Ritual Process: Structure and Anti-Structure*. London: Routledge and Kegan Paul.

Uvnäs-Moberg, K., 1999. Physiological and endocrine effects of social contact, in *The Integrative Neurobiology of Affiliation*, eds. C. Carter, I. Lederhendler & B. Kirkpatrick. Cambridge, MA: MIT Press, 245–61.

Van Gennep, A., 1960. *The Rites of Passage*. London: Routledge and Kegan Paul. Original work published in 1908.

Vanhaeren, M., F. d'Errico, C. Stringer, S. L. James, J. A. Todd, & H. K. Mienis. 2006. Middle paleolithic shell beads in Israel and Algeria. *Science* 312 (5781), 1785–8.

Watanabe, J. M. & B. B. Smuts, 1999. Explaining religion without explaining it away: trust, truth, and the evolution of cooperation in Roy A. Rappaport's 'The obvious aspects of ritual'. *American Anthropologist* 101, 98–112.

Whybrow, P., 1984. Contributions from neuroendocrinology, in *Approaches to Emotion*, eds. K. Scherer & P. Ekman. Hillsdale, NJ: Erlbaum, 59–72.

Yellen, J. E., A. S. Brooks, E. Cornelissen, M. J. Mehlman & K. Stewart, 1995. A Middle Stone Age worked bone industry from Katanda, Upper Semliki Valley, Zaire. *Science* 268 (28 April), 553–6.

PART II

PLAYING WITH BELIEF AND PERFORMANCE IN ANCIENT SOCIETIES

8

MAYA SACRED PLAY: THE VIEW FROM EL PERÚ-WAKA'

DAVID FREIDEL AND MICHELLE RICH

I had one other encounter with Don Pablo and talking stones. One day in the summer of 1989, after he had done some work on the camp kitchen, I found a clear glass marble in the area. Thinking it belonged to Don Pablo and was one of his saso'ob, the 'lights' he used when focusing on spiritual forces, I took it next door to him that evening. He took the marble and inspected it carefully. "Yes," he said finally, "this is a stone of light." Then he smiled, "However, it won't speak until it has been soaked in maize gruel, sak-a', and then it will only speak Maya." (Freidel, Schele & Parker 1993, 179)

PLAY AND RITUAL: MODERN PERSPECTIVES

Sometimes a marble is just a marble, but sometimes it is not just a toy. The marbles left in the dusty main road of Yaxuna village in north-central Yucatán in the summer of 1989 were certainly toys to begin with. The boys of the village amused themselves with games of marbles on the uneven surfaces, gambles that required expertise and were like games of marbles elsewhere vying for the ownership of the marbles. Maya boys play marbles this way everywhere and they are good at it. So, what is the relationship between the casting of marbles as a gambling game and the casting of tokens to divine the future or understand a present circumstance? Don Pablo de la Cruz does not cast his tokens;

he arranges them carefully on his altar, his 'field', and he looks through them and listens to them (Figure 8.1). But elsewhere in the modern world of people who speak Mayan languages, adepts do cast tokens, count them and arrange them with swift, graceful motions of their hands (Freidel et al. 1993, 224–30). For Maya archaeologists, there are many kinds of artefacts represented in the record which probably served as divining tokens and also tokens for gaming and gambling. Other objects, such as whistle figurines, likely functioned both as toys and ritual instruments.

The relationship between play and ritual is enduringly complex in the Maya world. In another example from Yaxuna, young boys play the role of frogs during the 'bring Chahk' rain ceremonies. They process around the field altar with bigger boys who play Chahk'ob, the rain gods, and then sit on rocks at the four corners of the altar. While the older boys sprinkle water on them from small, phallic-shaped gourds and make the sound of thunder, the young boys make the sounds of the night after the rains arrive, mimicking the croak of frogs and the buzz of insects (Figure 8.2). There is quite a bit of giggling during this activity. Meanwhile, Don Pablo stands before the altar oblivious, praying sonorously to the rain gods, to the true god and to the spirits of the place. The ritual continues deep into the night. At one juncture, the best hunter among the older boys is sent off into the dark and the others are tasked with tracking him down and bringing him back to the altar, to bring Chahk, the rains. It is the game

101

Figure 8.1 Don Pablo with marble *sastunob* light stones for divining. Photograph by Dan Buettner.

of 'hide and seek'. And for the traditional Catholic faithful of Yaxuna, it is heartfelt prayer and ritual.

As playful as this hunt may seem, the rain ceremony today in Yaxuna and elsewhere in Yucatán involves the sacrifice of animals, particularly chickens, whose flesh is offered along with sacred maize breads during the course of the ritual. The hide-and-seek game associated with the rain ceremony can allude to animal hunting, particularly deer, and to the capture of warriors draped in animal hides for sacrifice as depicted on ancient bas-reliefs from the Yaxuna area (Schele & Freidel 1990, 354–5). This example illustrates one of the many connections between the past and the present in the Maya world. In antiquity, Maya rulers played the god Chahk, among other deities. A fourth-century king discovered in a burial at Yaxuna, for example, was wearing *Spondylus spp.* Sprocket-decorated ear flares diagnostic of Chahk (Figure 8.3; Stanton et al. 2010).

Today, baseball is the most popular game in Yucatán, but in pre-Hispanic times, the Maya played a variety of games with solid latex rubber balls. The earliest ballcourts in Yucatán date to the first

millennium BC (Robles Castellanos & Andrews 2003), and there is a Preclassic ballcourt in the ancient city of Yaxuna adjacent to the northern acropolis where the Chahk king was discovered (Stanton et al. 2010; see also Taube, Chapter 17, this volume). In a broad sense, the examples presented here illustrate the pervasive and intertwined nature of play and ritual in contemporary Maya society, and allude to the deep history of this connection, thus setting the stage for the remainder of our exploration of Maya sacred play.

THE MAYA CREATION STORY, THE BALLGAME AND ANIMAL SYMBOLISM

Despite his sometimes controversial beliefs, Joseph Campbell (1988, 48) wisely articulated the idea that myths are public dreams. In a communal context, the spectacle re-enactment or tangible reimagining of myth is a critical element which reinforces a similarly shared understanding among often disparate groups of people participating in the same social and political network. What is a toy whistle in the hands of a child in the kitchen of a humble home can be an offering made by adults in the ceremonies of the city plaza. Yet the public performance of myth – from monumental representations of kings as Chahk or the Maize God erected on public plazas to hand-held portable items shared in domestic contexts – can have multiple implications. These objects and performances can simultaneously bolster notions of sameness and strengthen community identity, while also highlighting social difference and reinforcing hierarchy. This type of multivalency is seen in both play and ritual, which seem to fall along a spectrum of formality from spontaneous improvisation to rule-bound enactment, and the tension between these expectations can be not only entertaining, but even cathartic. Indeed, that would seem to be precisely the goal in many instances of public spectacle performed by ancient Maya leaders seeking to strengthen their charisma (Inomata 2006). Spectacle of the kind represented by ballgames and funerary proceedings, among other ceremonial occasions, clearly engaged the kind of enactment of public dreaming Campbell imagined in his view of

Figure 8.2 A mid-1980s Cha-Chahk rain ceremony at Yaxuna in Yucatán. Photograph by Debra Selsor Walker.

Figure 8.3 Fourth-century AD Maya king buried with the Spondylus ear flares of Chahk, visible at far right. Burial 23, Yaxuna. Photograph by Jeanne Randall.

myths. We will return to some of these themes, but here we continue our consideration of cross-cutting notions of play and myth.

Playful boys are featured in the famous eighteenth-century creation story called the *K'iche' Popol Vuh* from highland Guatemala (Tedlock 1985; Christenson 2003). In this story, the Maize God and his twin brother are defeated by the Death Lords in a series of ballgames played with the rubber ball, invented by 1600 BC (see Taube, Chapter 17, this volume). The Death Lords place the severed head of the sacrificed Maize God on a tree growing from the 'dusty court' as a warning to others not to challenge their power. The head spits on the hand of a maiden, engendering twin sons of the Maize God named

Hunahpu and Xbalanque. These twins also eventually play ball against the Death Lords, and win this match with the help of magical animals. Hunahpu and Xbalanque then voluntarily submit to sacrifice by the Death Lords so that they can be reborn as fish-men magicians who ultimately defeat the Death Lords decisively. Along the way, they transform their elder brothers into monkeys and these two deities, known as Monkey Scribes, become the patrons of both scribes and artists. This creation story undoubtedly constitutes a redaction of a myth cycle that was thousands of years old, and multiple lines of archaeological evidence suggest it was factored into the foundation of Classic Maya politics and religion. Within the Popol Vuh creation story are many episodes of play beyond the ballgame contests and, as already noted, often these exchanges feature animals. These episodes of play include divining by the gods to chart the ways to create the universe, contests between the human-form gods and the macaw spirit companion of the original old creator god, contests between the sons of the Maize God and animals in the maize fields, and gambling between these boys and the Death Lords. These scenarios imply the same type of supernaturally themed cognitive connections between animals and culture referenced by Lyvia Morgan (Chapter 14, this volume) in her discussion of bull sports as a ritualized transition for young men approaching manhood portrayed in the art of Ancient Egypt and the Aegean. These are worlds in which the lines between sacred and secular play are more connective than divisive.

We are still exploring our understanding of the sacred relationship between play, ritual and animals, and are open to suggestions, but, as outlined in the anecdotes of this preamble, we are convinced that these associations were as complex in the experience of the ancient Maya as they are among modern Maya. In the case of the ancient Maya, this is more than merely a reasonable hypothesis. The ancient word for spirit companion, *way* (pronounced like *why*), is intimately linked in Mayan languages to sleep and the dream state (Houston and Stuart 1989; Freidel Schele & Parker 1993, 188–93; Grube & Nahm 1994). The *way* creatures are often animals with extraordinary powers and human characteristics. Karl Taube (2003a, 476) has suggested Classic Maya *way* characters are frequently depicted as hideous, frightening deathly beings, jaguars and other wild forest creatures that clutch bowls of bones, eyeballs, severed hands and other gore as their food. *Way* spirits are indeed macabre and death-related in many scenes painted on Classic-period Maya polychrome vases. Yet there is at least one example where we believe a *way* deer spirit is not cursing, but rather healing. This is illustrated in the narrative figurine scene discovered in El Perú-Waka' Burial 39 (Freidel, Rich & Reilly 2010), which will be addressed shortly (Figure 8.4).

It is also the case that interaction with magical animals in the context of the Maya creation myth, as well as the existence of *way* spirits, illustrates a

Figure 8.4 The deer *way* spirit praying over the penitent dead king. Narrative figurine scene, Burial 39, El Perú-Waka'. Ministerio de Cultura y Deportes de Guatemala and Museo Nacional de Arqueología y Etnología de Guatemala. Photograph by Jenny Guerra. Courtesy of the El Perú-Waka' Regional Archaeological Project.

further notion: animals factor deeply into human play and ritual practice. While some animal species carry out certain forms of play (see Burghardt, Chapter 3, this volume; Bateson, Chapter 4, this volume), we observe that people relate to animals in a complex fashion, incorporating them into play, ritual and belief systems in such a way that animals cannot replicate. In light of this, we have elaborated on the theme of this volume by exploring the relationships between play and ritual, as well as representations of animals in ritualized contexts, in ancient Maya society using archaeological evidence from the Classic period (ca. AD 250–900) city of El Perú-Waka', Petén, Guatemala.

MAYA SACRED PLAY: THE VIEW FROM EL PERÚ-WAKA'

The ancient toponym for the city of Waka' was deciphered by Simon Martin (2000), which translates as 'Wakwater' or 'Wak-place'. Stanley Guenter (2007, 23), via the continued study of epigraphic and iconographic materials, proposed that 'Wak' refers to either a centipede or similar creature, or its jaws or teeth. As such, the name of the royal dynasty at El

Figure 8.5 As depicted on a Late Classic-period Codex-style vase, scribes make offerings to a Monkey Scribe seated on a cushioned throne. Note the centipede maw at the tip of his tail. Photograph by Justin Kerr.

Perú-Waka' references centipedes, and may suggest Waka's royalty had a particular affection for or focus on the aforementioned Monkey Scribe gods, whose tails end in centipede maws (Figure 8.5).

The dynastic kings and queens of Waka' participated in the great wars of the Classic period as key vassals to aspiring emperors, particularly the Snake dynasty king, Yuhknoom Ch'een the Great of the city of Cakalmul, but also his successor, Yuhknoom Yich'aak K'ahk'. Divining, conjuring with dice and tokens, consorting with animal-spirit companions, as well as ballgame play were expressed in central ritual performances as evidenced in the archaeological, epigraphic and iconographic record at Waka'. Many of these activities were represented in miniature images and figurines. Contextual analyses at other Classic-period Maya cities show that figurines, often also functional whistles or ocarinas, and other musical instruments were associated with the intimate settings of household kitchens and were likely toys for family entertainment (Triadan 2007). At Waka', however, figurines have been excavated in several ritually charged, elite primary contexts. This is one aspect in which the medium of the message bridges from the public arena of the mighty to the homes of their sustaining followers, demonstrating that the interweaving between ritual and play was a vital web of common experience in this complex society.

The city centre of Waka' covers approximately one square kilometre of hilltops and levelled land along an escarpment next to the San Pedro Mártir River in north-western Petén, Guatemala. Archaeological research has been conducted by the El Perú-Waka' Regional Archaeological Project (PAW) since 2003 (Navarro-Farr & Rich 2014). The city was founded in the Preclassic period, at least by 200 BC, and it flourished until the ninth or early tenth century AD (Eppich 2011; Marken 2011). Waka' has two major public foci: first, a western centre built around two long east–west oriented plazas, which is surrounded by an impressive concentration of elite residential groups. It features west-facing temples and pyramids at the eastern end of the plazas, including Waka's principal public shrine, Structure M13-1 (Navarro-Farr 2009). The palace acropolis anchors the western end of the centre and faces east (Lee 2012). Adjacent to the palace acropolis is the city's masonry ballcourt, built and used in the Late Classic period (Meléndez 2007). The second civic-ceremonial location is the tripartite Mirador Group to the south-east of that western centre, which is comprised of two large pyramids and a smaller temple group atop a natural rise levelled in antiquity (Rich 2011).

With regard to the themes of play and ritual, we briefly address relevant evidence from the palace complex in the west, particularly Structure L12-4 (Lee 2012); the main city temple, Structure M13-1 at the eastern end of the centre (Navarro-Farr 2009); and Structure O14-04 in the Mirador Group (Rich 2011). These localities have all produced significant archaeological evidence bearing on the way that the people of Waka' thought about play, ritual and animals, but we will especially focus on artefacts from Burial 39's mortuary assemblage discovered inside Structure O14-04.

The Ballgame at Waka's Royal Palace

The royal palace acropolis, researched from 2003–6 by David Lee, anchors the north-western end of the centre, and is adjacent to the Late Classic ballcourt excavated by Juan Carlos Meléndez. Lee discovered 14 carved masonry stair-tread blocks portraying portions of ballplayer scenes in a late version of the Classic period palace stairway. His research demonstrated these treads originated from an earlier, unknown stairway and were reset in this location. As argued by Lee and epigrapher Stanley Guenter (2010), several of the carved treads depict the most famous Late Classic king of Waka', named K'inich Bahlam II, and his overlord, emperor Yuhknoom Yich'aak K'ahk' of the previously mentioned Snake dynasty, sometime after AD 687 (Figure 8.6).

From El Perú Stela 33 we know that K'inich Bahlam II had been placed in power by the previous Snake dynasty emperor, Yuhknoom Ch'een the Great. The carving on the stair treads evidently portrays him engaged in play at the base of a staircase with Yuhknoom Ch'een's successor, named as part of his reaffirmation of his vassal status to this new Snake lord. K'inich Bahlam II and Yich'aak K'ahk' are both sporting royal ballplayer regalia, including elaborate headdresses. K'inich Bahlam (on left) is wearing a Waterlily Jaguar headdress, a creature that has multiple connotations, including a battle deity and a *way* spirit. Ballgame play was a major ritual means of sustaining political and military alliances among Late Classic kingdoms, cross-cutting *ritual* and *game* as defined by Vanghelis Kyriakidis (Chapter 18, this volume), particularly with regard to the concept of risk. It is not surprising to see a king depicted as wearing the Waterlily Jaguar headdress on the stair block which dates to a period of great political strife in the southern Maya lowlands.

These scenes related to alliances between overlords and vassals are well represented in the Classic period of western Petén, and it is clear that the deadly serious business of military alliance was celebrated in sacred play. While Waka's real ballcourt is near the palace acropolis, sculptured tread stairways of other sites in western Petén, such as La Corona located north of Waka', demonstrate that rituals of ball playing and likely of sacrifice alluding to creation myths took place on stairways as often as in actual ballcourts (Miller & Houston 1987). The animal headdresses worn by royal performers in these scenes link

Figure 8.6 Two Maya rulers engaged in a dynamic ballgame scene. Stair blocks excavated at the El Perú-Waka' royal palace. Ministerio de Cultura y Deportes de Guatemala. Photograph by Patrick Aventurier. Courtesy of the El Perú-Waka' Regional Archaeological Project.

the ritual play of ball represented in them to animal headdresses worn by warriors in battle. Furthermore, the broad connotations of the creation myths which feature the death lords also connect these performers to the death-related *way* spirits. This conflation of play, ritual, animal representations, myth and sacrifice could generate just the kind of tension alluded to earlier with its cathartic appeal.

Signs of Sacred Play in Surface Deposits

K'inich Bahlam II and ball playing are also represented at the grand stairway of the main temple in the city centre, Structure M13-1. In 2012, Olivia Navarro-Farr and her colleagues discovered the fragments of the preserved upper half of a stela that likely depicts K'inich Bahlam II embedded into the walls of the final stairway of this building (Navarro-Farr, Pérez Robles & Menéndez Bolaños 2012). Unfortunately, the headdress portrayed on this stela is not preserved. On well-preserved Stela 33, however, K'inich Bahlam II wears a water monster headdress with a tied waterlily diadem, so his performance incorporating animal allusions is consistent. Earlier excavation at this important temple conducted by Navarro-Farr from 2003–6 exposed a palimpsest of Late to Terminal Classic period ritual deposits (Navarro-Farr, Freidel & Arroyave Prera 2008; Navarro-Farr 2009). The massive deposits appear to have been layered onto Structure M13-1 over a long period of time – both during and following the demise of Waka's royal court. They also appear to be the offerings of ordinary people who continued to worship at this temple building, located at the east end of Plaza 2. The deposits, made in this tumultuous era, are of particular interest here, and in addition to broken ceramic vessels, include a wide array of artefacts. Among these are ceramic figurines, whistles and other musical instruments relevant to ritual play and performance. Some of these artefacts, perhaps once even children's toys, were transformed into ritual objects of memory in their final use, during what were, probably at best, uncertain times (see Watkins, Chapter 10, this volume, for a discussion of ritual and collective memory as a means to sustain cultural identity).

Figure 8.7 Ballplayer figurine wearing a deer headdress. Ministerio de Cultura y Deportes de Guatemala. Photograph by Patrick Aventurier. Courtesy of the El Perú-Waka' Regional Archaeological Project.

Ceramic figurine fragments were also found in other areas at the site. For example, one of these fragments, recovered near the surface in test excavations associated with a series of small structures adjacent to Plaza 2 (Pérez Robles 2003, 258), depicts a haughty individual, likely a king, wearing the thick, padded belt of a ballplayer and a large deer headdress in profile (Figure 8.7). It is possible that this elaborate figurine fragment, along with others found in the test excavations, washed downslope from Plaza 2, but it is also the case that figurine fragments are found in diverse contexts in the Maya world, for example as components of architectural construction fill, including in small buildings.

The Royal Mortuary Assemblage in Burial 39

Structure O14-04 is the second largest building within Waka's Mirador Group (Rich, Piehl & Matute 2006; Rich, Matute & Piehl 2007) and is architecturally similar to Structure M13-1. The royal mortuary assemblage in Structure O14-04's Burial 39, excavated by co-author Rich and her colleagues (Rich, Matute & Piehl 2007; Rich 2011), provides several points of discussion in regard to sacred play. The tomb's elaborate elite artefacts and its location in one of the grandest temple-pyramids at the site convey that the interred individual was a ruler of Waka' and also signify the wealth of Classic-period nobility. Burial 39 was located under the floor of a distinctively Early Classic style of stairway shrine atop the pyramid's frontal platform. This frontal platform, called an *adosada*, is an architectural feature noted at the highland Mexican city of Teotihuacan. Thirty-three ceramic vessels were recovered, and the various types identified by PAW ceramicist Keith Eppich suggest indicate interment occurred between AD 600 and AD 650 (Rich et al. 2010). This suggests the tomb possibly contains the immediate predecessor of the aforementioned Waka' king K'inich Bahlam II and dates to the reign of Calakmul's Yuhknoom Ch'een the Great, who ruled Calakmul from AD 636–86, and was likely the overlord of Waka' from at least 657 until his death. We documented unequivocal evidence that the tomb was re-entered in antiquity through the roof, in

approximately AD 770–820. During the re-entry, the interred individual was covered with carefully laid flat stones, after which the western side of the tomb's vault and the capstones were intentionally collapsed into the chamber. Subsequently, the chamber was filled with a matrix containing rocks and miscellaneous artefacts, but also with what can only be categorized as trash (Rich 2009). Many of the objects comprising the original mortuary assemblage were damaged when the tomb chamber was infilled, particularly the ceramic artefacts, a number of which have been restored.

One of the most fascinating components of the mortuary assemblage is the elaborate ritual tableau of 23 ceramic figurines, placed at the feet of the ruler (Figure 8.8). The narrative figurine scene depicts the resurrection ceremony of a deceased king kneeling as the penitent Maize God being cured of death by a magical deer or *way* spirit. His transformation into a healed and reborn ancestor is aided and witnessed by a presiding king, queen and royal courtiers, as well as a cluster of supernatural performers in the centre of the circular arrangement (Freidel et al. 2010).

Claire Halley (Chapter 9, this volume) offers an illuminating discussion of circular space in ritualized contexts as a symbol and metaphor providing a

Figure 8.8 The narrative figurine scene from Burial 39, El Perú-Waka'. Ministerio de Cultura y Deportes de Guatemala and Museo Nacional de Arqueología y Etnología de Guatemala. Photograph by Ricky López Bruni. Courtesy of the El Perú-Waka' Regional Archaeological Project.

Figure 8.9 Figurine king as a ballplayer wearing a Monkey Scribe headdress. Narrative figurine scene, Burial 39, El Perú-Waka'. Ministerio de Cultura y Deportes de Guatemala and Museo Nacional de Arqueología y Etnología de Guatemala. Photograph by Jenny Guerra. Courtesy of the El Perú-Waka' Regional Archaeological Project.

Figure 8.10 The monkey-shaman figurine. Narrative figurine scene, Burial 39, El Perú-Waka'. Ministerio de Cultura y Deportes de Guatemala and Museo Nacional de Arqueología y Etnología de Guatemala. Photograph by Michelle Rich. Courtesy of the El Perú-Waka' Regional Archaeological Project.

setting for individuals to forge and renew bonds – a pursuit surely intended to be conveyed in this resurrection tableau. Although not communal in the egalitarian sense Halley discusses, the scene exhibits the complex interplay between ritual and play in Maya culture and ritual: two women gesture as dancers; one of the men is carrying a ball for the ballgame; and the living king presiding over the funerary ritual is certainly a ballplayer, for he is outfitted in garb appropriate for such a match (Figure 8.9). He also wears a monkey headdress and a limpet shell pectoral called an *oyohualli* carved in the form of a vagina (Coe 1973).

The later Aztecs, according to Michael Coe, would combine these elements in ribald farces featuring monkeys and female genitalia, and this idea of sex play was part of ancient Maya ritual in ways that still need to be elucidated. The king's monkey headdress also likely alludes also to the Monkey

Scribe gods, who, as mentioned earlier, have tails that end in centipede heads, and are also represented in the Popol Vuh. Karl Taube (2003b) has cogently suggested that scribal lords are linked to centipedes because the cosmic centipede maw leads into the underworld, the land of the dead and divine. Scribes, through their capacity to read, can access the words of the dead and the divine. But it is also the case that Waka' means Centipede Water, and the kings of Waka' were Holy Centipede Lords. The king in this figurine scene surely represents just such a lord.

The monkey theme carries over into the cluster of performers, where a seated shaman is portrayed as an old monkey woman (Figure 8.10). She is carrying several objects under her arm which we believe may be a set of stick dice and a divining board, instruments of her conjuring craft. One of her companions is a male dwarf figurine who wears a large deer headdress, echoing the figurine depicted in Figure 8.7, and he carries a conch shell trumpet with which to call forth the deer spirit. This may be the *Chijchan*, the snake/deer spirit companion of the Snake dynasty kings and of Yuhknoom Ch'een the Great, Calakmul's ruler, in particular. The penitent deceased king is prayed over by a magical deer, possibly another *Chijchan*. This magical deer spirit is adorned with a blue-green painted *Ik* jewel around its neck (Figure 8.4). Identical artefactual jade pectorals exist, likely worn by royals, carved as effigy shells with *Ik* glyphs depicted on them (see Finamore & Houston 2010, 122–3, pls. 40–1). The *Ik* glyph denotes wind, breath or spirit, and greenstones such as jade have been cogently argued by Karl Taube (2005) to be a material embodying breath and spirit, and thus, life. We propose, therefore, that this *way* spirit wearing the *Ik* pendant is resurrecting the deceased king, rather than cursing him.

Circumstantial evidence of both an archaeological and epigraphic nature may support the hypothesis that the presiding king in the figurine scene actually represents the aforementioned Yuhknoom Ch'een the Great, the king who certainly oversaw the accession of K'inich Bahlam II, as attested by El Perú Stela 33. As intentionally arranged in the ceremony represented by the figurines, this king was placed next to the queen figurine, who is flanked on the other side by the kneeling deceased king and deer *way* spirit. Iconographically and temporally, it is possible this queen figurine represents Lady K'abel (Figure 8.11), the wife of K'inich Bahlam II and the probable daughter of Yuhknoom Ch'een the Great.

In terms of written history, Lady K'abel is the most important ruler of Waka' during the Late Classic period. As previously mentioned, the *Chijchan* is the snake/deer spirit companion of the Snake dynasty kings and of Yuhknoom Ch'een the Great in particular. As such, the deer curing the deceased king of death may represent the spirit companion of either Yuhknoom Ch'een the Great or Lady K'abel.

The queen figurine carries a battle shield on her left arm that is unlike any other in the Maya corpus, as it has a stick element attached to it that points upwards. This is not a product of the conservation process conducted by Licda. Griselda Pérez Robles, PAW archaeologist, and Lynn Grant, head conservator at the University of Pennsylvania Museum of Archaeology and Anthropology, to restore the

Figure 8.11 The queen figurine. Narrative figurine scene, Burial 39, El Perú-Waka'. Ministerio de Cultura y Deportes de Guatemala and Museo Nacional de Arqueología y Etnología de Guatemala. Photograph by Jenny Guerra. Courtesy of the El Perú-Waka' Regional Archaeological Project.

figurines after they were crushed in the ancient infilling of the tomb chamber; rather, it is the actual placement of the element on the shield by the Maya craftspeople who fashioned the figurines from clay. Lady K'abel does carry a battle shield on El Perú Stela 34, a well-preserved stela raised in AD 692. Artefacts generally interpreted by Maya archaeologists and art historians to be divining mirrors are paired with sticks in several painted vase scenes, and while we agree that mirrors were used for divining, we suggest they were not only for looking, but also for casting. The battle shield carried by the queen figurine may have served a dual function of a divining board, because the surface of the miniature shield is painted with distinctive geometric lines similar to the calculating and divining surfaces noted by Anthony Aveni (2005) along the southern side of the Pyramid of the Sun at Teotihuacan (Freidel & Rich 2015).

As Karl Taube (2004) has noted, a well-preserved Late Classic scene on a polychrome vessel shows a lord throwing elements directly onto a small table and not into the adjacent brazier as might be appropriate if it was a burnt offering. We suggest this scene represents divination casting of tokens such as practised widely on small tables and on boards in the Maya area today. The Conquest-Period game of *Patolli* used such lined boards and casting tokens – large, flat beans called *patoles*. *Patolli* was thought to have a relationship to divinatory and solar cycles (Soustelle 1964). A number of other artefacts found in Burial 39 are suggestive of small objects that may have served as divinatory casting tokens, including spangles or flat beads fashioned from *Spondylus spp.*, and 64 miniature spindle whorls (Masson, Freidel & Rich 2016). The quantity of spindle whorls and their context in this tomb may point to a function other than prosaic cloth manufacture, such as tokens for divinatory casting. Interestingly, weaving and its implements, such as the spindle, are particular insignia of the goddess *Chahk Chel*. This goddess, called *Ix Chel* at the time of the Conquest, was the protector of the shaman and blessed their divining instruments according to the clergyman Diego de Landa. But the most remarkable potential set of gaming devices in the tomb was composed of elaborately carved and painted bone sticks. Stick dice are still used for gaming today in Mexico, and while the subject has not received the study it deserves, there is every reason to believe that the pre-Hispanic people of the region also used sticks for gaming and divination. The carved sticks in Burial 39 have a variety of ends that include birds, flowers and hands holding masks (Figure 8.12).

Stick bundles are common regalia for scribes in painted Maya vase scenes, and stick bundles appear in settings suggesting that they are part of tribute and commercial negotiations. Lady K'abel wears a stick in her hair on El Perú Stela 34, and similarly, the figurine queen wears stick bundles in her headdress, reinforcing the activity suggested by the stick and divining board shield.

Additionally, we have evidence that gaming or divining sticks might not have been the exclusive prerogative of the royalty at Waka'. In 2005, Juan Carlos Ramírez discovered a set of carved bone sticks in a burial in one of the plazas north-east of

Figure 8.12 Carved bone from the El Perú-Waka' Burial 39 stick bundle. Ministerio de Cultura y Deportes de Guatemala and Museo Nacional de Arqueología y Etnología de Guatemala. Photograph by Denis Paz. Courtesy of the El Perú-Waka' Regional Archaeological Project.

the palace. One of these sticks has a brief glyphic text on it and another has an ornamented end. These differ from the Burial 39 sticks in being pointed on one end like styluses, but they are related.

Moreover, one of two dwarf boxers in the narrative figurine scene wears what might be a stick bundle on his headdress (Figure 8.13). Karl Taube has suggested (pers. comm., 2010) that the other boxer's headdress (Figure 8.14) is adorned with a distinctive obsidian sacrificial knife of a kind favoured at Teotihuacan, but this decorative element may possibly represent an abstracted centipede maw depicted in the *pars pro toto* ('part for the whole') style. If we are right, then a ritual boxing match that may have been part of the funeral games might have pitted a champion representing the Wak dynasty and its new king, K'inich Bahlam II, against a champion representing Lady K'abel.

Whatever the final answer to the question concerning the motifs of the boxer headdresses, it is clear

Figure 8.13 Boxer dwarf with stick bundle adorning helmet. Narrative figurine scene, Burial 39, El Perú-Waka'. Ministerio de Cultura y Deportes de Guatemala and Museo Nacional de Arqueología y Etnología de Guatemala. Photograph by Jenny Guerra. Courtesy of the El Perú-Waka' Regional Archaeological Project.

Figure 8.14 Boxer dwarf with helmet supporting what may be a Teotihuacan-style sacrificial knife or an abstracted centipede maw. Narrative figurine scene, Burial 39, El Perú-Waka'. Ministerio de Cultura y Deportes de Guatemala and Museo Nacional de Arqueología y Etnología de Guatemala. Photograph by Jenny Guerra. Courtesy of the El Perú-Waka' Regional Archaeological Project.

that funeral games such as ritualized boxing (Taube & Zender 2009) accompanied the resurrection of this king, as the Maize God was resurrected following the ballgames of *Xibalba* (the Maya underworld) in the Popol Vuh.

Christina Halperin (2014, 200–3), in her important recent synthesis of Maya figurines, underscores the complex relationship between ritual and play. She notes the presence of figurines in public monumental contexts, as well as households, and this invites the subtitle of her book, "Intersections between State and Household". Her wide-ranging review of figurine contexts shows clearly that these artefacts occur frequently in above-surface contexts (both common and public), midden especially, and rarely in burials and cached offerings. She arrives at the conclusion that figurines generally appear to be commodities available to all and not privileged 'inalienable' things worthy of special treatment in curation or disposal. Testament to play or ritual in their casual dismantling

and discard in public places, figurines bring clues to the witnessing of the humble devout to the pomp of state ceremony. While in general we do agree with this conclusion, her analysis puts into bold relief the figurine scene from Waka's Burial 39. Carefully made in royal workshops, featuring an array of Maya elites and an animal of extraordinary power and presence engaged in a resurrection ritual, the figurine scene we describe transcends the custom highlighted in Halpern's book, elevating the disposable ordinary to the status of inalienable and eternal icon.

CONCLUDING THOUGHTS ON MAYA SACRED PLAY AT WAKA'

Synthesizing the rich information addressing Maya sacred play deserves far more research than presented here. The opportunity to participate in the symposium from which this volume was developed, and the contributions of other participants – those cited and others who were not cited in the present chapter – opened new avenues of thought regarding how we conceive of the potential ways that play, ritual and representations of animals may have intertwined in lives of ancient Maya people, as they continue to among modern Maya we know and with whom we have worked. In addition to the abundant ballgame imagery and animal depictions available in the Maya artistic corpus, the text of the Popol Vuh creation myth clearly highlights those topics. Using archaeological evidence from Waka', we addressed the various themes at hand, yet many examples remain to be explored. For example, the performers at the centre of the narrative figurine scene in Burial 39 allude to sacred buffoonery in the deformed bodies of the dwarves, and are depicted boxing, trumpeting and carrying writing implements along with a hunchback scribe (see Taube & Taube 2009 for a related discussion of Maya figurines, ritual clowning and aesthetics). These figurines were arranged around the seated singing shaman. Commensurate with this imagery, Lady K'abel is depicted on El Perú Stela 34 performing with a court dwarf, who played his musical rattles while she danced, and it makes sense to us that a conjuring and healing ceremony would be accompanied by such characters. The monkey-faced singing shaman (Figure 8.10) is a strange and powerful figurine completely different from the rest in shape and execution. She is hollow and filled with bright red cinnabar, a symbol of life force and blood often found painted on the bones of deceased royalty, but she is not unique. Daniela Triadan (2007) found a similar monkey-faced old woman figurine cradling a child in a domestic context at the site of Ceibal south of Waka', and she concluded that it was a child's toy. Like the marble discovered in the dusty road of Yaxuna that ended up in a gourd cup of clear liquor on Don Pablo's altar as a light stone, some artefacts bind playful things in sacredness and remind us that the human imagination is not easily constrained by the categories of reason. Indeed, it is the breaching of such categories that inspires liminal experience often expressed through play and ritual.

ACKNOWLEDGEMENTS

The authors would like to thank Colin Renfrew and the MacDonald Institute for Archaeological Research for extending the offer to colleagues 'from across the pond' to participate in this symposium, as well as Michael Boyd, Iain Morley, Patricia Duff and others for their tireless work organizing conference details and patience during the process of assembling this volume. None of the interpretations presented herein would have been possible without the expertise of many generous colleagues who have participated or collaborated over the years with the El Perú-Waka' Regional Archaeological Project; the permission and endorsements of the Ministerio de Cultura y Deportes de Guatemala and Museo Nacional de Arqueología y Etnología de Guatemala; and the support of various funders, including the National Science Foundation (Graduate Research Fellowship Program grant awarded to Rich); the Foundation for the Advancement of Mesoamerican Studies, Inc. (FAMSI grant #07087 awarded to Rich); and project-wide support provided by the Jerome Glick Foundation, a National Geographic Scientific Research Grant, and PACUNAM – Fundación Patrimonio Cultural y Natural Maya.

REFERENCES

Aveni, A., 2005. Observations on the pecked designs and other figures carved on the south platform of the pyramid of the sun at Teotihuacan. *Journal for the History of Astronomy* 36(122), 31–47.

Campbell, J., 1988. *The Power of Myth*, New York: Random House.

Christenson, A., 2003. *Popol Vuh: The Sacred Book of the Maya*. Winchester, England: O Books.

Coe, M., 1973. *The Maya Scribe and His World*. New York: Grolier Club.

Eppich, K., 2011. Lineage and State at El Perú-Waka': Ceramic and Architectural Perspectives on the Classic Maya Social Dynamic. Unpublished PhD Dissertation, Southern Methodist University.

Finamore, D. & S. Houston, 2010. *Fiery Pool: The Maya and the Mythic Sea*. New Haven, CT: Yale University Press.

Freidel, D. A., M. Masson & M. Rich, 2016. Imagining a complex Maya political economy: Counting Tokens and currencies in Image, Text and the Archaeological Record. *Cambridge Archaeological Journal* 27(1), 29–54.

Freidel, D. A. & M. Rich,2015. Pecked circles and divining boards: calculating instruments in ancient Mesoamerica. In *Cosmology, Calendars, and Horizon-Based Astronomy in Ancient Mesoamerica*, eds. A. Dowd & S. Milbrath. Boulder: University Press of Colorado, 249–64.

Freidel, D. A., M. Rich & F. K. Reilly III, 2010. Resurrecting the Maize King. *Archaeology* 63(5), 42–5.

Freidel, D. A., L. Schele & J. Parker, 1993. *Maya Cosmos: Three Thousand Years on the Shamans' Path*. New York: William Morrow & Co. Inc.

Grube, N., & W. Nahm, 1994. A census of Xibalba: a complete inventory of way characters on Maya ceramics, in *The Maya Vase Book, Vol. 4.*, eds. B. Kerr & J. Kerr. New York: Kerr Associates, 686–715.

Guenter, S., 2007. On the Emblem Glyph of El Peru. *The PARI Journal* 8(2), 20–3.

Halperin, C. T., 2014. *Maya Figurines: Intersections between State and Household*. Austin: University of Texas Press.

Houston, S. D. & D. Stuart, 1989. The *Way* Glyph: Evidence for 'Co-essences' among the Classic Maya. *Research Reports on Ancient Maya Writing* 30. Washington, DC.: Center for Maya Research.

Inomata, T., 2006. Plazas, performers, and spectators: political theatres of the Classic Maya. *Current Anthropology* 47(5), 805–42.

Lee, D., 2012. *Approaching the End: Royal Ritual in the Palace Group at El Perú-Waka', Petén, Guatemala*. Unpublished Ph.D. Dissertation, Southern Methodist University.

Lee, D. F. & S. P. Guenter, 2010. *Ballgame panels from El Perú-Waka' in regional perspective*. Paper presented at the 75th Anniversary Meeting of the Society for American Archaeology, 14–18 April, St. Louis MO.

Marken, D., 2011. *City and State: Urbanism, Rural Settlement, and Polity in the Classic Maya Lowlands*. Unpublished PhD Dissertation, Southern Methodist University.

Martin, S., 2000. Nuevos datos epigraficos sobre la guerra Maya del clasico, in *La Guerra entre los Antiguos Mayas: Memorias de la Primera Mesa Redondo de Palenque 1995*, ed. S. Trejo. Mexico City: INAH, 105–24.

Meléndez, J. C., 2007. *Excavaciones en la Plaza 4 del Sitio Arqueológico El Perú, Petén: Cronología y Función*. Unpublished Licenciatura Thesis, Universidad de San Carlos de Guatemala.

Miller, M. E., & S. D. Houston, 1987. The classic Maya ballgame and its architectural setting: a study in relations between text and image. *RES: Anthropology and Aesthetics* 14, 47–66.

Navarro-Farr, O. C., 2009. *Ritual, Process, and Continuity in the Late to Terminal Classic Transition: Investigations at Structure M13-1 in the Ancient Maya Site of El Perú-Waka', Petén, Guatemala*. Unpublished PhD Dissertation, Southern Methodist University.

Navarro-Farr, O. C., D. A. Freidel & A. L. Arroyave Prera, 2008. Manipulating memory in the wake of dynastic decline at El Perú-Waka': Termination at abandoned Structure M13-1. In *Ruins of the Past: The Use and Perception of Abandoned Structures in the Maya Lowlands*, eds. T. W. Stanton & A. Magnoni, Boulder: University Press of Colorado, 113–46.

Navarro-Farr, O. C., G. Pérez Robles & D. Menéndez Bolaños, 2012. Operación 1: Excavaciones en la Estructura M13-1. In *Proyecto Regional Arqueológico El Perú-Waka': Informe No. 10, Temporada 2012*, ed. J. C. Pérez. Report presented to the Instituto de Antropología e Historia, Guatemala, 3–91.

Navarro-Farr, O. & M. Rich (eds.), 2014. *Archaeology at El Perú-Waka': Ancient Maya Performances of Ritual, Memory and Power*. Tucson: University of Arizona Press.

Perez Robles, G., 2003. ES: Excavaciones de Sondeo en las Plazas 1, 2, 3, y 4. In *Proyecto Regional Arqueológico El Perú-Waka': Informe No. 1, Temporada 2003*, eds. H. Escobedo and D. Freidel. Report presented to the Instituto de Antropología e Historia, Guatemala, 257–82.

Rich, M., 2009. *Refuse or Ritual? An Examination of the Problematic Deposit of Artifacts in the Tomb Fill of Burial 39, El Perú-Waka', Guatemala*. Paper presented at the 74th Annual Meeting for the Society for American Archaeology, Atlanta, GA.

Rich, M., 2011. *Ritual, Royalty and Classic Period Politics: The Archaeology of the Mirador Group at El Perú-Waka', Petén, Guatemala*. Unpublished PhD Dissertation, Southern Methodist University.

Rich, M., D. Freidel, F. K. Reilly III & E. K. Eppich, 2010. An Olmec-style figurine from El Perú-Waka', Petén, Guatemala: a preliminary report. *Mexicon* 17(5), 115–22.

Rich, M, V. Matute & J. Piehl, 2007. WK-11: Excavaciones en la Estructura O14-04. In *Proyecto Arqueológico El Perú-Waka': Informe No. 4, Temporada 2006*, eds. H. L. Escobedo & D. A. Freidel. Report presented to the Instituto de Antropología e Historia, Guatemala City, 217–57.

Rich, M., J. Piehl & V. Matute, 2006. WK-11A: Continuación de las Excavaciones en el Complejo Mirador, Estructura O14-04. In *Proyecto Arqueológico El Perú-Waka': Informe No. 3, Temporada 2005*, eds. H. L. Escobedo & D. Freidel. Report presented to the Instituto de Antropología e Historia, Guatemala City, 225–74.

Robles Castellanos, F. & A. P. Andrew, 2003. Proyecto Costa Maya: reconocimiento arqueologico de la esquina noroeste de la peninsula de Yucatan, *in Simposio de Investigaciones Arqueologicas en Guatemala (2003)*. Guatemala: Ministerio de Cultura y Deportes; Instituto de Antropologia e Historia, 47–66.

Schele, L. & D. Freidel, 1990. *A Forest of Kings, the Untold Story of the Ancient Maya*. New York: William Morrow & Co. Inc.

Soustelle, J. 1964. *Daily Life of the Aztecs*. Harmondsworth: Pelican.

Stanton, T. W., D. A. Freidel, C. K. Suhler, T. Ardren, J. N. Ambrosino, J. M. Shaw & S. Bennett, 2010. *Excavations at Yaxuná, Yucatán, Mexico.* Oxford: Archaeopress.

Taube, K., 2003a. Ancient and contemporary Maya conceptions about field and forest. In *The Lowland Maya Area: Three Millennium at the Human-Wildland Interface*, eds. A. Gomez-Pompa, M. F. Allen, S. L. Fedick, & J. J. Jimenez-Osornio,. New York: Food Products Press, an Imprint of the Haworth Press, Inc., 461–92.

Taube, K., 2003b. The maws of heaven and hell: the symbolism of the centipede and serpent in classic Maya religion. In *Antropología de la Eternidad: La Muerte en la Cultura Maya*, eds. A. Ciudad Ruiz, M. H. Ruz Sosa & M. J. Iglesias Ponce de León. Madrid: Sociedad Española de Estudios Mayas, 405–42.

Taube, K., 2004. Structure 10L-16 and its early classic antecedents: fire and the evocation and resurrection of K'inich Yax K'uk' Mo'. In *Understanding Early Classic Copan*, eds. E. E. Bell, M. A. Canuto & R. J. Sharer, Philadelphia: University of Pennsylvania Museum of Archaeology and Anthropology, 249–95.

Taube, K., 2005. The symbolism of jade in classic Maya religion. *Ancient Mesoamerica* 16, 23–50.

Taube, R. & K. Taube, 2009. The beautiful, the bad and the ugly: aesthetics and morality in Maya figurines. In *Mesoamerican Figurines: Small-Scale Indices of Large Scale Social Phenomena*, eds. C. T. Halperin, K. A. Faust, R. Taube & A. Giguet. Gainesville: University Press of Florida, 25–50.

Taube, K. & M. Zender, 2009. American gladiators: ritual boxing in ancient Mesoamerica. In *Blood and Beauty: Organized Violence in the Art and Archaeology of Mesoamerica and Central America*, eds. H. Orr & R. Koontz. Los Angeles, CA: Cotsen Institute of Archaeology Press, 161–220.

Tedlock, D., 1985. *The Popol Vuh: The Mayan Book of the Dawn of Life.* New York: Simon and Schuster, Inc.

Triadan, D., 2007. Warrior, nobles, commoners and beasts: figurines from elite buildings at Aguateca, Guatemala. *Latin American Antiquity* 18(3), 269–94.

9

COMMUNAL PERFORMANCE AND RITUAL PRACTICE IN THE ANCESTRAL PUEBLOAN ERA OF THE AMERICAN SOUTHWEST

CLAIRE HALLEY

This chapter begins with a brief discussion of the role of communal performance in contemporary Puebloan groups located in the Four Corners region of the American Southwest. By highlighting the multiple intentions of such practices including religious, secular, social and political ends, I present communal performance as an integrative device used to create a sense of community identity as well as an instrumental mechanism integral to the proper functioning and well-being of Puebloan society. Against this ethnographic background, I argue that the structuring role of communal performance has deep roots in Puebloan lifeways. Focusing on the period AD 500–700, when the first village communities began to appear in the Southwest, I consider architectural and iconographic evidence to examine the role communal performance, specifically the circle dance, played in creating and embodying ritual frameworks and ideas of community identity in the Ancestral Puebloan era.

Through crowds of spectators, the visitor sees masses of rhythmically moving bodies arrayed in colourful costumes and paraphernalia. Excited children run through the village, their laughter mingling with the voices of singers and the repetitive sounds of bells, rattles and drums. The smells of freshly baked bread, burning piñon, and steaming stews permeate the air. Together, the careful ritual preparations, the group movement sequences, the closely interrelated dance and music, the costumes, and the audience itself create a performance that communicates important images and messages to performer and observer alike. (Sweet 1985, 15)

CONTEMPORARY PUEBLOAN COMMUNITY PERFORMANCE

Jill Sweet's description of a contemporary communal performance at Tewa Pueblo, New Mexico, captures something of the atmosphere, excitement and expectation generated by such events. The sights, sounds and smells combine to create a sensuous experience for all participants whilst the preparations and execution of the performance generate a shared sense of intention, forging and sustaining social bonds.

Communal performance is an intrinsic and integral component of life not just in Tewa Pueblo but in the numerous contemporary Puebloan communities based in the American Southwest. The movements, actions, gestures, music, stories, costumes, musical instruments and paraphernalia all reflect religious beliefs, values and attitudes meaningful within the respective community, creating and reflecting ideas of identity. On one level, performances may be joyful, exuberant celebrations, full of fun and laughter, but this belies the serious and critical purpose of communal performance. Collective memory and worldview are important components involving the re-enactment of creation stories, including the emergence of the people from the underworld to the earth's surface and their subsequent migrations to find the 'centre place'. Performers also impersonate heroes and villains, spirits and animals to personify and enact an elaborate and complex belief system. Such performances reinforce ideals of community identity whilst adherence to the rules of performance in terms of setting, timing, dance steps, costume and music is necessary to appeal to and appease deities. Although the attributes of ritual behaviour have been variously characterised and described (e.g. Durkheim 1912; Turner 1969, 1982, 1990; Lange 1976; Beeman 1993; Bell 1997, 138–69; Rappaport 1999, 24; Marcus 2007, 48), the organisation, enactment and symbolism of Puebloan communal performance encompass the essential attributes of what we understand to be ritual and ritualised behaviour using practices that are time-structured, repetitive and formalised (Renfrew 2007, 109).

In many contemporary Puebloan groups such as the Hopi and Zuni, play is an integral component of religious practice and performance. Clowns and clowning societies have a key role in public ceremony. At Hopi, clowns represent unformed and uncultured humans and serve to remind the community of their antecedents and what humanity was like before learning the proper way to behave (Waters [1963] 1977). Clowning behaviour contradicts the formality and invariance that scholars such as Rappaport and Bell argue are key indicators of ritual behaviour. Clowns reverse normal conventions and behave in ways that, in normal circumstances, are taboo. Their behaviour and actions are unpredictable and certainly lack formality or decorum. Clowns may eat the inedible or speak and act in opposites. Clowns may single out certain individuals in the crowd who have broken social conventions for ridicule (Parsons [1939] 1996). This anarchic behaviour provokes shocked laughter from the crowd as they enjoy this perverse spectacle. These antics and mockery have a serious purpose. The chaotic, rule-breaking, unpredictable and extreme behaviour of clowns acts to reinforce the rules and norms of behaviour expected from members of the community (Hieb 1972). By breaking the rules, clowning serves to impose discipline and order.

Communal performance in contemporary Puebloan society encapsulates multiple meanings and intentions. Through observation and interview anthropologists such as Grimes (1976), Kurath (1967), Kurath and Garcia (1973), Spicer (1939) and Tedlock (1992) recognised the multiplicity of meanings, roles, beliefs, norms and values embodied in these events although some practices and meanings are restricted knowledge and not shared with outsiders. Religious, secular, social and political objectives are enacted through these events, which are at once entertaining, serious and playful. Communal performances in contemporary Puebloan society have a functional and instrumental purpose, not just in terms of religious practice and belief, but also in creating and framing community identity and membership.

Community performance has a long tradition in the Puebloan world. In the remainder of this chapter, I explore the earliest archaeological evidence for such events in Ancestral Puebloan society ca. AD 500–700. I make the case that it is possible to reconstruct something of the nature of past performance from architectural and iconographic remains. Architectural data offer an insight into the nature and scale of communal performance, but this analysis is incomplete without considering how people may have used these spaces. The iconographic depiction of communal performance in ceramics and rock art can be used to people these spaces, providing a snapshot of past practice and the types of dance form used. Based on these data, I argue that it is possible to consider the emotional, ideational and sensory experience of communal performance to provide an insight into how ritual and symbolic meanings were formed and maintained.

THE ARCHAEOLOGY OF PERFORMANCE

Performance is of the moment; activities such as music, drama, dancing or storytelling leave few traces once the event is over (Schechner 1994, 619). For the archaeologist, detecting the material remains of communal performance can be problematic (as noted by Renfrew, Chapter 2, this volume). For some time this area of enquiry seemed beyond archaeological exam-ination. Even though scholars cannot hope to recre-ate past performances with their inherent, nuanced meanings, to ignore these activities is to overlook a potentially rich repository of data which have the potential to reveal how social bonds and ritual frame-works were embodied. In recent work, scholars such as Inomata 2006; Inomata and Coben 2006; Pearson and Shanks 2001 and Soar 2010 have used the generic term of *performance* as a lens to consider the creation and negotiation of identity, belief, symbolism, social and political relationships in the past.

For the purpose of this chapter, I have limited the discussion to a constituent of communal per-formance – dance – and to one form – the circle dance. Dance is acknowledged as a cross-cultural phenomenon that appears in almost every time and type of community from the earliest periods of human development (Sachs 1952; Kraus 1969; Bland 1976; Lange 1976; Cass 1993). Dance is a purpose-ful, intentionally rhythmical and culturally patterned sequence of bodily movement, distinct from ordi-nary, daily practice (Hanna 1979). People dance to fulfil a range of intentions, e.g. explaining religion or myths, creating or recreating social roles, worshiping or honouring deities or spirits. The power of dance lies in its multisensory, emotional, cognitive, concep-tual and symbolic capacity to communicate inchoate ideas in visible form (Hanna 1987).

Circle dancing is a powerful and effective means of achieving social integration (Garfinkel 1998). Individuals create the form with their bodies by join-ing hands and moving in step, in the same direction, at the same tempo. The synchronicity and unifor-mity of movement creates feelings of group solidarity (Royce 1977; McNeill 1995). Through cooperation and collective action, individuality is subsumed by the embodiment and experience of uniformity and solidarity. Thus circle dancing is a sensory and physi-cal manifestation of social integration and equality; using a term coined by Inomata (2006, 807), it is a 'spectacle of unity'.

Garfinkel (2003) argues that religious cere-monies were a key device for creating community unity. Garfinkel develops this theme in this volume by considering the cognitive message of group sol-idarity conveyed by the use of identical masks by ceremonial participants in the proto-historic Near East. I too use the premise of ritual activity as a gen-erative activity in communal life, though I draw on architectural and iconographic data to argue that human practice and bodily experience create a cog-nitive, emotional and physical expression of ritual and communality. Experience of place and move-ment are the conduits for transcendent ritual expe-rience for "feeling through the body" (Morris & Peatfield 2002) inchoate ideas of social integration, bonding, community and identity.

EARLY COMMUNAL PERFORMANCE IN THE AMERICAN SOUTHWEST

At the end of the sixth century AD, Ancestral Puebloan people began to experiment with new lifeways expressed in subsistence, settlement patterns, architecture and material culture. There was a shift from a semi-nomadic, hunter-gatherer existence to a more settled, agrarian lifestyle. Instead of living in small pit houses scattered singularly or in twos and threes across the landscape, people began to build larger homes and aggregate together. Large village communities of up to 30 or more habitations were formed, and within each settlement the first example of a communal facility was built.

Although separated by time and distance, there are interesting parallels to be drawn with the devel-opments seen in the early Neolithic in South-West Asia around 12,000 BP (Watkins, Chapter 10, this volume). Here too, the adoption of a more settled, agrarian lifestyle corresponded with the develop-ment of large communities and the first examples of public buildings used for communal ritual. In the American Southwest, these socially integrative build-ings (Adler 1989) were large (floor area in excess of 50m²), circular, subterranean or semi-subterranean structures usually covered by a roof. Within each communal structure there were a limited number of internal features such as an encircling bench, central firepit or roof support posts. The Neolithic public buildings in South-West Asia had little floor space for rituals to be enacted and Watkins (Chapter 10, this volume) argues that the community focus was on making and remaking communal buildings rather than using these facilities for religious ceremony. In contrast, the communal structures of the America Southwest were designed with a clear and usable floor space, providing room for the community to gather together.

Architecture

Public architecture as humanly created space reflects cultural norms and values and provides a means for reproducing these. As Tuan (1997, 102) explains:

> Architectural space can define and make vivid sensations such as interior/exterior, open and closed, darkness/light, private and public. The built environment clarifies social roles and relations. People know who they are and how they ought to behave when the arena is humanly designed rather than nature's raw stage. Architecture teaches. … In the absence of books and formal instruction, architecture is a key to comprehending reality.

Given the recursive relationship between human practice and the built environment, an examination of the size and shape of a performance space can provide an indication of the scale and form of interactions that it was designed to facilitate. The size, shape and internal layout of communal spaces guide and shape movement, arrange and organise individuals and provide participants with a physical, experiential and cognitive expression of ritual and community.

The earliest settled communities in the American Southwest such as Broken Flute Cave in the Prayer Rock District (Morris 1959, 1980), Shabik'eshchee Village (Roberts 1929), Site 29SJ423 (Windes n.d.a) and Juniper Cove (Cummings 1953; Gilpin & Benallie 2000, 162–7) (Figure 9.1) each had a public building at its centre. Summary data (Table 9.1) including the size, form and internal features of these communal buildings are presented here together with a schematic floor plan of a typical communal structure (Figure 9.2).

The four communal structures have a number of common characteristics. They are large, circular, cleared floor areas, able to accommodate significant numbers of people although there are differences between the facility at Broken Flute Cave and the other three structures. These are explored later in this chapter.

Broken Flute Cave is a narrow, long, ledge some 76 metres above a valley floor. It is one of at least

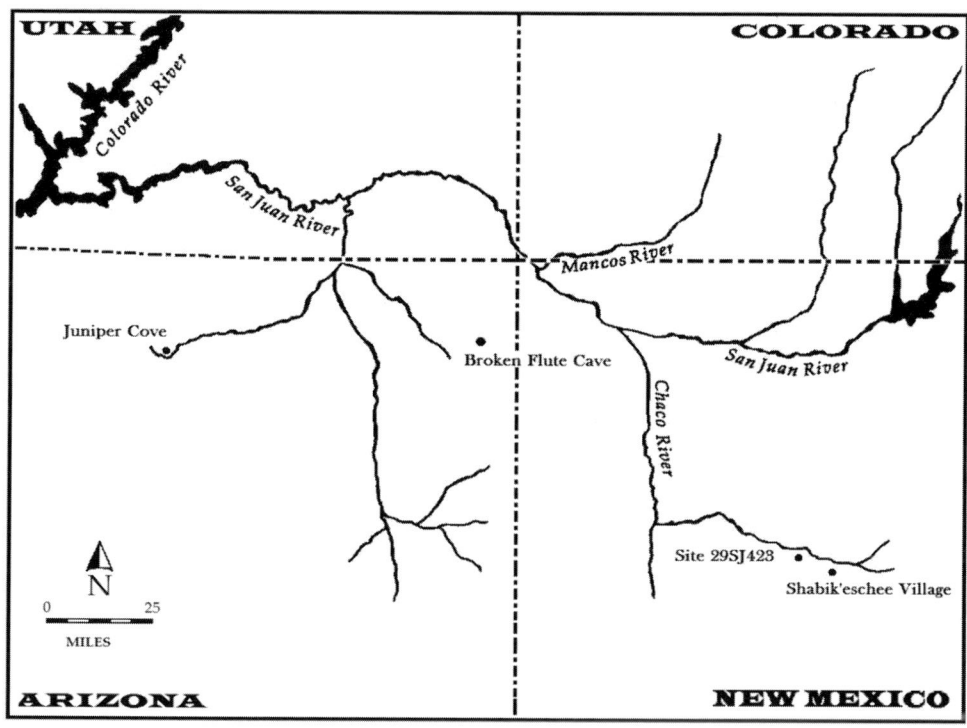

Figure 9.1 Map of the Four Corners region of the American Southwest showing the location of Basketmaker Sites. (Redrawn and adapted from Altschul & Huber 2000, fig. 7.1)

Table 9.1 Size, form and internal features of communal structures in early Ancestral Puebloan settlements

Site	Date AD	Shape	Floor Area m²	Roof	Hearth	Bench	Roof Support Posts (4)
Broken Flute Cave	623–40	Circular	132.73	No	No	No	No
Shabik'eshchee Village	550–700	Circular	116.90	Yes	Yes	Yes	Yes
Site 29SJ423	521–57	Circular	89.76	Yes	Yes	Yes	Yes
Juniper Cove	666–78	Circular	95.03	Yes	Yes	Yes	Yes

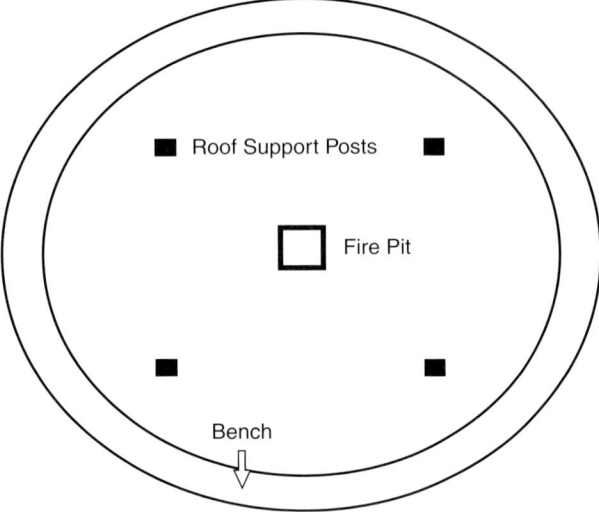

Figure 9.2 Schematic floor plan of a typical Ancestral Puebloan communal structure ca. AD 500–700.

12 inhabited caves in the Prayer Rock District of north-eastern Arizona, excavated in the 1930s by Earl Morris. On the western side of the cave, Morris excavated 16 small (5 metres in diameter) semi-subterranean pit houses. Removed from these habitations, on the eastern side of the cave was a large (13 metres in diameter), roughly circular structure formed by the placement of upright sandstone slabs in the cave floor surface. There was no formal entrance; it appears one just stepped over the slabs. Neither were there any internal features such as a firepit or bench. This was a clear, open floor space with unrestricted access.

The 'special' function of this large circular structure is emphasised by the concentration of rock art on the eastern cave wall, which includes the depiction of small, stick-like human figures in procession, holding sticks or staffs. Evidence from the western, domestic half of the cave indicates that musical performance was an integral part of social life in this community. Broken flute fragments (after which the cave was named), as well as four complete wooden flutes, were found under the floor of a pit house.

The large, clear floor area of the structure at Broken Flute Cave indicates this space was used as a gathering place, the form implying that circle dancing may have been part of the performance repertoire of this community. With a circumference of just over 40 metres, up to 80 hand-holding individuals (allowing 0.5 metres per person) could take part in a circle dance. As the structure was not roofed, the sights and sounds generated by performance activities could be seen and heard by people elsewhere in the cave or from valley floor below.

The location, size, shape, prominent position and accessibility of the structure at Broken Flute Cave suggest that it was a communal facility designed to emphasise access and inclusivity for actions and practices such as circle dancing meant to create bonds and solidarity. There are no obvious architectural features which segregate participants, reinforcing the egalitarian nature of relationships or, at least, the need to emphasise the experience and conception of inclusivity, social bonding and equality through communal performance.

The communal facilities at Juniper Cove, Shabik'eshchee Village and Site 29SJ423 differ from those found at Broken Flute Cave. These three large circular buildings were excavated out of the ground to form subterranean or semi-subterranean, roofed structures. Entrance was gained by descending a ladder placed in a central opening in the roof. Within the interior, a central hearth provided light in the dark, enclosed structure, an encircling bench around the interior wall could accommodate an audience and four posts placed at the cardinal directions supported the roof. Despite these internal features, these communal facilities are still characterised by large and relatively clear floor areas. A bench could have been used to demarcate space between audience and performers, organising individuals, imposing roles and configuring movement, encounter and experience. In contrast to Broken Flute Cave, the way space was conceived and experienced in these three communities may have been generative or reflective of changes in social relationships. The circular shape of these facilities underpinned ideas of solidarity, cohesion and social bonding, providing a backdrop against which emerging differentiation in participation between performers and audience was played out, perhaps creating or reflecting the emergence of asymmetrical social relations. The experience of being in a circular building inculcated an idea of order and epitomised political realities (Bradley 2012).

The circular communal buildings at the centre of these first settled communities became an established feature of later Ancestral Puebloan communal life. During the apogee of this culture, the Classic Bonito period (AD 1020–1100), large, circular, semi-subterranean structures based on the design and layout of these early communal structures were one of the defining features of the society. Called Great Kivas and defined as a "chamber specially constructed for ceremonial purposes" (Kidder 1927, 490), these facilities were constructed in the centre place of this community, Chaco Canyon, and were replicated in more than 100 communities in the Four Corners region of the Southwest. Though there have been changes in building style, variety and form over the years, semi-subterranean buildings with ceremonial and ritual functions are still found at the centre of contemporary Puebloan settlements providing facilities for settlement-wide events such as feasting, dance and ritual activities.

As a social construct, architecture reflects cultural norms, values and beliefs (Kus 1983). The study of communal spaces and changes through time offers an impression of the function and scale of these buildings and an indication of their changing role in public life, but this interpretation is incomplete unless we fill these locales with people and think about the practices and interactions that took place within and around these spaces. The iconographic portrayal of such events provides a snapshot of past practice and has the potential to inform our interpretation of the role and interactions of participants and the nature of ritualised behaviour.

Iconography

My starting point for the analysis of the iconography of communal performance is based on the assumption that the action, including the form, context and paraphernalia depicted, is an idealised, symbolised portrayal of real-life events (Morris & Peatfield 2002). A potential difficulty in interpretation lies in recognising a dynamic activity on a static medium and the identification of communal or dance activity, as opposed to fighting, hunting or other activities. I used the methodology established by Garfinkel (1998, 2003) to identify the iconographic depiction of dance, focusing on groups of human figures in rows or holding hands. Dancing figures were identified by body position, body ornamentation and the use of paraphernalia such as musical instruments, sticks, wands together with the relationship or proximity of one figure to another.

It is likely there were many diverse forms of community performance practices in the past. The data from architectural and iconographic evidence are a useful means to identify at least some of these and comment on why particular forms and settings were chosen and what implications these decisions had for ritual practice. The iconographic depictions presented herein are not a direct result of dance or communal performance (Longstreet 1968; Garfinkel 1998), but represent the transformation of real practices into idealised and abstract images which are comprehensible to the artist and the wider community to which they belong.

The choices involved in this process, what to depict and how, are reflective of the underlying ideals and values embodied in community performance. The external, physical action of the circle dance expresses and symbolises intellectual ideas of solidarity whilst the internal experience of the dance reflects how embodied action impacts the emotional and psychological state. Thus the depiction of dance is a means to convey the holistic and transcendent ritual experience of synchronous body movement (Turner 1969, 1982, 1990; Morris & Peatfield 2002).

Ceramics

The depiction of humans (and lifeforms generally) on ceramics in the American Southwest was rare in the period from AD 500–700. Ceramic decoration at this time was characterised by geometric and/or abstract designs. Nevertheless, in the small number of vessels depicting human forms from this time period, there is consistency in the method of depiction. The bowl shown here is a typical example (Figure 9.3).

In this example, 14 figures have been arranged around the interior circumference of the bowl. The figures hold hands and form a circle. There are no details or decoration on any of the individual forms and no distinctions in dress, posture or body size. There is no individuality and no one figure stands out, though gender differences are emphasised. Females are depicted with large hair whorls on either side of their head. This 'butterfly' style was used by unmarried Hopi girls until recently (Roediger 1961, 18). Mummified human remains recovered from the Ancestral Puebloan period attest to this hairstyle being used by females in antiquity (Hays 1988, 8). Males are shown with a one-horn headdress or feather plume on the side of their head.

The depiction of performance activities on ceramic vessels can not only suggest something about the shape and form of the dance, but can also imply something about the architectural setting of these events. I argue that the depiction of circle dancing provides support for placing such performances within the circular communal spaces found in early settled communities. A round object such as a bowl provides an apt object to accentuate the shape and form of a circle dance. The placement of the figures on the interior, rather than the exterior of the bowl, provides support for placing this activity within circular communal structures. If we consider that the wall of the bowl represents the enclosing, encircling walls of the communal structure, then the figures are depicted dancing inside the structure. The subterranean form of the building is emphasised by looking down into the bowl to see the figures. The decoration and physical properties of the bowl were being used as a metaphor to represent the activities and to provide a reminder of the events that took place here with all their inherent meaning. It is possible that circle dancing could have taken place in a number of different locales, including the open air; it is clear that during this time period, the experience of the circle, whether through engagement with architecture or through enactment in a circle dance, ensured that participation, integration and collective ritual practice were physically, emotionally and cognitively produced and experienced.

Rock Art

In contrast to the rarity of human forms in ceramic decoration, humans are a common feature of rock art design (Hays 1988, 5). In early depictions, humans are large, static, front-facing, broad-shouldered

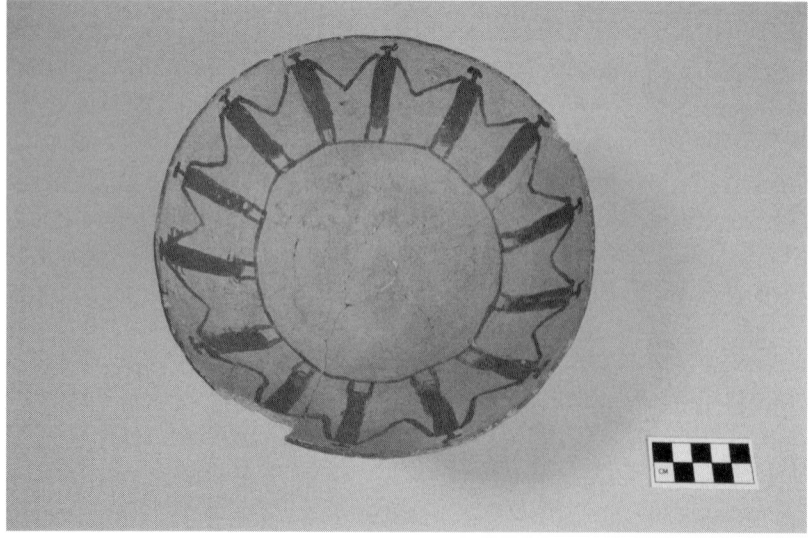

Figure 9.3 Hand-holding figures La Plata black-on-white bowl AD 600–850, Tohatchi Flats, New Mexico.
UCM No. 9509. Copyright University of Colorado Museum of Natural History.

figures up to one metre in height. These figures are often interpreted as shamans and are usually adorned with jewellery, necklaces, headdresses, earbobs and body decoration (Grant 1978; Schaafsma 1980). Coinciding with the formation of large, settled communities and the first public architecture, there was a significant change in rock art style. Human figures were shown as smaller, less elaborately decorated, more anonymous characters. Humans were no longer static, but portrayed in animated poses such as walking, running, playing the flute, hunting, in procession or performing circle dancing. If design composition communicates social ideas, then this change in style appears to indicate a general emphasis away from the individual and individuality to indistinct human forms interacting together. The emphasis of such composition is not the identification of particular individuals, but the depiction of a coordinated group in action.

The circumference of a round ceramic vessel is a useful medium to portray circle dancing; the shape of the vessel emphasising and expressing circular movement and form (see also Garfinkel, Chapter 11, this volume). A flat rock surface is a less satisfactory medium and requires some ingenuity and appreciation of perspective to depict circle dancing. The five examples of circle dancing shown here each demonstrate a different technique to express this dance form.

In the first example (Figure 9.4), humans are anonymous; apart from variations in size there is no differentiation between them. The focus of the design is on the circular form created by the figures rather than the figures themselves. To the right of the circle dance is a large figure (almost twice the size of the largest in the circle). This individual is playing the flute and could be interpreted as a human or deity providing musical accompaniment to the dance.

In the second example (Figure 9.5), three dynamic, hand-holding figures are represented, apparently dancing over a circle. The circle could represent the form of the dance and/or a circular performance area.

The artists responsible for the examples (Figures 9.6 and 9.7) use perspective created by the height and placement of the human form to introduce the idea of circularity into their depictions. In Figure 9.6, the central human is smaller than the two on either side whilst the ground surface, implied by the placement of the feet of the three individuals, creates a half circle. This image could be an attempt to depict an open circle dance.

Figure 9.7 could be interpreted as a single human holding up three others or as an attempt to represent four figures holding hands, joined together in a circle dance.

In all the examples, the dancing figures are anonymous (apart from the flute player who

Figure 9.4 Flute player and hand-holding figures.
Birch Creek, Utah.
(Image reproduced with permission from Slifer 2007, pl. 6)

Figure 9.5 Three figures – circle dancing.
Panel 4, South Shelter, Falls Creek,
Colorado.
(Reproduced from Powell et al. 1998,
figs. 3–4, with permission of History
Colorado)

Figure 9.6 Three figures – circle dancing.
Wall north of Terrace III, North Shelter,
Durango, Colorado.
(Reproduced with permission of the
Carnegie Institute from Daniels 1954,
fig. 113a)

provides musical accompaniment). No individuality is expressed and there is no apparent demarcation in roles, all of which echoes the depiction of hand-holding circle dancing in ceramics.

DISCUSSION

The images of circle dancing in ceramics and rock art can provide an insight into the type of communal ritualised performance activity practised in the sixth/ seventh centuries in the Southwest, and from these images we can also examine the ideational concepts this practice may have embodied and consider the architectural setting of these events.

Circle dancing limits individual movement. Hand-holding restricts arm gestures whilst movement requires unity in action; individuals must coordinate their bodily action with others to side-step together in time, in the same direction (Garfinkel 2003, 42–3). This simple type of movement does not require any great skill or practice and means that everyone can join in, emphasising the participative qualities of the dance. By joining the circle and

Figure 9.7 Four circle dancers.
Panel 28-7-31, Carrizo Canyon, New Mexico.
(Reproduced with permission courtesy of Hadlock Collection (H0412), Salmon Ruins Museum, Library and Research Collection)

moving in time with others, an individual accepts and submits to a collective social order. The depiction of males and females in equal numbers in the ceramic example discussed previously (Figure 9.3) is repeated in other examples from the time period (not illustrated) and emphasises the need for the contribution of both men and women in creating and maintaining community at this time.

The uniformity of appearance of individuals engaged in circle dancing emphasises collective action and equality between the participants. No one individual is emphasised in these depictions; rather, it is the collective form and action that is accentuated. The decision to minimise individuality in depictions established and reflected ideational concepts of equality, integration and collective action that underlined the experience of circle dancing.

Participation, integration and social bonding were physically, emotionally and cognitively produced and experienced through circle dancing. The form and physical action of the dance created a commonality of experience forging and maintaining social bonds and establishing communal ritualised practice. As such, the dance represented and was constitutive of belonging. This idea of participation

in village-level performances as a ritual activity to express solidarity, commitment and belonging has resonance in contemporary Puebloan society, as Sweet (1985, 25) explains:

> For the Tewas, beauty is found in the power of group movement, in repetitive and understated choreography and song composition, and in a serious, respectful, and dedicated performance. The motion of the entire group together is more important and more beautiful than the performance of any individual. … A single dancer must not destroy the illusion of the group moving as one.

The earliest architectural data from this period identified possible arenas for circle dancing at the semi-subterranean communal structures at Shabik'eshchee Village, Site 29SJ423 and Juniper Cove and at the open, surface structure at Broken Flute Cave. Ethnographic data record circle dancing taking place inside semi-subterranean communal ritual structures and outdoors in plaza areas with both men and women taking part at Zuni, Isleta, Taos and Keres Pueblos (Parsons [1939] 1996, 388, 531). Stephens (1936, 95–6) describes a Hopi war dance he observed in 1893 which included circle dancing by men and women:

> The drummer squats, drumming in the middle of the court, and beside him sits *Pa'hakola* who knows the songs and leads the singing. Choshon'niws and one or two other old men also sit beside the drummer. The ten formed a segment of a circle, facing the drummer, and moved around sideways with a light stamping motion, sinistral, and singing as they moved.

The depiction of circle dancing on the ceramic vessel (Figure 9.3) can also imply something about the setting of these events. As noted earlier, the round shape of the bowl provides an apt medium to highlight the shape and form of the dance. The decoration and physical properties of the vessel may have been used as a metaphor to represent the circular communal structure where these performances took place. The bowl then served as a reminder of these events and the cognitive and ideational concepts circle dancing embodied.

The combination of architectural data, iconography and ethnographic source provides a rich repository of data to explore the role of performance in communal ritual. The study of communal spaces and places offers an impression of the scale and potential interactions between participants whilst iconographic representation allows us to fill these spaces with people and to think about dance form.

CONCLUSION

Communal performance is a means of collective expression motivated by ritual, secular or social ends. Such performances involve prior organisation and preparation together with agreement on the proper time and place, the appropriate dance movements, musical accompaniment and paraphernalia fulfilling the attributes or components outlined by Bell (1997, 138–69), Rappaport (1999, 24) and Marcus (2007, 48) for ritualised action. Although the material evidence for past ritual performative actions can be difficult to identify in the archaeological record, a combination of architectural and iconographic data together with ethnographic accounts can provide an insight into the nature and form of past communal performance.

There may be many reasons why people choose to come together and participate in communal events. In the American Southwest, the inclusive, large, circular public performance spaces built at the centre of the earliest communities reflected the need to create and enact a sense of social solidarity and community among individuals and households who had begun to aggregate together for the first time. Circle dancing was an important component by which people forged social bonds and created a sense of community and identity through synchronous bodily movement and the sensuous experience of others' participation. Inchoate ideas of bonding, integration, equality, community and identity acquired substance through the symbolism of the circle. Through movement, depiction and architectural form, these abstract ideas were materialised and experienced. The central role of communal performance is not just evident in the Ancestral Puebloan era, but remains a central component of contemporary Puebloan life, establishing and maintaining identity, belief and social life, as this final quote from Jill Sweet (1985, 24) demonstrates:

> [P]erformances make explicit and implicit statements about Tewa society, not only reflecting social roles, relationships, and responsibilities but also helping to establish, shape and reinforce them. The village performances are arenas for demonstrating how the Tewas interact socially and what it means to be a member of Tewa society.

REFERENCES

Adler, M. A., 1989. Ritual facilities and social Integration in non-ranked societies, in *The Architecture of Social Integration*. Occasional Paper of the Crow Canyon Archaeological Center No. 1, eds. W. D. Lipe & M. Hegmon. Cortez, CO: Crow Canyon Archaeological Center, 35–52.

Altschul, J. H. & E. K. Huber, 2000. Economics, site structure, and social organisation during the Basketmaker III period: a view from the Lukachukai Valley, in *Foundations of Anasazi Culture: The Basketmaker-Pueblo Transition*, ed. P. F. Reed. Salt Lake City: University of Utah Press, 145–60.

Beeman, W. O., 1993. The anthropology of theater and spectacle. *Annual Review of Anthropology* 22, 369–93.

Bell, C., 1997. *Ritual: Perspectives and Dimensions*. Oxford: Oxford University Press.

Bland, A., 1976. *A History of Ballet and Dance*. London: Barrie & Jenkins.

Bradley, R., 2012. *The Idea of Order: The Circular Archetype in Prehistoric Europe*. Oxford: Oxford University Press.

Cass, J., 1993. *Dancing Through History*. Englewood Cliffs, New Jersey (NJ): Prentice Hall.

Cummings, B., 1953. *The First Inhabitants of Arizona and the Southwest*. Tucson, AZ: Cummings Publication Council.

Daniels, H. S., 1954. Pictographs. Appendix A, in *Basketmaker II Sites near Durango, Colorado*, eds. E. H. Morris & R. F. Burgh. Washington, DC: Carnegie Institution of Washington, 87–102.

Durkheim, E., 1912. *The Elementary Forms of Religious Life*. New York: Free Press.

Garfinkel, Y., 1998. Dancing and the beginning of art scenes in the early village communities of the Near East and Southeast Europe. *Cambridge Archaeological Journal* 8 (2), 207–37.

Garfinkel, Y., 2003. *Dancing at the Dawn of Agriculture*. Austin: University of Texas Press.

Gilpin, D. & L. Benallie Jr., 2000. Juniper Cove and early Anasazi community structure west of the Chuska Mountains, in *Foundations of Anasazi Culture: The Basketmaker-Pueblo Transition*, ed. P. F. Reed. Salt Lake City: University of Utah Press, 161–74.

Grant, C., 1978. *Canyon de Chelly: The People and the Rock Art*. Tucson: University of Arizona Press.

Grimes, R. L., 1976. *Symbol and Conquest: Public Ritual and Drama in Santa Fe*. New York: Ithaca: Cornell University Press.

Hanna, J. L., 1979. Toward a cross-cultural conceptualisation of dance and some correlate considerations, in *The Performing Arts: Music and Dance*, eds. A. R. Blacking & J. W. Kealinohomoku. The Hague: Mouton Publishers, 17–45.

Hanna, J. L., 1987. Dance: dance and religion, in *The Encyclopedia of Religion*. 2nd edition, ed. M. Eliade. New York: Macmillan Co, 436–46.

Hays, K. A., 1988. Human Figures in Anasazi Ceramic Vessels: Basketmaker III to Pueblo IV. Submitted as a term paper for Anthropology 426. Manuscript on file at the Arizona State Museum, Tucson.

Hieb, L. A., 1972. Meaning and mismeaning: toward an understanding of the ritual clown, in *New Perspectives on the Pueblos*, ed. A. Ortiz. Albuquerque: University of New Mexico Press, 163–96.

Inomata, T., 2006. Plazas, performers, and spectators: political theaters of the Classic Maya. *Current Anthropology* 47, 805–42.

Inomata, T. & L. S. Coben (eds.), 2006. *Archaeology of Performance: Theaters of Power, Community, and Politics*. Lanham, NY: AltaMira Press.

Kidder, A. V., 1927. *An Introduction to the Study of Southwestern Archaeology*. New Haven, CT: Yale University Press.

Kraus, R., 1969. *History of Dance in Art and Education*. Englewood Cliffs, NY: Prentice Hall.

Kurath, G. P., 1967. Drama, dance and music, in *Social Anthropology (Handbook of Middle American Indians)*, ed. M. Nash. Austin: University of Texas Press, vol. 6, 158–90.

Kurath, G. P. & A. Garcia, 1973. *Music and Dance of the Tewa Pueblos*. Santa Fe: University of New Mexico Press.

Kus, S. M., 1983. The social representation of space: dimensioning the cosmological and the quotidian, in *Archaeological Hammers and Theories*, eds. J. A. Moore & A. S. Keene. New York: Academic Press, 277–98.

Lange, R., 1976. *The Nature of Dance. An Anthropological Perspective*. New York: International Publications Service.

Longstreet, S., 1968. *The Dance in Art*. Alhambra, CA: Borden Publishing Company.

Marcus, J., 2007. Rethinking ritual, in *The Archaeology of Ritual*, ed. E. Kyriakidis. Los Angeles: Cotsen Institute of Archaeology, University of California, 43–76.

McNeill W. H., 1995. *Keeping Together in Time: Dance and Drill in Human History*. Cambridge, MA: Harvard University Press.

Morris, C. & A. Peatfield, 2002. Feeling through the body, in *Thinking Through the Body: Archaeologies of Corporeality*, eds. Y. Hamilakis, M. Pluciennik & S. Tarlow. London: Kluwer Academic/Plenum Publishers, 105–20.

Morris, E. A., 1959. Basketmaker caves in the Prayer Rock District, Northeastern Arizona. PhD Department of Anthropology, University of Arizona, Tucson.

Morris, E. A., 1980. *Basketmaker Caves in the Prayer Rock District, Northeastern Arizona*. Anthropological Papers of the University of Arizona 35. Tucson: University of Arizona Press.

Parsons, E. C., [1939] 1996. *Puebloan Indian Religion*. Lincoln: University of Nebraska Press.

Pearson, M. & M. Shanks, 2001. *Theater/Archaeology*. London: Routledge.

Powell, S., S. J. Cole, S. K. Hath & S. Brown, 1998. *Basketmaker Images at Falls Creek Shelters, Southwestern Colorado*. Denver: Colorado Historical Society State Historical Foundation.

Rappaport, R. A., 1999. *Ritual and Religion in the Making of Humanity*. Cambridge: Cambridge University Press.

Renfrew, C., 2007. The archaeology of ritual, of cult, and of religion, in *The Archaeology of Ritual*, ed. E. Kyriakidis. Los Angeles: Cotsen Institute of Archaeology, University of California, 109–22.

Roberts, F. H. H., Jr., 1929. *Shabik'eshchee Village: A Late Basketmaker Site in the Chaco Canyon*. (Bulletin 92. Bureau of American Ethnology). Washington, DC: Smithsonian Institution.

Roediger, V. M., 1961. *Ceremonial Costumes of the Pueblo Indians: Their Evolution, Fabrication, and Significance in the Prayer Drama*. Berkeley and Los Angeles: University of California Press.

Royce, A. P., 1977. *The Anthropology of Dance*. Bloomington: Indiana University Press.

Sachs, C., 1952. *World History of the Dance*. London: George Allen & Unwin Ltd.

Schaafsma, P., 1980. *Indian Rock Art in the Southwest*. Albuquerque: University of New Mexico Press.

Schechner, R., 1987. Drama – performance and ritual, in *Encyclopaedia of Religion Vol. 4*, ed. M. Eliade. New York: MacMillan, 436–49.

Schechner, R., 1994. Ritual and performance, in *Companion Encyclopaedia of Anthropology: Humanity, Culture and Social Life*, ed. T. Ingold. London: Routledge, 613–47.

Slifer, D., 2007. *Kokopelli: The Magic, Mirth and Mischief of an Ancient Symbol*. Salt Lake City, UT: Gibbs Smith.

Soar, K., 2010. Circular dance performances in the prehistoric Aegean, in *Ritual Dynamics and the Science of Ritual Vol. 2, Body, Performance, Agency and Experience*, ed. A. Michaels. Wiesbaden, Germany: Harrassowitz, 137–56.

Spicer, R. B., 1939. The Easter Fiesta of the Yaqui Indians of Pascua, Arizona. MA thesis, Department of Anthropology, University of Chicago.

Stephens, A. M., 1936. *Hopi Journal of Alexander M. Stephen*. New York: Columbia University Press.

Sweet, J. D., 1985. *Dances of the Tewa Pueblo Indians: Expression of New Life*. Santa Fe, NM: School of American Research Press.

Tedlock, B. 1992. *The Beautiful and the Dangerous: Encounters with the Zuni Indians*. New York: Viking.

Tuan, Y., 1997. *Space and Place: The Perspective of Experience*. Minneapolis: University of Minneapolis Press.

Turner, V. W., 1969. *The Ritual Process: Structure and Anti-Structure*. Chicago, IL: Aldine.

Turner, V. W., 1982. *Celebration: Studies in Festivity and Ritual*. Washington, DC: Smithsonian Institute Press.

Turner, V. W., 1990. Are there universals of performance in myth, ritual and drama?, in *By Means of Performance. Intercultural Studies of Theatre and Ritual*, eds. R. Schechner & W. Appel. Cambridge: Cambridge University Press, 8–18.

Waters, F., [1963] 1977. *Book of the Hopi*. London: Penguin Books.

Windes, T. C., (n.d.a.) *Early Pueblo Occupations in the Chaco Region: Excavations and Survey of Basketmaker III and Pueblo I sites, Chaco Canyon, New Mexico*, in prep. Vol. 1. Reports of the Chaco Center No. 14. Santa Fe, NM: Division of Cultural Research, National Park Service.

ARCHITECTURE AND IMAGERY IN THE EARLY NEOLITHIC OF SOUTH-WEST ASIA: FRAMING RITUALS, STABILISING MEANINGS

TREVOR WATKINS

In the first section of this book, issues concerning ritual and play have been discussed from different theoretical perspectives. It should be clear at the outset that the present author comes from a quite different direction, entering this field as a questioning prehistoric archaeologist, fascinated by extraordinary phenomena emerging from current and recent excavations at some of the earliest permanently settled sites in South-West Asia. These earliest settlements date from the very end of the Pleistocene (in regional archaeological terms, the Epi-Palaeolithic period) and the early millennia of the Holocene (the aceramic, or pre-pottery, Neolithic period). This period in South-West Asia has been the field laboratory where, for more than 50 years, researchers have concentrated on investigating the beginnings of cultivation and herding, the emergence of the first domesticated plants and animals and the relationship between these and climatic and environmental changes or demographic pressures. Arguably, the social transformation of small-scale, mobile hunter-gatherer bands of the Upper Palaeolithic into the large, permanently co-resident, early Neolithic communities is equally significant, and antedates the establishment of farming economies. In recent years a number of archaeologists have begun to focus on the extraordinarily vivid imagery and architecture of the early Neolithic period (Hodder 1990). In his influential book whose title encapsulates his thesis, Jacques Cauvin (1994, 2000) sought to explain the rich imagery that accompanied this social transformation: he

argued that the imagery represents "la naissance des divinités", and that it was accomplished by virtue of a "révolution des symboles". Cauvin was writing at a time when newly discovered archaeological sites were beginning to produce dramatic monumental architecture and vivid examples of symbolic imagery; coincidentally, there was a surge of research and exciting ideas about human cognitive evolution and gene-culture co-evolution.

We now have a series of early Neolithic sites in central and south-east Turkey, north and west Syria, Israel and Jordan that have produced fascinating imagery, enigmatic sculptures, monumental architecture and much evidence of elaborate ritual behaviours: and we also have a great deal of new research in the fields of cognitive and evolutionary psychology. My concern has been to bring some of these new cognitive and co-evolutionary ideas into contact with the new archaeological material (Watkins 2004a, 2004b, 2006, 2008, 2009, 2010a, 2010b, 2012, 2015; Sterelny & Watkins 2015). In particular, I want to explore how the impressive displays of symbolism and ritual performance that emerged as part of this great social transformation functioned in the context of the new, large, permanent communities that created them. I shall argue that the extraordinary levels of symbolism in architecture, artefacts and ritual functioned in the service of the construction and sustenance of a new and extraordinary kind of community and identity.

I start from the idea that the dynamic of hominin brain and cognitive evolution has been in the direction of sustaining larger and more cohesive social groups, the social brain hypothesis (Dunbar 1998, 2003). Most of the work on human cognitive evolution has been concerned with the long-term process that has differentiated the hominins from their closest living primate cousins and their postulated last common ancestor; until recently, accounts of that evolutionary narrative ended around 30,000–50,000 years ago, with the beginnings of representational two- and three-dimensional art. The social, cultural and economic transformation around the Pleistocene–Holocene boundary in South-West Asia and in the early Holocene in other parts of the world has tended to fall between two stools: on the one hand, it has not found a place in the long-term narratives of human evolution (with the exception of the final publications of the Lucy to Language project – Dunbar 1998, 2003; Dunbar et al. 2014; Gamble et al. 2014, and on the other hand, it cannot be treated in a uniformitarian manner as if it were contemporary or recent history. In evolutionary terms, a remarkably rapid and quite dramatic transformation in human affairs took place in South-West Asia from the Upper Palaeolithic (45,000–20,000 BC), through the Epi-Palaeolithic (20,000–10,000 BC) and the Neolithic (10,000–6000 BC). In some ways, what emerged (large populations living together in networks of permanent settlements) can be recognised as fundamental to how people live today; but in other ways, the new social and cultural systems are quite different from contemporary societies and not readily explicable in terms of contemporary experience.

I have taken the view that some of the hunter-gatherer groups living at relatively high population densities in resource-rich zones of South-West Asia in the final Pleistocene (the archaeological Epi-Palaeolithic) took the path of increasing their reliance on storable plant food resources and investing more labour and skill in hunting small mammals, birds, fish, reptiles and amphibians in order to support living in larger, more stable and less mobile groups. This is a version of Kent Flannery's (1969) broad spectrum revolution hypothesis, as reviewed and revised first by Mary Stiner (2001), and more recently by Melinda Zeder (2012). Zeder in particular comprehensively demolishes the arguments for explaining the shift in subsistence strategy in terms

of adaptive response to external environmental pressures, and argues that it was a complex form of "eco-system engineering intended to promote resource productivity" in optimal resource zones. She concludes by pointing to niche construction theory as a promising framework within which to investigate the broad-spectrum revolution (see also Zeder 2016). I endorse her tentative conclusion on the potential of niche construction theory as the evolutionary framework for understanding the processes at work in this period, and I set the changes in subsistence and settlement strategy in the context of furthering the evolutionary trend to larger and more cohesive and stable social groups (Sterelny & Watkins 2015; Watkins 2015).

If it were simply a matter of finding better ways to increase the resources in order to sustain larger social groups that moved less frequently and trended towards sedentism, we could relate the changes in settlement strategy with the innovations in subsistence strategies. But that would leave the question of explaining why these groups invested quite unprecedented levels of attention and effort in more and more elaborate and expensive cultural activities that seem to serve no straightforward economic, ecological or ergonomic purpose. Since Émile Durkheim's ([1912] 1995) *The Elementary Forms of the Religious Life*, anthropologists have generally accepted that shared beliefs and ritual practices help to sustain social cohesion. It would make sense, therefore, to think of the increased levels of symbolic and ritual activity as necessary to sustain social cohesion in the increasingly large communities of the Epi-Palaeolithic and early Neolithic. However, the scale, variety and complexity of these symbolic activities is a step-change from anything that we see from earlier periods, so we are left with the problem of explaining why such a massive expenditure of time, labour and resources and amplification of symbolic and ritual activities were necessary.

At one end of the spectrum of cultural elaboration there are relatively simple practices that took place at the household level, such as making white lime plaster and recoating the walls and floors of houses, interring a deceased member of the community in a shallow grave below a house floor or a courtyard surface or removing and curating the skull from such a burial. At Çayönü, in south-east Turkey, the living floors of the monumental houses were constructed in mud-brick upon a massive, stone-and-mud, ground-level substructure (Schirmer 1990; Özdoğan 1999). When a new house replaced an old one, the superstructure of the old house was demolished, and a new substructure was constructed directly on top of the foundation courses of the old one. It would surely have been simpler to build a completely new house alongside the old, or to reuse the foundations of the old house. At Qermez Dere, a small, very early aceramic Neolithic settlement in north Iraq, the houses were (semi-) subterranean, with frequently re-plastered side-walls and floor surfaces (Watkins 1990). When a new house was deemed necessary, the roof of the old house was removed, and the subterranean chamber was filled with soil, stones and occupation debris. But the cavity within which the new house was to be formed was excavated on almost exactly the same spot. And the same process of back-filling and re-excavating was repeated.

At the other end of the spectrum, we know of large and complex buildings that must have been communal enterprises. They were circular structures that were constructed below ground level, with signs of elaborate, non-domestic use. The earliest occur in settlements of the early Natufian (that is, early

in the late Epi-Palaeolithic in the southern Levant). Structures such as 'abri 131' at Mallaha (Eynan) in northern Israel, with its sequence of structured depositions (Valla 1988, 2008), and the large, complex structure at Wadi Hammeh 27 in Jordan, with its careful deposition of many kinds of discard, including human body parts and a dismantled relief-decorated monolith (Hardy-Smith & Edwards 2004; Edwards 2009), can be understood as the forerunners of the series of early aceramic Neolithic (between 10,000 and 8,500 BC) examples that have come to light. Such a large, central structure, full of strange and elaborate features, existed at the settlement of WF16 in Wadi Feynan, southern Jordan (Finlayson et al. 2011; Mithen et al. 2011), surrounded by smaller structures, some of which are interpreted as communal storage facilities. Several settlements in the Euphrates Valley in north Syria dating to the same early aceramic Neolithic date possessed different forms of central, communal building that was subterranean and circular, unlike the domestic and other structures.

The second in a sequence of three such communal buildings (Figure 10.1) at the settlement of Jerf el Ahmar, on the Euphrates in north Syria, required the excavation of a cylindrical pit 7 metres in diameter and 3 metres deep (more than 100 cubic metres of soil in total) (Stordeur et al. 2000; Stordeur

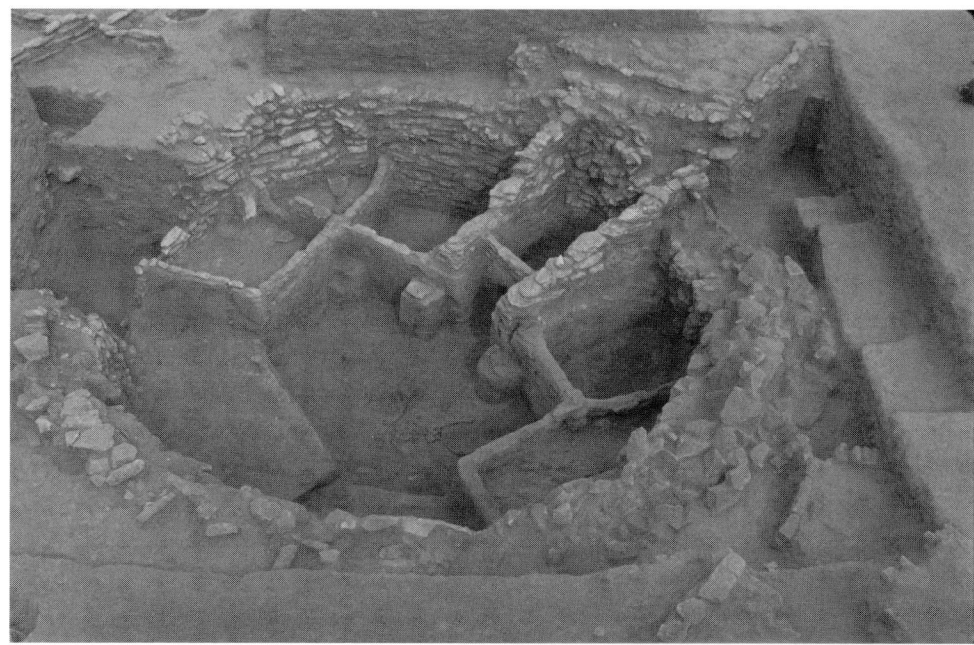

Figure 10.1 The second of the communal buildings at the centre of the village at Jerf el Ahmar, north Syria.

2015). Its predecessor was similar in size and internal arrangements, but was found, badly eroded, only as the rising waters behind a dam began to flood the site. The sides of the cavity were lined with a stone retaining wall within which a closely spaced series of wooden posts was incorporated to support a roof; extending around two thirds of the interior, a series of door-less cells was constructed, and all the internal walls and floors given a mud-based finish; more posts were set at intervals, so that a 30 square metre wooden roof structure could be formed over the whole structure. The cells have produced evidence that they were used for the (communal) storage of cereals and lentils (Willcox & Stordeur 2012). At the end of its use-life, the cells were emptied, a decapitated female body was thrown into the middle of the floor, the roof was disassembled and set on fire, and finally the cavity was completely refilled with soil. The successor to that building was also circular and subterranean, but, unlike its predecessors, it had no internal subdivisions. Around the base of its perimeter wall there was a broad, low 'bench', whose front edge was made up of six large limestone slabs carved with a simple pattern of low-relief pendant triangles along their top edge; and between each pair of slabs stood a pine-tree-trunk, roof-supporting post set in a lime-plaster 'sleeve'. At the end of its life, it too was completely dismantled and obliterated (buried?). At the nearby, contemporary settlement of Tell 'Abr 3, salvage excavations revealed a series of three, very similar, circular, subterranean communal structures, with a broad bench around the base of the perimeter wall (Yartah 2004, 2005). In one of them, the skulls and horns of wild cattle had been deposited within the bench.

It is clear that the construction of these large, subterranean structures required a substantial organised labour force and community collaboration (setting aside the site at the centre of the settlement, and laying out other buildings around it; obtaining the building materials, especially the main roof support timbers, in a region where pine trees were not locally available), not to mention their final dismantling and obliteration. Against that, it is worth noting that none of these structures had a doorway or a staircase for access to the interior; they were presumably entered from the roof. And none of them provided

Figure 10.2 Enclosure D at Göbekli Tepe, south-east Turkey. Work is still in progress at one of a cluster of four large, circular enclosures at the south-east edge of the site. The central pillars stand in sockets in pedestals cut from the living rock floor of the enclosure. Part of Enclosure C, the upper parts of whose central pillars were deliberately smashed, is visible at the top right.

much internal space within which the community might gather for whatever purpose. That there were ritual activities within these structures is indicated by the deposition of a spread-eagled and decapitated corpse, and, in two instances, the deposit of a human skull in a emptied posthole, or a niche cut at the base of a mud wall, as part of the closure and burial of one of the series of structures at Jerf el Ahmar. There are indications of ritual acts as part of the construction of at least one of the structures at Tell 'Abr 3; there, it took the form of the deposition of animal parts within the bench as it was being formed.

The most extraordinary example of architectural elaboration and communal effort is the whole site of Göbekli Tepe, in south-east Turkey (Schmidt 2000, 2006, 2011, 2012) (Figure 10.2). In the first place, it is worth noting that the site, which consists of a very substantial mound, 300 metres in diameter, and 15–17 metres tall, exists on a bare, limestone mountain

Figure 10.3 Pillar 31, one of the central pair of pillars in Enclosure D, Göbekli Tepe (with one of the peripheral pillars in the background). An arm can be made out in light relief, and the fingers of both hands almost meet on the 'stomach' of the figure. Around its middle, there is a belt, with a buckle at the front, from which a fox pelt hangs. Around its 'throat' (immediately below the wooden brace to which the steel stabilising hawsers are fixed), the faceless figure wears a band on which there is a pendant in the form of a horned animal head. One of the peripheral monoliths can be seen in the background, set into the stone 'bench' at the foot of the enclosure wall.

ridge; that is to say, its location is well chosen from the point of view of occupying a prominent position in the landscape, where there were large amounts of horizontally bedded limestone for building construction and the many large monoliths, but the immediate environs are completely unhelpful for supporting a permanently settled community. Those parts of the site that have been excavated to date belong in the early aceramic Neolithic period; the composition and date of the core of the mound is yet to be investigated. Excavation has revealed a cluster of massive, stone-built circular structures (there is one, smaller, rectangular structure dating around 8300 BC, and a number of other, smaller structures

close to the surface of the mound that are yet to be fully investigated). The circular structures seem to have been constructed in huge, cylindrical cavities, more than 20 metres in diameter, excavated at least 5 metres into the side of the pre-existing mound. Each monument consists of several concentric walls built of coursed stone and mud mortar, each of which may represent a retaining wall in successive downsizings of the overall structure.

In the centre of each enclosure stood a pair of tall, T-shaped monoliths, the largest of which stand 5.5 metres tall. Set into the surrounding wall, there are about a dozen more T-shaped monoliths, somewhat smaller than the central pair. The monoliths are variously decorated with raised reliefs. Some have a pair of human arms with the fingers of the hands meeting on the 'stomach' of the figure. Some have some kind of a pendant on a band around the 'neck'. The two largest monoliths wear decorated belts around their middles, with a prominent buckle at the front, from which is suspended a fox skin, with its hind legs and tail dangling (Figure 10.3). These monoliths were clearly intended as anthropomorphs, although none has any facial feature. Some monoliths have a single, male, wild animal – a bull, a boar or a fox or wolf – executed in raised relief on their flanks. Others have a number of creatures, from a repertoire that includes wild male animals, as well as spiders, scorpions, snakes or birds with long legs. A few monoliths are covered below the 'head' with a complex carpet of reliefs.

At the end of their use-life, each of these huge enclosures was deliberately filled with hundreds of tons of debris that includes large amounts of chipped stone tools and the debris from their manufacture, fragmented bone that is the residue from cooked meat (but not those parts that are discarded when an animal is butchered), and practically no carbonised plant remains or the heavy stone equipment used in food preparation. Contra Banning's (2011) attempt to reconfigure the structures as domestic and the site as a settlement, there is no evidence that the enclosures were used as houses, or that the site was a place of permanent residence. And, despite careful excavation and investigation of the deposits at the base of the fills of the enclosures, there is no trace of the installations that typify a domestic environment, or of any activities of any kind on their smooth, hard floors.

The investment of labour, skill, time, logistical thought and imagination at sites such as Çayönü, Jerf el Ahmar or Göbekli Tepe is extraordinarily impressive. The ability of the new, permanently co-resident communities of the early Neolithic to collaborate and coordinate their labour, and to develop and sustain complex worlds of imagery and meaning makes them very different from the archetypal notion of the mobile hunter-gatherer band, or the 'village-farming' cluster of simple huts. We are now beginning to learn that the communities of south-east Turkey and north Syria shared a repertoire of symbolic imagery, and were using what may be termed a lexicon of ideograms in a form of non-textual writing (Morenz & Schmidt 2009). Klaus Schmidt (2006, 2012), the excavator of Göbekli Tepe, has surmised that the site served as the religious central place for a regional confederacy, similar to the amphictyonies or leagues that were formed among Greek city-states in the Archaic and Classical periods.

Clearly, we archaeologists are challenged to revise our ideas concerning the nature of the societies of this period. I have proposed that the developments in architecture and imagery were an essential component in the formation and maintenance of the emergent large-scale communities. There are good evolutionary reasons for humans to live in larger, more socially cohesive groups: the larger and more cohesive the group, the more secure the transmission of culture and the maintenance of the stock of cultural capital; also, the larger and more cohesive the group, the better able it is to accumulate tested innovations in a context of increasing congestion and competition in the landscape (Shennan 2000, 2001; Powell, Shennan & Thomas 2009). Larger social groups and networks are also more effective in generating and assimilating cultural innovations; it therefore follows that we can expect that, as group and network size increases, the rate of cultural innovation and accumulation of cultural traits will accelerate, in a positive feedback loop that makes for further increase in group size, network scale and population density. Conversely, groups that become too small or too isolated can become vulnerable to the loss of cultural skills (Henrich 2004).

At some stage, the growth of group size and network scale on the one hand, and the generation of cultural complexity on the other, must have begun to outrun the pace at which biological evolution operates. At that point, if we accept Dunbar's correlation of neo-cortex ratio with social group size for primates and hominins in particular, modern humans would run up against the natural limit on the size of social network imposed by the size of the neo-cortex, and in particular the frontal lobe (proposed by Dunbar on the basis of a variety of evidence to be around 150 people); that is the number of people with whom an individual can maintain a knowledge of the web of relationships among them and a direct relationship of sufficient depth so as to know who can be trusted to give freely support when needed, or who would be one's best ally when it comes to manipulating a third party (Aiello & Dunbar 1993; Dunbar 1998, 2004; Dunbar et al. 2010). With larger co-resident communities, the need for close cooperation and for conforming to behavioural conventions was much greater: but at the same time individuals could know only a proportion of their fellow-citizens well enough to trust. By this time, however, modern humans had come to depend on culture and their ability to adapt to new situations by cultural means (for example, as *Homo sapiens* expanded rapidly across South and South-East Asia and into Australasia). Adapting by cultural means involved the development of new or more complex forms of material culture, but it also involved a quite new use of material culture to create and deploy material systems of symbolic representation. This line of argument is important in the context of the recognition that ethnographically documented communities are symbolically constructed (reflecting the title and the thesis of Anthony Cohen's (1985) important book on the symbolic construction of community).

Between 120,000 and 70,000 years ago, *Homo sapiens* groups had begun to wear material signs such as red ochre colouring and perforated marine shells indicative of personal identity. Sterelny (2011) is at pains to show that this should be understood as 'low amplitude' signalling by the individual within the group. By the Upper Palaeolithic (after 50,000 years ago), groups in the Levant had begun to develop distinctively different chipped stone tool-making traditions, though it is unlikely that these functioned as distinguishing markers of different communities.

In the Epi-Palaeolithic of the southern Levant (the only region of South-West Asia where the period has attracted sufficient levels of investigation), the microlithic traditions became more and more regionally diverse, and cultural change moved faster: by contrast with earlier periods, specialists recognise three cultural sub-periods within the approximately 10 millennia of the Epi-Palaeolithic, and the late Epi-Palaeolithic (Natufian) can itself be further subdivided by means of its changing lithic tradition into three sub-sub-periods. Within the Natufian, different groups seem to have lived different lifestyles, and individual Natufian sites can produce their own material culture traditions (Belfer-Cohen & Goring-Morris 2013).

The new large, permanently co-resident communities of the early aceramic Neolithic had populations of several hundred, a scale order larger than the mobile hunter-gatherer bands of the Upper Palaeolithic. I argue that such large communities were viable because their members had learned to capitalise on their cognitive and cultural capacity for symbolic culture to build environments (literally) in which individuals could trust and cooperate effectively with so many people with whom they were not closely familiar. When confronted with the cognitive limitation of managing meaningful relationships in excess of 150 people, they increased their capacity for symbolic modes of constructing community identity expressed in the things that they made, used and exchanged (Figure 10.4), a process that was already well under way in the Upper Palaeolithic period (Gamble 1998, 1999).

An effective way of describing this richer symbolic cultural world is in terms of a qualitatively enhanced facility in cultural niche construction. Niche construction has been recognised among many species, and a good case has been made for cultural niche construction playing an important part in human evolution (Laland, Odling-Smee & Feldman 2000; Sterelny 2007, 2011; Odling-Smee & Laland 2009; O'Brien & Laland 2012). Laland, Odling-Smee & Feldman (2001, 22) define niche construction thus: "Organisms frequently choose, regulate, construct and destroy important components of their environments, in the process changing the selection pressures to which they and other organisms

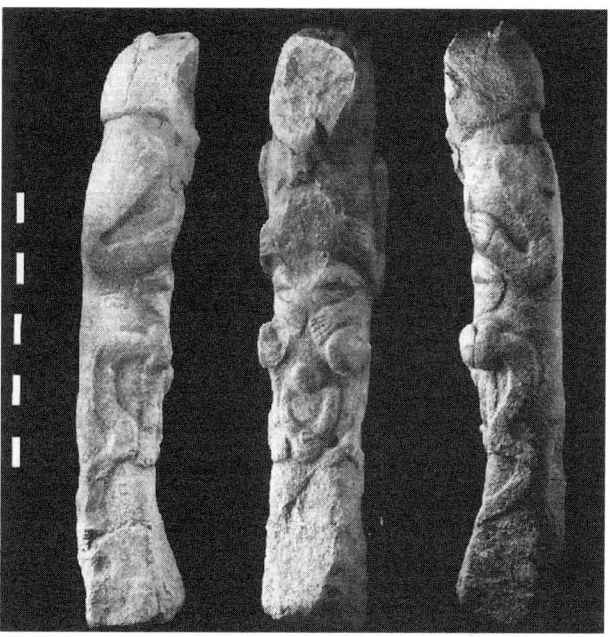

Figure 10.4 Göbekli Tepe. Three views of a complex stone sculpture. It was found incorporated into a wall, deliberately defaced. The head at the top of the sculpture seems more like a bear than a human, and the claws on its forepaws (or fingers on its hands) are ambiguous. It holds a second figure (whose face has also been removed), which in turn holds a third figure. On either side there appears the familiar, schematised snake motif. The scale is 1 metre.

are exposed." The importance of niche construction theory within general evolutionary theory is that it makes the evolutionary process a two-way process, potentially a positive feedback loop between the organism and the niche that it constructs: the organism affects the niche, and the niche affects the selection pressures on the organism, often continuing through the generations. Beavers constructing dams and lodges or birds building nests are among the many examples of niche construction; for humans, making fires with which to cook, creating clothing and shelters to protect the body, and cultivating plants and herding animals are equally elements of niche construction that enable us to speak of cultural niche construction (Laland et al. 2001; Laland & O'Brien 2011; Odling-Smee & Laland 2011). But the human cultural niche construction facility went further than such material measures; it is argued that the developmental environment within which children learn and begin to practise the large and complex body of cultural knowledge that they need as adults is an advanced form of cultural niche construction (Odling-Smee & Laland 2009; Kendal 2011; Sterelny 2011).

Arguably, something new was happening within the cultural niches that these first large, settled communities were creating for themselves (Sterelny & Watkins 2015; Watkins 2015). Living together in permanent settlements no doubt affected the developmental environment of children, just as it also intensified the dangers of contagious diseases, thereby affecting the inherited immunities of populations. But the built environment was also made with meaning; the architecture shaped the way that people lived their lives and the sculptures shaped the way that people shared their understanding of many complex things. The shaping of the symbolic cultural, or cognitive, niche constituted the formation of many powerful positive cognitive feedback loops; niche construction became cultural niche construction, which became "runaway cultural niche construction" (Rendell, Fogarty & Laland 2011), with as much formative influence on cultural evolution as niche construction had on human genes. The significant change, I would emphasise, was that cultural niche construction began to build niches that physically embodied cultural information that constituted a significant element in the cognitive development of the members of the community and the formation of ideas and beliefs.

It will help us to understand these extravagant architectural monuments if we bear in mind the importance of ritual and collective memory in the sustaining of community. Jan Assmann has discussed why collective memory is the essential underpinning of cultural identity (1995), just as personal memory underpins the sense of individual identity. Assmann therefore speaks of "cultural memory": cultural memory "preserves the store of knowledge from which a group derives an awareness of its unity and peculiarity", defining who 'we' are, and how 'they' are different. He shows us how cultural memory "always relates its knowledge to an actual and contemporary situation", and argues that the communicated meaning and shared knowledge is objectified and stabilised in spoken words, ritual actions or – importantly for our purposes in the present context – in

visual form. And he concludes that the knowledge preserved in cultural memory is both formative (educative, civilising and humanising) and normative (in that it provides rules of conduct) (Assmann 1995, 130–2).

Collective memory is memory that is distributed and shared among the individuals of a community. And memory functions through acts of memory. Our episodic memory, however, starts from re-experiencing images from our past; it is about feeling and emotion, rather than fact. Indeed, in his own essay on memory in a recent book, Pascal Boyer (2009, 3) notes that remembering events in one's personal history is akin to thinking about future events; both involve imagination, as does thinking about imaginary events or persons, whether past, present or future. Autobiographical memory involves "previous experience inserted into present consciousness" (Corballis 2011, 83); but then, it involves a nested structure, whereby the 'event-specific knowledge' is set in the context of a 'general event', which in turn fits within a 'lifetime period'. In other words, it is structured recursively. And it is perhaps significant, therefore, to note that the settlements, their houses and their communal buildings also exhibit a complex and recursive structuring. For example, the great circular enclosures of Göbekli Tepe are structured into the pre-existing mound, and then, within each enclosure, they are structured around the circle of about dozen monoliths that attend on the larger central pair of anthropomorphic monoliths; in turn, the monoliths bear a variety of sculpted images. Someone of those to whom Göbekli Tepe belonged might therefore comprehend the monolith in terms of the images that it bore on its surface, and then in terms of the monoliths placed among the other monoliths within the enclosure, and ultimately in terms of the enclosure's situation within the site of Göbekli Tepe. If the individual's sense of self depends on autobiographical memory, it follows that shared and collective memory, distributed among the individuals who form the collective, is essential to community identity. And it similarly follows that the collective memory of the community is based on the foundation of shared acts of remembering that are affective and "imagistic" (one of Whitehouse's (2004) contrasting modes of religiosity).

In his discussion of collective acts of memory, Connerton (1989) particularly emphasises the central role of 'commemorative ceremonies' and 'bodily acts'. In common with many people thinking about ceremony and ritual, I believe Connerton, Whitehouse and Lawson and McCauley pay little or no attention to the point that very often there is a proper and special place where ceremonies or rituals should take place, indeed, to which rituals should be directed. I believe that the monumental buildings and the sculptures were settings specially designed and equipped for a purpose; but rather than being the stage-sets where rituals could be played out, I wrote of them as "theatres of memory" (Watkins 2004a). On further reflection I think that these early Neolithic constructions operated in several different ways. I would now suggest that we see the architecture of the communal buildings as effectively the framing of the context, and the sculptures and their imagery within the communal buildings as the fixing of contextualised meanings. The analogy from which this view is derived is elaborate and nested symbolism of medieval Christian cathedrals and churches, with all their sculptures and other imagery. This leads to the observation that Whitehouse's "doctrinal" mode of religiosity (Whitehouse 2004; Whitehouse & Hodder 2010) does not have to depend on the written word, or the carefully institutionalised oral memory, for we see in these structures and their imagery a material and non-verbal, non-textual mode of sharing meaning. Whitehouse contrasts the doctrinal mode, which is mostly associated with large-scale, modern (in evolutionary terms) societies, with an "imagistic" mode whose impact derives from "sensory pageantry", and the emotional, even traumatic effects on participants. It seems to me that the structures, the monoliths and the imagery at Göbekli Tepe combine the doctrinal with the sensory pageantry of the imagistic, whether in terms of visual and spatial impact (the experience of standing in one of the enclosures among the towering monoliths is extraordinary), or in the memory of participating in the achievement of their making. McCauley and Lawson (2002, 9) comment that rituals can remain stable through periodic repetition, while the meanings that individual participants and witnesses associate with them can vary greatly. I suggest that the scale of these first permanent communities required that communal rituals be sustained and transmitted through the making of material meaning.

Not all rituals serve religious purposes, of course. Indeed, in the early Neolithic of South-West Asia religious rituals are very hard to find. In the case of Göbekli Tepe, it is reasonable to infer that the major T-shaped monoliths represent what McCauley and Lawson would call "culturally postulated superhuman agents". A number of the large T-shaped monoliths exhibit bent human arms on their broad, flat surfaces, and a pair of hands with fingertips meeting each other on one of the narrow faces. It therefore follows that the horizontal T-bar represents the head of a highly schematised anthropomorphic standing figure. However, these heads lack facial features, whereas psychologists tell us that the eyes and then the facial features are the focus of our visual attention. The sculptors at Göbekli Tepe and at Nevalı Çori were well able to sculpt human heads, of which there are plenty of examples at a smaller scale than the great monoliths. These monoliths, then, may be postulated to be anthropomorphic but inscrutable divinities, perhaps the first culturally postulated superhuman agents.

In an important essay on a key moment in the evolution of religion, Atran and Henrich (2010) seek to show how several strands come together in the evolution of pro-social religions, that is religions that promote among their adherents concern for others and behaving in ways to help or benefit other people. They are not the first, of course, to note the coincidence of such pro-social religions and large-scale societies, but what they seek to do is set the development of such demanding religions into the context of the emergence of societies that require commitment of cooperation and altruistic behaviour among large numbers of people who are not kin-related or well known to one another. They set out to show how "the cultural evolution of pro-social religions and the historical rise of large-scale civilisations involve the dynamic interaction of the by-products of adaptive cognitive mechanisms (e.g. minimally counterintuitive beliefs and overextended agent concepts), adaptive learning heuristics (e.g. emulation of successful and prestigious individuals), credibility-enhancing ritual displays (e.g. self-sacrifice and costly commitments to seemingly preposterous beliefs), and cultural group selection for those packages of rituals, devotions, and beliefs that best sustain in-group prosocial norms (e.g. monumental undertakings, sacred values)" (Atran & Henrich 2010, 19). Their theoretical and ethnographically based model seems to apply well to the early aceramic Neolithic situation of South-West Asia, as large, permanently co-resident communities developed extensive networks of sharing and exchange, and collaborated in the creation of the monuments of Göbekli Tepe. It suggests new lines of enquiry into the nature of these earliest permanent communities, as do the recent publications of Joyce Marcus and Kent Flannery, whose foundations are based on their work on the long sequence of prehistoric settlement of Mexico (Marcus & Flannery 2004; Flannery & Marcus 2012). It seems that at the end of the Epi-Palaeolithic and in the early Neolithic of South-West Asia a critical stage was reached in the emergence of networks of large-scale, permanent communities, coupled with the emergence of a form of 'prosocial' religion in which culturally postulated supernatural agents for the first time have an important role.

Several authorities have discussed the apparent relationship between large-scale communities and very prominent and demanding religious beliefs and practices. There is a very attractive line of argument that explains the emergence of corporate subscription to demanding rituals as a necessary new kind of vehicle for costly commitment displays (for example, Henrich 2009; Bulbulia & Frean 2010; Bulbulia & Sostis 2011). Henrich (2009, 247–8) argues that the cultural conservation and particularly the transmission of altruism require costly acts. He quotes research on altruism and cultural learning that shows that people willingly model their behaviour and ideas on those of members of their community whose costly acts of commitment he terms "credibility enhancing displays" (CREDS). Atran and Henrich (2010, 23–5) explain how participation in ritual performances that involve costly displays may exploit modern human evolved psychology to deepen commitment to supernatural agents and to religious communities. Bulbulia and Sosis (2011) set their discussion in the context of signalling theory, and particularly the role of costly signalling of

commitment in promoting general prosociality. The costly demands of religious rituals provide opportunities for credibility enhancing displays for their leading participants, in addition to their capacity for arousal, focusing group attention, exciting memory and corporate strengthening (Bulbulia & Sosis 2011, 365). This kind of costly signalling works well within a community where the individual has the opportunity to observe the behaviour of others over time, learning whose behaviour and beliefs provide the best model; but it follows that costly signalling does not work in communities that are too large or too dispersed to allow for the sustained interaction between individuals that accommodate the necessary observation and learning processes. At this point, Bulbulia and Sosis (2011, 373) turn to cultural niche construction theory, arguing that it allows the possibility of creating "exogenous designs that express and synchronise the cooperative motives" of a large community of people who rarely come into contact with one another. They call this sophisticated form of cultural niche the "cooperative niche", since one can imagine that it can "evolve to strongly govern the behaviour of cooperative populations, offloading strategic control from individuals to the information properties of their worlds" (2011, 380). There is not space to elaborate these ideas properly in terms of the communal architectural projects and powerful imagery of the earliest Neolithic that has been mentioned; but I am sure that the archaeology and the ideas fit together very well, defining a new and powerful form of cultural niche that permits the formation and maintenance of the first large-scale communities and networks of communities.

One of the most impressive aspects of the Göbekli Tepe enclosures, populated as they are with many T-shaped monoliths, is the way that they almost crowd out the ordinary human visitor. The central pairs of monoliths are much taller than an ordinary human, and the largest pair seem gigantic. While the overall dimensions of the enclosures are impressive on paper, the space in the interior is very limited because the central monoliths are mounted in slots in a broad stone pedestal; the remaining floor area would hardly accommodate a dozen or so people. The excavators have tried in vain to isolate any trace of activity or use in the interior at the base of the back-fill deposits. There is a further reason for thinking that the interior of the enclosures was not much used, for the central monoliths were only very precariously balanced in their vertical positions. The bases of the monoliths do not fit closely in the slots carved in the stone pedestal, and they drop into their slots by less than 10 centimetres. In effect, the central monoliths seem to have been balanced in position.

With most of the communal buildings at the centre of settlements, as with the great circular enclosures at Göbekli Tepe, it is the scale of effort and logistical skill in their construction and then in their burial that is impressive, while their use between those framing events remains practically invisible. But they do share another characteristic in the attention that was given to reworking, reshaping or refurbishing them. This characteristic is also a feature of domestic architecture. It was remarked in the houses at Qermez Dere in north Iraq at the beginning of the early aceramic Neolithic (Watkins 2004a), and is a conspicuous feature of the very different houses at Çatalhöyük in central Turkey at the transition from the aceramic Neolithic to the ceramic Neolithic (Hodder & Cessford 2004; Cutting 2005; Matthews 2005; Hodder & Pels 2010). Especially in the context of the well-studied site of Çatalhöyük, we can imagine the routines of everyday life punctuated by many rituals or ceremonies of different kinds and different scales: the once-in-two-or-three-generations rituals that surrounded the demolition of an old house and its rebuilding as new on the stumps of the old walls; the rare and exciting hunting excursions, followed by many people sharing a great feast of beef from wild cattle; the occasional burial rituals, when a body was prepared and laid to rest in a shallow pit below the plastered sleeping platform; and the frequent resurfacing of all the walls and the floor of a house with a thin coat of almost white marl plaster, which might be followed by the execution of painted designs or scenes, or the embedding of an animal's skull and jawbone in a wall.

I would argue, therefore, that through the medium of architecture, sculpture and imagery, and the repeated rituals of building, maintenance, reconstruction and final closure, the first large-scale communities forged the collective memory that affirmed their collective identity and assured their pro-sociality. These constructions of memory and identity took place at the level of the household, at larger scales of social groups within the settlement, as well as the co-resident community of several hundred people. At a higher level again, the extended community of groups who came together at Göbekli Tepe to build enclosures and populate them with massive sculptures full of a rich corpus of imagery asserted their corporate identity through the monuments that they created, modified or recreated. In addition, their actions demonstrated a shared and complex image of a cosmos in which, for the first time, supernatural agents played a part. The general correlation between formalised religions centred on supernatural, in some sense anthropomorphic, agents and large-scale societies has frequently been remarked upon, whether in the early cities of southern Mesopotamia, the pharaonic kingdom of Egypt or later civilisations; it is suggested here that we can detect the beginnings of the emergence of such ideas in South-West Asia around the Pleistocene–Holocene transition. Further, I believe that it is possible to argue that these earliest Neolithic communities were at the beginning of the emergence of a doctrinal mode of complex religiosity that was anchored in the making of symbolic material culture, rather than the reading of verbal or the reciting of written instruction.

What is most striking about the evidence of ritual practice as I have sketched it is its concern with making and remaking buildings, sculptures, figurines, signs or paintings, rather than with religious ceremonies taking place in those buildings or before those images. This suggests that the repeated performances of making and remaking buildings, of feasting or of interring bodies within the settlement were themselves the ritual performances essential to the forging of collective memory and the sustaining of collective identity. Their repetition was important because it necessarily involved remembering, and at the same time, it mediated the transmission of meaning down the generations. And those rituals that were religious (that is, rituals that involve the presumption of supernatural agents) illustrate the point that shared religious practice is the basis of making shared religious belief, to the extent that the making and installing of a sculpted stone image may be understood as the making of belief – truly make-believe, which is where the social play of children and ritual meet.

REFERENCES

Aiello, L. & R. I. M. Dunbar, 1993. Neocortex size, group size and the evolution of language. *Current Anthropology*, 36, 184–93.

Assmann, J., 1995. Collective memory and cultural identity. *New German Critique*, 65, 125–33.

Atran, S. & J. Henrich, 2010. The evolution of religion: how cognitive by-products, adaptive learning heuristics, ritual displays, and group competition generate deep commitments to prosocial religions. *Biology Theory*, 5(1), 18–30.

Banning, E. B., 2011. So fair a house: Göbekli Tepe and the identification of temples in the pre-pottery Neolithic of the Near East. *Current Anthropology*, 52(5), 619–60.

Belfer-Cohen, A. & A. N. Goring-Morris, 2013. Breaking the mould: phases and facies in the Natufian of the Mediterranean Zone, in *Natufian Foragers in the Levant: Terminal Pleistocene Social Changes in Western Asia*, eds. O. Bar-Yosef & F. R. Valla Ann Arbor, Michigan: International Monographs in Prehistory, 542–61.

Boyer, P., 2009. What are memories for? Functions of recall in cognition and culture, in Memory in Mind and Culture, eds. P. Boyer & J. W. Wertsch Cambridge: Cambridge University Press, 3–28.

Bulbulia, J. & M. Frean, 2010. The evolution of charismatic cultures. *Method & Theory in the Study of Religion*, 22(4), 254–71.

Bulbulia, J. & R. Sosis, 2011. Signalling theory and the evolution of religious cooperation. *Religion*, 41(3), 363–88.

Cauvin, J., 1994. *Naissance des divinités, naissance de l'agriculture: la révolution des symboles au Néolithique*. Paris: CNRS editions.

Cauvin, J., 2000. *The Birth of the Gods and the Origins of Agriculture*. Cambridge: Cambridge University Press.

Cohen, A. P., 1985. *The Symbolic Construction of Community*. Chichester & London: Ellis Horwood, and Tavistock.

Connerton, P., 1989. *How Societies Remember*. Cambridge: Cambridge University Press.

Corballis, M. C., 2011. *The Recursive Mind: The Origins of Human Language, Thought, and Civilization*. Princeton, NJ: Princeton University Press.

Cutting, M., 2005. The architecture of Çatalhöyük: continuity, household and settlement, in *Çatalhöyük Perspectives: Reports from the 1995–99 Seasons*, ed. I. Hodder London; Cambridge: British Institute at Ankara; McDonald Institute for Archaeological Research, 151–70.

Dunbar, R. I. M., 1998. The social brain hypothesis. *Evolutionary Anthropology*, 6(3), 178–90.

Dunbar, R. I. M., 2003. The social brain: mind, language, and society in evolutionary perspective. *Annual Review of Anthropology*, 32, 163–81.

Dunbar, R. I. M., 2004. *The Human Story: A New History of Mankind's Evolution*. London: Faber.

Dunbar, R. I. M., 2009. The social brain hypothesis and its implications for social evolution. *Annals of Human Biology*, 36(5), 562–72.

Dunbar, R. I. M., C. Gamble & J. A. J. Gowlett, 2010. *Social Brain, Distributed Mind*. Oxford: Oxford University Press & British Academy.

Dunbar, R. I. M., C. Gamble & J. A. J. Gowlett, 2014. *Lucy to Language: The Benchmark Papers*, Oxford: Oxford University Press.

Durkheim, E. 1995. *The Elementary Forms of Religious Life* [1912 *Les formes élémentaires de la vie religieuse*]. New York: Free Press.

Edwards, P. C., 2009. The symbolic dimensions of material culture at Wadi Hammeh 27, in *Proceedings of the 5th International Congress on the Archaeology of the Ancient Near East*, eds. J. Córdoba, M. Molist, C. Pérez, I. Rubio & S. Martínez Madrid: Universidad Autónoma de Madrid, 507–20.

Finlayson, B., S. J. Mithen, M. Najjar, S. Smith, D. Maričević, N. Pankhurst & L. Yeomans, 2011. Architecture, sedentism, and social complexity at pre-pottery Neolithic A WF16, southern Jordan. *Proceedings of the National Academy of Sciences*, 108(20), 8183–8.

Flannery, K. V., 1969. The origins and ecological effects of early domestication in Iran and the Near East, in *The Domestication and Exploitation of Plants and Animals*, eds. P. J. Ucko & G. W. Dimbleby. London: Duckworth, 73–100.

Flannery, K. V. & J. Marcus, 2012. *The Creation of Inequality: How Our Prehistoric Ancestors Set the Stage for Monarchy, Slavery, and Empire*. Cambridge, MA: Harvard University Press.

Gamble, C., 1998. Palaeolithic society and the release from proximity: a network approach to intimate relations. *World Archaeology*, 29(3), 426–49.

Gamble, C., 1999. *The Palaeolithic Societies of Europe*. Cambridge: Cambridge University Press.

Gamble, C., J. Gowlett & R. Dunbar, 2014. *Thinking Big: How the Evolution of Social Life Shaped the Human Mind*, London: Thames & Hudson.

Hardy-Smith, T. & P. C. Edwards, 2004. The garbage crisis in prehistory: artefact discard patterns at the early Natufian site of Wadi Harnmeh 27 and the origins of household refuse disposal strategies. *Journal of Anthropological Archaeology*, 23(3), 253–89.

Henrich, J., 2004. Demography and cultural evolution: how adaptive cultural processes can produce maladaptive losses – the Tasmanian case. *American Antiquity*, 69(2), 197–214.

Henrich, J., 2009. The evolution of costly displays, cooperation and religion: credibility enhancing displays and their implications for cultural evolution. *Evolution and Human Behavior*, 30(4), 244–60.

Hodder, I., 1990. *The Domestication of Europe: Structure and Contingency in Neolithic Societies*. Oxford: Basil Blackwell.

Hodder, I., 2005. Socialization and feasting at Catalhoyuk: a response to Adams. *American Antiquity*, 70(1), 189–91.

Hodder, I. & C. Cessford, 2004. Daily practice and social memory at Catalhoyuk. *American Antiquity*, 69(1), 17–40.

Hodder, I. & P. Pels, 2010. History houses: a new interpretation of architectural elaboration at Çatalhöyük, in *Religion in the Emergence of Civilization: Çatalhöyük as a Case Study*, ed. I. Hodder. Cambridge: Cambridge University Press, 163–86.

Kendal, J., 2011. Cultural niche construction and human learning environments: investigating sociocultural perspectives. *Biological Theory*, 6(3), 241–50.

Kuhn, S. & M. Stiner, 2007. Body ornamentation as information technology: towards an understanding of the significance of early beads, in *Rethinking the Human Revolution: New Behavioural and Biological Perspectives on the Origin and Dispersal of Modern Humans*, eds. P. Mellars, K. V. Boyle, O. Bar-Yosef & C. Stringer Cambridge: McDonald Institute for Archaeological Research, 45–54.

Laland, K. & M. O'Brien, 2011. Cultural niche construction: an introduction. *Biological Theory*, 6(3), 191–202.

Laland, K. N., J. Odling-Smee & M. W. Feldman, 2000. Niche construction, biological evolution, and cultural change. *Behavioral and Brain Sciences*, 23(1), 131–75.

Laland, K. N., J. Odling-Smee & M. W. Feldman, 2001. Cultural niche construction and human evolution. *Journal of Evolutionary Biology*, 14(1), 22–33.

Marcus, J. & K. V. Flannery, 2004. The coevolution of ritual and society: new 14C dates from ancient Mexico. *Proceedings of the National Academy of Sciences of the United States of America*, 101(52), 18257–61.

Matthews, W., 2005. Life-cycle and life-course of buildings, in *Çatalhöyük Perspectives: Reports from the 1995–99 Seasons*, ed. I. Hodder. London; Cambridge: British Institute at Ankara; McDonald Institute for Archaeological Research, 125–50.

McCauley, R. N. & E. T. Lawson, 2002. *Bringing Ritual to Mind: Psychological Foundations of Cultural Forms*. Cambridge: Cambridge University Press.

Mithen, S., B. Finlayson, S. Smith, E. Jenkins, M. Najjar & D. Maričević, 2011. An 11,600 year-old communal structure from the Neolithic of southern Jordan. *Antiquity*, 85(328), 350–64.

Morenz, L. D. & K. Schmidt, 2009. Grosse Releifpfeiler und kleine Zeichentäfelchen, in *Non-textual Marking Systems, Writing and Pseudo Script from Prehistory to Present Times*, eds. P. Andrássy, J. Budka & F. Kammerzell Göttingen: Lingua Aegyptia – Studia Monographica, 13–31.

O'Brien, M. J. & K. N. Laland, 2012. Genes, culture, and agriculture: an example of human niche construction. *Current Anthropology*, 53(4), 434–70.

Odling-Smee, F. J. & K. N. Laland, 2009. Cultural niche construction: evolution's cradle of language, in *The Prehistory of Language*, eds. R. Botha & C. Knight Oxford: Oxford University Press, 99–121.

Odling-Smee, J. & K. Laland, 2011. Ecological inheritance and cultural inheritance: what are they and how do they differ? *Biological Theory*, 6(3), 220–30.

Özdoğan, A., 1999. Çayönü in Neolithic in Turkey. *The Cradle of Civilization, New Discoveries*, eds. M. Özdoğan & N. Başgelen Istanbul: Arkeoloji ve Sanat Yayınları, 35–63.

Powell, A., S. Shennan & M. G. Thomas, 2009. Late Pleistocene demography and the appearance of modern human behavior. *Science*, 324(5932), 1298–301.

Rendell, L., L. Fogarty & K. N. Laland, 2011. Runaway cultural niche construction. *Philosophical Transactions of the Royal Society B: Biological Sciences*, 366(1566), 823–35.

Schirmer, W., 1990. Some aspects of the building in the 'aceramic Neolithic' settlement at Çayönü Tepesi. *World Archaeology*, 21(3), 363–87.

Schmidt, K., 2000. Göbekli Tepe, southeastern Turkey. A preliminary report on the 1995–1999 excavations. *Paléorient*, 26(1), 45–54.

Schmidt, K., 2006. *Sie bauten die ersten Tempel. Das rätselhafte Heiligtum der Steinzeitjäger*, Munich: Beck.

Schmidt, K., 2011. Göbekli Tepe, in *The Neolithic in Turkey. New Excavations and New Research – The Euphrates Basin*, eds. M. Özdoğan, N. Başgelen & P. Kuniholm Istanbul: Arkeoloji ve Sanat Yayinlari, 41–83.

Schmidt, K., 2012. *Göbekli Tepe. A Stone Age Sanctuary in South-Eastern Anatolia*, Berlin: ex oriente & ArchaeNova e.V.

Shennan, S., 2000. Population, culture history, and the dynamics of culture change. *Current Anthropology*, 41(5), 811–35.

Shennan, S., 2001. Demography and cultural innovation: a model and its implications for the emergence of modern human culture. *Cambridge Archaeological Journal*, 11(1), 5–16.

Sterelny, K., 2007. Social intelligence, human intelligence and niche construction. *Philosophical Transactions of the Royal Society B: Biological Sciences*, 362(1480), 719–30.

Sterelny, K., 2011. *The Evolved Apprentice: How Evolution Made Humans Unique*. Cambridge, MA: MIT Press.

Sterelny, K. & T. Watkins, 2015. Neolithization in south-west Asia in a context of niche construction theory. *Cambridge Archaeological Journal*, 25(3), 673–91.

Stiner, M. C., 2001. Thirty years on the 'Broad Spectrum Revolution' and Paleolithic demography. *Proceedings of the National Academy of Sciences of the United States of America*, 98(13), 6993–6.

Stordeur, D., 2015. *Le village de Jerf el Ahmar (Syrie, 9500–8700 av. J.-C.): L'architecture, miroir d'une société néolithique complexe*, Paris: CNRS Éditions.

Stordeur, D., M. Brenet, G. Der Aprahamian & J.-C. Roux, 2000. Les bâtiments communautaires de Jerf el Ahmar et Mureybet, horizon PPNA (Syrie). *Paléorient*, 26(1), 29–44.

Valla, F., 1988. Aspects du sol de l'abri 131 de Mallaha (Eynan), Israel. *Paléorient*, 14(2), 283–96.

Valla, F., 2008. *L'homme et l'habitat: l'invention de la maison durant la Préhistoire*, Paris: CNRS Editions.

Watkins, T., 1990. The origins of house and home? *World Archaeology*, 21(3), 336–47.

Watkins, T., 2004a. Architecture and 'theatres of memory' in the Neolithic South West Asia, in *Rethinking Materiality: The Engagement of Mind with the Material World*, eds. E. DeMarrais, C. Gosden & C. Renfrew Cambridge: McDonald Institute of Archaeological Research, 97–106.

Watkins, T., 2004b. Building houses, framing concepts, constructing worlds. *Paléorient*, 30(1), 5–24.

Watkins, T., 2006. Architecture and the symbolic construction of new worlds, in *Domesticating Space: Construction, Community, and Cosmology in the Late Prehistoric Near East*, eds. E. B. Banning & M. Chazan Berlin: ex oriente, 15–24.

Watkins, T., 2008. Supra-regional networks in the Neolithic of Southwest Asia. *Journal of World Prehistory*, 21(1), 139–71.

Watkins, T., 2009. Ordering time and space: creating a cultural world, in *Proceedings of the 5th International Congress on the Archaeology of the Ancient Near East*, eds. J. Córdoba, M. Molist, C. Pérez, I. Rubio & S. Martínez Madrid: Univer-sidad Autónoma de Madrid, 647–59.

Watkins, T., 2010a. Changing people, changing environments: how hunter-gatherers became communities that changed the world, in *Landscapes in Transition: Understanding Hunter-Gatherer and Farming Landscapes in the Early Holocene of Europe and the Levant*, eds. B. Finlayson & G. Warren London: Levant Supplementary Series & CBRL, 104–12.

Watkins, T., 2010b. New light on Neolithic revolution in South-West Asia. *Antiquity*, 84(325), 621–34.

Watkins, T., 2012. Household, community and social landscape: building and maintaining social memory in the early Neolithic of southwest Asia, in *'As Time Goes By' Monuments, Landscapes and the Temporal Perspective. Socio-Environmental Dynamics over the Last 12,000 Years*, eds. M. Furholt, M. Hinz & D. Mischka Kiel: Bonn: Rudolf Habelt, 23–44.

Watkins, T., 2015. The cultural dimension of cognition. *Quaternary International*, 405(Part A), 91–7.

Watkins, T., K. Dobney & R. M. Nesbitt, 1995. *Qermez Dere, Tel Afar*, Interim Report No. 3, Edinburgh: Department of Archaeology, University of Edinburgh.

Whitehouse, H., 2004. *Modes of Religiosity: A Cognitive Theory of Religious Transmission*, Walnut Creek, CA: AltaMira Press.

Whitehouse, H. & I. Hodder, 2010. Modes of religiosity at Çatalhöyük, in *Religion in the Emergence of Civilization: Çatalhöyük as a Case Study*, ed. I. Hodder Cambridge: Cambridge University Press, 122–45.

Willcox, G. & D. Stordeur, 2012. Large-scale cereal processing before domestication during the tenth millennium cal BC in northern Syria. *Antiquity*, 86(331), 99–114.

Yartah, T., 2004. Tell 'Abr 3, un village du Néolithique précéramique (PPNA) sur le Moyen-Euphrate. Première approche. *Paléorient*, 30, 141–58.

Yartah, T., 2005. Les bâtiments communautaires de Tell 'Abr 3 (PPNA, Syrie). *Neolithics: A Newsletter of Southwest Asia Neolithic Research*, 1/05, 3–9.

Zeder, M. A., 2012. The Broad Spectrum Revolution at 40: resource diversity, intensification, and an alternative to optimal foraging explanations. *Journal of Anthropological Archaeology*, 31(3), 241–64.

Zeder, M. A., 2016. Domestication as a model system for niche construction theory. *Evolutionary Ecology*, 30(2), 325–48.

DANCING WITH MASKS IN THE PROTO-HISTORIC NEAR EAST

Yosef Garfinkel

General Thoughts on Ritual Behaviour

Before going into the details of my particular topic, dancing with masks in the proto-historic Near East, I will make a general comment on the main topic of this volume: the importance of play and ritual in religious studies. Definitions of religion, its origin and development and its connection to society and ecology have been extensively addressed by anthropologists, from the founding fathers of the discipline up to today (see, for example, Tylor 1871; Frazer 1911; Durkheim 1912; Radcliffe-Brown 1922; Evans-Pritchard 1937; Malinowski 1948; Lévi-Strauss 1962; Bloch 1989; Rappaport 1999). It is not my intention here to summarize the different approaches to religion, as this has been done in numerous introductions to anthropology (see, for example, Grimes 1985; Morris 1987; Glazier 1997; Bowie 2000), and archaeologists have also written on the matter quite extensively from their own point of view (see, for example, Renfrew 1985; Marcus & Flannery 1994; Mithen 1996; Verhoeven 2002; Kyriakidis 2007). For our purposes, religion can be defined as the picture that people in a certain culture have in mind about the world, supernatural powers and the role of the individual in that system.

As summarized by Rappaport in the introduction to his monumental book *Ritual and Religion in the Making of Humanity*: "No society known to anthropology or history is devoid of what reasonable observers would agree is religion. … Given the central place that religious considerations have occupied in the thoughts and actions of men and women in all times and places, and given the amount of energy, blood, time and wealth that have been spent building temples, supporting priests, sacrificing to gods and killing infidels, it is hard to imagine that religion, as bizarre as some of its manifestations may seem, is not in some way indispensable to the species" (1999: 1–2).

There are probably hundreds of definitions in scholarly literature for the terms *religion*, *cult* and *ritual*. As a matter of fact, even in a given culture different individuals offer different interpretations of their own common religion. Some aspects of religion may intentionally be left vague, and some religions have 'secret societies' in which parts of the religion remain unavailable to large segments of the society. So, if religion is such an abstract entity, how can millions or even hundreds of millions of people classify themselves as belonging to a particular religion? How can such a paradoxical situation exist? The reason is that in practice, all these people share the same rituals. Thus, what is held in common by all is not the grand abstract concept, but the specific paraphernalia and performance involved in ritual ceremonies. The rituals are direct and authentic representations of any religion, the actual manifestation of the abstract ideology. Indeed, the importance of rituals has been emphasized by many scholars (see, for example, Turner 1969, 1982, 1990; Schechner

1987, 1994; de Coppet 1992). This is most fortunate from an archaeological point of view, as rituals have usually left behind cultic paraphernalia that can be unearthed and analyzed.

The great power that religion has over its believers, involving aspects of the emotional and irrational, is virtually unknown in other kinds of human behaviour. Many of the studies mentioned earlier in this chapter have tried to decipher the secret of this power, but have not arrived at clear-cut answers. In this context, I would like to introduce a term that originated in the discipline of biology but is commonly used in sociobiological research – *pheromone*. My main argument is that the function of religion in human society is similar to that of pheromones in the animal kingdom. The term comes from the Greek *pherein* (to transfer) and *hormon* (to excite) and was first introduced and defined by Karlson and Lüscher: "Pheromones are substances which are secreted to the outside by an individual and received by a second individual of the same species in which they release a specific reaction, for example, a definite behavior or developmental process" (1959). Unlike hormones, which are produced and function within the individual organism, pheromones communicate between individuals. In insects, they function on a wide scale: to release aggregation, trail-following, dispersion, sexual behaviour, oviposition, alarm and the regulation of social insect colonies. Pheromones are the main mechanism in the control of caste differentiation in bees, ants etc. In mammals, pheromones are involved, for example, in social hierarchies and territorial behaviour (Birch 1974).

The functional similarity of pheromones to religion in human society is striking. To paraphrase the definition of Karlson and Lüscher, religion is a substance that is secreted to the outside by individuals and received by another individual of the same religion in which it releases a specific reaction. An important aspect of religion is that it has an effect *only* on people of that particular religion. Just as bee pheromones are ineffective on ants, we can see that only members of a certain religion obey its rules. A Christian will eat pork, which is prohibited to Jews and Muslims. Jews and Christians consume alcohol and consecrate it in their rituals, while it is altogether forbidden to Muslims. Asceticism exists

as a religious institution in Christianity, but not in Judaism or Islam. These examples clearly show that what is considered a major taboo in one religion is a routine practice in another. Highly esteemed values for members of one religion are meaningless or even despised by members of another. To summarize, religion, like pheromones, creates a powerful reaction in its members, but is completely ineffective outside that circle. Hence, religion is a mechanism for the coordination and control of groups of peoples. A community that practises religion is more efficient over time and survives better than a community without it (Rappaport 1971, 1999).

Religion is a rather abstract term. What archaeologists actually study is the relics of cultic rituals, which leave behind clear-cut data and traces of repeated patterns of behaviour. Such rituals are often extravagant events that leave specific remnants, such as their location (cult structures, caves, mountain peaks), paraphernalia (figurative art, symbols of divine powers, special vessels), food consumption (cooking installations, animal bones, serving vessels), special clothing, body ornaments, musical instruments and so on. The elaborate ritual stimulates the individual's senses: sight (colours, elaborate art objects, special clothing of the participants, body gestures, fire), hearing (speech, reading, singing, music), smell (incense, smoke, flowers), taste (eating, drinking) and touch (touching other participants or sacred objects). Ritual activity is thus a multilayered sensory experience that leaves a strong impact on the participants in the event and endures in their memories.

DANCE AND RITUALS

Many scholars struggle with the definition of dancing. Dance experts even debate about how to recognize dance today when you see it (Hanna 1979). Dancing is described in Webster's Dictionary of 1965 as "rhythmic movement having as its aim the creation of visual designs by a series of poses and tracing of patterns through space in the course of measured units of time, the two components, static and kinetic, receiving varying emphasis and being executed by different parts of the body in accordance with temperament, artistic precepts, and purpose." Elsewhere dance has been defined as "a complex form of communication that combines the visual, kinesthetic, and aesthetic aspects of human movement with (usually) the aural dimension of musical sounds and sometimes poetry. Dance is created out of culturally understood symbols within social and religious contexts, and it conveys information and meaning as ritual, ceremony, and entertainment. For dance to communicate, its audience must understand the cultural conventions that deal with human movement in time and space" (Kaeppler 1992, 196).

For me, dance is a rhythmical movement that is not associated with any functional everyday activity of subsistence or technology. If we take dance as a means of non-verbal communication, it is not limited to human behaviour. It has been observed in insects (the bee dance) and in courtship interactions of various birds and mammals (von Frisch 1967; Wilson 1975, 176–241, 314–35). The use of body movement to convey a message is well known in the animal world in many other cases, such as aggression and submission. Hence, dance as a non-verbal mode of communication seems to be a very early form of human behaviour, predating speech and languages.

As observed by ethnographers and dance experts, dance is closely associated with cultic rituals in traditional societies all over the world, in Africa, Asia, Australia and America (see, for example, Sachs 1952; Lange 1976; Royce 1977; Hanna 1987). As summarized by Spencer (1985, 38): "Dance is not an entity in itself, but belongs rightfully to the wider analysis of ritual action, and it is in this context that one can approach it analytically and grant it the attention it demands. In a very important sense, society creates the dance, and it is to society that we must turn to understand it." The power of dance in rituals probably derives from its ability to act simultaneously in several different ways:

1. Coordination of the society. The importance of dance as a means of social interaction among traditional societies has been stressed by some of the most influential anthropologists of the twentieth century: Radcliffe-Brown (1922, 246–56) and Evans-Pritchard (1928). Evans-Pritchard (1928, 446), for example, observed that dance is essentially a joint and not an individual activity and that we must therefore explain it in terms of social function, that is to say we must determine what is its social value. Hanna (1979, 23–4) wrote that the purpose of dance can be understood also in terms of the larger social structure, the standardized social form through which conceptualization and action occurs. This aspect was analyzed in great detail in the book *Keeping Together in Time: Dance and Drill in Human History* (McNeill 1995). As is evident from ancient depictions (Garfinkel 2003), dance is an activity through which society instils collective discipline in its members: people gather in the same place at the same time, stand in the same circle, move in the same direction and perform the same body gestures. The participants in the dance accept the rules of the community, which is achieved not through fear, but through bodily activity – a form of group therapy.

As human behaviour became more and more complex over time, the practices that coordinated bands of apes were no longer adequate. This is when 'cultural pheromones' came in, in the form of dance, rituals and speech. Dance, as a non-verbal mode of communication known in insects, birds and mammals, may be the earliest of all.

2. Multisensory experience. Dancing involves most of the senses: sight (viewing the participants and their body gestures), hearing (listening to singing and music), touch (holding other participants) and smell (the sweat of participants). Drops of sweat from the dancer may reach his lips or those of others, creating a salty taste. This extensive sensory perception reaches the quantity and quality that are desirable for cultic rituals.

3. Self-expression for individuals. While anthropologists tend to emphasize the social dimension of dance, the individual dancer should not be overlooked. In traditional societies dance ceremonies last for hours, or even the entire night (see, for example Katz 1982). Even today, people can dance for hours in clubs. This extravagant expenditure of energy has no utilitarian purpose, as in hunting or cultivation. The dance is an opportunity for the individual to demonstrate his strength, endurance, vitality and sexual attractiveness. In this respect the human dance and the animal courtship dance are quite similar.

A major component of every religion and cultic ritual is the connection with supernatural powers which, according to that religion, control the world. The dance performed during rituals is the way in which each individual expresses his worship, respect and adoration of the supernatural powers. The rhythmical and ecstatic movement, sometimes leading to trance (see later in this chapter), is the contribution of each individual to the religious ceremony. The dance is the equivalent of the prayers and animal sacrifices that appear later in complex societies.

Another physiological aspect seems to be involved in dancing for long hours. The physical stress leads the body to release endorphins (Fraioli et al. 1980). This natural hormone helps the body to overcome the pain and exhaustion caused by extreme physical exertion and to create feelings of euphoria.

4. Dance and trance. An important observation is that after hours of rhythmical circular dancing, a few of the participants often fall into a trance. The trance is understood as a form of contact between the community and supernatural powers, in other words, a mystical and irrational event, the core of religious experience. Indeed, altered states of consciousness in religious contexts have been documented in more than 400 different human societies (Bourguignon 1973).

These four aspects of dance clearly explain its power on both the community and the individual levels. The extravagant expenditure of energy in the dance has direct physical consequences (release of endorphins and trance), results that are both emotional and irrational.

It has been suggested that dance was already practised during the Palaeolithic era (Louis 1955; Blacking 1976; McNeill 1995, 13–35; Garfinkel 2010; Morley 2013). Indeed, we can argue for very early roots of dancing in human behaviour, based on several criteria:

1. The widespread appearance of dance in every human society known today, including hunter-gatherer societies like the San of South Africa and Australian Aboriginals.
2. The central role of dance in current hunter-gatherer societies as demonstrated, for example,

by the many dancing activities of the San of South Africa (Marshall 1969; Biesele 1978; Katz 1982) is a clear indication that dance must have been a primary form of human behaviour in prehistory.

3. Dancing figures and musical instruments appear in the earliest *Homo sapiens* sites in Europe (Garfinkel 2010; Morley 2013).

Ancient human dancing is a neglected topic of study. Articles dealing with dance are seldom found (but see Halley, Chapter 9, this volume), while books are almost non-existent (but see Morley 2013). The study of dance by archaeologists is challenging for two main reasons:

1. Dancing does not leave visible remains and the chances of finding footprints in a circle or a group of human skeletons trapped and buried during a dance are minimal. Until relevant data become available we are dealing with a very fragmentary record.
2. Modern archaeological and anthropological research evolved in Western civilization, which is dominated by a Christian point of view. Unlike most of the other religions, its attitude to dance is negative. In the New Testament the term is mentioned only once, in the extremely dramatic dance of Salome which concluded with the beheading of John the Baptist (Mark 6: 21–6). In contrast, the Old Testament records dozens of instances of dancing, using 10 different verbs (Gruber 1981). Dance is not part of any official Christian liturgy. Western scholarship's lack of awareness of the importance of dance in human activity must be seen against this background.

Attempting to recognize dance in artistic depictions that have survived from prehistoric times, 40,000–5,000 years ago, is not a simple task. During my systematic research on Neolithic and Chalcolithic dance, it became clear that the depiction of dancing reflects a strict adherence to discipline, dictating the form of the performance (Garfinkel 1998, 2003):

1. The posture of all the figures is the same.
2. The figures are all dressed identically (or are all nude).

3. When holding objects, such as sticks, all the figures hold identical objects.
4. All the figures turn in the same direction.
5. The distance between one figure and the next is uniform.

As I have already dedicated a book-length study (Garfinkel 2003) and various articles (Garfinkel 1998, 2000, 2005, 2010) to dance, I present and discuss here a new topic: dancing with masks.

THE MASK

The mask is an object that covers the face. There is no other medium in performance paraphernalia that embodies such great power. Among the large variety of accessories used in human display, such as hairdo, headgear, make-up, earrings and jewellery, tattoos and other skin decorations, clothing, belts, shoes and other accessories, masks have an unparalleled effect. This power is apparently derived from two properties. First, the mask occupies the face, the major means of human expression and communication. The positions of the eyes, mouth and cheeks directly reflect the basic human emotions, such as happiness, sadness, anger, fear, disgust or surprise. The mask can magnify these emotions. Second, the mask has a double effect; it conceals the real and reveals a new reality instead, merging reality and illusion and exposing fantasies and hidden truths.

The number of studies devoted to the history, ethnography and other aspects of the use of masks is so vast that a comprehensive survey cannot be presented in the framework of this chapter. Three main genres, however, can be defined:

1. Studies relating to masks from the perspective of museology, surveying masks as art objects in accordance to geographical regions (see, for example, Gregor 1937; Garfield & Wingert 1966, 75–80; Hartmann 1967; Höpfner 1969; Lommel 1972; Sorell 1973; Glotz 1975; Mack 1994; Hahner-Herzog et al. 1998).
2. Studies seeking a more specific context for the mask from the historical or anthropological perspective (see, for example, Boaz 1890; Harley 1950;

Holas 1952; Valentine 1961; Guiart 1966; Lucas 1973; Lévi-Strauss 1975; Ottenberg 1975; Adler 1982; Napier 1986; Emigh 1996; Mamczarz 1999).
3. Studies presenting the observations of an anthropologist who has spent a period of time with a remote tribal community and, among many other aspects, dedicated a few paragraphs to the uses of masks in that specific community (see, for example, Birket-Smith 1953; Gerbrands 1978; Emmons 1991; Whitehouse 1995).

In general, there are three basic uses of masks:

1. Performance Masks. An actively used object hangs on the human face during various displays, such as religious ceremonies and theatre (Pernet 1987, 1992). The practical use of a mask requires attachment to the face in a way that enables the wearer to see, breathe and speak. Thus, such masks are life-size and have openings for the eyes and mouth, as well as attachment devices. The opening at the mouth enables both breathing and speaking. Exceptional examples in this category are late Egyptian masks that have such small openings for the eyes that the masked person needed a second person to guide them (Sweeney 1993; Wolinski 1986).

One can distinguish between two basic situations in performance masks. In the first, all the masks used in a given performance are identical. This situation usually characterizes religious rituals and, according to ethnographic observations, is very common in ceremonies conducted by tribal communities. The second situation is when different types of masks, reflecting a variety of personas, are used in a performance. This situation is typical of high-level drama usually carried out in formalized theatres. The aspects of masks, performances and theatre have been discussed by various scholars, but are beyond our current scopes (see, for example, Brockett 1969, 1991; Beeman 1993; Emigh 1996).

2. Funerary Masks. The mask as a burial accessory is placed on the face of the corpse and left in the tomb. Archaeological examples of these have been reported from Egypt (Middle Kingdom and onwards), Mycenaean Greece, the Phoenicians, the Punic civilization of North Africa, the Balkans of the mid-first millennium BC and the Near East in the third–fourth centuries AD (Schliemann 1880, 219–23; Cintas 1946, 37–55; Culican 1975; Taylor 1994; Curtis 1995; Theodossiv 1998, 2000; Dayagi-Mendeles 2002, 156–60; see also Freidel and Rich, Chapter 8, this volume, regarding the Maya). Since the dead have no need to see, breathe, speak or conduct a performance, funerary masks do not usually have openings for the eyes or mouth, or devices for attachment. As these masks are usually made of gold and silver or other precious materials, they should be considered as status symbols used by the ruling classes to emphasize their power.

3. Protective Masks. These are items used as magic artefacts. They may be used as amulets or fixed into architectural features and provide protection against evil forces (Harley 1950, 9; Bédouin 1961, 94–5; Lommel 1972). Harley, who studied the use of masks in Liberia, gave the following description of this kind of mask: "Each man of importance in the community has one of the small carved wooden masks called *ma*, just big enough to fit into the palm of his hand. No one but the owner was supposed to see it except when high ritual required him to show it. A woman must never be allowed to see it or hear its name. The *ma* needed a sacrifice of a chicken each new moon. It was prayed to every morning by its owner, with a short petition for good luck and protection from witchcraft, which was supposed to be the cause of accidents" (1950, 9).

Masks in this category, like those in the previous case, are not performance paraphernalia. Thus, miniature items without openings for the eyes and mouth or attachment devices clearly belong to this category. In the archaeological record such items are known as early as the seventh millennium BC, such as the miniature stone mask from the Pre-Pottery Neolithic B (PPNB) site of Nevali Çori (Hauptmann 1999, fig. 19). Later examples are Phoenician masks from Dor or in the Punic civilization of North Africa (Cintas 1946, 49, fig. 72; Stern 1976).

Is it possible to find evidence for the use of masks as early as the Upper Palaeolithic period in Europe? There are isolated figures that may be interpreted as humans wearing masks, like the so-called sorcerer from the cave of Les Trois Frères, France

(Leroi-Gourhan 1967, pl. 57) and other seemingly masked figures on the walls of caves (Gimbutas 1989, 176, fig. 275). There are also 21 carefully shaped and perforated stag skulls from the Mesolithic site of Star Carr in East Yorkshire in England, which have been understood as masks (Clark 1954, 168–75). Nonetheless, since masks are not reported today in the ethnography of hunter-gatherer communities, the interpretation of the Upper Palaeolithic material as presenting masks is speculative.

In contrast, a systematic appearance of masks is seen in the early village communities of the proto-historic Near East, around 9,000–5,000 years ago. In this region four different kinds of evidence for the use of masks have been uncovered: real masks made of stone and clay, depictions of people wearing masks, depictions of masks on pottery vessels, and finally anthropomorphic figurines wearing masks. The aim of this chapter is twofold:

1. To present the relevant data, which have never been assembled. Some items are published here for the first time.
2. To place the use of masks in a broader context by referring to ethnographic observations. Some cross-cultural patterns in the use of masks can be discerned.

THE DATA: MASKS IN THE PROTO-HISTORIC NEAR EAST

The information on masks in the proto-historic Near East is derived from four different sources: actual masks, depictions of people wearing masks, depictions of masks and figurines wearing masks. Each of these groups is presented and some relevant artefacts are shown in the accompanying figures.

1 Stone and Clay Masks

Nine masks made of either stone or clay have survived from these earliest periods. Some were uncovered in systematic archaeological excavations, while others were found on the sites' surface. Four other stone masks are reported from private collections

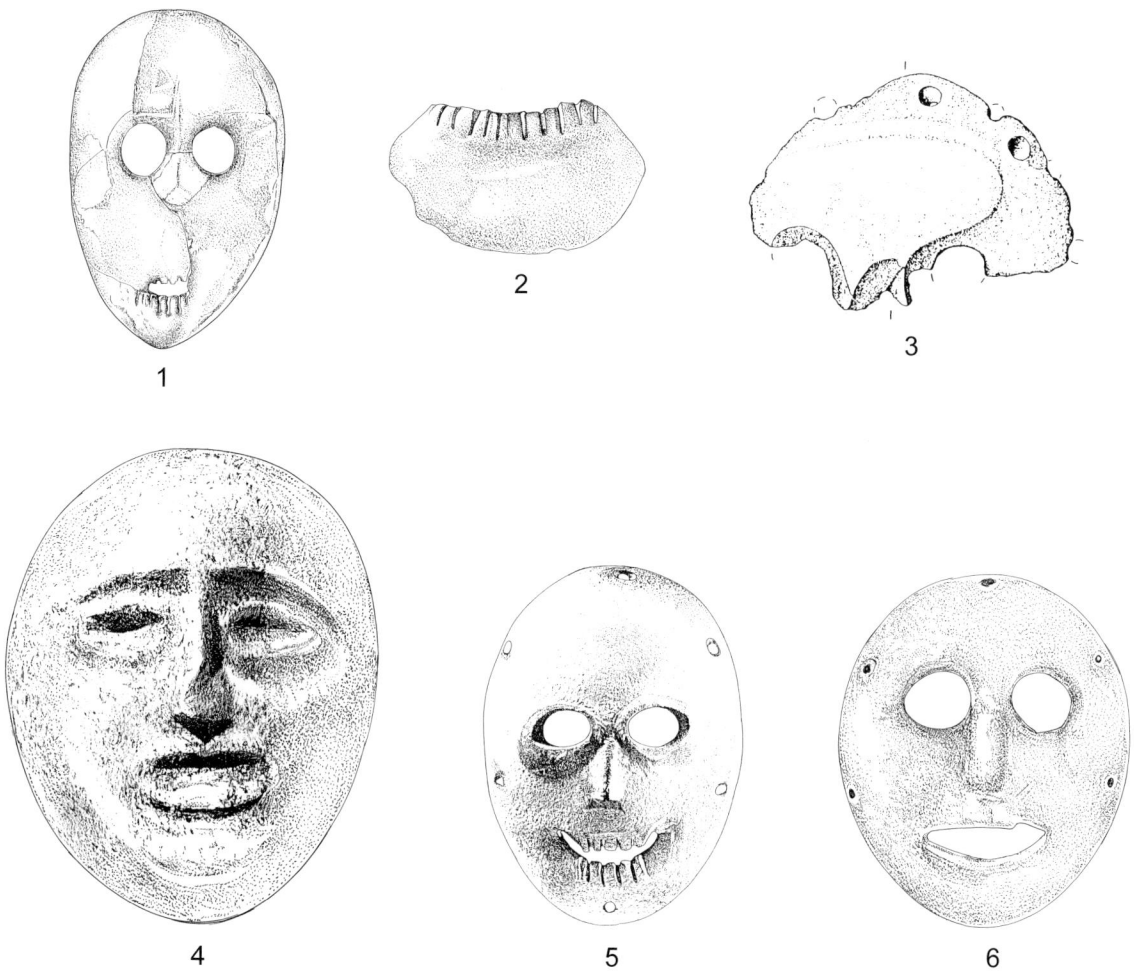

Figure 11.1 Stone masks from the Pre-Pottery Neolithic B of the southern Levant.

No.	Site	Reference
1	Nahal Hemar Cave	Bar-Yosef & Alon 1988, pl. X1
2	Nahal Hemar Cave	Bar-Yosef & Alon 1988
3	Basta	Nissan, Muheisen & Gebel 1987, fig. 16:1, pl. X2
4	Khirbet Duma	Ornan 1986, 18–20
5	Er-Ram	Barkay & Noy 1987
6	Unknown	Perrot 1979

and will not be discussed here. The data are presented in chronological order. Previously suggested interpretations of various scholars are also included.

a. Nahal Hemar Masks (Figure 11.1:1–2). Nahal Hemar is a small cave site located in the Judean Desert, some 10 miles west of the Dead Sea, and dated to the PPNB of the seventh millennium BC (Bar-Yosef 1985; Bar-Yosef & Alon 1988). A very rich cultic assemblage was found here, including

fragments of two masks, anthropomorphic plastered statues, modelled human skulls, anthropomorphic bone figurines and a zoomorphic figurine. The cave was apparently used for the final disposal of cultic objects (Garfinkel 1994).

Two stone masks were found at the site (Bar-Yosef & Alon 1988; Yizraeli-Noy 1999, nos. 121–2; Bar-Yosef 2003). The better-preserved mask is almost complete, made of limestone, oval in shape and life-size (26.5 by 17.2 cm). The edge of the mask is pierced by 18 holes running around its circumference. They were used to attach the mask to the human face. The mask was carved and well smoothed on both surfaces and varied in thickness between 13 and 21 mm. Residual scratches indicate that it was scraped with flint tools and that the polishing was facilitated with sand. In a few areas a fine coating of plaster filled incisions. The facial features include a short, protruding ridge representing the nose, two rounded holes depicting the eyes and an opening for the mouth, which is depicted with two rows of four teeth each. The mask is painted with wide stripes of various colours: red, red-brown, green, light buff, black asphalt and white plaster. Some of the stripes are arranged in a radial pattern, a feature that can be found on large-scale plastered statues of the same period (Noy 1988). Some patches of asphalt carry the imprint of hair, and the mask probably represented male features with moustache and beard. Evidence of repainting indicates that it was repeatedly reused in ceremonial activities.

The second item comprises only the lower part of a mask, including the chin and the lower jaw. It is carved on limestone and well smoothed. Twelve teeth are incised across the mouth, still bearing traces of asphalt. A small stain of bright red ochre is visible on the chin (Bar-Yosef & Alon 1988, 23). From its size it is clear that the complete item was life-size as well.

These earliest masks were not connected to performance activity. Bar-Yosef wrote: "It may seem unlikely that the stone masks were placed on the face during cult ceremonies. Stone masks are unknown in ethnographic research, but the ability to endure pain during religious ceremonies is so great in primitive societies, that wearing a heavy stone mask did not require an exceptional effort" (Bar-Yosef 1985, 14). Later, Bar-Yosef and Alon suggested that the masks demonstrate an additional expression of the 'ancestor cult', already alluded to in discussions of the modelled skulls of the PPNB (1988, 27). Arensburg and Hershkovitz, who studied the modelled skulls from the Nahal Hemar Cave, noted that the decoration was limited exclusively to the cranial vault, while on the other PPNB skulls the faces were reconstructed. Hence, they suggested, the faces of the Nahal Hemar skulls could have been replaced by the limestone

masks (1988, 54). In other words, these masks were understood as funerary items.

b. Basta Mask (Figure 11.1:3). Basta, located in southern Jordan, is one of the largest PPNB village sites. A preliminary report stated: "An outstanding find is the fragment of a stone mask made of porous limestone" (Nissan et al. 1987, 109, fig. 16:1). In the published drawing one can see an upper part of a mask with the upper parts of the eyeholes and a series of small perforations on the item's periphery. Further data on this poorly preserved mask were presented later (Hermansen 1997). The object was found in Area A in an unclear context that is nevertheless datable to the late PPNB. Hermansen's description states that the object may have been subjected to harsh treatment, since the edges of the recovered fragment are broken and there are large scars on the recto that may have been caused by more or less systematic destruction. He understood the small perforations as devices for tying the object onto something or attaching something to it, such as feathers, leaves, straw or the like.

One should note that the published section of this mask is thick and, if the drawing is accurate, the back part has not been removed as is usual in masks, leaving no space for the human face. What has been described as large scars on the recto created by systematic destruction may be chisel marks from the manufacturing process. The mask was probably broken in antiquity and discarded, thus finding its way into an 'unclear context'. Further investigation of this fragment is needed.

c. Khirbet Duma Mask (Figure 11.1:4). This item was found on the surface of Khirbet Duma in the southern Judean hills. It was originally in the private collection of Moshe Dayan and is now in the Israel Museum (Perrot 1979, fig. 20; Ornan 1986, 18–20; Yizraeli-Noy 1999, no. 124). The mask is made of limestone, oval in shape and life-size (22.3 by 15.2 cm, 1.13 kg). The facial features include a short protruding ridge representing the nose, two oval holes depicting the eyes and an elongated opening for the mouth, depicted with two rows of five teeth each. Six holes were drilled on the mask's rim for attachment. Typologically, it is quite similar to the

Nahal Hemar items and is thus dated to the PPNB of the seventh millennium BC. Ornan assumed that the absence of an opening for the nose, the location of attachment holes in the lower part of the mask and the weight of the mask did not allow actual use by a living person. She concludes that the holes could have been used to attach the item to a wall, pillar or statue. The holes could also have been used for attachment of hair or a headdress.

d. Er-Ram Mask (Figure 11.1:5). This was the first Neolithic stone mask reported from the Near East. It was purchased at Er-Ram, north of Jerusalem, but was not initially recognized as Neolithic (Chaplin 1890). Only some 100 years later, when the Nahal Hemar masks were found, was it correctly dated (Gophna, Lev-Yadon & Lifschitz 1986; Barkay & Noy 1987; Bar-Yosef & Alon 1988, 26–7). The mask, which is now in the collections of the Palestine Exploration Fund in London, has been described in great detail by various scholars (Barkay & Noy 1987; Bienert 1990). It is made of limestone with red limonitic inclusions, oval in shape and life-size (18.6 by 14.3 cm, 1.770 kg). The mask was carved into the shape of a human face at the front and back, with an emphasized chin. It has no openings for the eyes and nose or attachment holes. This is probably because it was not completed, as the right eye is incised more deeply in the attempt to bore through the stone.

e. A Mask in Paris (Figure 11.1:6). This mask was purchased in the antiquities market, said to have been found in the Judean Desert, and is now in the collection of the Musée de la Bible et Terre Sainte, Paris (Perrot 1979, fig. 26; Amiet 1980, no. 160; Starcky 1984; Bar-Yosef & Alon 1988, 26, pl. XI:2; Yizraeli-Noy 1999, no. 125). It was carved in a similar way to the other stone masks described previously in this chapter, made of limestone and life-size (17.8 by 14.0 cm). The mask has rounded holes for the eyes, a toothless mouth and five small attachment holes on its rim. Some black stains can be observed on the item. Based on its style, it should be dated to the PPNB of the seventh millennium BC. Amiet described the item as a "funerary mask" without further explanation (1980, 443).

f. Masks in Private Collections. Three stone masks, quite similar to the aforementioned items, have been reported from a private collection (Yizraeli-Noy 1999, nos. 123, 126, 127). A fourth similar mask was recently (June 2012) on sale at Christies. These masks surfaced in the antiquities market and may be either forgeries or illegally excavated in unknown sites. We will not take them into consideration here.

g. Nevali Çori Mask (Figure 11.2). This site is located in the Euphrates Valley of Turkey. In the PPNB settlement a miniature stone mask was found. This item is about 4.5 cm in diameter and has neither openings for the eyes or mouth nor attachment devices (Hauptmann 1999, fig. 19, personal communication). The site is characterized by intensive cultic and artistic activities and the mask is part of this assemblage (Hauptmann 1993).

h. Hierakonpolis Masks (Figure 11.3). In the excavations at the Predynastic site of Hierakonpolis, Upper Egypt, two clay masks have been discovered in a cemetery used for burial during the phases of Naqada I (early fourth millennium BC) and Naqada III (middle–late fourth millennium BC). The preliminary report indicates: "There were the life-size, straw-tempered pottery masks found in the robber's trench, one to the south of Tomb 16 and one to the east" (Adams 1999, 30). Tomb 16 is dated to the Naqada III period, but since the masks were found in a robber's trench, their relationship to this tomb is not certain. In any case, since the cemetery was used only during Predynastic times, the masks can be generally dated to the fourth millennium BC.

The better-preserved item is missing its upper left side. It comprises an oblique elongated eye, a central nose with depressions for the nostrils and a semicircular mouth. The second item is a fragment with a complete right eye, part of the left eye and a nose with nostril depressions. The lower part is completely missing. The two items are similar in their rhomboid shape and facial features. Although thousands of Predynastic graves have been excavated in Egypt over the past 120 years, this is the first time that such artefacts have been reported.

The excavators concluded: "Until further excavation has thrown more light on the contents of

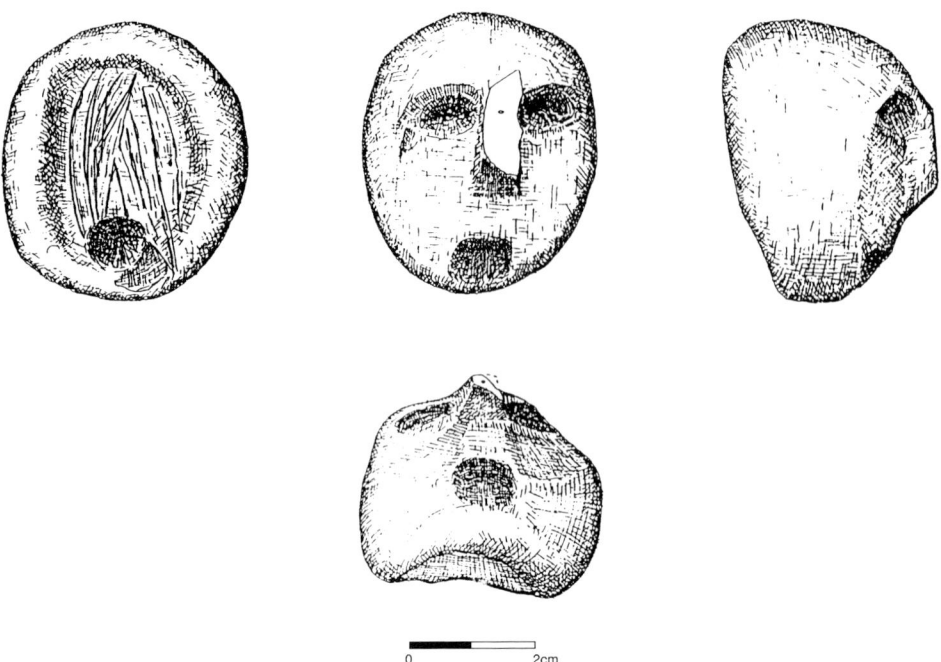

0   2cm.

Figure 11.2 A miniature stone mask from Nevali Çori (Hauptmann 1999, fig. 19).

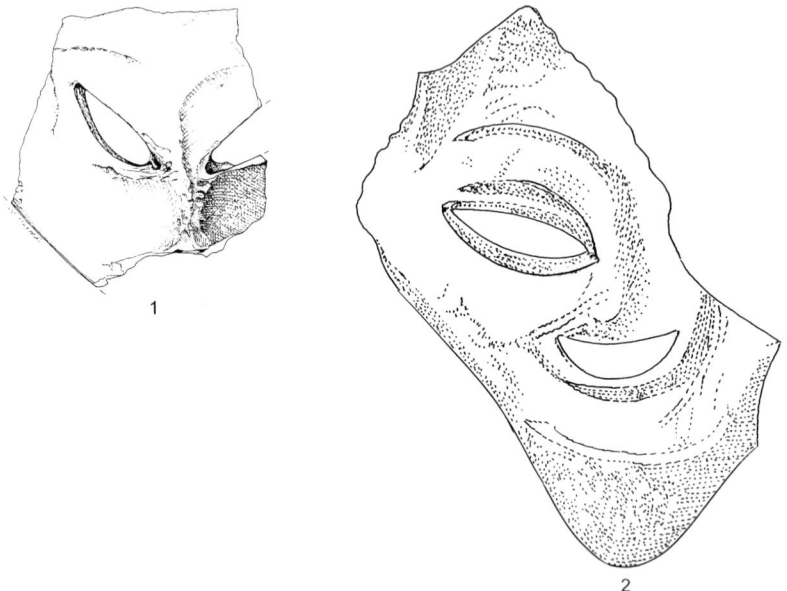

Figure 11.3 Pottery masks from Predynastic Egypt.

No.	Site	Reference
1	Hierakonpolis	Adams 1999, 31
2	Hierakonpolis	Adams 1999, 31

Tomb 16, we will not know if the masks were worn by the mourners as part of the elaborate funeral ceremony, or were made for use by the deceased" (Adams 1999, 31).

There are clearly three different groups of masks from the proto-historic Near East. Small differences can be found within each group of masks, but this should not surprise us, since the masks were hand-made rather than mass-produced. The first group, from the southern Levant, consists of six stone arte-facts dated to the PPNB of the seventh millennium BC. The stone masks were engraved from blocks of limestone. The items are all oval in shape, with rounded openings for the eyes; the mouth has an opening as well and usually has teeth; and a series of small holes on the item's circumference served for attachment. The second group consists of one item, the miniature rounded stone mask from Nevali Çori in the northern Levant. The third group consists of two pottery masks from Predynastic Egypt, dated to the fourth millennium BC. The pottery masks were modelled in clay and then fired. These masks are rhomboid in shape and have nostril depressions and elongated eyes.

The proto-historic stone and pottery masks unearthed in the Near East have commonly been interpreted as funerary items (Amiet 1980, 443, no. 160; Bar-Yosef 1985; Ornan 1986, 18–20; Arensburg & Hershkovitz 1988; Bar-Yosef & Alon 1988, 27; Adams 1999, 31). Some of the masks were indeed found with human skulls at the Nahal Hemar Cave and the Hierakonpolis cemetery. Nevertheless, masks were not associated with many PPNB graves and plastered or painted skulls found at various sites. The Nahal Hemar Cave was not a regular bur-ial ground and no complete human skeletons were found there. Hence, the site did not function as a cemetery, but was apparently used for the final dis-posal of the masks among other unwanted cultic objects, including decorated skulls, plastered statues, anthropomorphic figurines and a zoomorphic figur-ine (Garfinkel 1994).

Nevertheless, at Hierakonpolis the masks were found in a cemetery, an undisputed funerary con-text. However, in this case three aspects should be taken into consideration. Firstly, many thousands of Predynastic graves have been excavated over the years, at a considerable number of sites, but only two masks have been found so far; thus, the funerary use of masks was not a regular habit in Predynastic Egypt. Secondly, it is well known that Predynastic grave goods included a wealth of daily objects; thus, the masks probably belonged to the deceased during his life. Thirdly, these masks have openings for the eyes and mouth, features that do not typically occur in funerary masks.

In conclusion, it is most likely that the stone and clay masks from the proto-historic Near East were not burial accessories but performance masks used during various public ceremonies, as we shall see in the following discussion.

2 Depictions of People Wearing Masks

Beside the actual masks described earlier, there are a number of depictions from the proto-historic Near East that show human figures holding masks (one example) or wearing masks (several examples). In these depictions the masks are exag-gerated into an unrealistic size or shape or resem-ble animal heads. While in this period the human figure is usually depicted as a silhouette without any internal details, in the case of masks the eyes and sometimes the mouth openings are shown, an indication that masks are involved. Such depic-tions are reported from various sites and are usu-ally painted on pottery vessels. In one case they are engraved on basalt stone and at another site they are painted on walls.

My discussion starts with the painted sherds from Tepe Djowi, which are the best examples of this motif. The other examples are organized in chrono-logical order, from early to late:

a. Tepe Djowi (Figure 11.4). This site is located on the Susiana Plain, Khuzistan, western Iran and is dated to the second half of the sixth millennium BC (Le Breton 1947; Dollfus 1983). Two pottery sherds from the same vessel deriving from the earlier exca-vations depict a row of anthropomorphic figures holding masks. Due to its fragmentary state, this scene was overlooked and its unique importance remained unrecognized. For purposes of clarification, the

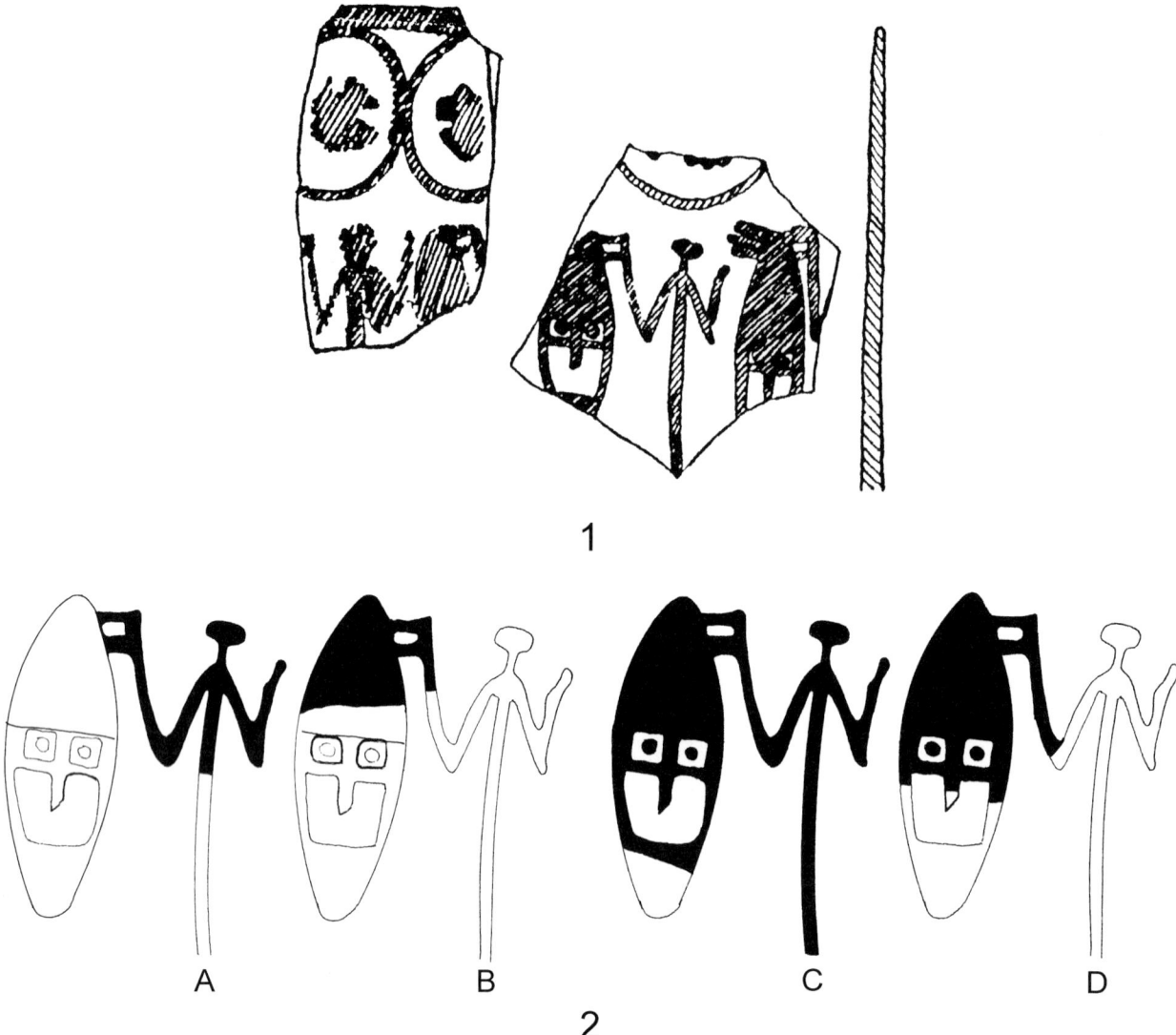

Figure 11.4 Painted pottery sherds with people holding masks from Tepe Djowi, Iran.

technical drawing (Figure 11.4:1) is presented with a schematic reconstruction (Figure 11.4:2). One can recognize four identical anthropomorphic figures (A–D), each holding a large mask. Of Figure A, only the upper part of the body has been preserved. Of Figure B, only part of the hand and the upper part of the mask have been preserved. Figure C, as well as a large part of the mask, has survived completely. Of Figure D, like Figure B, only the hand and part of the mask can be seen. It is possible that another painted pottery sherd from Choga Mish (Alizadeh 2008, pl. 19:c) bears the same motif.

The human figures are presented with their hands raised, each hand in a V-shape and the two hands together creating a W-shape. This body position is well known from various sites in the Khuzistan region of western Iran (Garfinkel 2000; 2003, 164–71). Masks with the same style of face were also found in this area in Choga Mish (Figure 11.8:1–2)

b. Dhuweila (Figure 11.5:1): This is a small campsite located in the Eastern Desert of Jordan. Some rock carvings were found in a PPNB layer dated to the eighth millennium BC. The carving was visible on stone slabs unearthed in the archaeological sediment. Most of the carvings depict animals, but one basalt slab displays a row of four human figures

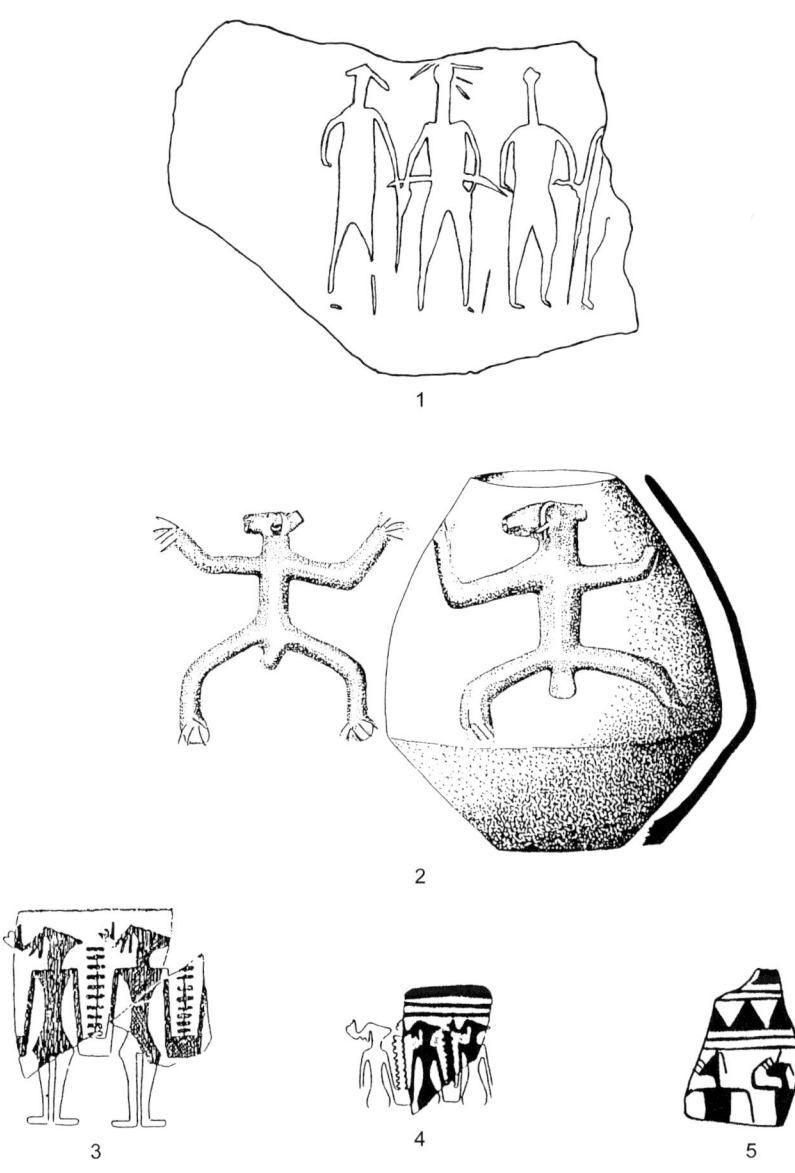

Figure 11.5 Depictions of masked people from the Neolithic and Chalcolithic Near East.

No.	Site	Reference
1	Dhuweila	Betts 1987; Garfinkel 2003, fig. 7.6a
2	'Ein el Jarba	Kaplan 1969, fig. 7; Garfinkel 2003, figs. 8.28–8.29
3	Tall-i Bakun A	Herzfeld 1932, fig. 1; Garfinkel 2003, fig. 9.32:a
4	Tall-i Bakun A	Alizadeh 1988, fig. 6:1; Garfinkel 2003, fig. 9.32:b
5	Tall-i Regi	Stein 1936, pl. XXV:19, Garfinkel 2003, fig. 9.32:e

presented *en face*, standing in a line and holding hands (Betts 1987; Betts et al. 1998, fig. 7.1). The bodies are relatively thin and tall with long necks, quite similar to each other. No specific gender characteristics are shown, but the general impression is that they are all male.

Each figure's head is portrayed somewhat differently. The head of the figure on the left is elongated like an animal's head. The second figure from the left seems to have a hat or a coiffure. The third has a very small head, and the head of the fourth figure has unfortunately been broken off. The heads

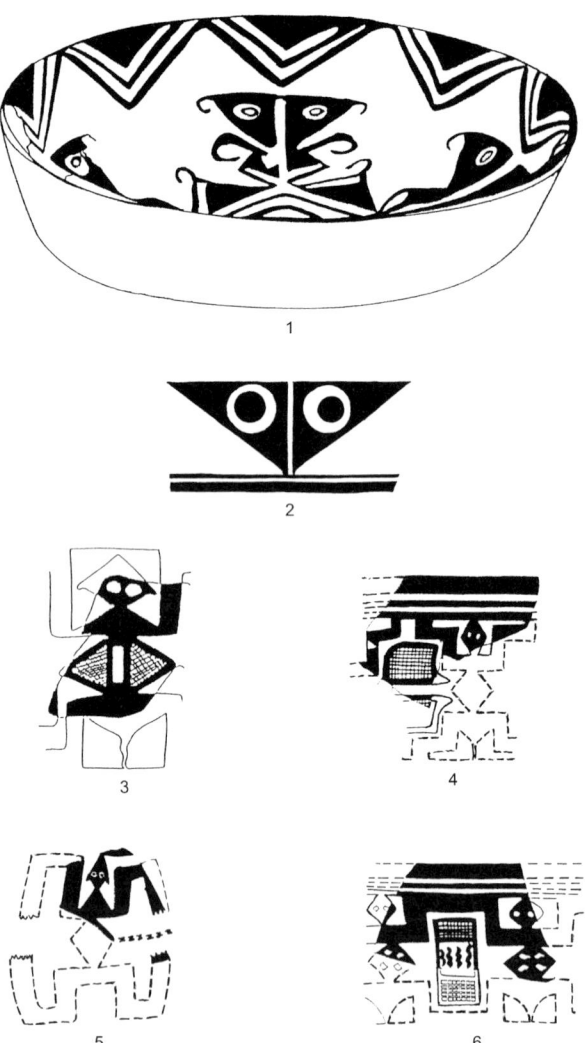

Figure 11.6 Depictions of masked people and masks from the Neolithic and Chalcolithic Near East.

No.	Site	Reference
1	Hacilar	Uzunoglu 1993, 67; Garfinkel 2003
2	Tepe Gawra	Tobler 1950, no. 450; Garfinkel 2003
3	Tall-i Bakun A	Langsdorff & McCown 1942, pl. 68:1; Garfinkel 2003, fig. 9.30a
4	Tall-i Bakun A	Langsdorff & McCown 1942, pl. 67:13; Garfinkel 2003, fig. 9.34b
5	Tall-i Bakun A	Langsdorff & McCown 1942, pl. 68:1; Garfinkel 2003, fig. 9.30b
6	Tall-i Bakun A	Langsdorff & McCown 1942, pl. 68:1; Garfinkel 2003, fig. 9.30c
7	Tall-i Bakun A	Langsdorff & McCown 1942, pl. 68:1; Garfinkel 2003, fig. 9.30d

are proportionally very small and give a generally non-human impression. Combinations of human bodies with non-human heads in the art of the proto-historic Near East have been interpreted as demons, demons with ibex horns, masked persons and bird-headed men (Herzfeld 1941, 30; Porada 1965, 32; Barnett 1966; Kaplan 1969;Fukai, Horiuchi & Matsutani 1974, 51). It seems to me that rather than being mythological demons, the figures at Dhuweila represent masked individuals. As mentioned earlier, actual masks have been discovered in contemporary PPNB sites in the Levant.

c. Hacilar (Figure 11.6:1). This site is located in central Anatolia and dated to the late seventh millennium BC (Mellaart 1970). An exhibition catalogue presents a carinated bowl that is described as "not an excavated find". The published photograph does not show the entire scene, but the supplementary text clarifies that the inner side of the bowl is divided into quarters "within each of which is depicted a stylized figure in abstract rectilinear form: Two of the figures, on opposite sides of the floor, have heads in the shape of inverted triangles, with rings, probably representing hair, hanging from the points. Eyes are round in shape. Upper arms are thick, forearms curl inwards in a spiral. Hips are triangular in shape. Legs are shown in cross bands. The two other figures have similar heads, but their arms are not shown. The figures resemble women" (Uzunoglu 1993, 67, item A-73).

The depiction on this bowl presents four figures in a circle, a classical dance configuration. The heads of these figures are grotesquely emphasized, indicating the usage of masks.

d. Domuztepe. This is a large village site located in south-east Turkey. From the Halafian culture, dated to the late sixth and early fifth millennia BC, a few fragments of the same vessel are decorated with a row of human figures wearing masks that imitate a horned animal, either goat or ibex (Carter 2012, 119, fig. 14a–b).

e. 'Ein el Jarba (Figure 11.5:2). This site is located in the Jezreel Valley of northern Israel. It is ascribed to the Wadi Rabah culture, generally dated to the sixth millennium BC, parallel to the Halafian culture (Garfinkel 1999, 104–52). A complete hole-mouth jar associated with a burial was discovered at the site (Kaplan 1969, 16; Meyerhof & Mozel 1981, 114; Garfinkel 1999, photo 62). Two large identical human figures modelled in clay were applied to both sides of the upper part of the jar. The heads are depicted in profile and facing left, thus indicating clockwise movement around the jar. The bodies are presented *en face*. Each figure has a masked animal head. The arms are stretched upwards, partly horizontal and partly

vertical, and end in fingers. The legs are separated, also partly horizontal and partly vertical, and end in toes. A projection below the loins indicates male gender. Three aspects of this depiction are especially noteworthy: 1) The dynamic body position of the figures indicates dancing. 2) The positions of the two figures on the vessel create a circle, a very prominent feature of dancing. 3) The figures are identical.

f. Tall-i Bakun A (Figures 11.5:3–4, 11.6:3–6). This site is located near Persepolis in Fars, Iran and dated to the first half of the fifth millennium BC. Various expeditions have worked at the site and large quantities of painted pottery with a remarkable wealth of designs have been unearthed. Two different painted styles depict human figures wearing masks. One group is characterized by standing human figures with stylized heads that look like animal heads (Figure 11.5:3–4). The second group is characterized by the depiction of human body parts as geometric shapes, creating a kind of 'Cubist' impression. Masked figures are a relatively common motif (Figure 11.6:3–6; Herzfeld 1932; Langsdorff & McCown 1942; Alizadeh 1988). The figures are presented in rows of identical figures, sometimes with linked arms and legs. Each individual is presented *en face* with raised arms, partly horizontally and partly vertically. The legs are separated, with their upper part horizontal and their lower part vertical. The grotesquely emphasized head and eyes indicate that the figures are wearing masks.

g. Tall-i Regi (Figure 11.5:5). This site is located near Khusu in Fars, Iran and is generally dated to the mid-fifth millennium BC. Sherds collected from the site's surface include a small sherd painted in a naturalistic style (Stein 1936, 201–2, pl. 25:27). The item includes the upper part of two human figures with elongated heads standing in a row, facing left. Their arms are bent, one upwards and touching the face and the other downwards.

h. Tuleilat el-Ghassul (Figure 11.7). This site is located in the lower Jordan Valley near the Dead

Figure 11.7 Wall paintings depicting masked people and a mask from Late Chalcolithic Tuleilat el-Ghassul.

No.	Site	Reference
1	Tuleilat el-Ghassul	Bienkowski 1991, 6; Garfinkel 2003, fig. 12.7b
2	Tuleilat el-Ghassul	Vincent 1935, fig. 18

Sea, Jordan. It was excavated by various expeditions and wall paintings depicting masked persons, dated to the Late Chalcolithic period of ca. 4,500–4,000 BC, were found during the excavations of the 1930s and the 1970s. The finds of the earlier excavations included fragments of four identical, heavily styled anthropomorphic heads with emphasized eyes and elongated noses (Mallon et al. 1934, 134, pls. 67–70). In the later excavations of the site a wall painting depicting a row of three people was found, each of the three wearing the same type of mask (Bienkowski 1991, 6). Altogether, seven human figures were reported from Tuleilat el-Ghassul, all of them with the same type of mask. It has been suggested that these masked figures were associated with shamanistic activity (Gilead 2002). However, since all the masks are identical, they apparently depict the community rather than an individual person.

3 Depictions of Masks

In this category, unlike the previous group, masks are shown as independent objects and are not associated with human figures. This motif is known mainly from proto-historic sites in Iran and on pottery vessels.

a. Choga Mish   (Figure 11.8:1–3). This site is located on the Susiana Plain, Khuzistan, western Iran. Large-scale excavations were conducted at this multi-period site during the 1960s and 1970s. Depictions of masks appear on a number of pottery sherds, dated to the fifth millennium BC (Delougaz & Kantor 1996, 236, pl. 217:I). Additional examples with the same motif were published in the second final excavation report (Alizadeh 2008, fig. 42:Q–R, pl. 19:D, I–J).

b. Khazineh   (Figure 11.9:1, 3–6). This site is located in southern Mesopotamia, in the Deh Luran

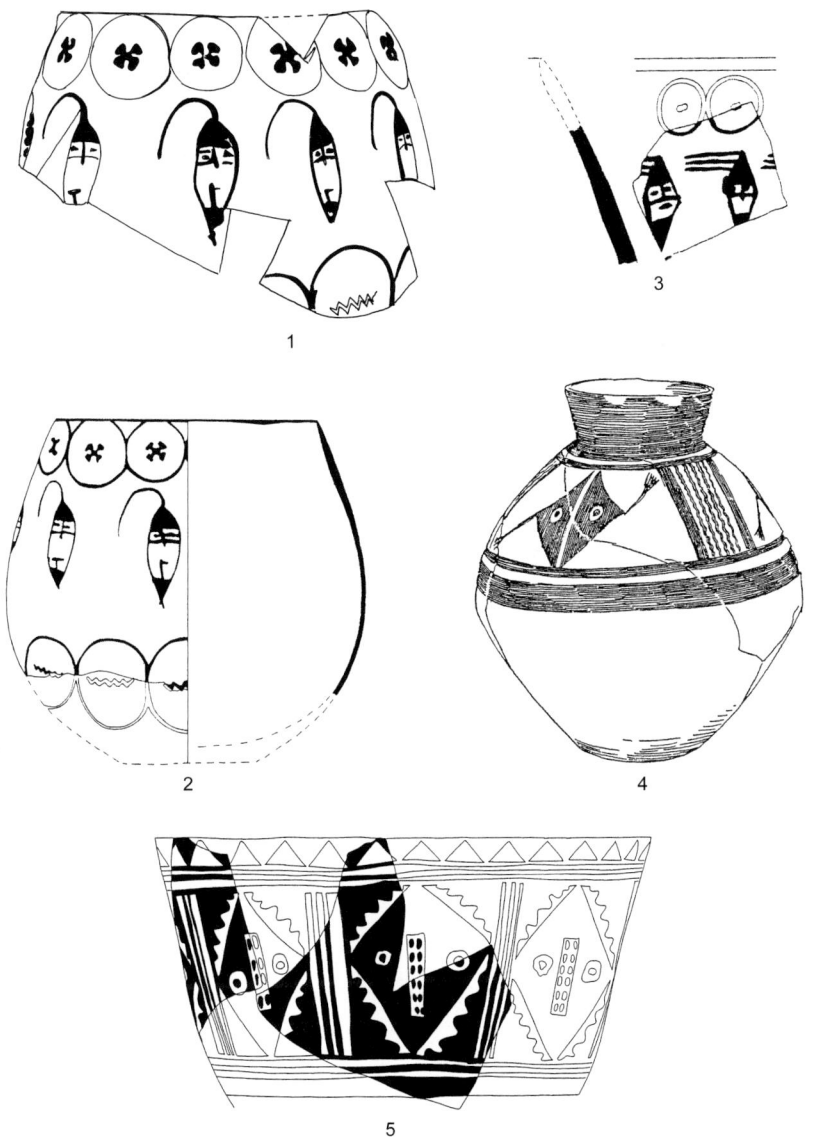

Figure 11.8 Painted pottery sherds depicting masks from Chalcolithic sites in the Near East.

No.	Site	Reference
1	Choga Mish	Delougaz & Kantor 1996, pl. 58A
2	Choga Mish	Delougaz & Kantor 1996, pl. 176:U
3	Choga Mish	Delougaz & Kantor 1996, pl. 176:T
4	Tall-I Bakun A	Herzfeld 1941, fig. 31
5	Tall-I Bakun A	Langsdorff & McCown 1942, pl. 34:1

Plain of western Iran. It has been excavated twice, at the beginning of the twentieth century and during the 1960s (Gautier & Lampre 1905; Hole, Flannery & Neely 1969, 68). It is dated to the second half of the sixth millennium BC. Only the first expedition reported items that are of relevance to us, each

depicting a single mask or a few identical masks in a horizontal row around the vessel.

c. Tepe Giyan (Figure 11.9:2). This site is located in Luristan, western Iran. A large sounding was carried out here in the early 1930s, including

Figure 11.9 Painted pottery sherds depicting masks from Chalcolithic sites in the Near East.

No.	Site	Reference
1	Khazineh	Gautier & Lampre 1905
2	Tepe Giyan	Unpublished, collection of the Musée de Louvre
3	Khazineh	Gautier & Lampre 1905
4	Khazineh	Unpublished, collection of the Musée de Louvre
5	Khazineh	Unpublished, collection of the Musée de Louvre
6	Khazineh	Gautier & Lampre 1905
7	Domuztepe	Campbell 1999, 3

a deep sounding about 20 meters below the top-soil (Contenau & Ghirshman 1935). In the storage rooms of the Musée de Louvre, Paris, I discerned an unpublished sherd from these excavations that is of relevance to our subject. It is a fragment of a bowl of Black-on-Buff Ware with a complex decoration. It was first painted with a rectangular 'structure'. After this, two rounded bulbs of clay were applied to the surface next to the 'structure' on its right. These were then painted, and finally the vessel was fired.

The applied decoration creates emphatic eyes in relief that have a much stronger effect than merely painted eyes.

d. Tall–i Bakun A (Figures 11.8:1, 11.8:5). This site is located near Persepolis in Fars, Iran and is dated to the first half of the fifth millennium BC. Various publications show pottery vessels with depictions of masks (Herzfeld 1932, fig. 31; Langsdorff & McCown 1942, pl. 34:1). The depictions are sometimes rather schematic and it is quite hard to recognize the motif (Langsdorff & McCown 1942, pl. 33:14, 16).

e. Tepe Gawra (Figure 11.6:2). This site is located in central Mesopotamia. From Stratum XV of the fifth millennium BC, a rim fragment of a pottery bowl with a painted design was reported. No illustration of the item itself was published, but a schematic composition showing a triangle-like stylized human head with two large emphasized eyes was presented (Tobler 1950, pl. CXLIX:450). This head is quite similar to the heads of the aforementioned bowl from Hacilar (Figure 11.6:1).

f. Domuztepe (Figure 11.9:7). This site has been described earlier in this chapter. From the Halafian culture, dated to the late sixth and early fifth millennia BC, a few fragments of pottery vessels are decorated with a row of masks (Campbell 1999, 3; Carter 2012, figs. 13a lower, 13b). One complete mask and half of another are preserved on the item presented here in Figure 11.9:7.

4 Figurines Wearing Masks

Three-dimensional depictions of human figures clearly wearing masks are known from the ancient Near East. Such examples have been unearthed in the deposits of the sanctuary of Apollo at Kourion, Cyprus, dated to the mid-first millennium BC (Young & Young 1955, pl. 11, 814, 816, 825; Karageorghis 1971). It has been suggested from time to time that Neolithic or Chalcolithic figurines that have unrealistic heads or faces, or human figures with animal heads, are actually wearing masks (Sorell 1973, 7). A systematic approach to this claim, based

on figurines from south-east Europe, has been developed by Gimbutas (1982, 57–66), but lies beyond the geographical boundaries of our presentation. In the proto-historic Near East such claims have been made for some specific items, as noted later in this chapter. However, such cases have sometimes been interpreted as figures of demons (Porada 1965, 32; von der Osten-Sacken 1992).

a. Sha'ar Hagolan. This site, dated to the sixth millennium BC, is located in the central Jordan Valley, Israel, and produced one of the richest assemblages of prehistoric art ever unearthed in the Near East. A large number of both clay figurines with elongated heads and diagonal eyes and pebble figurines with either horizontal or diagonal eyes has been found. It has been suggested that the items with diagonal eyes represent masked figures (Stekelis 1972, 30; Yevin & Mozel 1977).

b. Iran. A copper statue of a human figure with a goat's head has been understood as a masked figure (Barnett 1966).

c. Items from South-East Europe. It is quite common to interpret human figurines with 'strange' heads as people wearing masks (Gimbutas 1982, 57–66).

From these data, some patterns of behaviour can be discerned:

1. In almost all cases a number of masks are represented, whether actual masks or depictions. In Nahal Hemar two such items were found. Two masks were found in the same location at Hierakonpolis, Egypt. It is plausible that the three Neolithic stone masks in a private collection were found together as well. The pottery vessels from various sites and the wall paintings from Tuleilat el-Ghassul always depict a number of masks or masked persons performing together. This indicates that the masks were used in public ceremonies.

2. In any given assemblage, all the figures usually wear the same type of mask. In the Nahal Hemar Cave the two masks, at least the parts that have survived, are typologically identical. All of the

three Neolithic stone masks in a private collection are quite similar. The same can be said for the various depictions of masks on pottery sherds. It thus seems likely that in any given ceremony all the participants were wearing identical masks.

3. In the depiction of masks, or people wearing masks, information on the location of the ceremony is occasionally given. In these cases the people or masks are shown near a net-covered geometric feature. Such items are commonly interpreted as structures, temples in this case (Figure 11.9:1–2; Garfinkel 2000, 2003, 54–7).

This interpretation is supported by later examples from the ancient Near East, in which most of the performing masks or depictions of masked persons are associated with temples. Such examples are known from Late Bronze Age Hazor (Yadin 1972, 73, pl. XVa–b), Late Bronze Age Enkomi and Kition in Cyprus (Nys 1995), Iron Age Tell Qasile (Mazar 1980, 84–5), the first-millennium BC sanctuary of Apollo at Kourion, Cyprus (Young & Young 1955; Karageorghis 1971) and the Ptolemaic temple of Hathor at Dendera, Egypt (Wolinski 1986; Sweeney 1993). In no case are masks shown on dead bodies in mortuary ceremonies or hanging on structures; they are always associated with human figures.

4. A very small number of masks has survived from the proto-historic Near East: nine from the southern Levant and only two from Predynastic Egypt. In Iran and northern Mesopotamia, where mask depictions are quite common, no actual masks have been found. Why are masks so rare in the archaeological record? It seems likely that masks were generally made of organic, perishable materials, and hence have not survived.

5. In the depictions of masked persons, they are associated with movement and dancing poses. Masks are sometimes depicted on pottery vessels with the hair in a somewhat upright position. On round pottery vessels we have a circle of masks with the hair indicating a turning movement in a circle of dancing. Even the direction of movement (counter-clockwise) can be deduced.

6. The masks from Nahal Hemar, thanks to the dry climate of the region, preserve evidence of rich,

painted decoration as well as the attachment of hair. The performance mask was a composite artefact and was elaborately decorated.

7. Much energy was invested in the manufacture of the stone masks, including delicate carving to create the openings for the eyes and the toothed mouth, as well as the drilling of small attachment holes. The mask from Basta, which was broken during work, and the two unfinished items from Er-Ram and the private collection clearly indicate that their manufacture was not easy. It was probably executed by specialists.

8. The use of masks seems to have a gender dimension. It is usually male figures who are depicted with masks. In ethnographic observations of non-state societies, it is the men who are usually involved with the preparation and use of masks.

In conclusion, the archaeological data indicate that multiple masks were used simultaneously in any given event, that the masks were basically identical, that they were usually made of organic materials, and that they were associated with dancing, sometimes near structures (temples).

DANCING WITH MASKS IN TRADITIONAL SOCIETIES

Masks and mask-like effects (headgear or heavy face decoration) are very common in traditional societies and are known from almost every part of the globe.

Africa: Masks have been reported from large parts of Africa and are extensively used in tribal ceremonies (see, for example, Lommel 1972, 9–54; Balandier & Maquet 1974, 225–8; Segy 1976; Adler 1982). However, masks are not used in ritual ceremonies of the urban Islamic communities of North Africa or by the San hunter-gatherers of South Africa.

Asia: Masks are known from various parts of Asia, including Ceylon, India, Papua New Guinea, Indonesia and Siberia (see, for example, Valentine 1961; Höpfner 1969; Lommel 1972, 77–124; Emigh 1996). A large body of data is available on the use of masks in Papua New Guinea. The Awanga wear a woven face mask with a white shell over the nose; photographs of a number of such masked figures can be seen in the publication by Whitehouse (1995, figs. 12, 15, 17).

In the urban societies of the Far East, masks are used in a more restricted way, mainly in specific festivals and theatre or theatre-like situations (see, for example, Lucas 1973; Tribhuwan & Savelli 2003). We have no examples of an entire community dancing with identical masks. Masks do not form an integral part of Islamic or Jewish rituals. During his excavations at Khorsabad in Iraqi Kurdistan, Henry Frankfort witnessed a ceremony including music, dance, special dress, headgear and heavy face decoration. This non-Islamic ritual was interpreted by him as a relict from much earlier times, originating in the traditions of the ancient Near East (Frankfort 1934).

North and Central America: The Native Americans frequently used masks. A well-known group is the masks of the Northwest Coast, from Alaska, Canada and Washington State, treated extensively by many scholars (see, for example, Boaz 1890; Lommel 1972, 125–40; Lévi-Strauss 1975; Emmons 1991, 337–80). Masks are known from other parts of North America (Lommel 1972, 141–56) and from Central America (Lommel 1972, 167–78); in a photograph of the Tarascos Indians from Mexico, one can see a group of people who all have the same hair dress, the same mask and the same clothing, and all hold an identical stick in their hands. Some of the North American tribes were complex hunter-gatherers, showing that masks were not restricted to agricultural communities.

South America: In remote areas, outside the strong influence of Christian urban societies, masked performances are still carried out by local Indian tribes (Lommel 1972, 157–66).

Oceania: The traditional societies of Melanesia and Polynesia produced and used masks on various occasions (Lommel 1972, 56–60). In a drawing made in 1789, a boat from the Sandwich Islands with 10 identically masked rowers is depicted.

Australia: Australian Aboriginals, like many other hunter-gatherer societies, do not use masks. However, they quite often use headgear and heavy face decoration in their ceremonies. Such examples can be seen in photographs taken by Spencer at the beginning of the twentieth century. In one case a male group is performing a dance and the figures are painted in almost identical fashion (Vanderwal 1982, 38–9). In another case a female group is dancing, and again the entire group is painted in the same pattern (Vanderwal 1982, 40–1). In each of these ceremonies the participants are identical in their appearance and the accessories used.

Europe: Masks are known in Europe; they are not part of the Christian liturgy but are used in specific carnivals (Lommel 1972, 197–212; Glotz 1975) or in theatre performances (Mamczarz 1999).

From this short survey, it is clear that when masks are used in the popular domain rather than specialized theatre, they are usually associated with tribal communities. A clear pattern emerges from the various observations on masks used in tribal communities:

1. Masks are used in public ceremonies and a large number of such items is used simultaneously.
2. In the ceremony all the masks are usually identical (see, for example, Ottenberg 1975, figs. 64, 69, pl. XV; Adler 1982, frontispiece; Emigh 1996, fig. 6).
3. The items are usually made of perishable materials. There are three possible main reasons for this: a) it is easier to work with wood, leather and other organic materials than to sculpt a stone item; b) the use of a large variety of materials, with different colours and textures, enables a rich and extravagant result; c) the final item is lightweight, making it easier to use.
4. The masks are generally used during long ceremonies.
5. They must be practical, enabling the wearer to see, breathe and speak. Since ritual performances usually include dancing and singing, the mask must be attached to the face in a stable and comfortable manner during the entire ceremony.
6. Mask performance is associated with dance, a connection that is reinforced by almost all ethnographic observations (see discussion in Sorell 1973, 117–57). Movement has always been an essential

means of giving additional meaning and potency to the mask (Sorell 1973). Dance, as observed by many scholars, is an important component in every tribal community (see, for example, Sachs 1952; Lange 1976; Hanna 1987; Garfinkel 1998, 2003).

DISCUSSION

From the analysis of the data presented so far, consisting of actual masks, depictions of masks or people wearing masks, together with ethnographic observations, the following conclusions emerge:

1. From the ethnographic data, it is clear that many hunter-gatherers do not manufacture or perform with masks. This was observed both with regard to South Africa and for Australian Aborigines. However, note that amongst complex hunter-gatherers, such as some Native American groups, this was common (see earlier in this chapter). It is also noteworthy that the Mesolithic people at Star Carr were hunter-gatherers and also evidently made use of masks. However, Palaeolithic material culture so far contains no masks or unequivocal depictions of human figures wearing masks (though figurines do universally lack individually-identifying facial features).

2. Urban cultures do not use masks as part of the official rituals in churches, synagogues or mosques. There are certain festivals during which masks may be worn, but they are restricted to a very specific day or place. In the same way, we have few examples of people wearing masks in the art of the ancient Near East. On cylinder seals from Mesopotamia, of which we have thousands of examples, there are no clear human figures wearing masks. I am aware of only one seal that may depict a masked person, represented in a body motion suggesting dancing near a musical instrument (Amiet 1961, no. 1443).

3. Masks are well documented in tribal communities all over the world. The Neolithic and Chalcolithic communities of the proto-historic Near East shared a similar socio-economic organization: they were no longer hunter-gatherers, but had not yet developed urban societies. It is in this particular phase that we see the appearance of masks, in the form of actual masks or depictions of people wearing masks, in the archaeological record.

4. In the ample photographic documentation of mask performances in tribal communities, all the participants usually wear identical masks (see, for example, Emigh 1996, fig. 6). In the same way, the stone masks of the PPNB are very similar to each other, as are the two Predynastic pottery masks from Egypt. The Neolithic and Chalcolithic depictions of masks or human wearing masks also show identical masks in any given scene. This is unlikely to be a coincidence and must represent an important aspect of mask performances.

It seems to me that the main unanswered question is why both recent and ancient tribal communities frequently used masks, and why the masks were identical. In order to answer this question, we need to understand the qualities of masks and dance in tribal communities.

Masks are an extremely important component in many dances and festivals the world over (Sachs 1952, 131–8; Napier 1987; Cohen 1998, vol. 4:286–306). The unique contribution of masks to public ceremonies has been described as follows: "Masks may be indicated as the most expressive sign of festival, since they have an especially complex and important symbolic value. In fact, they 'mask', i.e. hide, the identity of the person wearing them, but at the same time they reveal another persona by bringing to the outside what in daily life is an invisible entity, a hidden double personality, or a secret dream. Furthermore, masks manifest artifice itself; they signal by their mere presence that a representation is being held, a symbolic message is being conveyed" (Napier 1987, 211).

The tremendous energy created during tribal ceremonies is a tool creating unity and ethnic identity. It is thus a dramatic and ecstatic experience. The message conveyed is 'group' or 'community' rather than 'individual'. The use of identical masks intensifies this message. The wearing of the masks eliminates the individuality of the participants and creates instead a group whose members are identical.

REFERENCES

Adams, N. 1999. Unprecedented discoveries at Hierakonpolis. *Egyptian Archaeology* 15: 29–31.

Adler, A. 1982. *La mort est le masque du roi. La royauté sacrée des Moundang du Tchad*. Paris: Payot.

Alizadeh, A. 1988. Socio-economic complexity in southwestern Iran during the fifth and fourth millennia B.C.: the evidence from Tall-i Bakun A. *Iran* 26: 17–34.

Alizadeh, A. 2008. *Chogha Mish II. Final Report on the Last Six Seasons of Excavations, 1972–1978*. Oriental Institute Publications 130. Chicago: The Oriental Institute.

Amiet, P. 1961. *La glyptique mésopotamienne archaïque*. Paris: Centre National de la Recherche Scientifique.

Amiet, P. 1980. *Art of the Ancient Near East*. New York: Abrams.

Arensburg, B. & Hershkovitz, I. 1988. Nahal Hemar Cave, Neolithic human remains. *'Atiqot* 18: 50–8.

Balandier, G. & Maquet, J. 1974. *Dictionary of Black African Civilization*. New York: Leon Amiel.

Barkay, G. & Noy, T. 1987. On R. Gophna et al.: A forgotten mask from Er-Ram in the land of Benjamin. *Qadmoniot* 77–8: 57 (Hebrew).

Barnett, R. D. 1966. Homme masqué ou dieu-ibex? *Syria* 43: 259–76.

Bar-Yosef, O. 1985. *A Cave in the Desert: Nahal Hemar* (Catalogue No. 258). Jerusalem: Israel Museum.

Bar-Yosef, O. 2003. Early Neolithic stone masks. In Özdoğan, M., Hauptmann, H. & Başgellen, N. (eds.) *From Village to Cities. Early Villages in the Near East*. Studies Presented to Ufuk Esin, pp. 73–86. Istanbul: Arkeoloji ve Sanat Yayinlari.

Bar-Yosef, O. & Alon, D. 1988. *Nahal Hemar Cave*. 'Atiqot 18 (English series). Jerusalem: Israel Department of Antiquities and Museums.

Bédouin, T.-L. 1961. *Les masques*. Paris: Presses Universitaires de France.

Beeman, W. O. 1993. The anthropology of theater and spectacle. *Annual Review of Anthropology* 22: 369–93.

Betts, A. V. G. 1987. The hunter's perspective: 7th millennium BC rock carvings from eastern Jordan. *World Archaeology* 19: 214–25.

Betts, A.V. G. et al. 1998. *The Harra and the Hamad. Excavations and Explorations in Eastern Jordan*. Sheffield: Sheffield Academic Press.

Bienert, H. D. 1990. The Er-Ram mask at the Palestine Exploration Fund, London. *Oxford Journal of Archaeology* 9: 257–61.

Bienkowski, P. 1991. *Treasures from an Ancient Land. The Art of Jordan*. Merseyside: Alan Sutton Publishing Ltd.

Biesele, E. M. 1978. Religion and folklore. In Tobias, P. V. (ed.). *The Bushmen. San Hunters and Herders of Southern Africa*, pp. 162–72. Cape Town and Pretoria: Human and Rousseau.

Birch, M. C. 1974. *Pheromones*. Frontiers of Biology, Vol. 32. Amsterdam and London: North-Holland Publishing Company.

Birket-Smith, K. 1953. *The Chugach Eskimo*. Copenhagen: National Museum.

Blacking, J. 1976. Dance, conceptual thought and production in the archaeological record. In Sieveking, G. de G., Longworth, I. H. & Wilson, K. E. (eds.) *Problems in Economic and Social Archaeology*, pp. 3–13. London: Duckworth.

Bloch, M. 1989. *Ritual, History and Power*. Monographs on Social Anthropology 58. London: London School of Economics.

Boaz, F. 1890. *The Use of Masks and Head-Ornaments on the North-West Coast of America*. Leiden: S.N.

Bourguignon, E. (ed.) 1973. *Religion, Altered States of Consciousness, and Social Change*. Columbus: Ohio State University Press.

Bowie, F. 2000. *The Anthropology of Religion*. Oxford: Blackwell.

Brockett, O. G. 1969. *The Theater: An Introduction*. New York: Holt Rinehart and Winston.

Brockett, O. G. 1991. *History of the Theatre*. Boston: Allyn and Bacon.

Campbell, S. 1999. Domuztepe 1999. *Anatolian Archaeology* (Research Reports of the British Institute of Archaeology at Ankara) 5: 2–3.

Carter, E. 2012. On human and animal sacrifice in the Late Neolithic at Domuztepe. In Porter, A. M. & Schwartz, G. M. (eds.) *Sacred Killing. The Archaeology of Sacrifice in the Ancient Near East*, pp. 97–124. Winona Lake, IN: Eisenbrauns.

Chaplin, T. 1890. A stone mask from Er-Ram. *Palestine Exploration Fund Quarterly* 23: 268–9.

Cintas, P. 1946. *Amulettes puniques*. Tunis: Institut des Hautes Etudes de Tunis.

Clark, J. G. D. 1954. *Excavations at Star Carr. An Early Mesolithic Site at Seamer near Scarborough, Yorkshire*. Cambridge: Cambridge University Press.

Cohen, S. J. (ed.) 1998. *International Encyclopedia of Dance*. 6 vols. New York: Oxford University Press.

Contenau, G. & Ghirshman, R. 1935. *Fouilles du Tepe Giyan*. Paris: Librairie Orientaliste Paul Geuthner.

Coppet, D. de. (ed.) 1992. *Understanding Rituals*. London: Routledge.

Culican, W. 1975. Some Phoenician masks and other terracottas. *Berytus* 24: 47–87.

Curtis, J. 1995. Gold face-masks in the ancient Near East. In Campbell, S. & Green, A. (eds.) *The Archaeology of Death in the Ancient Near East*, pp. 226–31. Oxford: Oxbow.

Dayagi-Mendeles, M. 2002. *The Akhziv Cemeteries. The Ben-Dor Excavations, 1941–1944*. IAA Reports 15. Jerusalem: Israel Antiquities Authority.

Delougaz, P. & Kantor, H. J. 1996. *Chogha Mish I. The First Five Seasons of Excavations 1961–1971*. Oriental Institute Publications 101. Chicago: The Oriental Institute.

Dollfus, J. 1983. Tepe Djowi: contrôle stratigraphique, 1975. *Cahiers de la Délégation Archéologique Française en Iran* 13: 17–131.

Durkheim, E. 1912. *The Elementary Forms of Religious Life*. New York: Free Press.

Emigh, J. 1996. *Masked Performance. The Play of Self and Other in Ritual and Theatre*. Philadelphia: University of Philadelphia Press.

Emmons, G. T. 1991. *The Tlingit Indians*. Seattle: University of Washington Press.

Evans-Pritchard, E. E. 1928. The dance. *Africa* 1: 446–62.

Evans-Pritchard, E. E. 1937. *Witchcraft, Oracles and Magic among the Azande*. Oxford: Oxford University Press.

Flannery, K. V. 1972. The cultural evolution of civilizations. *Annual Review of Ecology and Systematics* 3: 399–426.

Fraioli, F,. Moretti, C., Paolucci, D., Alicicco, E., Crescenzi, F. & Fortunio, G. 1980. Physical exercise stimulates marked concomitant release of β-endorphin and Adrenocorticotropic Hormone (ACTH) in peripheral blood in man. *Experientia* 36: 987–9.

Frankfort, H. 1934. A Tammuz ritual in Kurdistan. *Iraq* 1: 137–45.

Frazer, J. G. 1911. *The Golden Bough: A Study in Comparative Religion*. London: Macmillan.

Frisch, K. von 1967. *The Dance Language and Orientation of Bees*. Cambridge, MA: Belknap Press of Harvard University.

Fukai, S., Horiuchi, K. & Matsutani, T. 1974. *Telul eth Thalathat*, Vol. III. *The Excavation of Tell V*. The Tokyo University Iraq-Iran Archaeological Expedition Report 15. Tokyo: The Institute of Oriental Culture.

Garfield, V. E. & Wingert, P. S. 1966. *The Tsimshian Indians and Their Arts*. Seattle: University of Washington Press.

Garfinkel, Y. 1994. Ritual burial of cultic objects, the earliest evidence. *Cambridge Archaeological Journal* 4: 159–88.

Garfinkel, Y. 1998. Dancing and the beginning of art scenes in the early village communities of the Near East and Southeast Europe. *Cambridge Archaeological Journal* 8/2: 207–37.

Garfinkel, Y. 1999. *Neolithic and Chalcolithic Pottery of the Southern Levant*. Qedem 39. Jerusalem: Institute of Archaeology, Hebrew University.

Garfinkel, Y. 2000. The Khazineh painted style of western Iran. *Iran* 37: 57–69.

Garfinkel, Y. 2003. *Dance at the Dawn of Agriculture*. Austin: Texas University Press.

Garfinkel, Y. 2005. Dancing diamonds. *Iran* 43: 117–33.

Garfinkel, Y. 2010. Dance in prehistoric Europe. *Documenta Praehistorica* 37: 205–14.

Gautier, J. E. & Lampre, G. 1905. Fouilles de Moussian. *Mémoires de la Délégation Archéologique en Perse* 8: 59–148.

Gerbrands A. A. 1978. Talania and Nake, master carver and apprentice: two woodcarvers from the Kilenge (western New Britain). In Greenhalgh, M. & Megaw, V. (eds.) *Art in Society. Studies in Style, Culture and Aesthetics*, pp. 193–205. London: Duckworth.

Gilead, I. 2002. Religio-magic behavior in the Chalcolithic period of Palestine. In Oren, E. D. & Ahituv, S. (eds.) *Studies in Archaeology and Related Disciplines. Aharon Kempinski Memorial Volume*, pp. 103–28. Beersheva: Ben-Gurion University.

Gimbutas, M. A. 1982. *The Goddesses and Gods of Old Europe 6500–3500 B.C., Myths and Cult Images*. Berkeley: University of California.

Gimbutas, M. A. 1989. *The Language of the Goddess*. London: Thames and Hudson.

Glazier, S. D. (ed.) 1997. *Anthropology of Religion: A Handbook*. Westport/London: Praeger.

Glotz, S. (ed.) 1975. *Le masque dans la tradition européenne*. Binche: Musée international du carnaval et de masque.

Gophna, R., Lev-Yadon, S. & Lifschitz, N. 1986. A forgotten mask from Er-Ram in the land of Benjamin. *Qadmoniot* 75–6: 82–3 (Hebrew).

Gregor, J. 1937. *Masks of the World. An Historical and Pictorial Survey of Many Types and Times* (republished 1968). New York: Benjamin Blom Inc.

Grimes, R. L. 1985. *Research in Ritual Studies: A Programmatic Essay and Bibliography*. Metuchen, NJ: Scarecrow Press.

Gruber, N. I. 1981. Ten dance-derived expressions in the Hebrew Bible. *Biblica* 62: 328–46.

Guiart, J. 1966. *Mythologie du masque en nouvelle-Calédonie*. Publications de la Société des Océanistes No. 18. Paris: Musée de l'Homme.

Hahner-Herzog, I., Kecskési, M., Vajda, L. & Gabriel, J. W. 1998. *African Masks from the Barbier-Mueller Collection, Geneva*. Munich: Prestel.

Hanna, J. L. 1979. Toward a cross-cultural conceptualization of dance and some correlate considerations. In Blacking, J. & Kealinohomoku, J. W. (eds.) *The Performing Arts. Music and Dance*, pp. 17–45. The Hague: Mouton Publishers.

Hanna, J. L. 1987. Dance and religion. In Eliade, M. (ed.) *Encyclopedia of Religion*, Vol. 4:203–12. New York: MacMillan.

Harley, G. W. 1950. *Masks as Agents of Social Control in Northeast Liberia*. Cambridge: Peabody Museum, Harvard University.

Hartmann, G. 1967. *Masken südamerikanischer Naturvölker*. Berlin: Museum für Völkerkunde.

Hauptmann, H. 1993. Ein Kultgebäude in Nevali Çori. In Frangipane, M., Hauptmann, H., Liverani, M., Matthiae, P. & Mellink, M. (eds.) *Between the Rivers and Over the Mountains*, pp. 37–69. Rome: Universita di Roma.

Hauptmann, H. 1999. The Urfa region. In Ozdogan, M. & Basgelen, N. (eds.) *Neolithic in Turkey*, pp. 65–86. Istanbul: Arkeoloji ve Sanat Yayinlari.

Hermansen, B. D. 1997. Art and ritual behaviour in Neolithic Basta. In Gebel, H. G. K. & Rollefson, G. O. (eds.) *The Prehistory of Jordan, II. Perspectives from 1997*, pp. 333–43. Studies in Early Near Eastern Production, Subsistence, and Environment 4. Berlin: ex oriente.

Herzfeld, E. 1932. *Iranische Denkmäler*. Berlin: Dietrich Reimer and Ernst Vohsen.

Herzfeld, E. 1941. *Iran in the Ancient East*. London: Oxford University Press.

Holas, B. 1952. *Les masques Kono (haute-Guinée Française). Leur rôle dans la vie religieuse et politique*. Paris: Librairie Orientaliste Paul Geuthner.

Hole, F., Flannery, K. V. & Neely, J. A. 1969. *Prehistory and Human Ecology of the Deh Luran Plain. An Early Village Sequence from Khuzistan, Iran*. Memoirs of the Museum of Anthropology, No. 1. Ann Arbor: University of Michigan.

Höpfner, G. 1969. *Masken aus Ceylon*. Berlin: Museum für Völkerkunde.

Kaeppler, A. L. 1992. Dance. In Bauman, R. (ed.) *Folklore, Cultural Performances, and Popular Entertainments*, pp. 196–203. Oxford: Oxford University Press.

Kaplan, J. 1969. 'Ein El-Jarba. Chalcolithic remains in the Plain of Esdraelon. *Bulletin of the American Schools of Oriental Research* 194: 2–39.

Karageorghis, V. 1971. Notes on some Cypriote priests wearing bull-masks. *Harvard Theological Review* 64: 261–70.

Karlson, P. & Lüscher, M. 1959. Pheromones: a new term for a class of biologically active substances. *Nature* 183: 55–6.

Katz, R. 1982. *Boiling Energy. Community Healing among the Kalahari Kung*. Cambridge, MA: Harvard University Press.

Kyriakidis, E., ed. 2007. *The Archaeology of Ritual*. Los Angeles: Cotsen Institute of Archaeology UCLA Publications.

Lange, R. 1976. *The Nature of Dance. An Anthropological Perspective*. New York: International Publications Service.

Langsdorff, A. & McCown, D. E. 1942. *Tall-I-Bakun A, Season of 1932*. The University of Chicago, Oriental Institute Publications 59. Chicago: University of Chicago Press.

Le Breton, L. 1947. Note sur la céramique peinte aux environs de Suse et à Suse. *Mémoires de la Mission Archéologique en Iran* 30: 120–219. Paris: Presses Universitaires de France.

Leroi-Gourhan, A. 1967. *Treasures of Prehistoric Art*. New York: H. N. Abrams.

Lévi-Strauss, C. 1962. *The Savage Mind* (republished in 1976). London: Weidenfeld and Nicolson.

Lévi-Strauss, C. 1975. *The Way of the Masks*. Seattle: University of Washington Press (English edition 1982).

Lommel, A. 1972. *Masks: Their Meaning and Function*. London: Paul Elek Books.

Louis, M. 1955. Les origines préhistoriques de la danse. *Cahiers Ligures de Préhistoire et d'Archéology* 4: 3–37.

Lucas, H. 1973. *Java Maskem. Der Tanz auf einem Bein*. Kassel: Erich Röth-Verlag.

Mack, J. 1994. *Masks. The Art of Expression*. London: British Museum Press.

Malinowski, B. 1948. *Magic, Science and Religion and Other Essays*. London: Souvenir Press.

Mallon, A., Koeppel, R. & Neuvill, R. 1934. *Teleilat Ghassul I: Compte rendu des fouilles de l'Institut Biblique Pontifical 1929–1932*. Rome: Pontifical Biblical Institute.

Mamczarz, I. 1999. *Le masque et l'âme: de l'improvisation á la création theâtrale*. Paris: Klincksieck.

Marcus, J. & Flannery, K. V. 1994. Ancient Zapotec ritual and religion: an application of the direct historical approach. In Renfrew, C. & Zubrow, E. B. W. (eds.) *The Ancient Mind. Elements of Cognitive Archaeology*, pp. 55–74. Cambridge: Cambridge University Press.

Marshall, L. 1969. The medicine dance of the !Kung bushmen. *Africa* 39: 347–81.

Mazar, A. 1980. *Excavations at Tell Qasile Vol. 1. The Philistine Sanctuary: Architecture and Cult Objects*. Qedem 12. Jerusalem: Institute of Archaeology, Hebrew University of Jerusalem.

McNeill, W. H. 1995. *Keeping Together in Time. Dance and Drill in Human History*. Cambridge, MA: Harvard University Press.

Mellaart, J. 1970. *Excavations at Hacilar*. Edinburgh: The British Institute of Archaeology at Ankara.

Meyerhof, E. & Mozel, I. 1981. A new interpretation of the applied figurines on the jar from Ein el-Jarba, near Tell Abu Zureiq, Israel. *Bollettino del Centro Camuno di Studi Preistorici* 8: 114–16.

Mithen, S. 1996. *The Prehistory of the Mind: A Search for the Origins of Art, Religion and Science*. London: Thames & Hudson.

Morley, I. 2013. *The Prehistory of Music: Human Evolution, Archaeology, and the Origins of Musicality*. Oxford: Oxford University Press.

Morris, B. 1987. *Anthropological Studies of Religion: An Introductory Text*. Cambridge: Cambridge University Press.

Napier, A. D. 1986. *Masks, Transformation and Paradox*. Berkeley: University of California Press.

Napier, D. 1987. Festival masks. In Falassi, A. (ed.) *Time out of Time, Essays on the Festival*, pp. 211–19. Albuquerque: University of New Mexico.

Nissen, H. J., Muheisen, M. & Gebel, H. G. 1987. Report on the first two seasons of excavations at Basta (1986–1987). *Annual of the Department of Antiquities of Jordan* 31: 79–119, 548–54.

Noy, T. 1988. A radial decoration on human face images from the PPNB Period. *Israel Museum Journal* 7: 109–12.

Nys, K. 1995. The use of masks in Cyprus during the Late Bronze Age. *Journal of Prehistoric Religion* 9: 19–34.

Ornan, T. 1986. *A Man and His Land. Highlights from the Moshe Dayan Collection* (Catalogue No. 270). Jerusalem: Israel Museum (Hebrew).

Osten-Sacken, E. von der 1992. Der Ziegen-'Dämon'. *Alter Orient und Altes Testament* 230. Neukirchen-Vluyn: Neukirchener Verlag.

Ottenberg, S. 1975. *Masked Rituals of Afikpo*. Seattle: University of Washington Press.

Pernet, H. 1987. Masks, theoretical perspective and ritual in non-literate cultures. In Eliade, M. (ed.) *Encyclopedia of Religion*, Vol. I, pp. 259–69. New York: MacMillan.

Pernet, H. 1992. *Ritual Masks: Deceptions and Revelations* (translated by L. Grillo). Columbia: University of South Carolina Press.

Perrot, J. 1979. *Syria-Palestine I*. Archaeologia Mundi. Geneva: Nagel.

Porada, E. 1965. *Ancient Iran: The Art of Pre-Islamic Times*. London: Methuen.

Radcliffe-Brown, A. 1922. *The Andaman Islanders* (reprinted with additions in 1948). Glencoe, IL: The Free Press.

Rappaport, R. A. 1971. The sacred in human evolution. *Annual Review of Ecology and Systematics* 2: 23–44.

Rappaport, R. A. 1999. *Ritual and Religion in the Making of Humanity*. Cambridge: Cambridge University Press.

Renfrew, C. 1985. *The Archaeology of Cult. The Sanctuary of Phylakopi*. London: British School of Archaeology in Athens Supplement 9.

Rollefson, G. O. 1983. Ritual and ceremony at Neolithic 'Ain Ghazal (Jordan). *Paléorient* 9/2: 29–38.

Rollefson, G. O. 1986. Neolithic 'Ain Ghazal (Jordan): ritual and ceremony, II. *Paléorient* 12/1: 45–52.

Royce, A. P. 1977. *The Anthropology of Dance*. Bloomington: Indiana University Press.

Sachs, C. 1952. *World History of the Dance*. New York: Seven Arts.

Schechner, R. 1987. Drama – performance and ritual. In Eliade, M. (ed.) *Encyclopedia of Religion*, Vol. 4:436–46. New York: MacMillan.

Schechner, R. 1994. Ritual and performance. In Ingold T. (ed.) *Companion Encyclopedia of Anthropology: Humanity, Culture and Social Life*, pp. 613–47. London: Routledge.

Schliemann, H. 1880. *Mycenae. A Narrative of Researches and Discoveries at Mycenae and Tiryns*. New York: Arno Press (new edition 1976).

Segy, L. 1976. *Masks of Black Africa*. New York: Dover Publications.

Sorell, W. 1973. *The Other Face. The Mask in the Arts*. London: Thames and Hudson.

Spencer, P. 1985. Introduction: interpretations of the dance in anthropology. In Spencer, P. (ed.) *Society and the Dance. The Social Anthropology of Process and Performance*, pp. 1–46. Cambridge: Cambridge University Press.

Starcky, J. 1984. Le Musée de la Bible et Terre Sainte. *Le Monde de la Bible* 36: 52–4.

Stein, A. 1936. An archaeological tour in ancient Persia. *Iraq* 3: 111–225.

Stekelis, M. 1972. *The Yarmukian Culture of the Neolithic Period*. Jerusalem: Magnes Press.

Stern, E. 1976. Phoenician masks and pendants. *Palestine Exploration Quarterly* 108: 109–18.

Sweeney, D. 1993. Egyptian masks in motion. *Göttinger Miszellen, Beiträge zur Ägyptologischen Diskussion* 135: 101–4.

Taylor, J. H. 1994. Masks in ancient Egypt: the image of divinity. In Mack, J. (ed.) *Masks: The Art of Expression*. London: British Museum Press.

Theodossiv, N. 1998. The dead with golden face: Dasaretian, Pelagonian, Mygdonian and Boeotian funeral masks. *Oxford Journal of Archaeology* 17: 345–67.

Theodossiv, N. 2000. The dead with golden face II: other evidence and connections. *Oxford Journal of Archaeology* 19: 175–210.

Tobler, A. J. 1950. *Excavations at Tepe Gawra*, Vol. II. Philadelphia: University of Pennsylvania.

Tribhuwan, R. D. & Savelli, L. 2003. *Tribal Masks and Myths*. New Delhi: Discovery Publishing House.

Turner, V. W 1969. *The Ritual Process: Structure and Anti-Structure*. Chicago: Aldine.

Turner, V. W. 1982. *Celebration: Studies in Festivity and Ritual*. Washington, DC: Smithsonian Institute Press.

Turner, V. W. 1984. Liminality and the performative genres. In MacAloon, J. J. (ed.) *Rite, Drama, Festival, Spectacle. Rehearsals toward a Theory of Cultural Performance*, pp. 19–41. Philadelphia: Institute for the Study of Human Issues.

Turner, V. W. 1990. Are there universals of performance in myth, ritual, and drama? In Schechner, R. & Appel, W. (eds.) *By Means of Performance. Intercultural Studies of Theatre and Ritual*, pp. 8–18. Cambridge: Cambridge University Press.

Tylor, E. B. 1871. *Primitive Culture: Researches into the Development of Mythology, Philosophy, Religion, Art and Custom*. London: Murray. Republished in 1958 as *Religion in Primitive Culture*. New York: Harper & Row.

Uzunoglu, E. 1993. Women in Anatolia from prehistoric ages to the Iron Age. In Renda, G. (ed.) *Woman in Anatolia. 9000 Years of the Anatolian Woman*, pp. 16–24. Istanbul: Turkish Republic Ministry of Culture.

Valentine, C. A. 1961. *Masks and Men in a Melanesian Society*. Lawrence: University of Kansas Publications.

Vanderwal, R. (ed.) 1982. *The Aboriginal Photographs of Baldwin Spencer*. South Yarra, Victoria: A Currey O'Neil Book.

Verhoeven, M. 2002. Ritual and its investigation in prehistory. In Gebel, H. G. K., Hermansen, B. D. & Jensen, C. H. (eds.) *Magic Practices and Ritual in the Near Eastern*

Neolithic. Studies in Early Near Eastern Production, Subsistence, and Environment 8, pp. 5–40. Berlin: ex oriente.

Vincent, L. H. 1935. Les fouilles de Teleilat Ghassul. *Revue Biblique* 44: 69–104.

Whitehouse, H. 1995. *Inside the Cult. Religious Innovation and Transmission in Papua New Guinea.* Oxford: Clarendon Press.

Wilson, E. O. 1975. *Sociobiology: The New Synthesis.* Cambridge, MA: Belknap Press of Harvard University.

Wolinski, A. 1986. Ancient Egyptian ceremonial masks. *Discussions in Egyptology* 6: 47–53.

Yadin, Y. 1972. *Hazor, the Head of all those Kingdoms.* London: British Academy.

Yeivin, E. & Mozel, E. 1977. A fossil directeur figurine of the Pottery Neolithic A. *Tel Aviv* 4: 194–200.

Yizraeli-Noy, T. 1999. *The Human Figure in Prehistoric Art in the Land of Israel.* Jerusalem: Israel Museum (Hebrew).

Young, J. & Young, S. 1955. *Terracotta Figurines from Kourion in Cyprus.* Philadelphia: University Museum.

12

RITUAL, MIMESIS AND THE ANIMAL WORLD IN EARLY CHINA

Roel Sterckx

The animal world is omnipresent in textual sources and archaeologically recovered artefacts, murals and funerary objects from pre-imperial and early imperial China (ca. ninth century BC–second century AD). The realm of the zoomorphic is embedded early on in the Shang oracle bone script that includes numerous pictographs representing animals (Yang 2000b, 90, 114; Li 2002, 208–10; Figure 12.1). Zoomorphic motifs pervade Shang and Zhou bronze vessel décor; and scenes depicting hunts, animal combat and husbandry, as well as games involving animals, abound in Han period murals and on decorated ceramic bricks (Figure 12.2). Clay animal figurines are also commonly found in tombs (Figure 12.3). Most importantly, early China's masters of philosophy, its lexicographers, poets and historiographers drew intensively on images and behaviour observed in the animal world to draw moral analogies, construe philosophical arguments and construct taxonomies for human behaviour. The value of this textual record for our understanding of the relationship between ritual, play and animals is potentially revealing and rich, yet, at the same time, this source base also remains problematic and limited. It is revealing in that, as an aggregate record of human behaviour and thought, the information preserved in early Chinese texts must be anchored at least partly in guided observation of life and social communities in practice. It is limited in that it does not provide direct evidence for the prehistoric age, or at most does so in the form of ideologically coloured narratives of a utopian 'distant' past. In many cases these narratives

therefore provide mediated testimony at best as they were written by authors whose audience consisted mainly of statesmen and elites who were mostly preoccupied with the creation of social order and political rule during an age when China transformed from a polity of contending feudal states into a unified empire (221 BC).

When invoking the animal world, Warring States and Han texts blend biological and socio-religious models. Only rarely do observers dissociate the biological properties of animals from social perception. Both are complementary. Detached zoological inquiry in early China did not develop as a distinct branch of learning comparable to, for instance, the empirical and theoretical programme found in Aristotle. The general paradigm to emerge is one of contingency between the human and animal realm, that is, an understanding in which the boundaries between the human and the natural worlds are not necessarily always clear and distinct. Not infrequently human conduct – and its ramifications in social and political life – was thought to have a moral impact on the natural world at large. The boundaries of what was perceived to be distinctively 'human' or 'animalistic' were subject to change and permutation.[1]

Metaphor and analogy were much-used tools to describe animal behaviour and project it onto the human world, or vice versa. Yet behind the rhetorical veneer of anthropomorphic parallels and comparisons lurk signs indicating that a number of behavioural patterns among animals were interpreted as

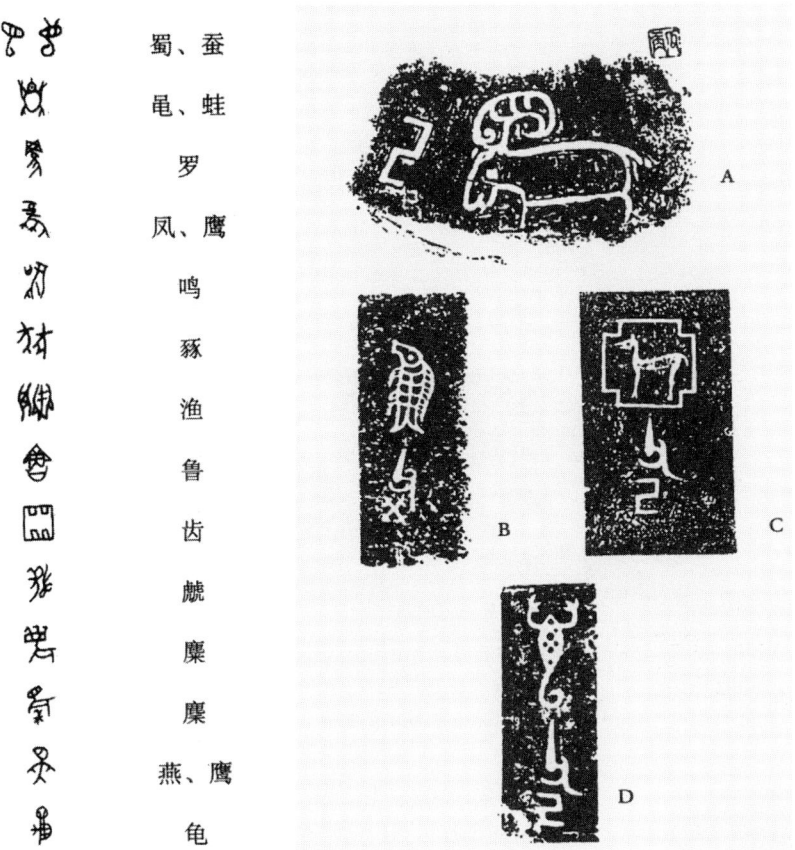

Figure 12.1 Left: zoomorph oracle bone graphs (Guo Fu 1999, 30). Right: bronze animal pictographs (Late Shang, early Western Zhou: Yang 2000b, 109).

meaningful models for prescriptive and regulated human behaviour. This is evident in at least three areas. First, the Chinese ritual canon shows that, not infrequently, animals were socialised into a world in which their behavioural, physical and anatomical qualities were described in terms of human virtues and ritual requirement. Second, the animal world inspired the orchestration of human forms of controlled violence. Finally, the origins of music, movement and dance were closely linked to animals.

Congruity between animal and human behaviour in early China manifests itself in both physical and conceptual forms of mimesis. The former includes re-enactment, imitation or mimicry of animal behaviour while the latter involves more abstract derivations of moral values from physical or biological features (e.g. physiognomy) through mechanisms such as analogy, allegory, metaphor, homology, inference, metonymic projection etc.[2] The hermeneutics operate in two ways: first, animal behaviour and links to habitat and environment are analysed following a sociology of human communities; second, human values, postures and feats of civilisation are inferred from patterns observed in the animal world.

RITUAL AND RITUAL PROPRIETY

Generally speaking, the classical Chinese textual tradition has a very limited vocabulary of 'play', both in terms of the space writers have devoted to describing or analysing the process, and in terms of available terminology in the classical Chinese language. In fact both graphs that are common in modern Chinese to refer to play today – *you* 游 and *xi* 戲 – are etymologically linked to the fluttering of military flags and the use of army banners (*Shuowen*, 7A.19b, 12B.38b). If we can draw any conclusions from etymology at all, these terms suggest at best that play denoted

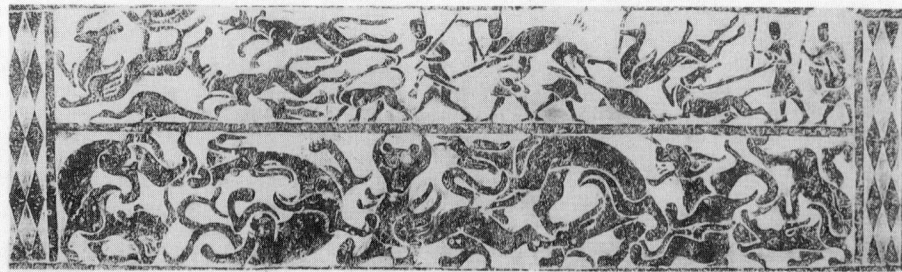

Figure 12.2 Top left: cockfight (Han; Zhengzhou; Li Song 2001, 208). Top right: hunting scene (Han; Shandong, Cangshan county, Qianyao; Xia Henglian 1996, 86). Bottom left: hunting and fishing scene (Han; Sichuan, Peng County; Xia Henglian 1996, 68). Bottom right: husbandry scene (Han; Shaanxi, Hengshan; Li Song 2001, 320).

Figure 12.3 Painted pottery figurines (Yangling pit no. 13; Shaanxi, Western Han; Shaanxi sheng kaogu yanjiusuo 2001, plate 21; courtesy of the Yangling Museum and Shaanxi Archaeological Institute).

some form of free movement within boundaries. By contrast, texts from the classical period are replete with discourse on 'ritual'. When early Chinese texts speak of 'ritual', they usually refer to the notion of *li* 禮. *Li* on the one hand refers to repeated, guided, rule-regulated behaviour; on the other hand, it covers the more abstract virtue of morally appropriate conduct and propriety. *Li* also represents the interplay of 'form and conduct', as well as 'etiquette' in

the narrow sense. In the eyes of most early Chinese thinkers, 'ritual' is a formal and performative concept, as well as a psychological disposition. It is noteworthy that the presence or absence of ritual 'propriety', on the one hand, is taken to be a marker that distinguishes human from animal nature while, on the other hand, outward feats of formal/ 'ritualised' behaviour were thought to apply to human and animal societies alike.

Let us turn first to moral distinctiveness. Several sources insist that what separates humans from animals is a sense for moral reasoning and ritual propriety. Xunzi 荀子 (ca. 335–ca. 238 BC), for instance, attributes humans' capacity to instruct and subdue physically superior animals to their sense for social organisation. This ability to form social flocks (*qun* 群, a graph that is etymologically related to a herd of sheep) is said to derive from man's capability to draw social distinctions (*fen* 分). Making social distinctions in turn originates from a sense for righteousness (*yi* 義, a character which, incidentally, also includes the grapheme for bovids/caprids; *Xunzi*, 9.164–5). The idea that a sense for propriety can serve as a tool to curb the supposedly animal aspects of man was based on the premise that animals were thought to be endowed foremost with physical power (*li* 力),

whereas humans possess an inborn sense of morality or 'ritual propriety (*li* 禮)'(e.g. *Guanzi*, 4.118). The philosopher Mencius (fourth century BC) remarks that humans' failure to reciprocate ritual propriety, benevolence and loyalty would put them on a par with birds and beasts (*Mengzi*, 5B.3b, 8B.5a–b). The *Spring and Autumn of Master Yan* (a late Warring States text) notes that a morally cultivated gentleman who loses his sense for ritual propriety lapses to the level of common folk, and common folk without ritual propriety are equal to birds and beasts (*Yanzi chunqiu*, 2.170, 4.241). That animals (and petty humans) lack a sense for propriety can be seen when they group together and give in to instinctive physical intercourse as they fail to distinguish between young and old, species or kin. Deer, as one recurrent phrase intimates, lack ritual propriety because stag and calves mate with the same doe (*Yanzi chunqiu*, 1.6, 7.430; *Liji*, 1.11a; *Lüshi chunqiu*, 16.946).

Some Warring States and Han thinkers insist that the human capacity to organise oneself socially benefitted from the fact that humans, roughly, belong to one and the same species group as opposed to animals (cf. Sterckx 2005). For instance, the *Guanzi* notes that "relations among a flock of crows may seem good, but they are never really close." A variation on this theme is the observation that animals of prey do not flock together (*Guanzi*, 1.17; *Huainanzi*, 17.568; *Wenzi*, 1.37b). According to *Huainanzi* (ca. 139 BC), birds and beasts cannot form flocks because their species are different (*qi lei yi* 其類異), and tigers and deer cannot play about together because their physical strength is disproportionate (*Huainanzi*, 9.286). Animals are also said to lack a sense for kin affinity that reaches beyond their own species, which is why adopting a clan-name and upholding social distinctions based on gender and marriage are attributes that emancipate humans from a state of primordial bestiality (*Bohutong*, 9.401). Relationships of parenthood and pedigree among animals, to return to Xunzi, lack the integrity of a human father-to-son relation. A distinction between male and female exists among animals, yet it does not induce a separation between the sexes (*Xunzi*, 2.21).

While narratives that insist on the moral distinction between humans and animals are numerous, it is equally clear that a number of highly valued core human virtues were detected, in simile and metaphor, in the animal world. Ritualised behaviour in the animal world was taken to inspire human gestures and performance. Some examples: On several occasions the disgorging of food by certain birds (translating the expression *fan bu* 反哺 'reverse feeding') is interpreted as a sign of their sense of filial piety, that is, an unconditional commitment to offer physical and moral sustenance to one's parents and elders. We have several references to filial bird behaviour, including one preserved in a verse of a prose-poem entitled 'Rhapsody on the Spirit Crows' ('Shen wu fu' 神烏賦), recovered in 1993 from tomb no. 6 in Yinwan, Jiangsu province (interment ca. 10 BC):

> Among all animals that can fly
> The crow is the most dignified.
> Its nature is to love to be humane.
> Repaying [their kindness] it nourishes its
>   [old] parents.
> It acts according to righteousness,
>   purity, vigour
> And always walks on the way of man.
> (Sterckx 2002, 251, n. 63; van Ess 2003, 612)

Reversely, the cuckoo's habit of having its eggs hatched by other birds, or the owl's instinct to devour its own mother, are condemned as un-filial conduct (*Xinlun*, 6b, 21b–22a; *Shuowen*, 6A.66a). Instances of filial animal piety perpetuated after death are recorded. One legend held that elephants spontaneously tilled the tumulus of Emperor Shun, and that crows laboured the fields where Yu the Great was interred. Shun was a legendary sage ruler credited with, among other achievements, settling disputes among farmers, fishermen and crafts folk. Yu dredged rivers and controlled flood waters, thereby fashioning civilisation (*Han Feizi*, 15.795; Mencius, 2A.8, 6B.15; Lewis 2006, 38–47). Another group to attract the spontaneous attendance of animal acolytes were immortals. The legendary Pengzu, alleged to have lived 800 years, was associated with the presence of tigers. Another immortal was known as Zhuji Weng or 'The Old Man Who Beguiled Chickens.' One story tells how he raised chickens for more than 100 years, giving surnames and styles to his birds, and summoning them by name. In his reclusion, he was said to be flanked permanently by hundreds of white cranes and peacocks (Kaltenmark 1953, 82–3, 127–8).

A sense of place and origins is highlighted among certain species. For instance, as a sign of benevolence, the fox upon death is said to turn his head towards the mound where it was whelped (*Liji*, 7.1a; *Huainanzi*, 10.325; *Bohutong*, 9.433; *Shuowen*, 10A.36a). Animals also show emotions or respond to human feelings such as sadness and mournfulness. In the *Analects*, Confucius' disciple and paragon of filial piety, Master Zeng, notes that "When a bird is about to die its call is mournful, when a man is about to die his words are good" (*Lunyu*, 8.4). Compassionate mountain birds come fluttering down in response to Master Zeng's unhappy cries (*Yantie lun*, 5.143). When the king of Linjiang (mid-second century BC) kills himself, several tens of thousands of swallows pick up earth in their beaks to pile up his grave mound (*Shiji*, 59.2094; *Hanshu*, 53.2412). Swallows also descend to fill up the burial pit of Empress Ding (consort of Aidi, r. 7–1 BC) after an order had been issued to desecrate her tomb (*Hanshu*, 97B.4004). Members of the Yang clan are associated with the appearance of spirit birds from the late Western throughout the Eastern Han. According to one story, days before the burial of Yang Zhen (d. AD 124) a big bird perched in front of his coffin, wailing and shedding tears. When the burial was over it flew off. Later a stone bird statue was erected at the tomb site and his funerary cortège of birds was immortalised in stone on Yang's stele (*Hou Hanshu*, 54.1759–60, 54.1767–8; Sterckx 2002, 293, n. 144).

In reading these stories, we must of course be aware of the literary and rhetorical contexts in which many of these narratives were cast. Yet the sheer volume of discourse in early Chinese texts that analyses animal behaviour either as a metaphorical referent to human values or, more importantly, as behaviour that was partly inspired in response to human conduct – or even political events – suggests that dismissing all of it simply as analogical reasoning or anthropomorphism may be untenable. Even if one would opt to do so, it is hard to dismiss that some analogies appear to be firmly based on observations of actual animal behaviour. I will discuss movement and sound in more detail later. First we turn to three other areas in which such projections appear: descriptions of the ritual gift exchange, the portrayal of ritual sacrifice and origin narratives of violence.

In stipulating when, how and what animals were to be used in sacrificial procedures and ritual exchanges, ritual codes infer interesting data with reference to animal behaviour. To be sure these texts are mainly concerned with establishing differentiae, status and hierarchies within human society. Yet, in their justification of why certain animals were to be selected and differentiated for ritual purposes, they start from the premise that certain modes of animal behaviour were symbolically or 'ritually' meaningful. For instance in a chapter entitled 'Gifts to Superiors' in a Han work known as the *Luxuriant Dew of the Spring and Autumn Annals* we are reminded that in presenting gifts to superiors or friends, a minister should use a lamb and a senior officer a goose. The text justifies the use of these particular animals by linking their natural behaviour to the social conduct desired of the human officer in question:

> A goose is of the same kind as the honourable man. An honourable man stands above the people and must, in a reserved manner, follow the order of first and last. He ought to be reverent and possess the capability of controlling rank and order. Therefore a senior official uses the goose as a gift. A lamb has horns but does not use them; it sets out preparations but never uses them; and it resembles someone who likes benevolence. When one catches a lamb it does not cry; when one slaughters it, it does not wail. It resembles someone who dies for righteousness. When lambs feed from their mother, they have to kneel to get (to the milk). This resembles someone who knows the rites. Therefore the word for 'sheep' (*yang* 羊) also means 'propitious' (*xiang* 祥). Hence a minister uses it as a gift. (*Chunqiu fanlu*, 16.394)

Similar examples occur elsewhere. They include the common officer who is associated with the pheasant because it cannot be inveigled by food or subjected by force, and common people who are associated with the tame duck that cannot fly off (*Shuoyuan*, 19.485; *Bohutong*, 8.356–57; *Liji*, 5.25a). The analogies inferred here are based on more or less plausible observations: the goose serves as an image for orderly conduct, a lamb evokes the idea of subservience by administrators. The image of the morally accomplished person who "stands above the people" may allude to the idea that geese on seasonal passage fly at higher altitudes than common birds. "Following the order of first and last" refers to the image of geese flying in formations, a concept also seen when precision formations of flying birds are used to name army formations (*Zuozhuan*, 1429; *Mozi*, 31.342; *Han Feizi*, 1.43).

To be sure it is not possible to establish the cognitive sequence in which these sorts of parallels may have come into being. Is it biology that inspires the imagination of a ritual category, is it an understanding of the formalities of ritual that is used to explain certain forms of locomotion among animals, or a mixture of both processes? To claim that meaning construction here is entirely devoid of empirical observation may be too strong. But it is equally clear that by explaining animal conduct in function of their possible use within a ritual order, the interpreter has not only transformed the lamb and the goose into social creatures, but also allows room for polysemy in description, since each social usage of a specific species can lead to new or slightly adapted explanations of its behaviour. So while in the passage cited previously a goose was linked to a ruler's capability to control rank and order, elsewhere it is singled out as the ideal wedding gift on account of its sense for orderly and subject obedience:

> As for the use of the goose as a present [at marriage], it is chosen on the basis of its seasonal (migration to) the south and (return to) the north and its never missing regular timing. This illustrates that a girl should not be deprived of her right time. (The goose) is also a bird that follows the *yang* (sun), as in the principle of a wife's duty to follow her husband. Furthermore (geese) are chosen on the basis of (their characteristic of) forming rows and ranks in flight and while resting. This clarifies the rites of marriage according to which old and young have their proper

order and do not trespass upon each other. (*Bohutong*, 10.457)

These examples deal with animals used as a medium in the gift exchange. Animals were also central to sacrifice as animal victims. The offering of sacrifice constituted the single most important performative act in early Chinese religious practice (one could argue that this continues to be the case up to the present day). Leaving aside the intricate mechanics of the sacrificial exchange (cf. Sterckx 2002, 58–61; 2011, 83–166), it is noteworthy that, according to some, sacrificial obligation itself could be observed in the animal world. Calendrical texts note that the hunting season was to be declared open only when the game animals themselves displayed their innate moral disposition. Hence fishermen are allowed to start fishing only when "otters sacrifice fish". One may explain the image of sacrifice (*ji* 祭) here simply as a metaphor. Alternatively, as at least one commentary does, one can take the image of sacrifice here as based on observation: there is an abundant catch, as a result of which remains of prey are scattered around on the riverbanks as if the otters were sacrificing to the four directions. Likewise hunts were to start only "when wolves sacrifice prey". And the nets were set out only "when doves transformed into eagles", one way of saying that seedeaters assume a carnivorous condition (*Liji*, 12.5b, 14.14a, 16.13a, 17.1b; *Lüshi chunqiu*, 9.467). So the opening and closure of the hunting season here is said to accord with the hunter's respect for the game animals' innate sense of sacrifice. The hunter interprets regulated sacrificial behaviour among his game animals as the sanctioning voice for the timing of his catch and, by extension, as a strategy to prevent these predatory animals from preying upon humans as their sacrificial meat.

It is worth noting that while animals may be seen to display cultic behaviour (e.g. as in predators leaving remnants of prey as some sort of thanksgiving offering), and while they function regularly as spirit mediums (and occasionally as tutelary spirits), on balance, organised zoolatry takes a minor share. In fact the few references that survive and involve the cultic worship of animals occur mostly in a context in which such activities are condemned as unorthodox and challenging the canonised sacrifices (Sterckx

2002, 59–61). This is not to say of course that these practices did not exist. Little may have survived in textual records partly because the court-based compilers of the majority of our sources did not grant canonical authority to organised animal worship. At any rate, the early Chinese pantheon in pre-Buddhist times appears to have been far less zoomorphic than its counterpart in Ancient Egypt, Greece, Rome or Gaul.

Contrary to the demonstrations of orderly conduct illustrated earlier, the origins of social disorder and the display of violence were also linked to the animal world. This is evident both in comments on animal psychology as well as through various forms of enactment. We should note that early Chinese texts do not contain a uniform origin myth of animal domestication, that is, a doctrine crediting humans with universal supremacy over the animal world that was shared by most schools of thought. While several tales and origin myths acknowledge the domestication of the animal world as a civilising process in which humans distinguish themselves from bestiality, other accounts insist on various forms of primitive naturalness and advocate human–animal harmony over cultural edifice or civilisation (Sterckx 2002, 93–6). Human behaviour is explained, on the one hand, as an emancipatory conquest over animal instinct, but, on the other hand, it is emphasised that human communities are doomed to relapse to bestiality when social, political or indeed cosmic circumstances are not right. The *Huainanzi* for instance explains human recourse to the military and violence as an extension of what happens in the natural world:

> All beasts that have blood and *qi* are equipped with teeth and horns. They have claws in front and paws behind. Those with horns gore, those with teeth bite, those with poison sting, and those with hooves kick. When they are happy they play with one another; when they are angry they injure one another. This is their Heaven [born] nature. Humans have instincts for clothing and food, yet [material] things are insufficient to satisfy them. Thus they flock together in communities in various locations. When their divisions are not equal, and when demands are not fulfilled, they fight. When they fight, the strong threaten the weak and the brave attack the cowardly. (*Huainanzi*, 15.489; Major et al. 2010, 580–1)

Several activities exemplified how the origins of violence and the command thereof were linked to the observation of animal nature. These included staged combats with wild animals in pens, bullfighting and bull-grappling and hunting (Figure 12.4). At

Figure 12.4 Top: fight with tigers (Rubbing of a Han mural; Nanyang, Henan; Xiao Kengda 2010, 253). Bottom: bull fight (rubbing of a Han mural; Nanyang, Henan; Xiao Kengda 2010, 253).

the same time these events also functioned as ritual forms of military training, as did, for instance, horse polo in later imperial times (Sterckx 2012, 36). Reference to wrestling and animal-fighting games occurs across several Warring States, Qin and Han texts (cf. *Zhanguo huiyao*, 27.270–4). One among these has received considerable interest as it appears to have been an enactment of an animal fight by human actors. The so-called horn-butting game (*jue di xi* 角抵戲) had fighters put on horns thereby imitating butting bulls or goats. The game, on record first for the Qin (208 BC), may have been part of a series of wrestling games that were popular by Han times. The catalogue of the Han imperial library includes the title of a work, now lost, entitled *Hand Wrestling* ('Shou bo' 手搏, in six scrolls) that may have contained descriptions of this and similar games (*Hanshu*, 30.1761). The first literary account of these horn-butting matches is preserved in a post-Han work but we have several murals from the period possibly depicting the game (Figure 12.5; Yang Xiangdong 2000a, 129–34; Du 2010, 177–9).

Several explanations of *juedi* have been offered, ranging from the suggestion that it originated in a military dance to the idea that it was an enactment of the battle between the mythical figures of the Yellow Emperor and Chiyou, god of war (Loewe 1994, 236–48). Horn butting and the wearing of a cap named after a horned beast (the *xiezhai*) also appears to be linked to legal procedure as several sources credit this creature with an innate sense of justice (*Han guan yi*, 1.16a–b; *Duduan*, 2.14b; *Lunheng*, 52.760). While evidence is not conclusive, the horn-butting game, as Mark Lewis has suggested, was most likely not simply a military exercise or a demonstration of skills for the purpose of entertainment. It may have been a ritual display symbolising that humans, i.e. the sage ruler or emperor, were able to command cosmic powers through the ritual enactment of animal combat or the staged subduing of wild animals (Lewis 1990, 150–60).

Regardless of the exact purpose and audience the horn-butting game may have served, it is clear that the observation of the movements of animals within their respective biotope prompted interpretation. Reference to shamanic animal impersonation and the mimicry of animal postures to forge

magical powers is well documented. In Shang oracle bone and Zhou bronze inscriptions the graph for the legendary master of music and dance, Kui 夔, represents, according to some scholars, a pictogram of an ape-like creature or a shaman disguised in animal skin and wearing a mask (Figure 12.6; Eno 1990, 196). Adopting animal postures to tackle demonic illness may have been believed to generate apotropaic effects comparable perhaps to those produced by exorcistic animal dances, often involving masks (Sterckx 2002, 187–9). Treatises on physical cultivation likewise contain gymnastic animal postures and therapeutic animal pantomimes. Manuals found at Mawangdui (Changsha, Hunan province) describe sexual positions and movements such as the "roaming tiger", "cicada clinging", "monkey's squat" and "rabbit bolts". "Guiding and pulling" exercises depicted on a chart found at Mawangdui and described in a manuscript excavated from a tomb at Zhangjiashan (Jiangling, Hubei, mid-second century BC), mention animal postures such as the "bird stretch" and the "bear ramble" (*Mawangdui*, vol. 4, 95, 155, 165, 116–17; *Zhangjiashan*, 285–99; Figure 12.7). These titles may have been no more than imaginative names for these exercises, yet it is plausible they grew out of a belief that imitating animal postures had therapeutic effects on the body. A critical comment in the *Huainanzi* confirms this when it condemns these exercises as examples of a lower level of spiritual perfection: "If you huff and puff, exhale and inhale, blow out the old and pull in the new, practice the Bear Hang, the Bird Stretch, the Duck Splash, the Ape Leap, the Owl Gaze, and the Tiger Stare. This is what is practiced by those people who nurture the body. They are not practices of those who polish the mind [i.e. the perfected person]" (*Huainanzi*, 7.230; Major 2010, 250). Yet, despite such comments, the great Daoist authors of the period appear to have used every opportunity to describe their ideal of the superior or perfected person through incisive analogies with the animal world. So the same *Huainanzi* notes in a different chapter that humans, like animals, ought to stick to what their natural propensities enable them to do best:

The movement of armoured bugs [e.g. molluscs, turtles] facilitates rigidity; the movement of asexual bugs [e.g. bees and wasps] facilitates poisonous stinging. The movement of black and brown bears facilitates seizing and grasping; the movement of rhinos and oxen facilitates butting and goring. No animals abandon their strong points to use their shortcomings

[*and neither should humans therefore*]. (*Huainanzi*, 16.553; Major 2010, 663)

Likewise, the most ingenious voice(s) in early Daoist literature, i.e. the authors(s) behind the *Zhuangzi* (fourth to second century BC), clearly seem to have

Figure 12.5 Top left: wrestling (*juedi*?) scene (Dahuting tomb. no. 2, Mixian county, Henan; late Eastern Han, ca. AD 160–90; Xiao Kengda 2010, 246). Top right: *juedi* as drawn in *Sancai tuhui* (AD 1565). Bottom: scene interpreted to represent *juedi* (Nanyang; Han; Loewe 1994, 240).

observed the play of primates to be able to produce the following moral tale:

The King of Wu was bobbing on the Yangzi river when he got off to climb a hill known for its monkeys. When the host of monkeys saw him, they all ran off in a fright, fleeing into the deep thickets. There was one monkey among them, however, that kept casually cavorting and saucily swinging through the branches, showing off its skills to the king. The king shot at it, but the monkey deftly grabbed the arrow. The king ordered his attendants to quickly get their shots in, and the monkey died forthwith. The king turned around to address his friend, Yan Buyi ("Mr Doubtless Composure"), "This monkey, by showing off his knack and relying on its agility, behaved in an arrogant manner to me, which is why it ended up perishing like this. Take heed of this! Ah, do not be haughty towards others by means of your looks." (*Zhuangzi*, 24.846–7)

Figure 12.6 Oracle bone graph for Kui 夔 (following Eno 1990, 196).

MUSIC AND DANCE

Monkeys bring us to music and dance. Perhaps nowhere is the ritual enactment of animal movements and sounds more clearly pronounced than in early Chinese narratives on the origins of music and dance (cf. Sterckx 2000). Music and dance were

Figure 12.7 Mawangdui 'Guiding and pulling' chart; courtesy of Wellcome Images (see also Lo 2012).

linked to the observation of sound and motion in the animal world. Tone, rhythm and melody were conceived of as embedded in the natural world. The skilful musician maieutically uncovered what was already there. He or she assumed the task of discovering and observing the patterning of sound and movement in nature to make these explicit in the form of melody, rhythm and dance.

The *Spring and Autumn of Mr Lü* (ca. 239 BC) records how, at the time of the legendary ruler Ge Tianshi, music originated when people waved oxtails and sang melodies while stomping their feet. Twelve pitch standards were created following the calls of the phoenix: six derived from the calls of the male phoenix, and six tones were based on the calls of the female (*Lüshi chunqiu*, 5.284). The phoenix was linked to the tuning of musical instruments and seen as the originator of wind-instruments. Its link to wind can also be seen in the cognate etymology of the characters *feng* (*b'ium) 鳳 'phoenix' and *feng* 風 (*pium) 'wind'. Phoenix calls were likened to that of pan-pipes, bells and drums (*Xunzi*, 21.389; *Lunheng*, 50.733). The transformation of wind into sound was also associated with the legendary emperor Zhuan Xu (fl.? 2514 BC), who commissioned Flying Dragon to give form to the sounds of the eight winds and then ordered Salamander to conduct by drumming with its tail on its belly (*Lüshi chunqiu*, 5.285). Scholars in East and West have and continue to speculate at length whether a 'real' zoological referent for the Chinese phoenix or dragon is identifiable. To no surprise, no conclusive evidence exists, so these statements embody an idea at most. However, we do find references to more generically identifiable species in definitions of musical tone. A passage in the *Guanzi* identifies musical tones as homophones of the cries of birds and beasts. It associates each note on the pentatonic scale with animal sound:

> Whenever one hears the *zhi* note,
> It sounds like a hog that has become aware
>   of being mounted by a smaller pig and
>   squeals in alarm.
> Whenever one hears the *yu* note,
> It sounds like the neighing of a horse in
>   the wilds.

> Whenever one hears the *gong* note,
> It sounds like the mooing of a cow that has
>   fallen into a pit.
> Whenever one hears the *shang* note,
> It sounds like a sheep that has become
>   separated from its flock.
> Whenever one hears the *jiao* note,
> It sounds like a pheasant ascending a tree
>   to crow.
> The sound is piercing in order to be clear
>   (*Guanzi*, 19.465; Rickett 1998, 263).

As the Zhuan Xu account suggests, drumming was also linked to the animal world. The image of a drumming reptile bears testimony to the use of reptile skins to cover drums. This practice has been traced to archaic times in the form of alligator drums excavated from Neolithic sites in Shanxi and Shandong (Liu Li 1996). One poem in the *Book of Odes* describes how King Wen (ca. 1099–1050 BC) celebrated the construction of his royal park with musicians rolling alligator drums (*Mao shi zhengyi*, 16E.7a). The same type of drum was used in the hunt (*Shiji*, 117.3014). Aquatic creatures and reptiles appear to be linked regularly to drumming or rhythmic motion. A thunder spirit said to "drum on its belly" is described in some sources as a hybrid with a dragon body and a human head (*Shanhaijing*, 13.329, 14.361; *Huainanzi*, 4.150). The use of reptile-skin drums and the image of amphibians stirring up rain and thunder were possibly inspired by the knowledge that amphibians move both on water and land and mediate between arid and moist zones. The aforementioned legendary music master, Kui, is not only associated with the origins of the drum, but also on record as an aquatic monster that rises from the Eastern Seas and generates rain and wind. He is skinned, made into a drum and played by the Yellow Emperor with the bones of Thunder Beast (*Shanhaijing*, 14.361; Sterckx 2000, 11–12).

The association of the zoomorph music master Kui with the origins of drumming and with the direction of the east is based on the identification of the east as a progenitor of movement, an idea some explained through paronomasia of the graphs *dong* 東 (*tung) and *dong* 動 (*d'ung) (*Shangshu da zhuan*, 1.3; *Chunqiu fanlu*, 16.414–15). Skins or hides were to be stretched on drums on the day when

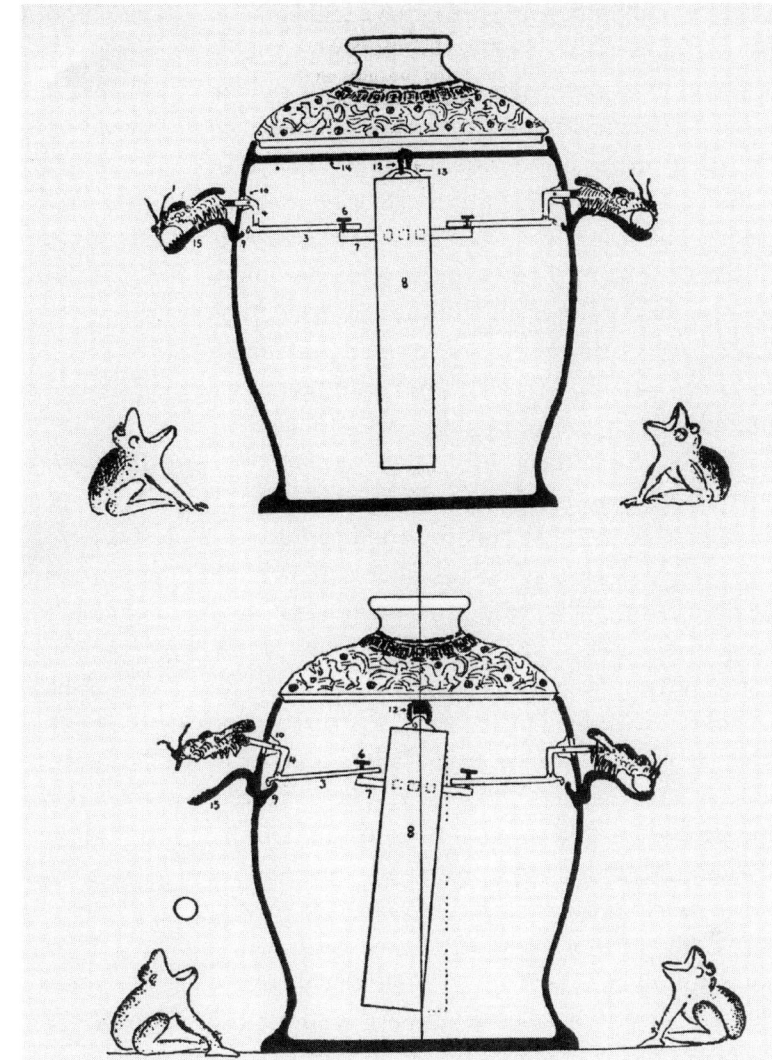

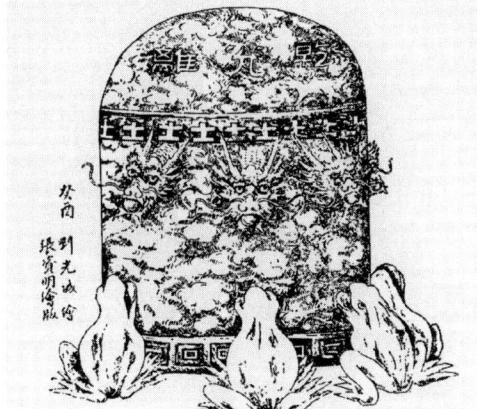

Figure 12.8 Left: drawing of Zhang Heng's seismograph (Needham 1954–, 628). Right: Zhang Heng seismograph mechanism (Needham 1954–, 629).

hibernating animals re-emerged. This was in early spring, when, following one commentator, hibernating animals could hear the thunder and started 'moving', precisely the effect drums were meant to cause (*Zhouli*, 40.24a). An early calendar confirms that alligators were caught in the second month to make drums (*Da Dai Liji*, 2.6a). In an act of sympathetic magic, beating drums covered in animal hides may have been believed to induce changes in climate or movement among the creatures or spirits that were addressed.

While animals were known to be receptive to thunder, their response to thunder was also presented as an act of drumming. Hence the observation of a pheasant 'drumming its wings' is taken as an indication of the emergence of thunder (*Da Dai Liji*, 2.3b–4a). The early Chinese were no doubt aware of certain animals' sensory prescience of thunder, rain, lightning or earthquakes (*Huainanzi*, 10.337, 18.618, 20.663). Zhang Heng's (AD 78–139) famous bronze seismograph illustrates the idea. It allegedly had an outer surface that was decorated with designs of mountains, turtles, birds and beasts. A bronze ball dropping from a dragon mouth into a toad underneath indicated a movement of the earth. The choice of reptiles and amphibians on the domed cover and body of the seismograph was inspired by the idea that these animals were capable of sensing motion and transmitting its vibrations (Figure 12.8; Needham, 1954–, vol. 3, 627–35).

In addition to associating drumming with animal motion, the movement of animals itself was seen as a source for musical resonance. The steeds that pulled Zhou royal carriages had bells attached to them so that the pace of the horse would regulate the tolling of the bells. By 'pacing' his horse, that is, controlling the unbound instinctive motion of the horse, the ruler's charioteer controls the sounds of the bells and hence, symbolically, the rhythm of the universe. Only when the pace of the horses was properly mastered by the driver would his ruler's reputation reverberate through the euphony of these bells (*Shuoyuan*, 16.384; *Xunzi*, 18.335; *Bohutong*, 12.588–9). Even the zoomorphic decoration of musical instruments may have been inspired by their link to sound and drumming. A technical treatise describing the design of animal motifs on clocks, bells, their stands and suspension bars classifies animals into five groups: those with firm layers of fat (oxen and sheep), animals with soft fat (pigs), 'naked' animals (i.e. short-haired species such as tigers and leopards), feathered animals and scaly species (dragons and snakes). The last three of these groups are said to be used as decoration on music stands. Next follows a list of animals used as decorative carvings on instruments and ritual vessels. They are differentiated according to their bone structure, locomotion and the way in which they produce sounds: animals that produce sounds by means of the throat (e.g. water-lizards), the mouth, the flanks (e.g. crickets), the wings, the thighs (e.g. grasshoppers) and the chest. Finally each animal sound is connected to an appropriate musical instrument. Naked animals, producing large and spacious sounds, are the appropriate decoration for the stands of bells. Birds, producing sounds that are light, rising and far-reaching, are appropriate decorations for stone chimes (*Zhouli*, 41.13a–16a; Sterckx 2000, 18–19). In other words, the sound produced by the instrument reflects the natural sounds of the animal(s) depicted on it.

Finally, like music, the origins of the dance were explained as mimetic and linked to animal movement. Several sources for example mention a magical rain dance associated with the southern state of Chu in which a one-legged bird (the *shangyang*) is imitated. Children performed the dance by leading each other two by two on a rope, bending one foot and jumping while shouting: "Heaven is about to send us a big downpour, the one-legged bird starts dancing" (*Shuoyuan*, 18.465; *Lunheng*, 43.649–50). Bird feathers used in dance were also associated with the procurement of seasonal fecundity. The performance of dragon dances whereby actors manipulated clay models of dragons to provoke rain may also be seen as another example of such imitative animal dances (*Bohutong*, 3.109; *Chunqiu fanlu*, 16.399–407).

CONCLUDING REMARKS

I end with another passage from the *Huainanzi*, the 21-chapter encyclopaedic anthology compiled under the auspices of an imperial kinsman and presented to Emperor Han Wudi in 139 BC as a comprehensive synthesis of all contemporary knowledge:

What *yin* and *yang* produce [from] the essence of blood and *qi* [are] creatures that have a mouthful of teeth and a head bearing horns, front claws or rear hooves, soaring wings or clutching talons that advance by wriggling or move by crawling. When happy they are harmonious, when angry they are quarrelsome; seeing benefit, they pursue it, avoiding harm, they withdraw from it; their instinctive responses in this respect are one. Although in their likes and dislikes they do not differ from people, nonetheless, though their claws and teeth are sharp, though their muscles and bones are strong, they cannot avoid being controlled by people [since] they cannot communicate their intelligence to one another, and their abilities and strength cannot be made to act as one. Each has its natural propensity that is not endowed or received from the outside. Thus their strengths have boundaries, and their accomplishments have limits. Now the wild goose follows the wind to fly in order to preserve its energy and strength. It holds straw in its mouth while soaring in order to fend off tethered arrows. Ants know how to build hills; badgers make their winding tunnels; tigers and leopards have lairs of grass. Wild boars have grassy nests, rows of felled trees, and burrowed holes that join one another in the manner of palaces and rooms; they provide protection to guard them from the rain and shield them from the hot sun. Thus even birds and beasts know ways to seek out and accord with what brings them benefit. (*Huainanzi*, 19.645–6; Major, 2010, 777–8; see also Major 2008)

This passage reminds us that, for all the socialising features Chinese literati may or may not have observed in the natural environment surrounding them or gleaned from canonical texts predating them in some cases by centuries, a recognition remains that a distinctive degree of cognition and intelligence separates humans from the animal world. Origin narratives may well link the mimicry of animal sounds to the beginnings of music, yet, to stay with *Huainanzi*, parrots' mimicking of human speech does not put them on a par with their owner who commands control over them and, one hopes, possesses a modicum of intelligent speech (*Huainanzi*, 16.524; Major 2010, 628). In the end, the analysis of the world remains firmly human-centred and a main undercurrent of early Chinese thought is one in which the natural world serves to a large degree as a utility for the explanation of human behaviour. Yet these texts show equally that animal behaviour was perceived in various modalities – directly and indirectly, positively and negatively – to inform certain forms of regulated human conduct. It is clear that a more or less advanced degree of abstraction and symbolism is at play in many of the explanations on offer. Yet, just as not all animal behaviour was understood as symbolically meaningful beyond its physical environment, not all identifications of bestiality in the human world were necessarily symbolic either. For instance, barbarians and tribes living on the periphery of the civilised 'Chinese' heartland were regularly referred to as animals: they dress in hides, eat raw meat and speak the "language of birds and beasts" (Sterckx 2002, 158–61; 2011, 20–1). Likewise, in their judgement of others, Chinese moralists did not refrain from mentally relegating those who lacked virtue and propriety to the world of birds and beasts. Even China's First Emperor had to succumb to the judgement of Han historiographers keen to point out that the man had the physiognomy of a beast: a puffed-out chest like a hawk, the voice of a jackal and the heart of a tiger or wolf (*Shiji*, 6.230).

Yet we need to remain very cautious in inferring that this rich bestiary documented in texts and illustrated in art is reflective of deeply rooted social or religious orientations that may somehow be linked to prehistoric times or early human society. To start exploring that line of thought would require a step-change in archaeological work on pre-Shang China, not in the least in the field of zoo-archaeology. It would also require a much more intensive dialogue between experts who work on the early historical age – who tend to be literate in the languages of the period, but fall short when it comes to analysing material evidence – and scholars working on pre-Shang China who tend to shy away from language and the written word. This chapter has drawn on data from a highly literate civilisation, a society that has left behind a copiously annotated and continuous textual canon that stretches across the first millennium BC and that, on many counts, does not fit past or revisionist definitions of so-called primitive society. The balance has been with textual sources for two reasons: first, its author has limited expertise in the analysis of material culture, and, secondly, it may help illustrate that the methodological hurdles that present themselves when examining ritual, play and its links to the animal world may not necessarily be of an entirely different order of magnitude when we rely on texts versus archaeological evidence.

Our understanding of patterns of human and animal behaviour as gleaned through a textual corpus (and one might argue art(e)facts) is concerned with *perceptions* of nature, *perceptions* of behaviour and *narratives* or *representations* of human-animal conduct that are deeply anchored in conventions of literary genre, ideology and, importantly, that were addressing an audience of mostly social elites. The same can be said of visual narratives, for instance, as they appear in tomb murals. These images are not value free, many express prescriptive conduct or desired behaviour, and many are in fact based on stories documented in the written canon (cf. Powers 1991). Importantly, they were not intended to be seen by the living once a tomb had been sealed.

Finally, we ought to be conscious of the fact that the contours of some of the core analytical concepts we use to scrutinise our evidence, such as there are 'ritual', 'belief', the 'sacred' versus the 'profane' etc., derive mostly from a Western academic canon (albeit one that has drawn on anthropological work). This complicates matters significantly when we are dealing with the Chinese tradition that has developed its own theoretical vocabulary. Take the case of 'ritual' or 'regulated' behaviour. It goes without saying that a historian, archaeologist, anthropologist, psychologist or ethologist would have no problem sourcing a gamut of Chinese historical data to fit the characteristics of what she or he would like to typify as ritual: repetition, performance, encoding, communication, formality, relative invariance, conformity, constraint, time, space, doxy, praxy etc. All of these elements are explicitly or implicitly present in the ways in which the Chinese tradition itself has conceived of behaviour that approximates the many definitions of 'ritual' on offer. I do not believe, however, that such definitions – often drawn from a paradigmatic smorgasbord of a-historicised and de-localised civilisations and societies – always adequately reflect indigenous and historically contingent conceptions. If measured in terms of volume, China has perhaps left behind more scholarly writings on *li* 'ritual' or 'regulated' behaviour than most other societies. Ritual specialists throughout more than 20 centuries of exegesis have been motivated to zoom in on the pragmatics, the philosophies and the economics of ritual. As late as the nineteenth century, literati were still elaborating commentaries on treatises that had attempted to define the contours of regulated behaviour 2,000 years earlier. Indeed, one could argue that scholarly debate about ritual and the ritual canon itself in dynastic China was one of its most enduring rituals. In the Chinese context, one could justifiably emend one anthropologist's contention that "ritual is the authority of repetition" (Feuchtwang 2010, 71) to read 'ritual is the authority of a repeated exegesis of its canon'. In trying to get our analytical vocabulary right for cross-cultural analysis in the case of ritual (let alone of what constitute 'sacred' versus 'profane' manifestations of ritual in different times and places), the existence of an indigenous scholarly preoccupation with the topic complicates issues in interesting ways. One would be hard-pressed, for instance, to find an acknowledgment in the Confucian ritual canon to the tune that ritual should or can be minimally defined as repeated performative action. Ritual in early China is intricately – indeed almost umbilically – linked with moral judgement. Performance without moral intent is repeatedly condemned in the Chinese ritual canon. To behave ritually implied to have a moral propriety that enables one to do so. This realisation must partly account for the generally negative attitude Confucian elites espoused towards play, sports and even leisure.

NOTES

1 Sterckx (2002) offers a detailed exposition of these themes. In a recent paper, Roderick Ptak has put some cogent question marks behind my thesis that a great deal of discourse on animals in early China was inspired by a preoccupation with nomenclature and textual exegesis rather than empirical or experimental enquiry (Ptak 2012, 9–11, 13). It is hard to disagree with Ptak's contention that hidden behind the 'literary' species in our sources there are biological and zoological realities. Ptak's critique, however, is an argument *ex silentio*. It is one thing to assume there may have existed, as he suggests, oral traditions we do not know about or indeed a class of specialist observers whose analyses did not get into the written record; it is, however, an entirely different proposition to infer from this that they did not end up in our texts because these specialists may not have been familiar with local writing systems or nomenclature (p. 11). Without more evidence of institutions or information on the sociological context in which zoological knowledge was transmitted, it remains problematic to infer the existence of a more vibrant interest in nature 'as such', especially when there is ample evidence for the transfer of technical knowledge in other areas during this period such as, for instance, medicine and astronomy.

2 'Mimesis' in its pre-Platonic sense, defined by Hermann Koller as 'performance', 'enactment', or 'impersonation' through rhythm and dance (rather than representation or imitation), seems the more apt category here for comparative purposes. See Koller (1954); and a critical review of Koller in Keuls (1978), chapter 1.

REFERENCES

Bohutong shu zheng 白虎通疏證. Edited by Chen Li 陳立 (1809–69). Beijing: Zhonghua, 1997.

Chunqiu fanlu yi zheng 春秋繁露義證. Edited by Su Yu 蘇輿. Beijing: Zhonghua, 1996.

Da Dai Liji jiegu 大戴禮記解詁. Edited by Wang Pinzhen 王聘珍. Beijing: Zhonghua, 1998.

Du Qingyu 杜庆余, 2010. *Handai tianzhuang yanjiu* 汉代田庄研究. Jinan: Shandong daxue.

Duduan 獨斷. *Han Wei congshu* edition.

Eno, Robert, 1990. *The Confucian Creation of Heaven. Philosophy and the Defense of Ritual Mastery.* Albany: State University of New York Press.

Feuchtwang, Stephan, 2010. *The Anthropology of Religion, Charisma, and Ghosts: Chinese Lessons for Adequate Theory.* Berlin & New York: De Gruyter.

Guo Fu 郭郛 et al., 1999. *Zhongguo gudai dongwu xue shi* 中国古代动物学史. Beijing: Kexue chubanshe.

Guanzi jiaoshi 管子校釋. Edited by Yan Changyao 顏昌嶢. Changsha: Yuelu shushe, 1996.

Han Feizi jishi 韓非子集釋. Edited by Chen Qiyou 陳奇猷. Gaoxiong: Fuwen, 1991.

Han guan yi 漢官儀. *Sibu beiyao* edition.

Hanshu 漢書. Beijing: Zhonghua, 1962.

Hou Hanshu 後漢書. Beijing: Zhonghua, 1965.

Huainanzi honglie jijie 淮南子鴻烈集解. Edited by Liu Wendian 劉文典. Taipei: Wenshizhe, 1992.

Kaltenmark, M., 1953. *Le Lie-Sien Tchouan*. Paris: Université de Paris; Publications du Centre d'Etudes Sinologiques de Pékin.

Keuls, Eva C., 1978. *Plato and Greek Painting.* New York: Columbia University Press.

Koller, H., 1954. *Die Mimesis in der Antike.* Bern: A. Francke.

Lewis, Mark E., 1990. *Sanctioned Violence in Early China.* Albany: State University of New York Press.

Lewis, Mark E., 2006. *The Flood Myths of Early China.* Albany: State University of New York Press.

Li Haixia 李海霞, 2002. *Hanyu dongwu mingming yanjiu* 漢語動物命名研究. Chengdu: Ba Shu shushe.

Li Song 李淞 ed., 2001. *Handai renwu diaoke yishu* 漢代人物雕刻藝術. Changsha: Hunan meishu chubanshe.

Liji zhushu 禮記注疏. *Shisanjing zhushu* edition; rpt. Taizhong: Landeng, n.d., vol. 5.

Liu Li, 1996. Mortuary ritual and social hierarchy in the Longshan culture. *Early China* 21, 1–46.

Lo, Vivienne ed., 2012. *Perfect Bodies: Sports, Medicine and Immortality.* London: British Museum Research Publications no. 188.

Loewe, M., 1994. *Divination, Mythology and Monarchy in Han China.* Cambridge: Cambridge University Press.

Lunheng jiaoshi 論衡校釋. Edited by Liu Pansui 劉盼遂. Beijing: Zhonghua, 1990.

Lunyu zhushu 論語注疏. Annotated by Xing Bing 邢昺 (932–1010). *Shisanjing zhushu* edition, vol. 8.

Lüshi chunqiu jiaoshi 呂氏春秋校釋. Edited by Chen Qiyou 陳奇猷. Shanghai, Xuelin, 1995.

Major, John S., 2008. Animals and animal metaphors in *Huainanzi. Asia Major* (third series), 21.1, 133–51.

Major, John S. et al., 2010. *The Huainanzi: A Guide to the Theory and Practice of Government in Early Han China.* New York: Columbia University Press.

Mao shi zhengyi 毛詩正義. *Shisanjing zhushu* edition, vol. 2.

Mawangdui Han mu boshu 馬王堆漢墓帛書 (1980–5). Edited by Mawangdui Han mu boshu zhengli xiaozu. Beijing: Wenwu.

Mengzi zhushu 孟子注疏. *Shisanjing zhushu* edition; rpt. Taizhong: Landeng, n.d., vol. 8.

Mozi jiaozhu 墨子校注. Beijing: Zhonghua, 1993.

Needham, Joseph M., 1954–. *Science and Civilisation in China.* Cambridge: Cambridge University Press.

Powers, M., 1991. *Art and Political Expression in Early China.* New Haven, CT: Yale University Press.

Ptak, R., 2012. *Birds and Beasts in Chinese Texts and Trade.* Wiesbaden: Harrassowitch.

Rickett, W. Allyn, 1998. *Guanzi. Political, Economic, and Philosophical Essays from Early China. Volume Two.* Princeton, NJ: Princeton University Press.

Shaanxi sheng kaogu yanjiusuo ed., 2001. *Han Yangling* 汉阳陵. Chongqing: Chongqing chubanshe.

Shangshu da zhuan 尚書大傳. *Congshu jicheng* edition.

Shanhaijing jiaozhu 山海經校注. Annotated by Yuan Ke 袁珂. Shanghai: Guji, 1980.

Shiji 史記. Beijing: Zhonghua, 1959.

Shuowen jiezi zhu 說文解字注. Annotated by Duan Yucai 段玉裁 (1735–1815). Taipei: Yiwen, 1965.

Shuoyuan jiaozheng 說苑校證. Edited by Xiang Zonglu 向宗魯. Beijing: Zhonghua, 1987.

Sterckx, R., 2000. Transforming the beasts: animals and music in early China. *T'oung Pao* 86, 1–46.

Sterckx, R., 2002. *The Animal and the Daemon in Early China.* Albany: State University of New York Press.

Sterckx, R., 2005. Animal classification in ancient China. *East Asian Science, Technology, and Medicine* 23, 26–53.

Sterckx, R., 2011. *Food, Sacrifice, and Sagehood in Early China.* New York: Cambridge University Press.

Sterckx, R., 2012. Animals, gaming and entertainment in traditional China, in Vivienne Lo ed., *Perfect Bodies: Sports, Medicine and Immortality* (London: British Museum Research Publications no. 188, 2012), 31–8.

van Ess, H., 2003. An interpretation of the Shenwu Fu of Tomb no. 6, Yinwan. *Monumenta Serica* 51, 605–28.

Wenzi 文子. *Sibu beiyao* edition.

Xia Henglian 夏亨廉 et al. (1996). *Handai nongye huaxiang zhuanshi* 汉代农业画像砖石. Beijing: Nongye chubanshe.

Xiao Kengda 萧亢达, 2010. *Handai yuewu baixi yishu yanjiu* 汉代乐舞百戏艺术研究. Beijing: Wenwu chubanshe.

Xinlun 新論. Attributed to Huan Tan 桓譚 (43 BC- AD 28). *Sibu beiyao* edition.

Xunzi jijie 荀子集解. Edited by Wang Xianqian 王先謙 (1842–1918). Beijing: Zhonghua, 1997.

Yang Xiangdong 杨向东, 2000a. *Zhongguo gudai tiyu wenhua shi* 中国古代体育文化史. Tianjin: Tianjin renmin chubanshe.

Yang, Xiaoneng, 2000b. *Reflections of Early China: Decor, Pictographs, and Pictorial Inscriptions*. Seattle and London: The Nelson-Atkins Museum of Art and University of Washington Press.

Yantie lun jiaozhu 鹽鐵論校注. Compiled by Huan Kuan 桓寬 (1st century BC), annotated by Wang Liqi. Beijing: Zhonghua, 1996.

Yanzi chunqiu jishi 晏子春秋集釋. Edited by Wu Zeyu 吳則虞. Beijing: Zhonghua, 1962.

Zhangjiashan Han mu zhujian (tomb no. 247) 張家山漢墓竹簡 (二四七號墓). Beijing: Wenwu, 2001.

Zhanguo huiyao 戰國會要. Edited by Yang Kuan 楊寬 and Wu Haokun 吳浩坤. Shanghai: Shanghai guji, 2005.

Zhouli zhengyi 周禮正義. *Shisanjing zhushu edition*, vol.3.

Zhuangzi jishi 莊子集釋. Edited by Guo Qingfan 郭慶藩. Taipei: Guanya, 1991.

Zuozhuan: *Chunqiu Zuozhuan zhu* 春秋左傳注, edited by Yang Bojun 楊伯峻. Beijing: Zhonghua, 1995.

13

MANIPULATING THE BONES: EATING AND AUGURY IN THE MALTESE TEMPLES

Caroline Malone

Few social occasions demand greater effort in terms of playacting and ritual behaviour than feasts. These may require clothes to demonstrate status and affiliation, and the participants must play a role that is almost theatrical, employing special manners and rituals in the public consumption of food. The food served is also different, special and imbued with symbolic values through its presentation, preparation and the manner of its disposal. This chapter explores the nature of play in feasts and special celebratory meals and the multiple symbols used in the components of the feast, combined with the playacting involved in one context of European prehistory. The drama of formal eating involves not only the place and its paraphernalia (the space, table, dishes, cutlery and lighting), but also the food (alive, dead and cooked) and its presentation. Much of the consumption is structured and organised as if part of a dramatic performance such as the order of the dishes and their ingredients (for example, soup, followed by fish and meat), the way they are served and the participation of the guests involved. There will be first feeders, high tables, and such formalities are the very stuff of drama and playacting, combined with ritual action in the mannered, repeated and deeply embedded order of action. Status is especially important for both the guest and the host, and dramatists and writers have long parodied dinner parties as mirrors of society in a given place and time. Patronius' Satyricon and his depiction of "Dinner at Trimalchio" (Sullivan 2011) is just one splendid example of dramatic excess and pomp in the Roman world. For prehistory, insight into the tastes of a society is difficult, although plenty of evidence survives that might hint at the drama and play of competitive feasting.

INTRODUCTION

Animal flesh figures large in human feasts, since celebratory eating and feasting invariably focuses on meat, not veg, and few grand meals are served without animal flesh of some form. In some traditional societies, the 'steak' may be delivered alive, to be despatched in public view as part of the drama of the feast. The differing values attached to wild or domesticated animals, be it for their breeding, power, rarity, taste and so on adds to the significance of meat. In contrast, far less public symbolism or celebration seems to be attached to non-meat foods in such societies, or at least of a nature that surfaces in archaeological evidence. Animal-based food privileges archaeology with a wealth of bony remains from feasting and sacrificial encounters, enriched further by hearths, cooking equipment, serving dishes, carving implements and rubbish. All too often these data have been disregarded as mundane, and artefact evidence favoured instead for interpreting ritual in the form of altars, images and pottery vessels. In this chapter, I argue that the manipulation of animal remains and animal symbolism within competitive feasting and ritual play offers important insights into the manner of human–animal relationships, religion and art.

One hundred years ago, Sir Themistocles (Temi) Zammit investigated the buried prehistoric temples of Tarxien on Malta, and recorded the clearance of the many spaces and rooms of one of the most complex ritual buildings surviving from European prehistory. Zammit noted the dumps of carefully secreted animal bones and horns in the buildings and collected samples. Later lost, those bones were never studied, and these data have been ignored. In contrast, wonderful animal representations – figurines, friezes and decorated pottery which accompanied the palaeozoological material – have dominated the interpretation of this island culture, in tandem with an obsession for 'goddess' figurines. The richness of the imagery provides a tantalising insight into the role of animals in a feasting context, and the possible aspects of animal 'play' and drama involved in early Malta's apparently lavish feasting activities.

Zammit kept site diaries of his work between 1915–19, in which he charted the distribution patterns of bones and artworks at the excavation site of Tarxien (Zammit 1915–19, 1930). From my systematic study, a new understanding of the manipulation of animal bones in the temple context becomes possible, allowing insight into the theatrical and visual manipulation of a feast in prehistoric times. Within the wider prehistoric setting of a deteriorating environment and irreversible social change that was under way in Neolithic Malta, the relationship between food symbols, subsistence and survival was played out intensively and graphically.

The Maltese Temple Setting

The theme of animals and play offers an enticing opportunity to review the role of animals in the feasting practices of prehistoric Malta. Rarely in the archaeological context do we think of animals as more than sources of food, traction-transport and general economic benefit. The ritual dimension of animals in prehistory is varied, and typically characterised by Palaeolithic cave paintings, animal deities of Ancient Egypt, the bull games of Minoan Crete and the demonic animal symbols inscribed on Viking metalwork. The remarkable context of the megalithic prehistoric temples of Neolithic Malta, however, provides a different and rich exploratory source of material. Here the manipulation of animals in the theatrical and symbolic expression of ritual drama and human belief is combined. It is expressed in the layout and decoration of deliberate arenas of theatre and in the disposal of feasting rubbish in a manner that enables a reconstruction of prehistoric ritual 'play' – a play that combined scarce and treasured food resources in a controlled drama. As Bateson (Chapter 4, this volume) describes, playfulness is a positive mood state, and one can presume that the prospect of feasts in prehistory might promote a positive, cooperative and optimistic sense of well-being, especially in an island world where food was in short supply.

Ritual activity focused on animals is often associated with early prehistory and hunter-gatherer-herding peoples, for whom animals were the principal source of subsistence. In contrast, the close relationship between farmers and their animals is rather overlooked by archaeologists. The long breeding histories of many stock lines and the importance of herds/flocks to early and traditional farmers was always important, and animals held prestige and embodied wealth. The slaughter of precious stock, especially the larger animals, was likely to be a highly ritualised and dramatic event. It required a large gathering of people to consume the meat and dispose of the carcass within hours, if not days of despatch. Such despatch required a feast and a party and engendered much ritual play and theatre. Even today, we can identify the deeply embedded human instincts that emerge with the hunting/ritual slaughter of animals-fish-birds and their often flamboyant consumption, enhanced by special dress, weapons, places and behaviour. When there were few animals to hunt, as in the case of island Malta, the domestic creatures took the place of wild or dangerous prey and became the *persona dramatica* of food, feast and foray instead. When this stock was slaughtered for feasts, their identities were probably celebrated by symbolic displays of their horns and bones, and not simply consumed and disposed of. One can imagine competitive farmers presenting their ever-larger and finer bulls, rams and boars for ostentatious sacrifice and feast in the milieu of competitive community ritual. The depiction of bulls in particular, may be deeply embedded Indo-European myth, and reflected the wider Neolithic world that arrived in Malta (Rozwadowski 2001, 65–86).

EARLY MALTA

The archipelago of Malta and Gozo represents one of the smallest and most isolated archipelagos of the Mediterranean. These islands cover barely 316 km², and the rocky limestone presented a challenging landscape for the Neolithic settlers who arrived between 5500–5000 BC from neighbouring Sicily. From the initial findings of pollen studies (Hunt and Schembri 1999; Carroll et al. 2004, 2012), it seems likely that the landscape the first settlers encountered was relatively verdant, with a substantial soil cover partly made up of loess. This supported an open, wooded environment that offered potential for intensive use, in spite of the islands' small size. Agricultural productivity was limited by scale and the lack of perennial streams or rivers: it resulted in dependency on springs and rainfall.

Armed with axes and fire, those early settlers soon laid waste to the woodlands, cutting and burning their way towards rapid soil loss and a progressive erosion of natural resources. They brought the standard stock animals with them, cattle, sheep-goat and pig, together with dog and perhaps cat. Wild animals on the islands may have included small rodents, birds and (?imported) deer. The imported domestic animals required grazing land and fodder, and goats especially may have made a rapid and perhaps catastrophic impact on the vegetation of the landscape. We still have much to learn about the prehistoric environment ([1]), but within centuries, the Maltese islands were degraded, a process that has continued almost unabated over succeeding millennia. Humans, being the resourceful creatures they are, responded to these changes through intensification, first maximising their food production of terrestrial foods – plant cultivation and managed stock animals through breeding and husbandry. Terrace systems to retain soil were then developed; how early we still cannot

be sure, but probably from the second millennium BC. By the late Bronze Age, a wider world system had emerged, and boats plied between Sicily, Italy and the wider Mediterranean; perhaps even foodstuffs were moved around. Before that moment, the Maltese islands remained a remote and economically precarious place – at least 80 km from Sicily across an unpredictable sea. Over time felling resulted in insufficient mature trees to build many large seagoing boats, and from the archaeological evidence, the contacts between Malta and its neighbours seem to have been spasmodic and small-scale. The impact of such 'remoteness' was the development of a strong local identity expressed in distinctive material culture and unique megalithic buildings. A continuing question is why the early Maltese culture invested heavily in ritual theatre in special 'temple-like' buildings focused on the display, despatch and consumption of precious stock animals. Was the outcome serious religious 'theatre' with spiritual goals? Or was the outcome socially competitive parties, playacting and feasting in a celebration of fertility or a religious food frenzy?

FOOD AND THE VALUE OF ANIMALS

Maltese Neolithic farming was small scale, broadly based on the mixed Mediterranean model of cereals, pulses and domestic animals (Jarman, Bailey & Jarman 1982; Barker 1985, 2000, 2006; Halstead 1989, 1996), and it has received little study until now. Farmed food dominated, and like most of the Neolithic communities of Europe, Maltese farmers rarely exploited marine foods, in spite of being surrounded by productive seas. Our assessment of a small sample of faunal remains (see Barber et al. 2009) is insufficient to draw solid conclusions, but it shows that ovicaprids were better adapted to the dry Mediterranean conditions, and were the mainstay of meat in the subsistence diet. The rough macchia-type terrain and meagre seasonal rain was suited to grazing of stubble after harvest by agile, small beasts able to graze on the spiny vegetation on the rocky hillsides or to exploit the reeds and seaweeds. Pigs and cattle were present in significant numbers, and they probably exploited the scarce lush and lightly wooded zones of Malta. The meat of adult cattle or pigs was sufficient for a communal feast, and unsurprisingly bull images dominate the zoo-art of Temple Period Malta (as in Minoan Crete, see Marinatos, Chapter 15, this volume). These farm animals represented the only significant meat source in a space-limited island where wild animals were not present, so images of sheep and pigs or bulls (Figure 13.3: 2, 3, 4, 7, 13, 14, 16) may be seen as symbols of wealth. Meat animals were also the closest equivalent to a walking bank balance in a non-monetary society, especially one with no prospect of accumulating other forms of wealth in a resource-poor island.

The Brochtorff-Xaghra Circle faunal sample (ca. 7,000 fragments; see Barber et al. 2009) may not be representative of typical daily life or feasting, since animal remains were associated with human burials and represented funerary offerings. The selection of animals nevertheless reflects the relative frequency of the contemporary Neolithic farm animals of Malta, with 45 sheep-goat individuals representing the greatest number but not the most meat. Instead, the much lower numbers of individual pigs (15) and cattle (14) represented the more valuable meat of the Temple Culture community, who ritually disposed of the least meat-bearing bones (lower limbs, hooves, teeth/mandibles and skulls) in the burial complex. These recognisable bones may have been emblematic of meaningful animal offerings without any significant loss of precious nutrition, and their placement could symbolise mortuary feasts eaten elsewhere. Given that sheep jaws were found with several female burials and a boar's head with a male, gender and status may also have been inferred by the offering. Fragmented but recognisable, some 38 horn cores of cattle and ovicaprids were retrieved from the more peripheral burial zones of the cave complex (Figure 13.1a). Sheep-goat offerings contrasted from the cattle-pig remains, since meat-bearing torso parts were afforded prime place in the burials, whilst nutritionally negligible feet, skull, teeth and lower limb bones were strewn in peripheral zones. Some deposits were distinguished by right or the left side bones from the carcass, and sidedness may have been significant. Importantly too, almost none (less than 0.5%) of the animal bones recovered from the site had been burnt (and possibly not even cooked), which implies that the carcass parts taken to the

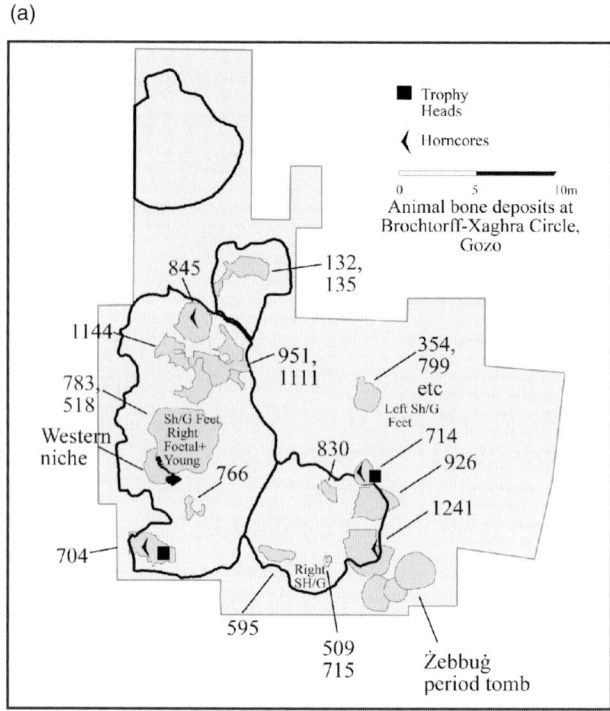

Figure 13.1 (a) Plan of Brochtorff Xaghra Circle animal bone deposits and horn cores. (Drawing – author).

funerary site were butchery off-cuts that were used to embody the animals of a feast that took place elsewhere or raw cuts.

When compared with the temple complexes, mortuary sites are unlikely foci for food remains, and in order to explore how the ancient Maltese dealt with food and the likely shortages that they probably encountered, we need to re-examine the faunal evidence from the Maltese temples. Here we are thwarted by the scantly published results from Skorba (excavated 1958–63), which produced a mass of bones from a temple-settlement site that extended over many phases (Trump 1966, 53). Material is now being reanalysed (Darvill, pers. comm.). At Tarxien (the most significant excavation of Neolithic remains in the twentieth century), the diary records of excavation reveal a little more, but no faunal study was ever undertaken, and most of the finds were subsequently lost. The ongoing study of a prehistoric temple deposit by the Italian team at Tas-Silġ under the Phoenician temple complex presents exciting new opportunities to assess ritual rubbish in situ (Cazzella & Reccia, pers. comm., 2012; Fiorentini, D'Oronzo & Colaianni 2012).

There are cross-cultural parallels in the ways that different animals and their various body parts are used as symbols in mythology and religious ritual. Skulls of deer, cattle and ovicaprids were used to embellish ritual places (for example, the shrines and altars of Çatal Hüyük and the horns of consecration at Mycenae (Evans 1901), the nine gold-banded drinking horns from the Iron Age Hochdorf burial (Aldhouse-Green et. al. 2005, 125)), to mark burial sites of cattle farmers (contemporary Madagascar), or to imply hunting prowess and social status in nineteenth-century baronial houses. Heads and horns signal animal personalities and successful hunts or herding, and their display occurs throughout human history. More symbolically, hybridised animal-human characters are portrayed through manipulated bones such as the Mesolithic Star Carr (Yorkshire) (Clark 1954, 123; Legg & Rowley Conwy 1988) and the deer antler-skull frontals used as headdress paraphernalia for ritual and dance, or in the antlered shamanic figure in the ice-age Trois Frères cave in Ariège, France. In pre-historic Malta, the lack of wild horns and antlers was replaced by emblematic domestic animal horns in ceremonial ritual and feasting.

Maltese culture in the Neolithic period developed what appears to be an unprecedented level of sophistication in terms of architecture and artistic representation. Neighbouring Sicily and southern Italy had neither comparable buildings to the Maltese temples nor the artistic paraphernalia. But whilst these contemporaneous neighbours don't appear to have invested in lavish structures and art, they certainly developed sophisticated and novel subsistence strategies such as milk processing and other secondary products (Ashley et al. 2007).

Malta's subsistence stability was significant in that it almost certainly underpinned the socio-economic impetus that provoked the building and use of its so-called temples, together with consolidation of the development of its ritual world. Until now, interpretations to explain these building have focused on the extravagant and artistic aspects – chiefly hierarchies, priests, goddess and sun worship, amongst various propositions. But perhaps the answer is far more mundane and related to the economy and to the availability of food, its redistribution, its storage and the ceremonial despatch of precious domestic animals.

The megalithic 'temples' of Malta need some explanation. They are some of the most sophisticated stone-built structures of early Europe and are architectural in design and scale (Evans 1971; Trump 1983; Bonanno 1990). The structures were built to a canon of set, repeating forms of oval-shaped, partially hidden rooms opening from a central corridor (clover-leaf shaped). The rooms were enclosed within high walls and covered by stone corbels and slab roofs. The main corridor opened onto an arena-like forecourt and many temples had stone 'display benches' built into the façade. Distinct areas within the 'temple' were hidden spaces organised for storage, altars and ritual refuse disposal. In many instances, quantities of symbolic objects and containers were stored, displayed or hidden inside the structures in specific locations (Malone 2007). Finally, the temple buildings (and there were normally several adjacent structures) partly surrounded a large, level forecourt. Several examples survive, and today they suggest a theatrical space, a stage with a backdrop, on which the actors could play out their roles. If indeed the temples were ancient theatrical spaces, then we can talk of playacting and ritual drama in a securely Neolithic context.

ZAMMIT AND THE EXCAVATIONS AT TARXIEN

One key source of information are the original excavation diaries of Temi Zammit, and it is possible to extract a range of overlooked but general economic information relating to bones, serving vessels and hearths. From 1915 until 1919, during the height of World War I, Zammit conducted excavations at the site that was to reveal the remarkable temples of Tarxien in the village of Paola. He had a little excavation experience from his salvage work at the neighbouring hypogeum site of Hal Saflieni, which he completed after workmen had all but emptied the contents. His methods were probably typical of the time, and involved supervision of local, untrained workmen, paid by the day to clear the site over several weeks at a time, while funds lasted. The notebooks take the form of a diary with typical entries identifying a room or area under excavation (letters for rooms provide identification; see plans depicted

(b)

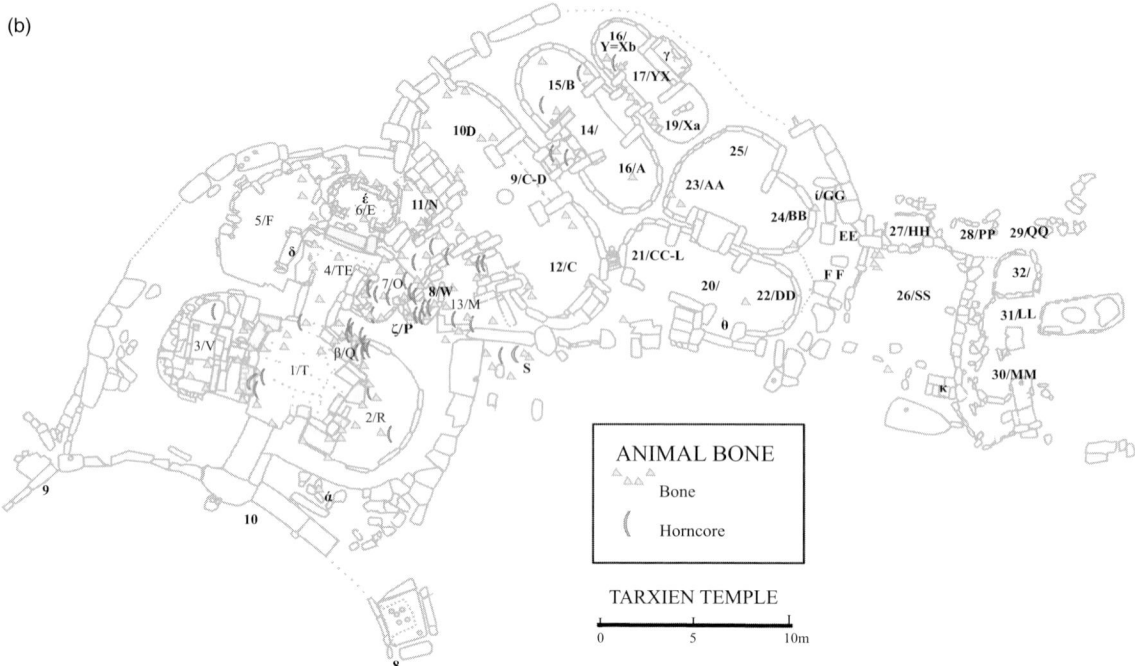

Figure 13.1 (b) Tarxien temple (rooms numbered according to the Evans 1971 format, and Zammit's alphabetic system) animal bone plots and horn cores, as recorded in Zammit's excavation notebooks (1915–19). (Drawing – Author)

(c)

Figure 13.1 (c) Tarxien temple pottery-stone vessels, fragments and other artefacts recorded in Zammit's excavation notebooks (1912).

in Figure 13.1b–c). The descriptions are brief, sometimes noting the approximate level below the surrounding field, or whether conservation of walls and stones took place. Quantities are vague – typically "several boxes of sherds collected" or "bones and stones and pots". Zammit habitually recorded the excavation areas by letters, and he further identified internal features by more A, B and C identifiers, sometimes sketching the context, but assuming the letter would identify the correct position. In many cases, this is not now possible. Few excavators at the time bothered with survey of a site until it was cleared, and we have no surviving measured plans of excavation trenches or sections, just graphic sketches of various rooms and niches. Photos were taken, showing the progress of excavation, and sometimes there are captions, but no scales or directions were included to pin-point the positions. Invariably, more interest was taken in the artefacts than in the archaeological context and its association with soil, colour, levels, directions or method of excavation. Inevitably, vital data are lost to us today on the detail of the site. The significance of the Tarxien temples was as the first and most extensive twentieth-century prehistoric excavations in Malta, even if many data are not preserved.

WHERE WERE THE BONES AND WHY?

The Zammit's excavation diaries of Tarxien have enabled me to plot the general location of many of the bone deposits of animals found in the temple. The notes, when read carefully, reveal an unexplored facet of the temples and their ancient activities that show feasting activities took place, and resulted in the disposal of cattle, sheep-goat and pig bones within the temple structures. These remains seem to have been encountered almost daily in the excavations, and a plot of their recorded distribution allows us to explore how animals may have featured in the ritual activities, and in the feasting and storage of materials in the many nooks and crannies of the temple rooms. The potential for faunal study was not understood in the earlier decades of the twentieth century, and few samples were retained for study – indeed, there was no formal study, simply a note of encounters. The standard of Zammit's recording is very variable and by the later years of the Tarxien clearance, he seems to have spent less time on the site and almost no bones were noted in the eastern temple area, whilst the finds of the early years were recorded in enthusiastic detail with sketches and lists. Some bones were even sketched or photographed, but generally, Zammit seems to have thought the animal bones were part and parcel

of the temple deposit. He rarely speculated about the significance of species or of the treatment or significance of the body parts. A typical entry is that for 15 May 1916 on page 42 of Notebook 12, where he notes:

> In the brown soil to the extreme left close to space W a large horn ... of ox is found about 1ft from the pavement. (National Museum of Archaeology Archive, Valletta)

Space W and its pavement can be roughly identified through the notes, which provides some spatial understanding. Significantly, over the 65 years since the work at Tarxien, no modern excavation recorded or retrieved much animal bone either, leaving a void in our understanding of the zooarchaeological record (Trump 1966; Evans 1971; Cilia 2004). Zammit set a standard for archaeological work in Malta that provided the benchmark for his successors, and his methods were not questioned or improved upon for decades. Subsequently, few scholars understood or examined the zooarchaeological record or its potential to reveal the economic and ritual activities of the early Maltese culture. At a time when archaeological recording was becoming systematic and had access (between the 1930s–1960s) to the palaeoeconomic ideas of Graham Clark and other scholars (see Jarman et al. 1982), even the 1960s work at Skorba remained incomplete and unquestioned (see Trump 1966, Appendix III).

Zammit's diary notes also observed the locations of pottery and stone vessels. The majority were finely made vessels and were not the cooking and food storage variety, but instead were types designed for the display, presentation and consumption of feasts. Decorated and elaborate in form, these vessels must have transmitted significant information to users and viewers about their role in the serving of food and drink (Evans 1953, 1971, figure 21, 5). Ceramic and stone vessels made up the assemblage of containers, which vary in size from miniature to out-sized. A range of forms (discussed by Evans 1953, 1971 and Trump 1966) included a standardised offering bowl with lugs and a rounded base, and this seems to have dominated the feasting equipment. In one or two excavated instances, caves and hollows were crammed with the ritual rubbish formed of discarded bowls (Ggantija North Cave, Evans 1971, 173, 214), so it is likely that the ceremonial offerings, once eaten, were formally disposed of within the 'sacred' feasting area. Likewise, remains may have been considered ritual rubbish, given the recorded observations of burnt bones littering Hagar Qim in the 1840s clearance (Evans 1971, Plan 18A, rooms 11, 14, 7, 8; and the nineteenth-century dumps in the eastern building). Early twentieth-century excavators encountered further bones and horns at several sites (Ashby et al. 1913; Zammit 1927), and as this material was not disposed of outside the buildings, this pattern might imply the importance of bone remains as ritual rubbish symbolic of past feasts and offerings. The records of Tarxien's bones therefore provide a tantalising insight to a once rich source of elusive evidence and a general parallel to the Gozo data discussed earlier in this chapter. Given the paucity of Maltese faunal collections or records, little progress on precise skeletal parts, relative ages or meat potential of the creatures deposited in the temples is now possible. Instead, another thread of indirect evidence is the graphic record of animals in reliefs, models and incised representations (showing domestic stock, birds, fish, reptiles and strange monstrous creatures). Zoomorphic images have even greater antiquity than those of human images in much of Europe, but generally scholars have seized on the human forms and developed elaborate theories to explain them (Gamble & Moser 1998; Jones 2011). The Temple Culture developed particularly distinctive and often obese figurative art forms, of different scales and of varying posture, nakedness and gender. From Vance and other scholars in the nineteenth century, to Zammit, and then Marija Gimbutas in the later twentieth century, these obese forms became the focus of discussions on Maltese art and religion. In contrast the animal imagery and its interpretation has been largely ignored.

ANIMALS IN EARLY MALTA

The animal representations in prehistoric Malta occur as small personal ornaments, pendants and talismans, as carved and modelled images and engravings, sometime as modelled handles of pottery vessels or as statuettes, and in rare cases, as larger reliefs carved into temple walls. The categories making up this animal art include domestic, marine-subterranean, birds and hybrid-monstrous creatures. The present assemblage has few wild mammals, but displays a distinct separation between edible, warm-blooded, domestic mammals, feathered wild birds and reptilian, cold-blooded creatures. These animal representations may have been manipulated as part of elaborate gameplay, acting out processions, masquerades and carnivals, used as toys, or as proxies and talisman of memory. The relief art from Tarxien (see Figure 13.3) includes a cavalcade of domestic stock, apparently processing in line to the temple (sheep, goat and pig) and suggest graphically the temple's function as a site of display, despatch and feasting. The Buġġiba temple by the sea (see Evans 1971, 109–12) appears, albeit on scarce evidence, to have had a marine focus represented by a fish relief (Figure 13.3: 5.6) and model (Figure 13.2: 6). (Sadly, this temple was almost obliterated without record by the building of the scandalous 'Dolmen Hotel' that now surrounds it). Imagery at the temples varied, with Hagar Qim focused on humans and curious monstrous semi-human images, Mnajdra focused on humans and cattle, and Ggantija including a carved snake relief on a pillar, whilst its neighbour Santa Verna included snails. The rich assemblage collected from the burial site of Hal Saflieni had human figures, cattle, birds, fish and reptiles.

Domestic animal images appear in various forms and scales, from miniature models, ornaments, pendants and engravings in various contexts, to stone reliefs in temples-tombs of more than a meter in length. Several ceramic vessels have bulls on them, including fine spotted ones (Figure 13.3: 9, 11), and some sherds depict pigs and birds, whilst modelled sheep/goat heads occur on handles of drinking cups. The Hal Saflieni Hypogeum yielded many of the most significant zoomorphic objects, modelled, carved and incised, and often of small size, such as the string of small bull pendants carved from hard stone, each represented with horns and a tail (Figure 13.3: 7, 8).

The presence of marine and subterranean animal images provides a different focus for discussion,

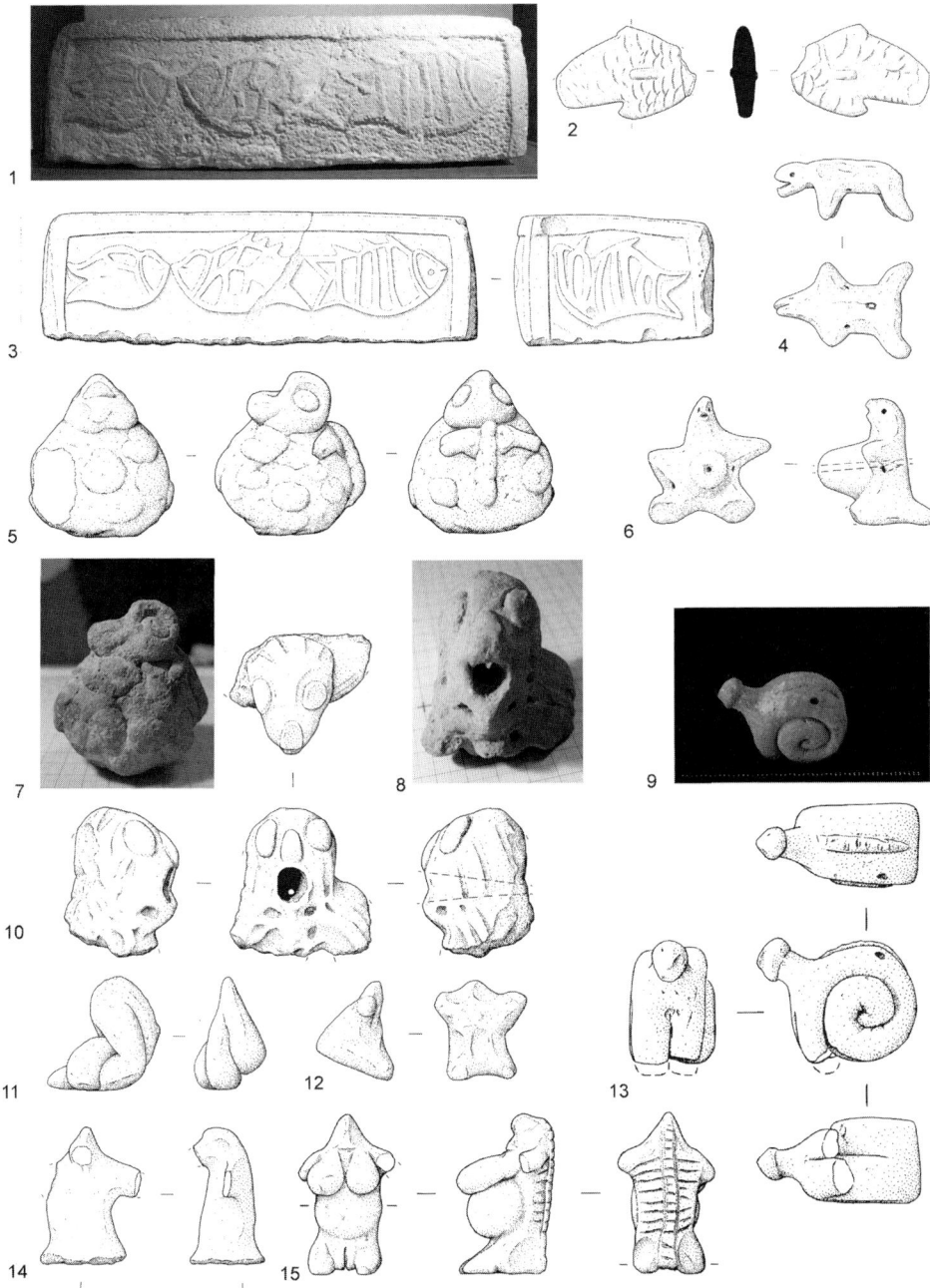

Figure 13.2 Animal images from Malta of the marine and subterranean category from Maltese Temple Period sites (various scales). (1), (3): Stone fish frieze from Buġġiba; (2): Clay model fish from Hal Saflieni; (4): Clay lizard from Hal Saflieni; (5), (7): Clay turtle from Mnajdra; (6): Clay figurine from Hal Saflieni; (8), (10): Clay sea monster? From Hagar Qim; (9), (13): Clay snail from Brochtorff Circle; (11): Clay twist 'foetus' from Mnajdra; (12): Clay figurine from Mnajdra; (14): Clay figurine from Tarxien; (15): Clay grotesque figurine with exposed backbone and distended belly from Mnajdra. (Drawings and Photos – author, by kind permission from the National Museum of Archaeology, Valletta).

since there were apparently negligible marine foods in the diet of Neolithic people on Malta (as revealed by the isotope programme conducted on the human bones from Gozo – see Lai, O'Connor & Tykot 2009, 335–40). It is likely that terrestrial food supplies were precarious throughout Maltese pre-history, especially with a likely rising population, so the lack of marine exploitation in a bountiful sea is strange. The pattern of marine-food avoidance follows a trend found across Neolithic Europe, and

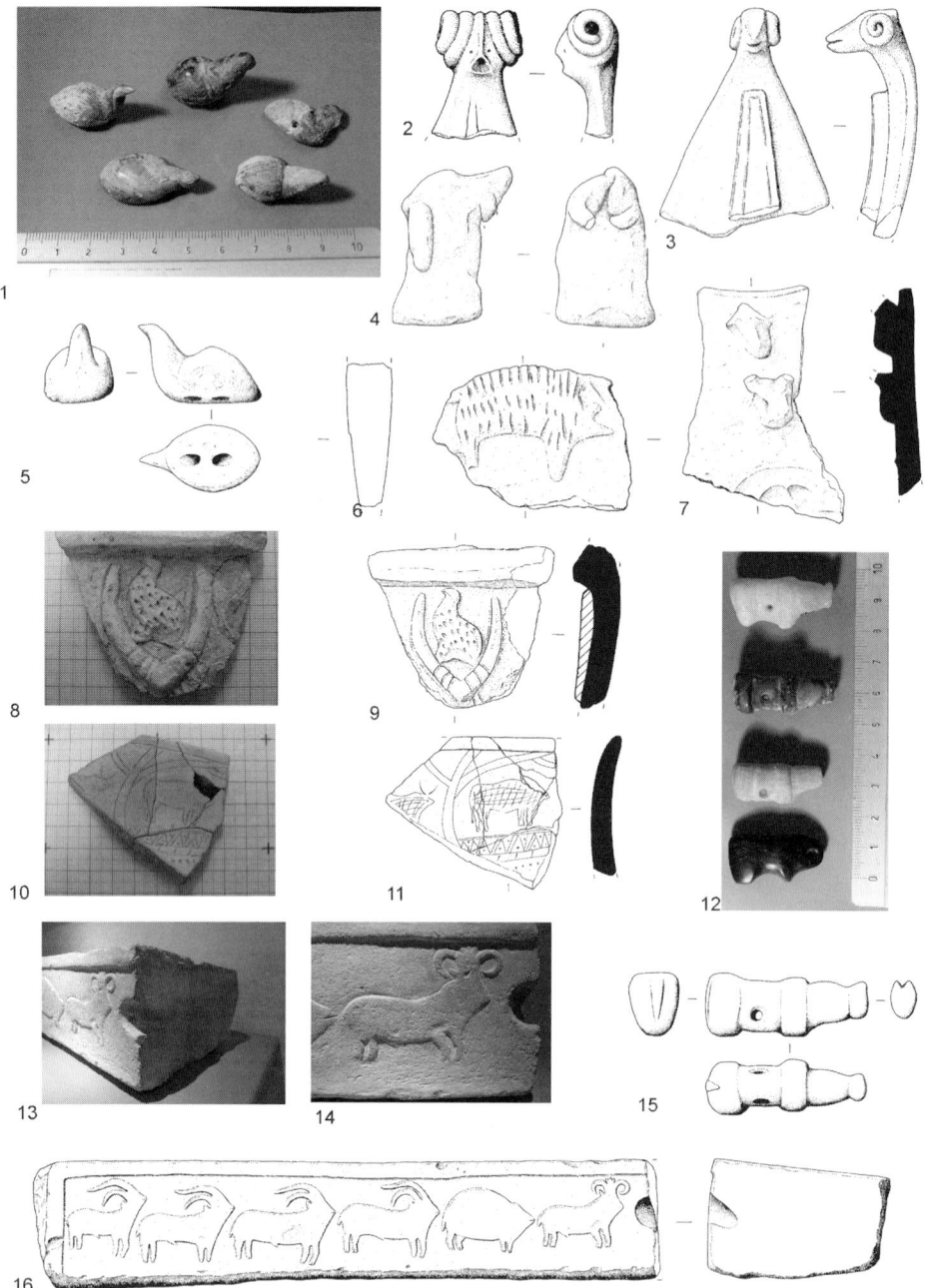

Figure 13.3 Domestic animals and birds from temple sites (various scales): (1), (5): Bird-shaped 'v' perforated buttons carved from shell and stone; (2), (3): Sheep head handles, Tarxien; (4): terracotta goat model, Mnajdra; (7): modelled animal head ceramic fragment, Buġgiba; (8), (9): Pottery sherd with modelled bull horns and bird, Tarxien; (10), (11): Rim sherd with incised cattle-bulls, Tarxien; (12), (15): stone cattle-bulls beads, Hal Saflieni; (13), (14), (16): Stone frieze of male animals, approximately 1 metre in length, Tarxien. (Drawings and Photos – author, by kind permission from the National Museum of Archaeology, Valletta).

could be associated with widespread dietary traditions and prohibitions. There is limited evidence that marine creatures were routinely consumed for food (remains are only known from the Bronze Age onwards), but in Malta, fishy, cold-blooded, reptilian

and mysterious creatures were depicted on figurines and reliefs (Figure 13.2). Fish (Figure 13.2: 1, 2, 3, 10), snakes, lizards (Figure 13.2: 4), turtles (Figure 13.2: 5, 7) and snails (Figure 13.2: 13) are rarely encountered in Neolithic art in Europe, but in Neolithic Malta, the notion of a marine and underworld environment was portrayed. In contrast, snakes were widely portrayed as seductive, evil and deathly creatures, from the Garden of Eden to Minoan snake goddesses. In Gozo, a snake was carved on a prominent megalithic upright at the Ggantija temple, and this imagery reminds the writer of the intervention made by Gordon Burghardt (Chapter 3, this volume). He presented graphically the snake-handling rituals still conducted by a sect of Christians in the southern United States, who include the handling of numerous poisonous snakes in their weird interpretation of religious practice. In Malta, reptilian-marine creatures were undoubtedly part of the ceremonial practices and cosmology – symbolic perhaps of death, hibernation and subterranean dimensions, since these creatures may disappear under water or underground to reappear in the sun to soak up energy – a process that could imply a certain magical or spiritual quality in the minds of the early Maltese.

Located strategically between North Africa and Europe, Malta was and is an important stopover for migrating birds (now virtually 'hunted' out of existence). In prehistory, the flocks of migrating birds passing in spring and autumn must have provoked ideas of connections to the outside world(s). Bird hunting/trapping would provide food and sport, a notion still deeply rooted in Malta today, especially in an island bereft of game since the arrival of human residents. Bird representations on personal ornaments and pottery provide a sense of their importance. A wonderful group of ducks from Hal Saflieni is represented on buttons carved from shell and stone (Figure 13.3: 1, 5) and were burial ornaments. One pot fragment depicts a bird perched between the horns of a bull (Figure 13.3: 8, 9), perhaps echoing a mythical story or game played out in early Maltese culture, a parallel to the bull-jumping games of Crete (see Marinatos, Chapter 15, and Spivey, Chapter 16, this volume).

The significance of birds and feathers in traditional societies is linked to notions of spiritual and 'out-of-body' flight to the heavenly ancestors and the sun (Devlet 2001) and the wearing of feathers in headdresses are seen as symbolic of shamanic powers. One stick figure found in the burial deposits

at Xaghra is shown wearing such a headdress or crown (Figure 13.4) and is a rare example of a headdress from Neolithic Malta. Zammit recorded at least five incidents of finding of 'bird bones', molluscs and fish vertebrae 'beads' in Tarxien's Bronze Age rather than Neolithic levels, which aroused scholarly curiosity in the first decades of the twentieth century. Bird bones with holes were suggestive of flutes; others were formed into handles for bronze awls and were also associated with carved bird pendants.

Alongside the distinctly animal or 'fishy' images (Figure 13.2: 8, 10), the Neolithic Maltese created highly imaginative hybrid characters – part human, part 'other'. Some are revolting creations of diseased humans, with distended stomachs and protruding spines and ribs, with reduced heads and extremities (see Figure 13.2: 6, 13). Schematic figures swathed in cloaks or shrouds (see Figure 13.2: 14, 15) and curious twists of clay (foetuses) (Vella Gregory 2005) (Figure 13.2: 11, 12) and a range of knobbed forms make up yet other images (Gimbutas 1982, 1991; Gimbutas & Dexter 2001; Malone 2007). One might question indeed, if these curious, amusing, revolting or crazy objects are actually amusing toys and playthings rather than serious symbolic paraphernalia.

FOOD AND FEAST

Cooking, burning and the serving of food and liquid were central to the symbolic activities preserved at Tarxien and the temples of Malta. Many food-focused installations were formed around prominent altars, firepits and hearths, often placed in the main line of sight within the central corridors, and visible from many points. In antiquity, in roofed, dark and stuffy buildings, the fires that burnt in them would have involved sensory responses to the visible flames, smoke, the smell of cooking or burning food, hot flames and crackling sounds. Tarxien more than any other temple preserves the positions of these hearths and firepits. The logical end point of the food chain of early Malta was consumed in these special locations, by flame and probably human appetite, leaving a slight archaeological trail behind it. The feasting and food was apparently focused on animals, and it

Figure 13.4 Brochtorff Circle stick figurine: carved from limestone, with feather (?) headdress. (Photo-Author).

seems very likely that stock animals were paraded, tied up to the stone tethers located in front of the main entrance and slaughtered in public view, butchered, presented on altars and cooked within the space of the temple. The meat was also cut and consumed within the precinct, as suggested by the innumerable ceramic bowls found everywhere and occasional lithic knives. The massive vessels and troughs encountered in parts of the temple site may have contained a communal stew or a brew consumed by the assembled company.

At Tarxien, Zammit recorded many of the room deposits in some detail. Here is an example of the clearance of space W (or room 8):

June 8th 1916
    Space B contains stones, soil, animal bones, many horns. Not burnt. B' under recess A full of soil at the entrance a fine pair of horns more bones and horns (ox and goat). (Zammit Notebook 12, Library Archive, National Museum of Archaeology, Valletta)

The records allow a plot of the information of animal bones and pottery to be constructed, which presents a general pattern of their distribution. Bones and discarded, burnt, ashy food offerings were dumped between the walls and immediately around the temple buildings – perhaps within what in prehistory was considered the sacred precinct. The plots suggest the south-west temple was the main focus of sacrificial activity, partly because of bones, and also because the structural elements of sculpture, reliefs and altars presented a theatrical, visual theme of animals and their entry into the temple. Firstly, Altar (Q) in Room 1–2/T-R preserves a remarkable mini-temple entrance, which contained an internal cupboard. This was accessed by a small, decorated stone slab, the space behind filled with faunal remains, including horns, of sheep-goat and cattle and flint knives (Figure 13.5: 1, 2, 4). Secondly, the extraordinary friezes of animals opposite in Room 3/V represent male and females in ordered rows. The male frieze (only half of the original slab survives – see Figure 13.3: 13, 14, 16) depicts a line of male animals that face to the right, led by a goat, and followed by sheep and pig. There was a tie hole in the centre of the original longer slab perhaps to tether the victim during ritual slaughter. Close to this, but actually facing it in its original position was another slab – intact, that represents two rows of (probably female) sheep-goats, all facing to the left. These constructions were 1.5 metres apart, and together with several other panels formed a unique, highly decorated room with a variety of vegetal-spiral-decorative friezes, panels and altars. At least three sets of horns were placed close to the entrance to this room (Room 1/T-3/ V) in primary stratigraphic levels (Figure 13.1b). Yet another horn was located to the north of the decorated slabs. Quantities of animal horns seem to have been concentrated on the right-hand side of the main corridor, becoming more frequent and denser as one progressed into the temple. Horns were secreted away in the hidden rooms, 7/O, ζ/P, 8/W and 13/M, where Zammit's notes indicate dozens of horns and dense bones. Room 13/M is very significant since this room contained a imagery of a pair of bulls and a sow with piglets carved in relief. Within three to four metres of these reliefs, some 16 horns/ pairs of horns were noted which represented a dense and symbolic concentration of bull-billy goat-ram consumption. Beyond this rather hidden area of the south-west temple, the few other recorded horns were clustered around the remarkable double spiral altar at the entrance to Room 14 and in the spaces behind this in the stone shelves of Rooms 15/B and 16/Y-Xb on the left (Figure 13.5: 3, 6, 7) in the northern-most middle temple.

Whilst horns are missing from the record of animal bones in the northern rooms of the south-west temple, the apse-shaped Room 6/E not only had a concentration of figurines (animal, human and temple models), but also, in the adjacent Room 5/F, a horizontal representation of a bull on a slab (hidden from view for some years – Vella pers. comm. and noted by Ugolini) (see Figure 13.1c for general location). Only one occurrence of horns was recorded outside the walls of the temple, outside the east wall of the south-west temple in the area Zammit called S. Figure 13.1a shows the distribution of both horns and bones (there are 49 instances of "horns" mentioned in the notes and 11 instances of "tusk"). Unfortunately, there are few surviving bones from these excavations, and what there are need further analysis.

At the temple site of Hagar Qim, an important freestanding altar was found in the middle of the nineteenth century (Figure 13.6: 8) placed beside a double spiral altar/blocking slab, and traditionally referred to as the "Floral" altar. It was thought to represent a pot plant with branches. The repeated carved decorations cover the four sides of a pillar (Figure 13.6: 3). They lie below a dished circular top, ideally formed for ceremonial slaughter or presentation of meat offerings. Originally, the altar was prominently placed on the principal line of axis on entry to the main temple, and this position, combined with its imagery, suggests to me that the altar was much more significant than a floral arrangement! Figure 13.6: 1 shows my reworking of this curious object, where stacked horn frontals (a range of horned stock animals is shown in Figure 13.6: 4, 5, 6, 7) have been overlaid on the photograph and diagram (Figure 13.6: 2). The animal rather than plant theme (closely connected to the thick layers of bones located close by) suggests a layered stack of curved horn-skull frontals, one above the other, secreted into a narrow niche. The drilled decoration around the suggested horn stack imitates the decoration found on many of the hidden cupboards and shelves within the Hagar Qim and Mnajdra temples. The altar decoration could hardly be a more graphic reference to horned animals, sacrifice and offering.

ENVIRONMENT AND FEASTS

Much has been written on the anthropology of feasts (Dietler & Hayden 2001), and there are common trends that emerge in traditional, and especially island contexts. Malta provides significant evidence that chimes with recent observations in regard to food and feasting. Neolithic Malta was economically marginal, a place where survival may have been precarious, especially when environmental fluctuations increasingly degraded a densely populated island. The maintenance of a reliable food supply would be a matter of paramount significance to that society, and its management closely linked to the power dynamics of its political structure. Doubtless, subsistence success was coupled with social competition and reflected in the tenure of limited farmland and food production, in the ownership and control of stock breeding, grazing and slaughter. Likewise, the organisation of food

Figure 13.5 Altars and hidden rooms at Tarxien: (1), (2), (4): The 'Q' altar. (4) shows the 'hatch' within which were secreted flint knives and a quantity of bones and horns. (3): Stone shelves. (5): The Bull reliefs in Room P. (6): Antiquarian photo (Zammit) of large bull horns in situ in Room M/O. (7): Highlighted photo (Zammit) of the Reliefs in Room P (from his original album). (8): Doorway in M/O looking towards shelves today. (Drawings and Photos – author, by kind permission of the National Museum of Archaeology, Valletta).

distribution or redistribution and competitive feasting was linked, probably to an emergent chiefdom society. These typically engage in economic controls, and in the munificent redistribution of resources in monumental centres. If we transpose this scenario to early Malta, then we could expect ritual practices that developed specifically around the control and consumption of food, the manner of its killing, cooking, serving and eating. Indeed, considerable ceremonial pomp and symbolism would be expected, and are well demonstrated in Malta. Anthropological and archaeological examples of distinctive isolated/island

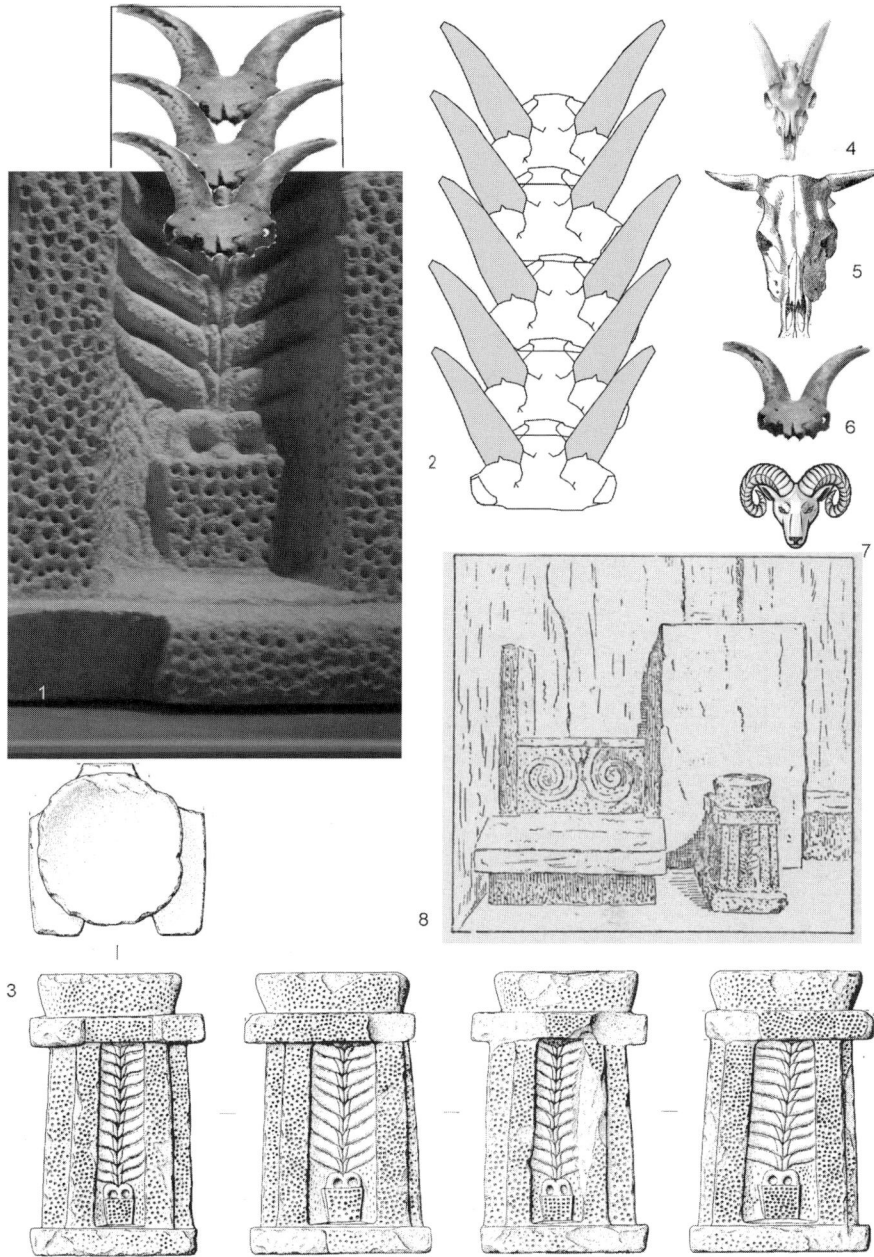

Figure 13.6 The Hagar Qim altar. (1) Annotated photograph to show possible arrangements of horns. (2): suggested manner of stacking skulls and horns. (3): The altar drawn from all sides. (4), (5), (6), (7): different horn shapes of ovicaprids and bovids. (8): The altar location in 1840 (after Vance). (Drawings and Photos – author, kind permission from the National Museum of Archaeology, Valletta).

societies (e.g. Hawaii-Polynesia: Green & Kirch 2001; Hayden & Villeneuve n.d. and 2011; British Columbia: Perodie 2001; Philippines: Junker 1999) further emphasise the role of extravagant structures (built and social) that developed specifically to deal with unpredictable food supplies. In such circumstances, social responses (seen ethnographically and archaeologically) involved competitive redistribution of food and seasonal feasts, elaborate ceremonial ritual and gift exchange and storage arrangements, often located in particular structures/places (Hayden 2014). These societies frequently focused on animal symbols to represent wealth and their walking bank accounts/larder, a prime means to status and power. Totemic symbols, large male animals and their horns, tusks and antlers were often represented, curated and worn as headdresses, ritualised costumes and ornament motifs. Female animals and their fertility were often represented as pregnant, fertile, lactating, submissive and under human control. Carnival-style processions represented animals and hybrid characters dressed up in animal-rich symbols (Insoll 2011) and from this, we might construe that such societies had distinct goals. Those could include the appeasement of animal spirits when slaughtered (an idea often cited for Palaeolithic cave art, sometimes called "sympathetic magic" in the manner of Abbé Brêuil and his followers (Brêuil 1952). The wearing of animal parts – feathers, claws, horns-antlers, teeth and tusks and so on (as necklace, headdress, image, skin etc.) – might imply that respected aspects of an animal's character (strength, fierceness, courage, virility, fertility, productivity, taste, appearance and so on) or gender were transferred to the wearer, often with shamanic powers (Nelson 2011). The special placement of animal parts in human graves or in special deposits might also imply that special powers or attributes were stored in respected places or transmitted to ancestral spirits. Some lineages may have adopted particular animals as emblematic of their clan and used symbolic body parts to emphasise this association.

In early Malta, we can trace aspects of these potential symbolic acts in the treatment of animals – whether domestic, wild or imagined. The animals represented the starting point for the community's wealth and means to a well-nourished life – the common domestic creatures were the foundation of the Temple Culture's ability for survival. Unglamorous though this revelation might be, Malta was a very marginal place, densely populated in a degrading environment, largely dependent on the management of three key animal food species. These creatures thus became the focus of ritualised drama and play in the business of food and feast; their collective personalities and spirits were part and parcel of the ritual life of Malta. In front of each of the major excavated temples, large tie holes, carved into stone slabs or bedrock, demonstrate how large animals, almost certainly bulls, were tethered in public view in the temple forecourt. Within the temples, smaller tie holes have been identified close to altars for smaller animals. The tie holes were the locations of ceremonial slaughter, an important component in the drama of the play that underpinned feasting at these sites.

SYMBOL AND COSMOLOGY – ANIMALS AND ART: LOCATING AND POSITIONING SYMBOLS IN RITUAL PLACES

The theme of this volume, 'play, ritual and belief', provokes alternative ideas about the components of the Temple Culture in Malta and the potential to see the evidence in a new way. The employment of 'play', or at least competitive games involving animals, was evident in several complex, palace-type societies, as described by Spivey (Chapter 16, this volume). At a simpler level of social organisation, as in early Malta, we can assume that people and their animals were closely associated; indeed, notions of animal identities would be embedded in that of the community, so bringing the farmyard into the "temple" as part of wider ritual belief would have been logical and important. Virtually everything to do with food and feast involves animals caught or 'tamed' in preparation for slaughter, breeding, presentation and so on, and often requires the performance of some ritual in the process. The graphic friezes of animals from Tarxien and the visual references to farm animals imply that these creatures had special status in ceremonial or carnival-style events. As described earlier in this chapter, horn cores and hooves seem to have been quite frequent at the Brochtorff Circle deposits. One interpretation is that animal skin shrouds complete with hooves and head covered some corpses (Malone et al. 2009, 335). An alternative idea could be that some people dressed up as animals and wore horn cores and skull frontals in ceremonial 'play' and playacting, a process of metamorphosis into bestial form, the wearer zoomorphically transfigured and granted a virtual entry into demarcated 'animal' spaces or worlds. Playing the animal perhaps imbued the individual with special power or insight through rites of passage. Acting as an animal, in touch with the animal world, could have been a powerful medium for shamanic-style 'master of the animals' rituals, and involved communing with animals (Berkert 1979).

The Tarxien material provides some indications that animal bones and artworks of bulls, sheep, goat and pig may have formed distinct spatial patterns, as suggested by Figure 13.1b. Room 3/V especially, on the left of entry to the south-west temple contained a concentration of horns, bones, images and human representations. Room 2 opposite this space suggests more extreme segregation, with an immense anthropomorphic statue, and the animal offerings in Altar Q (containing a concentration of bones, horns, flints and an animal figurine jammed in the wall behind). The secret, hidden rooms immediately behind Altar Q (7/O, 8/W, 13/M, 5/P, 8/W) all contain a mass of animal rubbish, preserved beneath the later Bronze Age burials which were also concentrated in that specific area, and initially was the deposit that seized Zammit's interest. In particular, the horns, some of which Zammit described as from bulls and noted the dimensions, were placed in hidden stone shelves (Figure 13.5: 3, 6) and at the entrance steps in and out of the rooms. What did this apparently intentional arrangement symbolise?

PLAYING RITUAL – ANIMAL POWER AND IDENTITY

The limitations of detailed knowledge of early Malta inhibit much speculation about the role of animals. However, new leads encourage me to delve into these important data. Studies on the changing environment and degrading landscape of early Malta (Hunt, pers. comm. and 1997; Hunt and Schembri 1999; Carroll et al. 2004, 2012; Fenech 2009) ([1]) suggest a fertile island when first colonised, with thick, partly loess soil, supporting a mixed Mediterranean woodland-scrub vegetation. Very rapidly, that vegetation was cleared for farming, and soil erosion took place, in tandem with the slight, but significant rise of Mediterranean sea levels. For a tiny island archipelago, such changes were potentially catastrophic, reducing the viable land surface and soil fertility at an alarming rate. How much and how far this process affected the population we cannot yet know (although current research is tackling such questions). One reaction was a focus on crops and stock, perhaps breeding animals for specific purposes, and

to increasingly revere and symbolise their power, value and food potential. Scholars have long speculated about the role and function of the temples which are unique in almost every way to Malta (Trump 1976, 1983, 2002; Bonanno 1990; Cilia 2004; Grima 2007, 2008; Malone 2007; Malone & Stoddart in prep). Orientation of the structures with reference to the sun and the horizon has been suggested (Ventura 2004), whilst fertility dominated the ideas of Gimbutas (Gimbutas 1989). More mundane, but more easily comprehended is the notion that the social role of the temples was part of an elaborate form of control over food production and its redistribution (Malone & Stoddart 2012–13). We contend that this emerged from an intensively competitive, chiefly social structure that emerged in response to declining food reliability. Some of the dated human bones from the Brochtorff-Xaghra Circle indicate declining levels of animal protein in the diet during the later Temple Period, in contrast to those of earlier populations. The pre-temple Zebbug period community had statistically better health and nutrition, although on the basis of this sample we cannot yet jump to conclusions about food availability (Malone et al. 2009). The main rebuilding of the temples seems to have taken place just as populations seem to have expanded, with concomitant growth of both social and the internal complexity of the temple buildings. The animal images too, are largely a product of the final Temple Period elaboration and decoration of temple space. With the large numbers of bones and horns, it might be construed that feasted animal food was plentiful and routine, but the very fact that animals became a focus of religion, of elaborate altars, of carefully secreted bone caches in special places and decoration might imply the very opposite. Perhaps the animals became so restricted in a drier, poorer landscape where every last scrap of fertile land was given over to cropping, that ritual slaughter and feasting resulted. Even grain seems to have had a role in the temples, with querns and rubbing stones installed for processing grain for the feasts. One can imagine the huge vessels (and there are several from Tarxien alone) being employed for some soup or stew that was prepared for a very large gathering, the contents decanted into the smaller, almost identical offering bowls in some form of feasting or feeding. The scale of the vessels, mirrored in the representations of human and animal figures, ranged from miniature to enormous, from plaything to the monumental. Model-making is sometimes regarded as play, although serious adult model-makers with train sets and dolls' houses might not consider it so. But there is a serious element here, since in creating an imaginary world, at whatever scale, there is scope for the participant to become transformed, for revelation and for the rehearsal of special moves or actions before the main event took place.

Alternatively, the small miniatures were game pieces, playing out imaginary, mythical or competitive games, or enacting processions, slaughter and feast. Such objects could be seen as instructive and part of the education of young people (see Kyriakidis, Chapter 18, this volume).

Play and animals and their role in the emergence of society in early Malta was a response to the physical character of the restricted and insular place, and its population perhaps engaged in complex competitive ceremonial and feasting. The food itself was projected into artistic, ritualised, ceremonial spectacle to be participated in, celebrated and observed. The temple layout was specifically designed for dramatic revelation combined with hidden mysteries. Playacting, probably dancing and music and genuine drama based on animal myths and shamanic ideas, potentially was at the heart of the food and feast, organised with much symbolism and leaving a trail of archaeological hints in its wake.

In a traditional society, where there was fluidity in the social hierarchy, ambitious individuals might cement their influence for a time through hosting lavish and impressive feasts (Dietler 2011). Renfrew (1973) first speculated that the distribution of the temple clusters across Malta and Gozo might be indicative of an emerging chiefdom society, focused on competitive units. This idea is still attractive, although perhaps with more analysis of the differences between each of the clusters, the temples might be distinguished one from another by complex rituals that involved many loci for different, perhaps seasonal ceremonies, foods and concerns. Control (and the power it gave) of larger land units, more animals, farmhands and inevitably, food, would always have been a major 'driver' in the motivations

of an emerging chiefly society. Making scarce food accessible to all the 'stakeholders' controlled through ceremonials, festival and fun would have been a convenient mechanism to ensure maximum benefit for the host, and presumably future productive power. That such events were pleasurable, functional and possibly spontaneous further confirms the notion of 'play' as defined by Renfrew (Chapter 2, this volume) and Burghardt (Chapter 3, this volume).

CONCLUSIONS

This volume seeks to explore how play and animals may be involved in ritual. In early Malta, we have some particular insights into a very specific context, where the key components for these criteria seem to be present. The temple buildings provided a theatre stage, with opportunities for dramatic revelation, performance and occasion. The inclusion of large animals, tethered to the forecourt for public display and despatched, were part of an elaborate, deeply rooted ritual. The likely roleplaying adopted by participants, the dressing-up, costumes, formalities, structured behaviour and organisation required for a temple feast, was doubtless pleasurable, playful and competitive in a game-playing sense. Whether such events were seasonal, regular or developed in response to extreme conditions is a question now under active investigation of environment and archaeology. But if the art, architecture, zooarchaeological remains, space and context were not part of a drama of survival ritual, then it is hard to see what else they could be. Zammit began the story; now new investigation has taken up his narrative with the aim of placing this particular cultural milieu in context.

NOTE

(¹) A European Research Council grant is currently funding a programme of environmentally focused research in Malta, led by the author and colleagues, 2013–18, and will attempt to reassess and test the many assumptions made here through dating, vegetation reconstruction, population study, palaeoeconomy and new archaeological prospection.

ACKNOWLEDGEMENTS

The author thanks Stephen Ashley and Jason Gibbins for preparing the original artefact drawings, and Sharon Sultana and the staff of the National Museum of Archaeology in Valletta for enabling study of material and the Zammit diaries in 2006. Thanks also to The John Templeton Foundation: Cambridge-Templeton Consortium – who funded that study through a grant ('Explorations into the conditions of spiritual creativity in Prehistoric Malta'). The author also thanks an anonymous reviewer for constructive suggestions for improvements to this chapter. Needless to say, any shortcomings are those of the author alone.

REFERENCES

Aldhouse-Green, M. & S. Aldhouse-Green. 2005. *The Quest for the Shaman: Shape-Shifters, Sorcerers and Spirit Healers of Ancient Europe*. London, Thames & Hudson.

Ashby, T., R. N. Bradley, T. E. Peet & N. Tagliaferro. 1913. Archaeological investigations in Malta. *Papers of the British School at Rome* VI, 1–127.

Ashley, S., J. Bending, G. Cook, A. Corrado, C. Malone, P. Pettitt, D. Puglisi, R. Redhouse & S. Stoddart. 2007. The resources of an upland community in the fourth millennium BC. In Fitzjohn, M. (ed.), *Uplands of Ancient Sicily and Calabria. The Archaeology and Landscape Revisited*. Accordia Specialist Studies on Italy. University College, London. Vol 13. London, 59–80.

Barber, G., D. Redhouse & S. Stoddart. 2009. *The animal bone*, in Malone, C. et al. (eds.), pp. 330–5.

Barker, G. 1985. *Prehistoric Farming in Europe*. Cambridge: Cambridge University Press.

Barker, G. 2000. Hidden prehistoric landscapes: an Italian perspective. *Journal of Mediterranean Archaeology* 13 (1), 100–2.

Barker, G. 2006. *The Agricultural Revolution in Prehistory: Why Did Foragers Become Farmers*. Oxford: Oxford University Press.

Bonnano, A. 1990. *Malta: An Archaeological Paradise*. Second ed. Valletta, Malta, M. J. Publications.

Breuil, H. 1952. *Four Hundred Centuries of Cave Art*. Montignac: CEDP.

Burkert, W. 1979. *Structure and History in Greek Mythology* (section entitled 'Shamans, Caves and the Master of Animals'). Berkeley: University of California Press. (Reprinted in Narby, J. & F. Huxley (eds.). 2001. *Shaman through Time: 500 Years on the Path to Knowledge*. London, Thames and Hudson, 223–6).

Carroll, F. A., K. Fenech, A Bonanno, C. Hunt, A. M. Jones & P. J. Schembri. 2004. The past environment of the Maltese islands: the Marsa cores, in *Exploring the Maltese Prehistoric Temple Culture. 2003 Conference in Malta (CD-ROM)*, ed. L. Eneix. Sarasota, FL: EMPTC.

Carroll, F. A., C. O. Hunt, P. J. Schembri & A. Bonanno. 2012. Holocene climate change, vegetation history and human impact in the Central Mediterranean: evidence from the Maltese Islands. *Quaternary Science Review* 52 (2012) 24–40.

Cazzella, A. & G. Recchia. 2012. Tas-Silġ: the Late Neolithic megalithic sanctuary and its re-use. *Scienze dell'Antichita* 18, 15–38.

Cilia, D. 2004. *Malta before History. The World's Oldest Freestanding Architecture*. Sliema: Miranda Publishers.

Clark, J. G. D. 1954. *Excavations at Star Carr: An Early Mesolithic Site at Seamer near Scarborough, Yorkshire*. Cambridge: Cambridge University Press.

Devet, E. 2001. Rock art and the material culture of Siberian and Central Asian Shamanism. In Price, N. (ed.), *The Archaeology of Shamanism*. London: Routledge.

Dietler, M. 2011. Feasting and fasting. In Insoll, T. (ed.), *The Oxford Handbook of The Archaeology of Ritual*. Oxford: Oxford University Handbook, 179–94.

Dietler, M. & B. Hayden, 2001. *Feasts: Archaeological and Ethnographic Perspectives on Food*. Washington, DC: Smithsonian Institution Press.

Earle. T. 1997. *How Chiefs Come to Power: The Political Economy in Prehistory*. Stanford, CA: Stanford University Press.

Evans, A. 1901. Mycenaean tree- and pillar-cult and its Mediterranean relations. *The Journal of Hellenic Studies* 31 (107), 135–8.

Evans, J. D. 1953. The prehistoric culture sequence of the Maltese archipelago. *Proceedings of the Prehistoric Society* 19, 41–94.

Evans. J. D. 1971. *The Prehistoric Antiquities of the Maltese Islands*. London: Athlone Press.

Fenech, K. 2009. *Human Induced Changes in the Environment and Landscape of the Maltese Islands from the Neolithic to the 15th Century AD as Inferred from a Scientific Study of Sediments from Marsa, Malta*. Oxford: BAR (Int. Series) 1682.

Fiorentini, G., C. D'Oronzo & G. Colaianni. 2012. Human-environmental interaction in Malta from the Neolithic to the Roman period: archaeobotanical analyses at Tas-Silġ. *Scienze dell'Antichita* 18.

Gamble, C. S. & S. Moser. 1998. *Ancestral Images: The Iconography of Human Origins*. Cornell, NY: Cornell University Press.

Gimbutas, M. 1982. *The Goddesses and Gods of Old Europe 6500–3500 BC. Myths, Cults and Images*. London: Thames and Hudson.

Gimbutas, M. 1989. *The Language of the Goddess*. New York: HarperCollins Publishers.

Gimbutas, M. 1991. *The Civilisation of the Goddess: The world of Old Europe.* San Francisco, CA: Harper Collins.

Gimbutas, M. & Dexter, M. (ed.). 2001. *The Living Goddess.* Oakland. University of California Press.

Green, R. & P. Kirch. 2001. *Hawaiki, Ancestral Polynesia: An Essay in Historical Anthropology.* Cambridge: Cambridge University Press.

Grima, R. 2007. Landscape and ritual in Late Neolithic Malta. In Barrowclough, D. & C. Malone (eds.), *Cult in Context. Reconsidering Ritual in Archaeology.* Oxford: Oxbow, 35–40.

Grima, R. 2008. Landscape, territories, and the life-histories of monuments in Temple Period Malta. *Journal of Mediterranean Archaeology* 21 (1), 35–56.

Halstead, P. 1989. The economy has a normal surplus: economic stability and social change among early farming communities in Thessaly, Greece. In *Bad Year Economics: Responses to Risk and Uncertainty.* Halstead, P. & J. O'Shea (eds.), Cambridge: Cambridge University Press.

Halstead, P. 1996. Pastoralism or household herding? Problems of scale and Specialisation in early Greek animal husbandry. *World Archaeology* 28 (1), 20–42.

Hayden, B. 2014. *The Power of Feasts: From Prehistory to the Present.* Cambridge: Cambridge University Press.

Hayden, B & S. Villeneuve. n.d. *Preliminary report on feasting in Futuna.* www.sfu.ca/archaeology-old/dept/fac_bio/hayden/reports/futuna.pdf (accessed January 2015). www.sfu.ca/archaeology-old/dept/fac_bio/hayden/reports/futuna.pdf

Hayden, B. & S. Villeneuve, 2011. A century of feasting studies. *Annual Review of Anthropology* 40(1), 433–449.

Hunt, C. O. 1997. Quaternary deposits in the Maltese islands: a microcosm of environmental change in Mediterranean lands. *Geojournal* 41(1), 3–11.

Hunt, C. O. & P. J. Schembri, 1999. Quaternary environments and biogeography of the Maltese Islands. In Mifsud, A. & C. Savona Ventura (eds.), *Facets of Maltese prehistory,* Malta: The Prehistoric Society of Malta, *Mediterranean Archaeology* 21/1: 35–56.

Insoll, T. 2011. Sacrifice. In Insoll, T. (ed.), *The Oxford Handbook of the Archaeology of Ritual.* Oxford: Oxford University Handbook, 15–165.

Jarman, M. R., G. N. Bailey & H. N. Jarman. 1982. *Early European Agriculture: Its Foundation and Development.* Cambridge: Cambridge University Press.

Jones, A. 2011. *Biographies in Stone: Place, Memory and the Prehistory of Sculpture.* In Bonnaventura, P. & A. Jones (eds.), *Sculpture and Archaeology.* Farnham: Ashgate Publishing.

Junker, L. L. 1999. *Raiding, Trading, and Feasting: The Political Economy of Philippine Chiefdoms.* Honolulu: University of Hawaii Press.

Lai, L, T. O'Connor & R. Tykot. 2009. Diet and environment in Maltese prehistory. In Malone et al. 2009. Chapter 11, 335–40.

Legg, A. J. & P. A. Rowley-Conwy. 1988. *Star Carr Revisited.* London: Centre for Extra-Mural Studies, Birkbeck College, University of London.

Magro Conti, J. & P. C. Saliba (eds.), 2007. *The Significance of Cart-Ruts in Ancient Landscapes.* Malta: Midsea Books Ltd.

Malone, C. 2007. Ritual, space and structure – the context of cult in Malta and Gozo. In Barrowclough, D. & C. Malone (eds.), *Cult in Context.* Oxford: Oxbow Books, 23–34

Malone, C. 2008. Metaphor and Maltese art: explorations in the Temple Period. *Journal of Mediterranean Archaeology* 21 (1), 81–109.

Malone, C., G. Ayala, M. Fitzjohn & S. Stoddart. 2004. Under the volcano. *Accordia Research Papers.* University College London, London, 97–21.

Malone, C. & S. Stoddart. 2012–13. Ritual failure and the temple collapse in IIIrd millennium BC Malta. In Koutrafouri, V. (ed.), *Ritual Failure.* Amsterdam: Sidestone Press.

Malone, C. & S. Stoddart (eds). in prep. *The Art of Ritual in Prehistoric Malta.* Cambridge: Cambridge University Press.

Malone, C., S. Stoddart, D. Trump, A. Bonanno, T. Gouder & A. Pace. (eds.) 2009. *Mortuary Customs in Prehistoric Malta: Excavations at the Brochtorff-Xaghra Circle, Gozo, 1987–1994.* Cambridge: McDonald Institute Monographs.

Nelson. S. M. 2011. Gender and religion in archaeology. In Insoll, T. (ed.), *The Oxford Handbook of the Archaeology of Ritual.* Oxford: Oxford University Handbook, 195–207.

Perodie, J. 2001. Feasting for prosperity: a study of southern northwest coast feasting. In *Feasts: Archaeological and Ethnographic Perspectives on Food, Politics, and Power.* M. Dietler & B. Hayden (eds.), 185–214. Washington, DC: Smithsonian Institution Press.

Renfrew, A. C. 1973. *Before Civilisation.* Harmondsworth: Penguin Books.

Rozwadowski, A. 2001. Sun gods or shamans? Interpreting the 'solar-headed' praxis of Central Asia. In Price, N. (ed.), *The Archaeology of Shamanism.* London: Routledge.

Sullivan, J. P. 2011. *The Satyricon by Petronius* (translated by J. P. Sullivan). Harmondsworth: Penguin Classics.

Trump, D. H. 1966. *Skorba.* Oxford: Society of Antiquaries of London. Monographs XXII.

Trump, D. 1976. The collapse of the Maltese temples. In Sieveking, G, Longworth, I. & Wilson, K. E. (eds.), *Problems in Economic and Social Archaeology.* London: Duckworth, 605–9.

Trump, D. 1983. Megalithic architecture in Malta. In Renfrew, A. C. (ed.), *The Megalithic Monuments of Western Europe*. London: Thames and Hudson, pp. 64–76.

Trump, D. 2002. *Malta: Prehistory and Temples*. Malta: Midsea Books Ltd.

Ventura, F. 2004. *Temple Orientations*. In Cilia, D. (ed.), 307–26.

Vella Gregory. I. 2005. *The Human Form in Neolithic Malta*. Valletta: Midsea Books Ltd.

Zammit, T. 1915–19. Archaeological Field Notes: Notebook numbers 11, 12, 13, 14: 1915–19. Archive Manuscripts, Library, National Museum of Archaeology, Malta.

Zammit, T. 1927. *The Neolithic Temples of Hagar Qim and Mnajdra, and the Miska Reservoirs*. Empire Press, Valletta. Malta.

Zammit, T. 1930. *The Tarxien Temples*. Oxford: Oxford University Press.

PART III

THE RITUAL IN THE GAME, THE GAME IN THE RITUAL

PLAY, RITUAL AND TRANSFORMATION: SPORTS, ANIMALS AND MANHOOD IN EGYPTIAN AND AEGEAN ART

LYVIA MORGAN

Play, with its connotations of exuberance and entertainment, is also a feat of cooperation and competition when preparing the young for the physical and mental vicissitudes of approaching adulthood. This is the context in which we most frequently encounter play in the art of the ancient world. Play is thereby ritualized in both form and function, since the training of mind and muscles leads to the process of transformation from youth to maturation or, in the case of Egypt, from maturity to regeneration.

The notion of the transformative power of ritual, clearly evident within rites of passage involving initiation into adulthood or specific social groupings, is fundamental to all performative rites (Turner 1969, 1988; Grimes 2003; Mitchell 2006, 2007; Garwood 2011; Renfrew, Chapter 2, this volume). Equally, the ritualization of 'play' in its broadest sense as an underlying cultural phenomenon (Huizinga 1955) is at the heart of all performance, whether it be athletic contests of games, sport or hunt, cultural presentations of dance, music and theatre or ceremonial and cultic rites. The boundaries between these 'categories' of performance are permeable (Turner 1982, 1988; Schechner 1988), and (in the ancient world especially) each encompasses aspects of the others. What distinguishes between them are the primary contexts and the perceptions of the participants and the audience.

In this chapter, I propose that notions of male initiation or ritualized transition through social performance, though not explicit, underlie images of games, bull sports and hunting in Egyptian and Aegean art. In such images, the process of male transformation – the transition to a new or renewed state – is imbued with efficacy through symbolic parallels and performative action. It is with wall paintings and reliefs, with their symbiotic relationship to architectural space and their ability to juxtapose and narrate, that the programmatic role of images in the realm of ritual is revealed (Morgan 2016). In the greater part of this chapter, I will analyze relationships between agonistic games, warfare, bull sports and hunting in Egyptian art. In the latter part of the chapter, I will turn to the Aegean, specifically wall paintings from Akrotiri, Thera, in the iconographic programmes of which boys, animals, play and ritual are interwoven in the creation of meaning. In attempting to understand cognitive patterns of the past, the method used here is contextual, relating image, space, orientation and human movement. Meanings are seen as cumulative, generated through juxtapositions of elements in a visual, spatial and kinaesthetic syntax.

PLAY, RITUAL AND TRANSFORMATION IN ANCIENT EGYPT

The words 'play' and 'ritual' may be relatively new as discrete conceptual categories, and clearly are culture-specific in their linguistic range of meanings.

While this is not the place to delve into comparative linguistics, some comments on how such concepts are discernible in the Ancient Egyptian language may be useful here. Ancient Egyptian had no generic word for either 'play' or 'ritual'; instead, certain words defined particular games, particular rituals. The closest to a generic term for 'play' is ⌈◎𓈖𓆓𓏛 *sḫmḫ-ib*, loosely translated as 'amusement' ('to amuse'), literally "to have the heart forget" (Erman & Grapow 1930, 252–3; Faulkner 1981, 241; Decker 1992, 2). This word encompassed a wide range of activities, as we shall see. Ritual was a fundamental part of Ancient Egyptian existence, crucial not only to individual and social well-being, but to the very maintenance of cosmic order. Again, there is no generic word in the language for 'ritual', though the concept is linguistically implied (Thompson 2001, 326). Closest, are the words 𓈖𓏭𓏛 *nt-ꜥ* (Faulkner 1981, 142), translated as "custom" / "rite", and 𓈖𓏭 *irt ḫt* (Faulkner 1981, 25+182), translated as "doing things". Both are classified with the sign for 'abstract idea', perhaps referencing a sense of obligation, yet both describe performative actions and hence agency.

Initiation and transformation are central concepts in Ancient Egyptian thought, as expressed in mortuary texts. These texts, or spells, were designed to actualize the transition from this life to the next through ritual utterances and secret knowledge. As far as I am aware, (with the exceptions mentioned later in this chapter) there are no surviving texts that refer explicitly to the transition between childhood and adulthood in life. However, in the mortuary texts the notion of initiation is implied in the word 𓂋𓏛𓀀 *bs* (Erman & Grapow 1926, 473–4; Faulkner 1981, 84), involving 'secret' knowledge linked to the notion of 'emergence' and rebirth, and it is hard to believe there was no parallel conception of transformation from one state to another in the passage of life. A number of mortuary spells, written in secret language, aimed to transform the person through what Jan Assmann has called "initiatory examinations" (2005, 351–5). The word that defines the transformative power of such spells is 𓇋𓀠𓏤 *sꜣḫ*, translated as 'transfigure' (Erman & Grapow 1930, 22–3) or 'spiritualize' (Faulkner 1981, 210), and also applied to the wrapped mummy, who awaits transfiguration into a radiant spirit (*akh*) through the process

of ritual (Quirke 1992, 159; Taylor 2010, 20, 24) and is, therefore, in a liminal state (cf. Turner 1967, 1969). Assmann's interpretation of these spells as "initiatory examinations" draws from an anthropological understanding of rites of passage in life, in which initiations rely on ritual to effect transformation. "All cultic ceremonies presupposed such a transformation. Truly great things happened" (Assmann 2005, 397).

Initiation is, indeed, a controlled process usually undertaken in relative secrecy in hidden places, whether interior or exterior, away from the eyes of the opposite sex and the uninitiated (Van Gennep 1960; La Fontaine 1985; Garwood 2011). As such, explicit representation of the more intimate rituals is not to be expected. Yet initiation is also about performance and the final integration into adult society is often accompanied by public theatricality (Turner 1982, 1988). Such performances are, in certain contexts, represented in visual images.

In Egyptian art, a rare representation of the process of bodily transformation as an actual part of initiation appears in a painted wall relief from the 6th Dynasty tomb of Ankh-ma-Hor at Saqqara. Two naked boys are shown being circumcised (Janssen & Janssen 1990, 90–1; Roth 1991, 62–72; Nunn 2002, 169–71; Halioua & Ziskind 2005, col. pl. on p. 91). Roth draws attention to the accompanying text citing the men in the scene as *ka*-priests (mortuary priests responsible for the nourishment of the spirit of the deceased within the ritually animated *ka*-statue), and interprets the occasion as the initiation of two young sons of the tomb owner into membership of a group (phyle) with priestly duties (Roth 1991, esp. 65–6). These associations clearly link the act of circumcision (only rarely referred to in texts) with ritual and imply initiation into an adult community.

But if references to physiological changes are striking in their rarity or discretion, depictions of bodily preparation for adulthood in the form of performative play are implied in scenes of children's and young men's games (Decker 1992; Decker & Herb 1994; Tyldesley 2007). Many of these are agonistic, contact sports (Decker & Herb 1994, LI–N2, pls. CCI–CCCXXIII). Games unequivocally played by children appear in wall reliefs from five Old Kingdom

Figure 14.1 Tomb of Ptahhotep, East Wall. Drawing after Harpur & Scremin 2008, Figs. 5-6. © Oxford Expedition to Egypt.

tombs, three in situ (Harpur 1987, 111–12; Harpur & Scremin 2008, 196), notably those of Mereruka (Duell 1938, pls. 162–5; Kanawati et al. 2011, pls. 20–2, 76, 79–80) and Ptahhotep and Akhethetep (Davies 1900, pls. XXI, XXIII–XXIV; Harpur & Scremin 2008, pls. 122–3, 126–7, 230–2, figs. 6–7, 9) at Saqqara, both of which include a separate tomb chapel for the son of the main tomb owner, who in both cases was the vizier (highest-ranking official) to the king. In the tomb of Mereruka, the games appear in the ceremonial chapel of the father, adjacent to his *ka*-statue, amidst autobiographical scenes and strategically placed around the entrance to the tomb chapel of the son (Meriteti). Both boys' and girls' games are depicted. In the tomb of Ptahhotep and Akhethetep, the games occur in the single-roomed tomb chapel of the son, Ptahhotep [II] (Figures 14.1, 14.2a–e). Only boys' games are depicted. Ptahhotep stands in large scale watching the scenes, and beside him in each case is the diminutive figure of one of his own sons. In both cases, therefore, the referent for the games is the observation of the adult father, and the sons are depicted as children, despite being mature at the time of the father's death. Several of the boys' games in these two tombs are agonistic in character,

and include the pretend capture of a bound prisoner (also a boy) (Figure 14.2d). The same game of capture is depicted in the partially preserved tomb of Khenti-ka (James & Apted 1953, pl. XI) and in the tomb of Idou (Simpson 1976, 24–5, pl. XXIVa, fig. 38 upper register). In the former, there may have been a circumcision scene in association, and the accompanying inscription states that *ka*-priests were involved, implying a ritual association with the children's games (Roth 1991, 70–1). In the latter, the games, which include two stick-fighters with lotus blossoms in their hair, are connected with the festival of the goddess Hathor. Capart (1931) interpreted the game of capture on a fragment from a tomb in Giza (now in the British Museum), which he related to the scenes in the tombs of Mereruka and Ptahhotep, as a form of ritual dramatization connected with circumcision which took place, he argued, at the celebration of the reaching of the 'age of virility' of the tomb owner's son. Drawing on this interpretation, Roth further concludes that initiation into phyles is the referent for the ritual actions of such games. The broader implication of this is that ritualized activities involving circumcision and games transformed the boy into a man responsible for ritual action.

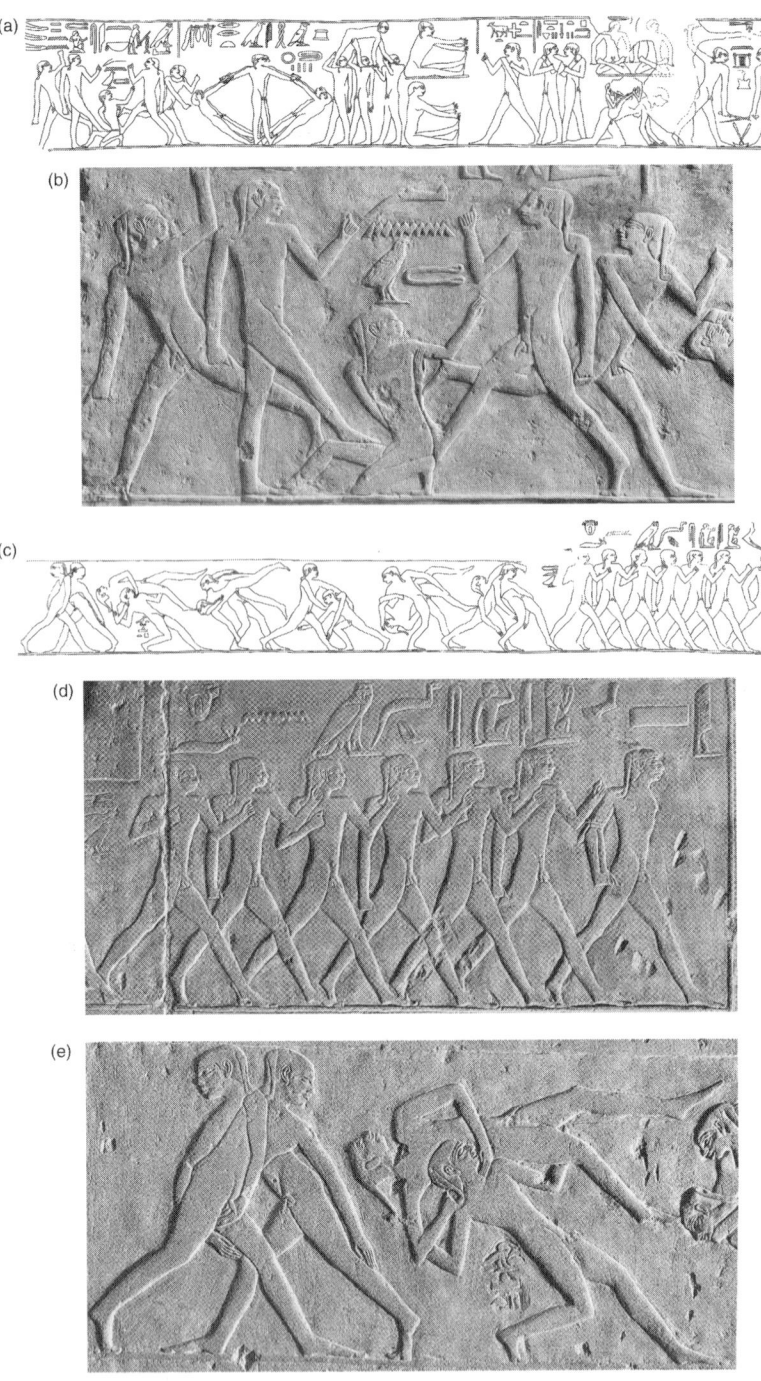

Figure 14.2 (a) Children's games, left side of the east wall, Tomb of Ptahhotep. Drawing after a detail in Harpur & Scremin 2008, fig. 5 / 7. © Oxford Expedition to Egypt. (b) Prisoner game, left side of the east wall, Tomb of Ptahhotep. Harpur & Scremin 2008, pl. 122. © Oxford Expedition to Egypt. (c) Children's games, right side of the east wall, Tomb of Ptahhotep. Drawing after a detail in Harpur & Scremin 2008, fig. 6 / 9. © Oxford Expedition to Egypt. (d) Prisoner game, right side of the east wall, Tomb of Ptahhotep. Harpur & Scremin 2008, pl. 230. © Oxford Expedition to Egypt. (e) Wrestling, right side of the east wall, Tomb of Ptahhotep. Harpur & Scremin 2008, pl. 231. © Oxford Expedition to Egypt.

The most complete series of scenes of boys' games comes from the east wall of the tomb of Ptahhotep. The games are physically challenging and mostly agonistic (Figures 14.1–14.2). The boys' nakedness and partially shaved heads with side-lock signify their extreme youth (Janssen & Janssen 1990, 26–7, 37–8). A further significant distinguishing feature, barely visible today with the loss of paint on the stone reliefs, is the colour of their skin, which was rendered yellowish-brown in contrast to the red-brown of adult men (Harpur & Scremin 2008, 296–9 re. pls. 122–7 and 319–20 re. pls. 230–3). They are uncircumcised and no doubt prepubescent. Their games are social, either in pairs – wrestling (Figure 14.2e), stick-fighting (Figure 14.2a, right) – or in groups, including spinning, acrobatics and pretend warfare with the capture of a prisoner. The 'prisoner' game is here divided into two, implying separate but related activities. In one, on the extreme left of the wall, the captors kick the prisoner as he crouches on the ground (Figure 14.2b). In the other, on the extreme right of the wall, the bound prisoner is marched off by the captors (Figure 14.2d). The same two parts of the game appear in the tomb of Mereruka, there in a continuous strip uninterrupted by other games (which appear above), with the kicking scene on the right, the marching on the left (Duell 1938, pls. 162–3; Kanawati et al. 2011, pls. 20, 21b, 76, 79). The associated inscription calls the team of boys "gazelles" (Decker 1992, 121), likening their agility to that of animals. The direction of the hieroglyphic inscriptions in both tells us that the kicking precedes the marching. That the boy prisoner is equated with adult foes is evident from the Ptahhotep inscription, the ancient equivalent of a speech bubble, in which the captors exclaim *"The foreigner approaches! Listen to his (pounding) heart!"* (Harpur & Scremin 2008, 297, 319, pl. 230).

The boys' games are juxtaposed in the surrounding registers with agricultural and hunting pursuits of adult males (Figure 14.1). On the left (north) side of the wall, immediately beneath the children's games, an acrobatic pose is adopted by a man pressing grapes in a register devoted to viticulture. The spinning game of the boys above is accompanied by the inscription *"Pressing the grapes"* (Harpur & Scremin 2008, 297), evoking the dizziness of wine and, in the juxtaposition of the images, linking youthful and adult forms of 'amusement'. A deeper implication is that the spinning game was played in association with festivities celebrating the vintage, which in the context of the tomb, in which wine was desired for the afterlife (the man pouring water at the beginning of the viticulture scene is identified as a *"ka-servant"*), adds a ceremonial dimension to the activity. Balancing and vaulting games (both also depicted in the tomb of Mereruka) follow. Towards the right of the register are two boys locking arms (Figure 14.2a), perhaps in a preliminary stage to fighting. Finally, on the far right of the register are two boys with sticks, with the inscription *"Throwing darts for Shesemu, god of the vintage"*, again linking the games with the viticulture scene below (Harpur & Scremin 2008, 298),

and, in referring to the god as the recipient of the game, to ritual.

In the lowest register on this side of the wall (Figure 14.1, left), depicting the return from fishing and fowling in the marshes, is another game, involving fighting with sticks from small boats, played by mostly clothed (one naked) adult men who are fowling (cf. Decker & Herb 1994, O1-O47, pls. CCCXXIV–CCCXXXVII). Play, agriculture and the hunt for birds are cognitively linked through bodily motion and sticks, the youths naked, the adults clothed.

In the middle lies a hunting scene (Figure 14.1, left), in which one man tethers horned animals (right), wearing a belt-like loincloth, and another, accompanied by two hunting dogs and wearing a distinctive striped garment, points, either to instruct his dogs or, more likely, with a magical gesture of protection at a bull attacked by a lion. The bull defecates in fear or death throes, as the lion's mouth closes on his muzzle. While the lion attacks the bull, hunting dogs, implying the presence of man, attack ungulates. Yet this is no mere hunt, but rather a philosophical comment encapsulating the cycle of life, with scenes of mating and birth in the midst of those of carnage and death. The scenes are watched by the large-scale figure of the tomb owner, accompanied by his small-scale son, naked but for a necklace, and shaved with side-lock. The accompanying inscription tells of Ptahhotep "Viewing every good thing that pleases ['amuses'] the heart" [𓉼𓏤𓈖𓏏𓆰 *sḥmḫ-ib*] (Harpur & Scremin 2008, 293, pl. 104, fig. 5), linking play and the hunt in words as in images.

On the right side of the wall the theme continues (Figure 14.1, right), this time with a text that has Ptahhotep (vizier to the king) "seeing the tribute, the contributions of the fortresses and cities of north and south". At the top are the naked boys with hair-locks, playing at wrestling and pretend war (Figure 14.2c–e). To the left of the 'prisoner' game (Figure 14.2d), is a row of six pairs of boy wrestlers (Figure 14.2e), apparently unique in Old Kingdom private tomb reliefs, though two blocks from royal funerary complexes depict adult male wrestlers (Harpur & Scremin 2008, 320). The aim of the wrestling game here appears to have been to upturn the opponent to fall onto his head. Traces of colour indicate that one of each pair was painted red-brown, so no doubt the other was yellow-brown to affect a contrast. Both in each pair are, however, children.

Immediately beneath the agonistic games is the return from the hunt (Figure 14.1, right): a hunter in a striped garment leading his dogs, men carrying live animals, and on the right a lion and leopard captured in cages, pulled on sledges by hunters in belt-loincloths. Horned animals (also from the hunt) are brought in the register below, cattle and waterfowl at the bottom, and in the middle, corresponding to the position of the hunt and mating, is a birthing scene of a calf. Taken as a whole, the programme juxtaposes youth and age, play and work, animals and men, life and death, not as contrasts but as a continuum.

In the Middle Kingdom, scenes of agonistic games occur in prominent positions in tomb chapels at Beni Hasan. These were the tombs of local chiefs (governors), whose inscribed titles link them to the king. In the tombs of Baqt III (15), Khety (17), and Amenemhet (2), the east wall, directly opposite the entrance and hence the primary focal point, juxtaposes several rows of pairs of wrestlers in the upper part of the wall with rows of soldiers attacking a fortress, fighting and slaying their enemies in the lower part (Newberry 1893, pls. XIV, XVI (No. 2); 1894, 43–50, pl. V (No. 15); pl. XV (No. 17); Shedid 1994, pls. 21, 43–5 (No. 15); pls. 53–5 (No. 17); pls. 24, 114, 117 (No. 2). Cf. the poorly preserved tomb No. 14, Newberry 1893, 85, pl. XLVII). In each of these tombs, as in others at Beni Hasan, the adjacent north wall held a scene of hunting in the desert, and on the other side of the wrestling, in the south-east corner of the room, each included a vintage sub-scene. It is as though the vertical arrangement of the east wall of the tomb of Ptahhotep had been unfolded, retaining the games as the pivotal scene. To this scene is now added, in place of the pretend games of the 'prisoner', real warfare.

Tomb 15, the tomb of Baqt III, contains an astonishing 220 pairs of wrestlers across the entire length of the wall of six registers (Figure 14.3a–c). The depictions are detailed, each pair in a different hold. It is unclear whether we are looking at a manual of positions, with continuous fights between a limited number of protagonists, or a mass wrestling match, but there is continuity between some of the poses, suggesting sequences of moves by a series of contestants. The ritualized tone of the event is demonstrated by the first pair at top left, as the paler-skinned figure holds out his belt (reminiscent of a modern judo belt, but without chromatic distinctions of rank), before putting it on in preparation for the fight. The belt signals that this is formal play, while the contestants' nakedness is an idiom pertaining, in certain contexts, to childhood (in other contexts, to the vulnerability of defeat). Tonal differentiations of the figures (darker and paler ochre) are, in this case, an idiomatic device to distinguish the bodies from their entanglement, but may also reference age distinctions. In the three rows beneath this agonistic activity, the scene changes to warfare as men, now clothed and armed, attack a fortress. In the bottom row are pairs of men, stick-fighting, elsewhere associated with the playing of war-like games. Similarly, at the far right, pairs of men fight like wrestlers. Details of the warfare therefore refer back to the sports above, emphasizing, if the striking juxtaposition were not enough, the direct relationship between the two. Yet this relationship is more than a simple equation between preparation and event, youth and maturity; it highlights the fundamental link between ritualized play and the appropriation of adult power. Other forms of sport and play flank the wall: on the north wall, amongst activities of crafts and music, are the male 'amusements' of hunting in the desert (occupying the entire top register), fishing and fowling, and jousting by boatmen, and the female 'amusements' of dancing, playing ball and performing acrobatics. On the south wall, towards the western end, following scenes pertaining to the needs of the deceased including the processional transport of his statue, are games involving clothed men (Figure 14.4). In one register is a group of men with sticks, one pair aiming at a target on the ground, a game played by two of the boys in the tomb of Ptahhotep (Figure 14.2a, right). Beneath this is what appears to be a version of the 'prisoner' game discussed earlier, and beneath that a row of men playing board games (referencing the journey to the afterlife). Above all these are men with sticks goading bulls to fight, a scene that will be discussed in the next section of this chapter.

(a)

(b)

(c)

Figure 14.3 (a) Wrestlers. Detail of registers 1–2 of the East wall, Tomb of Baqt III (No.15), Beni Hasan. Shedid 1994, detail of fig. 43 (colour). © Abdel Ghaffar Shedid. (b) Drawing of the East wall in the Tomb of Baqt III (No.15), Beni Hasan. Newberry 1893, pl.V. (c) The East wall in the Tomb of Baqt III (No.15), Beni Hasan. Shedid 1994, fig. 21 (colour). © Abdel Ghaffar Shedid.

Games are clearly an integral and significant part of the overall programme, their distribution and orientation carefully planned, with special prominence given to hunting in the desert and especially to wrestling juxtaposed with battle. Such associations highlight play in the context of male transition within ritualized space. In terms of narrative content, wrestling, prominently displayed on the central wall opposite the entrance and with more space allotted than to any other activity,

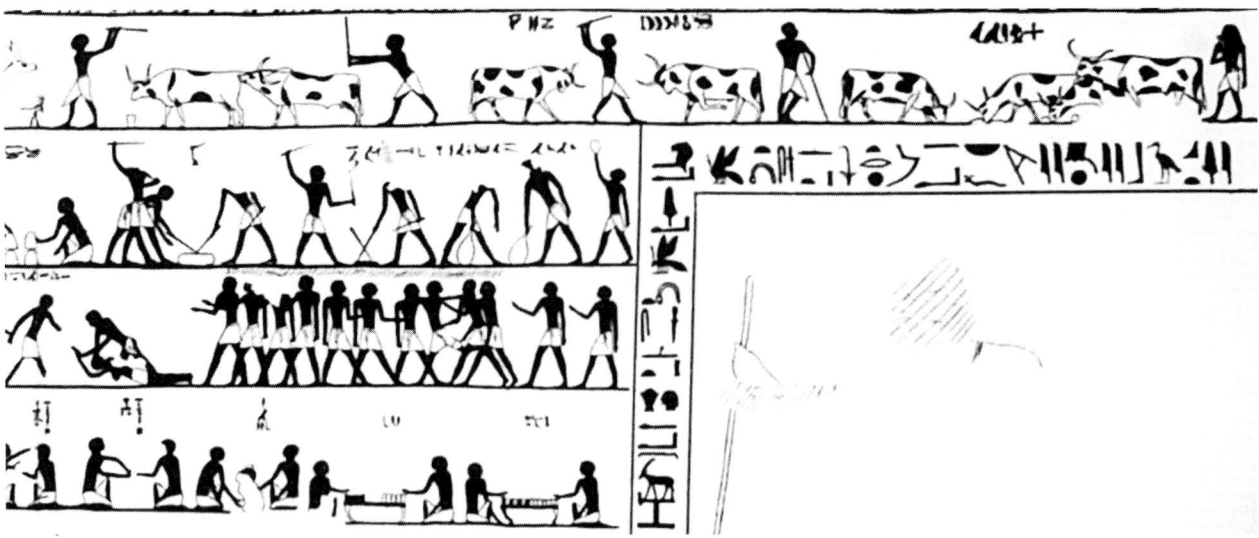

Figure 14.4 Drawing of part of the South Wall in the Tomb of Baqt III (No.15), Beni Hasan. Newberry 1893, detail of pl. VII.

implies the pivotal role of agonistic sports in the acquisition of skills needed for the masculine pursuits of hunting and warfare. In terms of the wider programmatic meaning, it is through the efficacy of such images that the tomb owner is transformed to his eternal state.

BULL-GRAPPLING AND BULL SPORTS IN EGYPTIAN ART: ANIMALS AND MALE POWER

Bulls were a potent symbol of power in Ancient Egypt. While lion hunts were always royal in conception, the capture of wild bulls was, prior to the New Kingdom, a visual theme applicable to the governing elite, before it became an exclusively royal trope. As with lion hunts, the goal was not food, but magical conquest of wild, chaotic forces and, for the bull, ultimately ritual sacrifice.

Old and Middle Kingdom tombs show that the capture of a wild bull for sacrificial purposes involved grappling and lassoing the animal in a team effort. In the tomb of Mereruka, Figure 14.5, several stages are depicted, the animal tussled by the horns and held by the tail, before being roped (Kanawati et al. 2010, pls. 17 (col), 69–70). On the left, one man holds a horn, two hold the legs, while a fourth vaults the bull, holding on simultaneously to a horn and the

tail. The latter's action hardly seems warranted in the context of capture, and the man is naked but for a belt. In another of the groups, the animal is roped by two men, while a third is suspended above the bull, holding on to one horn while anchoring his feet against the other.

The acrobatic movements of a man vaulting a bull on the south wall of the Middle Kingdom tomb of Baqt I at Beni Hasan (No. 29), Figure 14.6a, is exactly mirrored in the posture of the man pressing grapes in the tomb of Ptahhotep, which, as we saw, is directly associated with the boys' games (Figure 14.1, left). Here the bull is roped by two men, held by the tail by another and by the legs by two more. The athletic man leaps over the horns, hands outstretched before him in what appears to be a somersault. In these examples, the bodily movements of the capturer signal the play element of the task in their visual correspondence to acrobatics. This is bull-grappling, but strikingly akin in both bodily movements and aim to bull-leaping (Figures 14.11–14.12). This wall contains a remarkable series of related images. In the top register of the right half of the wall, corresponding to the bull-grappling on the left, are six pairs of wrestlers (Figure 14.6b). The figures are naked except for a belt. Their presence in pairs directly parallels pairs of fighting bulls in the fourth register below and the second register of the left side beneath the bull-grappling. Games are therefore directly associated not only with bull-grappling

Figure 14.5 Detail of bull-catching. Tomb of Mereruka, A1, south wall. Duell 1938, Part I, pl. 20.

Figure 14.6 (a) Cattle scenes, including bull-catching (top register), bull-sports (2nd register, left), and a lion hunting a bull (4th register). South wall, east side, Tomb of Baqt I (No. 29), Beni Hasan. Newberry 1893, pl. XXXI, detail. (b) Wrestling, herding and bull-sports. South wall, west side, Tomb of Baqt I (No. 29), Beni Hasan. Newberry 1893, pl. XXXII, detail.

involving athletic vaulting, but also with fighting between bulls, also a ritualized form of sport. Such an association, as we saw, appears on the south wall of Tomb 15 at Beni Hasan at the top of four partial registers of games (Figure 14.4). Three of these are agonistic, two with men, and the one with bulls. On a larger

scale, the tomb owner (whose image is mostly lost) watches the stick-fighting and the 'prisoner' game to his left, while the scene with the bulls surmounts the frame of his large-scale image. In terms of both the immediate surroundings, with its stick and 'prisoner' games, and the predominance of wrestling as the focal

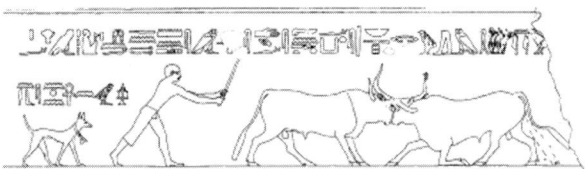

Figure 14.7 Details of bull sports in Middle Kingdom tombs. (a) Tomb of Senbi, Meir. After Blackman 1914, pl. xi. (b) Tomb of Khety, Beni Hasan. After Newberry 1894, pl. xii.

point of the tomb, the bullfight is a motif closely identified with male agonistic games.

In Egyptian art, bull sports take the form of animal against animal, rather than man against animal as in the familiar bull-leaping scenes of Aegean art.[1] Such sports – one bull pitting its horns against the horns of another – appear within the iconographic programmes of tombs from the late Old Kingdom through to the beginning of the New Kingdom (Vandier 1969, 58–62, 219–24; Kanawati 1991; Galán 1994). They occur in association with one or more scenes of masculine endeavour: bull-grappling, hunting, wrestling and other agonistic games. Such scenes are always watched by a large-scale standing figure of the tomb owner. The action of the sport appears to involve men bringing two bulls to face one another, then goading them by hitting them on the horns with a stick to provoke aggression (Galán 1994). Goading with sticks and the actual bullfight are both illustrated in the 12th Dynasty tomb of Senbi at Meir (Figure 14.7a, read from right to left). In the fight, the herdsman is accompanied by a hunting dog, conceptually linking bull sports with the hunt.

These tombs belonged to local chiefs, responsible for the governance of their *nome* (district), who had a close relationship, even kinship, to the king. They were, therefore, 'rulers' in the wider sense of the term. Galán (1994) has convincingly demonstrated that the point of the bull sports as represented in the tombs is to symbolically identify the tomb owner with one of the bulls, as leader of its herd. He (the chief as bull) is forced to defend his status as

regional social leader on earth against his opponent, thereby claiming his right to maintain his position in the Underworld. Both bulls represent leaders of their herds, and having been urged to 'charge', the winner is identified as a 'victorious *ka*-bull'. In terms of the bulls, the winner is the one most suitable for breeding, a point graphically illustrated in the tomb of Khety at Beni Hasan (Figure 14.7b) through the juxtaposition of fighting with mating. In terms of the tomb owner, the analogy highlights not only the chief's supreme leadership, but also his virility, associated epithets referencing sexual prowess and the power for procreation. The bull sports therefore facilitated the transformation of the tomb owner, for leadership and virility were vital factors for a successful transition to rebirth in the afterlife.

In the tomb of Baqt I (29) (Figures 14.6a–b), the pairs of fighting bulls directly parallel the pairs of human wrestlers, which in turn relate to the capture of the bull with the acrobatic vaulting. The entire sequence of scenes relates to cattle and the symbolic significance of wild animals in relation to male dominance. At the centre of the lowest register on the left is a lion hunting a bull. To the left of this sub-scene there was a hunter, now virtually destroyed (Newberry 1894, 35). Simultaneously, the lion hunting a bull echoes the theme of dominance of man against bull, bull against bull, man against man. Completing the cycle of death and life, mating is anticipated next to the hunt and a calf is born next to the bullfight. Watched by the male tomb owner, with male attendants, the games, human and

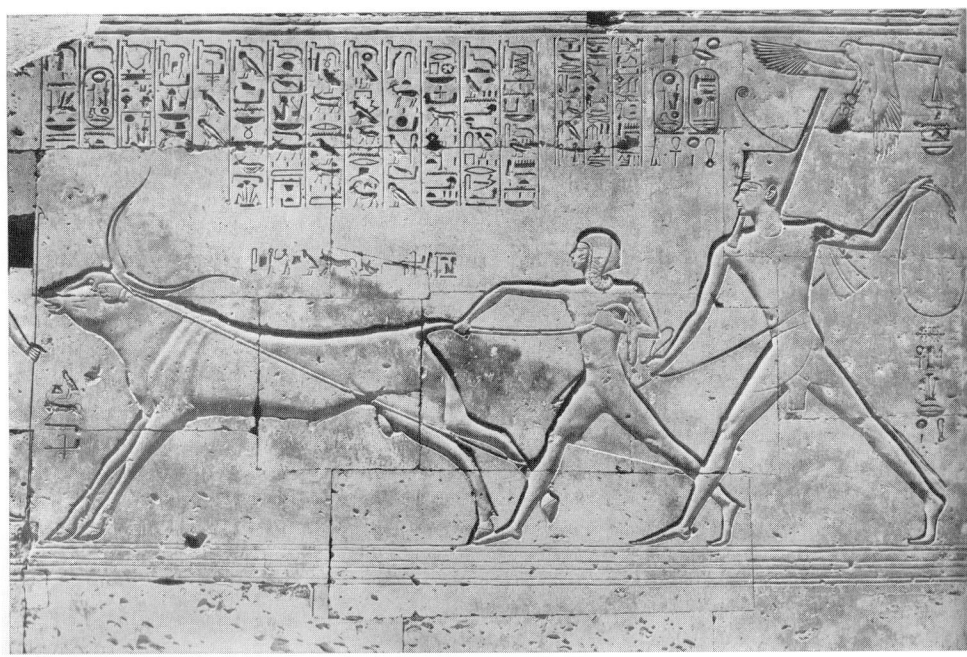

Figure 14.8 Rameses II and Prince Amen-ḥirkhopshef capturing a bull. Incised relief from the east end of the north wall of the 'Corridor of the Bull', Temple of Seti I, Abydos. Lange & Hirmer 1968, pl. 224. © Hirmer Fotoarchiv.

animal, proclaim the strength, agility and force of masculinity.

In the New Kingdom, the theme of the capture of a wild bull is, like that of the lion hunt, exclusively royal. Depictions of the capture of wild bulls with a rope (a technique going back to prehistoric times) appear on temple walls, defining the ritual significance of the act through its context. Images and texts proclaim the vigour of the king. In the Temple of Seti I at Abydos, an evocative scene in incised relief on the north wall of the 'Corridor of the Bull' shows Rameses II and the young prince Amen-ḥirkhopshef lassoing a bull (Figure 14.8) (Mariette 1869, pl. 53; Decker & Herb 1994, J126, pl. CLXXXI). The placement of such a scene in the interior of a temple dedicated to cult highlights the ritual significance of the action. In reality, such an activity, if it took place, could only have done so out of doors. The many ritual scenes on the walls of the temple were organized according to routes connected with the 'daily ritual' for the gods (David 1981), and it has been noted that the 'Corridor of the Bulls' led to a large open space behind the temple suitable for ceremonial events (O'Connor 2009, 55). The scene implies that the capture of the bull is

itself an offering (even prior to sacrifice), as facing the scene in front of the bull stands the funerary god Wep-wa-wet and another unidentified deity, while the inscription cites the king as saying "I have lassoed (for thee) the bull of Upper Egypt," followed by claims of sacrificial slaughter (David 1981, 112). Next to this scene is an image of the king slitting the throat of a sacrificial animal.

As in the bull-grappling scenes in the Old and Middle Kingdom (Figures 14.5–14.6), the lassoed animal is held by horns, leg and tail. The king manipulates the lasso, which links horns with leg, while the prince, who wears the side-lock of youth, grabs on to the animal's tail. In Egyptian art, the bull's tail was symbolically appropriated and worn by kings as a sign of virility and power in overcoming the wild beast. Both the king and the prince stride forward in a posture associated, in other contexts, with the ritual run made by the king at his Jubilee (*heb-sed*) festival (Decker & Herb 1994, A1–A307, pls. I–LIII). Indeed, the motif of the king running was prevalent throughout the reliefs of the Corridor, and some of these scenes have been associated with the Jubilee as well as with hunting rituals (David 1981, 113–15). Running is thereby defined as a rite and the 'amusements' of the hunt are unequivocally ritualized. The *heb-sed*, theoretically held every 30 years of reign, was a 'Festival of Renewal' designed to rejuvenate the physical and magical powers of the king (Bleeker 1967, 91–123). The ritual run was a magical act of renewal, akin to an initiation, in which the king's show of youthful vitality deemed him fit to continue to protect the cosmos. What is significant about this particular image is that the task of capturing the bull with the vitality of a run is undertaken by both father and son. The corridor in which the image appears leads off the Gallery of the Lists, which is filled with inscriptions detailing the ancestral kings of Egypt. There is, therefore, in the image as in the architectural context, a distinct reference to royal lineage. Highlighting this link is the inscription above the scene of lassoing the bull, which refers to the prince as "Great heir-apparent of the entire land" (David 1981, 112). The multivalent symbolism of the image implies both the appropriation and sustaining of the king's power to dispel chaotic forces (the bull), and the initiation of royal youth into manhood and the lineage of that power, in the presence of the gods.

RITUALIZED PLAY AND ROYALTY IN EGYPTIAN NEW KINGDOM ART

Hunting of dangerous animals, which had metaphorical significance in Egypt (as elsewhere in the ancient world) was a vital part of the ideology of kingship (Altenmüller 1967, 1980; Houlihan 1996; Germond & Livet 2001). Conceptually, the hunt was a way of expelling chaos and ordering the universe. In societies with agriculture and domestic animals in which hunting no longer carries with it the necessity of providing meat, the hunt is invested with significance beyond the utilitarian, as a form of ritually charged play. Hunting scenes in Old and New Kingdom multi-chambered tomb chapels are frequently placed near the entrance, in that liminal zone between this life and the next, to ensure that malevolent forces that might infiltrate the eternal abode are dispelled. In royal hunts, wild bulls and lions are the ultimate prey, animals that were never hunted for the provision of food, but always for ritual purposes, to

be vanquished through magic (*heka*) as much as by (supra)human courage and skill.

On a series of commemorative scarabs, Amenhotep III boasts of having captured 96 wild cattle in a single expedition and, in his first 10 years as king, having killed 102 lions (Decker 1992, 15, 151–2, fig. 115). Yet Egyptian symbolic thought was multivalent, and the very power of those two animals was paralleled with (divinely inspired) royal supremacy. Significantly, Amenhotep's hunting park was located at the site of his Jubilee temple (Houlihan 1996, 72). One of the royal epithets of the New Kingdom was 'powerful bull', while throughout dynastic Egypt the king was identified with the lion (think of the sphinx), man having appropriated the power of the beast through the ritual of the hunt.

For the king, agonistic contact is reserved for the most powerful of adversaries, in the hunting of wild bulls and lions or the capture of enemy chiefs. His divine as much as his royal status places him above participation in the actions of wrestling, boxing or stick-fighting. Yet, alongside the (relatively rare) scenes of such sports in the New Kingdom, metaphorically or actually, the divine king is present, watching, just as the viziers, local governors and kinsmen of the king watch the children's and young men's games on the walls of Old and Middle Kingdom tombs.

In the tomb of Meryra (Steward to Nefertiti) at Amarna, wrestling, stick-fighting and what may be boxing are shown taking place in the presence of the king (Davies 1905, pls. XXXVII–XXXVIII; Wilson 1931, 211–12; Decker & Herb 1994, L28/M3/N2, pl. CCCIX). A clear, and otherwise unique, instance of boxing appears in the Theban tomb of Khereuf (TT 192), who was (perhaps not coincidentally) also Steward to a Great Royal Wife, Amenhotep III's Queen Tiye, as well as 'hereditary prince and governor' (Fakhry 1943, 484; Nims et al. 1980). Alongside the six pairs of boxers are 'stick'-fighters (Figure 14.9a), who use as their weapons stems of papyrus, the ideogram for which signifies 'young' and 'fresh', clearly indicating the ritualized nature of the sport and the symbolic association with renewal (Nims et al. 1980, 47, 63–4, pls. 59–63; Decker 1992, 85–8; 2006, 72–7, figs 72–4, col.; Decker & Herb 1994, M2, pl. CCCXV–CCCXVI (stick-fighters), N1, Pls. CCCXXII–CCCXXIII (boxers)). The plants as sticks refer to

(a)

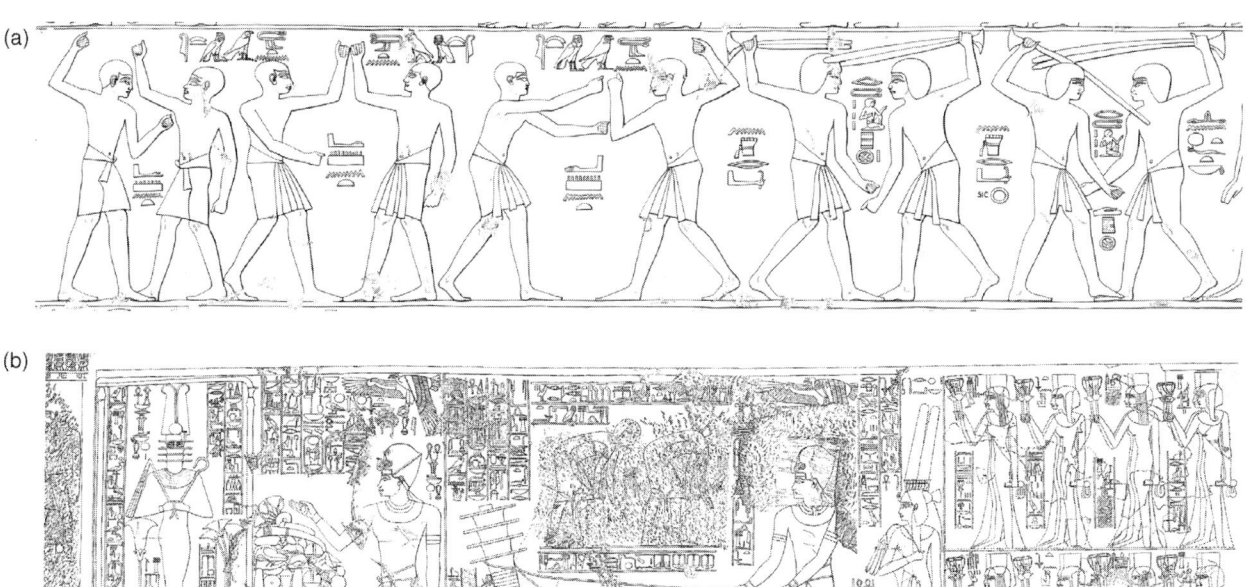

(b)

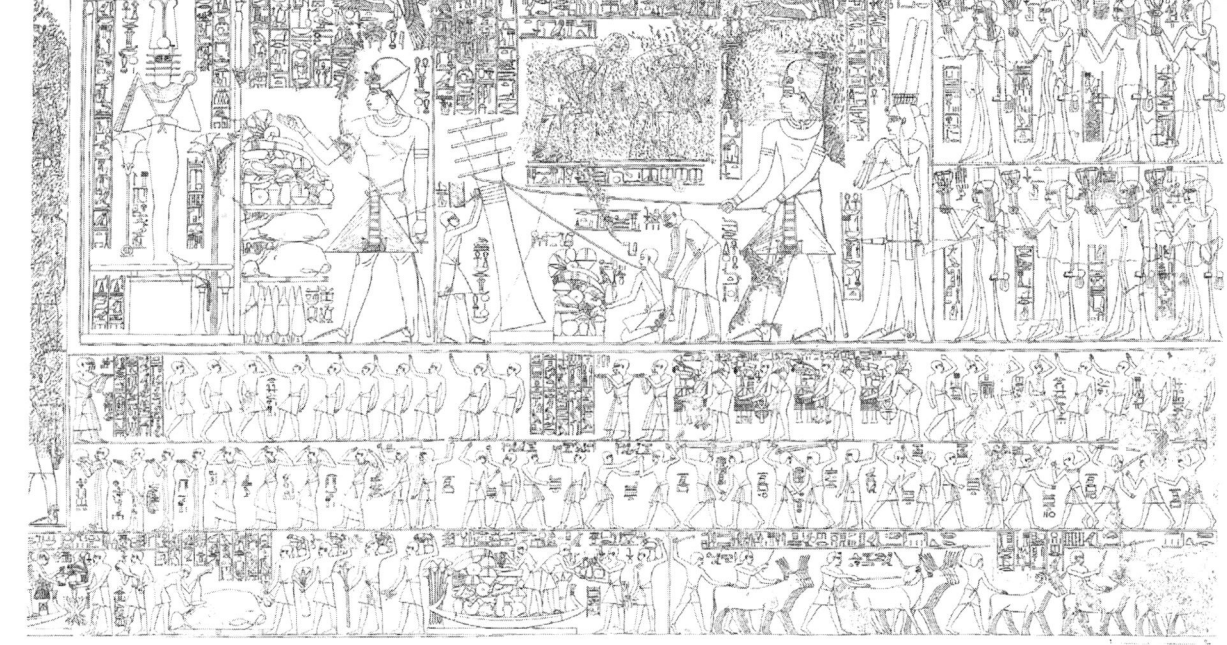

Figure 14.9 (a) Boxing and stick-fighting with papyrus. Detail from the Tomb of Khereuf (TT 192) at Thebes. After Nims et al. 1980, pl. 47 (detail). Courtesy of the Oriental Institute of the University of Chicago. (b) Scenes from the Portico, Tomb of Khereuf (TT 192) at Thebes, showing Amenhotep III raising the djed pillar before Osiris, and, below, dancers and stick fighters. Nims et al. 1980, pl. 47. Courtesy of the Oriental Institute of the University of Chicago.

the mythological conflict between Horus and Seth, as documented in texts (Piccione 1999, 338–44). The inscriptions identify the contestants as priests, 'ritualists' or men of 'Pe' and 'Dep' (i.e. ancestral), and over the heads of the boxers is written "Horus Appearing in Truth has prevailed" (Nims et al. 1980, 64), unequivocally situating the ritualized sport within the context of a god central to Egyptian kingship. The sports are held on the occasion of the raising of the *djed* pillar (symbol of the resurrection of the god Osiris) on the occasion of the *heb-sed* festival of Amenohotep III, the purpose of which was to magically renew the powers of the king (Figure 14.9b).

The ritualized playing of contact sports in the context of the rejuvenation and deification of the king is apparent in two later monuments. In the 19th Dynasty Theban tomb of Amenmose (TT 19), pairs of wrestling and stick-fighting men appear next to a depiction of a barque statue shrine of the deified Thutmose III (Porter & Moss 1960, 33–4 (3); Decker 1992, 82, fig. 51; Decker & Herb 1994, L30/M5, pl. CCCXVI), clearly linking the action with the cult of the (here long deceased) king. This, as with the tomb of Khereuf, demonstrates the role of the elite tomb owner in rituals designed to renew and uphold divine kingship through performative action.

In the mortuary temple of Rameses III at Medinet Habu in Thebes, the role of agonistic sports within the ideology of kingship is defined by the architectural and iconographic programme of the temple. Within the complex, facing on to the western side of the first court, was a royal palace. In the centre of the façade was a 'Window of Appearances' for the king to watch ceremonial performances taking place in the court, receive tribute and distribute rewards (Nelson 1932, pls. 111–12; Hölscher 1941, 37–41, pl. 3; Decker & Herb 1994, L34/M9, pls. CCCXI, CCCXIX, G; Decker 2006, figs. 82–3, 87–92, col.). Surrounding the window, beneath scenes of the smiting king and sculpted prisoners' heads, was a row of wrestling and stick-fighting games between Egyptians and foreigners (Figure 14.10a–b), no doubt

(a)

(b)

Figure 14.10 (a) Detail of wrestlers and stick-fighters from beneath the 'Window of Appearances' of the Mortuary Temple of Rameses III at Medinet Habu, Thebes. Detail from Nelson 1932, pl. 112. (b) Reconstruction of the 'Window of Appearances' of Rameses III on the façade of the temple palace, showing wrestlers and stick-fighters beneath the heads of enemies and the smiting king. Temple of Rameses III at Medinet Habu, Thebes. Nelson 1932, pl. 112.

reflecting events that took place in the court (Wilson 1931; Hölscher 1941, 40–1; Piccione 1999, 345–6). The games are watched on either side by princes, courtiers and foreign ambassadors.

This scene, articulating the place designated for the king's appearance, implies that wrestling and stick matches were staged within the temple precincts, as part of the cult of the divine king. Within this first court and around the exterior walls and pylons of the temple are scenes of pharaonic power over enemies (Nelson 1930, 1932; Lange & Hirmer 1968, pls. 253–4; O'Connor 2012, 249–69, fig. 6.11), symbolically protecting the outer articulation of the ritual space within. On the interior side of the east tower (next to the palace) is a tiered scene, in which the king in his chariot attacks desert animals above and wild bulls below (Nelson 1932, pls. 116–17, 130; Decker & Herb 1994, J128–129, pls. CLXXXIII–CLXXXV). On the north exterior wall, scenes of battle are paralleled with a royal lion hunt (Nelson 1932, pl. 35; Decker & Herb 1994, J127, pl. CLXXXII). Each group of hunted animals is equated with a specific enemy (O'Connor 2012, 268–9). The symbolic significance of the temple cult centred on the rejuvenation of the king and his divine rebirth, analogous on the cosmic scale to the repeated renewal of the sun (O'Connor 2012, 251–2), the ultimate power of transformation.

In programmes in which hunting and warfare are juxtaposed, the two activities are virtually interchangeable in their symbolic resonance. Yet within this ideology, the notion of ritualized play in the sense of performance is never far from the surface, even when games themselves are not present in the iconographic programme, as they explicitly are at Medinet Habu. Here, the power of divine kingship over the chaotic forces of the cosmos, as manifest in wild animals and enemies, is echoed in the theme of contact sports apparently staged within the temple precincts as part of the cult of the divine king. Wrestling and stick-fighting are depicted as ritualized sports, ones that had magical and symbolic significance, since with the efficacy of the image the outcome was never in doubt. We shall return to this theme of the efficacy of images of ritualized play in the concluding section of this chapter.

RITUALIZED PLAY AND WILD ANIMALS IN AEGEAN ART

Throughout the ancient world, appropriation of bovine and leonine power was a theme prevalent in the imagery of rulership. This is surely reflected in the Aegean, where lion hunting would hardly have been the norm but was nonetheless depicted in elite contexts, as on the famous inlaid dagger from Shaft Grave IV at Mycenae (Marinatos & Hirmer 1960, pls. XXXV–XXXVI; Morgan 1998, 172–80). In Aegean art, it is, however, bull sports that most clearly define the ritualized play of young men in relation to wild animals (Marinatos, Chapter 15, this volume), a theme related to that of the hunt (cf. Marinatos 1989; 1993, 212–20; Morgan 1998). Just as in Egypt, physical flexibility and agility were prerequisites for a successful manhood, and acrobatics, such as those performed in bull-leaping, were perfect preparation. An acrobat winds his way around the pommel of a sword from Mallia on Crete, his body echoing that of bull-leapers, here in the context of a weapon (Marinatos & Hirmer 1960, pl. 69; Morgan 1998, pl. 4).

Initiation of youths into manhood is most likely the theme of two stone vessels from Ayia Triada on Crete, the 'Chieftain Cup' (Koehl 1986) and the 'Boxer Rhyton' (Säflund 1987; Militello 2003; Marinatos 2005; Platon 2008). The rhyton, a ritual vessel with a hole in the base for libations, is organized in registers (a format familiar from Egyptian wall paintings and reliefs) (Figure 14.11a–d). As with other stone vessels, it has exclusively male iconography and was clearly ceremonial in function (Marinatos 2005). A scene of bull-leaping, in which a leaper or grappler is suspended above the horns, is juxtaposed with three rows of boxers and wrestlers, distinguished as young elite males (with long hair and necklaces) and warriors (in helmets). The registers have been read from bottom to top, as ascending age and status of the contestants, from youths with bare feet and heads below, to young men in boots and helmets with, in the top register, plumes (Säflund 1987, 230–2). Play in the form of combat sports and challenges of man against animal intimate preparation of young males for warfare in adulthood.

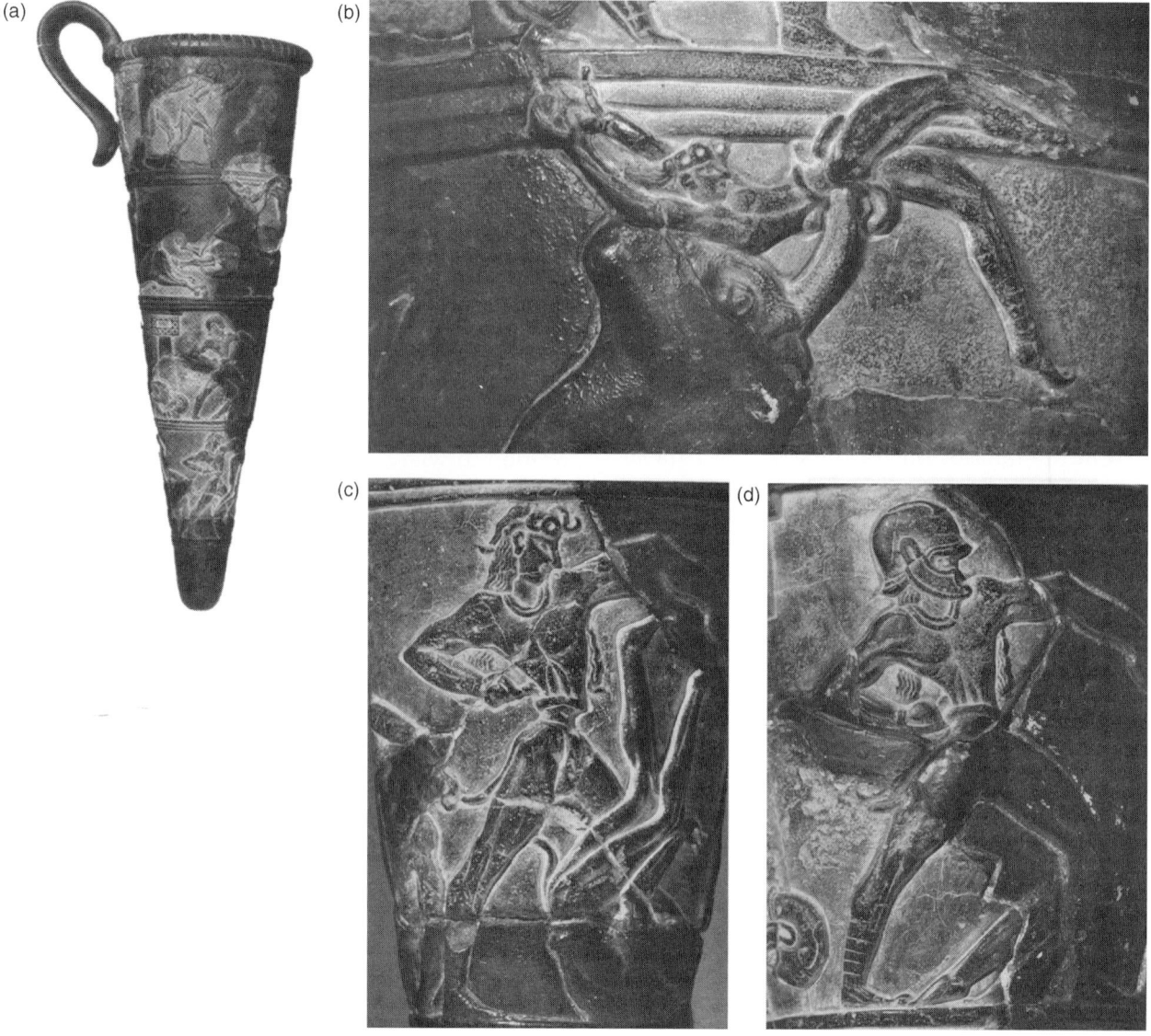

Figure 14.11 (a) Serpentine rhyton (libation vessel) carved with scenes of bull-leaping, boxing and wrestling, from Ayia Triada, Crete. Marinatos & Hirmer pl. 106. © Hirmer Fotoarchiv. (b–d) Details of the serpentine rhyton (libation vessel) carved with scenes of bull-leaping, boxing and wrestling, from Ayia Triada, Crete. Marinatos & Hirmer pl.107. © Hirmer Fotoarchiv.

The two registers flanking the scene with the bull have pillars of a form that reference shrine and palatial architecture.

These echoes between Egyptian and Aegean art, of male prowess through ritualized bull sports and hunts involving lions, provide a framework for interpretation of the fragments of Aegean wall paintings found in a dump outside a small palace (Palace F) at Tell el Dabᶜa in the eastern Delta of Egypt (Figure 14.12). In what was no doubt a series of friezes, bull-leaping, bull-grappling and acrobatics

performed by young men were juxtaposed with scenes of hunting (Bietak, Marinatos & Palyvou 2007; Marinatos 2010; Morgan 2010a, 2010b). The palace, from its architectural form, was ceremonial (Bietak 2007, 41), and the painted programme may have functioned within the context of a royal audience chamber (Morgan 2010a). The theme that unites these images is that of human (male) and animal (feline) prowess through acrobatic play and hunting involving horned animals. A direct parallel is set up between the power of young men over

Figure 14.12 Bull leaper. Fragment from a wall painting from Palace F at Tell el Dabᶜa, Egypt. Colours digitally restored by Clairy Palyvou. Bietak, Marinatos and Palyvou 2007, p. 95 (colour).

bulls through play and the power of both men and felines in the hunt against prey.

Notably, the young man vaulting over one of the bulls in Figure 14.12 is distinguished by having yellow skin, rather than the usual red (as are two other, more fragmentary, figures: Bietak et al. 2007, 97 (A21), 100 (A30), fig. 59). The bull sports in the wall paintings from Knossos involve figures that are red-skinned and white-skinned, and, though originally interpreted as male and female respectively, both, wearing the masculine attire of loincloths with codpieces, represent males, apparently with different roles (Marinatos, Chapter 15, this volume). The lighter-skinned males in the Tell el Dabᶜa painting may be seen as younger. Light versus dark is a symbolic distinction between the sexes, which is sometimes (not invariably) extended to young boys in the colour yellow, as we saw in Egyptian art and will see again at Akrotiri, Thera. Lacking the bodily maturity of a man, the boy is distinguished by a lighter tone, identifying him as within the sphere of childhood. The young bull-leaper's hair is long, as was usual in Minoan art for males engaged in ritualistic activities, but the blue reveals that his head was partially shaven. The partially shaven head and partial locks reveal that he is a youth in transition.

Representations of children or youths in Aegean art, though they appear in other media (Rutter 2003; Papageorgiou 2008), are uncommon in wall paintings outside Thera. Their occurrence in several of the almost life-size paintings of Akrotiri on Thera is therefore notable. Boys or youths appear in the West House, carrying bundles of fish (Doumas 1992, pls. 18–23) in juxtaposition with a miniature frieze depicting a maritime-based festival, the boys' presence interpreted as initiatory (Papageorgiou 2000); in Beta 1, in a ritualized boxing match (Figure 14.13a); and in what appears to be initiation rites in Xesté 3 (Figure 14.14). Nakedness, shaven heads with hair locks at various stages of growth, and, in one case yellow skin colour, are the defining features, along with distinctions between proportions of bodily form according to age (E. Davis 1986; Doumas 1987, 2000; Withee 1992; Morgan 2000; Papageorgiou 2000; Chapin 2007, 2009). In all cases, their context is ritual; in one, it is explicitly ritualized play.

The boxing boys and antelopes, from a small room adjacent to what is identifiable as a sacred repository, sets up a clearly definable parallel between young men and animals (Figure 14.13a–b) (Morgan 1995, 180–4). Boxing in Aegean art (Coulomb 1981), relatively infrequently depicted compared to bull-leaping, appears to be in the context of ritual. It has been suggested that the sport was played at festivals culminating in ceremonial contests associated with male initiation (Platon 2008; cf. Marinatos 2005). Besides this painting, in what was almost certainly a shrine (Marinatos 1984, 106–12), boxing is predominant, as we saw, on the Ayia Triada stone rhyton, a vessel designed for libations,

Figure 14.13 (a) Boxing Boys. Wall painting from the south wall (adjacent to the Antelopes) of Beta 1 at Akrotiri, Thera. Doumas 1992, pl. 79 (colour). (b) Boxers and Antelopes. Wall paintings from the south and west wall of Beta 1 at Akrotiri, Thera. Courtesy of the Archaeological Society at Athens.

Figure 14.14 Boys. Wall paintings from Room 3b, ground floor, Xeste 3. Doumas 1992, pl. 109 (colour).

and recurs on fragments of other stone vessels from Knossos. Significantly, boxing is performed by male figurines of clay, left as dedications at the peak sanctuary at Kophinas on Crete (Platon 2008, 97).[2] In the painting, it is clear from their body proportions and shape and their shaved heads with locks that the boxing boys are young. Almost naked, their select body coverings display status and the significance of the sport: jewellery, a belt-loincloth and the world's earliest known boxing glove. Facing one another, eyes locked, bodies matched in their agonistic pose, they engage in a ritualized fight. On the adjacent walls were pairs of antelope (partially hybridized with the Cretan wild goat), linked to the boys through the wavy background. One antelope turns his head to face the other, eyes locked, ears and tails raised in the communicative movements of ritualized aggression. Play-fighting, involving species-specific signals that communicate non-aggressive intent, is the most common form of social play in animals (Burghardt 2006, 87–96; see also Burghardt, Chapter 3, this volume; Bateson, Chapter 4, this volume; Smith, Chapter 5, this volume). Young antelope, like other horned ungulates, engage in ritualized mock fights in preparation for adulthood, which involve precisely the bodily signals displayed here in what is known as the 'proud posture' (Schenkel 1966, esp. 187–8, 193–9; Bere 1970, 50–1, 56–7). While adult males fight to establish social dominance and mating advantage, the young play by mimicking adult behaviour. Why the Theran painters chose to depict antelope is an intriguing question, since the species was not native to the islands; the choice reflects the web of contacts linking Egypt and the Aegean. What is apparent is that the principle of agonistic behaviour amongst horned animals and its specific application to young male animals and hence to play was understood. Most likely such behaviour would have been observed in the Cretan wild goat, the agrimi, as well as amongst fallow deer (cf. Lorenz (1966) 2002, 111). In the juxtaposition of the pairs in this mural painting, a symbolic, mimetic parallel is set up between human and animal play, framed within a process of ritualization applicable to both (Huxley 1966), in which conflict is channelled into safe mode through symbolic action (Lorenz (1966) 2002) as the young prepare for adulthood.

More complex in its range of images is the iconographic programme of Xesté 3 at Akrotiri (Figures 14.14–14.15). A unique group of paintings has survived (fallen from the walls) from several rooms in the cultic east side of the building (Doumas 1992, 126–75, pls. 93–137; Vlachopoulos 2008a, 2008b;

Papageorgiou in press a, b; see also Marinatos, Chapter 15, this volume). Architecture and images together form the ritual space for human action (Palyvou 2005, 54–62; Vlachopoulos 2010; Paliou, Wheatley & Earl 2011). The dominant themes of the interior spaces are of initiation of young girls (Marinatos 1984, 61–84) and of young boys (Doumas 2000; Morgan 2000; Vlachopoulos 2007) and the natural and supernatural worlds of nature and the goddess. Boys and girls were separated from one another in Rooms 3b and 3a of the ground floor, and the scene with the goddess was on the first floor above 3a (Figure 14.15, plan).

Relevant to this chapter are the young males (Doumas 1992, pls. 109–15), who are clearly distinguished in their ages, ranging from a small boy to adolescents, are naked and have shaved heads (the stubble rendered in blue) with a few locks of hair (Figure 14.14). This practice was common in the ancient world, as we saw in Egypt, as well as in later times in North Africa, China, Japan and elsewhere. In a seminal paper, the anthropologist Edmund Leach wrote of the widespread custom of shaving the head and cutting of hair locks, as a frequent feature of what van Gennep called the 'separation' stage of initiatory rituals, in which the initiates move from one stage of life to another through a series of bodily transformations (Leach 1958; cf. Karageorghis 1990).

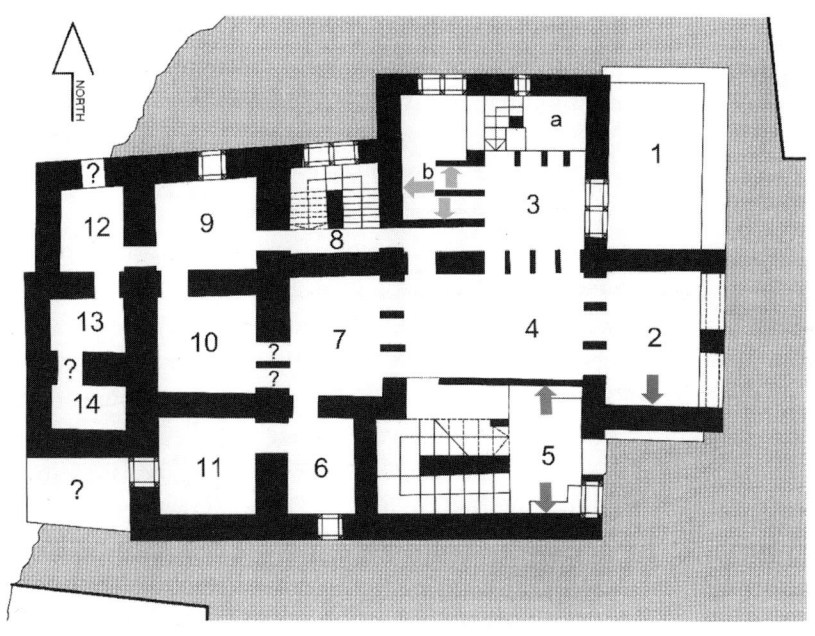

Figure 14.15 Plan of Xeste 3. After Palyvou 2005, fig. 62. Arrows show the positions of the boys in Room 3b, the bull- and goat-grapplers in the Vestibule Room 5, and the animals in Room 2. Courtesy of Clairy Palyvou (with arrows added).

While shaved heads and nakedness are indexes of life practices, other distinguishing features rely on artistic idiom through colour. Inside the eyes are blue lines for some of the younger figures, red for some of the older (Davis 1986). The artists, in portraying youth and age, thereby meld ritual practice with colour symbolism. This is most apparent in the case of the youngest child in the painting (Figure 14.14, left), who is further distinguished by his yellow skin colour, like the young bull-leaper at Tell el Dabᶜa, and like boys in Egyptian art. The colour yellow implies that the boy is as yet without the bodily maturity of a man.

Nakedness and partially shaved heads with individual locks link these youths with those in the Beta 1 paintings of boxing boys and antelopes. In Xesté 3, the association between youths and animals is more distributed, but no less cogent. Specific animals recur in different paintings throughout the building. Monkeys are involved in forms of human play in Room 2 on the first floor (Doumas 1992, pls. 95–6; Rehak 1999). One plays a musical instrument, two others wield swords, while a fourth apparently claps his hands. Here we have entered the mythic sphere, in which human play is appropriated in animal mimesis, expressive of a system of beliefs. At the same time, rhythm, music and dance-like motion frequently accompany ritual, and the painting lies near the threshold to the inner room with the scene of the goddess, in which a monkey as intermediary makes an offering to the deity. Ducks and dragonflies also recur, as motifs on the necklace of the goddess in Room 3a on the first floor (Doumas 1992, pls. 122, 125–6), living in a marsh with reeds in the adjacent Room 3b (Vlachopoulos 2000, 2008a, 2008b) and alongside animals (perhaps a hunt) in Room 2 on the ground floor (Vlachopoulos 2008a, 451). They are, I propose, significant to the theme of initiation, as creatures that physically metamorphose from youth to maturity (Morgan 2016). The marsh scene in Room 3b lay immediately above the boys in Room 3b of the ground floor, a correspondence that is worthy of note, as both allude to transformation. Male mallards both mature and rejuvenate through transformation of their plumage, in a process that is essential to breeding;

dragonflies, too, mature through metamorphosis. The mallard ducks in the painting are identifiable by their plumage as male. Several stages of maturity are depicted: chicks (without dimorphism), male juveniles and mature drake (Vlachopoulos 2008a, pls. 41.31, 41.28–29, 41.30). They present a striking parallelism with the images in the room beneath, in which different stages of male maturation are defined through symbolic and actual transformations – skin colour, height, head shaving, hair growing, from nakedness to clothes – in boys, youths and a single man (Doumas 1992, pls. 109–15). The boys uniquely reference transitions, while in a form of visual mimesis, the ducks and dragonflies allude to the process of bodily transformation in the process of maturation. The recurrence of duck and dragonfly associated with what may be a hunt in Room 2 on the ground floor is, therefore, significant.

Preliminary publication of the wall paintings from the entrance vestibule – the first to greet those who entered the building – has revealed a striking new emphasis within the iconographic programme. Two young men rope a bull, while another two tackle the horns of a goat (Papageorgiou in press b; Vlachopoulos 2008a, figs. 41.3–41.6). In Room 2, near this vestibule, were animals, as yet unidentified, but initially thought to be a lion attacking a horned prey (Vlachopoulos 2008a, 451, figs. 41.7–41.9). This emphasis on horned animals is reflected in an adjacent building, considered an annex, in which a hoard of animal horns was recently found in a deposit that was surely related to the ritual action of Xesté 3 and to the iconography of the vestibule wall paintings (Vlachopoulos 2007, 108–9; 2010). The scenes of horn-grappling and hunting draw attention to the theme of male initiation through association between young men and wild animals (cf. Vlachopoulos 2007, 109; Papageorgiou 2008, 94). As these vestibule paintings, along with those of the reed landscape in Room 3b on the upper floor, are still part of an extensive programme of conservation and study at Akrotiri, full consideration of the iconography must wait.[3] For the purposes of this chapter, however, it is important to draw attention to the association between bull-grappling, horns and hunting at the entrance to the building with what have been widely identified as scenes pertaining to initiation rites in the interior of the building. These associations signal in a concrete way, through distribution in ritual space, the link between sports, animals and the process of maturation of young men.

THE TRANSFORMATIVE POWER OF RITUALIZED PLAY: TOWARDS CONCLUSIONS

The transformative power of ritualized play, especially through the conquest and appropriation of animal power, was a widely shared ideology within the ancient world. While games were surely played by children and adults in daily life, it is the ritual context of play that is memorialized in the monuments.

Through juxtapositions, parallel postures and specific placements and orientations of images on the walls of Egyptian tomb chapels and temples, cognitive links are drawn between boys and young men, athletic and agonistic games, bull-grappling, bull sports, hunting and warfare (pretend and actual, children's and adults'). These interrelated activities are, by virtue of their context in tomb or temple as well as in the resonances of images and text, clearly grounded in ritual. In the Old Kingdom tomb of Ptahhotep, we saw that children's physical, mostly agonistic games are connected both with a vintage festival dedicated to the god Shesemu and with hunting and by implication rebirth. In the contemporary Tomb of Idou, such games are connected with the festival of Hathor, a goddess associated with fertility and kingship and manifested in bovine form. In Middle Kingdom tombs, wrestling is associated with warfare, hunting, bull-grappling and bull sports whose aim is to magically transition the virility and leadership of the tomb owner into the afterlife.

In the New Kingdom, contact sports are associated with divine kingship, while kings themselves are displayed appropriating the animal powers of bull and lion in hunts that magically ensure their fitness to defend the universe from chaos. As we saw at Medinet Habu, wrestling and stick matches were apparently staged within the temple precincts, as part

of the cult of the king as protector of cosmic order. This relationship between contact sports and the divine king is apparent in the Tomb of Amenmose, in which scenes of ritualized sports are juxtaposed with the shrine of the deified king, and in the Tomb of Khereuf, where they appear in the context of the *heb-sed* festival aimed at magically renewing the powers of the king. A different but deeply significant sportive activity is the royal run, associated with the rejuvenation of kingship. In the Temple of Seti I, Rameses II and his son are shown running while lassoing a sacrificial bull, simultaneously evoking the *heb-sed* festival of the king with the initiatory animal conquest by the prince. These interrelated activities – games, bull-grappling, bull sports, hunt – depicted within the ritual context of tomb or temple and associated with rites and festivals, rejuvenation and the transition to the afterlife, define 'play', what the Egyptians called 'amusements', as a series of performative actions initiating transformation to a new or renewed state of being.

In Aegean art, bull-leaping is the quintessential sport of young men within a palatial context. At Tell el Dabᶜa, an Egyptian palace with Aegean paintings, bull-grappling, bull-leaping, acrobatics and hunting were combined into a unified programme in what may have been a royal audience chamber within a ceremonial palace. Registers of bull-leaping and wrestling wrap around the Ayia Triada rhyton, a vessel used in ritual for libations. Young boxing boys and sparring antelopes appear in mimetic parallel in the wall paintings from Beta 1 at Akrotiri, recalling both the juxtapositions of wrestling with bullfights in Middle Kingdom tombs and the Old Kingdom textual reference to boys playing agonistic games as 'gazelles'. Both this and the Xesté 3 paintings specifically link youths with horned animals, the former in the context of play, the latter in the context of grappling and the hunt. Beta 1 was almost certainly a shrine, and Xesté 3 unequivocally so, with its uniquely recognizable depiction of a goddess and its iconographic programme suggestive of initiatory rites.

While the particular forms of these actions and their contexts are quintessentially Egyptian or Aegean, the range of associations between childhood and manhood and the symbolic appropriation of animal power can be viewed through a wider lens pertaining to the transformative power of play. In early urban and some indigenous pastoral societies, maturation to manhood frequently involved encounters with wild animals, whose strength and prowess must be appropriated or vanquished through contact sports or hunting. This is the wider context in which we might view bull-grappling and bull-leaping, as a form of initiation into manhood, closely allied with hunting. In complex palatial societies, such encounters with wild animals draw on the ritualization of long-established traditions reaching back to earlier times in which society may have been organized differently.

Bull sports as a form of initiation can still be seen today amongst the Hamar in southern Ethiopia (Parry 2007). Integration into adult male society involves bodily preparations and transformations, including nakedness and the shaving of part of the head, for the culminating performative action of leaping onto the backs of a row of several bulls (held by tails and horns by men), before landing on the ground beyond, transformed through ritual action into a man, ready for marriage. Hunting of wild animals is in many African societies associated with the acquisition of power and maturation (e.g. Bloch 1992; Morris 1998, 2000), and is seen as 'a rite of transformation' comparable to physical processes like smelting and to the social and biological processes of initiation and procreation (Herbert 1993; Morris 1998, 62). Initiation rites in such societies are cumulative over time, and may include circumcision, shaving of the head, fighting, acrobatic display, herding of cattle and hunting. The culminating rituals that consolidate the transformation into manhood involve a series of physical actions by the youths that test the limits of the body and the courage of the mind in theatrical performances and confrontations with wild animals.

Viewed in terms of the tripartite schema of rites of passage put forward by van Gennep, it is the last – integration into adult society – that sports as public spectacles appear to embody. Yet transition is built into the task and fundamental to the outcome. Such spectacles are equivalent to the return from the hunting of dangerous animals by young men with horns, pelts, tails, etc., as testimony to their courage

and prowess and witness to their transformation into the mature status of heroic men.

In focusing on ritualized play in ancient art, contact sports (wrestling, stick-fighting, boxing), bull sports and hunting have been seen to play a significant role in society as rituals of transition. Underlying such socially constructed actions is the notion of the transformative role of courage, agility and physical danger. Trials involving the appropriation of animal power carry with them the premise of culture controlling the wild, order conquering chaos. In bull-grappling and bull-leaping the player physically interacts with the animal, as wrestlers and boxers do with each other. In the hunt, man and animal are parallel adversaries.

Physical transformations indicative of youth, whether as indexes of symbolic features in life (head shaving, hair locks, nakedness) or purely as a symbolic visual idiom (colour), define some players of contact sports as immature boys. In one case, such physical transformations are portrayed in what appears to be a unique glimpse of secluded male initiation rituals. These indicators of extreme youth are sometimes carried over into the public performances of bull sports, suggesting a transitional stage of maturity in the players. Hunters are at the height of their masculine prowess, no longer youths, initiated through their actions into manhood. In the wall paintings of Akrotiri, several youths are physiologically and culturally distinguished. The boys are in all cases symbolically associated with animals, either through direct parallelism of ritualized play associated with social learning, or trials of skill and strength in the appropriation of power, or physiological transformation in the process of maturation.

What are the conceptual implications for these iconographic juxtapositions between youths and animals, especially in the realm of ritualized play? What form of relationship is expressed in the desire to appropriate the power of wild animals? Association is implicit in all symbolic parallels, while identification takes us to another level of relationship, and may be the crux of ritualized play. In particular, the symbolic comparison between mock fighting of antelopes and combat sport of boys raises the larger question of whether in the ancient world a notion equivalent to our concept of culture might have been extended to significant animals. What form of comparison was being made here? Was it simply a mimetic parallel, or the identification of imitative behaviour across species, or did the artist see conceptual similarities in the educative role of play? The portrayal of monkeys playing musical instruments and wielding swords, a mind-set linked to theriomorphism, implies a cognitive link between animals and culture, albeit in the supernatural order of things. Such reflections are worth considering in the context of the ritualized play of bull sports and its parallelism with the hunt. All such scenes belong within a wider conceptual framework. As I believe underlies the programmes discussed here, that framework incorporates physiological and sociological transformation. The multivalent associations between the various components of all the murals discussed in this chapter, each set within its ritually charged architectural space, reveal fundamental links between what for us are linguistically discrete notions. Play, ritual and belief are inextricably interwoven, not as separate concepts, but as part of the totality of the ancient worldview.

NOTES

Many thanks to Colin Renfrew for inviting me to join the Symposium, to Michael Boyd and Iain Morley for their organizational and editorial skills, and to all the participants of the Symposium, whose stimulating papers and discussions, in and out of the lecture hall, made for a fascinating and memorable few days in Cambridge. My thanks to Orly Goldwasser and Stephen Quirke for helpful advice on aspects of Ancient Egyptian language, to Stuart Laidlaw for assistance with illustrations and to Nanno Marinatos and Doan Morgan Vassaf for their perceptive comments on drafts of this chapter.

1 An exception, no doubt informed by Aegean bull sports as represented in the palace of Tell el Dab^ca, is a scene on an 18th Dynasty wooden box from Kahun (Decker & Herb 1994, R4.2, pl. CDIII).

2 Thanks to Evangelos Kyriakidis for drawing my attention to these clay statuettes in discussion at the Symposium.

3 I am grateful to Andreas Vlachopoulos for showing me the newly conserved paintings at Akrotiri in August 2010 and to both him and Irini Papageorgiou for kindly providing me with updated information in August 2012.

The paintings of the vestibule are being studied for publication by Irini Papageorgiou (in press b); while the animals in Room 2 on the ground floor and the ducks in Room 3 on the first floor are subjects of study by Andreas Vlachopoulos. The analysis of the male component of the programme presented in this chapter appears more fully in Morgan 2016, written after this chapter.

REFERENCES

Altenmüller, H. 1967. *Darstellungen der Jagd im alten Ägypten*. Hamburg – Berlin: Verlag Paul Parey.

Altenmüller, H. 1980. Jagd. *Lexicon der Ägyptologie* III, 224–32.

Assmann, J. 2005. *Death and Salvation in Ancient Egypt*, translated by D. Lorton. Ithaca, NY – London: Cornell University Press.

Bere, R. 1970. *Antelopes*. London: Arco Publishing.

Bietak, M., N. Marinatos & C. Palivou, 2007. *Taureador Scenes in Tell el-Dab'a (Avaris) and Knossos*. (Österreichische Akademie der Wissenschaften Denkschriften der Gesamtakademie 43, Untersuchungen der Zweigstelle Kairo des Österreichischen Archäologischen Institutes 27). Wien: Verlag der Österreichischen Akademie der Wissenschaften.

Blackman, A. M. 1914. *The Rock Tombs of Meir, I*. London: Egypt Exploration Fund.

Bleeker, C. J. 1967. *Egyptian Festivals. Enactments of Religious Renewal*. Leiden: E. J. Brill.

Bloch, M. 1992. *Prey into Hunter. The Politics of Religious Experience*. Cambridge: Cambridge University Press.

Burghardt, G. M. 2006. *The Genesis of Animal Play. Testing the Limits*. Cambridge, MA – London: MIT Press.

Capart, M. J. 1931. Note sur un fragment de bas-relief au British Museum. *Bulletin de l'Institut Français d'Archéologie Orientale* XXX (1931), 73–5.

Chapin, A. P. 2007. Boys will be boys: youth and gender identity in the Theran frescoes, in *Constructions of Childhood in Ancient Greece and Italy*, eds. A. Cohen & J. B. Rutter. (*Hesperia* Supplement 41). Princeton, NJ: The American School of Classical Studies at Athens, 229–55.

Chapin, A. P. 2009. Constructions of male youth and gender in Aegean art: the evidence from Late Bronze Age Crete and Thera, in *Fylo: Engendering Prehistoric 'Stratigraphies' in the Aegean and the Mediterranean. Proceedings of an International Conference, University of Crete, Rethymno 2–5 June 2005*, ed. Katerina Kopaka. (*Aegaeum* 30). Liège and Austin: Université de Liège and University of Texas at Austin, 175–82.

Coulomb, J. 1981. Les boxeurs minoen. *Bulletin de Correspondance Hellénique* 105, 27–40.

David, R. 1981. *A Guide to Religious Ritual at Abydos.* Warminster: Aris & Phillips.

Davies, N. de Garis, 1900. *The Mastaba of Ptahhotep and Akhethetep,* Part I. London: Egypt Exploration Fund.

Davies, N. de Garis, 1905. *The Rock Tombs of El Amarna, Part II. The Tombs of Panehesy and Meryra II.* London: Egypt Exploration Fund.

Davis, E. N. 1986. Youth and age in the Thera frescoes. *American Journal of Archaeology* 90:4, 399–406.

Decker, W. 1992. *Sports and Games in Ancient Egypt.* New Haven, CT: Yale University Press.

Decker, W., 2006. *Pharao und Sport.* Mainz am Rhein: Verlag Philipp von Zabern.

Decker, W. & M. Herb, 1994. *Bildatlas zum Sport im alten Ägypten. Corpus der bildlichen quellen zu Leibesübung, Spiel, Jagd, Tanz und vervandten Themen.* Leiden: Brill.

Doumas, C. 1987. Ἡ ξεστή 3 καί οἱ κικινοκέφαλοι στήν τής Θήρας, in *ΕΙΛΑΠΙΝΗ, Τόμος τιμητικός γιά τόν Καθηγητή Νικόλαο Πλάτωνα,* eds. L. Kastrinaki, G. Orphanou & N. Giannadakis, Iraklion: Municipality of Iraklion, 151–9.

Doumas, C. 1992. *The Wall-Paintings of Thera.* Athens: The Thera Foundation, Petros M. Nomikos.

Doumas, C. 2000. Age and gender in the Theran wall paintings, in *The Wall Paintings of Thera. Proceedings of the First International Symposium, Petros M. Nomikos Conference Centre, Thera, Hellas, 30 August – 4 September 1997, Vol. II,* ed. S. Sherratt. Athens: Thera Foundation – Petros M. Nomikos and The Thera Foundation, 971–81.

Duell, P. 1938. *The Mastaba of Mereruka,* Part I. Chicago: University of Chicago Press.

Erman, A. & H. Grapow, 1926/1930. *Wörterbuch der Aegyptischen Sprache.* Vol. 1 / Vol. IV. Leipzig: J.C. Hinrichs Buchhandlung.

Fakhry, A. 1943. A note on the tomb of Kheruef. *Annales du Service des Antiquités de l'Égypt* xlii (1943), 449–508.

Faulkner, R. O. 1981. *A Concise Dictionary of Middle Egyptian.* Oxford: Griffith Institute, Ashmolean Museum.

Galán, J. M. 1994. Bullfight scenes in ancient Egyptian tombs. *Journal of Egyptian Archaeology* 80, 81–96.

Garwood, P. 2011. Rites of passage, in *Oxford Handbook of the Archaeology of Ritual and Religion,* ed. T. Insoll. Oxford: Oxford University Press, 261–78.

Germond, P. & J. Livet, 2001. *An Egyptian Bestiary.* London: Thames and Hudson.

Grimes, R. L. 2003. *Deeply into the Bone. Re-inventing Rites of Passage.* Berkeley – Los Angeles – London: University of California Press.

Halioua, B. & B. Ziskind, 2005. *Medicine in the Days of the Pharaohs.* Cambridge, MA – London: The Belknap Press of Harvard University Press.

Harpur, Y. 1987. *Decoration in Egyptian Tombs of the Old Kingdom. Studies in Orientation and Scene Content.* London – New York: KPI.

Harpur, Y. & P. Scremin, 2008. *The Chapel of Ptahhotep. Scene Details.* Oxford: Oxford Expedition to Egypt.

Herbert, E. W. 1993. *Iron, Gender, and Power: Rituals of Transformation in African Societies.* Bloomington: Indiana University Press.

Hölscher, U. 1941. *Medinet Habu,* Vol. III, Part I. Chicago: The University of Chicago Oriental Institute Publications.

Houlihan, P. F. 1996. *The Animal World of the Pharaohs.* London: Thames and Hudson.

Huizinga, J. 1955. *Homo Ludens. A Study of the Play Element in Culture.* Boston: The Beacon Press.

Huxley, J., ed. 1966. *Ritualization of Behaviour in Animals and Man.* Philosophical Transactions of the Royal Society of London, Series B, Vol. 251, Biological Sciences, London.

James, T. G. H. & M. R. Apted, 1953. *The Mastaba of Khentika called Ikhekhi.* London: Egyptian Exploration Society.

Janssen, R. M. & J. J. Janssen, 1990. *Growing up in Ancient Egypt.* London: Rubicon Press.

Kanawati, N. 1991. Bullfighting in ancient Egypt. *Bulletin of the Australian Centre for Egyptology* 2, 51–8.

Kanawati, N., A. Woods, S. Shafik & E. Alexakisi, 2010 and 2011. *Mereruka and His Family, Part III:1 and Part III:2. The Tomb of Mereruka.* The Australian Centre for Egyptology: Reports 29 and 30. Oxford: Aris and Phillips.

Karageorghis, V. 1990. Rites de passage at Thera: some Oriental comparanda, in *Thera and the Aegean World III, Proceedings of the Third International Congress Santorini, Greece, 3–9 September 1989, Vol. One,* ed. D. A. Hardy. London: The Thera Foundation, 67–71.

Koehl, R. B. 1986. The Chieftain Cup and a Minoan rite of passage. *Journal of Hellenic Studies* 106, 99–110.

Lange K. & M. Hirmer, 1968. *Egypt. Architecture, Sculpture, Painting in Three Thousand Years.* London – New York: Phaidon.

La Fontaine, J. S. 1985. *Initiation. Ritual Drama and Secret Knowledge Across the World.* Harmondsworth: Penguin Books.

Leach, E. R. 1958. Magical hair. *The Journal of the Royal Anthropological Institute of Great Britain and Ireland* 88:2 (Jul.–Dec), 147–64.

Lorenz, K. (1966) 2002. *On Aggression.* London – New York: Routledge.

Mariette, A. 1869. *Abydos: description des fouilles exécutées sur l'emplacement de cette ville* Vol. 1. Paris: Imprimerie nationale.

Marinatos, N. 1984. *Art and Religion in Thera.* Athens: D. and I. Mathioulakis.

Marinatos, N. 1989. The bull as an adversary: some observations on bull-hunting and bull-leaping. *Αφιέρωμα ατον Στυλιάνο Αλεξίου, Ariadne* 5: 23–32.

Marinatos, N. 1993. *Minoan Religion. Ritual, Image and Symbol.* Columbia, SC: University of Carolina Press.

Marinatos, N. 2005. The ideals of manhood in Minoan Crete, in *Aegean Wall Painting: A Tribute to Mark Cameron,* ed. L. Morgan. London: British School at Athens Studies 13, 149–58.

Marinatos, N. 2010. Lions from Tell el-Dab'a. *Ägypten und Levante / Egypt and the Levant* 20, 325–55.

Marinatos, S. & M. Hirmer, 1960. *Crete and Mycenae.* London: Thames & Hudson.

Militello, P. 2003. Il rhytòn dei Lottatori e le scene di combattimento: battaglie, duelli, agoni e competizioni nella Creta neopalaziale. *Creta Antica* 4, 359–401. English abstract: "The Boxer Rhyton and the Scenes of Fighting, War, Combat, and Competition in Neopalatial Crete," p. 401.

Mitchell, J. P. 2006. Performance, in *Handbook of Material Culture,* ed. C. Tilley, W. Keane, S. Küchler, M. Rowlands & P. Spyer. London: Sage Publications, 384–401.

Mitchell, J. P. 2007. Towards an archaeology of performance, in *Cult in Context. Reconsidering Ritual in Archaeology,* ed. D. A. Barrowclough & C. Malone. Oxford: Oxbow Books, 336–9.

Morgan, L. 1995. Of animals and men: the symbolic parallel, in: *Klados. Essays in Honour of Professor J. N. Coldstream,* ed. C. Morris. London: Institute of Classical Studies, 171–84.

Morgan, L. 1998. Power of the beast: human-animal symbolism in Egyptian and Aegean art. *Ägypten und Levante / Egypt and the Levant* 7, 17–31.

Morgan, L. 2000. Form and meaning in figurative painting, in: The Wall Paintings of Thera. Proceedings of the First International Symposium, Petros M. Nomikos Conference Centre, Thera, Hellas, 30 August - 4 September 1997, Vol. II, ed. S. Sherratt. Athens: Thera Foundation - Petros M. Nomikos and The Thera Foundation, 925–46.

Morgan, L. 2010a. A pride of leopards: a unique aspect of the Hunt Frieze from Tell el-Dabᶜa. *Aegypten und Levante / Egypt and the Levant* 20, 263–301.

Morgan, L. 2010b. An Aegean griffin in Egypt: the Hunt Frieze at Tell el-Dabᶜa. *Aegypten und Levante / Egypt and the Levant,* 20, 303–23.

Morgan, L., 2016. The transformative power of mural art: ritual space, symbolism, and the mythic imagination, in *Metaphysis: Ritual, Myth and Symbolism in the Aegean Bronze Age, Proceedings of the 15th International Aegean Conference, Vienna, 22–25 April 2014 (Aegaeum 39),* eds. E. Alram-Stern, F. Blakolmer, S. Deger-Jalkotzy, R. Laffineur & J. Weilharnter. Leuven-Liège: Université de Liège, 187–197.

Morris, B. 1998. *The Power of Animals. An Ethnography.* Oxford – New York: Berg.

Morris, B. 2000. *Animals and Ancestors. An Ethnography.* Oxford – New York: Berg.

Nelson, H. H. 1930. *Medinet Habu I. Earlier Historical Records of Rameses III.* The University of Chicago Oriental Institute Publications Vol. VIII. Chicago: University of Chicago Press.

Nelson, H. H. 1932. *Medinet Habu II. Later Historical Records of Rameses III.* The University of Chicago Oriental Institute Publications Vol. IX. Chicago: University of Chicago Press.

Newberry, P. E. 1893/1894. *Beni Hasan. Part I / Part II.* London: Egypt Exploration Fund.

Nims, C. I., L. Habachi, E. F. Wente & D. B. Larkin, 1980. *The Tomb of Kheruef. Theban Tomb 194.* The Epigraphic Survey in cooperation with The Department of Antiquities of Egypt. Chicago: Oriental Institute of the University of Chicago.

Nunn, J. F. (1996) 2002. *Ancient Egyptian Medicine.* London: British Museum Press.

O'Connor, D., 2009. *Abydos. Egypt's First Pharaohs and the Cult of Osiris.* London: Thames and Hudson.

O'Connor, D. 2012. The Mortuary Temple of Ramesses III at Medinet Habu, in *Ramesses III. The Life and Times of Egypt's Last Hero,* eds. E. H. Cline and D. O'Connor. Ann Arbor: University of Michigan Press, 209–70.

Paliou, E., D. Wheatley & G. Earl, 2011. Three-dimensional visibility analysis of architectural spaces: iconography and visibility of the wall paintings of Xesté 3 (Late Bronze Age Akrotiri). *Journal of Archaeological Science* 38, 375–86.

Palyvou, C. 2005. *Akrotiri Thera: An Architecture of Affluence 3500 Years Old.* Philadelphia, PA: INSTAP Academic Press, Prehistory Monographs 15.

Papageorgiou, I. 2000. On the *Rites de Passage* in Late Cycladic Akrotiri, Thera: a reconsideration of the frescoes of the 'Priestess' and the 'Fishermen' of the West House, in *The Wall Paintings of Thera. Proceedings of the First International Symposium, Petros M. Nomikos Conference Centre, Thera, Hellas, 30 August – 4 September 1997, Vol. II,* ed. S. Sherratt. Athens: Thera Foundation – Petros M. Nomikos and The Thera Foundation, 958–70.

Papageorgiou, I. 2008. Children and adolescents in Minoan art, in *From the Land of the Labyrinth. Minoan Crete, 3000–1100 B.C. Essays,* eds. M. Andreadaki-Vlazaki, G. Rethemiotakis & N. Dimopoulou-Rethemiotaki. Hellenic Ministry of Culture – Archaeological Museums of Crete, 89–95.

Papageorgiou, I., in press (a). Η πορεία προς την ενηλικίωση στο προϊστορικό Ακρωτήρι, *ΑΛΣ* 8 (2011–12). 'Coming age in prehistoric Akrotiri, Thera'.

Papageorgiou, I., in press (b). Προθάλαμος Ξεστής 3: "Η επάνοδος των κυνηγών" Εισαγωγικές παρατηρήσεις με αφορμή δύο νέες τοιχογραφίες από το Ακρωτήρι, in: Χρ. Ντούμας (επιμ.), *Ακρωτήρι Θήρας. 40 χρόνια έρευνας.* 'The vestibule of Xeste 3: "The return of the hunters". Introductory remarks on two "new" wall-paintings from Akrotiri, Thera', in *Akrotiri, Thera: Forty Years of Research (1967–2007),* C. Doumas, ed.

Parry, B. 2007. *Tribe,* Series 2: Hamar. Produced and directed by J. Smith, J. Clay, S. Robinson, G. Johnston, presented by B. Parry. A BBC Wales / Discovery Channel co-production, originally transmitted 2006, DVD 2007.

Piccione, P. A. 1999. Sportive fencing as a ritual for destroying the enemies of Horus, in *Gold of Praise: Studies on*

Ancient Egypt in Honor of Edward F. Wente, eds. E. Teeter & J. A. Larson. Studies in Ancient Oriental Civilization 58, Chicago: Oriental Institute of the University of Chicago, 335–49.

Platon, L. 2008. Athletics and sports, in *From the Land of the Labyrinth. Minoan Crete, 3000–1100 B.C. Essays*, eds. M. Andreadaki-Vlazaki, G. Rethemiotakis & N. Dimopoulou-Rethemiotaki. Hellenic Ministry of Culture – Archaeological Museums of Crete: New York, 96–9.

Porter B. & R. L. B. Moss, 1960. *Topographical Bibliography of Ancient Egyptian Hieroglyphic Texts, Reliefs and Paintings. The Theban Necropolis. Part I. Private Tombs*. Oxford: Clarendon.

Quirke, S. 1992. *Ancient Egyptian Religion*. London: British Museum Press.

Rehak, P. 1999. The Monkey Frieze from Xeste 3, Room 4: reconstruction and interpretation, in *Meletemata: Studies in Aegean Archaeology Presented to Malcolm H. Wiener as He Enters His 65th Year. Vol. III*, eds. P. P. Betancourt, V. Karageorghis, R. Laffineur, & W.-D. Niemeier. Liège and Austin: Université de Liège (Histoire de l'art et archéologie de la Grèce antique) and University of Texas at Austin (Programs in Aegean Scripts and Prehistory), 705–9.

Roth, A. M. 1991. *Egyptian Phyles in the Old Kingdom: The Evolution of a System of Social Organization*. Chicago: Oriental Institute of the University of Chicago.

Rutter, J. 2003. Children in Aegean prehistory, in *Coming of Age in Ancient Greece. Images of Childhood from the Classical Past*, eds. J. Neils & J. H. Oakley. New Haven, CT – London: Yale University Press, 30–57.

Säflund, G. 1987. The *Agoge* of the Minoan youth as reflected by palatial iconography, in *The Function of the Minoan Palaces. Proceedings of the Fourth International Symposium at the Swedish Institute in Athens, 10–16 June, 1984*, eds. R. Hägg & N. Marinatos. Stockholm: Swedish Institute in Athens.

Schechner, R. (1988) 2003. *Performance Theory*. London – New York: Routledge.

Schenkel, R. 1966. On sociology and behaviour in impala (*Aepyceros melampus suara Matschie*). *Zeitschrift für Säugetierkunde* 31, 177–205.

Shedid, A. G. 1994. *Die Felsgräber von Beni Hassan in Mittelägypten*. Mainz am Rhein: Philipp von Zabern.

Simpson, W. K. 1976. *The Mastabas of Qar and Idu, G7101 and 7102*. Boston: Department of Egyptian and Ancient Near Eastern Art, Museum of Fine Arts.

Taylor, J. H. ed., 2010. *Journey through the Afterlife. Ancient Egyptian Book of the Dead*. London: British Museum.

Thompson, S. E. 2001. Cults, in *The Oxford Encyclopedia of Ancient Egypt*, ed. D. B. Redford, Vol. 1. Oxford: Oxford University Press, 326–33.

Turner, V. 1967. *The Forest of Symbols. Aspects of Ndembu Ritual*. Ithaca, NY – London: Cornell University Press.

Turner, V. 1969. *The Ritual Process. Structure and Anti-Structure*. New Brunswick, NJ – London: Aldine Transaction.

Turner, V. 1982. *From Ritual to Theatre. The Human Seriousness of Play*. New York: PAJ Publications.

Turner, V. 1988. *The Anthropology of Performance*. New York: PAJ Publications.

Tyldesley, J. 2007. *Egyptian Games and Sports*. Princes Risborough: Shire Egyptology.

Vandier, J. 1969. *Manuel d'Archaeologie Égyptienne*, I. Paris: Picard.

Van Gennep, A. 1960. *The Rites of Passage*. Translated M. B. Vizedom & G. L. Caffee. Chicago: University of Chicago Press.

Vlachopoulos, A. G. 2000. The reed motif in the Thera wall paintings and its association with Aegean pictorial art, in *The Wall Paintings of Thera. Proceedings of the First International Symposium, Petros M. Nomikos Conference Centre, Thera, Hellas, 30 August – 4 September 1997, Vol. II*, ed. Susan Sherratt. Athens: Thera Foundation – Petros M. Nomikos and The Thera Foundation, 631–56.

Vlachopoulos, A. G. 2007. Mythos, logos and eikon. Motifs of early Greek poetry in the wall paintings of Xeste 3 at Akrotiri, Thera, in *Epos. Reconsidering Greek Epic and Aegean Bronze Age Archaeology*, ed. S. P. Morris & R. Laffineur, (*Aegaeum* 28). Liège and Austin: Université de Liège and University of Texas at Austin, 107–18.

Vlachopoulos, A. G. 2008a. The wall paintings from the Xeste 3 building at Akrotiri: towards an interpretation of the iconographic programme, in *Horizon. Ορίζων: A Colloquium on the Prehistory of the Cyclades*, eds. N. Brodie, J. Doole, G. Gavalos & C. Renfrew. Cambridge: McDonald Institute for Archaeological Research, 451–65.

Vlachopoulos, A. G. 2008b. Ἡ "Τοιχογραφία τοῦ Δονακῶνος" ἀπὸ τὸ κτήριο Ξεστὴ 3 τοῦ Ἀκρωτηρίου, in *Ακρωτήρι Θήρας. Τριάντα χρόνια έρευνας 1967–1997*, ed. C. Doumas. Athens: Archaiologiki Etaireia, 261–86. English summary: The wall-painting of the reed bed and building Xeste 3 at Akrotiri, p. 286.

Vlachopoulos, A. G. 2010. L'espace rituel revisité: Architecture et iconographie dans la Xestè 3 d'Akrotiri, Théra, in *Espace civil, espace religieux en Égée durant la période mycénienne: Approches épigraphique, linguistique et archéologique. Actes des journées d'archéologie et de philologie mycéniennes tenues à la Maison de l'Orient et de la Méditerranée*, eds. I. Boehm & S. Müller-Celka. Lyon: Travaux de la Maison de l'Orient et de la Méditerranée 54, 173–98.

Wilson, J. A. 1931. Ceremonial games of the New Kingdom. *Journal of Egyptian Archaeology* 17, 211–20.

Withee, D. 1992. Physical growth and aging characteristics depicted on the Thera frescoes, *American Journal of Archaeology* 96, 336.

15

BULL GAMES IN MINOAN CRETE: SOCIAL AND SYMBOLIC DIMENSIONS

NANNO MARINATOS

This chapter discusses various aspects of Minoan bull games: the nature of the sport, the gender and status of the participants, the role of the palace in the organisation and execution of the games and the deity to which the games were dedicated. The first part presents the iconographical evidence; the second investigates the sport in its cultic and comparative context with a glance at the civilisations neighbouring Crete in Anatolia and Syria.

DEFINITION

What are the bull games of Minoan Crete?[1] The assumption here will be that this sport had rules and an end-goal, as well as ritual and ideological dimensions. There is no doubt that it was a very popular and spectacular performance to judge by the fact that it was represented in a variety of artistic media: wall paintings, gold rings, seal stones, precious stone vessels. The games were performed in Crete during its palatial period, from about 2000 to 1375 BC, but they were *not* unique to this island since we find evidence (to be discussed later in this chapter) also from Syria, Anatolia and the Mycenaean mainland. This fact must be stressed because all too often the sport has been singled out as peculiar to Minoan civilisation (Kyle 2007, 45), whereas some scholars have attempted to associate it with the legend of the Minotaur. It will be argued here, by contrast, that Minoan Crete was a cosmopolitan culture with international contacts and therefore shared certain of its religious rituals and court ceremonies with its neighbours in the Near East. We shall return to this subject.

A few words must be said about the occurrence of the sport on the Mycenaean mainland before the Minoan bull games are discussed. There is indeed evidence of bull games there – they are represented in the frescoes of Mycenae, Tiryns and Pylos and on a sarcophagus from the area of Thebes (Immerwahr 1990). It is not entirely certain, however, that these Mycenaean representations reflect the actual practice of the sport, and it is possible that these kingdoms, smaller than Knossos, imitated the grand Cretan palace art for ideological reasons. This issue is beyond the scope of this chapter. My concern here will be the rules and symbolism of the games as practised during the palatial period of Crete until the fall of Knossos ca. 1400/1375 BC.

THE TWO GROUPS OF THE SPORT AND THEIR FUNCTION

A further clarification is necessary for the comprehension of bull games. Sometimes the sport is referred to as 'bull-leaping' (Younger 1976), a slightly misleading designation since the games *do not consist of bull-leaping alone,* but involve also *grappling the bull.* In other words, we have two distinct activities performed by two distinct age groups, each having its

Figure 15.1 Taureador panels from Knossos. After Bietak, Marinatos & Palyvou 2007.

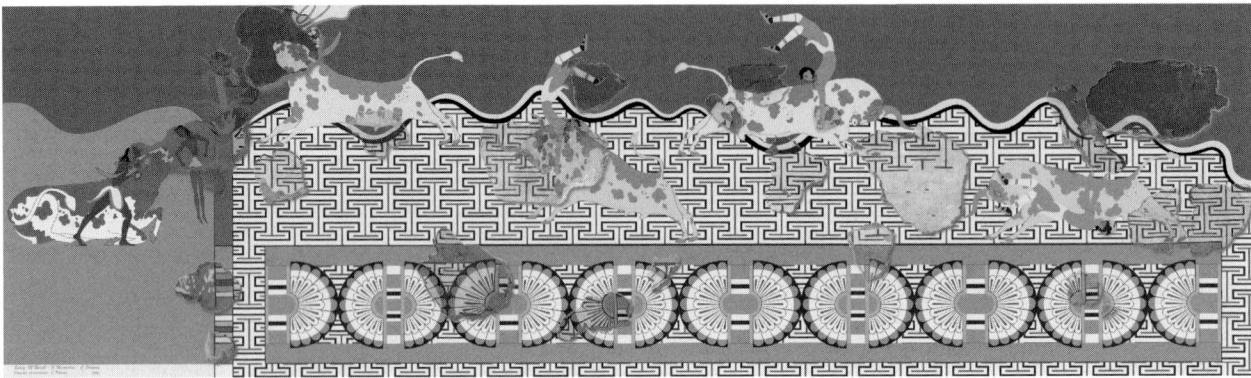

Figure 15.2 Tell el Dab'a panel. Restoration by Bietak et al. 2007.

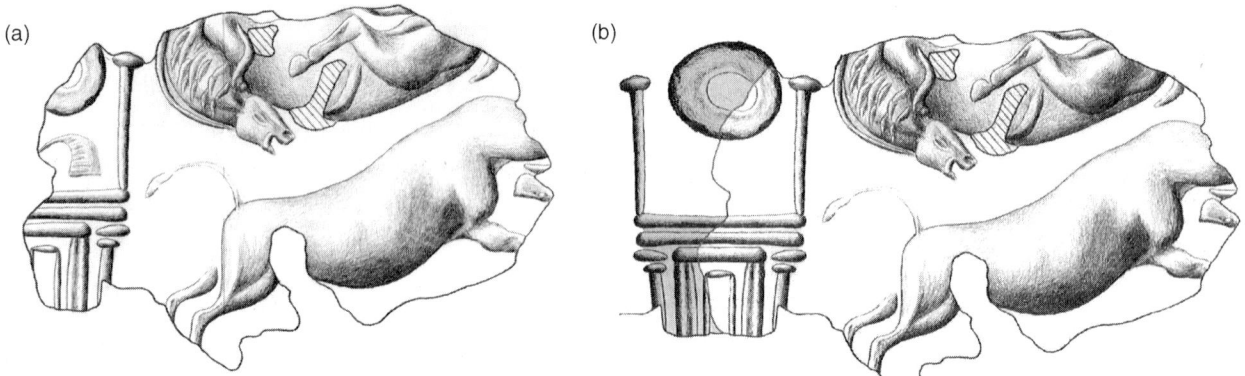

Figure 15.3 (a, b) Akrotiri ring impressions and slightly restored version with bull games in front of a palace. Pini 2004, CMS VS3, 404. Courtesy CMS.

own task, but both aiming at a common goal: to tire out the bull and subjugate it. No females took part, as will be argued subsequently.

How can we distinguish between the two groups? The differentiation is easy because the figures have two sizes and, in the case of Knossian frescoes (Figure 15.1), two hues of skin colour, red and white. The first group is rendered red and consists of acrobats. They are smaller in size than the white figures and may well have been teenagers or very young adults, hence they were agile and flexible. Their role was to perform somersaults of various types over

the galloping animal (Younger 1976; Laughlin 2004); they leapt over the back of the bull, or over his side and thus displayed their bodily skill whilst confusing the animal. Some leaps, such as the side-leap, were low-risk tasks, whereas bolder leaps required jumping from the front over the bull's head. This task must have been reserved for the most experienced leapers.

The second group consists of grapplers who are rendered with lighter skin, white on the Knossos murals (Figure 15.1) and yellow on the Tell el Dab'a ones (Figure 15.2). The colour was possibly a mark of distinction and rank. In other words, the lighter the colour, the higher the rank. In any case, the white figures are not only larger and more muscular than the leapers, but also more elaborately ornamented (Figures 15.1–15.2). What was the task of the grapplers? They would hang on to the bull's horns or around his neck and body and arrest his impetus, thus facilitating the leaper's task (Figure 15.3) (Evans 1930, 218–19; Bietak, Marinatos & Palyvou 2007, 64, figs. 65–7, 83, 92, 84, 93–5, 95, 116, 100). In short, the grapplers' task was both dangerous and vital to the safety of the leaper. The skill required speed, precision and knowledge of animal behaviour as well as considerable muscular strength and, most of all, courage.

This hypothesis will now be tested on the best known of the Knossos murals, the Taureador panels. It must be mentioned, in parenthesis however, that bull games and hunts decorated almost all the major entrances of Knossos such as, for example, the west and north porticoes (Evans 1930, 158–91). The most celebrated and frequently illustrated scene is one Taureador panel from the east quarters because it was completely restored by Evans' artist, Emile Gilliéron senior (Evans 1930, 203–32). But here we shall also look at the lesser-known panels of this composition which were identified and restored on paper by Mark Cameron (Hood 2005, 56, 71, 79–80). In the 1990s, these fragments were re-studied by Clairy Palyvou and myself in the storerooms of the Heraklion museum, and we enhanced Cameron's restorations (Figure 15.1). One of the most important results of our study was the realisation that *all the white figures* without exception were larger and more muscular than the leapers (Bietak et al. 2007, 115–26). We also verified that they wore ornaments, necklaces, armlets and bandeaux around their curly coiffures, whereas the red leapers did not. Finally, we ascertained that the white figures wore boots, whereas the leapers were all barefooted. In sum, the grapplers are clearly distinguished as larger, older adults wearing more ornaments. It was the aforementioned adornments and the light skin of the grapplers that misled Sir Arthur Evans to identify them as women. The bandeaux and the curls of the hair especially seemed very feminine to him:

> They wear bands around their wrists and double necklaces – one of them beaded – and, in the case of some of the figures, blue

and red ribbons round their brows. But perhaps their most distinctive feature is the symmetrical arrangement of short curls over their foreheads and temples, already noticed in the case of the female 'cow-boy' of the Vapheio cup. (1930, 212)

Evans was misled by one additional feature: one of the white figures of the restored taureador fresco seemed to him to have a swelling in the chest area, and he took this to be a breast. However, a better explanation of this feature is that it represents developed chest muscles and a bulky chest, such as might distinguish a young adult from a teenage leaper. There is suspicion that the nipple of this bulky figure may have been touched up by the restorer, Emile Gilliéron senior (Evans 1930, 208). This possibility cannot be excluded given the vivid hue of the paint.

In sum, the white figures/grapplers *cannot have been women* given their costume of phallus-sheaths. Evans had a possible answer, arguing that the women wore male costumes only for this special occasion, but this is not so convincing. It is also worth noting that Evans was thrown off on account of certain ivory statuettes of women leapers that were in circulation in the market in the 1920s. The latter are now considered forgeries by most scholars (Lapatin 2002, 108–19); to date there is *no single Minoan statuette* stemming from an excavated context that represents a female leaper. This is surely an argument against the possibility of female taureadors.

THE TELL EL DAB'A TAUREADOR PANEL AND ITS KNOSSIAN DERIVATION

More evidence about the Minoan bull games came to light between 1990 and 1993, when the Austrian archaeologist Manfred Bietak excavated a set of mural fragments in the Delta of Egypt. They decorated the walls of the palatial compound of Tuthmosis III, near the modern village of Tell el Dab'a. Among the fragments were several pieces with representations of bulls and leapers. Were they Egyptian or Cretan? There is no doubt the murals were executed by Knossian artists, despite objections expressed by scholars (Shaw 2009). The arguments in favour of Knossian artists are the following (although this does not mean that some version of the games was not practised in Egypt. On this subject, see Morgan, Chapter 14 in this volume).

The first argument is the technique of painting on wet plaster and organising the space by imprinting a string to define the borders: this exact method is found at Knossos and Akrotiri, Thera. A second argument concerns details of clothing and ornament which reveal intimate knowledge of Minoan life and custom, as well as understanding of Minoan artistic convention. For example, the yellow grappler wears a Minoan seal-bracelet (Figure 15.2): only an artist trained in the Minoan tradition would understand such a detail. Third, there is evidence of religious 'idiom' (Morgan 1985; see also Marinatos 2007b). Take this example: the Taureador panel from Tell el Dab'a is framed by a half-rosette frieze in its lower level. This ornament is typically Knossian and makes best sense if the palace of Knossos was the model that inspired the representation. Otherwise, the half-rosette would have no meaning to the uninitiated artist or the Egyptian spectator and I assume that even the latter would have recognised that something Knossian was depicted.

The rosette is associated with the palace also on ring-engravings. On a ring-impression found at Akrotiri, Thera but made by a Knossian ring and imprinted on Cretan clay, we see the following scene, which is presented here in the original and in a slightly restored version (Figures 15.3 a, b). Two bulls are depicted in an unrealistic, contorted position as though they are in pain and confusion; to the right of the animals we see a palace façade recognisable by its gate and a circle which must be a rosette (Pini 2004, no. 404; Marinatos in Bietak et al. 2007, 130, fig. 122). If palace and rosette constituted an idiomatic formula, how could a non-Knossian artist come to associate the bull games with half-rosettes at Tell el Dab'a?

Evans understood that the half-rosette was charged with special meaning when he found a stone frieze *in corpore* in the west court of the palace and realised then that it ornamented its façade (Evans 1935, 223, fig. 172). He then pointed out that the symbol was imitated by Mycenaean magnates at the palaces of Mycenae and Tiryns and thus emblematised Knossian presence.

The practical identity that is at times discernible in the material suggests, indeed, that in some cases at least, these reliefs were actually exported from the Knossian workshops, as the alabaster frieze of Tiryns seems to have been at a later date (Evans 1928, 596).

Finally, it is to Evans that we owe the insight that the rosette had a symbolic and religious significance (1928, 590–6; Marinatos 2007b, 2010, 131–9).

To return to the Tell el Dab'a Taureador panel, the excavator M. Bietak rightly concluded that a Knossian painter and his team was invited to Egypt and was asked to decorate the Egyptian royal palatial compound with scenes of bull games and half-rosettes as well as other scenes of hunting which are not of our immediate concern. The presence of bull-leaping in an Egyptian palace suggests commonality of ideologies and strategies between the two courts, perhaps an alliance or intermarriage.

Some more details of the Tell el Dab'a Taureador panel must be discussed now. In a computer restoration, undertaken by Clairy Palyvou and myself (Bietak, Marinatos & Palyvou 2007, 48, 53, 56–7) (Figure 15.2), we attempted to combine all the relevant fragments by placing them against the maze pattern, a convenient grid. In this way, we could restore the minimum number of animals, combining fragments of same-colour bulls whenever possible. Four animals were put together, galloping in ring fashion on the maze. The latter we interpreted as a court. Most human figures are yellow and there is evidence of a fallen man. Where preserved, the yellow figures have jewellery. Two of them clearly hang on to the bull's neck or his body: they are therefore grapplers rather than leapers (Bietak et al. 2007, 53, fig. 54).

There was a separate scene on the Tell el Dab'a taureador panel which gave a most important clue as to the end-goal of the games because it represents the defeat of a bull (Figure 15.4), namely the final and climactic episode of the bull games. It is significant that this act takes place under a palm, to which we shall return. For the moment, we observe that the broken-down beast is held fast by one man, whilst a youth of slighter frame than the grappler (hence younger) jumps up and down in joy and triumph. This scene confirms that there was close collaboration between older and younger

Figure 15.4 Tell el Dab'a Taureador panel detail. The subjugation of the bull. After Bietak et al. 2007.

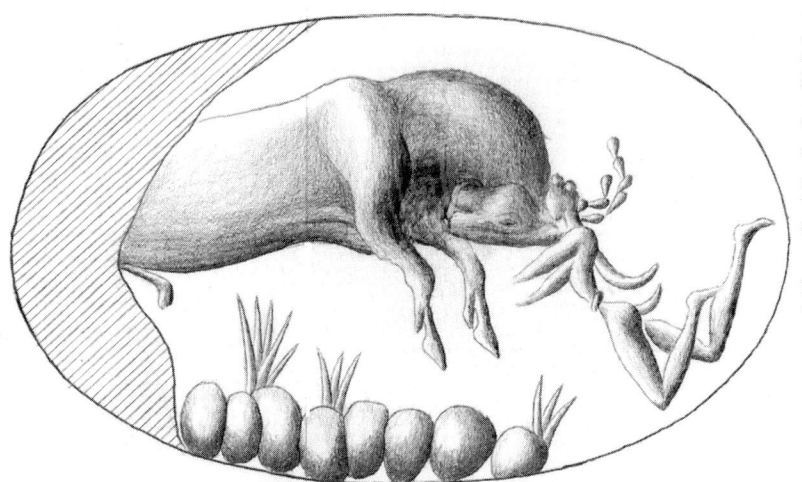

Figure 15.5 Bull grappler tossed by a bull in the wild. Ring impression from Akrotiri made by a Knossian ring Pini 2004, CMS VS3, 395. Courtesy CMS.

Figure 15.6 Tiryns Ring. Sakellariou, CMS I 179. Courtesy CMS.

men, grapplers and leapers, and that they celebrated together. The breaking down of the beast was the achievement of the grappler, who performed the task with bare hands and *without use of* weapons. In fact, to date, no representation exists that shows the bull as being stabbed in clear connection with the sport. Finally, let us note that the achievement of the bull grappler and the defeat of the bull were emblematised on rings, as we can ascertain from preserved Minoan impressions (Figures 15.5, 15.6). The emblematising of the sport constitutes further evidence that the games were associated with the Cretan aristocratic elite.

THE PLACE OF PERFORMANCE

Next we turn to the question of *where* the games were performed. Evans gave the very plausible answer that they were held in the vicinity of the palace, perhaps in the central court (1930, 182–201). He was right that the events take place very close to the palace, as the following evidence shows.

Many of the bull-leaping scenes are associated with architectural façades adorned with half rosettes and pillars (see Figures 15.3 a, b). At Knossos, a set of mural fragments stemming from the Ivory Deposit depicts pillars adorned with double axes and a bull's head.[2] In another painting, stemming from a room north of the central court, the fragments represent a palace façade adorned with so-called sacral horns and a half rosette; other fragments found in the same deposit depict crowds. This makes it likely that the subject of this last fresco was a performance held in front of the palace watched by large crowds. It is most plausible that the answer is the bull games (Evans 1930, 61–2). Some fresco fragments of bull games originated in the west magazines and depict an acrobat above a coursing bull (Evans 1930, 209, fig. 143). In sum, numerous representations of bull games existed in the palace and ranged from magnificent reliefs (such as those of the northern entrance) to the miniatures of the west magazines. It is reasonable to assume that the palace advertised its connection with the sport and that the games were held in its vicinity. This idea has been confirmed by the Tell el Dab'a Taureador mural since the bull games there

take place in a court represented by the maze pattern (Figure 15.2) (Bietak et al. 2007, 85; Shaw 2012).

There is a second reason why it is likely that the palace was involved in the sport. It alone would have afforded the considerable expense of training the youthful acrobats and the grapplers, providing the animals and procuring food for the crowds. Or, to ask the question differently, would the royal elite miss an opportunity to offer a popular spectacle to its people? Evans perceived this lucidly and added the further argument that the palace trained the youths to leap and to catch their fellow acrobats (1935, 207). As an analogy he spoke of the Spanish court games under the patronage of Isabella of Spain in the sixteenth century AD. This palatial culture helped him imagine how such a spectacle might be organised.

> Mutatis mutandis, then, it is allowable to compare their participation in these sports of the arena that needed such skill and strength with the appearances of personages of the highest rank as protagonists in the Spanish bull-fights. Moorish princes had adopted the native custom, and in the list of their arenas, as of that at Granada, were already famous. The Cid Campeador … is traditionally said to have played his part as a champion in the arena. (227–8)

In this citation, Evans has taken the matter further than I have so far by suggesting, through analogy, that the games gave an opportunity to the aristocratic youths of Knossos to display their skill and bravery in the social arena. It is a very reasonable suggestion. The youths in question were likely to be the leaders of tomorrow because of their bravery and courage. They took the risk of losing their lives, a possibility which must have excited the admiration of the people.

Another major question is why accidents are so often depicted and this fact may have something to do with the ethos of bravery. Human grapplers, in particular, are emblematised as heroic when they are shown as being tossed by a charging bull on gold rings (Figure 15.5) (Pini 2004, 395). Accidents are depicted also on Knossian frescoes (see Figure 15.7), on the Tell el Dab'a Taureador mural (Figure 15.2), on the stone rhyton from Hagia Triada, on the Vapheio cup etc. (Bietak et al. 2007, 128, fig. 120).

If we compare the accidents in the sports of ancient Greece, we shall perhaps gain some perspective. The winners of the games were most often aristocrats: Peisistratus, Miltiades, Alcibiades, and others (Herodotus 6.103.2) who gained prominence and political power in Athens *because of the way they competed* in the most dangerous of all sports, the chariot races. In Sophocles' *Electra*, Orestes supposedly loses his life during such a chariot race (Soph. *El*. 45–76). Is it possible that bull games had a similar role in Knossian society? Namely, the best young men were singled out through participation in the sport. Of course, since the games were dangerous, some of these noble men would have lost their lives. They – and those who survived – were admired all the more for their courage.

AKROTIRI

We shall next consider some new evidence which stems from the town of Akrotiri, on the island of Thera, just north of Crete. The building is less exalted than the palace of Knossos, or the Egyptian residence of Tuthmosis III at Tell el Dab'a, but it is nevertheless one of the major ones in the town. It was called Xeste 3 by its excavator, Spyridon Marinatos, although its exact function is yet to be understood. Most scholars agree that it had a religious character since it is one of the few that has yielded a fresco of a seated goddess flanked by a monkey and griffin (another such painting existed in sector A in the same town). For our purposes, the murals of the entrance of Xeste 3 are of interest because they represent men wrestling animals, a bull and a goat, respectively (Papageorgiou in Doumas 2012, 12–13, pl. 12).

The human figures are life-sized and must therefore have made an impression on the incoming visitor to the building (we are reminded that the north and west entrances of the palace of Knossos were likewise decorated by bull-grappling scenes). But to return to Thera, the protagonists on the murals are clearly youths, as shown by their partly shaved heads. Yet they are not likely to be young teenagers since they are muscular. We also notice a further

element: on one of the two murals, the youths *work together* in order to subjugate a young bull. On the other, two youths grapple a goat and they do it in unison and perfect collaboration. Such is their coordination that they give the impression of twins. We must notice, however, that the Theran representations are *not* bull games, but mere grappling scenes. Bull games proper, we suspect, were a prerogative and obligation of the Knossos palace and it alone.

I also note here in parenthesis that I designate the culture of Akrotiri as *Minoan*, by which term I mean a specific cultural and ideological expression and not geographical location or ethnic origin of the inhabitants.

THE DIVINE PATRONESS AND HER SYMBOLS: HALF-ROSETTE AND PALM

We shall consider next whether there was divine patronage of the games. Indeed, dedication of games to a deity was common practice in antiquity, and we need not wonder why this was the case (see Spivey, Chapter 16 in this volume). Divine sanction always legitimises human hierarchy and gives the palace further authority. As well, endorsement by a higher power comes in handy in case there are human casualties (Burkert 1996, 80–98). Evans thought that the patroness was "the great Minoan Goddess herself, as the impersonation of the spirit of the race", and we shall see that he was correct also in this case (1935, 207).

The most important indication of the divine patronage of the games is the presence of the half-rosette symbol that we have already discussed in connection with its adornment of palace façades (Evans 1921, 444, fig. 322; Lang 1969, pl. 78, no 8A3; Immerwahr 1990, pl. XVI). Note in addition that half-rosette friezes were visually associated with bull-catching in nature on the façade of the tomb of Atreus at Mycenae (Marinatos & Hirmer 1960, 166; Bietak et al. 2007, fig. 91), and with bull games on a signet ring from the mainland (Dakoronia et al. 1996, 517; Bietak et al. 2007, fig. 49). It is arguable that the rosette is associated with bull games because the patron goddess of the games is represented by the rosette.

Indeed, the case that the half-rosette is the emblem of the enthroned female deity of Crete and Mycenae is easy to make. Incontrovertible evidence stems from a gold ring found at Tiryns (Figure 15.6). The seated divinity there receives libations from a group of leonine butlers and below her is a frieze of half-rosettes. Since the half-rosette is associated *both with the divinity and with the bull games* the following visual formulas are established.

Bull-games + half-rosette
Palace + half-rosette
Goddess + half-rosette

On the basis of the formulas, an explanation for the half-rosette as representing the female divinity may be proposed. In other words, I suggest the following hypothesis:

The *half-rosette is the emblem of the goddess and she is the patroness of the bull games.*

It is worth repeating that the rosette could not be purely ornamental because of its consistent symbolic associations with religious objects and the divinity in Minoan art (Marinatos 2010, 131–9).

There is a second clue about the identity of the divinity of the bull games, and it leads to the same conclusion, namely that she is a female deity. The clue is given by the palm under which the bull subjugation takes place (Figure 15.4). The palm is always the sacred tree of female deities in Crete as well as in the Near East and Egypt: Ishtar and Hathor are both associated with the cult of palms (Danthine 1937; Marinatos 1984; Teissier 1996, 98). Even in the Hebrew Bible, we read that the prophetess Deborah gives her responses under a palm tree (Robertson Smith 1927, 196), a highly interesting passage given the fact that also in Minoan art the goddess is shown seated under a palm (Marinatos 2007 in Bietak et al., 146–7).

We return now briefly to the Tell el Dab'a Taureador panel. The defeat of the bull takes place under a palm tree, and this is surely not an accident. Rather, it provides one more clue that the bull games were celebrated in honour of a goddess whose emblem was the split rosette and the palm. Evans right when he said that the Minoan goddess overlooked the bull sports (1935, 23).

Our first goal has now been accomplished. We have discussed the performance of bull games, the arena in which they took place, the palace's role, the crowds of spectators who watched them, the role of the aristocratic youths who distinguished themselves as bull grapplers and leapers and the patron goddess represented by the split rosette and the palm tree. We must now turn to the broader context of bull games in the Near East and test the hypothesis of their symbolism against the Near Eastern evidence.

BULL GAMES AND RELIGIOUS SYMBOLS IN ANATOLIA AND SYRIA

As far as the symbolism of the half-rosette is concerned, it has already been noted that it originated in the palace of Knossos in MM III (Evans 1928, 591, fig. 368). Note, however, that the full rosette is not unique to Crete, but has many parallels in Syrian glyptic in the early second millennium where it signifies the sun or a star and often refers to Ishtar (Tessin 1996, 101, 111; Marinatos in Bietak et al. 2007, 145–50; Marinatos 2010, 131–4). A variant of the full rosette is its abstract version, the 'split rosette' of the dado of the throne room at Knossos. Its shape has exactly the same form as the Hittite hieroglyph for 'god' (Figure 15.7). Coincidence of form between Minoan and Hittite is very unlikely, and although some scholars have been sceptical of the existence of a *koine* between the Near East, Egypt and Crete, the commonality of symbols is hard to dispute: there are just too many examples for coincidence (Marinatos 2010, 131–9).

In fact, the similarity of the Minoan half-rosette to the Hittite determinative for 'god' was pointed out already by the German Hittitologist Helmut Bossert in 1932. The observation went unnoticed until it was taken up again by Helga Reusch in her discussion of the iconography of the throne room at Knossos (1958, 349–51). On the basis of this observation, both German scholars drew the conclusion that the symbolism of the half-rosette is the same in both Anatolia and Crete and that it reveals the divine aspect of the throne at Knossos. It must be added here in parenthesis that the origin of Hittite hieroglyphs is Luwian and that the signs in question are attested

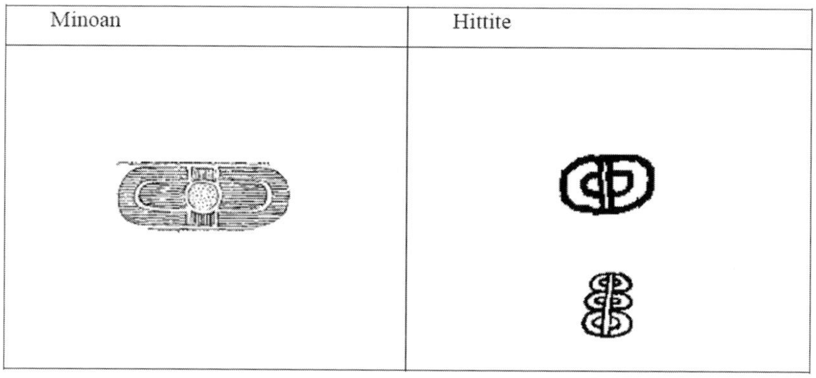

Minoan	Hittite

Figure 15.7 Hittite hieroglyph for God. After Marinatos 2010, 135, fig. 10.7.

Figure 15.8 Syrian seal. After Collon 1994, 86, pl. 1, no. 4

on royal seals already in the early Hittite period of the seventeenth/sixteenth centuries BC. A chronological association between Minoan and Anatolian ideograms during the palatial era of Knossos is thus entirely possible. In sum, the hypothesis that the half-rosette signifies 'deity' is reinforced by the Anatolian connection.

The next question is whether bull games were practised in Anatolia. The answer is yes – a Hittite relief vase with bull games was found there (Sipahi 2000, 67; Aruz 2008, 139, fig. 280). On the vase, we see a bull moving forward (but not galloping) whereas above him is an acrobat performing a somersault. To his left is another acrobat who, having already performed this task, is about to jump off. In front of the bull are men who bear musical instruments. If music accompanied the performance, a ritual character to the event in the context of a festival is most likely (Sipahi 2000).

Even more interesting is the evidence from a group of Syrian seals, dating to the period of Hammurabi or a little later to the eighteenth or seventeenth century BC (Collon 1994, 81–8; Aruz 2008, 139–41, figs. 279–84). Because these seals predate the

Knossian frescoes, a derivation from Cretan iconography must be excluded. Note, however, that a clay figurine from the Messara Tombs, representing a bull and two grapplers hanging from his horns, dates to the era of the first Minoan palaces and is contemporary with the Syrian seals (Evans 1928, 260, fig. 155).

On one Syrian seal (Figure 15.8), the representation consists of a charging bull trampling on a fallen man. A grappler is apparently trying to get hold of his horns, but has missed the opportunity, whereas a leaper, hovering above the bull, seems more successful. Behind the bull is another figure with a raised arm; he may be trying to catch the leaper, or perhaps he is encouraging him with shouting (Collon 1994, 86, pl. 1, no. 4). This representation has great similarities with certain Minoan scenes, especially a fresco from Knossos as restored by Marinatos and Palyvou (compare Figures 15.8, 15.9). On both we see a grappler, a leaper and a fallen man who is trampled by the wild animal. On the Knossos fresco, the position of the fallen man is attested by a single large fragment, but the posture is impossible to imagine in any other way. The comparison shows that the double specialisation of leaper and grappler was not unique to Crete, but was also practised in Syria. As well, we note that accidents are represented in both cultures, no doubt an allusion to the high danger posed by the sport.

Another Syrian seal (Figure 15.10) yields information about the religious nature of the bull games in Syria. It includes multiple sub-scenes, the bull games being only one small section of the composition in the upper left corner. A leaper performs his task above a charging bull, whereas behind him stands a helper with a raised arm. There is no reason

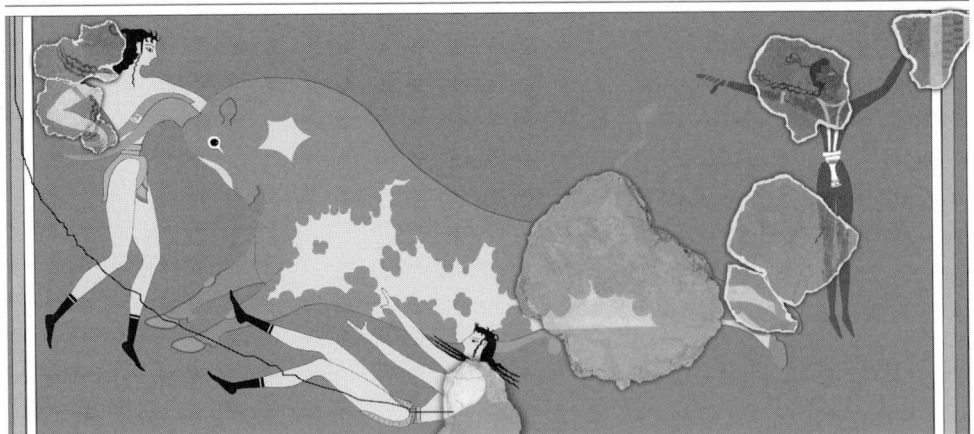

Figure 15.9 Fallen grappler. Knossos panel after Marinatos and Palyvou.

Figure 15.10 Syrian seal. After Collon 1994, pl. 2.5.

to designate the latter as female, as has been suggested by Dominique Collon (1994, 82). The most interesting feature of the scene is this: a man, bigger in size than the leaper, stands in front of the bull and draws his bow. Presumably he is ready to shoot his arrow if the animal gets out of control. He is the equivalent to the grappler of the Minoan scenes, the responsible partner of the leapers and ready to help in a case of emergency. His high status is denoted by a pointed cap which is normally worn by high-standing officials or royal personages. What is most interesting for our purposes is that an enthroned goddess and two male gods are present as well. Consequently, it is legitimate to draw the conclusion that the *Syrian bull games were presided over by gods in Syria*.

In one final example from Syrian seals (Figure 15.11), the religious associations between bull games and deity are most evident. In the city of Alalakh, the excavator Leonard Wooley (1955, 258–68) found a clay envelope stamped by a cylinder seal (Collon 1994, 86, pl. 1, no. 2; Aruz 2008, 296, fig. 282). The scene consists of two acrobats on a bull flanking an *ankh*, an Egyptian solar religious symbol. The composition is clearly a product of Egypto-Syrian syncretism (Tessier 1996). The most interesting feature for our purposes is that the religious content of the scene is testified by an accompanying inscription where the owner of the seal is identified as the *servant of the solar goddess Hepat*. This would appear to suggest that a formal connection existed between the solar deity and the bull games, perhaps presided over by this 'servant of the solar goddess'.

By combining Anatolian, Syrian and Minoan bull game scenes, we have confirmed the hypothesis

Figure 15.11 Seal impression from Alalakh. After Collon 1994, pl. 1.2.

that, stylistic differences apart, Minoan and Near Eastern bull games had a lot in common. In both regions, we see a differentiation of skills and teamwork between groups; we also see accidents. The games are dedicated to a goddess and possibly her son, the storm god.

A question of a more general nature is the connection between Crete and its neighbours in the Near East. It is my belief that such connections between cultures were not forged by trade alone, but resulted from cooperation between royal courts (Marinatos 2010,186–91). Only a traffic of ideas conducted between elites and royal families – involving perhaps also intermarriages – justifies similarity of symbols and customs, such as we see in the arts. Ideologies are seldom forged without the intervention of elites and without the use of transferable monuments, such as seals. In any case, it is difficult to imagine the spreading of these practices by travelling merchants alone.

CONCLUSIONS ABOUT RITUAL AND GAMES

Some more general conclusions about the nature of the Minoan bull games as a human ritual are the following.

A. We have seen that the overall strategy of the bull games was to subjugate the bull and this was accomplished by teamwork. The 'coach' would have been an experienced ex-leaper and grappler who instructed his colleagues to work together and coordinated the two teams. The success of the games would have been dependent on strict discipline such as would ensure maximal safety for the leaping youths. Thus, the freedom of movement that we see on the frescoes and which leads certain scholars to speak of a 'bull-dance' must be carefully re-evaluated in terms of the rules that governed the sport (Laughlin 2004). Without adhering to rules, the games would have been too dangerous to practise and quite unpredictable in their outcome. The greatest responsibility lay on the shoulders of the grapplers who saw to it that the younger men were not injured.

B. There is a difference between this sport and the competitive sports of ancient Greece. Since the Minoan men did not compete with each other but with the animal, cheating and competition were out of place (for cheating in races, see Antilochus' apology in *Iliad* 23, 590). What was rather encouraged in the bull games was cooperation between humans; this was essential for confusing and combating the wild bull.

C. What is the relation between ritual and sport? The settings of the Minoan and Near Eastern scenes suggest a formal arena, or a court, as well as the context of a festival during which the deity, or deities, would have been imagined as present. In this sense, the bull games are ritual and Renfrew's theoretical definition and discussion in this volume (Chapter 2) is justified. Some further questions arise. In some sense, the bull games constitute a primeval ritual of communication and competition between species. They also reflect a contest between man and beast whilst reinforcing the human instinct to establish hierarchy in nature. The ultimate goal was not just a display of human skill, but a demonstration of the supremacy of man over beast (see also Morgan, Chapter 14 in this volume).

Notes

1 For the Near Eastern representations, see Marinatos (2007a), with further references. For a bull hunt in Egypt, see Decker (1992), and see *Sport und Spiel* 1987, 160–1, fig. 118.
2 Ivory Deposit at Knossos, and fresco from Mycenae: Evans 1930, 207, fig. 141. See also Maria Shaw's reconstruction.

References

Aruz, J. 2008. *Marks of Distinction, Seals and Cultural Exchange Between the Aegean and the Orient*, 139–41, Corpus der Minoischen Mykenischen Siegel, Beiheft 7, Marburg: von Zabern.

Bietak, M., N. Marinatos & C. Palyvou. 2007. *Taureador Scenes in Tell el Dab'a (Avaris) and Knossos*, by M. Bietak, N. Marinatos & C. Palyvou. Vienna: Österreichische Akademie der Wissenschaften.

Burkert, W. 1996. *Creation of the Sacred: Tracks of Biology in Early Religions*. Cambridge, MA: Harvard University Press.

Collon, D. 1994. Bull Leaping in Syria. *Egypt and the Levant* 4, 81–8.

Dakoronia, P., S. Deger-Jalkotsy & A. Sakellariou (eds.), 1996. *Corpus der minoischen und mykenischen Siegel Supplementum 2, Die Siegel aus der Nekropole von Elatia-Alonaki*. Berlin: Mann.

Danthine, H. 1937. *Le palmier-dattier et les arbres sacrés dans l'iconographie de l'Asie occidentale ancienne*. Paris: Geuthner.

Doumas, Ch. 2012. "Οι εργασίες στο Ακρωτήρι κατά τα έτη 2009 και 2010", ΑΛΣ 7, 2009–10, Athens.

Evans, A. 1921. *The Palace of Minos: A Comparative Account of the Successive Stages of the Early Cretan Civilization as Illustrated by the Discoveries at Knossos, volume 1*. London: Macmillan.

Evans, A. 1928. *The Palace of Minos: A Comparative Account of the Successive Stages of the Early Cretan Civilization as Illustrated by the Discoveries at Knossos, volume 2*. London: Macmillan.

Evans, A. 1930. *The Palace of Minos: A Comparative Account of the Successive Stages of the Early Cretan Civilization as Illustrated by the Discoveries at Knossos, volume 3*. London: Macmillan.

Evans, A. 1935. *The Palace of Minos: A Comparative Account of the Successive Stages of the Early Cretan Civilization as Illustrated by the Discoveries at Knossos, volume 4*. London: Macmillan.

Hood, S. 2005. Dating the Knossos frescoes, in L. Morgan, ed., *Aegean Wall Painting*. London: British School at Athens Studies 13, 45–82.

Immerwahr, S. 1990. *Aegean Painting in the Bronze Age*. University Park: Pennsylvania State University Press.

Kyle, D. G. 2007. *Sport and Spectacle in the Ancient World*. Oxford: Blackwell.

Lang, Mabel 1969. *The Palace of Nestor at Pylos in Western Messenia. v. II, The Frescoes*. Princeton : University Press.

Lapatin, K. 2002. *The Mysteries of the Snake Goddess*. Boston and New York: Houghton Mifflin Company.

Loughlin, E. 2004. Grasping the bull by the horns. Minoan bull sports, in S. Bell & G. Davies, eds., *Games and Festivals in Classical Antiquity*. Proceedings of the conference held in Edinburgh 10–12 July 2000. BAR International Series 1220. Oxford: Archaeopress, 1–9.

Marinatos 1984. The Date-palm in Minoan Iconography and Religion. *Opuscula Atheniensia* 15, 115–22.

Marinatos, N. 2007. Bull-leaping and royal ideology, in *Taureador Scenes in Tell el Dab'a (Avaris) and Knossos*, by M. Bietak, N. Marinatos & C. Palyvou. Vienna: Österreichische Akademie der Wissenschaften, 127–32.

Marinatos, N. Rosette and palm on the bull frieze from Tell el Dab'a and the Minoan solar goddess of kingship, in *Taureador Scenes in Tell el Dab'a (Avaris) and Knossos*, by M. Bietak, N. Marinatos & C. Palyvou. Vienna: Österreichische Akademie der Wissenschaften, 145–9.

Marinatos, N. 2010. *Minoan Kingship and the Solar Goddess: A Near Eastern Koine*. Champaign: University of Illinois Press.

Marinatos, S. N. & M. Hirmer. 1960. *Crete and Mycenae*. London: Thames & Hudson.

Morgan, L. 1985. Idea, idiom and iconography, in P. Darcque & J.-C. Poursat, eds., *L'iconographie Minoenne (Bulletin de correspondance hellénique Supplément XI)*. Athens: École française d'Athènes, 5–19.

Morgan, L. 2010. An Aegean griffin in Egypt: the hunt frieze at Tell el-Dabᶜa, *Aegypten und Levante / Egypt and the Levant* 20, 303–23.

Pini, I. 2004. *Corpus der minoischen und mykenischen Siegel Supplementum 3,1. Kleine Griechische Sammlungen.*

Reusch, Helga, 1958. Zum Wandschmuck des Thronsaales in Knossos, in *Minoica. Festschrift zum 80. Geburtstag von Johannes Sundwall*, ed. Grumach Ernst. Deutsche Akademie der Wissenschaften zu Berlin: Akademie Verlag, 334–58.

Robertson Smith, W. 1927. *Lectures on the Religion of the Semites: The Fundamental Institutions*. New York: Macmillan.

Sakellarakis, J. A. 1982. *Athen, Nationalmuseum, Band I Supplementum (Corpus der Minoischen und Mykenischen Siegel I Suppl.)*. Berlin.

Sakellariou, A. 1964. *Die Minoischen und Mykenischen Siegel des Nationalmuseums in Athen (Corpus der Minoischen und Mykenischen Siegel I)*. Berlin.

Shaw, M. C. 2009. A bull-leaping fresco from the Nile Delta and a search for patrons and artists. *American Journal of Archaeology* 113, 471–7.

Shaw, M. C. 2012. New light on the labyrinth fresco from the palace at Knossos. *Annual of the British School at Athens* 107, 1–17.

Sipahi, T. 2000. Eine athletische Reliefvase von Hüsyindede Tepesi. *Istanbul Mitteilungen* 50, 63–85.

Teissier, B. 1996. *Egyptian Iconography on Syro-Palestinian Cylinder Seals of the Middle Bronze Age*. Göttingen: University Press.

Wooley, C. L. 1955. *Alalakh: An Account of the Excavations at tell Atchana in the Hatay, 1937–1949*. Oxford: Oxford University Press, 258–68.

Younger, J. 1976. Bronze Age representations of bull-leaping. *American Journal of Archaeology* 80(2), 125–37.

16

EPIC GAMES

NIGEL SPIVEY

A Greek vase in Copenhagen's National Museum serves to introduce, in visual terms, the problem addressed in this chapter (Figures 16.1 and 16.2). It is not, at first sight, a distinguished example of its type: a sixth-century BC amphora, gathered in J. D. Beazley's *Attic Black-Figure Vase-Painters* among the category of 'Group E', with its subject laconically itemized as "A, fight, with chariot. B, victor lifting tripod".[1] The description suggests a pair of stock scenes. Yet it is precisely the pairing of images on this vase that makes it significant for historians. The amphora was produced in Athens, and probably first used as a container of wine, perhaps at a *symposion* or formal drinking party; eventually, like many of its sort, the vase ended up in an Etruscan tomb. 'Mass-produced' it may have been (relatively speaking). But its images lead us to questions that are of particular interest to the understanding of the motives for 'play' in antiquity, and the ideology of formal sporting contests in ancient Greece.

It is routine practice, in the study of Greek painted pottery, to speak of a vase having a 'Side A' and a 'Side B': but of course this does not deny the possibility (or, perhaps, probability) that the vase's decoration may be iconographically coherent – in other words, that both sides are 'twinned', or part of the same picture. In the case of this vase, viewers are overtly prompted to connect the separate scenes. One side ('A') does indeed represent some episode of combat: a warrior aboard a four-horse chariot stands poised to launch his spear at an opponent who has fallen over backwards, as if under the

rearing horses (Figure 16.1). And there is little doubt that on the other side ('B') we see a moment of athletic victory: four naked men, with garlands, appear to acclaim a fifth, who stoops to lift a large, two-handled tripod-cauldron, typically a prize awarded for sporting triumph (Figure 16.2). The figures are not labelled, so we cannot presume that the artist intended to evoke specific scenes from the heroic past – though both the mode of fighting (from a chariot) and the athletic prize (a large metal tripod) could well belong to the ambience of Homer's epic poetry. The cue for the viewer to associate the two images, nonetheless, seems obvious. It is the prominent motif emblazoned on the shield of the fallen warrior: an unusual blazon or *episêma*, yet unmistakably a two-handled tripod, similar to that featured in the scene of athletic victory. As if to dispel any doubt that this tripod as a shield-badge is a sportsman's tripod, a further unusual motif is included: a pair of *haltêres* – the handheld weights Greek athletes used to give impetus in jumping. So the implicit message of the shield is that its bearer is an athlete.

The inference to be drawn from a clear linking element between the two scenes on this vase may be rather melancholy. One day a man gathers glory on the sports field; another day he is toppled into the dust of the battlefield. Beyond such fatalism, the images may simply affirm a set of expectations: that the athlete is a warrior, and the warrior an athlete. In this broader sense, the vase anticipates a sentiment we find in a third-century AD monograph on 'Gymnastics' – that there was a time

Figure 16.2 'Side B' of the same vase.

Figure 16.1 'Side A' of an Athenian black-figure amphora, mid-sixth century BC, from Vulci. Copenhagen, National Museum inv. Chr.VIII.322.

II

when war was regarded as practice for athletics, and vice versa (Flavius Philostratus, *Gymnastikos* ch. 43: Philostratus is explicitly referring to an archaic or proto-historic period, albeit ill-defined).[2] But to modern sociologists (notably Norbert Elias), such complementarity is problematic, if the development of sport is historically conceived in terms of "transformations of aggressiveness", or "the organization of violence-control".[3] According to this view, an athlete may be a warrior *manqué* – but a warrior would hardly use his jumping-weights as an offensive symbol. Testing one's prowess at jumping should be some kind of substitute for fighting, or sublimation of fighting: at least, that is the theory. So how are we to understand the pairing of warrior and athlete here? The aim of this chapter is to conclude by returning to the vase with a clear and plausible answer to that question – and, with regard to the broader theme of this volume, implicitly to assess how closely an ancient paradigm of 'play' translates to its ostensible emulation in modern times (i.e. 'the Olympics').

It was George Orwell who gave perhaps the most memorable expression to a trope that has since repeatedly served journalists and commentators – and a trope that was already built into the descriptive parlance of many games ('attack', 'defence', etc.). Reporting a series of ill-tempered football matches between teams from Britain and the Soviet Union, shortly after the Second World War, Orwell declared that "serious sport", for all its high-minded ideals of fairness and character-building, was nothing more than "war minus the shooting".[4]

The definition of sport as war "minus the shooting", like any cliché, begs for academic qualification. One problem is that within the wider context of 'play' as a factor in human evolution and culture, the likeness tends to tautology – recalling that in Johan Huizinga's account of *Homo ludens*, the agonistic 'play spirit' manifests itself in the formal conduct of war no less than in competitive sport.[5] More particularly, anthropologists would query any necessary link implied by the analysis of sport as mock combat. One piece of ethnographic research, by Richard

Sipes, is often cited as refutation of the theory that humans are innately aggressive and have developed games in order to channel their aggression.[6] Sipes did not deny a synchronic rapport between "war-like" societies and "risk exercise" sports, but proposed that it be regarded as a "culture pattern", not a "drive discharge". A chorus of scientists from various disciplines subsequently affirmed the biological principle behind this reasoning, in the 'Seville Statement on Violence', adopted as an official declaration by UNESCO in 1989. The view prevails among social scientists and psychologists, as evident notably in recent work from Steven Pinker.[7]

To accept the "culture pattern" as a model does not, however, simplify our understanding of the historical relationship between sport and warfare. At first sight, the connections ought to be easy to make: if 'playing' is always a transitive activity, i.e. we play *at* something, then a variety of sports and games, from chess to rugby, may be seen as simulations of physical conflict. The regulated development of these activities denotes something more than 'rough-and-tumble'. Certain sports, such as boxing, clearly appear to be substitutions for what Huizinga would call "original violence": that is, they are 'restrained' and relatively 'safe' versions of contests that might otherwise lead to serious injury or death. But an almost random consideration of particular historical situations warns against presuming more direct forms of correlation. Jousting, for example, was a conspicuous pastime in Elizabethan England – when wars were no longer decided by knights tilting at each other on horseback (though the romantic ideal lingered).

So what about institutional athletic contests as they evolved in Archaic and Classical Greece? Here, at first sight, the nexus between sport and warfare seems close and explicit. A Greek lexicon immediately signals the connection: the Greek *agôn*, root-source of our 'agony', denotes a contest that could be either outright war or athletic games. The linkage was more than just lexical. Within programmes of Greek athletic contests there were of course the formal 'heavy' disciplines of hand-to-hand combat – boxing, wrestling and the notoriously violent *pankration*, the 'all-strength event' or 'all-in fighting'. Aside from these, there was the phenomenon of the *hoplitodromos*, a race in which all competitors were

Figure 16.3 Panathenaic amphora, early fifth century BC, from Campania. Naples, Archaeological Museum inv. 81.293. (After *CVA Italia* 20, pl. 3.3).

encumbered with items of infantry panoply and weapons (Figure 16.3).

This 'race in armour' may not have remained a lasting feature of the Classical athletic repertoire. Nevertheless, it is worth remembering that many contests took place within sacred precincts heavily stocked with trophies and memorials of actual warfare: the quantity of arms and armour recovered from Olympia, in particular, is striking (Figure 16.4). Athletic training was firmly established in the militaristic constitution of Sparta; while from Athens, ideological visions of the perfect state – the best known being Plato's *Republic* – made clear that the good citizen practised sport regularly in order to stay ready for military service.[8] Medical authority came to vouchsafe for the transferable skills involved: so ballgames, for example, were recognized as beneficial for developing coordination (O'Sullivan 2012).

To point out that neither the Spartans nor the Athenians figure large in the athletic victory lists of the ancient Olympics is one way of sounding another caveat about any necessary symbiosis of sport and war.[9] But there were sceptics of the connection long ago. A seventh-century BC Spartan poet declares: "I

Figure 16.4 View of the storeroom of Olympia Museum: some of the 200-plus helmets recovered from the site (cf. H. Frielinghaus, *Die Helme von Olympia*, Berlin: De Gruyter 2011).

take no account of a man for his prowess at running or wrestling. … No man is good in war unless he can take the sight of bodily slaughter and is able, at close quarters, to lunge at the enemy. This is excellence." (Tyrtaios Fr. 12). Later, the Athenian playwright Euripides gives voice to a (comic) diatribe on the civic redundancy of athletes, which equates to their uselessness on a battlefield. *"Will they go into battle waving a discus, or break through a barrage of shields and scatter an enemy with their fists alone?"* (Euripides Fr. 282, 19–21). Even Plato acknowledged that fulltime training for athletics per se rendered citizens prone to illness and somnolence; his sentiment finds echo in the corpus of Hippocratic wisdom.[10] One could add a number of mordant comments from Roman sources, to the effect that prize-winning athletes proved feeble when tried with the actual rigours of professional soldiering (Spivey 2012, 25–8).

"A voluntary attempt to overcome unnecessary obstacles" is one definition of a game; add the element of physical exertion, to the point of exhaustion, then it becomes 'sport'.[11] The programme of the Olympic festival, and other 'contests' (*agônes*) of the Panhellenic athletic 'circuit' (*periodos*), was certainly voluntary in participation, artificial in its difficulty, and exhausting (frequently on the occasion of competition and invariably during the prerequisite training): there is no problem in defining ancient athletics as sport. Situate these contests within sanctuaries, and the 'play' element of ritual becomes gloriously transparent – a gift to Huizinga's broad synthesis of 'civilization'. But what were the athletes at Olympia, Delphi and elsewhere playing *at*? We know about the prizes, and what those were worth in terms of personal and familial repute (*kudos*) and symbolic value: however, describing the prizes answers a different enquiry (what were they playing *for*?). It is precisely the 'pretend-play' or mimetic quality of ancient athletics that demands elucidation. The Greek games were *like* something. What was it?

By way of illustrating the problem we face here, it is enough to wonder about the raison d'être of just one ancient athletic 'event' – throwing the javelin. The javelin was thrown then, as it is now, for distance rather than accuracy. But in what respects was this a 'martial art'? Impressionistically, hardly at all. The Classical Greek infantry-soldier – the hoplite – was armed with a thick-shafted spear (*dory* [*doru*]): this was for jabbing, not throwing, and was quite different from the slender and aerodynamic javelin (*akôn*, or *akontion*) deployed within the fivefold challenge of the pentathlon. Vice versa, the javelin could not

Figure 16.5 Detail of an Athenian red-figure cup, ca. 490 BC. Getty Museum inv. 85.AE.25. (After *Greek Vases in the J. Paul Getty Museum* vol. 5, Malibu 1991, 102).

serve a hoplite, for it was a stick of sharpened elder-wood, launched not only by a run-up, but also by a coil of cord around the shaft and attached to the thrower's index finger, imparting spin. A red-figure drinking cup (Figure 16.5) shows the action, uncannily similar to javelin-throwing techniques today.

I say 'impressionistically', because the foregoing summary bypasses certain historical doubts and nuances regarding hoplite warfare; at least in its early phase, when soldiers may have carried two spears, one of which was for launching at a distance.[12] Yet in any case, Greeks of the Classical period must have been well aware that the javelin-throw was once, so to speak, a transferable skill – that is, that throwing a lance or spear had once been part of battlefield practice, in the proto-historic 'Homeric world'. This weapon, for which the words *dory* and *egchos* are used, was customarily fashioned from cornel or ash and tipped with a metal point. It might be used at close quarters; more frequently, in epic encounters, it was hurled with force sufficient to pierce a substantial shield. The distance might not be great – Homer's heroes like to exchange some aggressive banter before they make a cast; a chariot could serve as a platform for the throw (or simply as a 'taxi' to some suitable open terrain), and indeed a chariot might contain the target. In any case, the poet, ad nauseam, relishes the effects of a successful throw. *"Diomedes cast. His spear, steered by Athena, struck Pandaros on the nose beside the eye and passed through his white teeth. His tongue was shorn off at the root by the relentless bronze, and the point emerged at the base of his chin. He toppled from his chariot."* (*Iliad* 5.290).

These heroes, as we know very well, served as paragons of 'manliness' (*andreia*); a status that endured over centuries, sustained in no small part by the fact that canonized versions of Homer's epics formed the 'core curriculum' of Greek 'youth-rearing' (*paideia*). The exemplary presence of Homeric heroes in Greek education and society is epitomized by Aristotle's tutoring of young Alexander 'the Great'; Pythagorean doctrines of reincarnation and metempsychosis were among the earliest of a series of Greek philosophies offering the hope that the soul of Achilles could be accommodated in another body. Beyond schooling and philosophy, however, a more exact mode of emulation developed.

Which brings us to a core proposal: that the regular Panhellenic ('All-Greek') Games may be seen as the formalized development of tests to define who was most akin to the heroes of Homer – who could claim to be 'best of the Achaeans'. I have remarked, en passant, that every Olympic festival was like a 'civilian' rehearsal of the Trojan war (Spivey 2011, 37). The rest of this chapter serves to expound and expand that remark. To view Greek athletics as mimetic of epic combat is not only a key to understanding the fierce, occasionally fatal, nature of competitive commitment in ancient Greece. It also reveals a peculiar consequence of the historical development of hoplite warfare – a mode of settling disputes that is one of the defining features of the Greek city-state, and an important aspect of the process described (by Colin Renfrew et al.) as 'peer polity interaction' – if often abrasive interaction.[13]

III

Disregarding the "certain historical doubts and nuances regarding hoplite warfare" mentioned earlier, we may summarize as follows. Hoplite battles were in theory – and perhaps quite often in practice – efficient forms of dispute resolution. The drilled forces of opposing city-states gathered at a mutually convenient site, at a generally convenient time – not when all hands were needed for harvest, for example. Each warrior wore a panoply of armour suited for fighting in the formation of a phalanx: a full bronze helmet (offering virtually no scope for lateral vision), a body corselet, and greaves, also bronze, protecting the lower leg. A large circular shield, of bronze and wood, was carried in such a way as to both cover its bearer and overlap with the shield of the soldier next to him. The principal offensive weapon was, as remarked, a stout spear, about eight foot (almost 2.5 m) long, to be thrust (underarm) at the enemy when the formations clashed; a short sword would also be carried, for the eventuality of further fighting at close quarters. At the sound of a signal, each phalanx advanced at a measured pace. Obviously, those fighting 'in the front line' (*en promachois*) took the most immediate risk of becoming casualties: they would be impelled forwards by those behind during the final 'shove' (*ôthismos*). If one side broke ranks en route, then the battle was more or less over; in any case, once a phalanx lost cohesion, its members had little option but to scatter in retreat – and the prevailing side could then claim victory. Pursuit was hardly necessary: a collection of enemy accoutrements (especially helmets, discarded for the sake of swift escape) would suffice as proof of success, and serve to stack as the marker (*tropaion*) of victory. (Our 'trophy', therefore, derives from the ancient Greek word for defeat, rout or 'turnaround' – *tropê* – on the battlefield.)

By contrast, the Trojan war as presented by Homer – a siege prolonged over a decade – could hardly be classified as 'efficient dispute resolution', whether that dispute arose over the possession of a beautiful woman (the romantic motive) or control of the Dardanelles – a realist's take on some actual conflict at Troy ca. 1250 BC. Nonetheless, Homer's evocation of warfare, for all that it notoriously mingles

diverse elements of 'heroic' and historic practice, indicates a system bound by well-defined protocols of victory and defeat, and entailing – relatively speaking – limited numbers of casualties. The opposing forces may have been numerous, but in general, it seems that only a chosen few from each side engaged in mortal combat. I say 'a chosen few': the process of choice, too, was formalized, as we see in Book 7 of the *Iliad*, where Hector emerges from Troy's citadel and challenges any of the Greeks to a duel. After some collective hesitation, nine volunteers respond, and Nestor, the grand old man of the Greek contingent, decrees that a 'drawing of lots' (*klêros*) shall be held to determine which one of them goes forward. Each man marks his own lot – a sign on a potsherd, we suppose, though Homer does not specify – and puts it into Agamemnon's helmet for the draw; the great(er) Ajax is picked.

Pausanias describes a group of bronze statues once dedicated by 'the Achaeans' close to the Temple of Zeus at Olympia as representing this episode of sortition (5.25.8–10). Made by the fifth-century sculptor Onatas of Aegina, the nine volunteers stood with their shields and spears on one base (a semi-circular platform has been recovered): only Agamemnon's statue was identified by inscription, but others seem to have been recognizable, if only by their shield emblems – Pausanias notes that the figure of Odysseus had been removed (by Nero) – while on a separate base stood the image of old Nestor.

We shall come back to this statue-group, to ask why it was suitable as a dedication at Olympia. (Incidentally, the same group makes claim as a possible provenance for the celebrated Riace Bronzes). But what ensues, according to Homer? The sequence of events is telling. Ajax buckles on his armour, and sallies forth, brandishing 'like a tower' an enormous shield (*sakos*) made up of eight layers (seven of hide, one of bronze). He approaches the Trojan champion, issues a brief defiant speech, and invites Hector to make the first spear-throw. Hector, after replying with no less spirit, launches his spear. It is a good throw, but not quite powerful enough, piercing just six layers of the mighty shield. So it is the turn of Ajax to throw. His spear penetrates not only Hector's shield, but also his corselet. Hector dodges the impact, however. Each hero then retrieves his spear (this seems to be a mutual courtesy), and tries something else. Ajax makes a lunge that draws blood. Hector steps back, and picks up a large rock, which he lobs: its impact makes the central boss on the shield of Ajax ring loud. Ajax finds an even larger rock, and throws it with such force that Hector's shield crumples, and Hector is knocked to the ground. Both heroes are then about to engage with their swords when two 'heralds' (*kêrykes*) – one from the Greek, one from the Trojan side – intervene, holding out their staffs as if referees. Speaking on behalf of both, the Trojan Idaeus calls for a halt to the fight. Hector and Ajax have each shown their mettle, so honour is satisfied; but now it is getting dark (Il.7. 279–282).

"Bad light stops play" … and it does seem rather like play, with Idaeus addressing the two combatants as "dear boys" (*paide philô*). Hector magnanimously acknowledges his respect for Ajax, and the opponents swap trophies: Hector giving Ajax his silver-studded sword, Ajax giving Hector his splendid purple belt. Each re-joins his fellows, to much happiness and back-slapping.

Such a mode of theatrical single combat, along with its element of gift-exchange, broadly squares with what we can infer from images and material remains of Mycenaean practice – or at least, the Late Bronze Age milieu we suppose Homer to be evoking. The evidence from Mycenaean graves, and indeed from Early Iron Age sites such as Lefkandi, adds some historical plausibility to the rhapsode's vision. Shields, whether articulated into a rectangular, circular or 'figure of eight' shape, were both heavier and more manoeuvrable than the regular hoplite form, and suited to one-on-one fighting, or hunting (arguably the shield described for Ajax resembles one featured on the Lion Hunt dagger from Mycenae). Helmets and other items of panoply seem designed as marks of individual distinction; chariots provided suitably conspicuous mobility-aids for a warrior-champion (accepting the view that these vehicles were not so much items of tactical use as status symbols: indicators of the aristocratic *right* to fight: Greenhalgh 1973).

We can broaden our perspective. The tenth-century burial at Toumba (Lefkandi), with its associated architecture, has been categorized as indicative of a 'Big Man' society. The skeletons in Schliemann's shaft graves at Mycenae were those of physically large specimens (for the time). And Homer notoriously described his heroes as formidable hulks (with hugely carnivorous appetites to match). The poet likes to calibrate the distance between his contemporary audience and the heroic past by imagining a combatant easily lifting (for offensive purposes) a boulder that nowadays could not even be budged by several men (e.g. *Iliad* 5. 302–4). Say that these heroes are 'larger than life', and we enter the mentality of hero-cult, from the eighth century BC onwards: size mattered, and so it is documented that when the bones of prehistoric fauna were discovered in Classical antiquity, such gigantic relics would be treasured as body-parts once pertinent to the likes of Ajax or Theseus (Mayor 2000; Boardman 2002: 33–43).

One is tempted to say that 'it goes without saying' that these big strong men were also good at sport. But here it is important to emphasize that in Homer's day – following the consensus that there was an Ionian rhapsode, equating to the historical reputation of 'Homer', who composed for recitation the *Iliad* and the *Odyssey*, approximately between 750–700 BC – no institutional organization of sport yet existed. Never mind the traditional date of 776 BC for the first Olympiad: if formalized contests were then established – and so far nothing has been excavated at Olympia to indicate as much – they were so petty that Homer had never heard of them.[14] No stadium was yet built, at Olympia or anywhere else: if Homer's heroes want to stage a race, they must improvise a track ad hoc. The gymnasium had still to be invented, so training was unheard of. Athletics might be one way of demonstrating social status, but it had not become a way of life.

I have commented elsewhere on the episode in the *Odyssey* when Odysseus, shipwrecked and destitute among the Phaeacians, attests his heroic pedigree by throwing a discus further than any of the rather arrogant local youth can manage (Spivey 2011, 21–3). Of the athletics described in detail in *Iliad* 23, further exegesis is not necessary, except to recall the occasion and its constituent events. These are funerary games, expressly organized by way of respect for the hero Patroklos by the 'big man' Achilles, who loved him (Figure 16.6).

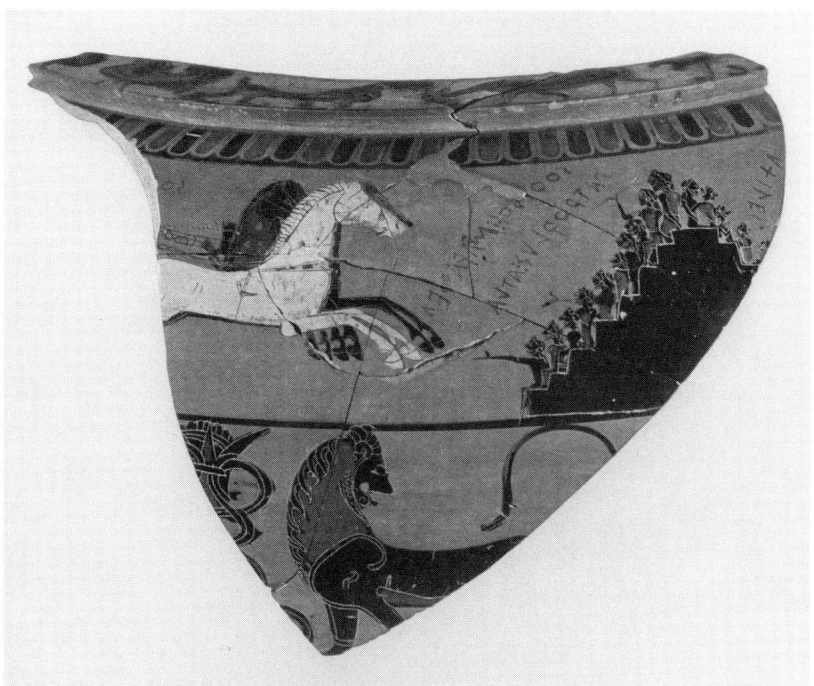

Figure 16.6 Fragment of an Athenian black-figure dinos by Sophilos, ca. 570 BC. From Pharsalos (Thessaly). Athens, National Archaeological Museum, inv. 15.499. (After M. Robertson, *Greek Painting*, Geneva 1959, 58).

The challenges are chariot racing, boxing, wrestling, foot-race, armed combat (the first to draw blood), throwing a lump of unworked iron (it is the prize too), archery – and throwing the spear. As it happens, the last test does not take place: there are just two contestants, and Achilles already has a pair of prizes, which he allots with due diplomacy. Again we note the words used by Homer for what would have been thrown. Both *egchos* and *dory* here seem interchangeable, though *dory chalkeon*, "spear of bronze" (*Il.* 23. 896) may define the *egchos* as normally too heavy to be thrown (depending, of course, upon its owner's prowess: Achilles famously wields a spear that others, including Patroklos, cannot manage).[15] Neither weapon, so far as we can tell, was like the slender javelin later used in formal athletics.

A brief excursus into semantics is needed at this point. We speak of 'Olympic *Games*' – and we have just described Book 23 of the *Iliad* as relating the 'funerary *games*' of Patroklos. But the ancient Greek term for what happened at Olympia, and in honour of Patroklos, was either *athla* (pl.) – as inscribed, archaically (*ATLA*) and in retrograde on the fragment illustrated in Figure 16.6 – or, more commonly, *agôn*. 'Contest', 'struggle', 'showdown' – whether used of athletics, the battlefield or the law courts, this word *agôn* carries into English usage due to

associations of exertion and distress for the sake of some outcome or prize. Radically different words were reserved for 'games' where little or nothing was at stake: *paignia*, or *paidia*, denoting something done for fun, the antithesis of earnest zeal (*spoudê*).

Paidia has overtones of childishness, yet amusements thus classified were open to adults. Indeed, in the further elaboration of Trojan-themed epic by poets subsequent (and inferior) to Homer – works that survive only fragmentarily – it seems there was a character called Palamedes who took credit for having codified such non-agonistic 'games'. Some scholars like to invoke his name when discussing a series of scenes showing Ajax and Achilles at a board-game – of which the best-known example is the noble amphora in the Vatican by Exekias, with each hero calling out his score, and both either just returned from the battlefield, or else supposed to be there (Figure 16.7).

Pesseia (or *petteia*, in Attic Greek) is the name for this particular pastime: a substantial quantity of Athenian vases show a pair of hoplites engaged in it, usually reckoned similar to draughts or backgammon.[16] There appears once to have been a sculptural group on the Athenian Akropolis representing such players, and various theories have been suggested as to its original significance; eventually, I suspect,

Figure 16.7 Detail of an Athenian black-figure amphora by Exekias, mid-sixth century BC, from Vulci. Vatican Museums, inv. 344.

artists simply enjoyed the imaginative contrast it displayed – warriors armed but off guard, absorbed in an activity that does no harm whatsoever to them or anyone else (Ajax and Achilles are on the same side, but that does not preclude their rivalry as fighters).

So we see that epic heroes may, in their spare time, play games of the sort that amused ordinary mortals. But ordinary mortals could not become heroes by playing games like this. Categorically, more strenuous effort was required.

IV

The 'carry-over' from sports field to battlefield may not have been widely acknowledged in antiquity, but one instance deserving our notice concerns a pentathlete called Phayllos, from the Greek colony of Croton, in south Italy. Recorded as several times a victor in the Pythian Games, and attributed with a remarkable long jump of some 55 feet (more than 16 metres), he not only provided a warship to the Greek fleet facing the Persians and Phoenicians at the battle of Salamis in 480 BC, but staffed and commanded it – with distinction (Herodotus 8.47; Strauss 2005, 199). A statue was subsequently dedicated in his honour upon the Athenian Akropolis (Monaco 2007), and his name eventually became a byword upon the Athenian stage for sprinting speed

(thus Aristophanes, *Acharnians* 214–16). His celebrity, however, may already have been assured by the last decade of the sixth century – if he is the same Phayllos who appears as a pentathlete on several vases painted by Euthymides.[17]

One of these vases, a wine cooler, offers two scenes that again provoke contemplation as a thematic pair – mutually informative pendants (Figures 16.8 and 16.9). On one side (Figure 16.8), a couple of athletes (one of them labelled as Phayl[l]os) flourish the strigils necessary for scraping themselves down after exercise; nearby are the pick-axes they would use for softening up the ground before a wrestling-bout. The other side of the vessel (Figure 16.9) shows two wrestlers: one, denoted as Theseus, is applying some sort of arm-lock upon the other, named Kl[?yti]os. Whether this Klytios is a brother of Priam, or a Giant, or some other figure by that name obscure to us, does not matter much: what must be represented here is some legendary exploit of the Athenian hero-king Theseus. That the vase-painter approves the wrestling expertise of Theseus may be suggested by the inscription *euge naichi*, 'well done!' – more importantly, however, Euthymides invites viewers to elide the spheres of the mythical and the contemporary. Phayllos, the prize-winning athlete, is given a parallel visual status to Theseus, the hero. According to the conventional chronology of Athenian vase-painting, this image of Phayllos must predate his moment of

Figures 16.8 and 16.9 Drawings of scenes on an Athenian red-figure psykter by Euthymides, ca. 510 BC. Probably from Vulci. Turin, Museo di Antichità, inv. 4123. (After *Journal of Hellenic Studies* 35 [1915], pls. V and VI).

military glory at Salamis by some two decades or more. Yet it also forecasts such glory. Phayllos will prove that athletes are primed to perform heroically beyond the stadium and the wrestling-pit.

As is well-known, to be saluted as 'hero' in Classical antiquity was not merely an expression of praise and admiration. It was a form of cult practice, involving regular rites at special locations. From the archaeological and literary records of hero-cults established during the eighth century BC, it is a matter of debate whether Homer served as a prompt to such cults, or shaped his narrative in knowledge of their existence (Coldstream 1976; Whitley 1988). Some shrines of heroes, e.g. the Menelaion at Sparta, are demonstrably 'Homeric'; others, such as the barrow of Pelops at Olympia, belong to the wider web

of Hellenic mythology; still others, such as the *hêrôon* of Akademos near Athens, pertain to names that seem more or less obscure; while a few appear always to have been anonymous, soliciting dedications simply 'to the hero'.

Placing the practice of hero-cult within an 'archaeology of ancestors', and a means of creating continuity of cultural identity, ritual procedures, territorial occupation and so on, has come a long way since the days of Jane Harrison and the 'Cambridge ritualists' (Antonaccio 1995). Yet, as Leslie Kurke has shown, an intellectually old-fashioned resort to the Pacific-islander term *mana*, in its sense of magical, awesome and talismanic power, remains rather appropriate to the understanding of hero-cults in the Classical world; in particular, to the understanding of how a prize-winning athlete was subject to trans-figuration into a semi-divine being, or *hêmitheos* (Kurke 1993).

The phenomenon of heroizing athletes is first documented in the sixth century BC. According to Herodotus (5.47), a *hêrôon* was raised in honour of Philippos of Croton, an Olympic victor in 520 BC. Others followed in the fifth and fourth centuries, including cults attested for Euthymos of Locri, Cleomedes of Astypalaia, Theagenes of Thasos and Polydamas of Skotoussa (Fontenrose 1968; Bohringer 1979). Legends around such names were duly woven, some of them bizarre, causing some commentators to suppose that athletic victory in itself was not sufficient for heroization. Yet the wider 'celebrity status' accorded to triumphant athletes in the Classical world is striking. Conveyed by poetry of high calibre – the 'epinikian' odes of Pindar, Bacchylides et al. – and commemorative statuary, likewise calling upon the talent of such outstanding sculptors as Myron, Polykleitos and Lysippos – this was no ephemeral success. Beyond the symbolic wreath of leaves awarded at Olympia and other venues, city-states greeted returning victors with extravagant gestures (e.g. knocking down defensive city walls), and lasting benefits: cash bounties, pensions, meals at civic expense for the athlete and his descendants and so on.

That athletes symbolized good fortune, and performed 'thaumaturgic' services, either in person or by their images, is well documented. And, as Kurke shows, there are several attestations of their talismanic deployment on the battlefield – the best-known, or most spectacular, being the occasion when Milo of Croton, multiple winner of the Olympic wrestling title in the late sixth century BC, reportedly went ahead of a hoplite phalanx wearing his six Olympic crowns, wielding a knotty club and dressed in the guise of Herakles (the enemy turned and ran: Diodorus Siculus 12.9).

That episode, fantastic as it sounds, brings us to the point. The phalanx experience has been described as a "*brief* nightmare", in which "a man could focus all his courage upon one pure burst of frenzied activity" (Hanson 1989, 25). But the hoplite was part of a quintessentially collective dynamic: there was, "quite literally, no room for individual acts of valour"

(Bowden 1993, 53). Each man's bravery was certainly tested – but it was not cardinal to an outcome. Cohesion – the maintenance of a general esprit de corps – was more decisive to victory.

This is not to say that hoplites could not be heroes. The 192 Greeks who fell at the battle of Marathon in 490 BC were, as Thucydides noted (2.34), given an extraordinary burial at the site of Marathon; this was in markedly archaic fashion, and done so that the war-dead should thereafter be worshipped with the honours due to heroes. We also find grave monuments in Attica and elsewhere that take pains, with their epitaphic inscriptions, to define the deceased as one who was *promachos* – who served (voluntarily or not) as a 'front-line fighter'. Recognition of 'outstandingness' (*aristeia*) in the ranks was possible.[18] Nonetheless, by its very nature, the phalanx tended not to generate *kudos* for this or that individual. This was a highly appropriate effect, in the ideology of a democratic city-state (Crowley 2012).

So when Homer spoke of *kudianeira machê*, "battle that brings glory to men" (*Il*. 24.391), he did not have the hoplite experience in mind. He and his audience were imagining how battles were fought in the mythologized past – on a sublime level, transcendent of reality.

Exemplars of those heroic encounters were cast in bronze at Olympia by the mid-fifth century. Prominently located, just by the Temple of Zeus, was the group of Homeric heroes in bronze by Onatas to which we have already alluded, showing the drawing of lots to determine which of the Achaeans will meet Hector. This provided a paradigm for the sortition process whereby athletes at Olympia discovered, for example, whom they would meet in the first rounds of the boxing (Spivey 2012, 80–3). But the monument did more than provide a paradigm: it "fused the moment before the Homeric military *agôn* … with the assignment of lots for Olympic athletes" (Ajootian 2003, 159). The sanctuary enclosure at Olympia became not only a meeting-place for living athletes, but also an imaginative juncture of the present with the epic past. Hardly less prominent than the Achaean heroes, on the way to the Stadium, was an assemblage of statues dedicated by colonists from Apollonia in Illyria (Pausanias 5.22.2; Barringer 2009). These showed ten antagonists from

Homer's world: Achilles versus Memnon, Odysseus versus Helenos, Paris versus Menelaus, Achilles versus Diomedes, and Deïphobus versus Ajax. Zeus, with Thetis and Himera, completed the group: every competitor at the Games should never forget that victory came by way of divine allocation. But that, of course, was as Homer's heroes were aware – all too well.

Returning to the sixth-century BC vase with which this chapter began, we now see that the visual logic whereby a warrior is identified as an athlete is entirely consistent with Olympic ideology. How far the Greeks themselves were aware of a 'civilizing' rationale to their regular athletic contests remains arguable: Gabriel Herman, following Norbert Elias, has described such games as the "embodiment of transformed propensities to aggression and cruelty", and speaks of "the remarkable psychological metamorphosis undergone … during the transition from the Homeric society to the civic' (Herman 2006, 240, 281). The obligation upon citizens of the Classical *polis* to bear arms, and therefore to keep themselves physically prepared for military service, is not to be discounted (Pritchard 2013). All the same, these games *were* 'games': relatively harmless re-enactments of ancestral bids for glory, the epic imperative to decide who indeed was 'best of the Achaeans'.

NOTES

1 J. D. Beazley, *Attic Black-Figure Vase-Painters* (Oxford 1956), p. 135. Copenhagen, National Museum inv. Chr. VIII.322. Basic publication in *Corpus Vasorum Antiquorum, Denmark Fasc. 3* (Paris & Copenhagen 1928), pl. 101,2. I am grateful to Bodil Bundgaard Rasmussen and Nora Petersen at the National Museum for supplying the images of the vase used here. My thanks also to Paul Cartledge for his comments on this chapter.

2 *Meletên poioumenoi polemika men gymnastikôn, gymnastika de polemikôn erga*: "they regarded war as preliminary training for athletics, and athletics as preliminary training for war." On the context of this observation, see König 2009.

3 Elias 1986; see also Elias 1978 – an adapted translation of a chapter of his two-volume 1939 study, *Über den Prozess der Zivilisation* (Basel: Falken).

4 Originally published in *Tribune* magazine (December 1945), Orwell's piece is gathered in Vol. 4 of his *Collected Essays, Journalism and Letters*, eds. S. Orwell & I. Angus (Harmondsworth: Penguin 1970), 61–4; see further Spivey 2012, 1–4.

5 Huizinga 1970, 110–26. The agonistic protocols of Greek hoplite warfare have not gone unnoticed: see Vernant 1968.

6 Sipes 1973: essentially targeted against the theory the Austrian ethologist Konrad Lorenz articulated in his popular work *On Aggression* (first published 1963: issued as a 'Routledge Classic', London and New York 2002). See also Ferguson 1983.

7 Pinker's focus is not upon sport as a conduit for aggression, but he notes the historical outlawing of violent pastimes such as bare-knuckle fighting: "Though people have lost none of their taste for consuming simulated and voluntary violence, they have engineered social life to place the most tempting kinds of real-life violence off-limits" (Pinker 2011, 458).

8 Plato *Republic* 404b; *Laws* 830–1.

9 This is to set aside success in horse- and chariot-racing, at which both cities, especially Sparta, enjoyed more success.

10 Plato *Republic* 404a; echoed by the Hippocratic *Aphorisms* 1.3.

11 Connor 2012, 17 (in turn quoting from the work of Bernard Suits).

12 There is some iconographic evidence for the use of shorter and lighter spears, hurled with the aid of a 'throwing loop' – from the seventh century BC: see Snodgrass 1967, 57–8, and more generally van Wees 1994. That Homer amalgamates (by poetic licence) some aspects of 'heroic' and 'contemporary' warfare seems undeniable: thus van Wees 1997. Recent debate on various hoplite problems is collected in Kagan & Viggiano 2013.

13 "War can be a channel for communication as much as for destruction" (Renfrew 1986, 16).

14 The necessary qualification to this statement is that by the time that a *text* of Homer was established – probably by the mid-sixth century BC – formal contests were in existence. One vague allusion in the *Iliad* to organized chariot-racing may therefore be no more than an 'interpolation'. See Scanlon 2004; also Nagy 2015.

15 For the spear as "the weapon *par excellence* of the Homeric hero", and an outline of the rapport between poetry and archaeology here, see Lorimer 1950, 254–61.

16 On this image, with previous bibliography, see Mariscal 2011.

17 Hoppin 1917, 19ff.; note also *J. Paul Getty Museum Journal* 13 (1985), 168.

18 E.g. the anecdote about Aristodamos at Plataea (Herodotus 9.71), though this may count as an instance of madness rather than bravery.

REFERENCES

Ajootian, A., 2003. Homeric time, space, and the viewer at Olympia, in *The Enduring Instant. Time and the Spectator in the Visual Arts*, eds. A. Roesler-Friedenthal & J. Nathan. Oxford: Mann, 137–63.

Antonaccio, C., 1995. *An Archaeology of Ancestors: Tomb Cult and Hero Cult in Early Greece*. Lanham, MD: Rowman and Littlefield.

Barringer, J. M., 2009. The Olympia Altis before the Temple of Zeus. *Jahrbuch des Deutschen Archäologischen Instituts* 124, 223–49.

Boardman, J., 2002. *The Archaeology of Nostalgia*. London: Thames and Hudson.

Bohringer, F., 1979. Cultes d'athlètes en Grèce classique: Propos politiques, discours mythiques. *Revue des Études Anciennes* 81, 5–18.

Bowden, H., 1993. Hoplites and Homer: warfare, hero cult, and the ideology of the polis, in *War and Society in the Greek World*, eds. J. Rich & G. Shipley. London and New York: Routledge, 45–63.

Coldstream, J. N., 1976. Hero cults in the age of Homer. *Journal of Hellenic Studies* 96, 8–17.

Connor, S., 2012. *A Philosophy of Sport*. London: Reaktion.

Crefeld, M. van, 2013. *Wargames: From Gladiators to Gigabytes*. Cambridge: Cambridge University Press.

Crowley, J., 2012. *The Psychology of the Athenian Hoplite: The Culture of Combat in Classical Athens*. Cambridge: Cambridge University Press.

Elias, N., 1978. On transformations of aggressiveness. *Theory and Society* 5.2, 229–42.

Elias, N., 1986. The genesis of sport as a sociological problem, in *Quest for Excitement: Sport and Leisure in the Civilizing Process*, eds. N. Elias & G. Dunning. Oxford: Blackwell, 126–49.

Ferguson, R. B., 1983. Introduction: studying war, in R. B. Ferguson ed., *Warfare, Culture and Environment*. Orlando, FL: Academic Press, 1–81.

Fontenrose, J., 1968. The hero as athlete. *California Studies in Classical Antiquity* 1, 73–104.

Greenhalgh, P. A. L., 1973. *Early Greek Warfare: Horsemen and Chariots in the Homeric and Archaic Ages*. Cambridge: Cambridge University Press.

Hanson, V. Davis, 1989. *The Western Way of War: Infantry Battle in Classical Greece*. London: Hodder.

Herman, G., 2006. *Morality and Behaviour in Democratic Athens*. Cambridge: Cambridge University Press.

Hoppin, J. C., 1917. *Euthymides and his Fellows*. Cambridge, MA: Harvard University Press.

Huizinga, J., [1944] 1970. *Homo Ludens: A Study of the Play Element in Culture*. London: Paladin.

Kagan, D. & G. F. Viggiano eds., 2013. *Men of Bronze: Hoplite Warfare in Ancient Greece*. Princeton, NJ: Princeton University Press.

König, J., 2009. Training athletes and interpreting the past in Philostratus' *Gymnasticus*, in *Philostratus*, eds. E. Bowie & J. Elsner, Cambridge: Cambridge University Press.

Krentz, P., 2002. Fighting by the rules: the invention of the hoplite *Agôn*. *Hesperia* 71.1, 23–39.

Kurke, L., 1993. The economy of kudos, in *Cultural Poetics in Ancient Greece*, eds. C. Dougherty & L. Kurke. Cambridge: Cambridge University Press, 131–63.

Lorimer, H. L., 1950. *Homer and the Monuments*. London: Macmillan.

Mariscal, L. R., 2011. Ajax and Achilles playing a board game: revisited from the literary tradition. *Classical Quarterly* 61.2, 394–401.

Mayor, A., 2000. *The First Fossil Hunters: Paleontology in Greek and Roman Times*. Princeton, NJ: Princeton University Press.

Monaco, M. C., 2007. 'Un'isolata presenza occidentale sull'Acropoli di Atene: l'*anathema* di Faillo di Crotone., in E. Greco and M. Lombardi eds., *Atene e l'Occidente: I grandi temi*. Athens: Scuola archeologica italiana di Atene, 155–89.

Nagy, G., 2015. Athletic Contests in Contexts of Epic and Other Related Archaic Texts. Published online in *Classics@* 13: *Greek Poetry and Sport*.

O'Sullivan, P., 2012. Playing ball in Greek antiquity, in *Greece and Rome* 59.1, 17–33.

Pinker, S., 2011. *The Better Angels of Our Nature: A History of Violence and Humanity*. New York: Viking.

Pritchard, D., 2013. *Sport, Democracy and War in Classical Athens*. Cambridge: Cambridge University Press.

Renfrew, C., 1986. Introduction: peer–polity interaction and socio-political change, in *Peer–Polity Interaction and Socio-political Change*, eds. C. Renfrew & J. F. Cherry. Cambridge: Cambridge University Press, 1–18.

Scanlon, T. F., 2004. Homer, the Olympics, and the heroic ethos, in M. Kaila et al. eds., *The Olympic Games in Antiquity*. Athens: Atropos, 61–91 (also published online in *Classics@* 13: *Greek Poetry and Sport* [2015]).

Sipes, R., 1973. War, sports and aggression: an empirical test of two rival theories. *American Anthropologist* 75, 64–86.

Snodgrass, A. M., 1967. *Arms and Armour of the Greeks*. London: Thames and Hudson.

Spivey, N., 2011. Pythagoras and the origins of Olympic ideology, in *Thinking the Olympics: The Classical Tradition and the Modern Games*, eds. B. Goff & M. Simpson. London: Bristol Classical Press, 21–39.

Spivey, N., 2012. *The Ancient Olympics*, rev. edn. Oxford: Oxford University Press.

Strauss, B., 2005. *The Battle of Salamis: The Naval Encounter that Saved Greece – and Western Civilization*. New York: Simon and Schuster.

Vernant, J.-P. ed., 1968. *Problèmes de la guerre en Grèce ancienne*. Paris: Mouton.

Wees, H. van, 1994. The Homeric way of war: the *Iliad* and the hoplite phalanx, I and II, *Greece and Rome* 41, 1–18; 131–55.

Wees, H. van, 1997. Homeric warfare, in I. Morris & B. Powell eds., *A New Companion to Homer*. Leiden: Brill, 668–93.

Whitley, J. M., 1988. Early states and hero-cults: a reappraisal. *Journal of Hellenic Studies* 108, 173–82.

17

THE BALLGAME, BOXING AND RITUAL BLOOD SPORT IN ANCIENT MESOAMERICA

KARL TAUBE

One of the more frequently noted aspects of the rubber ballgame in Mesoamerica is its close relation to human sacrifice, especially in terms of decapitation. However, there tends to be little discussion of the underlying motivations and meanings of this violent act. In this study, I will discuss how human sacrifice and the ballgame relates to agricultural fertility and abundance, including the ritual flooding of ballcourts to denote them as sources of fertility and growth. This symbolic complex begins as early as the Olmec (ca. 1200–500 BC), who offered rubber balls to the sacred spring at El Manati and portrayed the feline Olmec rain god as a ballplayer. The Olmec also related the rain deity to ritual boxing, a widespread but little-studied sport in ancient Mesoamerica. The early Zapotec site of Dainzú features many monumental reliefs of ritual boxers wearing jaguar helmet masks, at times with the facial features of Cocijo, the Zapotec rain god. Among the Classic Zapotec, boxers wielded stone manoplas with jaguar faces while the contemporaneous Maya had similar manoplas with the visage of Chahk, the god of rain. Finally, I will note that the tradition of ritual boxing continues to this day in highland Guerrero, where youths dressed as jaguars engage in combat atop mountains, with their falling blood a potent form of fertile rain.

For any thorough discussion of ancient Mesoamerican culture, it is impossible to ignore the Mesoamerican ballgame, which is amply documented by pre-Hispanic scenes as well as actual ballcourts in Mesoamerica and, in fact, as far as the American Southwest (see Wilcox 1991). Among the most noted aspects of the rubber ballgame in Mesoamerica is its close relation to human sacrifice, especially in terms of decapitation. Along with being sport and competition, forms of the Mesoamerican ballgame also pertained to basic cosmic processes, including rain and the strength and vigour of the sun, especially in terms of human blood – due not only to injuries in the playing field, but also to the sacrifice of players. Along with the physical, human component of the ballgame, the courts themselves pertain to agricultural fertility, including the flooding of ballcourts to denote them as vital sources of growth and abundance.

In this study, I trace the symbolic complex of the ballgame with agricultural fertility to the early Olmec (ca. 1200–500 BC), often considered the 'mother culture' of ancient Mesoamerica, who offered rubber balls to the sacred spring at El Manatí and portrayed the feline Olmec rain god as a ballplayer. However, the Olmec also related their rain deity to ritual boxing, a widespread but little-studied sport in ancient Mesoamerica (Orr 1997, 2003; Chinchilla Mazariegos 2009; Taube & Zender 2009; Baudez 2011, 2012). In contrast to the thick, woven belts and knee pads of ballplayers, ancient Mesoamerican boxers tend to have protection or 'armour' on other parts of their bodies, including thick helmet masks. In addition, they often wield weapons inconsistent with the well-known form of the Mesoamerican ballgame, including handheld, solid stone *manoplas*, as well as rock spheres, in dimension very much smaller than ancient Mesoamerican rubber balls and often wrapped in cloth as handy 'saps' (Taube & Zender 2009). As with the ancient ballgame, it is obviously difficult to balance the importance of competitive sport versus sacred ritual for the ancient peoples of Mesoamerica, a charge that has been levelled at Marc Zender and myself in a recent publication by Claude Baudez (2012: 26):

> For these authors [Taube and Zender], the warriors were '[A]merican gladiators' or 'boxers' that were practicing a sport. The Mesoamerican ritual battle was neither a spectacle nor sport but rather a ritual (translation by author).

Nonetheless, as Zender and I discuss in our 'ritual boxing' paper, there very much was a sacred and ritual component to these events, especially in terms of rainmaking and offerings to the fertile earth. In addition, among contemporary communities of highland Guerrero, men and boys dressed as jaguars engage in boxing combat atop mountains, with their falling blood compared to fertile rain. These modern events inform us that in Mesoamerica, public sport and sacred ritual overlap in subtle and profound ways.

In contrast to other contributions to this volume concerning 'play', a central theme of this chapter concerns the symbolism of sacrificial blood, and any comprehensive discussion of the ancient Mesoamerican ballgame must acknowledge the importance of the very bloody decapitation of victims. Although some could perhaps view ancient Mesoamerican religion as bloodthirsty, it is actually 'life-thirsty', as human blood was considered a precious distillation of vital forces of nature. In Mesoamerican thought, our bodies are intensely refined and distilled microcosms of the world, with our blood metaphorically compared to the life-giving water of rain as well as streams and pools. The following account is from a contemporary Yukatek Maya native priest and curer, or *ah hmen*, from Yucatán:

> The water in the earth is like the blood in your veins. Your soul is your wind. ... It is

said that water is the blood of the earth. When you want to make a well, you must dig a well to reach the water inside the earth. Thus you reach the veins of the earth. It is like our body: the earth has a lot of veins where there is water, the blood of the earth. (de Jong 1999, 306)

Similarly, in a discussion of Mesoamerican rain gods, María del Carmen Anzures y Bolaños notes that

> water that falls from the sky as rain originates in springs and underground currents, from whence it ascends by evaporation, and then returns to earth as lifegiving drops to resurrect all of nature, which dies each year and returns to be reborn. For this reason it is said that water circulates through the veins of the earth as blood through the human body. (translation in Ortíz & Rodríguez 2000, 85–6)

As noted by Klein (1987, 295–6), human penitential blood promoted plant growth in ancient Mesoamerican belief: "the most archaic form of the practice [bloodletting] was directed toward agricultural fertility, with the grower's blood an analogue for precious water." Blood had nourishing as well as sustaining qualities, and in pre-Hispanic times gods were explicitly 'fed' blood, often with the liquid placed on the lips of sculptures. The Aztec *cuauhxicalli* bowls were sacrificial serving vessels for the sun to feed and drink hearts and blood, with similar offering bowls known for both the ancient Maya and the contemporary Huichol (see Taube 2009). Recent excavations have uncovered a magnificent sculpture of the Aztec earth goddess, Tlaltecuhtli, at the base of the Templo Mayor, the centre of Tenochtitlan and present-day Mexico City. The largest Aztec sculpture known, it features a strongly anthropomorphic Tlaltecuhtli drinking a massive spurt of blood from her cut-open womb, profoundly denoting the cycle of life – the earth being both a birth giver and a consumer of her original blood essence (for the *cuauhxicalli* as a womb, see Taube 2009). Rather than simply the sloppy aftermath of executions, sacrificial blood was the 'gasoline of the cosmic machine' for ancient Mesoamerica.

THE OLMEC BALLGAME

It is somewhat fitting that the term *Olmec* signifies 'the rubber people' in the Aztec language of Nahuatl, as they in fact were the first known Mesoamerican culture to use rubber. In fact, rubber is actually documented for the 'pre-Olmec' phase known as Ojochí (ca. 1600–1400 BC), when the Formative period, roughly equivalent to the Neolithic of Europe and the Near East, begins in this region. Located some 10 kilometres from the major Olmec site of San Lorenzo, Cerro El Manatí is a hill with a freshwater spring and pool at the base of its western side. Excavations directed by Ponciano Ortíz and Maria del Carmen Rodríguez (1994, 1999) within the spring mud uncovered rubber balls dating to the early Ojochí phase (Ortíz & Rodríguez 1999, 231, 242; 2000, 79). In addition, rubber balls corresponding to the later San Lorenzo phase (1150–900 BC) – the apogee of the Olmec at San Lorenzo – were also discovered, along with the remains of sacrificed human infants. Ortíz and Carmen Rodríguez (2000, 89) compared these infant offerings to contact period, sixteenth-century Aztec rites of children sacrificed to the rain gods at springs and on mountain tops (see also Sahagún 1950–82, II:1–2, 42–4; Schaafsma & Taube 2006). The presence of 14 rubber balls at Cerro El Manatí strongly suggests a close relation of the Olmec ballgame to water, rain and mountains, a theme consistent, as we will see, with ballgame symbolism of the later Classic and Postclassic periods. As the excavators Ortíz and Rodríguez (2000, 84) note:

> We are probably uncovering ancient rituals at El Manatí performed in honor of the 'Lord of the Mountain', controller of the rains, lightning and thunder, who held within himself a space filled with primordial waters from which flowed the springs that provided access to the mansion of the rain god.

As will be noted, although not palaces, ballcourts certainly were places of the gods of rain and lightning and served as symbolic springs offering access to both the moist underworld and the rain-thirsty sky above.

For the Early Formative period of San Lorenzo, there are many examples of ceramic figurines from San Lorenzo, Tlapacoya, Canton Corralito and other sites of ballplayers wearing thick belts and other protective devices, including small masks over the lower face and tall, helmet-like headdresses (see Coe 1965a, figs. 100, 151, 152, 157, 158; de Borhegyi 1980; Niederberger Bretton 1987, 243, fig. 126; Bradley 1991; Bradley & Joralemon 1993, 18–19; Whittington 2001, nos. 8–9; Cheetham 2009, 158, fig. 6.7). Frequently, the headdresses are conical with a hat-like encircling brim. In addition, ballplayer ceramic figurines often wear a circular element – probably a mirror – on their chest or waist. As for the pattern of Early Formative figurines wearing what appears to be an oddly thick 'mask' resembling a slab of leather across the lower face – much like face guards for many contemporary athletes – it will be mentioned that this may have been a special type of Mesoamerican ballgame perhaps more resembling hockey than the traditional Mesoamerican form played in ballcourts. Clearly enough, the masks and series of rings of protective padding on the limbs of these Early Formative figures are not the same as the belts or knee guards to strike a rubber ball, as is so well known for the later Classic Mesoamerican sport of the ballgame. Rather, this gear suggests a far more physical sport involving heavy protective padding and wooden sticks, as well as the rubber ball.

For the Olmec, depictions of ballplayers are not limited to diminutive figurines, but also appear in monumental stone sculpture, including Monument 34 from San Lorenzo (see Coe & Diehl 1980, 340–3). Although the head is missing, the figure wears the circular pectoral, a thick belt and leg bands just below the knees. Oddly, the shoulders are deeply socketed to receive separately carved arms. In addition, there is Tenochtitlan Monument 1 (Tenochtitlan referring to a part of San Lorenzo rather than the much later Aztec capital), portraying a figure kneeling atop another (see Coe & Diehl 1980, fig. 499). Although Matthew Stirling (1955, 8) suggested that the sculpture portrays the mythic copulation of a jaguar with a woman, the upper individual has no feline characteristics and is clearly a ballplayer with a thick belt, protective bands on the legs and the circular pectoral (see Taube 1992; Bradley & Joralemon 1993, 21). In

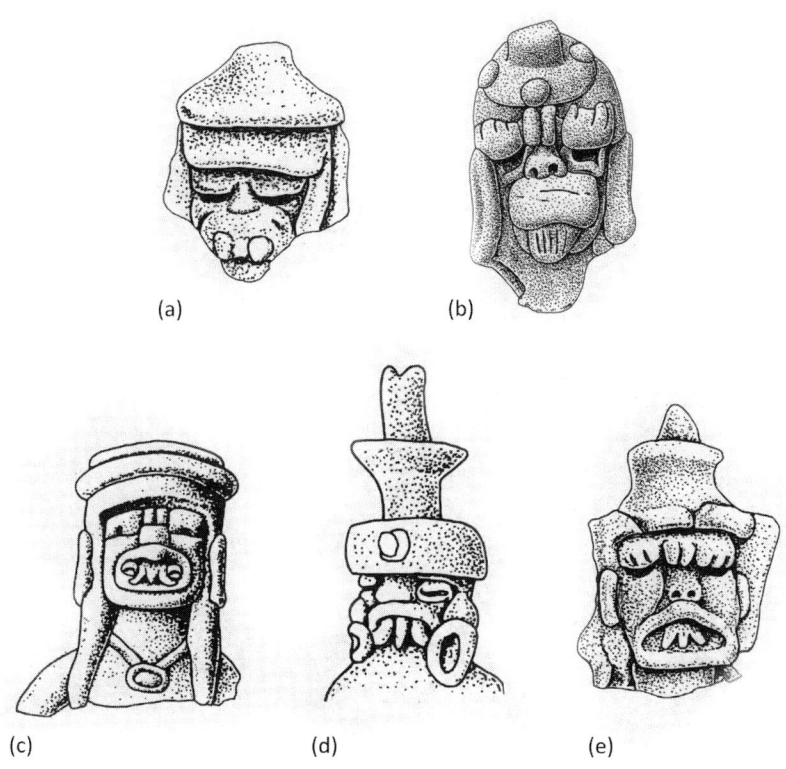

(a)   (b)

(c)   (d)   (e)

Figure 17.1 Early Formative figurines depicting the Olmec rain god as a ballplayer (drawings by author).

a) Olmec rain god with conical hat commonly found with ballplayers, San Lorenzo (after Coe & Diehl 1980, fig. 334).
b) Olmec rain god with conical hat, figurine head in the collection of the American Museum of Natural History, New York (from Taube 2009, fig. 3g).
c) Figurine fragment of Olmec rain god with pectoral commonly found with Early Formative ballplayers, Tlatilco (from Taube 2009, fig. 3e).
d) Olmec rain god with ballplayer headdress, Tlapacoya (from Taube 2009, fig. 3f).
e) Olmec rain god with deeply furrowed brow and ballplayer headdress (after Bradley 1991, fig. 4).

addition, the bound legs of the lower figure clearly indicate its status as a captive, and this scene may well be an especially early portrayal of the relation of the ballgame to human sacrifice (Taube 1992).

Located close to San Lorenzo, the Olmec site of El Azuzul featured a 'diorama' of four monumental sculptures consisting of a pair of virtually identical youths facing two seated jaguars (Cyphers Guillén 1994, figs. 4.8–4.12). Both young men lean forward while firmly grasping a staff or baton in their hands. Their dress recalls the ballplayer appearing atop the captive on Tenochtitlan Monument 1, as both have similar thick belts and a broad and long piece of fabric or leather hanging down the centre of their backs. Most importantly, the El Azuzul youths have what appears to be protective padding entirely covering their forearms and shins. In addition, with their chin straps and rope encircling the head, the headdresses of these figures strongly suggest protective helmets. In view of the probable protective padding and staffs, the pair of El Azuzul figures probably portrays an Early Formative form of stick ball, a theme to be further discussed in terms of the Middle Formative Olmec (900–500 BC).

It is noteworthy that a good number of Early Formative ballplayer figurines bear the visage of the Olmec rain god, a feline being typically displaying a snarling mouth with prominent canines, a deeply furrowed brow and 'L-shaped' eyes that turn sharply down at the sides of the face (Figure 17.1; see Taube 1995, 2009). Frequently, the eyes are virtually shut, much as if the rain god were crying tears of rain. In fact, if Aztec children offered to the rain god were to cry, it was believed that this would bring the rain:

When they took the children to be slain; if they wept and shed many tears, those who carried them rejoiced, for they took [it] as an omen that they would have much rain that year. (Sahagún 1950–82, II:2)

In a well-known diagram, Miguel Covarrubias (1946, fig. 4; 1957, fig. 22) posited that Mesoamerican rain gods derived from an Olmec jaguar prototype, with feline features still discerned in Classic and Postclassic rain deities of the Maya, Zapotec and Aztec (see also Taube 2004, fig. 14; 2009). Although not widely acknowledged, C. W. Weiant (1943, 97) made a similar

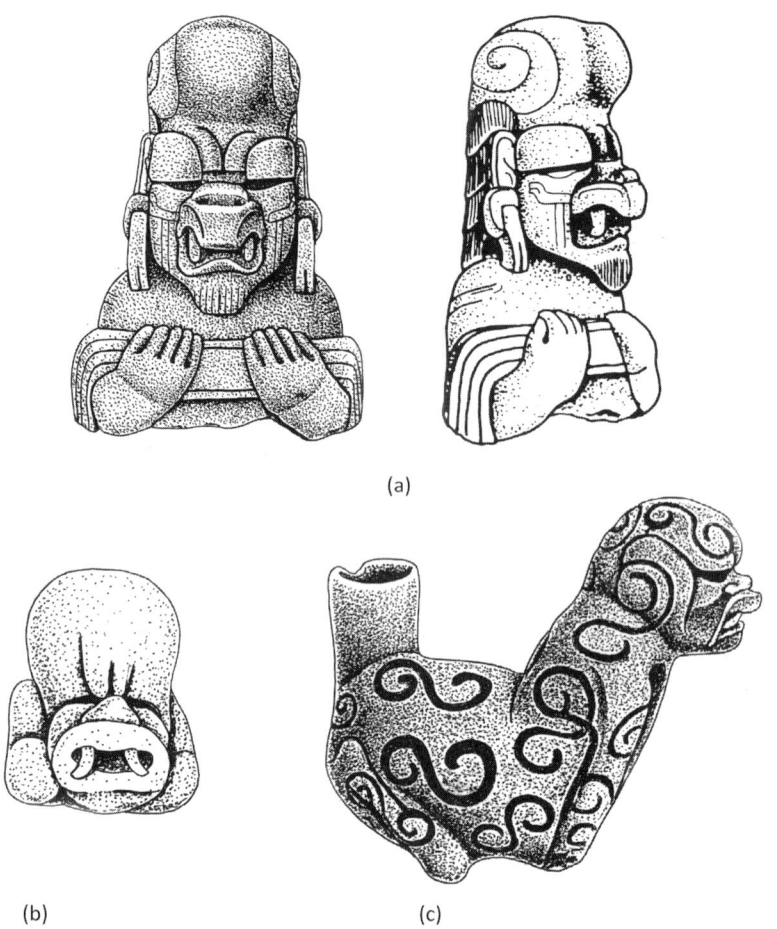

Figure 17.2 Middle Formative portrayals of the Olmec rain god (drawings by author).

a) Two views of a serpentine statuette of the Olmec rain god; note the furrowed brow and S-shaped cloud motif on brow (American Museum of Natural History, New York).

b) Ceramic figurine fragment of the Olmec rain god with slit eyes and furrowed brow, Tres Zapotes (after Weiant 1943, pl. 29, no. 4).

c) Effigy vessel of the Olmec rain god with S-shaped cloud scrolls on body (from Taube 1995, fig. 19b).

case based on a fragmentary Olmec figurine from Tres Zapotes: "This figurine bears unmistakable resemblance to the Zapotecan Rain God Cocijo as we find him on the earliest of the funerary urns." In addition, Weiant (1943) compared this figurine to the later central Mexican rain deity known as Tlaloc. As in other examples of the Olmec rain god, the figurine face has a furrowed brow, bears prominent fangs and has apparently shut eyes (Figure 17.2b).

Clearly enough, basing an interpretation of a crying Olmec rain god on only a sixteenth-century Aztec source is tenuous at best, but there is additional evidence that the Olmec compared the head of the rain deity to rain clouds, or 'thunderheads'. A stone statuette at the American Museum of Natural History in New York depicts the Olmec rain god with a bulbous brow marked with large swirling elements denoting clouds, as will be noted later in this chapter (Figure 17.2a). An Olmec ceramic vessel depicts another example of the Olmec rain deity with slit

eyes and a bulging brow marked with S-shaped cloud scrolls covering his entire body as well (Figure 17.2c). In Late Preclassic Maya monumental art dating to roughly the first century BC, the brow of the Maya rain god Chahk is frequently spiral and accompanied by other swirling clouds (see Taube 1995, figs. 15–16; 2009, fig. 5). In addition, although not documented for the Olmec, faces of the later Zapotec Cocijo and the central Mexican Tlaloc often appear on water jars, indicating that their heads are considered much like fertile clouds filled with water, a trope also found in pre-Hispanic images of Katsina rain spirits of the American Southwest (Schaafsma & Taube 2006).

As has been mentioned, the Olmec rain god is strongly feline, and in Mesoamerica, there are two great cats, the jaguar (*Panthera onca*) and the puma or mountain lion (*Puma concolor*). Whereas the cougar is perhaps the creature most feared in terms of human predation, the jaguar figures most prominently in Mesoamerican thought. Thus while the Olmec did

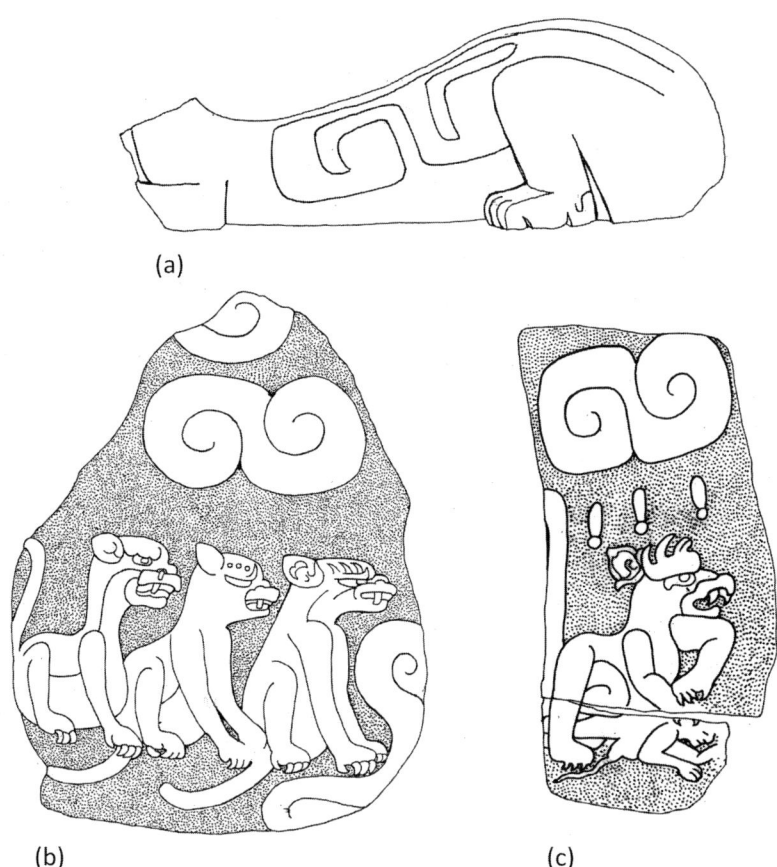

(a)

(b)   (c)

Figure 17.3 Olmec felines with cloud scrolls.

a) Early Formative Olmec feline with cloud scroll on back, San Lorenzo Monument 7 (after Coe & Diehl 1980, fig. 430).
b) Three felines with cloud scrolls, Chalcatzingo (drawing by author after González, Córdova & Buitrago 2011, 18–19).
c) Feline with human victim below a cloud with rain, Chalcatzingo (from Taube 1995, fig. 24c).

not carve spots on feline stone monuments – which were more than likely painted – Olmec murals from the cave sites of Juxtlahuaca and Oxtotitlan in Guerrero explicitly portray jaguars with their spotted pelage (see Grove 1970, figs. 13, 36). Although I will frequently refer to Mesoamerican portrayals of great cats as 'jaguars', note that, at times, they could well be pumas. For the aforementioned effigy vessel of the Olmec rain god with cloud scrolls, the deity adopts a seated feline pose and rears up on his arms or forelegs, with the spout being his upright tail (Figure 17.2c). The figure also recalls the aforementioned pair of Olmec jaguar monuments from El Azuzul, which are also sitting while leaning on their forelimbs (see Cyphers 1994, figs. 4.11, 4.12). Two recently discovered Olmec-style monuments from Zazacatla, a site on the outskirts of Cuernavaca, Morelos, portray the rain deity in a similar seated pose, although for one sculpture the arms clearly lean atop crossed human legs (see Aguilar and Mendoza 2007; Aguilar & Mendoza 2010, figs. 4.6, 4.7).

Aside from the Olmec rain god being strongly feline, jaguars are also portrayed with cloud and rain imagery in Olmec iconography. As noted by Kent Reilly (1994, 249), Monument 7 from San Lorenzo portrays a supine feline with a cloud scroll on its back (Figure 17.3a). Olmec-style petroglyphs from the highland site of Chalcatzingo, Morelos, explicitly depict supernatural jaguars with similar rain clouds, with Monument 31 portraying an S-shaped cloud shedding rain on a feline atop a dismembered human corpse (Figure 17.3c). At about the time of its discovery at Chalcatzingo, David Stuart and Stephen Houston (pers. comm. 1990) noted that in the Late Postclassic Codex Dresden, this S-form is glyphically labelled as *muyal*, meaning 'cloud' in Mayan languages. Although the S-shaped motif serves as a specific sign for clouds in Olmec and Maya iconography, this is by no means the only way that clouds were portrayed, which included the aforementioned convention of the Olmec rain god and Late Preclassic examples of the Maya Chahk portrayed as swirling 'thunderheads'.

Excavated and reconstructed in 2011, Chalcatzingo Monument 41 portrays three jaguars, the first atop a cloud scroll resembling the letter 'M' and another S-shaped cloud hovering above the entire group (Figure 17.3b). As in the case of Monument 31, their facial features strongly resemble the Olmec rain god, including the effigy vessel covered with S-shaped rain clouds (Figure 17.2c). Considering that this new relief is found on the western side of the hill in the general vicinity of Monument 31, it is conceivable that Monuments 31 and 41 constituted a set of four supernatural jaguars with rain clouds, recalling the strongly quadripartite nature of later Mesoamerican rain gods, including the Zapotec Cocijo, the Maya Chahk and Tlaloc of central Mexico, with four aspects of these gods oriented to the world directions. Considered as a group, the four Chalcatzingo felines suggest that the Olmec closely related jaguars to human sacrifice and rites of rainmaking. Clearly enough, in sacrificial ceremonies, it would be priests dressed as jaguars who were present rather than the beasts themselves (Taube 1995, 100). An Olmec-style cave painting at Juxtlahuaca, Guerrero, portrays a human figure with jaguar limbs and a tail brandishing a clawed instrument before a much smaller individual. Given its presence in the deep, dark zone of the cave, this scene could well portray a rain-making act.

At El Manatí, many carved wooden objects were found among the local Macayal phase corresponding to the Olmec apogee at nearby San Lorenzo, and aside from a series of human busts, staffs resembling bladed clubs were also discovered (see Ortíz & Rodríguez 1999, figs. 7–8). It is noteworthy that one offering contained two rubber balls as well as two of these staffs (Ortíz & Rodríguez 1999, 242–3). According to Ortíz and Carmen Rodríguez (2000, 88), the staffs may have been used in a form of the rubber ballgame, and note the staffs carried by Olmec figures on later Middle Formative Olmec monuments (ca. 900–500 BC):

> Personages carrying sceptres are also common on other, later stelae and have been interpreted as symbols of rulership, but they could be images of leaders or players of the ballgame.

One such monument is Stela 2 from the Middle Formative site of La Venta, featuring a frontally standing human figure, probably a ruler, flanked by six supernatural figures (Figure 17.4a). The central individual holds a staff diagonally across his body, which although possibly denoting a gesture of royal power and might, could also suggest a pose of defence and engagement with a facing opponent. All seven individuals on Stela 2 grasp sticks or clubs with curving ends, with the six flanking deities engaged in very dynamic movements perhaps indicative of battle or, more likely, competitive sports. The two beings at the viewer's lower left are looking *behind* and upwards, indicating that they are relaying a ball rather than battling aggressive adversaries on the opposite sides of the scene. With their fanged muzzles and narrowed eyes, these beings can be identified readily as the Olmec rain god. Aside from the two at ground line, the other four appear as if floating, much as if they are playing in the sky above. In addition, the club wielded by the principal central figure bears the visage of the same rain deity. Along with being for playing ball, such clubs could have had rain-making significance. According to the early colonial *Historia de los mexicanos por sus pinturas*, the Aztec rain gods had four great ceramic tubs storing different types of rain which were struck with staffs to create showers. The breaking of these vessels was the cause of lightning and thunder (Garibay 1979, 26).

The curving ends of the La Venta staffs resemble contemporary hockey sticks, recalling shinny sticks of native games of North America, as well as those of the Tarahumara of Chihuahua (Culin 1907, 616–47). In contemporary Michoacán, there is the Purepecha (Tarascan) ballgame of striking a burning ball with sticks having solid curving ends, strongly resembling the staffs appearing on La Venta Stela 2 as well as contemporary hockey sticks (see Uriarte 2001, fig 34). Clearly enough, the heavy and sharply turned end would be ideally suited for striking a ball at ground surface, much like a golf club, but unlike the contemporary sport, such sticks could be readily used as formidable weapons in serious engagements, making protective padding on the limbs a reasonable explanation for the arm and leg bands commonly found with Early Formative ballplayers.

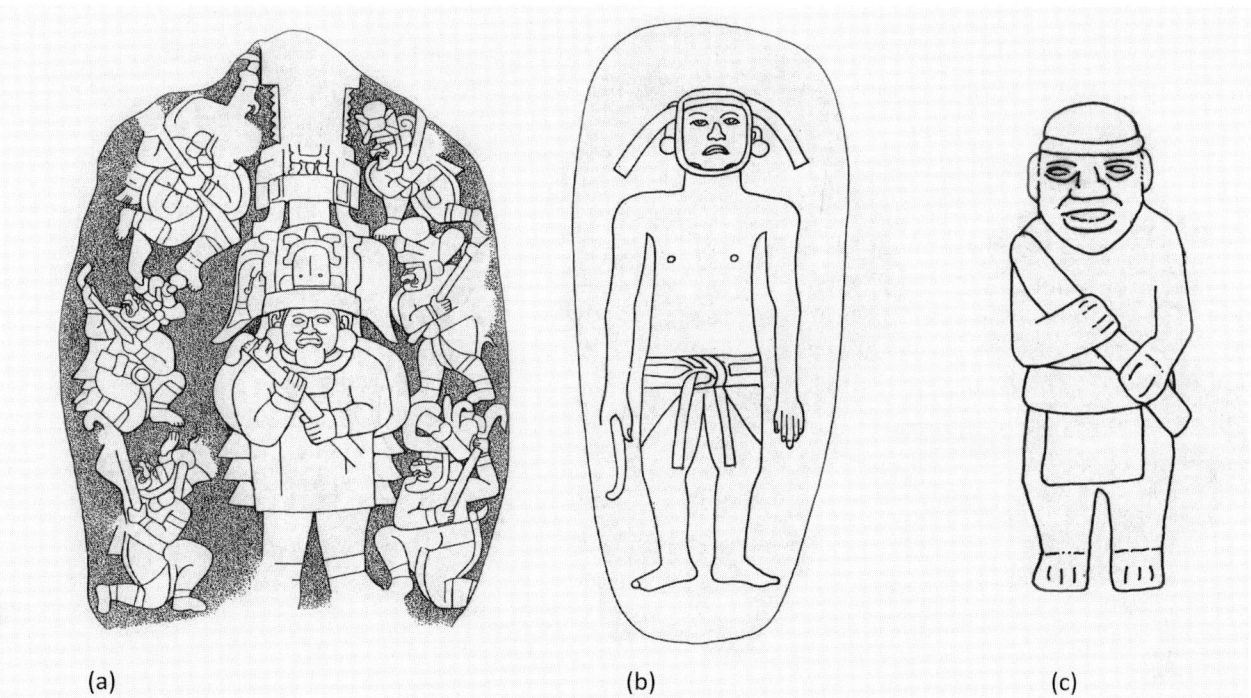

(a)   (b)   (c)

Figure 17.4 Probable depictions of sticks used in the Olmec ballgame (drawings by author).

a) Olmec ruler surrounded by six images of the Olmec rain god, all wielding curved sticks probably used in the ballgame, La Venta Stela 2.

b) Incised jadeite celt portraying Olmec ballplayer with curved stick (from Taube 2004, fig. 6a).

c) Jadeite figurine of ballplayer with probable curved bat (after Dunkelman 2007, no. 7).

Aside from La Venta Stela 2, the roughly contemporaneous Stela A at Tres Zapotes also depicts a frontally facing figure wearing an exceptionally tall headdress, and in the case of both stelae, this regalia recalls the aforementioned headdresses of Early Formative ballplayer figurines (see Figure 17.1). The central figure is flanked by two others who wield curving sticks, quite probably ballgame clubs (see Taube 2004, fig. 6b). In addition, a Middle Formative jadeite celt attributed to Río Pesquero in the Museo de Arqueología in Jalapa, Veracruz, bears an incised image of what is clearly a ballplayer, including a thick belt, chinstrap headdress and apron-like leggings still worn by ballplayers today in contemporary Sinaloa (Figure 17.4b). In his left hand he holds a curving baton which, as has been mentioned, is probably for striking the ball. A jadeite statuette in the Jay I. Kislak collection at the U.S. Library of Congress depicts a standing male holding a curving club diagonally across his abdomen, a pose virtually identical to La Venta Stela 2 (Figure 17.4c). Wearing a broad

headband as well as a thick belt, this figure probably is also a ballplayer.

If indeed stickball was the favoured rubber ballgame of the Olmec, this opens up greater avenues of thought to where it would be played. The 'traditional' well-known Mesoamerican ballgame is appropriate within the relatively closed areas of archaeologically documented ballcourts, and in scale corresponds well to the contemporary ballgame in Sinaloa, despite the fact that now only chalk markers and lines rather than long parallel structures delineate the circumscribed area. Kent Reilly (1999, 20–1) notes that with its two parallel mounds, Complex A at La Venta resembles a ballcourt. However, Reilly considers this unlikely, given the fact that the 'court' would be far larger than those known for Mesoamerican ballcourts, with an inner court space almost 90 meters long and 40 meters wide. However, considering the possibility that a hockey-like game could have been played, such dimensions would certainly be compatible with known contemporary forms of the sport.

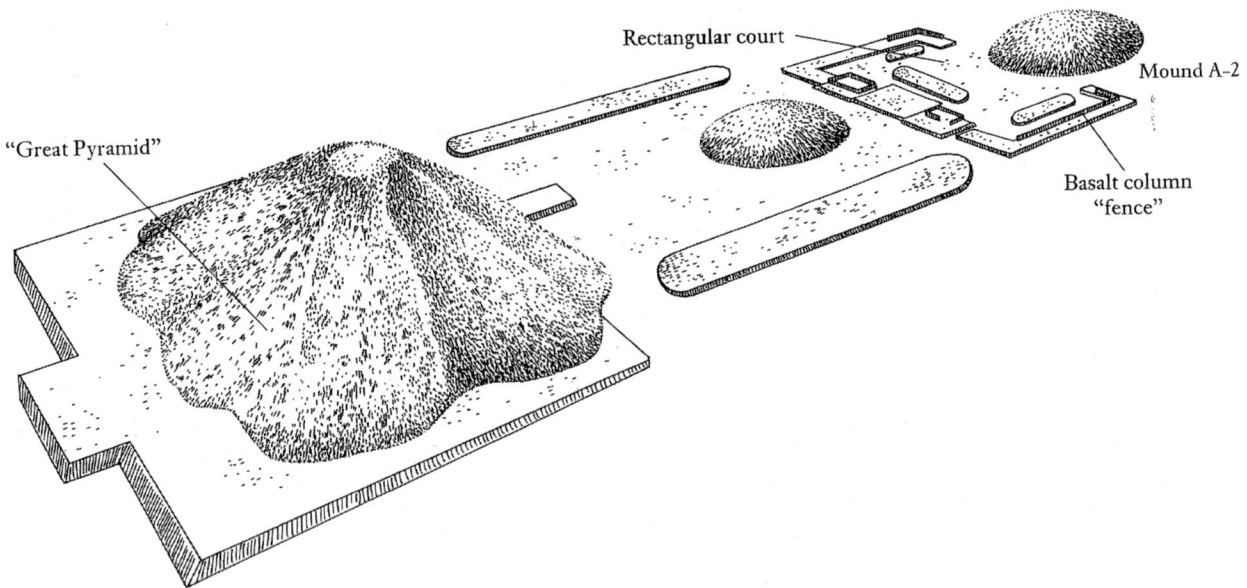

Figure 17.5 Complex C and A at Middle Formative La Venta (from Coe & Koontz 2008, fig. 46).

In addition, La Venta Mounds A2 and A4 create an avenue or 'alley' directly oriented to the first major Mesoamerican pyramid, Complex C (Figure 17.5). As will be noted, one of the striking conventions of Mesoamerican ballcourts is that they are frequently oriented to the central axis of pyramids which probably served as symbolic mountains of water and sustenance.

MOUNTAINS OF RAIN, COURTS OF WATER

It is important to note that as of yet, Mesoamerican-style ballcourts with two flanking structures having inner benches have not been documented for Early or Middle Formative Olmec sites, including San Lorenzo and La Venta. In fact, the first known ballcourt is still earlier at the site of Paso de la Amada in south coastal Chiapas. Almost 80 meters in length, only slightly less than Mounds A2 and A4 at La Venta, the court dates to the local phase known as Locona, roughly equivalent to the pre-Olmec phase of Ojochí at San Lorenzo (ca. 1400 BC):

> One of the striking aspects of this initial court is that the architectural elements – parallel mounds and low sloping benches flanking

a long narrow alleyway – are the essential characteristics of all later Mesoamerican ballcourts. (Blake 2011, 112)

Given the paucity of representative art at this very early date, including even a large corpus of ceramic figurines, we have little knowledge as to what form of ballgame was played in this court. The Middle Formative site of Teopantecuantitlan, located in highland Guerrero of western Mexico, features an ashlar masonry enclosed court with four images of the Olmec maize god (see Martínez Donjuán 2010). The interior floor of the enclosed court contains two low parallel mounds in its centre, and according to the excavator, Martínez Donjuán (2010, 60), they constitute 'a small, symbolic ballcourt'. A major stone aqueduct system both enters and exits the court near the north-western and north-eastern corners, respectively, strongly suggesting that this system was not simply for drainage as one exit would certainly suffice (Figure 17.6). Instead, the aqueducts on both sides of the sunken masonry court indicate that it was ritually flooded to form a pool, perhaps to celebrate the advent of the rainy season (Taube 2004, 11; Schaafsma & Taube 2006).

Although creating bodies of water in Mesoamerican ballcourts may seem radical, there is a remarkable effigy vessel graphically portraying this

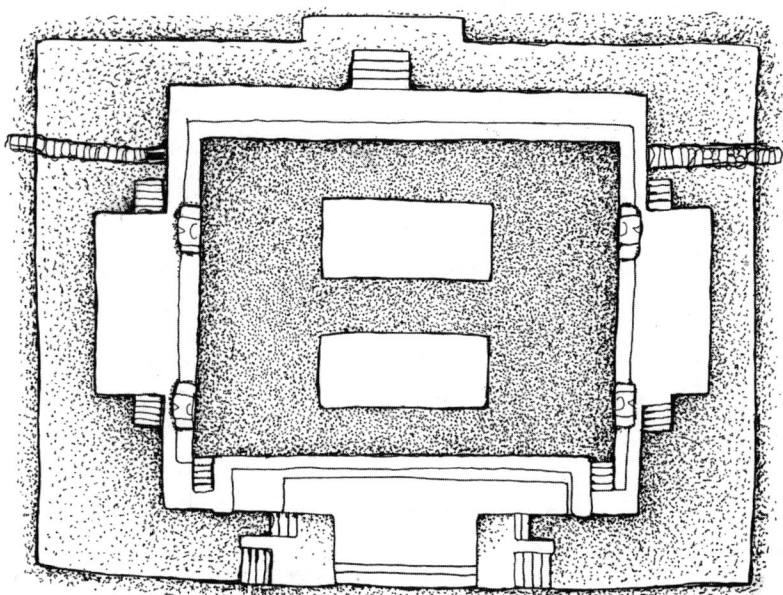

Figure 17.6 The sunken court at Teopantecuanitlan, Guerrero, note drains at north-east and north-west corners (drawing by author after Martínez Donjuán 1994, fig. 9.10).

very concept (Figure 17.7a). Stephan de Borhegyi (1980,4) noted that the piece is probably Late Preclassic Maya (ca. 100 BC) from highland Guatemala. Oddly, de Borhegyi did not mention that fluids would readily pour through 'drains' to fill the ballcourt, which was later noted by Whittington (2001, 164) in a catalogue concerning the Mesoamerican ballgame: "liquid poured into the spout would completely fill the I-shaped court, turning it into a mirror-like surface." Houston (1998, 359) compared this vessel to a rock carving at the Late Classic Maya site of El Planchon de las Figuras on the shore of the Lacantun River in Chiapas, where a channel was cut from a spring into a miniature sunken ballcourt (Figure 17.7b; note arrows for direction of flow). According to Houston (1998), this Maya tradition may relate to concepts of a symbolic well or spring in the centre of the courts, a theme to be further discussed later in this chapter: "Some of the channels connected with ballcourts may reflect the belief, documented in Postclassic Central Mexico, that the central hole of the court is a 'well,' a source of water for irrigation." Houston (1998) also calls attention to similar ballcourt *maquetas* at Las Palmas, Chiapas. For one example, clear I-shaped ballcourts alternate with simpler rectangular depressions (Figure 17.7c). The rectangular forms are probably also ballcourts of a type extensively documented in highland Guatemala, referred to as

a *palangana* or 'wash basin', which is "a rectangular enclosure with surrounding walls of even height and with no end zones" (Smith 1965, 91). Another *maqueta* at Las Palmas appears to portray a *palangana* ballcourt with prominent drains at opposite corners, recalling the drain system on two sides of the sunken court at Teopantecuantitlan (Figure 17.7d).

Such rock architectural models, or *maquetas*, are also widespread in highland Mexico, including the site of Plazuelas, Guanajuato, which has many depictions of architecture as well as cupules cut into boulders and outcrops (see Castañeda López 2008). Andrew Turner (pers. comm. 2012) notes that during storms, the architectural models and cupules fill with rainwater, surely pertaining to concepts of abundance and agricultural fertility. Although rain and water is the underlying theme, sacrificial blood may have been offered as well. Ruiz de Alarcon's early seventeenth-century account of idolatry in highland Guerrero suggests that penitential blood was offered in cupules cut into mountain outcrops ("little receptacles like saltcellars which they made in the rocks" (see Coe & Whittaker 1982, 81). In a recent publication, Eric Taladoire (2012) discusses three-dimensional as well as codical representations of Mesoamerican ballcourts, including other examples of *maquetas* from highland Mexico, including an example from Plazuelas. Following Houston, he

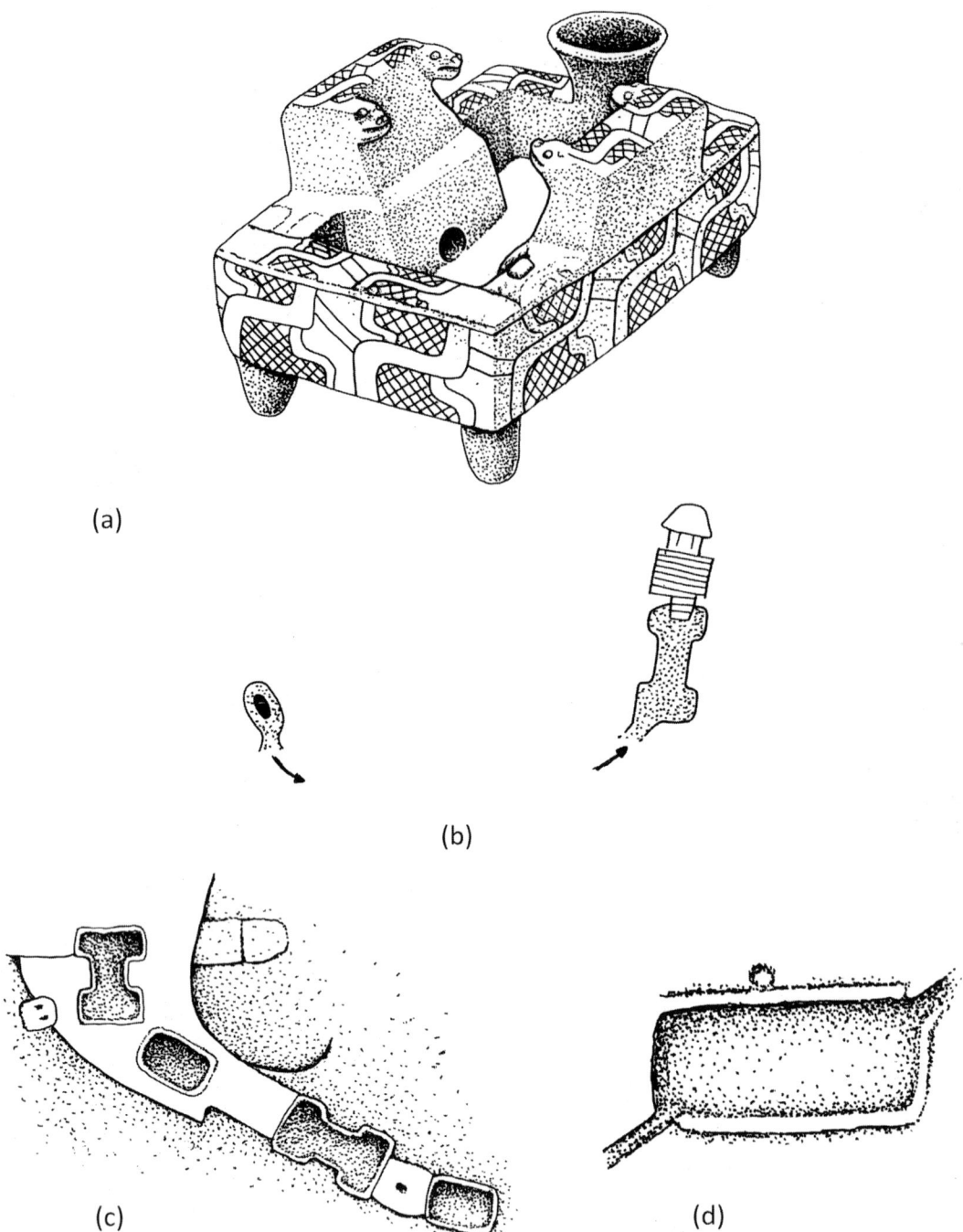

Figure 17.7 Miniature models, or *maquetas* in ancient Mesoamerica.

a) Late Preclassic Maya vessel portraying I-shaped enclosed ballcourt, note spout and drain for filling the object (drawing by author after Whittington 2001, no. 31).

b) Stone *maqueta* of ballcourt connected to water source, El Planchon de las Figuras, Chiapas (from Houston 1998, fig. 22, with stippling added by author).

c) *Maqueta* boulder outcrop carving of I-shaped ballcourts alternating with *palangana*-style courts, Las Palmas, Chiapas (after Navarrete et al. 1993, fig. 51).

d) *Maqueta* carving of *palangana* court with drains at two corners, Las Palmas, Chiapas (Navarrete et al. 1993, fig. 50).

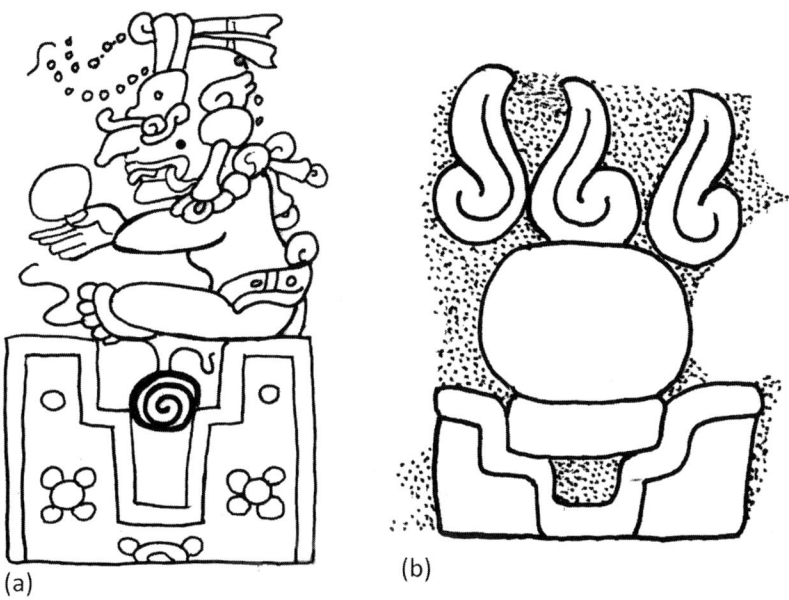

Figure 17.8 Portrayals of ballcourts with burning rubber balls (drawings by author).
a) The Maya rain god Chahk seated atop a ballcourt with a burning rubber ball, Codex Dresden p. 41a.
b) Burning rubber ball in a stepped ballcourt, detail of Early Classic vessel from the Escuintla region of southern Guatemala, Denver Art Museum.

notes that many of these ballcourt carvings seemed to have been intended to receive water, and illustrates a remarkably complex *maqueta* scene carved in bedrock at San Miguel Ixtapan, in the State of Mexico (Taladoire 2012, fig. 1). As noted by Taladoire (2012, 26): "the architectural representations could serve for rituals in which they were used for water or other liquids that would circulate through the courts" (translation by author).

In Mesoamerica, burning offerings of sacrificial blood and copal served to bring clouds of fertile rain. However, rubber constituted another favoured offering burned to ritually create rain clouds, as along with copal incense, rubber is the sap or 'blood' of trees (Ortíz & Rodríguez 2000, 91; Stone 2002, 23). In a discussion of magic in ancient Mesoamerica, Thompson (1970: 166) notes that "perhaps the most important example of 'like produces like' is the widely held belief that the black smoke of copal or rubber attracts the black rain clouds, and it is probably for that reason rubber plays such an important part in Tlaloc rites and paraphernalia." According to Stone (2002, 23), "rubber has strong conceptual parallels with the human body, especially with the

heart and blood." As is suggested from the offerings found in the spring at El Manatí, rubber balls could have closely related to rain and water symbolism. In fact, the Late Postclassic Codex Dresden portrays the Maya rain god Chahk seated atop a burning rubber ball within a ballcourt (see Figure 17.8a). An Early Classic Teotihuacan-style vessel from the Escuintla region of Guatemala portrays a rubber ball explicitly burning within a ballcourt, probably again referring to black clouds of burning rubber as dark, rain-laden clouds (Figure 17.8b).

A large stone *maqueta* from the Late Classic site of Xochicalco, Morelos, bears a complex portrayal of temple platforms, terraces and a ballcourt, as well as the aforementioned cupules, quite possibly an idealised three-dimensional rendering of the hilltop site itself (Figure 17.9). The *maqueta* features a principal stepped pyramid with a large cupule on its summit and, at its base, a ballcourt with a deeply carved channel at its opposite end for conveying liquid through the court, whether this be water, blood or some other fluid, such as *pulque*. Moreover, the recently excavated East Ball Court at Xochicalco (Figure 17.10a) is entirely enclosed, with a small horizontal drain at

Figure 17.9 Stone *maqueta* of temple complex and ballcourt. Note channel for liquid at close end of court, Xochicalco, Morelos (photograph by author).

the northern end and a larger vertical one at the opposite southern side, clearly serving as the exiting drain (Figure 17.10b). As in the case of the Olmec miniature ballcourt at Teopantecuantitlan, the two drains strongly suggest that this sunken court could have been ritually flooded, quite like the *maqueta* court from the same site. In addition, the sunken I-shaped ballcourt at Xochicalco is also notably similar to the aforementioned ceramic vessel portraying a ballcourt with drains.

It is widely recognised that the monumental art and architecture of Xochicalco exhibits strong Maya influence (e.g. Coe & Koontz 2008, 136–9). Thus the famed Temple of the Feathered Serpent portrays seated Maya-style rulers against the undulating bodies of great rattlesnakes covered with long quetzal plumes, a precious commodity squarely from the Maya area. In this regard, it is important to note that this structure is oriented directly to the East Ball Court below, that is, the direction of the Maya region. Although the documented context remains unpublished, a recently discovered ballcourt ring almost

surely came from the East Ball Court, as they were excavated at roughly the same time (Figure 17.11a–b). Although in the current museum display there is a bat on top and a pair of quetzal birds below, the original orientation was surely the opposite, with the pair of quetzals denoting the heavens and the upside-down hanging bat the deathly underworld below. In fact, I (Taube 2005, 38) have noted that in Classic Maya and Teotihuacan iconography, a pair of male quetzals serves as a symbol of the afterlife 'Flower World' paradise of the east. As with the quetzals, the bat probably also alludes to Maya traditions. In Classic Maya art, bats commonly appear with crossed bones on their wings, a theme probably related to the Camazotz, or 'death bat' of the K'iche' Maya *Popol Vuh*, who decapitates one of the Hero Twins in their epic ball-game battle with the lords of death (Figure 17.11c; see Recinos 1950, 149–50).

Enclosed I-shaped ballcourts similar to the East Ball Court at Xochicalco are relatively common at Late Classic and Postclassic sites in the Maya highlands of Chiapas and Guatemala (Smith 1961, 110–16; 1965, 89, 91; Taladoire 2001). Quite frequently, they are at the base of major architectural complexes, and as in the case of a Late Classic ballcourt at Chinkultic in highland Chiapas, it is hard to imagine how water would not collect during a tropical storm (Figure 17.12a, b). This is also the case for a *palangana* at San Juan las Vegas in the Chixoy Valley of highland Guatemala, where the sunken court is oriented parallel to a terraced hillside (Ichon 1988, fig. 49). In a discussion of enclosed ballcourts of highland Guatemala, Smith (1965, 91) noted that drains were virtually a necessity:

> it can be assumed that all courts that were completely enclosed had drains. In several such courts, where there has been sufficient excavation, water outlets were uncovered.

In another study, Smith (1961, 112) mentions that "[d]rains were found in the corners of the end zones" of several enclosed courts. Unfortunately, Smith does not specify if drains occurred at all four corners of a given court. If this were the case, such drains could have cosmic significance, with the water pouring out

Figure 17.10 The enclosed East Ball Court at Xochicalco, Morelos.

a) View of north end of court with small drain in centre (photograph by author).

b) View of sound end of court with larger vertical drain (photograph by and courtesy of Andrew Turner).

Figure 17.11 Ballcourt ring probably from the East Ball Court, Xochicalco (drawings by author).

a) Ballcourt ring with male quetzals with jade beads in mouth and inverted bat below (after photograph courtesy of Andrew Turner).
b) Detail of bat, note crossed bones on wings.
c) Maya bat with crossed bones of wings, detail of Late Classic vase from Chama region of highland Guatemala.

to the four inter-cardinal points. In Late Postclassic and early colonial Mexico, ballcourts are commonly portrayed in terms of four quarters marked with contrasting colours (see Figure 17.18).

Although Smith was somewhat vague concerning both the topographic orientation of highland Maya ballcourts and the specific placement of drains, recent archaeological investigations at the Late Classic site of Santa Rosa close to the city of Antigua, Guatemala, have documented a series of four drains in a *palangana* court (Robinson 2014, 162). Although not all the drains were found *in situ*, Robinson (2014) notes that they appear to have been on the east and west sides of the court. The site is atop a ridge, with the ballcourt at the lowest end of the monumental architecture. The court constitutes the southern end of the main plaza, and the other three sides are

structures atop a U-shaped platform, with the open side facing the ballcourt to the south. Higher up the ridge to the north, a large platform is directly oriented to the ballcourt and plaza. As will be noted, the pattern of a ballcourt at the lower end of a U-shaped complex with a larger central structure above is not present only in the Maya highlands, but in highland Mexico as well.

At the site of San Francisco, located in highland Guatemala east of the Ixil town of Nebaj, one architectural complex features a pyramidal platform with a court and central altar below leading down to a ballcourt with its alley oriented directly to the principal platform above, recalling the aforementioned Complex A and Complex C at Middle Formative La Venta (Figure 17.13a; cf. Figure 17.5). However, the San Francisco complex is especially

(a)

(b)

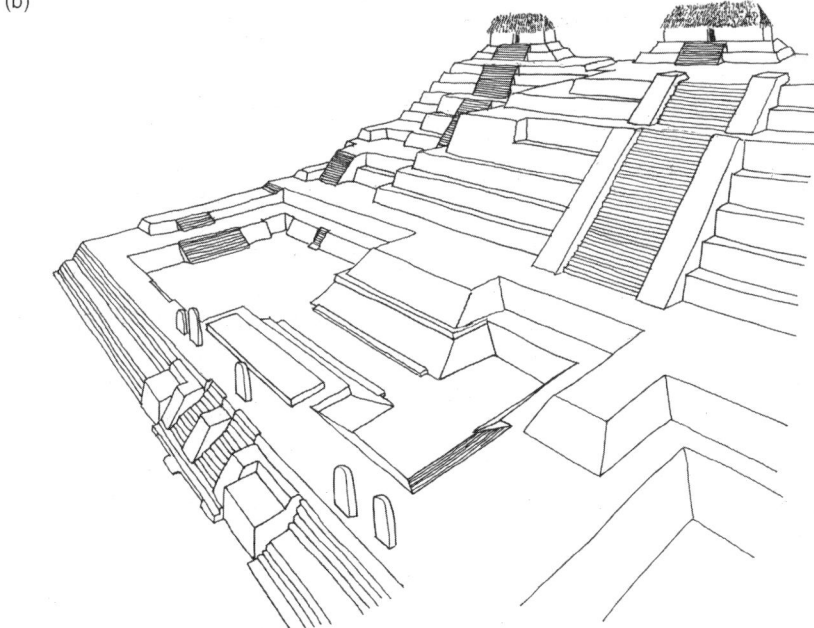

Figure 17.12 Enclosed I-shaped ballcourt at Chinkultic, Chiapas.

a) Recent view of enclosed court (photo by and courtesy of Caitlin Earley).

b) Reconstruction of ballcourt and associated temple structure (drawing by author after Taladoire 2001, fig. 127)

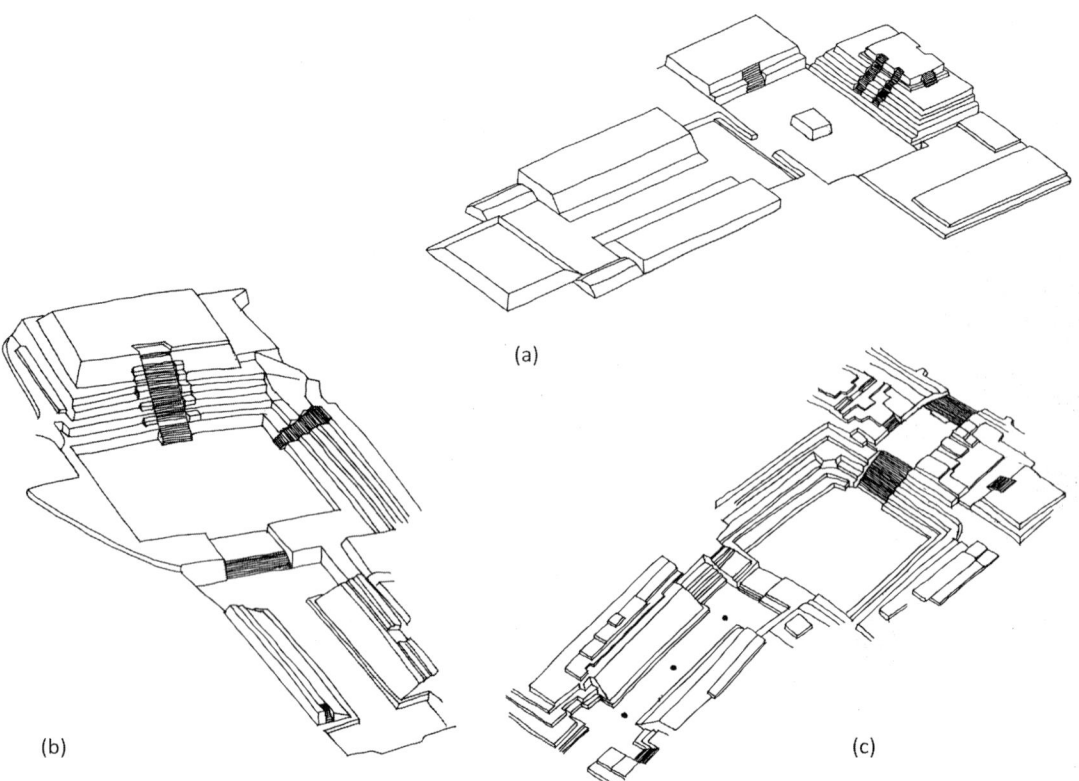

Figure 17.13 Comparison of I-shaped ball-court temple complexes from highland Guatemala and Cantona, Puebla (drawings by author and not to same scale).

a) Ball-court temple complex at San Francisco, Departamento del K'iche', Guatemala (after Burkitt 1930, plate 28).
b) Ball Court Group 6, Cantona (after García Cook & Merino Carrión, 1998, fig. 11).
c) Ball Court Group 7, Cantona (after García Cook & Merino Carrión, 1998, fig. 10).

similar to ceremonial architecture known for the massive Late Classic site of Cantona, located in a *malpaís* or 'badland' area of eastern Puebla, Mexico (Figure 17.13b–c). Remarkably, Cantona has no fewer than 24 ballcourts, and of these 12 are what García Cook and Merino Carrión (1998, 200) define as 'Cantona type', which share the following interconnected features: a major multi-tiered platform, one or two plazas below delineated by surrounding platforms that can contain a central altar and a ballcourt at the lowest, opposite end from the main pyramid, much like the aforementioned site of Santa Rosa. These complexes are strikingly similar to San Francisco, although I have no ready explanation for any historical contact between these two distant regions.

Many traits of Late Classic highland Maya ballcourts, including *palanganas* and courts abutting higher platform complexes, continued in highland Guatemala to the sixteenth-century contact period. The hilltop K'iche' Maya site of Chitinamit, or Hacawitz, has a ballcourt immediately below the principal complex supporting five platforms. However, rather than being oriented directly to the main platform stairway, the court alley is perpendicular, recalling the aforementioned Late Classic example at Chinkultic (see Fox 1991, fig. 12.2). In addition, Fox (1991, 224) notes that for the Kaqchikel capital of Iximche' that "[q]uite dramatically, both courts are sunken below the plaza surface." The impression received upon seeing these ballcourts could suggest a modern swimming pool as well as the Middle Formative enclosed court at Teopantecuantitlan. In their important study concerning the symbolism of the ballgame among the ancient Maya, Schele and Freidel (1991) note the close relation of ballcourts to caves and the underworld, which is entirely consistent with the netherworld court of Xibalba in the sixteenth-century *Popol Vuh*. Not only were ball-courts' symbolic pools or cenote-like caves filled, but actual courts were probably flooded, perhaps to dramatically celebrate the coming of the spring and summer rains.

In terms of the ritual flooding of Mesoamerican ballcourts, Steve Lekson (pers. comm. 2012) has pointed out to me that this is also a likely scenario in the arid American Southwest, with many courts apparently oriented to receive the flow of water. Indeed, James Holmlund (cited in Wilcox 1991, 119), notes that Hohokam ballcourts of southern Arizona, roughly contemporary with Classic-period Mesoamerica, are situated to the water flow from natural topography:

> One characteristic of this ballcourt which has been noted for other ballcourts, recently, is the fact that it was built perpendicular to the local slope. This serves a dual purpose: 1) It significantly reduces the amount of excavation to build a ballcourt, and 2) it deflects downslope water and sediment movement if a small upslope berm is maintained.

Located in northern Arizona close to Flagstaff, the pueblo site of Wupatki has an especially late form of masonry ballcourt, dating to roughly AD 1200 (see Lekson 2008, 157). The ballcourt is at the base of a steep wash beginning at the pueblo centre located atop a narrow mesa. When I visited the site in late November 2011, there was noticeable water in the court, in sharp contrast to the surrounding arid landscape. It is important to note that the 'flooding' of courts in both Mesoamerica and the American Southwest does not mean that they were filled with many feet of water, but that run-off entered and symbolically fertilised them as places of growth and abundance.

THE SYMBOLISM OF WATER AND RAIN IN MESOAMERICAN BALLCOURTS

Aside from the architecture and orientation of Mesoamerican ballcourts, pre-Hispanic iconography and early colonial texts also confirm that they were symbolic places of water. The Late Classic South Ball Court at El Tajín in northern Veracruz, Mexico, contains six bas-reliefs featuring some of the most complex scenes of rituals and symbolism pertaining to the Mesoamerican ballgame (see Koontz 2009, 37–68). All six panels depict pools of standing water, with the opposing central scenes both portraying the water inside a masonry structure backed by a maguey covered mountain (Figure 17.14a–b). The Classic Veracruz version of Tlaloc appears prominently in both central panels, with the southern relief portraying the rain deity letting blood from his penis onto a figure with a prominent fish headdress (Figure 17.14a). It has been suggested that this scene constitutes an early version of the Aztec myth in which gods let blood on the ground bones of the fish people killed in the flood to create the current race of mankind, although it should be noted that in the Aztec myth, the main protagonist is Quetzalcoatl rather than Tlaloc (Dellhale & Luykx 1986; Taube 1986). However, Tlaloc is prominently featured in an Aztec myth of the fall of Tollan appearing in the *Leyenda de los soles* (see Bierhorst 1992, 156–7). In this account, the last king of Tollan, Huemac, played ball with the Tlalocs (or Tlaloque), who wagered their precious jades and quetzal plumes if Huemac won. However, after having defeated the Tlaloque, Huemac refused their 'true' wealth, which is maize, and instead foolishly insisted on actual jewels and plumes. For this, Tollan was devastated by a four-year drought. Clearly enough, this episode relates the ballgame to the rain gods and, by extension, to agricultural wealth and abundance.

In early colonial Aztec manuscripts, there is reference to the town of Tlachquiyauhco, or 'place of the ballcourt rain', corresponding to the modern Mixtec community of Tlaxiaco in highland Oaxaca. In the Codex Mendoza, this toponym appears twice as an I-shaped ballcourt, or *tlachco*, containing raindrops (Figure 17.15a–b). H. B. Nicholson and Eloise Quiñones Keber (1991, 125, 128) note that the Tlachquiyauhco place name occurs in the Codex Telleriano-Remensis and the Codex Azcatitlan as well, again with ballcourts and drops of rain (Figure 17.15c–d). For one example in the Telleriano-Remensis, a dark cloud shedding rain hovers directly above the court (Figure 17.15c). However, probably

(a)   (b)

Figure 17.14 The middle panels of the South Ball Court at El Tajín (drawings by author).
a) Tlaloc letting his blood from his penis to a fish-man, Panel 5 (after Kampen 1972, fig. 24).
b) Tlaloc seated above a watery temple with another example of him lying atop a water pool in the temple, Panel 6 (after Kampen 1972, fig. 25).

the most explicit and elaborate Aztec reference to ballcourts and water is the late sixteenth-century account by Tezozomoc (1944, 11–14) in the *Crónica mexicana* concerning the legendary migration of the Aztec, or Mexica. While at the legendary place of Coatepec, the Aztec tutelary Huitzilopochtli created a spring in the centre of the *teotlachco*, or 'ballcourt of the gods', that flooded the land and made it a wonderful, verdant land of growth and fertility teeming with fish, shrimp and other aquatic creatures. The central spring in this miraculous court was referred to as *itzompan* or 'his place of skulls'. In order that the Aztec continue on their journey to Tenochtitlan, Huitzilopochtli sacrificed his half-sister Coyolxauhqui in the ballcourt and eventually destroyed the spring, causing the region to once again become a wasteland.

Directly adjacent to the east side of the Great Ball Court at Chichen Itza, there is a T-shaped platform ornamented with bas-reliefs of skulls horizontally pierced with poles, clearly referring to a *tzompantli* skull rack. This relates to an episode in the sixteenth-century *Popol Vuh*, where the severed head of the father of the Hero Twins, Hun Hunahpu,

is placed in a tree adjacent to the ballcourt (Taube 1994). Excavations atop and on the centre line of the *tzompantli* platform uncovered a large, fragmentary stone ring resembling the pair of rings from the Great Ball Court (see Salazar Otregón 1952, 39). However, Salazar Otregón (1952, 41) noted that it was probably placed horizontally as an altar atop the *tzompantli* platform. More recently, it has been described as "a [c]ircular altar that was probably used for sacrifices" (Sabloff 1998, 52–3). One side portrays two rings of small, swimming fish, thereby linking this sculpture to both skulls and verdant springs, in other words, the *itzompan*, and here in the centre of an Early Postclassic ball-court skull rack (Figure 17.16).

In a discussion of the Mesoamerican concept of a 'Lagoon of Primordial Blood' as a place of origin, Michael Oudijk (2011, 160) notes that folios 16r and 16v of the *Historia Tolteca-Chichimeca* are actually the same scene, and portray the Chicomoztoc mountain cave of human origin and emergence on one side and Tollan as a lush, verdant spring and a ballcourt on the other. As Oudijk (2011) points out, although the scenes are separated, the text unambiguously links them together:

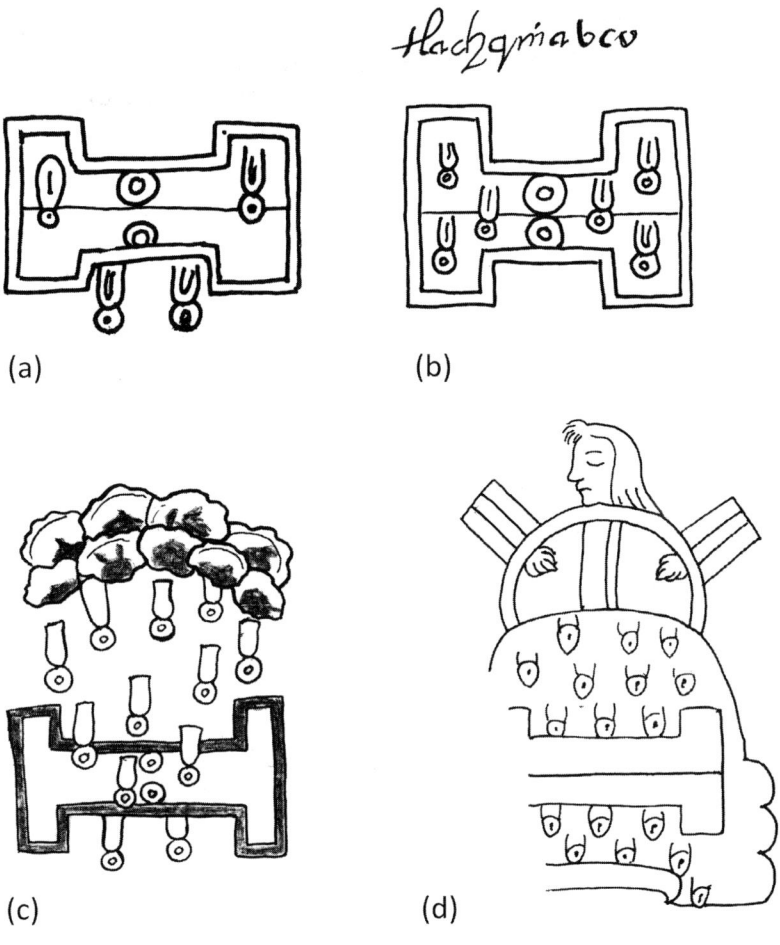

(a)   (b)

(c)   (d)

Figure 17.15 Early colonial portrayals of the place name of Tlaxiaco, Oaxaca, meaning 'ballcourt of rain' (drawings by author).

a) Ballcourt with raindrops, Codex Mendoza fol. 16r.
b) Ballcourt with raindrops with accompanying gloss 'tlachquialco', Codex Mendoza fol. 45r.
c) Tlaxiaco toponym with dark cloud raining into ballcourt, Codex Teleriano-Remensis, fol. 41r.
d) Tlaxiaco toponym with defeated warrior atop mountain with raining ballcourt, Codex Azcatitlan, plate XXII.

Figure 17.16 Stone ring with swimming fish discovered atop a *tzompantli* platform at Chichen Itza (drawing by Karl Taube after Salazar Otregón 1952, pl. 1).

Figure 17.17 Heart sacrifice within ballcourt, detail of *Selden Roll*, Coixtlahuaca region, highland Mexico (drawing by Karl Taube).

And here is where the curved hill is, where the blue water extends, where the white tules are, where the white reeds are, where the white willow raises, where the white-water sand extends, where the ballcourt of the nahuales is. (translation by Karen Dakin cited in Oudijk 2011, 160)

Clearly enough, the sacred mountain, spring and ballcourt constitute a version of the Huitzilopochtli account by Tezozomoc and in addition, the frequent orientation of ballcourts to pyramidal platforms at ancient Mesoamerican sites.

Aside from the Aztec migration account, there is an explicit reference to heart sacrifice in a ballcourt from the *Selden Roll*, an early colonial pictorial manuscript from the Coixtlahuaca region of highland Oaxaca. In one scene, a woman holds the heart of a supine male victim within a ballcourt, in essential opposition to the Aztec sacrifice of the goddess Coyolxauhqui during their legendary journey to Tenochtitlan (Figure 17.17).

The episode described by Tezozomoc is corroborated by other early colonial sources. For the Aztec 365-day calendar, the 20-day month of Panquetzalli was explicitly dedicated to Huitzilopochtli. During Panquetzalli, four captives were sacrificed in the ritual ballcourt known as the Teotlachco (Sahagún 1950–82, II:27, 145), recalling the slaying of Coyolxauhqui

in the ballcourt bearing the same name at Coatepec. In addition, the blood of the four victims was spread over the court surface: "When they had slain them, then they dragged them around the ballcourt. It was as if they painted it with [the victims'] blood" (Sahagún 1950–82, II:27, 145). Given the clear thematic overlap between blood and rain, this ritual practice probably also relates to the symbolic importance of water within courts. In addition, the *Crónica mexicana* mentioned the *itzompan* skull spring in the centre of the court. Long ago, Eduard Seler (1902–23, III:329) noted that page 19 of the Aztec Codex Borbonicus probably portrays this very place, this in the form of a skull and rubber ball spurting water in the centre of a ballcourt (Figure 17.18a). According to Stern (1949), for the parallel passage in the Aubin Tonalamatl, the circular element in the court centre is probably the *itzompan* spring (Figure 17.18b). However, Stern (1949, note 23) also mentions a striking scene in the Codex Colombino-Becker, which being Mixtec, probably has nothing to do with the Aztec migration account. In this case, water containing a marine shell can be seen coursing from the viewer's upper right through the court (Figure 17.18c). In addition, John Pohl (pers. comm. 2012) kindly pointed out a very similar scene in another page of the same manuscript, where a priest makes a fire offering in a ballcourt with a stream passing through it (Figure 17.18d). Although Stern (1949,

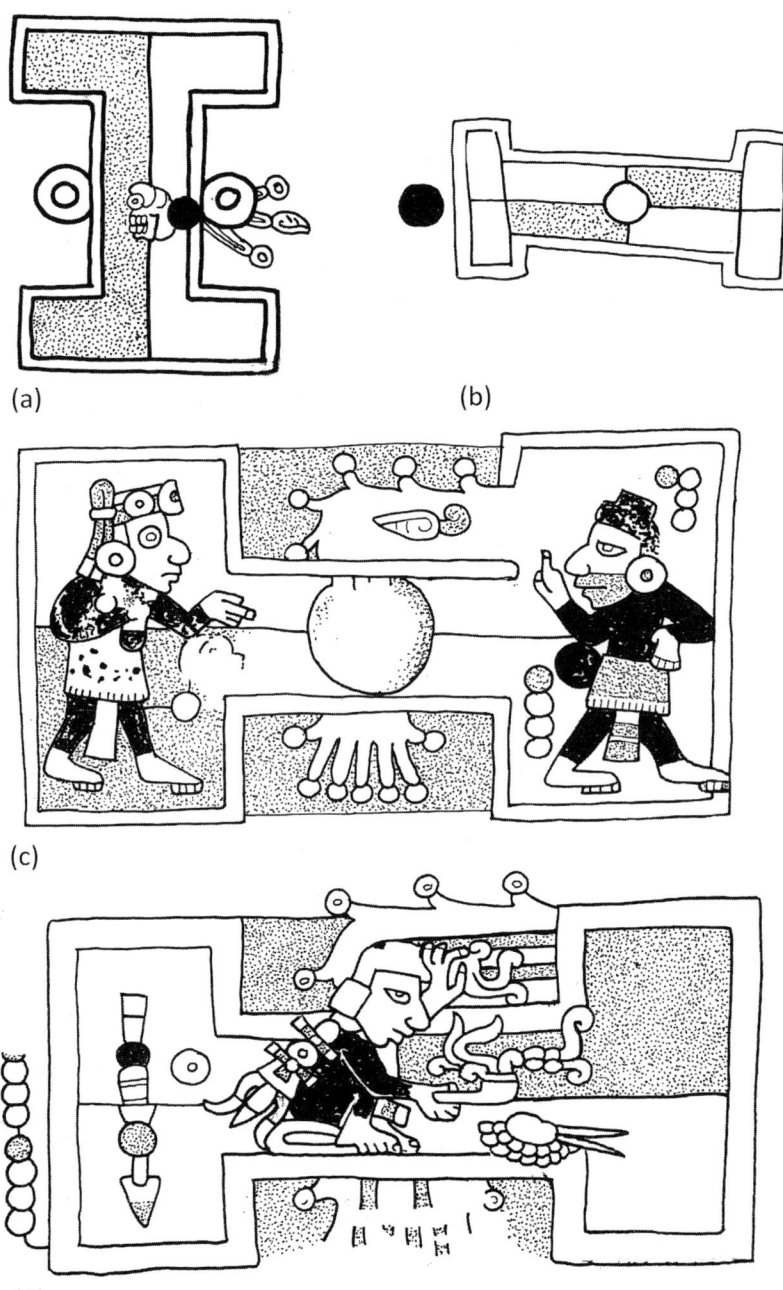

(a)

(b)

(c)

(d)

Figure 17.18. Late Postclassic and early colonial highland Mexican portrayals of ballcourts with central hole and water (drawings by author).

a) Aztec depiction of *itzompan* as a watery skull hole in the centre of the court, Codex Borbonicus, p. 19.
b) Ballcourt with a probable hole in the centre, Aubin Tonalamatl, p. 19.
c) Mixtec depiction of a watery ballcourt with a red element in the centre, possibly a version of the Aztec *itzompan*, Codex Colombino-Becker, p. 2.
d) Priest making a fire offering in a watery ballcourt, Codex Colombino-Becker, p. 6.

69) notes that the *Crónica mexicana* account of the mythic ballcourt at Coatepec could be "an allusion to a fundamental link between the *tlachco* [ballcourt] and water", he argues instead that the episode refers to the legendary wealth and abundance of nearby Tollan. However, given the symbolic relation of the ballgame and water to even before Olmec times, I would argue that there is indeed a fundamental link between the ballcourt and powers of rain and abundance.

Aside from codical scenes and early colonial accounts, ballcourts from the Maya region provide architectural evidence for a symbolic 'spring' in the court centre. In a detailed discussion of ballcourts from highland Guatemala, Smith (1961, 108) notes a round hole some 60 centimetres wide and 25 deep in the ballcourt at Chalchitan "in the plaster floor exactly in the centre of the playing alley". In the same publication, Smith (1961, 112) notes a similar feature in the enclosed ballcourt at the highland site of Xolchun: "In the exact centre of the early floor of the playing alley of the ballcourt at Xolchun, Department of Huehuetenango, there is a hole 20 cm. in diameter and 35 cm. deep. ... It is obvious that these enclosed courts must have had some method of disposing of water." Although Smith mentions the collecting of water as a logistical problem, surely this was part of their intended function. While Smith does not provide dates for the Chalchitan and Xolchun courts, they surely are within the range of the Classic and Postclassic periods (AD 250–1521). However, there is a far earlier example from northern Yucatán. Dating to roughly 600 BC, the ballcourt at Xanila contains a ring of stones in the alley centre (see Anderson 2012, fig. 2.5). Although Anderson (2012, 48), identifies this feature as an "altar", he notes that "the Xanila marker was made up of multiple rough cut pieces of stone arranged in a circle." Given the fact that there is no stone inside the ring, it probably delineated a shallow hole in the court centre, very like the much later courts at Chalchitan and Xolchun. However, there surely was a thematic overlap between solid stone ball-court markers and symbolic sources of water. As noted by Schele and Freidel (1991, 309), with its three stone markers bearing the Mesoamerican quatrefoil cave motif, "[t]he floor of the ballcourt at Copán was like a glass bottomed boat with windows that let one see into the watery Underworld."

Ritual Boxing in Ancient Mesoamerica

In recent research, it has been noted that aside from the ballgame, ritual boxing was also another important sport in Mesoamerica, especially in the southeastern regions of the Olmec, Zapotec and Classic Maya (Orr 1997, 2003; Chinchilla-Mazariegos 2009; Taube & Zender 2009; Baudez 2011, 2012). Moreover, as in the case of the ballgame, ritual boxing relates closely to rain ritual and in addition, jaguars, a tradition that can be readily traced to the Early Formative Olmec to contemporary highland Guerrero.

Monument 10 at San Lorenzo portrays the Olmec rain god wearing a headband and a very broad belt while holding a pair of objects in his hands (Figure 17.19a). These items are commonly termed 'knuckle-dusters' in Olmec studies (e.g. Coe 1965b, 764–5; Grove 1987), and according to Michael Coe (1965b, 765), they may have been used as "a fairly effective hand-weapon during close infighting". In support, Coe (1965b, fig. 1) notes that an Olmec stela from Padre Piedra portrays a standing Olmec figure apparently menacing a much smaller individual with this device. Clearly enough, "close infighting" could well relate to ritual combat, and it has been suggested that these were items used in boxing (Taube 2004, 63, 84; Taube & Zender 2009, 2010). As has been noted by a number of researchers, they were probably fashioned from cut conch, and in fact an actual pair of conch knuckle-dusters is on display in the Museo Regional de Tapachula, Chiapas (Taube 2004, 83; see Taube & Zender 2009, fig. 7.30a).

Along with San Lorenzo Monument 10, La Isla Monument 1 portrays another Olmec rain god wielding a pair of knuckle-dusters along with the broad belt and headband (see Gillespie 2000, figs. 9–11). Wearing the same protective gear along with the knuckle-dusters, this sculpture is so similar to that of San Lorenzo Monument 10 as to suggest that they formed a pair. However, a stone head fragment from Estero Rabón, close to San Lorenzo, depicts an Olmec rain god with very similar facial features as well as the headband, suggesting that there could well be additional monumental sculptures portraying the Olmec rain god as a ritual boxer (Figure 17.19b). Aside from San Lorenzo Monument 10 and La Isla Monument 1, a Middle Formative jadeite statuette also depicts the Olmec rain god with a deeply furrowed brow and apparently shut eyes grasping a pair of knuckle-dusters (Figure 17.19d). In addition, a miniature stone bench portrays the head of the Olmec rain god in profile within a knuckle-duster (Figure 17.19c). Considering their derivation from the sea, conch knuckle-dusters may have been identified with water and rain, and in fact they do resemble Olmec portrayals of rain clouds in profile (see Taube 2004, 83–4, fig. 38). However, if they were hand-held weapons, they could also have been considered symbolic rainmakers, with sprays of sweat and blood compared to falling rain.

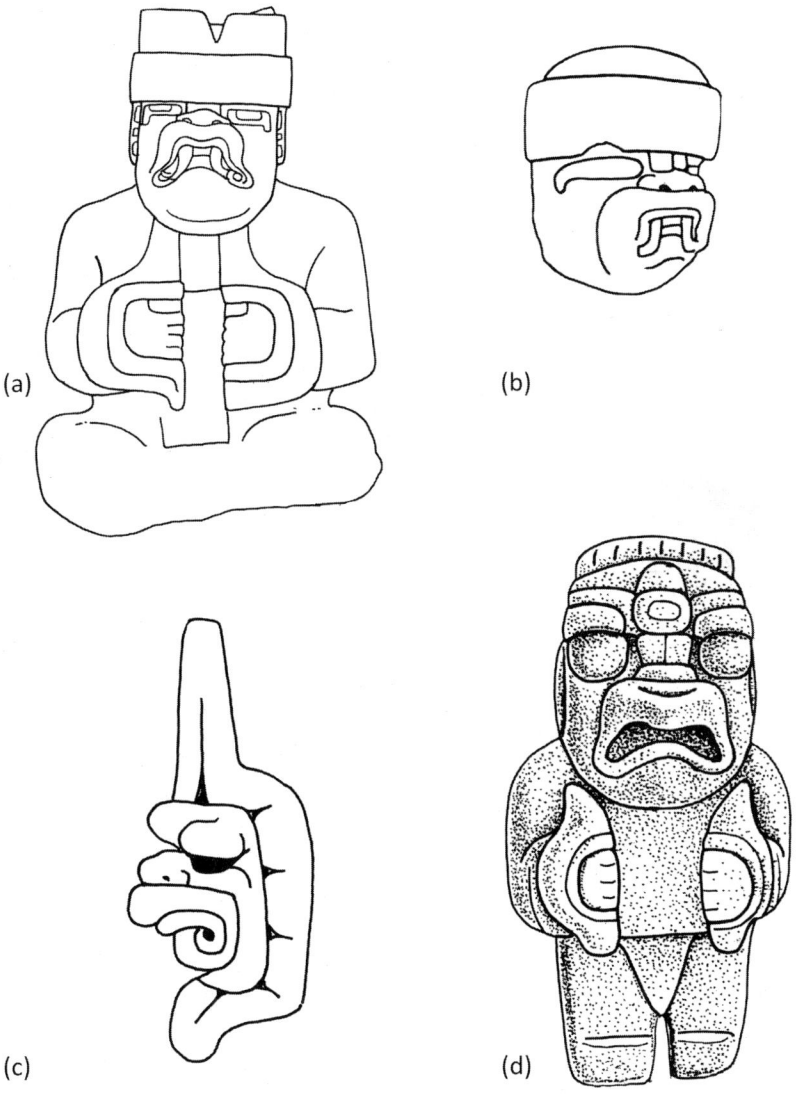

(a)

(b)

(c)

(d)

Figure 17.19 Portrayals of the Olmec rain god and 'knuckle-duster' weapons (drawings by author).

a) Early Formative Olmec rain god grasping two knuckle-dusters, San Lorenzo Monument 10 (after Coe & Diehl 1982, fig. 434).

b) Head of Olmec rain god with headband similar to San Lorenzo Monument 10, Estero Rabón Monument 15 (from Taube 2009, fig. 3a).

c) Face of Olmec rain god emerging from knuckle-duster, detail of miniature stone bench (after Guthrie 1995, no. 224).

d) Jade statuette of Olmec rain god grasping pair of knuckle-dusters (from Taube & Zender 2009, fig. 7.30b).

For ancient Mesoamerica, jaguars and pumas may have been considered the preeminent boxers, who readily kill and maim with their powerful clawed paws, typically in a devastating sideswipe motion. In fact, in contemporary Yukatek Mayan languages, including Yukatek and Itzaj, a common term for jaguar is *chak mo'ol*, meaning 'great paw'. Two serpentine statuettes in the collection of Dumbarton Oaks in Washington, DC – quite probably from the same workshop – portray standing figures combining human and jaguar characteristics often called 'transformation figures' in Olmec studies (Furst 1968). For the larger carving, the being is clearly more human, but still possesses a feline-like muzzle (see Taube 2004, 62–4). The figure is tightly flexed with

one powerful arm lowered defensively and the other raised as if to strike, and perhaps this pose led George Kubler (1962, 70) to suggest that he was a "middle age gladiator". The other statuette depicts a far more feline being with no apparent human characteristics aside from his bipedal stance and clearly pugilistic pose with his forearms extended at right angles to the body; the right arm is slightly lower, recalling the combative stance of the other piece.

In Oaxaca, ballcourts are well known for the Zapotec since at least the Late Formative period, that is, between 500 and 100 BC (Kowalewski et al. 1991). However, portrayals of the ballgame and ballplayers are notably rare in Zapotec art, with some of the few examples being Classic-period effigy vessels of seated ballplayers wearing heavy belts (see Whittington 2001, nos. 41–2). Of course, the bas-reliefs from the site of Dainzú, dating to roughly 100 BC, or Monte Albán II, often have been cited as portrayals of ballplayers (see Bernal 1968, 1969; Bernal & Seuffert 1979) but in fact they are not. The figures are masked and wear padding across the forearms and torso quite unlike the conventional garb of Mesoamerican ballplayers, including the cited Zapotec sculptures (Figure 17.20). In addition, they grasp small spheres in their gloved hands, with one relief showing two figures holding these items in the very same scene (Figure 17.20b). Of course, in the traditional ballgame of ancient Mesoamerica as well as its contemporary form in the state of Sinaloa in western Mexico, the rubber ball is never played with the hand. In watershed research, Heather Orr (1997; 2003, 83) notes that rather than playing the rubber ball game, the Dainzú figures are actually engaged in ritual combat with stone spheres and mentions that such objects were found both here and at Monte Albán. At Dainzú, full-figure reliefs of fighters are limited to a platform at the base of a mountain, but many heads of helmeted boxers are carved as petroglyphs on outcrops atop the same summit (see Orr 2003; Baudez 2011), suggesting a close relation between ritual boxing and mountain worship, a theme to be discussed later in terms of contemporary Guerrero. In addition, for both the mountain petroglyphs and the reliefs against the basal platform, many of the helmets are supplied with feline ears (Bernal & Seuffert 1979, 16). Moreover, two of the platform relief players have tails, quite probably alluding to jaguars as well (Figure 17.20c).

For the illustrated example of a player with a tail, the helmet displays a projecting snout and has an S-shaped scroll on the brow (Figure 17.20c). A monument from nearby Monte Albán portrays a very similar example, but along with the S-shaped motif, the muzzle is clearly fanged (Figure 17.20d). As Orr (2003, 84) astutely noted, this profile is that of Cocijo, the Zapotec god of rain and lightning. As will be recalled, for the Olmec and later Classic and Postclassic Maya, the S-shaped motif denotes a rain cloud, and this is certainly the case for the Zapotec for both Late Preclassic (Monte Albán II) and Classic periods, during which Cocijo appears

with the S-cloud motif. A pair of ceramic tubes from Cuilapan, Oaxaca, portray in all four Cocijos with S-shaped clouds as well as the exclamation (!) rain motif noted for both the Middle Formative Olmec and the contact period Aztec (Sellen 2002, 11). In addition, as noted by Weiant (1943, 97), early forms of Cocijo bear a striking resemblance to the Olmec rain god (Figure 17.21). A Monte Albán II effigy vessel portrays the head of Cocijo with S-cloud scroll ears, and its proportions strongly suggest an *olla* or water vessel (Figure 17.21d). As has been mentioned, in ancient Mesoamerica, the faces of rain gods appear on water vessels to denote them as symbolic, rain-filled clouds. Clearly enough, if Zapotec boxers dressed themselves as rain gods, pummelling their heads could only promise to bring rain, in human terms as sprays of blood and sweat.

In Classic-period Mesoamerica, one of the favoured weapons of ritual boxers was the *manopla*, a round stone with a loop-shaped handle that would entirely cover the player's fist. For both Teotihuacan and the Classic Maya, *manoplas* can appear as skulls with the mandible as the handle, quite probably a grim allusion to these objects as 'skull crackers' (Taube & Zender 2009, fig. 7.15). However, for the Classic-period Zapotec, a jaguar head with feline ears and a fanged muzzle is the favoured motif on stone *manoplas* (Figure 17.22c–e). For some examples, the exclamation-shaped element denoting liquid drops appears on the snout (Figure 17.22c–d). Such drops denote the blood of the opponent, much as if from the 'bite' of the jaguar. In addition, as has been noted for Monument 31 at Chalcatzingo, the jaguar's symbolic devouring of the combatant's blood was probably a rain-making act (see Figure 17.3c).

The remarkable Late Classic Zapotec murals from Tomb 5 at Huijazoo, Oaxaca, depict masked boxers wielding what appear to be stone *manoplas* (Figure 17.22a). The costume of the illustrated example includes a skull headdress, long bones and an inverted human trophy head, all suggestive of death and sacrifice and quite unlike the traditional gear of Mesoamerican ballplayers. For both series of boxers on the east and west walls of the main tomb chamber, the leading figure wears a feline headdress (see Miller 1995, fig. 80). In view of its orange colour and lack of spots, it is likely that in this case the feline is

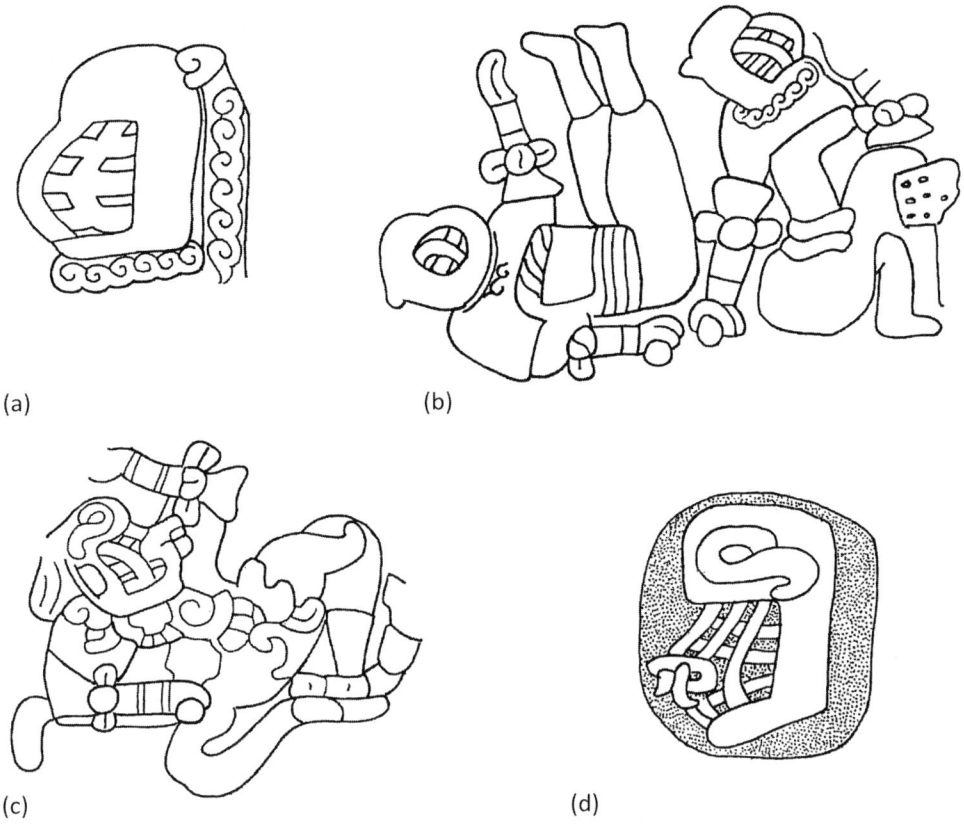

(a) (b)

(c) (d)

Figure 17.20 Late Preclassic Zapotec portrayals of helmeted boxers (drawings by author).

a) Boxer head with probable jaguar ear and cloud scrolls, Dainzú (from Taube & Zender 2009, fig. 7.4b).

b) Pair of helmeted boxers with probable jaguar ears and cloud scrolls wielding spheres with heavy gloves, Dainzú (from Taube & Zender 2009, fig. 7.4d).

c) Dainzú boxer with probable helmet of Cocijo with S-shaped cloud motif on brow; note probable feline tail (from Taube & Zender 2009, fig. 7.4e).

d) Monument portraying boxing helmet with fanged muzzle of Cocijo and S-shaped cloud on brow, Monte Albán (from Taube & Zender 2009, fig. 7.4a).

a puma rather than a jaguar. Although ritual boxing with stone *manoplas* is not documented by any contact period sixteenth-century account, such boxers probably do appear in the Late Postclassic Mixtec Codex Colombino-Becker, where men wearing heavy tunics wield white objects emitting great gouts of blood (Figure 17.22b, see Taube & Zender 2009, 191). The poses adopted by these figures are notably similar to the earlier Late Classic murals from Cerro de la Campana.

Reiko Ishihara-Brito recently informed me of a discovery of great importance in the Mixe region of eastern Oaxaca. Spelunkers in 2011 found near the Mixe community of San Isidro a cave system with over life-sized dried mud sculptures, including

jaguars, women with splayed legs and an apparent couple *in coito* (Ballensky 2012). Based on the style of the sculptures and associated ceramics, the figures probably date to roughly 200 BC, in other words, roughly contemporaneous to if not slightly earlier than Dainzú (Ballensky 2012, 8–9). In this brief preliminary report, Ballensky (2012, 8) provides images of a figure with a pronounced phallus next to a supine woman with splayed legs and a fully exposed vulva. In contrast to the other anthropomorphic sculptures, the male figure has what Ballensky describes as "animal facial features". In fact, with its fangs and furrowed brow, this figure can be identified as a local form of the Zapotec rain god, Cocijo, as the face is notably similar to a very early stone mask of Cocijo

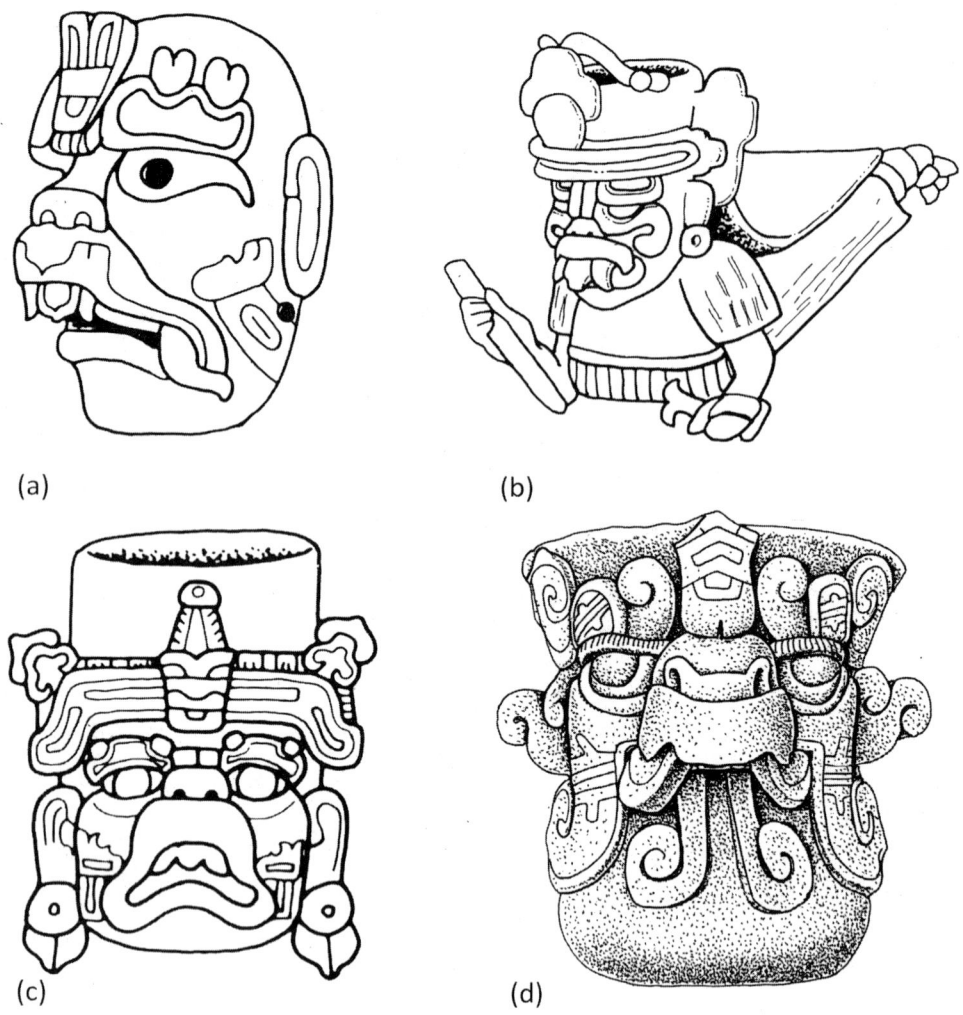

(a)

(b)

(c)

(d)

Figure 17.21 Early depictions of the Zapotec rain god, Cocijo (all drawings by author).

a) Stone mask of Cocijo, Peabody Museum of Archaeology and Ethnology, Harvard University (from Taube 2009, fig. 4d).

b) The Zapotec rain god, Cocijo, wielding weapons of lightning, San José Mogote (from Taube 2009, fig. 4b).

c) Early Zapotec Cocijo as rain jar, ca. 300 BC (from Taube 2009, fig. 4e).

d) Zapotec jar of Cocijo roughly 100 BC with rain cloud ears (from Taube 2009, fig. 4f).

in the Peabody Museum of American Ethnology and Archaeology at Harvard (see Figure 17.21a). Ballensky (2012, 8) notes that this sculpture is "a male ball-player" due to the small sphere in this upraised right arm. However, in light of Dainzú and many other aforementioned scenes in ancient Mesoamerican art, it is probably more correct to view this sculpture as an image of the rain god wielding a stone sphere for combat. The pronounced sexuality of this figure and the adjacent nude woman requires comment. In our paper concerning ancient Mesoamerican boxing, Marc Zender and I called attention to a Late Classic Maya vessel scene of the rain god Chahk grasping a stone *manopla* with his supernaturally large penis dragging on the ground below him. As we noted: "the significance of Chahk's prominent genitalia remains obscure, although it perhaps refers to the sexual virility of Chahk or boxers more generally" (Taube & Zender 2009, 186).

In view of the recently discovered cave sculptures from eastern Oaxaca, it seems that ritual boxing encompassed male virility as well as fertilising the earth. Among the contemporary Tarahumara, or Raramuri, of Chihuahua, the spring rites of Semana

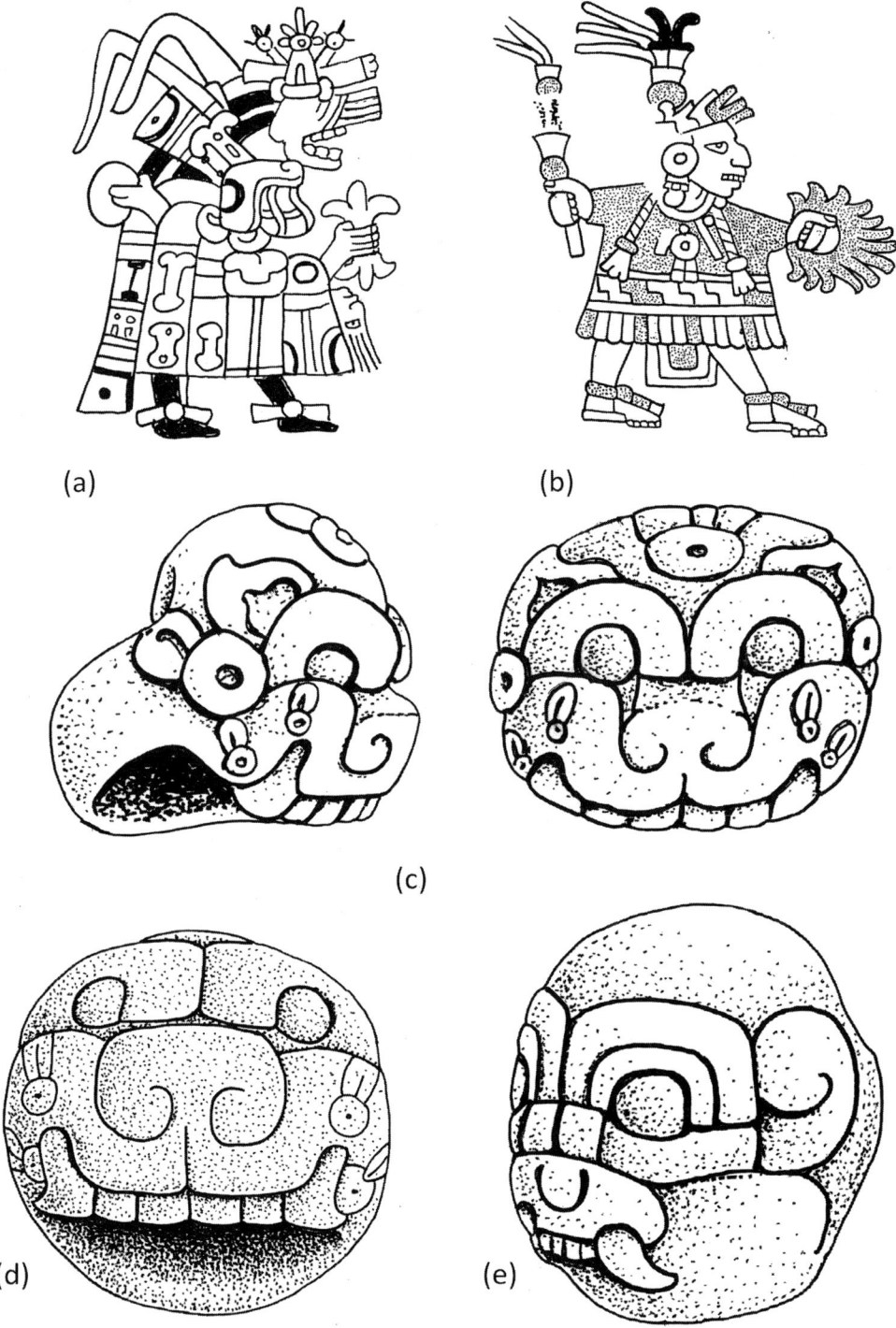

Figure 17.22 *Manoplas* of ancient Oaxaca (all drawings by author).

a) Masked boxer wielding probable *manopla*, Tomb 5, Huijazoo (from Taube & Zender 2009, fig. 17b).

b) Mixtec figure grasping probable *manopla* spurting blood, Codex Colombino-Becker, p. 12.

c) Late Classic Zapotec jaguar head *manopla* with probable drops on cheeks, attributed to Monte Albán (after Seler 1902–23, II:364).

d) Late Classic Zapotec jaguar head *manopla* with probable drops of blood on muzzle (from Taube & Zender 2009, fig. 17a).

e) Late Classic Zapotec jaguar head *manopla* (after Dunkelman 2007, no. 121).

Santa concern a ritual battle between two groups, the *soldados* and *fariseos*, concerning the resurrection of Christ and world renewal. Raúl López (1981) documented that for one community, the culmination and climax of these pre-Easter celebrations were wrestling matches between the two opposing groups in a freshly turned community field accompanied by a pronouncedly ithyphallic wooden 'Judas' sculpture charged with supernatural sexual vigour. In the final match, the victor simulated copulation over his defeated foe. Although generally not well documented, human fertility also related to the fecundity of the earth in ancient Mesoamerica.

The most graphic portrayals of ritual boxing in ancient Mesoamerica appear in Late Classic Maya art, including ceramic figurines. A remarkable corpus of ceramic boxer figurines derives from the small site of Lubaantun in southern Belize (Joyce 1933). As in the case of Zapotec boxers from Dainzú and later Cerro de la Campana, they wear heavy helmet masks. For two examples illustrated by Joyce, pairs of athletes clearly share pugilistic blows with their heavily mitted hands (Figure 17.23b–c). It is more than likely that these 'mitts' are actually protective wrapping around a *manopla* or other stone or wood weapon. According to Norman Hammond (1976, 106), the Lubaantun figurines strongly suggest competitive fighting rather than simply the ballgame: "They are shown either just standing fully accoutred, or in a close active juxtaposition that might be reasonably called 'combat'." While Marc Zender and I were preparing our paper concerning ritual boxing, Hammond (pers. comm. 2005) called our attention to a Lubaantun figurine displaying a feline ear on the side of the helmet mask, immediately recalling the Dainzú boxers as well as still earlier images of the Olmec rain god as a probable boxer (Figure 17.23a).

Aside from Lubaantun, a pair of helmeted boxer figurines wielding spheres was discovered recently in a remarkable ceramic figurine group from a Late Classic royal tomb at El Peru, located in the northern Peten of Guatemala (see Finamore & Houston 2010). Along with a third blowing a conch trumpet, the two figures are clearly dwarves, with one helmet displaying Teotihuacan shell goggles and a curved sacrificial blade and the other, a large panache of quetzal plumes, perhaps alluding to the Maya, where these feathers originate. In other words, this pair of dwarf boxers may represent an oppositional, dualistic contrast between the Maya and central Mexico. Mary Miller (pers. comm. 2015) notes that in terms of their body proportions, it is likely that many of the boxer figurines from Lubaantun are also dwarves (see Joyce 1933, pl. 3: nos. 5, 8, 11; pl. 7: nos. 15–22; pl. 8: nos. 1, 4, 5). One could readily place the theme of gladiatorial dwarves in the concept of play and humour, but combatants could have deep symbolic meaning as well, as in Mesoamerica, both children and dwarves are closely related to rain and agricultural fertility, much as if they were seed-like embodiments of germination and growth.

Aside from figurines, a number of Classic Maya vases portray scenes of ritual boxing, with one depicting a match between men dressed as the rain god Chahk and an opposing team with helmets denoting the jaguar god of the underworld, or JGU, complete with spotted jaguar ears (Figure 17.23d). Although the items in their hands resemble *manoplas*, the small, circular elements atop the weapons suggest the spikes of conch shells, recalling the knuckle-dusters of the earlier Formative Olmec. Another Late Classic vessel portrays a pair of boxers wearing spotted jaguar helmet masks while wielding what are obviously conches in their right hands, with the other hands heavily wrapped around a round object, probably a *manopla* (Figure 17.23e). One of the figures has wrapping covering much of his torso, recalling the Olmec rain god figures from San Lorenzo and La Isla (Figure 17.19a; Gillespie 2000, fig. 11).

As in the case of the Olmec and Zapotec, the Classic Maya also identified ritual boxing with jaguars, a theme surely relating to hand-held stone weapons as symbolic 'great paws'. A small stone carving in the regional museum in Retalhuleyu in the southwestern piedmont of Guatemala portrays a human hand grasping a round object, recalling the balls held by the Dainzú boxers (Figure 17.24a). The piece has a deeply carved groove near the thumb for grasping, with the other digits fitting into the other grooves of the fingers. In other words, this piece is a weapon portraying the very same device. As in the case of hand-held stone spheres, such an object would only be used in broad, swiping motions, much like the paw of a great cat. In Late Classic Maya texts

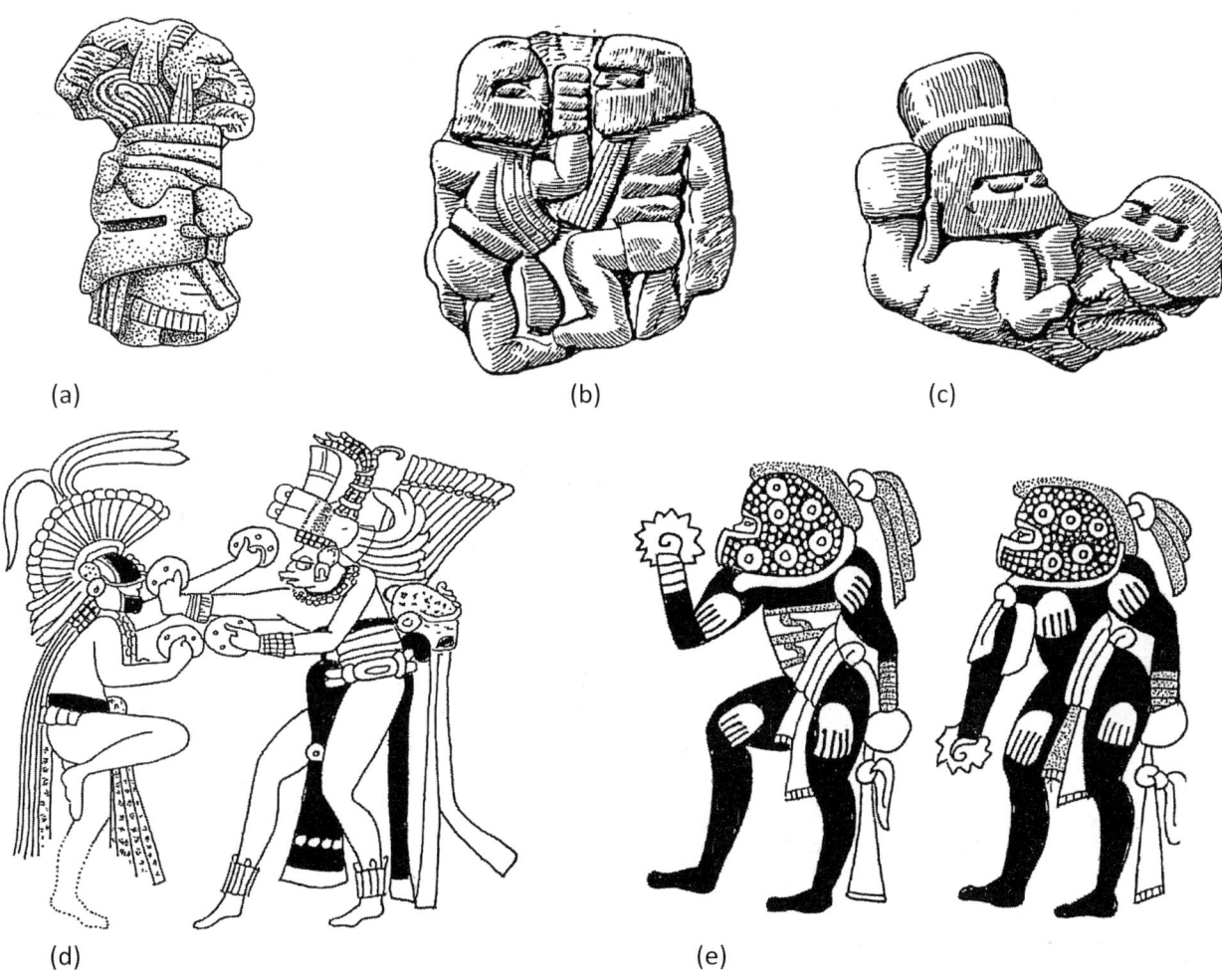

Figure 17.23 Late Classic Maya portrayals of helmeted boxers.

a) Figurine fragment of masked boxer with jaguar ear, Lubaantun (drawing by author after photo courtesy of Norman Hammond).

b) Ceramic figurine portraying boxers, Lubaantun (from Joyce 1933, pl. 8, no. 1)

c) Figurine fragment of helmeted boxers, Lubaantun (from Joyce 1933, pl. 8, no. 5).

d) Boxer wearing helmet mask of the jaguar god of the underworld fighting another dressed as the rain god Chahk, detail of Late Classic Maya vase (drawing by author from Taube & Zender 2009, fig. 7.3a).

e) Boxers with jaguar helmets wielding conch and probable bound *manoplas*, detail of Late Classic Maya vase (drawing by author from Taube & Zender 2009, fig. 7.3b).

and iconography, there are many portrayals of jaguars grasping stones, including what are probably skull *manoplas* (Figure 17.24b–c).

Aside from jaguars, the Late Classic Maya Chahk also commonly wields a stone *manopla* along with his lightning axe (Figure 17.25a, c). As in the case of the Olmec and Zapotec rain gods, Chahk is strongly feline, but also aquatic as well. Thus rather than jaguar ears, he has Spondylus shells and fish barbells for feline whiskers (Figure 17.25a; see Taube

1995, 98–9). Along with the axe, the *manopla* was surely another symbol of thunder and lightning and the bringer of fertile rain. In fact, a number of Late Classic Maya vessel scenes portray *manoplas* as the head of Chahk – true 'thunderheads' creating rain through the shedding of blood (Figure 17.25b–c). As David Stuart (2010, 289) has noted, Late Classic Maya zoomorphic portrayals of stone have "a very strong resemblance to Chahk, the animate force of rain and storms". As Stuart (2010) suggests,

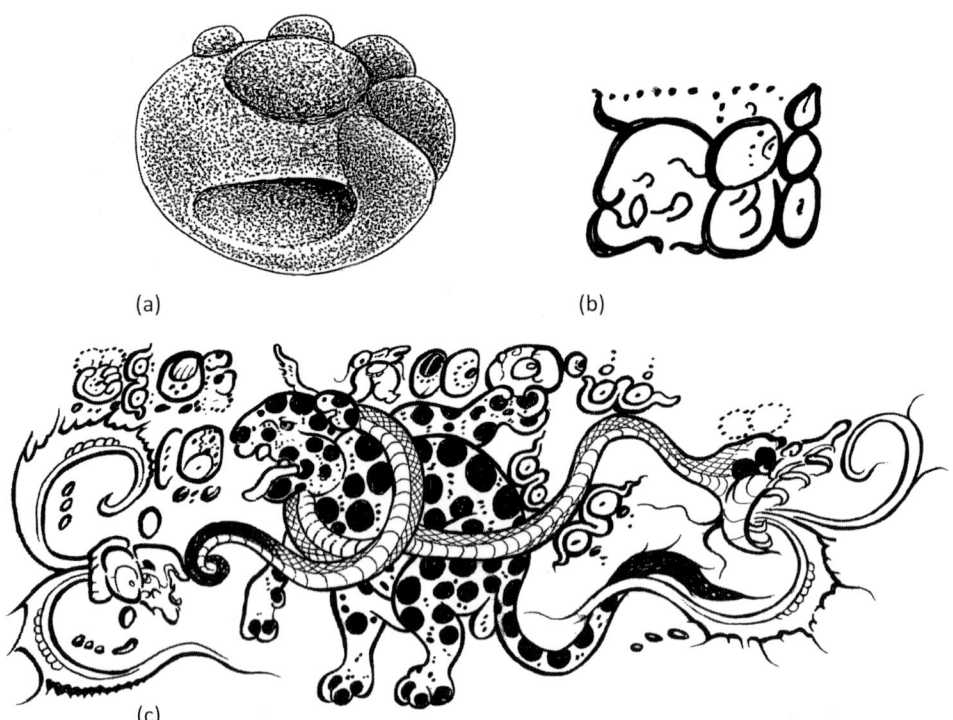

Figure 17.24 Jaguars and boxing stones.

a) Stone weapon of hand grasping a similar weapon, drawing by author of object in the Museo de Arqueología e Etnología, Retaluleu, Guatemala (from Taube & Zender 2009, fig. 7.24a).

b) Late Classic glyph of jaguar grasping stone (drawing by Marc Zender from Taube & Zender 2009, fig. 7.13g).

c) Jaguar wielding probable stone skull *manopla* (drawing by Marc Zender from Taube & Zender 2009, fig. 7.25c).

animate stones bearing the likeness of Chahk probably denote them as embodiments of lightning and I would suggest in terms of boxing, 'thunder stones'. Excavations in 2012 co-directed by Marcello Canuto of Tulane University and Tomás Barrientos of the Universidad del Valle uncovered more than 20 finely carved stairway panels with texts and scenes, including a pair featuring the local La Corona ruler facing a major king from Calakmul, Yuknoom Ch'een (see Stuart 2012). David Stuart (pers. comm. 2012) notes that the panel portraying the Calakmul ruler also bears the glyphic term *pitz*, the Mayan word for the rubber ball game. However, rather than playing ball, the two figures sit in royal ease and wear neither the thick belts nor kneepads known for the Classic Maya ballgame. Whereas the headdress of Yuknoom Ch'een is effaced, that of the local lord is of Chahk, and both rulers grasp Chahk head *manoplas* (Figure 17.25d–e). Rather than referring only to the rubber ball game, *pitz* may have been a more

inclusive term for competitive sports, including perhaps boxing as well.

A fragmentary stone *manopla* from Ek' Balam, Yucatán, features a figure holding his arm upwards with some sort of wrapping or padding covering his forearm (see Grube, Lacadena & Martin 2003, fig. 34). Although not a conventional pose for ballplayers, it is found with Classic Maya boxers (Figure 17.21b, e). The accompanying text describes the *manopla* as a *ub'aal pitz tuun*, or "his protector *pitz* stone" (Grube et al. 2003, 37–8). Among the Classic Maya, there may have been considerable thematic overlap between the ballgame and boxing, with boxing matches probably performed in ballcourts (Taube & Zender 2009, 175). A monumental bas-relief from a ballcourt at Piedras Negras portrays two ballplayers with belts and kneepads sparring with cloth-wrapped objects in their hands, perhaps *manoplas* or stone spheres used much like modern saps (Taube & Zender 2009, fig. 7.7). Of course, such boxing events in ballcourts would cause

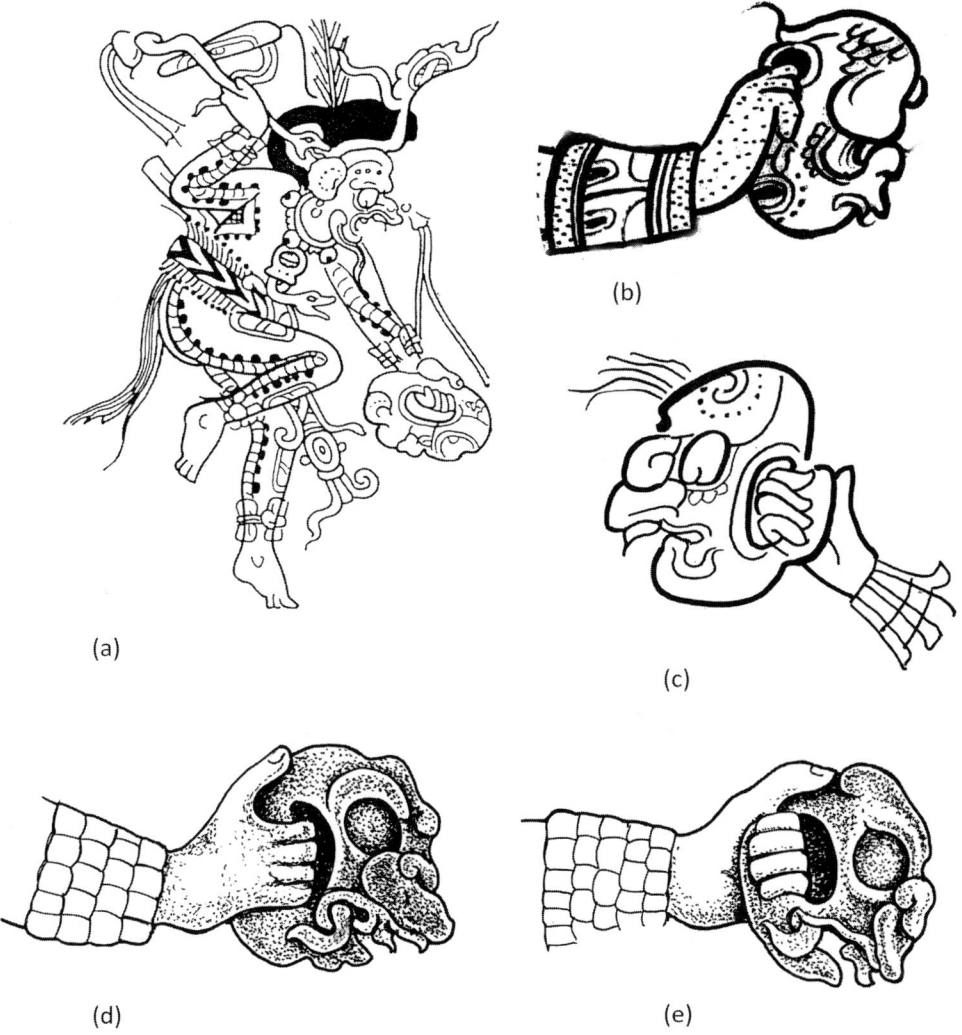

Figure 17.25 The Late Classic Maya rain god, Chahk, with stone *manoplas*.

a) Chahk wielding axe and stone *manopla*, detail of codex-style vessel (from Taube & Zender 2009, fig. 7.12b).

b) Stone *manopla* with probable head of Chahk (detail of drawing by Marc Zender in Taube & Zender 2009, fig. 7.26b).

c) Chahk head *manopla* wielded by Chahk, detail of codex-style vase (drawing by author after photograph by Justin Kerr in Kerr 1992, 459).

d)–e) Chahk head *manoplas* grasped by rulers from Calakmul and La Corona, details from recently excavated panels from La Corona, Guatemala (drawings by author).

the shedding of blood, again linking such courts to ritual rainmaking.

In her interpretation of the masked figures on the platform and hill at Dainzú, Orr (1997, 2003) called attention to rites of ritual combat currently performed in highland Guerrero. In the communities of Zitlala and Acatlán, fighters wearing jaguar helmet masks of heavy leather fight in early May as a petition for rain at the beginning of the spring rainy season (Sánchez Andraka 1983; Obregón

Téllez & Martínez Resclavo 1991; Calles Travieso 1994; Olivera 1994; Matías Alonso 1997; Dias Vasquez 2003; Zolrich 2008). For these public events, the shedding of blood is considered a symbolic rain-bringing act:

> These Tigré combats are part entertainment and part religious ritual. Many in the community believe that a fighter's spilled blood will help bring rain for the coming year's harvest. (Zolrich 2008, 46)

Figure 17.26 Ritual boxing in contemporary Guerrero (all photos by and courtesy of Sergio Garza).

a) Youths dressed as jaguars boxing atop Mount Pacho, Guerrero.

b) Adult male combatants fighting with rope 'saps', Zitlala, Guerrero.

c) Women with offerings ascending Mount Pacho for annual boxing event.

As has been discussed for the Mesoamerican ballgame, this contemporary boxing also involves mountain worship as well as ritual rainmaking. One of the places for ritual boxing is atop sacred hills, which, as Orr (1997, 2003) notes, recalls the petroglyphs of boxers on the hill directly above Dainzú (Orr 2003, 46, 48). During one recently recorded event, rites were performed at a sacred spring, reinforcing the underlying theme of water and agricultural abundance (see Zolrich 2008, 46, 48). The contemporary boxers wear leather gloves and jaguar masks bound and reinforced with baling wire. The jaguars' mouths serve as eye slits for the combatants, strongly resembling Late Classic Maya boxing helmets (Figure 17.26a, cf. Figure 17.23). For the town of Zitlala, men wear jaguar helmet masks that entirely enclose the head and fight with heavy rope clubs that can provide rib-cracking blows (Figure 17.26b).

In the illustrated images kindly provided to me by Sergio Garza, who accompanied Zach Zorich to document ritual combat in Guerrero in 2008, one can observe a wide array of emotions on the spectators' faces, from gentle bemusement for children boxing to trepidation and concern for an event several days later in Zitlala when masked men fought with the rope clubs (Figure 17.26a–b). In addition, whereas young boys do fight atop Mount Pacho, "the main attraction", according to Zorich (2008, 48), is the adult male fighters, surely not only for the spectators, but for rain-bearing clouds as well. It should also be noted that although the 'arena' of spectators at these events is typically men, women are also very much participants, and also ascend Mount Pacho with food and offerings (Figure 17.26c).

CONCLUSIONS

In terms of the topic of this volume, my contribution may seem the most divergent in terms of relating blood sport and violence to 'play'. However, in the natural world of animals, felines are well known for toying with their prey, especially if they are of diminutive size and have little opportunity for escape. In the perspective of the cat, this is indeed 'play', but obviously a captured mouse would offer a quite different opinion indeed. This is also true in terms of the ballgame and gladiatorial combat in ancient Mesoamerica, but here, as in ancient Rome, it was the far more detached audience rather than the athletes that observed this as play and even 'fun'. In this way, the ruling polity organising such events becomes the omnipotent creature enjoying the sport to its bloody conclusion.

The concept of entertainment surely relates to the cross-cultural belief – especially with state-level societies – that the concept of animals behaving as people is fundamentally amusing, as they satire with their obvious bestiality highly codified, formal norms of human behaviour. In a recent study, my wife and I noted examples of such animal/human humour for ancient Mesopotamia, Egypt and medieval Japan as well as among the Classic Maya (Taube & Taube 2009). The chapter in this volume by Roel Sterckx (Chapter 12) concerning animals and play in ancient China mentions a 'horn-butting game' (*juedi*) where the protagonists wear horned headdresses to evoke goats or bulls. For one illustrated scene, the competition seems much like a playful dance accompanied by musicians (see Figure 12.5, top right). With ritual boxing in contemporary Guerrero, it is clear that the jaguar costumes provide a signal of otherworldly fun decontextualized from daily life, a stark contrast to unmasked and well-known community members fighting it out publicly in town. As with bestial ritual clowns, it is likely that in ancient Mesoamerica, boxers dressed as jaguars were regarded with amusement as well as fear. From the play of animals to public human sport, such boxing events become something else, this being the ceremonial evocation of rain through human blood.

Aside from the obvious component of entertainment, both the ballgame and ritual boxing had an intensely religious aspect as well. Since the human body was a basic metaphor for the cosmos, blood was a most precious distillation of the waters of the world, including rain, pools and streams and the primordial salty sea. It is widely acknowledged that decapitation is a major theme in the ancient Mesoamerica ballgame. The sixteenth-century *Popol Vuh*, in addition to scenes of human skulls in rubber balls in the Maya area, as well as at El Tajín and Las Higueras in central Veracruz, clearly indicates that the severed head was metaphorically compared to the rolling ball. However, in terms of the ancient ballgame and ballcourts, there is another aspect to decapitation: it is the most efficient means of rapidly draining blood from the body. Although little discussed, it is more than likely that such rites of sacrifice were performed within the ballcourt, with the spurting blood covering much of the plastered surface, such as is described in the aforementioned account of the sacrifice of four individuals in the Aztec re-enactment of the killing of Coyolxauhqui in the mythic ballcourt of Huitzilopochtli. One scene from the South Ball Court at El Tajín graphically depicts decapitation in the court, with a sacrificial blade slicing the victim's throat (see Kampen 1972, fig. 23). Although fragmentary, it is clear that another El Tajín relief depicts decapitation within a ballcourt, along with a human skull within a ball (Kampen 1972, fig. 19a). In addition, the Great Ball Court at Chichen Itza has six panels portraying ballplayers decapitating an opponent, with the spurts of blood appearing as serpents and flowering vines (see Schele & Freidel 1991). Moreover, there is also the Great Ball Court Stone of Chichen Itza featuring the bloody decapitation of a ballplayer, as well as a rubber ball containing a skull (see Wren, Schmidt & Krochock 1989, fig. 1). The rounded form of the monument is notably similar to the seat occupied by the victim in the panel from the South Ball Court at El Tajín (see Kampen 1972: fig. 23). In addition, the Chichen Itza Great Ball Court Stone strongly suggests a ball seated halfway within a ring, immediately recalling the *itzompan* hole found in the Aztec account as well as in ancient ballcourts in the Maya region. Although purely conjectural at this point, the ballcourt rings on the central walls of Late Classic and Postclassic ballcourts may also evoke the concept of *itzompan* – a spring of fertility and abundance.

In view of architectural orientation, the abutting higher buildings as well as the presence of drains, many ballcourts seem to have been ceremonially flooded, including such Classic sites as Chinkultic and Xochicalco, as well as the Middle Formative, Olmec-style miniature court at Teopantecuantitlan. Although, it might seem far-fetched in terms of ancient architecture alone, Mesoamerican iconography and early colonial texts provide abundant evidence that ballcourts were considered verdant, watery places. In addition, their frequent orientation to a higher pyramid suggests that such a structure was considered a source of water and abundance, which would be vividly seen with the rain run-off pouring from the building into the court below. In this sense, the spring at the base of Cerro El Manatí may have been regarded as a symbolic ballcourt containing offerings of rubber balls as well as probable clubs for striking the ball.

In terms of boxing, an obvious arena would have been the ballcourt, and the aforementioned panel from Piedras Negras suggests a very strong overlap between ritual boxing and the ballgame, although at this point in time it is impossible to determine whether these were usually distinct sport events or perhaps to resolve disputes during a ballgame. Regardless, if ritual boxing or human decapitation were enacted in ballcourts, blood would have been sprayed or pooled. Leonard Ashby (pers. comm. 2013) pointed out to me the remarkable rapid spread of the colour of blood in water, as many have surely noticed while shaving. If courts were flooded even only slightly, human blood would rapidly render them as red pools. In view of the metaphor of flowing water as the veins of our bodies, in terms of flow channels and aqueducts at ancient Mesoamerican sites, where would the pounding and pulsing heart lie? It would surely be the ballcourt.

References

Aguilar, G. C. & V. M. C. Mendoza, 2007. Los señores de Zazacatla, Morelos. *Arqueología mexicana* 15(85): 16–19.

Aguilar, G. C. & V. M. C. Mendoza, 2010. Zazacatla in the framework of Olmec Mesoamerica. In *The Place of Stone Monuments: Context, Use and Meaning in Mesoamerica's Preclassic Transition*, J. Guernsey, J. E. Clark & B. Arroyo, eds., 77–95. Dumbarton Oaks, Washington, DC.

Anderson, D., 2012. The origins of the Mesoamerican ballgame: a new perspective from the northern Maya lowlands. In *The Ancient Maya of Mexico*, G. E. Braswell, ed., 43–64. Sheffield: Equinox.

Ballensky, T., 2012. Secret of Condoy: discovering Oaxaca's ancient mud sculptures. *NSS News*, September: 6–13.

Baudez, C.-F., 2011. Las batallas rituales en Mesoamérica: Parte 1. *Arqueología Mexicana* 19(112): 20–9.

Baudez, C.-F., 2012. Las batallas rituales en Mesoamérica: Parte 2. *Arqueología Mexicana* 19(113): 18–29.

Bernal, I., 1968. The ball players of Dainzú. *Archaeology* 21: 246–51.

Bernal, I., 1969. Stone reliefs in the Dainzú area. In *The Iconography of Middle American Sculpture*, 13–23. The Metropolitan Museum of Art, New York.

Bernal, I. & A. Seuffert, 1979. *The Ballplayers of Dainzú*. Akademische Druck, u. Verlagsanstalt, Graz.

Bierhorst, J., 1992. *History and Mythology of the Aztecs: The Codex Chimalpopoca*. University of Arizona Press, Tucson.

Blake, M., 2011. Building history in domestic and public space at Paso de la Amada: an examination of Mounds 6 and 7. In *Early Mesoamerican Social Transformations: Archaic and Formative Lifeways in the Soconosco Region*, R. Lesure, ed., 97–118. University of California Press, Berkeley and Los Angeles.

Borhegyi, S. F. de, 1980. The pre-Columbian ballgames: a pan-Mesoamerican tradition. *Milwaukee Public Museum Contributions in Anthropology and History* 1.

Bradley, D. E., 1991. A power player: the iconography of rulership and fertility on a Tlapacoya ballplayer. In *The Mesoamerican Ballgame*, G. W. van Bussel, P. L. F. van Dongen & T. J. J. Leyenaar, eds., 161–70. Rijksmuseum voor Volkenkunde, Leiden.

Bradley, D. E., & P. D. Joralemon, 1993. *The Lords of Life: The Iconography of Power and Fertility in Preclassic Mesoamerica*. The Snite Museum of Art, Notre Dame.

Burkitt, R., 1930. Explorations of the highlands of western Guatemala. *The Museum Journal* 21(1): 41–72.

Calles Travieso, R., 1994. *Atlzatzilistli*: Las ceremonias de petición de agua en Acatlán de Alvarez, Guerrero. In *Rituales agrícolas y otras costumbres guerrerenses (siglos XVI-XX)*, M. Matías Alonso, ed., 99–107. Centro de Investigaciones y Estudios Superiores en Antropología Social, Mexico City.

Castañeda López, C., 2008 Plazuelas, Guanajuato. *Arqueología Mexicana* 16(92): 44–7.

Cheetham, D., 2009. Early Olmec figurines from two regions: style as cultural imperative. In *Mesoamerican Figurines: Small Scale Indices Large Scale Phenomena*, C. Halperin, K. Faust, R. Taube & A. Giguet, eds., 149–79. University Press of Florida, Gainesville.

Chinchilla Mazariegos, O., 2009. Games, courts and players at Cotzumalhuapa, Guatemala. In *Blood and Beauty: Organized Violence in the Art and Archaeology of Mesoamerica and Central America*, H. Orr & R. Koontz, eds., 139–60. The Cotsen Institute of Archaeology, University of California, Los Angeles, Los Angeles.

Coe, M. D., 1965a. *The Jaguar's Children: Pre-Classic Central Mexico*. Museum of Primitive Art, New York.

Coe, M. D., 1965b. The Olmec style and its distributions. In *Handbook of Middle American Indians*, vol. 3, R. Wauchope, gen. ed., 739–75. University of Texas Press, Austin.

Coe, M. D. & R. A. Diehl, 1980. *In the Land of the Olmec: The Archaeology of San Lorenzo Tenochtitlan*, 2 vols. University of Texas Press, Austin.

Coe, M. D., & R. Koontz, 2008. *Mexico: From the Olmecs to the Aztecs*. Thames & Hudson, London.

Coe, M. D. & G. Whittaker, 1982. *Aztec Sorcerers in Seventeenth Century Mexico: The Treatise on Superstitions by Hernando Ruiz de Alarcón*. Institute for Mesoamerican Studies, State University of New York at Albany, Albany.

Covarrubias, M., 1942. Origen y desarrollo del estilo artístico 'Olmeca'. In *Mayas y Olmecas: Segunda Reunión de Mesa Redonda Sobre Problemas Antropológicos de México y Centro América*: 46–9, Tuxtla Gutiérrez.

Covarrubias, M., 1946. El arte Olmeca o de La Venta. *Cuadernos Americanos* 4: 154–79.

Covarrubias, M., 1957. *Indian Art of Mexico and Central America*, Alfred A. Knopf, New York.

Culin, S., 1907. *Games of the North American Indians*. Twenty-Fourth Annual Report of the Bureau of American Ethnology. Smithsonian Institution, Washington, DC.

Cyphers Guillén, A., 1994. San Lorenzo Tenochtitlan. In *Los Olmecas en Mesoamérica*, John Clark ed., 43–67. El Equilibrista, Mexico City.

de Jong, H. J., 1999. *The Land of Corn and Honey: The Keeping of Stingless Bees (Meliponiculture) in the Ethno-Ecological Environment of Yucatán (Mexico) and El Salvador*. Doctoral dissertation, Utrecht University, Utrecht.

Delhalle, J.-C. & A. Luykx, 1986. The Nahuatl myth of the creation of mankind: a coastal connection? *American Antiquity* 51(1): 117–21.

Días Vásquez, R., 2003. *El ritual de la lluvia en la tierra de los hombres tigre: Cambio sociocultural en una comunidad náhuatl (Acatlán, Guerrero, 1998–1999)*. Conaculta, Mexico City.

Dunkelman, A., 2007. *The J. Kislak Collection at the Library of Congress*. Library of Congress, Washington, DC.

Finamore, D. & S. D. Houston, 2010. *Fiery Pool: The Maya and the Mythic Sea*. Peabody Essex Museum, Salem.

Furst, P. T., 1968. The Olmec were-jaguar motif in the light of ethnographic reality. In *Dumbarton Oaks Conference on the Olmec*, E. P. Benson, ed., 143–74. Dumbarton Oaks, Washington, DC.

Fox, J. W., 1991. The lords of light versus the lords of dark: the Postclassic highland ballgame. In *The Mesoamerican Ballgame*, V. L. Scarborough & D. R. Wilcox, eds., 213–38. University of Arizona Press, Tucson.

García Cook, A., & B. L. Merino Carrión, 1998. Cantona: Urbe prehispánica en el altiplano central de México. In *Latin American Antiquity* 9(3): 191–216.

Garibay, A. M., 1979. *Teogonia e historia de los Mexicanos: Tres opúsculos del siglo XVI*, 3rd ed., Editorial Porrua, Mexico City.

Gillespie, S. D., 2000. The monuments of Laguna de los Cerros and its hinterland. In *Olmec Art and Archaeology: Social Complexity in the Formative Period*, J. E. Clark & M. Pye, eds., 94–115. Studies in the History of Art, vol. 58. National Gallery of Art, Washington, DC.

González, C. O. L., T. M. Córdova & S. G. Buitrago, 2011. El Monumento 41 o Triada de los Felinos, Chalcatzingo, Morelos. *Arqueología Mexicana* 19(111): 18–23.

Grove, D. C., 1970. *The Olmec Paintings of Oxtotitlan Cave, Guerrero, Mexico*. Studies in Pre-Columbian Art and Archaeology, no. 6. Dumbarton Oaks, Washington, DC.

Grove, D. C., 1984. *Chalcatzingo: Excavations on the Olmec Frontier*. Thames and Hudson, London and New York.

Grove, D. C., 1987. 'Torches', 'knuckle dusters' and the legitimization of Formative period rulership. *Mexicon* 9: 60–5.

Grube, N., A. Lacadena & S. Martin, 2003. *Chichen Itzá and Ek' Balam: Terminal Classic Inscriptions from Yucatan: The Proceedings of the Maya Hieroglyphic Workshop*, P. Wanyerka, ed., University of Texas at Austin, Austin.

Guthrie, J. (editor), 1995. *The Olmec World: Ritual and Rulership*. The Art Museum, Princeton University, Princeton, NJ.

Hammond, N., 1976. A Classic Maya ball game vase. In *Problems in Economic and Social Archaeology*, G. de G. Sieveking, I. W. Longworth & K. E. Wilson, eds., 101–8. Gerald Duckworth and Company, London.

Houston, S. D., 1998. Classic Maya depictions of the built environment. In *Function and Meaning in Classic Maya Architecture*, S. Houston, ed., 353–72. Dumbarton Oaks, Washington, DC.

Ichon, A., 1988. Le Peuplement Préhispanique. In *La Vallee Moyenne du Rio Chixoy (Guatemala): Occupation Préhispanique et Problèmes Actuels*. A. Ichon, D. Douzan-Rosenfeld & P. Usselmann, eds., 53–195. Editorial Piedra Santa, Guatemala.

Joyce, T. A., 1933. The pottery whistle-figurines of Lubaantun. *Journal of the Royal Anthropological Institute of Great Britain and Ireland* 63: 15–25.

Kampen, M. E., 1972. *The Sculptures of El Tajín, Veracruz, Mexico*. University of Florida Press, Gainesville.

Kerr, J., 1992. *The Maya Vase Book*, vol. 3. Kerr Associates, New York City.

Klein, C. F., 1987. The Ideology of Autosacrifice at the Templo Mayor. In *The Aztec Templo Mayor*, E. H. Boone, ed.: 293–370. Dumbarton Oaks, Washington, D.C.

Koontz, R., 2009. *Lightning Gods and Feathered Serpents: The Public Sculpture of El Tajín*. University of Texas Press, Austin.

Kowalewski, S. A., G. M. Feinman, L. Finsten & R. E. Blanton, 1991. Pre-Hispanic ballcourts from the Valley of Mexico. In *The Mesoamerican Ballgame*, V. L. Scarborough & D. R. Wilcox, eds., 25–44. University of Arizona Press, Tucson.

Kubler, G., 1962. *The Art and Architecture of Ancient America*. Penguin Books, Middlesex.

Lekson, S. H., 2008. *A History of the Ancient Southwest*. School for Advanced Research Press, Santa Fe.

López, R. A., 1981. Judas of the Napuchi Tarahumaras. In *Semana Santa in the Sierra Tarahumara: A Comparative Study in Three Communities*, J. G. Kennedy & R. A. López, authors, 65–77. Occasional Papers of the Museum of Cultural History, No. 4. University of California, Los Angeles.

Martínez Donjuán, G., 1994. Los Olmecas en el estado de Guerrero. In *Los Olmecas en Mesoamérica*, J. Clark, ed., 143–63. El Equilibrista, Mexico City.

Martínez Donjuán, G., 2010. Sculpture from Teopantecuanitlan, Guerrero. In *The Place of Stone Monuments: Context, Use and Meaning in Mesoamerica's Preclassic Transition*, J. Guernsey, J. E. Clark & B. Arroyo, eds., 55–76. Dumbarton Oaks, Washington, DC.

Matías Alonso, M., 1997. *La agricultura indígena en la Montaña de Guerrero*. Plaza y Valdés, Mexico City.

Miller, A., 1995. *The Painted Tombs of Oaxaca, Mexico: Living with the Dead*. Cambridge University Press, Cambridge.

Navarrete, C., T. A. Lee Jr. & C. Silva Rhoads, 1993. *Un catálogo de frontera: Esculturas, petroglifos y pinturas de la región media de Grivalva, Chiapas*. Universidad Nacional Autónoma de México, Mexico City.

Nicholson, H. B. & E. Quiñones Keber, 1991. Ballcourt images in central Mexican native tradition pictorial manuscripts. In *The Mesoamerican Ballgame*, G. W. van Bussel, P. L. F. van Dongen & T. J. J. Leyenaar, eds., 119–33. Rijksmuseum voor Volkenkunde, Leiden.

Niederberger Betton, C., 1987. *Paleopaysages et Archeologie Pre-urbaine du Bassin de Mexico*, 2 vols. Centre d'Etudes Mexicaines et Centramericaines, Mexico City.

Obregón Téllez, J. & M. Martínez Resclavo, 1991. *La montaña de Guerrero: Economía, historia y sociedad*. Instituto Nacional Indigenista, Mexico City.

Olivera, M., 1994. *Huemitl* de Mayo en Zitlala: Ofrenda para Chicomecóatl o para la Santa Cruz? In *Rituales agrícolas y otras costumbres guerrerenses (siglos XVI-XX)*, M. Matías Alonso, ed., 83–97. Centro de Investigaciones y Estudios Superiores en Antropología Social, Mexico City.

Orr, H., 1997. *Power Games in the Late Formative Valley of Oaxaca: The Ballplayer Carvings at Dainzú*. PhD dissertation, University of Texas at Austin.

Orr, H, 2003. Stone balls and masked men: ballgame as combat ritual, Dainzú, Oaxaca. *Ancient America* 5:73–104. Center for Ancient American Studies, Barnardsville.

Orr, H. & R. Koonst, 2009. *Blood and Beauty: Organized Violence in the Art and Archaeology of Mesoamerica and Central America*, The Cotsen Institute of Archaeology, University of California, Los Angeles, Los Angeles.

Ortíz, P. & M. del Carmen Rodríguez, 1994 Los espacios sagrados Olmecas: El Manatí, un caso especial. In *Los Olmecas en Mesomamérica*, J. E. Clark, ed., 69–91. El Equilibrista, Mexico City and Turner Libros, Madrid.

Ortíz, P. & M. del Carmen Rodríguez, 1999. Olmec ritual behavior at El Manatí: A sacred space. In *Social Patterns in Pre-Classic Mesoamerica*, D. C. Grove & R. A. Joyce, eds., 225–54. Dumbarton Oaks, Washington, DC.

Ortíz, P. & M. del Carmen Rodríguez, 2000. The sacred hill of El Manatí: A preliminary discussion of the site's ritual paraphernalia. In *Olmec Art and Archaeology: Social Complexity in the Formative Period*, J. E. Clark & M. Pye, eds., 297–337. Studies in the History of Art, vol. 58. National Gallery of Art, Washington, DC.

Oudijk, M. R., 2011. Elaboration and abbreviation in Mexican pictorial manuscripts. In *Their Way of Writing: Scripts, Signs, and Pictographies in Pre-Columbian America*, E. H. Boone & G. Urton, eds., 149–74. Dumbarton Oaks, Washington, DC.

Recinos, R., 1950. *Popol Vuh: The Sacred Book of the Ancient Quiché Maya*. University of Oklahoma Press, Norman.

Reilly, F. K., III, 1994. Cosmología, soberanismo y espacio ritual en la Mesoamérica del Formativo. In *Los Olmecas en Mesoamérica*, J. Clark, ed., 238–59. El Equilibrista, Mexico City.

Reilly, F. K., III, 1999. Mountains of creation and underworld portals: the ritual function of Olmec architecture at La Venta, Tabasco. In *Mesoamerican Architecture as Cultural Symbol*, J. K. Kowalski ed., 14–39. Oxford University Press, Oxford.

Robinson, E. J., 2014. The other Late Classic Maya: regionalization, defence, and boundaries in the central Guatemalan highlands. In *The Maya and Their Central American Neighbors: Settlement Patterns, Architecture, Hieroglyphic Texts, and Ceramics*, G. E. Braswell, ed., 150–74. Routledge, London.

Sabloff, J. A., 1998. Ancient Maya civilization in space and time. In *Maya*, P. Schmidt, M. de la Garza & E. Nalda, eds., 52–71. Rizzoli, New York.

Sahagún, F. B. de, 1950–82. *Florentine Codex: General History of the Things of New Spain*. A. J. O. Anderson & C. E. Dibble, trans. The School of American Research, Santa Fe.

Salazar Otregón, P., 1952 El tzompantli de Chichén Itzá, Yucatán. *Tlatoani* 5(4): 36–41.

Sánchez Andraka, H., 1983. *Zitlala: Por el mágico mundo indígena guerrerense*. Costa-Amic Editores, Mexico City.

Schaafsma, P. & K. Taube, 2006. Bringing the rain: an ideology of rain making in the Pueblo Southwest and Mesoamerica. In *A Pre-Columbian World: Searching for a Unitary Vision of Ancient America*, J. Quilter & M. Miller, eds., 231–85. Dumbarton Oaks, Washington, DC.

Schele, L. & D. A. Freidel, 1991. The courts of creation: ballcourts, ballgames and portals to the Maya otherworld. In *The Mesoamerican Ballgame*, V. L. Scarborough & D. R. Wilcox, eds., 289–315. University of Arizona Press, Tucson.

Seler, E., 1902–23. *Gesammelte Abhandlungen zur Amerikanischen Sprach- und Altertumskunde*, 5 vols. Ascher & Co., Berlin.

Sellen, A. T., 2002. Storm-god impersonators from ancient Oaxaca. *Ancient Mesoamerica* 13: 3–19.

Smith, A. L., 1961. Types of ball courts in the highlands of Guatemala. In *Essays in Pre-Colombian Art and Archaeology*, S. K. Lothrop, ed., 126–51. Harvard University Press, Cambridge, MA.

Smith, A. L., 1965. Architecture of the Guatemalan highlands. In *Handbook of Middle American Indians*, vol. 2, R. Wauchope, gen. ed., 76–94. University of Texas Press, Austin.

Stern, T., 1949. *The Rubber-Ball Games of the Americas*. Monographs of the American Ethological Society 17.

Stirling, M. W., 1955. *Stone Monuments of the Río Chiquito*. Bureau of American Ethnology, Bulletin 157. Smithsonian Institution, Washington, DC.

Stone, A., 2002. Spirals, ropes and feathers: the iconography of rubber balls in Mesoamerican art. *Ancient Mesoamerica* 13(1): 21–39.

Stuart, D., 2010. Shining stones: observations on the ritual meaning of early Maya stelae. In *The Place of Stone Monuments: Context, Use and Meaning in Mesoamerica's Preclassic Transition*, J. Guernsey, J. E. Clark & B. Arroyo, eds., 283–98. Dumbarton Oaks, Washington, DC.

Stuart, D., 2012. Notes on a new text from La Corona. *Maya Decipherment: A Weblog on the Ancient Maya Script* (Decipherment.wordpress.com/…/notes-on-a-new-text-from-la-corona, posted June 30, 2012).

Taladoire, E., 2001. The architectural background of the pre-Hispanic ballgame: an evolutionary perspective. In *The Sport of Life and Death: The Mesoamerican Ballgame*, E. M. Wittington, ed., 96–115. Thames and Hudson, London and New York.

Taladoire, E., 2012. Las representaciones bi y tridimensionales de juegos de pelota en Mesoamérica. *Arqueología Mexicana* 29: 18–27.

Taube, K. A., 1986. The Teotihuacan cave of origin: the iconography and architecture of emergence mythology in Mesoamerica and the American Southwest. *Res: Anthropology and Aesthetics* 12: 51–82.

Taube, K. A., 1992. Uses of sport, book review of *The Mesoamerican Ballgame* by V. Scarborough and D. R. Wilcox, *Science* 256: 1064–5.

Taube, K. A., 1993. *Aztec and Maya Myths*. British Museum Press, London.

Taube, K. A., 1994. The iconography of Toltec period Chichen Itza. In *Hidden among the Hills: Maya Archaeology of the Northwestern Yucatan Peninsula*, H. J. Prem, ed., 212–46. Acta Mesoamericana 7, Verlag von Flemming, Möckmühl.

Taube, K. A., 1995. The rainmakers: the Olmec and their contribution to Mesoamerican belief and ritual. In *The Olmec World, Ritual and Rulership*, G. Guthrie, ed: 82–103. The Art Museum, Princeton University.

Taube, K. A., 2004. *Olmec Art at Dumbarton Oaks*. Dumbarton Oaks, Washington, DC.

Taube, K. A., 2005. Representaciones del paraíso en el arte cerámico del Clásico Temprano de Escuintla, Guatemala. In *Iconografía y escritura teotihuacana en la costa sur de Guatemala y Chiapas*, O. Chinchilla & B. Arroyo, eds., 33–54. U tz'ib, Serie Reportes, Vol. 1, No. 5: Asociación Tikal, Guatemala City.

Taube, K. A., 2009. El dios de la lluvia Olmeca. *Arqueología Mexicana* 16(96): 26–9.

Taube, K. A. & R. B. Taube, 2009. The beautiful, the bad, and the ugly: aesthetics and morality in Maya figurines. In *Mesoamerican Figurines: Small Scale Indices Large Scale Phenomena*, C. Halperin, K. Faust, R. Taube & A. Giguet, eds., 236–58. University Press of Florida, Gainesville.

Taube, K., & M. Zender, 2009. American gladiators: ritual boxing in ancient Mesoamerica. In *Blood and Beauty: Organized Violence in the Art and Archaeology of Mesoamerica and Central America*, H. Orr & R. Koontz, eds., 161–220. The Cotsen Institute of Archaeology, University of California, Los Angeles, Los Angeles.

Tezozomoc, H. A., 1944. *Crónica mexicana*. Editorial Leyenda, Mexico City.

Thompson, J. E. S., 1970. *Maya History and Religion*. University of Oklahoma Press, Norman.

Uriarte, M. T., 2001. Unity in duality: the practice and symbols of the Mesoamerican ballgame. In *The Sport of Life and Death: The Mesoamerican Ballgame*, E. M. Wittington, ed., 40–59. Thames and Hudson, London and New York.

Weiant, C. W., 1943. *An Introduction to the Ceramics of Tres Zapotes, Veracruz, Mexico*. Bureau of American Ethnology, Bulletin 139. Smithsonian Institution, Washington, DC.

Whittington, E. M., ed., 2001. *The Sport of Life and Death: The Mesoamerican Ballgame*. Thames and Hudson, London and New York.

Wilcox, D. R., 1991. The Mesoamerican ballgame in the American Southwest. In *The Mesoamerican Ballgame*, V. L. Scarborough & D. R. Wilcox, eds., 101–25. University of Arizona Press, Tucson.

Wren, L., P. Schmidt & R. Krochock, 1989. The Great Ball Court Stone at Chichén Itzá. *Research Reports on Ancient Maya Writing* 25.

Zolrich, Z., 2008. Fighting with jaguars, bleeding for rain. *Archaeology* 61(6): 46–52.

18

RITUALS, GAMES AND LEARNING

EVANGELOS KYRIAKIDIS

INTRODUCTION

Rituals and games are two types of activities that, in archaeology, are very difficult indeed to distinguish. This in the past has led many, this author included, to support the view that these activities are very similar. Certainly it is true that both rituals and games are different ways to crystalise action. But I would now support further that we can distinguish between these two types of activity. In this chapter, I will compare the two and identify a number of differences which are symptomatic of one profound distinction between them: whereas participants in rituals have an overall passive 'intention-in-action', participants in games are constantly engaged actively. As will be argued, both rituals and games are strong learning mechanisms; yet this difference in engagement affects the ways that the two function as such, and therefore also affects the ways in which rituals and games can be used.

Firstly, however, a definition for the terms *ritual* and *game* should be offered.

Ritual is a category of action that has many definitions and almost every researcher uses the term in a different way. Although the lack of a single definition has occasionally been seen as a good thing (see Bell 2008, 277–88), this is a major hindrance to any meaningful study of this category of action. For the purposes of this chapter, I will employ my own definition of the term, which I have been using since 2004. According to this definition (Kyriakidis 2008, 289–94):

'Ritual' is an etic (Lett 1990, 127–9) *category that refers to set activities with a special (not-normal)*

intention-in-action, and which are specific to a group of people. Without intending to justify this definition, which I have done elsewhere (Kyriakidis 2008, 289–94), it is worth commenting that ritual being an *etic* category means that we can only use it for analytical purposes, as we shall indeed do here, and not expect that all performers are aware they are performing a ritual.

'Game' is, indeed, a set activity that is specific to a group of people and again has a special intention-in-action. Yet games, as we shall see, are 'set' in a different way from rituals, and they have a different 'special' intention-in-action.

A distinction is drawn here between game and play. I take the former to be set and often institutionalised, and the latter to refer to any playful activity, a larger category of action that includes games. This chapter will focus only on games and their relation to rituals.

These distinctions do not preclude, however, the possibility that the two activities can often occur together. It is possible to have a ritual package, such as a funeral, with games amongst its elements, such as the funerary games in Patroclus' funeral as described by Homer in *Iliad 23*. It is also possible to have games as packages, such as the sport of baseball, with mini-rituals as elements, such as the rituals baseballers perform before batting.

COMPARING RITUALS AND GAMES

The apparent similarity between the two types of action is mainly due to the fact that both are set, or '**crystallised**' activities, as I prefer to call them.

'Crystallised' action refers to those types of activity that we can most readily trace in archaeology; this is because of their repetitive nature, which is more likely to leave material patterns that will be traceable in the archaeological record.

By 'set' or 'crystallised' ritual activity, summarising Bell (1997, 138–69), we imply that it is a repeated, invariant, rule-governed, formal activity, with an 'air of tradition'. This is a common denominator of most, although not all rituals, and every trait is graded, i.e. it is a variable which can be present to a greater or lesser extent: there are some rituals that are not repeated, and therefore are not invariant (such as the coronation of Alfonso XI – Linehan 1994, 309–27); there are rituals that have no 'air of tradition' and so on. Yet all of these traits are important to and characterise most rituals.

This group of graded aspects of ritual defines the way in which ritual is set. For example, ritual has a predetermined goal and a predetermined (desired) outcome. While achievement of the desired 'result' in ritual is not a definitive criterion of ritual, the specific result desired is definitive of that ritual. This means that when the desired outcome is not achieved (whether immediately or deferred in time), the action fails to be classified as *that* ritual. If for example, an individual fails to succeed in a rite of passage, the rite has not occurred. If the animal to be sacrificed escapes, no sacrifice has been performed,[1] despite all the preparations and the attendance. If in a graduation ceremony no awards or diplomas are bestowed, no graduation ceremony has been performed. Symbolism is widely used in rituals.

Game is a different type of 'crystallised' activity. Most games are repeated, but are never invariant in their form or outcome. There is a finite set of possible results for a game, yet they are highly variable. They are always rule-governed, and this is perhaps their most important trait. Formality and the 'air of tradition' do not characterise a lot of them, though some make use of these traits. It is thus the aim for the participants of a game to achieve the game's predetermined goals (e.g. win), yet the outcome (whether or how and who will achieve these goals) is not predetermined. Finally, 'symbolism' or representation, as with rituals, is widely used in most games.

The *special intention-in-action* (for ritual, see Humphrey & Laidlaw 1994, 70–1) can be found both in games and in rituals. The rules of the games and of rituals separate them from the quotidian, and render them special. Very often this 'special' comes to mean non-contiguous (in the causality sense), irrational, illogical etc., to the etic observer, the outsider. The aims of the ritual (e.g. to make rain) or of the game (e.g. to achieve checkmate in chess) are achieved through non-contiguous means, departing from the everyday and following the internal rules of the ritual and game respectively.

This is related to and may result in what Bourdieu calls *doxa* (1972, 164, 167, 169). As Bloch (1989, 45) puts it, "you cannot argue with a song," and you cannot argue with a ritual either. When you decide to start the performance of a ritual, if you intend your action to be successful, you cannot alter significantly (with few exceptions) what you set out to do. Once you start, you choose to become a follower; you do not strategise your next move as you do constantly in a game; you do not need to make decisions along the way, but rather you follow a prescribed path.

In games, you intend to achieve their goal, and with every step you take you need to think and, within the rules, act independently. This affects the 'intention-in-action' that Humphrey and Laidlaw insightfully comment on (1994, 70–1) in their book on the ritual of the Jain Puja. Both ritual and games are special actions, in that they are separated from the mundane world, yet participants in ritual are *followers* who intend to be faithful to a prescribed path whereas participants in games are *players* who intend to actively achieve the game's goals (win). The latter are active (in being required to respond to unpredictable variation, which is central to the game), in comparison to the former, who are mostly passive (in being required to adhere to a prescribed set of actions with minimal intended variation). This, I believe, is the essence of the difference between the two types of activity, and it is connected to the different types of outcome the two have, as we have commented earlier in this chapter.

To recapitulate, both games and rituals are *special* (not mundane), *set* activities, being both repeated, rule-governed and making a wide use of

representation. They are entirely dissimilar, however, in that they have different ways of participation
(active vs. passive), and as a result are distinct in every
way, having ultimately different types of outcomes.

Risk

A further notable characteristic of rituals and games
which is of relevance here is that both are often associated with risk. Risk is a common attribute of all
games and a large number of rituals. The association
between games and risk is easier to demonstrate,
since their end is not predetermined. This means that
game participants do not know whether they will
achieve its goals (and win), nor do they know how
any other players will perform. In a game the future
is unknown. The fact that ritual is a set category with
a predetermined course of action may make it seem
free of risk. There are several reasons why this is not
the case.

Firstly, we mentioned that ritual is an etic category, i.e. an observer's category, not primarily an initiate's/insider's category. It is mainly for the observer
that ritual is a set category. For initiates, and especially lower-level or new initiates, rituals can often
give a false sensation of uncertainty as to what happens next. Only those who can see outside the box,
often in the higher echelons of initiation, may be
aware of ritual invariance.

Secondly, the successful performance of the ritual is not itself predetermined. It cannot be known
in advance whether a liturgy will be completed, or
whether a bull will be sacrificed. We are not abso-
lutely sure whether the Orthodox patriarch in
Jerusalem will come out of the inner chamber of the
Church of the Holy Sepulchre, apparently the tomb
of Christ, with the 'holy fire' the day before Easter as
he has been doing every year for the past millennium
(Peters 1985, 262). Ritual failure[2] commonly refers to
this type of uncertainty.

Moreover, ritual is often associated with risk,
although ritual itself may not be uncertain. There
may be uncertainty about whether a sacrifice is
going to be accepted by the gods, even if the performance of the sacrifice itself has been completed

successfully, or about whether the performance of
a divination ritual will have the desired result. It is
impossible to know that a magic spell will have the
intended effect when cast. In this respect, risk is not
part of the ritual but associated with it; it is an aftermath of ritual. It is this association with risk that is
the most common in rituals.

The first two categories correspond to Howe's
(2000, 69) intrinsic types of risk (will the performance of the rite be successful, will the ritual be a
ritual or not?), whereas the last category is extrinsic (will the gods appreciate the sacrifice or not?).
In games the risk is primarily of the intrinsic kind,
though there are occasions when extrinsic risk may
be involved (e.g. that the audience will not like it).

RITUALS AND GAMES AS LEARNING MECHANISMS

Due to the common features described previously
in this chapter, as well as some others, both types
of action constitute an agglomeration of learning
mechanisms. It was in this context that risk was
explained as an element of both rituals and games.
It goes without saying that some representatives of
each category are particularly powerful examples of
such mechanisms.

New Background and Learning

A first instance of this is that both in ritual and games
the participant enters a new world (metaphorically
'exits' the mundane world), with new rules and a
series of new experiences perceived through the
senses. Both games and rituals are made to be different; their rules are a departure from the everyday,
and the experiences they offer are also different. It is
the special intention-in-action that sets things apart
from the quotidian.

Creating a new setting makes it very likely that
new associations will also be created and that *blocking*
will be weakened. The concept of *blocking* (Kamin
1969, 242–59) refers to the process by which the
association of a reinforcer with a second stimulus is

blocked (or hindered) once there already has been an association between that reinforcer with another stimulus. For example, the association between a bell (stimulus) and food arriving (reinforcer) is hindered if there has already been an association between a light (a second stimulus) and food arriving (reinforcer). In other words, what you have learnt is difficult to change because of blocking. With a change of background or context associations between previously reinforced stimuli and new reinforcers are again possible, i.e. blocking is weaker. This means that the difficult task of changing one's habits or altering one's knowledge is easier because of this special environment that game players or ritual participants enter. In the new environment, as McLaren and colleagues (1994, 387–400) have shown, the bonds of conditioning are not as strong and new associations are more likely to take place. Once new conditioning takes place, however, generalisations to normal, everyday environments may transfer the new knowledge acquired (Ceci 1990, 178).

Furthermore, learning is stronger in new environments that games and rituals often provide because habituation is weaker. Habituation is often linked with blocking and means the lack of attentiveness when a stimulus appears (after several instances of repetition); we have all benefited from habituation when an annoying sound is repeated at length, and our brains just 'switch off' and stop paying any attention after a while. This lack of attentiveness also acts against learning, as the stimulus is not given attention. Yet, as McLaren and colleagues (1994, 387–400) have shown, the greater the variance in the 'background' or 'context', the less the habituation of the stimulus, and thus this stimulus is more easily associated with a reinforcer. In other words, the greater the departure from the everyday context that often both games and rituals provide to new players/performers, the more powerful the learning during that activity.

This change of environment can also confirm and fortify existing knowledge, because the more backgrounds one conditioning takes place in, the stronger the connection between stimulus and reinforcer becomes. This means that if something is known from everyday life and it is confirmed in the different environment of rituals or games, this piece of knowledge will be fortified.

In short, the changing background, or the 'special intention-in-action' provides for an environment where learning is possible and can be stronger, confirming or going against what was known from everyday life.

Other Common Ritual and Game Traits as Mechanisms for Learning

As mentioned earlier, both rituals and games are repetitive, rule-governed activities that make a wide use of representation or 'symbolism'. It goes without saying that *repetition* is one of the strongest learning mechanisms, forming the basis of classical conditioning, demonstrated experimentally since the times of Pavlov (1927; Rescorla 1967, 71–80). This does not need introducing here. But it is important to add that repetition forms a positive predisposition towards both rituals and games, making them familiar and consequently reassuring (Zajonc & Markus 1982, 125–7). And this reassuring environment makes for a more comfortable learning environment.

Rule governance is mainly responsible for setting both rituals and games apart from the mundane. It is also an independent learning mechanism as it limits possible action. In a rule-governed environment humans are much more likely to be able to extrapolate and then memorise the next possible step, much as an oral performer can more easily remember verse that has a rhythm, a rhyme and a certain formulaic system (Silk 1987, 14–21). Thus the ritual performer can memorise the ritual more easily when there are rules that bind the action, and similarly the game player can learn to strategise, but also learn the rules of the game better due to the fact that there are a finite number of possible next steps (Acker 1998, xv).

Symbolism or representation is a way to 'import' information into an activity in a powerful way. Although not widely recognised as a learning mechanism, *representation* facilitates learning as it creates material representatives of immaterial or remote signifieds. An icon of the crucifix in Christian church rituals and its participation in ritual creates a visual link between the participant and the crucifix in the

narrative, thus making it much easier for the participant to comprehend and internalise the respective
narrative, much like the representation of different
characters of varied in and out of game importance,
such as king, queen and pawns in chess.

Risk, or rather uncertainty, is recognised as a very
strong learning mechanism. Indeed, the aforementioned concept of blocking (Kamin 1969, 242–59)
in psychology was crucial for identifying the value
of uncertainty in conditioning (learning). Pearce and
Hall (1980, 532–52) have extensively argued that the
effects of 'blocking' do indeed take place, but due to
a different mechanism from the one just mentioned.
They have argued that the first time the light-
stimulus appears, there is heightened attention (and
therefore faster learning) on the part of the beholder,
due to the uncertainty of what this stimulus is to
be associated with. Once a stimulus (light) has been
associated with a reinforcer (food), then attention
is reduced and further associations are hindered.
According to Pearce and Hall, therefore, uncertainty
about what comes next is a mechanism that height-
ens attention and facilitates learning. Their argument
is too complicated to present here fully, but it suffices
to say that "the more uncertain an animal is about
a stimulus, the faster it learns about that stimulus"
(Dayan & Yu 2003, 176–7). Risk is therefore a strong
learning mechanism.

No matter whether one is a player or a follower,
both rituals and games (Csikszentmihalyi 1990,
72) often create a sense of effortless attending, what
Mihaly Csikszentmihalyi has termed *flow*, where
"one acts with a deep but effortless involvement that
removes from awareness the worries and frustrations
of everyday life. *Flow* assists attention and therefore
learning by helping to focus effortlessly, whilst creating 'a sense of deep enjoyment'" (49). *Flow* is a powerful learning tool that both rituals and games share.

Thus, both game and ritual are agglomerations
of mnemonic mechanisms for the various reasons
explained previously. Some also use *mood evocation*,
which makes for even more memorable experiences. Indeed a number of sensory arousal stimuli,
such as incense, muscle pain (Rose & Orlowski
1983, 131–5), vertigo (Gell 1980, 219–48), singing
or chanting (Bloch 1989, 45) and music in general

(Trainor & Trehub 1992, 464), are all good mood-
evoking mechanisms commonly employed by both
rituals and games. Music, in particular, has seen a
lot of study in the field, with the 'emotional meaning theory' asserting that music "elicits emotional
responses in listeners" (Krumhansl 1997, 336), with
good experimental backing (Goldstein 1980, 126–9).

Sensory arousal and mood evoking not only help
create an environment/background that is separated
from the everyday, but they also create more memorable experiences. More importantly, when they
occur at a certain level of intensity, they help learning directly. Above a certain level, however, learning speed decreases (Yerkes & Dodson 1908, 480–1).
This means that sensory arousal and mood evoking
that is the result of the aforementioned stimuli are
strong learning mechanisms, i.e. they are learning
mechanisms in three different respects. They cannot,
however, be considered crucial for our analysis here,
because they are deliberately used in only some, not
most rituals and games.

Conclusions

To sum up, both rituals and games are powerful
agglomerations of learning mechanisms and often
employ additional, very strong, mechanisms. Both
activities facilitate the absorption of related information in similar ways. However, there is one significant difference between the two activities, i.e. the
passive vs. the active participation, and this affects
the means of learning. Learning through ritual takes
place passively, without the need for, or even possibility of, constant engagement. Learning through
games implies a constantly engaged process.

This means that each activity lends itself as a
learning mechanism for different fields of knowledge and different types of people. Information that
should not be questioned at all, for example, such
as some religious or cultural information, or a leader's political authority, is best presented or absorbed
through ritual. Further research must be conducted
on the role of rituals in the teaching of individuals
with different social skills (most prominently individuals with autism).

Games are already gaining ground in school and university curricula, and there is a growing call for their more widespread use (Aldrich 2005; Salen Tekinbas 2007; Ferrera 2012), especially following the realisation that some of them, most prominently those called 'massively multiplayer online role-playing games' (MMO RPGs), have been particularly successful not only in passing information to participants, but also mobilising an enormous number of participants to action (issues beyond the scope of this chapter) (Gee 2003).

The power of rituals has not been discussed in recent education discourse to my knowledge, despite the fact that in some specific circumstances they may be appropriate. Designing a game or a ritual purely for educational purposes ought to be very well studied, however, due to the possibly unwanted information that may be absorbed by the participants.

NOTES

This chapter would not have been possible without the creative discussions and debates I have had over the years with several people, including Nicholas McIntosh, Colin Renfrew, Ian Hodder, Kate Plaisted-Grant, Caroline Humphrey and James Laidlaw, whom I would like to thank sincerely. Of course any mistakes remain my own. In particular, I would like to dedicate this chapter to Colin Renfrew on his eightieth birthday. He has been the person with whom I have conversed, with whom I have disagreed and from whom I have learned about ritual, more than any other.

1 Here the reader will notice that I do not mention the purpose of the sacrifice, e.g. for victory in battle, because even if no victory is bestowed, the sacrifice will have still taken place. In this and several other instances, the 'purpose' of the ritual is not part of the ritual nor its definitive trait.

2 It is important here to explain what is meant by ritual failure. A specific ritual, e.g. a Sunday church liturgy, can be seen as a category in its own right. Categories have specific traits that are necessary for an item's classification as such and are called definitive criteria: Sunday church liturgies have to occur both on a Sunday and in church; otherwise, if planned under that rubric and not satisfying these two conditions, they cannot be classified as such and will fail. A human sacrifice, to use an extreme, has two main ingredients, death and humans; if a rabbit is slaughtered instead, or if a human is involved but does not die, the intended ritual fails. There are also additional traits that are not crucial for membership in that category: the priest does not have to read all the hymns correctly to the letter in order for the Sunday church service to be classified as such. Failing in one of the non-crucial traits of ritual does not constitute ritual failure, but rather a deviation.

BIBLIOGRAPHY

Acker, P., 1998. *Revising Oral Theory: Formulaic Composition in Old English and Old Icelandic Verse* [Garland Studies in Medieval Literature 16]. New York: Garland Publishing.

Aldrich, C., 2005. *Learning by Doing: A Comprehensive Guide to Simulations, Computer Games, and Pedagogy in e-Learning and Other Educational Experiences.* San Francisco, CA: John Wiley and Sons Inc.

Bell, C., 1997. *Ritual Perspectives and Dimensions.* Oxford: Oxford University Press.

Bell, C., 2008. Response: Defining the need for a definition, in *The Archaeology of Ritual*, ed. E. Kyriakidis. Los Angeles, CA: The Cotsen Institute of Archaeology Publications, 277–88.

Bloch, M., 1989. *Ritual, History and Power: Selected Papers in Anthropology.* London: Athlone Press

Bourdieu, P., 1972. *Outline of a Theory of Practice*, translated by R. Nice 1977. Cambridge: Cambridge University Press.

Brabham, D., 2008. Crowdsourcing as a model for problem solving: an introduction and cases. *Convergence: The International Journal of Research into New Media Technologies* 14:1, 75–90.

Ceci, S., 1990. *On Intelligence: A Bioecological Treatise on Intellectual Development.* Cambridge, MA: Harvard University Press.

Csikszentmihalyi, M., 1990. *Flow: The Psychology of Optimal Experience.* New York: Harper and Row.

Dayan, P. & Yu, A., 2003. Uncertainty and learning. *Neuroscience* 49:2, 171–81.

Ferrera, J., 2012. *Playful Design: Creating Game Experiences in Everyday Interface.*, Rosenfeld.

Flad, R. 2008. Divination and power: a multiregional view of the development of oracle bone divination in early China. *Current Anthropology* 49:3, 403–37.

Gee, J., 2003. *What Video Games Have to Teach Us about Learning and Literacy.* New York: Palgrave McMillan

Gell, A., 1980. The gods at play: vertigo and possession in Muria religion. *MAN: The Journal of the Royal Anthropological Institute* (New Series) 15, 219–48.

Goldstein, A., 1980. Thrills in response to music and other stimuli. *Physiological Psychology* 8, 126–9.

Humphrey, C. & Laidlaw, J., 1994. *The Archetypal Actions of Ritual: A Theory of Ritual Illustrated by the Jain Rite of Worship* (Oxford Studies in Social and Cultural Anthropology). Oxford: Clarendon Press.

Kamin, L., 1969. Predictability, surprise, attention, and conditioning, in *Punishment and Aversive Behavior*, eds. B. Campbell & R. Church. New York: Appleton-Century-Crofts, 242–59.

Krumhansl, C., 1997. An exploratory study of musical emotions and psychophysiology. *Canadian Journal of Experimental Psychology* 51:4, 336–52.

Kyriakidis, E., 2002. *Ritual and Its Establishment: The Case of Some Minoan Open-Air Rituals*. PhD thesis, University of Cambridge.

Kyriakidis, E., 2005. *Ritual in the Aegean: The Minoan Peak Sanctuaries*. London: Duckworth.

Kyriakidis, E., 2008. The Archaeologies of Ritual, in *The Archaeology of Ritual*, ed. E. Kyriakidis. Los Angeles, CA: Cotsen Institute of Archaeology Publications, 289–306.

Lett, J., 1990. Emics and etics: notes on the epistemology of anthropology. In *Emics and Etics. The Insider/Outsider Debate*, eds. T. Headland, K. Pike & M. Harris (Frontiers of Anthropology vol. 7). Newbury Park, CA: Sage Publications, 127–42.

Linehan, P., 1994. The mechanisation of ritual: Alfonso XI of Castille in 1332. In *Riti e Rituali Nelle Società Medievali*, eds. J. Chiffoleau, L. Martines & A. Paravicini Bagliani. Spoleto: Centro Italiano di Studi Sull'Alto Medioevo, 309–27.

Marcus, J., 2006. The roles of ritual and technology in Mesoamerican water management, in *Agricultural Strategies*, eds. J. Marcus and C. Stanish [Monograph 50]. Los Angeles, CA: Cotsen Institute of Archaeology Publications, 221–54.

McLaren, I., Bennett, C., Plaisted, K., Aitken, M. & Mackintosh, N., 1994. Latent inhibition, context specificity, and context familiarity. *Quarterly Journal of Experimental Psychology* 47B, 387–400.

Nikolaidou, M., 2008. Ritualised technologies in the Aegean Neolithic? The crafts of adornment, in *The Archaeology of Ritual*, ed. E. Kyriakidis. Los Angeles, CA: Cotsen Institute of Archaeology Publications, 221–54.

Pavlov, I., 1927. *Conditional Reflexes*. New York: Dover Publications.

Pearce, J. & Hall, G., 1980. A model for Pavlovian learning: variation in the effectiveness of conditioned but not unconditioned stimuli. *Psychological Review* 87, 532–52.

Peters, F., 1985. *Jerusalem: The Holy City in the Eyes of Chroniclers, Visitors, Pilgrims and Prophets from the Days of Abraham to the Beginning of Modern Times*. Princeton, NJ: Princeton University Press.

Rescorla, R., 1967. Pavlovian conditioning and its proper control procedures. *Psychological Review* 74, 71–80.

Rose, S. & Orlowski, J., 1983. Review of research on endorphins and learning. *Journal of Developmental Behavioural Pediatrics* 4:2, 131–5.

Salen Tekinbas, K., 2007. *The Ecology of Games: Connecting Youth, Games, and Learning* (The John D. and Catherine T. MacArthur Foundation Series on Digital Media and Learning).

Silk, M., 1987. *Homer: The Iliad*. Cambridge: Cambridge University Press.

Trainor, L. & Trehub, S., 1992. The development of referential meaning in music. *Music Perception* 9:4, 455–70.

Yerkes, J. & Dodson, J., 1908. The relation of strength of stimulus to rapidity of habit-formation. *Journal of Comparative Neurology and Psychology* 18, 459–82.

Zajonc, R. & Markus, H., 1982. Affective and cognitive factors in preferences. *Journal of Consumer Research* 9, 123–31.

PART IV

FROM PLAY TO FAITH?
DISCUSSION

PLAY AND RITUAL: SOME THOUGHTS FROM A MATERIAL-CULTURE PERSPECTIVE

LAMBROS MALAFOURIS

The aim of this brief commentary is simply to bring together some of the main ideas and threads of evidence presented in this volume and use them to rethink how we know what we know and reflect on what it is that we know about play and ritual. I plan to do this mainly by focusing on some recurring themes (definitional, methodological, comparative and developmental) that I believe provide fertile ground for cross-disciplinary interaction. This cross-disciplinary interaction, which I see as one of the distinctive features of this book, will also help us to understand better the developmental and material basis of play and ritual as well as to shed new light on the nature of the relationship between them. In my review of those themes I adopt a material culture perspective. In particular, my underlying assumption is that the sort of things, physical qualities and objects we often classify in archaeology under the banner of material culture are extremely important for the constitution of both play and ritual; yet they remain slightly undermined in the study of either. As many chapters in this book demonstrate play and ritual essentially comprise culturally assembled embodied processes of joint attention, shared action and collective intentionality. Those culturally assembled processes (hard or soft), however, obey the enactive logic of practice which sets them apart from the representational logic of mere concepts and beliefs. That means that they need to be acted out or performed before they can be thought of or conceptualised. Thus, from a developmental and evolutionary

perspective, it makes little sense to speak of play or ritual in the absence of material bodies and things. I will return to exemplify that at the end of this chapter. For now I turn to a more basic point about definitions.

What is play? What is ritual? What is belief? One might think that interdisciplinary books, like this one, bringing together people from a broad range of scientific backgrounds, with different styles of thinking and epistemic predispositions, may not be the best place to ask for consensus over those hotly debated issues. I think this is not true. In fact, it is precisely interdisciplinary volumes like this one which provide the ideal context to test, expand and rethink our list of attributes and set of criteria. I believe we should make the most out of this opportunity, and thus I want to revisit some of those basic definitional issues. Let's focus, for instance, on the notion of play. As many chapters in this book point out, defining play is an extremely important analytical task if one wants to understand its different manifestations and possible evolutionary significance. It is also a very difficult task, and in some cases potentially misleading. To explain, a good definition can help us delineate the basic outline of the phenomenon we seek to understand and thus to guide our empirical investigations in the right direction. A poor definition, on the other hand, can be the cause of confusion and lead us to look for the wrong thing in the wrong place. Have we come up with the right working definition or set of criteria about play in this book then? Although I sense that no general agreement has emerged among the different chapters about the nature of play in humans and animals, there seems to be sufficient common ground to begin a fruitful discussion that can lead to a new, possibly more useful and applicable, definition of play. Patrick Bateson, to mention one specific example, makes a very interesting proposition: he writes that one way to overcome the ambiguity of play as a category is to distinguish between the different meanings of play by comparing the different manifestations of play at different developmental stages in humans and animals. I found his observation that social play in cats and other animals is replaced by object play around the seventh month of their life particularly interesting, especially if we contrast this with what we see in the case of humans (see, for example, Smith, Chapter 5, and Morley, Chapter 6, this volume). Similarly, Gordon Burghardt asks what might be a definition or criteria that will enable us to differentiate between pretend play in other animals. To this end he raises also the issue of intentionality and of the different levels of intentionality. I think it may be useful in this context to differentiate between intention in action and prior intention and maybe to consider the possibility of affordance learning from ecological psychology.

Of course, whatever the main types of play behaviour one chooses to recognise and focus on (e.g. locomotor, social, object or pretend) and whatever the precise criteria one uses to define play or ritual, they would be of little use in archaeology before one is equipped with the necessary methodology that will enable the identification of those features and behaviours in the material record. One question, then, is what kind of evidence we expect to find about play and ritual in early human societies. Another question is about what might be the most fruitful way to approach and interpret that evidence. Reading the different contributions in this volume, one can learn much about 'what it is' that we call play and ritual; maybe less about 'what it is' that we call belief. Still, it is the relationship between the three notions that raises the most challenging questions, and it is this relationship that this book helps us to understand better. For instance, what would count as an instance of play becoming a ritual? Gordon Burghardt (Chapter 3) discusses, from a comparative

perspective, the example of the captive Japanese monkeys that he observed at the Kyoto Primate Institute which have developed the habit of knocking stones together to make a sound on what looks like a repeated formalised performance. Moreover, the chapter by Colin Renfrew (Chapter 2) gives us an additional clue looking at the relationship between belief and ritual: it is ritual, Renfrew argues, that instantiates and thus precedes belief. In other words, it is not so much the belief but the performance of the belief that matters. And it is by focusing on that notion, namely performance, that we might be able to bridge the gap between play and ritual. I think that most of the chapters in this volume highlight, implicitly or explicitly, the significance of this 'performative element' in a number of different contexts of ritual action. For example, Yosef Garfinkel (Chapter 11) and Claire Halley (Chapter 9), discussing these issues in relation to dance, have also made some interesting suggestions about how one could make sense of the available evidence. Specifically, Halley combines evidence of the communal performative action of circle dance from the architecture and iconography of the American Southwest to emphasise the importance of embodiment and materiality for our understanding of how ritual practices and beliefs develop. Moreover, Garfinkel focuses on the impact of masks as powerful performance paraphernalia blurring reality and illusion. Tracing some of the earliest appearances of this phenomenon at the village communities of the proto-historic Near East, he combines the available archaeological remains (e.g. depictions of masks being worn, masks on vessels and anthropomorphic figurines bearing masks) with ethnographic observations about the use of masks in dances and festivals to construct an argument about the use of dance and mask performances in the creation of a sense of community and collective identity. Colin Renfrew suggests that if you are trying to identify specific instances of play and ritual in the past, essentially you are looking for a place. You are looking for the space, or some sort of spatial structure, in which congregation and collective play takes place. Sometimes this type of social theatre or arena is found also, at least to some extent, in other animals; but as archaeologists, we often need to look for aspects or dimensions of play and ritual that are not always visible or do not exist in other animals. A good example of that can be seen in the case of the visual representations and figurations of animals or humans from different places around the world discussed in the chapters in this book. From the magnificent frescoes of Akrotiri, Knossos and Tel El Daba (Lyvia Morgan, Chapter 14, this volume), to the impressive T-shaped anthropomorphic blocks and animal engravings from Göbekli Tepe (Trevor Watkins, Chapter 10, this volume), to the animal representations and figures from the Maltese temples (Caroline Malone, Chapter 13, this volume), to the wealth of material from Mesoamerica (Claire Halley (Chapter 9), David Freidel and Michelle Rich (Chapter 8) and Karl Taube (Chapter 17), this volume), a whole series of challenges is being raised for the archaeologist and anthropologist. Historical texts offer another potential source of comparative material and information which present their own challenges, and Roel Sterckx's chapter (Chapter 12) makes an interesting contrast between the 'lack of zoography' and the absence of an extended vocabulary of play in Chinese texts with what seems to be the case in other cultures, for instance, in ancient Greece.

I now turn to the last major theme of this book, which relates to a series of comparative, developmental and evolutionary considerations. From a comparative perspective, the evidence presented in many chapters makes clear that play is a behaviour present in many non-human animals. What remains less clear, however, is what kind of animals engage in which types of play. This also relates to the definitional issues I mentioned before. Important to point out in this respect, as Gordon Burghardt also underlines, is that play is an evolutionary heterogeneous phenomenon, possibly the product of 'convergent evolution'. This is something we need to be aware of when we decide where to look for possible manifestations of animal play. Burghardt's discussion also highlights the problem of 'anthropomorphism' in comparative and evolutionary studies. We need to be very careful each time human intelligence and behaviour is used as the measure or model for animal intelligence or behaviour. And the same applies, of course, in the case of play and ritual. I am not sure however, what a non-anthropomorphic approach

to play and ritual might be. Burghardt proposes the notion of 'critical anthropomorphism', but it is not very clear how exactly this notion might change the way we decide who plays and what kind of game. Maybe our recent tendencies to 'animali[se] humans' or 'humani[se] animals', if I may borrow the words of Raymond Tallis from his recent book *Aping Mankind* (2011), are parts of the same problem. This last point also relates to the broader question of continuity versus discontinuity between animal and human behaviour and cognition. Darwin famously argued that: the difference in cognition between humans and animals, great as it is, is one of degree and not of kind (1871, 105). I wonder what might be the relevant meaning of this statement in the context of play and ritual. If one wishes to underline the element of continuity, one could look at what we may call 'core' aspects of play, those which – as we have seen – are widespread phenomena in the animal kingdom. If on the other hand, we decide to explore the path of discontinuity, we should be focusing on what we call 'intentional', 'symbolic' or 'socio-dramatic' aspects of play. Pretence, joint intentionality and games, that is, rule-governed, conventional play activities would be key areas to look at in this case. Maybe a more useful question to ask in the context of this integrative volume is about difference in the light of similarity. Namely, given this evolutionary continuum between animal and human play or ritual behaviour what makes us humans so different?

Take, for instance, pretend play. Peter Smith (Chapter 5, this volume) argues that we may have precursors of pretend in some animals, but this is not the type of play that you expect to find in any developed sense in the animal world. In order to have pretend, Smith suggests, you need a pretender, a reality, and a mental representation that is projected onto reality, with awareness and intention on the part of the pretender. These are not capacities of the sort you expect to find in other animal species. Pretend develops in children around two years of age and is found in many non-Western societies. Right from the start, pretend is social in nature and thus not frequent in children with autism. So what might be the evolutionary significance of pretend? Iain Morley (Chapter 6, this volume) makes an interesting suggestion: looking at the developmental life history stages in apes and humans, he proposes that the early stages of pretend play in both species is predominantly imitative, and that the capacities on which pretend play relies and which it may aid in developing are those traditionally associated with the emergence of modern human intelligence. This brings us to another basic question: what is play for? Clearly the benefits are many if only indirect. As several chapters point out, besides being fun, play allows creative exploration, the acquisition and refinement of basic skills (e.g. physical coordination and muscular strength), affordance learning (that is, learning about the properties of making and using objects) and the development of social skills (finding out about how others think and behave). Moreover, it allows for all these avoiding the dangers of real-life situations. Patrick Bateson emphasises the benefits of playfulness in enhancing creativity, which he clearly and in my opinion correctly distinguishes from innovation. Last, Peter Smith, after rightly underlining the differing views on the value of play in different human societies, discusses a number of different hypotheses about the functional significance of pretend play in language development, creativity, theory of mind (ToM) etc. He examines three main proposals about the role of play in human development – namely, epiphenomenal (does not matter), equifinality (one of many factors) or essential (essential for development) – and finally concludes that play is useful but not essential for normal development. These are all, of course, issues worth looking into and developing further from an interdisciplinary perspective.

I end my response with a brief note on material culture. As mentioned at the beginning, one element or category of evidence that I suggest has not been sufficiently incorporated into the interdisciplinary study of play and ritual is that of materiality or material culture. That is, the world of things, objects and materials that surround us and mediate our thoughts and actions (Malafouris & Renfrew 2010; Malafouris 2013). But is it not material culture that most chapters in this book have been looking at and discussing, from different regions, periods and archaeological contexts? It certainly is. I should explain, thus, that the problem I am trying to point out here concerns more specifically our views about the role that this materiality might have played in

the context of play and ritual. In particular, I believe that most of the time, our approach to material culture has been one that ascribes to it an epiphenomenal, or at best, representational status. In other words, we view things as something that might be useful, informative or instrumental for play and ritual but which nonetheless, has little if any 'constitutive' power. This deeply entrenched construal, however, undermines the ontological significance of material things in the context of play and ritual. To illustrate that, consider the example of toys. What are toys for? I suggest that the use of toys is very important in child development for two main reasons. On the one hand, they play a major role in the emergence of collective 'we'- intentionality, and thus, in the developmental transition from primary or 'minimal' forms of play to secondary representational and meta-representational forms of play. Why is that? Toys provide the necessary material scaffold – gesture can play a similar role – for the passage from mere imitation to symbolic thinking which opens up radically new possibilities for meta-cognition. This brings us to the second and related reason that I suggest toys are important: The infant who is repeatedly pressing a plastic key, in addition to having fun, is also having a lesson in agency and causality. Through play the child becomes a self, a 'Me'. As the developmental psychologist Phillipe Rochat shows in his *Others in Mind* (2009), after the second year of life, an important transformation happens: the toy is no longer simply an object for the child to play with; it is now experienced as belonging to the child. In other words, it is owned. This new sense or claim of ownership is a major step in the development of selfhood. The act of playing with toys, which we should not forget are highly affective or emotive material objects, brings about the experiences of 'owning', but also of 'sharing', and thus helps delimiting and defining the self in relation to others.

At the core of infant child development, Phillipe Rochat writes, there is a tension between comfort and adventure: "On the one hand the child enjoys and depends on the care received by others. On the other hand, the child needs to exhaust all possibilities for action outside this dependency. This is a core conflict that sparks a whole dynamic in development, whether cognitive, social, or emotional. This existential dilemma young children start to grapple with during the first months will never really leave them in their journey through life and relationships. It is a *constitutive dilemma* of our psyche. The question for them will always be how to expand outside the primal bind without jeopardizing it, how to leave a secure base in order to explore beyond, without taking the risk of losing it?" (2009, 160). I think that play is the answer to this existential dilemma and that maybe later in life this same *constitutive dilemma* finds expression in the realm of ritual and religious belief.

REFERENCES

Darwin, C. (1871). *The Descent of Man, and Selection in Relation to Sex*. John Murray.

Malafouris, L. (2013). *How Things Shape the Mind: A Theory of Material Engagement*. Cambridge MA: The MIT Press.

Malafouris, L., & Renfrew, C. (Eds.) (2010). *The Cognitive Life of Things: Recasting the Boundaries of the Mind*. Cambridge: McDonald Institute for Archaeological Research.

Rochat, P. (2009). *Others in Mind – Social Origins of Self-Consciousness*. New York: Cambridge University Press.

Tallis, R. (2011). *Aping Mankind: Neuromania, Darwinitis and the Misrepresentation of Humanity*. Durham: Acumen.

20

BELIEVING IN PLAY AND RITUAL

ROBIN OSBORNE

This volume is a product of the project 'Becoming human: the emergence of meaning'. The stated aim of the symposium which preceded this volume, on 'Play, ritual and belief in animals and in early human societies', was "to investigate the extent to which 'play', interpreted in a wide sense, may underlie the development of ritual and of religion in early human societies".

The chapters presented in this volume certainly tell those of us who are not professionals in animal behaviour much more about "'play', interpreted in a wide sense". We now know very much more about the evidence for animals playing, and the case for thinking that playing is found even among spiders. We now know, too, much more about particular rituals and the archaeological evidence for them. We have seen ritual buildings and monuments of very different sizes and types, sculptures that show rituals or were the focus of rituals, paintings that depict rituals, and ways in which animal imagery has been good to think with in the context of rituals of various sorts.

But has reviewing aspects of play among animals and humans given insights into early ritual behaviour as reflected among human societies? The expectation that this would be the case was prompted by the thoughts that ritual is often involved in play and games, that make-believe is related to belief, and, on the other hand, that animal rituals, that is performative behaviour among animals, did not have to be 'meaningful' in order to serve a purpose.

How many of these thoughts have survived this investigation? Well, we have seen plenty of reasons

for thinking that there are many ways in which play and ritual differ. This has been extremely helpful, both in the context of the discussion here and more generally for our understanding of what is important about ritual. To put things at their most schematic, I would want to stress in particular the following:

- Rituals end the same way: 'I pronounce them man and wife'; play and games end differently, indeed, may have no obvious result.
- Rituals minimise the opportunity for chance (which is not to say that there may not be variable elements within them); play and games are not play if there is no chance element.
- The chance element in play and games may be a product of players making mistakes, of forced or unforced errors. Rituals do their best to eliminate the possibility of mistakes.
- Play is initiated when the animal or human involved is in a relaxed state – at least ideally – and on the face of it nothing is at stake; rituals are very frequently moments of high stress when some crucial things are at stake.

Have we learned something by emphasising differences in this way? One thing we should have learned, I think, is that both rituals and play define themselves by opposition, both to each other and to 'normal' life. Take play. It is hard to think of any circumstance where play might not in fact be purposive – even if we cannot in many cases demonstrate that it is. After all, play – and this is paradoxically true even of

316

solitary play – is essentially social. Those who play with others – even with imaginary others – seek to leave an impression on those others by the way that they play with them. However much the biochemistry of play makes it rewarding in its own right, as a result of the feel-good factor that it produces, we rarely will believe that those with whom we have playful relations (whether in playful banter or across the table-tennis table, and whether we are playing against them or on the same side) have not been trying to impress us. But as soon as talk comes under the sign of banter, or hitting balls in another person's direction comes under the sign of games, we are asked to imagine that 'the play's the thing', that nothing is 'meant personally' by the verbal or physical actions. To distort an observation made in the course of the symposium by Nicholas Humphrey, to signal that one is playful is to say 'pax' (and saying 'pax' is a reminder that that is the case) – that is, to signal that one is playful is to signal a change of circumstances and rules from the mundane to the special – as also in ritual.

By the same token, rituals also define themselves in opposition both to play and to 'normal' life. We talk of actors in a ritual as we talk of actors in a play. To take a part in a ritual is to cease to be a particular individual and to become the mouthpiece for a given role – just as in various play activities we perform roles. It is not John Smith who marries you, it is the registrar (or the priest). The registrar or the priest's performance of the role does not depend on who they are as persons, rather it depends on their having been through an earlier ritual. They can perform symbolic roles because they have acquired symbolic capital. So although rituals define themselves against play (serious against frivolous, goal-directed against aimless), they share the feature of defining themselves against 'normal life' – both in terms of their contrast to normal life, and in involving their own world in which actions that are part of the game or part of the same ritual nexus count, while actions outside the game or outside that ritual nexus do not.

But how important a shared feature should we take this common opposition to 'normal life' to be? It is worth thinking a bit more about what opposition to normal life is good for. This is not quite the same question as the question about what is the 'function' of play, with which contributions to this volume are quite heavily concerned, or what is the 'function' of ritual, with which they rather curiously are less concerned explicitly. It is to ask rather more broadly what sorts of abnormal conditions there is some advantage to signalling.

In the case of play, the abnormality that is signalled is arguably precisely the aimlessness. Signalling play rules out that what you see is what you get; it signals a performance in which less is happening than meets the eye; it denies that the actions performed have their customary significance – or indeed any significance at all; it rules out in advance interruptions that take the actions performed seriously. Play-fighting is an obvious case, but we have seen many other activities among animals which would invite intervention from other animals if they were not play – and it is not hard to multiply the examples with humans. 'Teasing' is the limit case here – deliberately withholding obvious signals of play so that the other person begins to react as if this were a serious situation and not play. The game here is precisely making others guess, despite the absence of unequivocal signals, that this is a game. Play tells others to suspend their belief.

In the case of rituals, the abnormality is, by contrast, precisely the goal-directedness. Signalling ritual also rules out thinking that what you see is what you get; it rules out in advance interruptions that assume that the only thing that is happening is the actions seen and the words heard. In a sense, ritual tells others to suspend their *dis*belief. In J. L. Austin's terms, it signals that these utterances are performative, that these actions are performative. That the words and the actions do more than meet the eye. That they are supercharged. That we have entered the realm of the symbolic. There has been some demurring here about whether Catherine Bell was right to think that all rituals involved sacred symbols. Put like that, we might indeed want to resist, but the very signalling of something as ritual lays claim to there being more happening than meets the eye, to the involvement of unseen powers. Those may not be 'sacred' as such; they may simply be the authority that comes from repetition itself or that is carried by certain actors because of the roles bestowed upon them (queen, archbishop). Bell did not in fact need 'sacred', for such power arguably belongs to every symbol. (When I was admitted as a junior unofficial Fellow at King's College Cambridge 35 years ago, it was with the words '*Ego Bernard Williams, praepositus huius collegii, auctoritate mihi commissa admitto te*' – Bernard had restored Latin on the grounds that his predecessor, the anthropologist Edmund Leach, had displayed a misunderstanding of ritual in abolishing it, and this formula signalled ritual, it signalled role-play and it signalled, supplied even, symbolic capital, authority mysteriously bestowed (*commissa* in the passive, with no subject expressed.))

If this scheme is right – that essentially play signals that less is happening than you might think, ritual signals that more is happening than you might think – then it is worth pressing a bit more what the circumstances are in which those signals can be sent with advantage. It has repeatedly been observed that play is a feature of young animals, more than mature animals, of children, rather than adults. Whether or not play is educative, in any straightforward sense, whether or not it in any way prepares the young for mature life, it is clearly vital that the actions performed by the immature in play are not mistaken for the same actions performed by the mature for real. Real fighting maims and kills. Those who really use a banana instead of a telephone are certified – along with those maintaining conversations with non-existent others. If individuals want to do these things without facing the consequences, they need some way of telling others that that is what they are doing. But equally with rituals. If we don't recognise that this is a ritual and that this woman has authority, then there is no special relationship created between this man and this woman. And, though it has not here been observed, I think, it is surely not by chance that rituals are as much a feature involving only the mature as play is a feature involving only the immature. Indeed, age has frequently been an important qualifier for ritual roles – and, as we have seen, rituals have been frequently a way of marking age.

Arguably, ritual is as helpful here in our understanding play as play is in understanding rituals. When we see a ritual, we know there is some sort of 'passage' being effected. When we see play, we know that nothing is being effected. Play is the marked term for unmarked action. Ritual is the marked term

for super-marked action. Whatever the actual consequences of play, that it was play renders them inconsequential – that is, even if one party to play gets hurt, 'he was only playing' absolves the other party of consequences. For all that no one denies that play serves some purpose, putting something under the sign of play denies that it can have the purpose that the same actions would have were they done under any other sign.

Play demands a community. It is only possible among a consenting group. And this ability to strike through actions, to render them as if they have not happened, is pretty clearly desirable as soon as one has any sort of group – as soon as two or three are gathered together, it may be desirable to bracket off some actions as not counting. But if there really were only two or three, it is hard to see that there would be much of a role for super-marked actions. Super-marked actions also demand a group of consenting individuals. But super-marked actions surely become needed only in relatively complex social circumstances. Some rituals produce hierarchy, and indeed reproduce it; others produce equality. But equality only needs to be produced in the face of hierarchy – we need situations where hierarchy has emerged for ritual to become appropriate, and it is in the fact of the accumulation of other forms of capital that possessing symbolic capital becomes vital.

It is not by chance that, using part of Gordon Burghardt's definition of play, play and ritual share being "behaviour … performed repeatedly in a similar, but not rigidly stereotyped form". The repetition of certain actions is, as Yosef Garfinkel observed in discussion, part and parcel of being a form of communication: communication is impossible without at least minimal repetition of at least similar actions, and communication is impossible to avoid once there is minimal repetition. More than that, repetition is vital to both play and ritual because both are comments upon actions. I have talked so far as if the norm is that actions are consequential, and play has to distinguish itself from this norm. But we might equally reckon that it is only distinguishing inconsequential versions of action as play that establishes the norm of consequentiality. But equally it is only distinguishing the super-consequentiality of ritual that establishes that other actions are not super-consequential – that when I say, "I'll bring that reference tomorrow," I don't establish a legal contract or incur the shame due to grossly immoral actions when I forget.

Of the three key terms within the title of the conference, *play*, *ritual* and *belief*, belief has received less consideration. This is hardly surprising. Very few people are comfortable with belief, and in my own neck of the woods, most scholars have attempted to remove questions of belief from discussion of Greek and Roman religion completely. But if we stop worrying about *religious* belief for a moment, I think the editors' suggestion that we link belief and make-believe is helpful.

I suggested earlier that play signalled to others that they should suspend their belief. What they might think was happening wasn't really happening. The actions they were observing had *a different ontological status*. And I suggested that something exactly similar happens with rituals – they signal that what you might think is happening is not *all* that is happening, that what is happening has *a different ontological status*. And just as the world of play is a simplified world, a world where only some rules count and all others are suspended, so too the world of ritual is a simplified world. Although, as we have variously heard, the stories that may be told to justify rituals and convince people that there is indeed a different ontological world, may be complicated, what is being communicated in rituals is commonly not itself subtle. Rituals simplify, they rely on putting actors into big categories and then making some simple change to the category: words that are spoken have a special force because heard by abstract, absent and/or supernatural powers, the unmarried man is made a married man; the prince becomes the king; the lawyer becomes the judge and is empowered to deprive people of liberty or even life; the assembly of members of parliament becomes authorised to pass laws that bind every member of the community.

Play and ritual are then, in my view, in many ways parallel, if going in opposite directions. The existence of the one makes easier the existence of the other. But is there any mileage in the idea underlying this volume that play underlies ritual? What we have discovered has certainly been helpful to us, I think, in discerning ritual and play in the archaeological record, even though few papers have devoted

much time explicitly to trying to do that. What we are looking for as sites of ritual and what we are looking for as sites of play are precisely similar. Both play and ritual demand that the actions that constitute them are set apart from the actions of the rest of life. Actions may be set apart, may set themselves apart, without involving any material object – the same actions may, indeed, set apart both play and ritual, as we have seen most clearly with the dance. And when any objects are involved, they need to be capable of marking actions as not ordinary actions. But that marking too may not distinguish play from ritual. Both play and ritual may involve marking a space as not an ordinary space – marking it as a playground or as a sanctuary.

When we find a space marked as not an ordinary space, we find space itself made to play a role. But it plays a role only for those who can recognise that it is marked. Knowledge is demanded here, but also belief. That a space is distinguished may be signalled by physical means, but that that space is a space where normal rules do not apply demands belief, just as recognising that the actions performed in play or ritual are not the actions of normal life also demands belief. The spaces of ritual and of play are spaces put under quotation marks, spaces of the always already. They are spaces of representation, of mimesis. For me, the most intriguing thought to come out of this volume concerns 'representation', mimesis – to use a word to which several contributors have resorted. For representations are by definition not the real thing, are always secondary. As soon as we are in a world of mimesis, we are in a world where belief, and the suspension of belief, is at issue. We may have to suspend our belief that this rag is a rag, because in this play the rag is a mouse. Or we may need to suspend our disbelief that this stone with carvings on it can have supernatural powers, because this stele is a god. And if we are to do that, we must also suspend our belief that this space is a room or a field or …

Archaeologists like to think of themselves as down to earth in more than just the literal sense. But to understand a world of ritual and play demands an acknowledgement that identifying traces of past activity may be a matter of belief. The ontological status of the traces of the past is not something inherent in the material itself; it was determined by the humans and animals who interacted with those traces. The possibility of ontological mutability is a prerequisite of mimesis, and is arguably something that juveniles of the species learn through play. In that sense, the editors of this volume seem to have been not simply right to insist that belief is *the* central issue, but also right to think that experience of play crucially prepared humans not just for ritual, but for the entry to a supernatural world that ritual can effect. And right, too, to think that it is only if we stop shying away from belief that we will understand the place of either play or ritual.

21

THE PENTAGRAM OF PERFORMANCE: RITUAL, PLAY AND SOCIAL TRANSFORMATION

IAIN MORLEY

The preceding chapters present a very rich diversity of material, spanning a wide range of disciplinary and intellectual approaches, and individually addressing the many different aspects of the large overarching theme of this book, outlined in the introductory chapters (Morley, Chapter 1; Renfrew, Chapter 2). Collectively they contribute in important ways to exploring the underlying concepts and evidence, and developing new ways of elucidating the topics of ritual, play and performance in prehistory.

This concluding chapter does not aim to summarise the full content and conclusions of the preceding chapters; these are introduced individually in the Introduction, and the richness and diversity of their content is such that their individual discussions and conclusions are best considered in their original context. This discussion has the modest, though not simple, aim instead of identifying common themes and synergies within the chapters, and of relating these to each other in the ambition of drawing out conclusions from the sum of their parts.

It is clear from the preceding discussions that play behaviours are a human universal; that they have a biological basis and have a long evolutionary history in a wide range of animals; that much of human play has close similarities with that in animals, but that some types of play behaviours are uniquely developed in humans; that the developed versions in humans rely on core higher cognitive functions that are also uniquely developed in humans; and that these higher cognitive functions underpin a wide range of behaviours that are distinctively human.

Clearly ritual behaviours can sometimes be recognised archaeologically in past societies, especially when those activities are structured and take place in dedicated contexts, and the same applies to ritualised play, in the form of games. The occurrence of non-ritualised forms of play in the past is harder to identify, though insight into their origins and importance in the past and present can be achieved through synthesis of archaeological, palaeoanthropological, ethological and psychological evidence.

As has been discussed in the Introduction (Morley, Chapter 1) and the opening chapter by Renfrew (Chapter 2), there are clear elements of structural similarity between human ritual behaviours and play behaviours in both humans and across a large range of animals (Bateson, Chapter 4; Huizinga 1955; Burghardt 2005 and Chapter 3, this volume). The subsequent chapters and discussions reveal that these similarities go beyond similarities of form, encompassing genuine interrelations in terms of the requisite underlying cognitive abilities, their processes, structures and the ends that they achieve, to the extent that in many human societies, past and present, ritual and play activities are intertwined and, in some cases, inseparable.

The discussion considers the following recurring themes:

- Some key distinctions between ritual and play activities;
- The possession and marking in both ritual and play of a different ontological status from the

'normal', 'everyday' versions of the activities that they encompass;

• The sharing of core cognitive foundations in both ritual and play;

• The shared roles that ritual and play fulfil;

• The relationships between ritual, play and other forms of activity as *performance*, and the perpetuation of play-based behaviours into adulthood;

• The discussion concludes by proposing that critical behaviours that are uniquely developed in humans are fundamentally interrelated as a 'pentagram of performance'.

DISTINCTIONS BETWEEN THE MANIFESTATION OF RITUAL AND PLAY BEHAVIOURS IN HUMANS

In addition to the structural and cognitive similarities between ritual and play behaviours discussed in the preceding chapters, and later in this chapter, several authors also articulate clear distinctions between them.

An obvious notable difference between ritual and play behaviours concerns the principal actors in the majority of examples. In animals and in humans, in most cases, play is carried out by juveniles, whilst most rituals, whether secular or religious, are carried out, or officiated at least, by adults. Furthermore, as Renfrew (Chapter 2) articulates, "many kinds of play involve actions or activities that are less highly structured than are those of ritual. The formalism of ritual is often lacking: play is often characterised by 'behavioural plasticity' (Pellegrini 2009, 47)."

For all the apparent structural and functional similarities between ritual and play, it is clear that strong cultural distinctions are often maintained between them, in various respects; the cultural conceptions of ritual and play activities, their roles and their value, is frequently very different. Whilst chapters in this volume provide clear examples of the converse (e.g. Freidel & Rich, Chapter 8; Halley, Chapter 9; Taube, Chapter 17; Morgan, Chapter 14; Marinatos, Chapter 15), it is clear that in many cultures – including modern Western society – play and some games are conventionally viewed as 'trivial'

or inconsequential, while rituals are viewed as serious and of considerable consequence. For example, Sterckx outlines that in classical Chinese, the meanings of the terms closest to 'ritual' and 'play' have very clear distinctions. The formal performative aspect of 'ritualised' behaviour was seen as being possessed by both animals and humans, but the presence of ritual 'propriety', or etiquette, distinguished the behaviour of humans. Aspects of play and performance of music and dance were seen as having their origins in mimesis of animal movement, but in the ritual context, according to the Confucian canon, performance was intricately related to moral judgement and intent – "To behave ritually implied to have a moral propriety that enables one to do so" (Sterckx, Chapter 12). In this context, ritual is much more than repeated performative action, and would also be perceived as contrasting fundamentally in this respect with play.

Such distinctions clearly have analogues in many other belief systems, where (for example) an officiating individual is considered to have a degree of moral or spiritual propriety and pre-eminence that in itself distinguishes the meaning of their actions from those of other individuals undertaking comparable actions (see also Osborne, Chapter 20). Sterckx cautions that the labels that we apply and the categories that we use in identifying behaviours (as having properties of ritual) may not reflect the conceptions of those activities that were (or are) held by the practitioners themselves when experienced in their cultural and historical context. Particular types of performative activities could be perceived as ritually efficacious by their practitioners precisely because of a definitive distinction from other performative activities – a distinction that is not necessarily perceivable in the *form* of the activities. But equally, these distinctions perceived by the practitioners can exist alongside their overlaps in form, function and perhaps foundations, without necessarily undermining their significance.

Bateson notes a significant difference in the *context of occurrence* (and preceding mood state) between exploratory 'playful' play and ritual: the former (as also noted by Burghardt 2005 and Chapter 3, this volume) is predicated on a positive mood state, and the instigation of spontaneous and flexible thought. Ritual activity, on the other hand, certainly does not rely on positive mood state, and is often instigated in times of heightened tension. Furthermore, spontaneous and flexible thought is often antithetical to ritual practices and goals.

However, both positive mood state and spontaneous and flexible thought are clearly important in other forms of performance and, especially, improvisation, and spontaneous and flexible thought could be argued still to be essential in rituals that seek to achieve altered states of consciousness (especially if participants are then expected to report on them).

The distinction between the perceived consequentiality of ritual and play activities is also noted by Osborne (Chapter 20). Ritual is generally serious, while play (amongst humans at least) may be viewed as frivolous (though not necessarily by its participants). As mentioned previously, this difference may be related to another that Osborne elaborates: that ritual is goal-directed while play is (often) aimless – at least as far as immediate-term aims are concerned (but see also Renfrew, Chapter 2, for discussion of the fact that ritual does not always feature immediate or direct consequences, and Bateson, Chapter 4; Smith, Chapter 5; Morley, Chapter 6; Dissanayake, Chapter 7, for examples of ways in which play is not aimless, even if not motivated by achieving ends). This could be articulated alternatively as play being perceived by its participants as an end in itself, rather than play lacking an end, whilst ritual is perceived as a means to an end (or ends).

Games, as a specialised subset of play, provide an informative exception. Games are frequently perceived as both an end in themselves and a means to an end; likewise they are frequently viewed as being far from frivolous by participants and spectators. Participation in structured games requires all of these abilities that are prerequisites for less structured play (see later in this chapter). Both play and games involve cooperative participation through engagement with an agreed set of parameters for the behaviour, whether codified in advance but agreed at the time (games with rules) or negotiated at the time in relation to pre-established parameters (improvisational role play). Also play and games have their roots in mimicking social situations and structures, though they are distinguished from each other in the same way – i.e. in featuring pre-codified rules/laws

(games) vs. more improvised 'navigation' of behaviour within established parameters, or non-codified social rules (play).

However, Smith (Chapter 5) outlines some important differences that exist between play and games in terms of their manifestation, if not the underlying abilities required. In particular, in terms of rule structure, games generally conform to publicly accepted expectations; games are constrained to follow certain procedure(s) and achieve certain outcome(s) (which are also publicly sanctioned); games can involve much larger numbers of participants (which I would argue is made possible by the widely accepted expectations); and games often involve an audience (the members of which, in addition to the participants, or *performers*, provide the public sanction and expectations).

Games do not *have* to have these characteristics, but the existence of the publicly sanctioned expectations and structures of games makes these characteristics possible. In this respect, games are distinct from other forms of play in the ways in which they can be manifest, but it is highly significant that in all of these respects games closely parallel rituals (Smith, Chapter 5). The 'ritualisation of play' as games is critical in several of the contributions to this volume (e.g. Morgan, Chapter 14; Spivey, Chapter 16; Freidel & Rich, Chapter 8; Taube, Chapter 17; see later in this chapter). Kyriakidis (Chapter 18) points out that "both rituals and games are repetitive, rule-governed activities that make a wide use of representation or 'symbolism'", their rule governance setting both apart from the mundane.

THE SPECIAL ONTOLOGICAL STATUS OF RITUAL AND PLAY

A marked, overarching structural commonality between play behaviours and ritual behaviours, noted repeatedly in the preceding contributions, is their incorporation of versions of 'everyday' behaviour in a context that demarcates them as distinct from the 'normal' version, with different meanings and consequences. Ritual and play behaviours, whilst incorporating behaviours carried out in everyday contexts, confer on those behaviours a different ontological status (Osborne, Chapter 20), and this is demarcated at the outset.

In play behaviours in animals and humans, these differences take various forms, including any or all of: familiar behaviours carried out in exaggerated (or 'supernormal') form relative to the 'normal' version, with repeated, repetitive occurrence, with transformations or exchanges of identity such as reversed social roles, and in a different context. In humans, these traits all frequently characterise ritual behaviours. In ritual contexts, versions of 'normal' behaviour that are exaggerated or supernormal, in form and significance, frequently have a central role, in which context repeated performance of particular actions and thoughts – within and between occasions – is fundamental to their perceived success. Likewise the adopting of alternate roles and personas which characterises much play is a core feature of many rituals.

In mammals such as monkeys, canids, felids and ursids (Bekoff & Allen, 1998, in Smith, Chapter 5, this volume), specific signals are made which indicate that a shift from the 'normal' version of behaviour to a non-normal, non-literal version (the 'play' version) is occurring (Smith, Chapter 5), under which circumstances different rules and consequences apply (Bateson, Chapter 4). There are also now amongst animals many examples of behaviours moving from one context to another, including the exploitation and exaggeration by animals of stimulus qualities that are 'supernormal' (Burghardt, Chapter 3).

Pretend play, which is uniquely developed in humans (Smith, Chapter 5; Morley, Chapter 6; Dissanayake, Chapter 7), requires intention to pretend on the part of the instigator, and awareness of this intention on the part of the play partner; these intentions, and understanding and acceptance of them, must be indicated, and this indication must in turn be understood.

Dissanayake (Chapter 7) argues comprehensively that play behaviours and ritualised behaviours have core specialised characteristics in common; these characteristics, which she refers to as *aesthetic* operations, signal to participants that the activities being carried out are not the 'ordinary' or 'everyday' versions of those behaviours. These characteristics are *stereotypy, repetition, exaggeration, elaboration* and *manipulation of expectations*, all of which can occur through

signals across all the major media of interpersonal communication – visual, vocal and gestural. They could be further argued to constitute performance, and to structurally link ritual, play, music and dance, as well as facilitating social learning, as the core foundation of the development of belief systems and the arts. These characteristics in common betray a shared heritage and, in Dissanayake's view, indicate that it is in play and ritualised behaviours that religious rituals have their evolutionary beginnings.

This parallel between ritual and play is strikingly manifest in the use of masks in ritual contexts. The donning of masks conspicuously demarcates the change from 'normal' and 'everyday' activity to a different realm of action and relationships (Garfinkel, Chapter 11), in both ritual and play. Masks effect transformations – they transform identity, either by hiding it or by imposing a new identity, and they thus transform social relationships amongst those interacting as, or with, mask-wearers. They can be distinctive, and distinct from each other, and impose a new, 'non-normal' social order or, when identical, they have the potential to function as a means of removing individuality and imposing commonality of appearance and experience (see the discussion of the roles of ritual and play later in this chapter). They actually physically manifest the *aesthetic operations* that characterise both ritual and play that are outlined by Dissanayake (Chapter 7; see earlier in this chapter) of *stereotypy, repetition, exaggeration, elaboration* and *manipulation of expectations*.

In Taube's discussion, the jaguar masks and costumes that are worn in the context of contemporary Guerrero ritual boxing demarcate this activity as distinct from daily life, and from 'normal' fights between individuals. In this context, "public sport and sacred ritual overlap in subtle and profound ways" (Chapter 17). Taube persuasively argues for clear ritual and cosmological significance to the Mayan boxing, ballgames and their courts – a synthesis of ritual and game – both in the past and in the present.

As in play-fighting, imaginative role play and games, the signalling of ritual (in the transition from 'normal life' to ritual context) "signals that these utterances are performative, that these actions are performative" (Osborne, Chapter 20). The notion of *performance* is, in my view, critical. Performers are enacting behaviours that have an ontologically different status from the 'normal' version of those behaviours. Participants in ritual, play, games, improvisation, drama, narratives etc., are unavoidably performers (Renfrew, Chapter 2; Morley, Chapter 6; Dissanayake, Chapter 7).

It is notable that this non-normal demarcation from 'normal' or 'everyday' versions of the behaviour, and from normal life, could be regarded as a characteristic of all forms of *performance*, whether ritual, play, games, music, dance, improvisation, or the rehearsal of social norms. Dance, for example, has been defined in a similar way as "purposeful, intentionally rhythmical and culturally patterned sequence of bodily movement, *distinct from ordinary, daily practice*" (Hanna 1979, in Halley, Chapter 9, this volume; emphasis added).

Osborne argues that a difference between ritual and play activities, however, is that the ontological status of the activities that follow this signalling also differ from each other in play and ritual, as well as differing from normal life. The "signalling of something as ritual lays claim to there being more happening than meets the eye, to the involvement of unseen powers" (or of unseen 'cause-and-effect') (Chapter 20). He emphasises that these unseen powers need not be 'sacred' (or supernatural), but can include the authority that certain performers hold because of the roles bestowed upon them, or the authority that arises from repetition of the ritual itself. In the case of play, on the other hand, he argues, what is signalled is that *less* is happening than meets the eye – relative to what the 'normal' versions of those behaviours represent.

Despite differences in the culturally attributed significance of the actions that follow, the social significance of that signalling of ontological difference from the 'normal' is equivalent. Individuals who in normal circumstances maintain conversations with non-existent others or use a banana as a telephone (Osborne, Chapter 20) are considered eccentric at best, with social consequences for them. In the words of Bateson (Chapter 4), "The player is to some extent protected from the normal consequences of serious behaviour." Both play and ritual require that participating individuals are able to signal that

what they are doing carries a different significance, or ontological status, form the 'normal' versions of those behaviours.

This is a powerful commonality between rituals and play. Both require the establishment at the outset that the following events occur outside the 'normal' rules. The priest (and congregation) is able to speak in prayer to an invisible entity, that cannot be perceived by others present, without fear of being subjected to the same judgements as an individual in a 'normal'/'everyday' context would be, because there is prior agreement that the present situation represents one in which a different set of shared understandings exists. The actions undertaken in ritual and play, and the spaces in which they take place, clearly require the establishment of this shared understanding, shared *belief*, that normal rules do not apply in that context. "They are spaces of representation, of mimesis. … For representations are by definition not the real thing, are always secondary. As soon as we are in a world of mimesis we are in a world where belief, and the suspension of belief, is at issue" (Osborne, Chapter 20).

SHARED COGNITIVE FOUNDATIONS OF PRETEND PLAY AND RITUAL BEHAVIOURS

The parallel between ritual and play goes beyond analogy to homology, since both play with imaginary entities and ritual engagement with entities who are similarly not attested in any 'normal' sensory way, but by convention and shared agreement, require the same underlying cognitive abilities – namely, anthropomorphisation, the creation of imagined entities, imitation and the sharing of beliefs – and, underpinning these, self-awareness, Theory of Mind and communication, which are central to both the establishment of a perception of shared belief and the creation of imagined anthropomorphic entities.

Indeed, it would appear that at least some of this suite of connected abilities (Theory of Mind and self-awareness, and communication by symbolic, representational means (Smith, Chapter 5)) exists, in a relatively simple form, in our closest relatives, the great apes. The simple types of pretend play in the great apes that are outlined by Smith, and which appear to rely largely on imitation, exist alongside the relatively simple (compared to humans) versions of self-recognition, Theory of Mind and elements of the abilities for linguistic-type communication that they also possess. Smith argues that the episodes of pretend play witnessed in our closest relatives, the great apes, are most likely to be by-products of the evolution of symbolic intelligence, which is supported by the development of the abilities for self-recognition, communication, tactical deception, imitation and visual-kinaesthetic matching. The existence of these abilities, and limited pretend play amongst our closest relatives, suggests that the potential for pretend play was present also in our last common ancestor with chimpanzees. The palaeoanthropological evidence analysed to date suggests that the first major changes in developmental life-history that would support development of complex *over-imitation* occurred in *Homo erectus*, and that the development of the critical *middle-childhood* phase of development, supporting the development of this into pretend play, occurred by the time of our last common ancestor with Neanderthals (Morley, Chapter 6).

As noted, imitative play, pretend play, relies on "some ability in visual-kinaesthetic matching – the ability to recognise the spatial or bodily similarity between their visual experience of another and their own kinaesthetic experience, and make some matching action to that observed" (Smith, Chapter 5, this volume; Mitchell 2007). These abilities for cross-modal matching, for *mimesis*, which in fact must include the auditory mode as well as visual and kinaesthetic (see Donald 2001), are also critical for participation in dance and music performance (Morley 2009, 2013, 2014 and references therein; Dissanayake, Chapter 7; see also Halley, Chapter 9). And these abilities required for role play and socio-dramatic play are also necessary prerequisites for ritual performance (Dissanayake, Chapter 7; Morley, Chapter 6).

ROLES OF RITUAL AND THE CONTRIBUTIONS OF PLAY

Play can clearly be identified as a component of ritual, whilst ritual has also been defined as a subcategory of play. The meeting of ritual and games in the Classical Greek athletic games can be viewed as imitative – mimetic – of epic combat (Spivey, Chapter 16). When such games are performed in a sanctuary (cf. also Freidel & Rich, Chapter 8; Taube, Chapter 17; Morgan, Chapter 14; Marinatos, Chapter 15; Halley, Chapter 9), "the 'play' element of ritual becomes gloriously transparent" (Spivey, Chapter 16). Meanwhile, as Burghardt (Chapter 3) observes, "in Sutton-Smith's (1997) magisterial discussion of the seven 'rhetorics' of play, festivals, rituals, social reversals (e.g. Mardi Gras) and other social scripts are incorporated into play." In this view, rituals are considered a subcategory of play (see also Renfrew, Chapter 2).

Whilst there are clear cases where play and ritual are distinguished from each other culturally (cf. Sterckx, Chapter 12, and earlier in this chapter), Morgan further points out that the concepts of play and ritual are culturally specific in their range of meanings and in many cultures may be relatively new as discrete conceptual categories. In her view, "Play, ritual and belief are inextricably interwoven, not as separate concepts, but as part of the totality of the ancient world view." Similarly, Freidel and Rich (Chapter 8) present numerous examples from both contemporary and past Mayan society that in their view illustrate "the pervasive and intertwined nature of play and ritual" which furthermore "allude to the deep history of this connection".

The intertwining of ritual and play in past and present cultural contexts is made possible – likely, even – because of their similarities in foundations, form and effects.

Play as Contributing to the Development of Social Cognition, Ritual and Belief Systems

As Burghardt (Chapter 3) puts it, "Play is ... considered by some leading play researchers as essential scaffolding for the development of moral behaviour and fairness/equity in animals as well as people (e.g. Bekoff & Pearce 2009), certainly a topic central to much discussion of religion." Play may thus "not only be of great importance in normative social and cognitive development and behavioural innovation, but also critical to an understanding of belief systems, religion and spirituality" (Burghardt, Chapter 3).

In considering the possible developmental and social functions of pretend play, Smith cites Alexander's (1989) argument that social-intellectual (pretend) play allows practice in "an expanding ability and tendency to elaborate and internalize social-intellectual-physical scenarios", using these to "anticipate and manipulate cause-effect relations in social cooperation and competition" (Alexander 1989, 480). Ritual practices would also appear to be predicated on the possession of these abilities, which, according to Alexander, are refined in the context of pretend play: namely, to conceptualise social-intellectual-physical scenarios and to anticipate and attempt to manipulate cause-and-effect relations in them, but via social cooperation.

Smith also outlines Harris' (2000) argument that the ability to imagine scenarios that transcend direct personal experience is nurtured in the context of pretend play, and that it is this ability that allows the learning of rule-based obligations and information from testimony alone. Children (and, in fact, humans of all ages) can learn and accept information "concerning events, processes, or entities that are difficult for them to observe first-hand – perhaps about other countries, other people, mythical or religious entities" (Smith, Chapter 5), and this ability is argued to be refined initially in the context of pretend play. This ability to imagine non-real-world scenarios and to accept the testimony of those in authority regarding the existence (and interpretation) of events, processes and entities that cannot be observed first-hand is clearly a necessary prerequisite for the acceptance of rules (including ritual rules), doctrine, cosmology and supernatural entities and phenomena.

This form of pretend play is described as *what if* play by Engel (2005) (Smith, Chapter 5), which exists alongside *what is* play. "Both involve pretence, but one [*what is* play] rests on plausible reconstructions of every day lived experience, while the other [*what if* play] rests on exploring implausible and often magical events and explanations" that go beyond everyday lived experience (Engel 2005, 524; in Smith, Chapter 5, this volume). Belief in deities and other supernatural entities and phenomena must be predicated on *what if* modes of comprehension.

Applying this model to the development of supernatural beliefs, the mental process of explaining otherwise unexplained phenomena in supernatural terms could actually be a consequence of overlaps between *what is* and *what if* play; in instances where comprehension of '*what is*' everyday lived experience is not complete, reconstructions of everyday experience must also rely on some *what if* elements. The ability to carry out *what if* narrative would actually be a necessary prerequisite for making connections between doctrine and ritual, as well as the initial construction of those belief systems.

Pretend play may thus be viewed as a crucible for the development of understanding of others' beliefs – and the beliefs of imagined entities – in the form of contributing to the development of Theory of Mind ability, understanding of agency, the ability to creatively imagine and accept testimony about scenarios beyond direct personal experience, to internalise rule systems and to relate these to each other. Furthermore, amongst humans, participation in collaborative play, even more so when it involves pretend, and yet more so when it involves role play, requires not only Theory of Mind and creativity, but the use of those abilities in this context requires the practice of fundamental social skills such as negotiation, concession, agreement and reciprocity.

Malafouris (Chapter 19) argues that in the context of play, toys and gesture provide a framework for collaborative intentionality, allowing symbolic thinking to emerge from imitation. These processes are as valid in other forms of performance as in play, and in the context of ritual in particular, gesture, embodied performance and the associated material culture surely provide an equivalent framework for the development of the symbolic conceptualisations relating to shared intentionality and shared belief in the supernatural.

Reiterating Social Structures, Roles and Beliefs

The development and reiteration of shared systems of belief and social identities is repeatedly discussed as a key role of ritual (e.g. Renfrew, Chapter 2; Freidel & Rich, Chapter 8; Marinatos, Chapter 15; Halley, Chapter 9; Watkins, Chapter 10). As has been discussed (and further later in this chapter), in the ritual context, transformations of roles and identities frequently occur, either solely for the duration of the ritual performance, in that special 'non-normal' context, in close parallel with socio-dramatic play, or on a permanent basis. Socio-dramatic play highlights the identification and understanding of roles and identities (Smith, Chapter 5) through their temporary adoption and exchange, and this seems frequently to be an important intended role and outcome of rituals.

Freidel and Rich (Chapter 8) argue that different types of both ritual and play activities seem to fall on a spectrum of formality which ranges from spontaneous improvisation at one extreme to rulebound formality at the other, and that the performances, of both ritual and play, and their associated objects, are importantly able to contribute to reinforcing a sense of sameness and community identity between participants, whilst at the same time being used to reiterate existing social structures (Freidel & Rich, Chapter 8). Halley (Chapter 9) elaborates how, in the case of many Puebloan groups, religious practice and performance feature play as an integral component; in this context. performance, music, gestures and mimesis are intimately related, representing and reiterating beliefs, values and attitudes; these reinforce ideals of community and identity within stipulated (spiritually sanctioned) rules. Similarly, the ritual 'sport' of the bull games of the Minoan and Near Eastern Bronze Age, in Marinatos' (Chapter 15) view, served to reiterate and reinforce existing cosmology and hierarchy between humans and nature.

Ritual practices constitute shared acts that create collective memory, which is essential to generating individual and collective community identity. Ritual activities – and games, music and dance (see also Morley 2009) – can contribute to the formation of the collective memory, and the collective memories, and thus community identity, can furthermore be reinforced in the crucible of repeated performance of those activities. This Watkins relates to Whitehouse's *Imagistic* and *Doctrinal* modes of religiosity (Whitehouse 2004, in Watkins, Chapter 10, this volume).

The ritual practices Watkins examines in the prehistoric Near East at Göbekli Tepe (Turkey) appear to prioritise the performance of the "making and remaking of buildings, sculptures, figurines, signs or paintings", rather than additional ceremonies within those spaces. These activities, plus those of feasting and of re-interring bodies in the settlements, Watkins argues, "were the ritual performances essential to the forging of collective memory and the sustaining of collective identity". The repetition of these acts of shared religious practice created shared religious belief, and in the creation of sculpted images of imagined entities, the creative and "social play of children and ritual meet" (Chapter 10).

Halley points out that *performance* has been argued, by scholars including Inomata (2006), Inomata and Coben (2006), Pearson and Shanks (2001) and Soar (2010), to be a key process through which "the creation and negotiation of identity, belief, symbolism, social and political relationships in the past" can be conceived (Chapter 9).

Through their *performance* play and ritual are linked, and it is in the performance that beliefs are created and reiterated. Performance reiterates and manifests beliefs and conventions, be they social conventions or cosmological frameworks. After all, a cosmological belief system is part of the "large and complex body of cultural knowledge" (Watkins, Chapter 10), social behaviour, values, rules and relationships that both children and adults must learn to understand and accept (not necessarily in that order) to function within their society.

Performance of shared religious practice is the basis of making (and perpetuating) shared religious beliefs, as the performance of shared social and creative play is the basis of making (and perpetuating) shared social beliefs. Play – and especially games – can reduce (social) stress by providing a mechanism/framework through which social tension/agonism can be resolved in a socially sanctioned way. Rituals can reduce social stress by providing a mechanism by which control can be exerted (or, at least, seem to be exerted) over events, and a structure through which shared values, beliefs and structures are reiterated and renewed.

The Performative and Transformative Power of Ritualised Play

Morgan (Chapter 14) argues that fundamental to all performative rites is their perceived transformative power, and that play, through embodied action leading to transformation, can become ritualised in form and function. Not only does play effect transformations from childhood to adulthood in longer-term ontogeny, Morgan provides detailed discussion of evidence that when performative play is perceived by a culture as effecting transformation in the immediate term, it becomes ritual itself.

Renfrew (Chapter 2) highlights a strong similarity between ritual and play activities in that whilst neither is actually functionally productive in an instrumental sense (cf. Rappaport 1999), both effect transformations in the world; these are transformations not of the material world, but of social realities.

Play, in the context of games and sports in a ritual or festival setting, is defined by Morgan (Chapter 14) as a series of performative actions initiating transformation to a new or renewed state of being. Morgan argues that within the ancient world, the transformative power of ritual play was a widely shared ideology, with transformation particularly effected through the appropriation of animal and adult power. Similarly, the material remains from the Tarxien temples of Malta suggest to Malone (Chapter 13) that "play, animals and ritual were intimately combined," perhaps incorporating dressing up as animals and transformation as ceremonial 'play'.

Agreeing closely with our original hypothesis, Morgan argues that "the ritualisation of 'play' in its broadest sense as an underlying cultural phenomenon (Huizinga 1955) is at the heart of all performance, whether it be athletic contests of games, sport or hunt, cultural presentations of dance, music and theatre or ceremonial and cultic rites," and that each of these forms of performance encompasses aspects of the others, with permeable boundaries between them.

Ritual and play are equivalent in their reliance on performance, and the importance of signalling the beginning of that performance (see earlier in this chapter), but different in the goal-orientedness of the performance – or to put it another way, the extent to which the performance constitutes an end in itself (play) or a means to an end or ends (ritual). Games, as a form of ritualised play, appear to fall in between play and ritual in this regard. Ritual behaviour could be argued to be a development of play structures that were already in place, incorporating a capacity to believe cause–effect relationships – thus allowing the attribution of ends/effects to means/ causes (whether correctly attributed or not).

As Bateson (Chapter 4) elaborates, a prolific form of adult (and juvenile) behaviour in both secular and religious contexts is the use of chemicals (including alcohol) and trance (through music and dance) to achieve the experience of alternative versions of normal perception, and to facilitate achievement of different versions of reality and/ or 'transformation'. These circumstances, Bateson argues, have a clear analogous link with play, and their effects may also "be relevant to the conditions in which rituals are established" (Chapter 4). In the respect of voluntarily generating circumstances that are demarcated as an alternative non-normal version of behaviour, this is in common with both play and ritual, and indeed achieving altered states of consciousness can have central roles in contexts of both ritual and leisure. This can result in the generation of "experiences that enable people to perceive things in a different way or connect previously unrelated bits of information" and "combine thoughts in novel combinations", which leads to "a general increase in the ability to deal with complexity and an increase in openness, such that the usual restraints that encourage humans to accept preconceived ideas about themselves and the world around them are challenged" (Chapter 4).

Play, innovation and creativity are thus argued to be closely related (see also Carruthers, 2002, and discussion in Morley, Chapter 6); this may be seen as a direct contrast to the aims of many rituals, which seek to reiterate particular tropes, norms, doctrine, cosmology and statuses (see earlier in this chapter). These often encourage humans to accept preconceived ideas about themselves and the world rather than seeking to challenge these. But in the case of some rituals, especially transformative ones, such as initiations, these effects can be very important. Rituals focused around achieving insight, spiritual contact, revelation or transformation, through an altered state of consciousness for example, may have a fixed structure, but their aim is the creation of a unique outcome in the form of a unique experience and creative narrative, and having induced questioning of accepted perceptions of reality, present a shared alternative version to be accepted by the participants. In these circumstances, innovation and creativity can be an important part of ritual on the part of the focal participants.

Pretend play has been argued (Göncü & Perone 2005, in Smith, Chapter 5, this volume; see also McConachie 2011, and discussion in Morley, Chapter 6) to continue into adulthood in the form of dramatic improvisations, poetry and dance. These are all "activities which enable development of representations of experiences with affective significance." (Smith, Chapter 5). To this list – which clearly links these different forms of performance – could be added ritual performance.

Watkins outlines the view from niche-construction theorists (Odling-Smee & Laland 2009; Kendal 2011; Sterelny 2011) that "the developmental environment within which children learn and begin to practise the large and complex body of cultural knowledge that they need as adults is an advanced form of cultural niche construction." It is possible that the perpetuation of play into adulthood, in the broader sense of games, improvisation, narrative and ritual, and its continued efficacy, could actually be because, in forming a key part of social learning in childhood, play then constitutes a key part of the cultural niche that we occupy as adults.

At the very least play behaviours exercise, and may contribute to the formation of, many of the critical cognitive abilities on which ritual practice and religious thought are predicated. But it seems likely too that the use of these faculties into adulthood for these purposes represents not just continuity in the *use of the forms of thought* that are *developed in the context of* play, but in many respects constitutes a continuity in the *patterns of behaviour themselves* that *gave rise to the development of those abilities*.

THE PENTAGRAM OF PERFORMANCE

Recurrent in the foregoing discussion are the processes of *performance* and *mimesis*, as underpinning core aspects of a range of behaviours that are uniquely developed in humans: play and ritual, which form our principal focus, as well as music, dance, narrative (including drama and poetry) and social learning. These activities appear to be closely related, and perhaps interdependent, in a variety of ways (Figure 21.1).

According to Nicolopoulou (2006), children's play and narrative are forms of *socially situated symbolic action* (in Smith, Chapter 5), a category which also includes ritual practice, visual representation, improvisation and some music and dance. In fact, *socially situated symbolic action* could be considered interchangeable with *performance*. Furthermore, in his analysis Malafouris (Chapter 19) avers that play and ritual both "essentially comprise culturally assembled embodied processes of joint attention, shared action and collective intentionality". Each of these elements requires significant cognitive abilities (discussed earlier in this chapter) which are thus in common between ritual and play. This description is actually also applicable to music, dance, drama, narrative and social learning. Joint attention, shared action and collective intentionality could be argued to together constitute *performance*, and in all cases this performance is culturally assembled via rules or conventions – on a continuum of stricture – that distinguish these behaviours from 'everyday' or 'normal' life. For McConachie (2011), "performance is an intentional, emotionally expressive, event-centred phenomenon involving pattern and attention in social interaction – i.e., a type of play – that entails conceptual integration" (p. 43). To McConachie, then, performance is a type of play; in turn, he considers (after Boyd 2009) that "rituals tied to religious beliefs are the evolutionary offspring of play and performance" (p. 45), in that they rely on the presence of the capacities that already underpin play and performance (Morley, Chapter 6).

Mimesis is performance, performance is representation, representation is mimesis, and the capacities for this are learned and developed in juveniles – and refined in later life – through play. In this

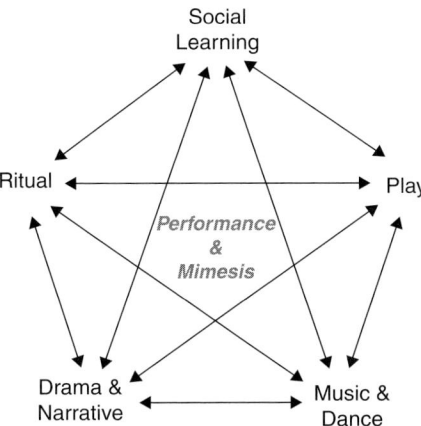

Figure 21.1 'The Pentagram of Performance'. It is proposed that the uniquely developed human behaviours of play, ritual, social learning, music and dance and narrative and drama are fundamentally interrelated in cognitive capacities that underlie them, the ways in which they function, the ends that they achieve and their mutual reliance in achieving these ends.

sense, as Osborne (Chapter 20) puts it, "experience of play crucially prepared humans not just for ritual, but for the entry to a supernatural world that ritual can effect."

In contributing to the initial proposal for this volume, and the symposium that gave rise to it, I proposed the hypothesis that ritual, play, music and dance, social learning and mimesis were all interrelated in fundamental ways, in terms of the ways in which they function, the capacities that underlie them, the ends that they achieve, and the extent to which they rely on each other in achieving their ends. We invited our contributors to explore the extent to which such proposed links are supported – or not – by evidence from cognitive evolution and historic (and prehistoric) cultural contexts. As explored in the foregoing discussion, the contributions to this volume allow us now to elaborate those connections, and to propose a more detailed illustration of their links, with the processes of mimesis and performance underpinning them all (Figure 21.1). It is hoped that this will provide a framework for the future exploration and elaboration of these relationships in human societies past and present, building upon the contributions made by the authors in this book.

REFERENCES

Alexander, R. D. 1989. Evolution of the human psyche, in *The Human Revolution*, eds. P. Mellars & C. Stringer. Edinburgh: Edinburgh University Press, 455–513.

Bekoff, M. & Allen, C. 1998. Intentional communication and social play: how and why animals negotiate and agree to play, in *Animal Play: Evolutionary, Comparative, and Ecological perspectives*, eds. M. Bekoff & J. A. Byers. Cambridge: Cambridge University Press, 97–114.

Bekoff, M. & Pierce, J. 2009. *Wild Justice: The Moral Lives of Animals*. Chicago, IL: University of Chicago Press.

Boyd, B. 2009. *On the Origin of Stories: Evolution, Cognition and Fiction*. Cambridge, MA: Belknap Press.

Burghardt G. M. 2005. *The Genesis of Animal Play: Testing the Limits*. Cambridge, MA: MIT Press.

Carruthers, P. 2002. Human creativity: its cognitive basis, its evolution, and its connections with childhood pretence. *British Journal of the Philosophy of Science* 53, 225–49.

Donald, M. 2001. *A Mind So Rare: The Evolution of Human Consciousness*. London: Norton.

Engel, S. 2005. The narrative worlds of *what is* and *what if*. *Cognitive Development* 20, 514–25.

Göncü, A. & Perone, A. 2005. Pretend play as a life-span activity. *Topoi* 24, 137–47.

Hanna, J. L. 1979. Toward a Cross-Cultural Conceptualisation of Dance and some Correlate Considerations, in *The Performing Arts: Music and Dance*, eds. A. R. Blacking & J. W. Kealinohomoku. The Hague: Mouton Publishers, 17–45.

Harris, P. L. 2000. *The Work of the Imagination*. Oxford: Blackwell.

Huizinga, J. 1955. *Homo Ludens: A Study of the Play Element in Culture*. Boston, MA: Beacon.

Inomata, T. 2006. Plazas, performers, and spectators: political theaters of the Classic Maya. *Current Anthropology* 47, 805–42.

Inomata, T. & Coben, L. S. (eds.), 2006. *Archaeology of Performance: Theaters of Power, Community, and Politics*. Lanham, MD: AltaMira Press.

Kendal, J., 2011. Cultural niche construction and human learning environments: investigating sociocultural perspectives. *Biological Theory* 6(3), 241–50.

McConachie, B. 2011. An evolutionary perspective on play, performance and ritual. *TDR: The Drama Review* 55, 33–50.

Mitchell, R. 2007. Pretense in animals: the continuing relevance of children's pretense, in *Play and Development: Evolutionary, Sociocultural and Functional Perspectives*, eds. A. Göncü & S. Gaskins. Hillsdale, NJ: Lawrence Erlbaum, 51–75.

Morley, I. 2009. Ritual and music – parallels and practice, and the Palaeolithic, in *Becoming Human: Innovation in Prehistoric Material and Spiritual Culture*, eds. C. Renfrew & I. Morley. Cambridge: Cambridge University Press, 159–75.

Morley, I. 2013. *The Prehistory of Music: Human Evolution, Archaeology, and the Origins of Musicality*. Oxford: Oxford University Press.

Morley, I. 2014. A multi-disciplinary approach to the origins of music: perspectives from anthropology, archaeology, cognition and behaviour. *Journal of Anthropological Sciences* 92, 147–77.

Nicolopoulou, A. 2006. The interplay of play and narrative in children's development: theoretical reflections and concrete examples, in *Play and Development: Evolutionary, Sociocultural and Functional Perspectives*, eds. A. Göncü & S. Gaskins. Hillsdale, NJ: Lawrence Erlbaum, 247–73.

Odling-Smee, F. J. & Laland, K. N. 2009. Cultural niche construction: evolution's cradle of language, in *The Prehistory of Language*, eds. R. Botha & C. Knight. Oxford: Oxford University Press, 99–121.

Pearson, M. & Shanks, M. 2001. *Theater/Archaeology*. London: Routledge.

Pellegrini, A. D. 2009. *The Role of Play in Human Development*. Oxford: Oxford University Press.

Rappaport R. A. 1999. *Ritual and Religion in the Making of Humanity*. Cambridge: Cambridge University Press.

Soar, K. 2010. Circular dance performances in the prehistoric Aegean, in *Ritual Dynamics and the Science of Ritual Vol.2, Body, Performance, Agency and Experience*, ed. A. Michaels. Wiesbaden, Germany: Harrassowitz, 137–56.

Sterelny, K. 2011. *The Evolved Apprentice: How Evolution Made Humans Unique*, Cambridge, MA: MIT Press.

Sutton-Smith, B. 1997. *The Ambiguity of Play*. Cambridge, MA: Harvard University Press.

Whitehouse, H. 2004. *Modes of Religiosity: A Cognitive Theory of Religious Transmission*. Walnut Creek, CA: AltaMira Press.

INDEX

aboriginals, Australian, 163, 164
abri 131, Mallaha (Eynan), 131
accidents, depiction of, 242–43, 245, 247
aceramic Neolithic settlement, 131, 133, 135, 138, 139
acrobatics, 214, 218, 225, 226, 231
adolescence, 66, 67, 68, 69, 75, 83, 84, 229
Aegean
    initiation in, 225
Aegean art
    boxing, 227
    representations of children and youths, 227
    transformative power of ritualized play, 231–33
Aegean Bronze Age art, 6, 211, 220
    Akrotiri, paintings from, 211
    initiation in, 104
    ritualized play and wild animals in, 225–31
aesthetic devices/operations, 94, 95, 324
affinitive behaviours and emotions, 88, 93
Africa, 60
    ape fossils, 77, 81, 83
    dancing with masks in, 162
    hunting in, 232
Akaike Information Criterion, 33
Akrotiri, Thera, 211, 227, 230, 232, 240, 313
    bull sports, 243
    ring impressions, 238f15.3 (a, b), 240, 241f15.5
    Xesté 3, 227, 229–31, 243
Alternate Uses Task, 48
alternation, 31
altruism, 137, 138
American Southwest
    Broken Flute Cave, 119–20, 125
    communal performance, 126
        ceramics, 122
        circle dancing, 124–26
        early, 118–19
        iconography, 121
        rock art, 122–24
    communal performance in
        architecture, 119–21
    Juniper Cove, 120
    Pueblo. See Pueblo, communal performance
    Shabik'eshchee Village, 120, 125
    Site 29SJ423, 120, 125

Analects, 174
analogies, 18, 29, 45, 50, 51, 72, 74, 88, 137, 170, 174
Anatolia, bull games and religious symbols in, 244–47
animal fighting, 177, *See also* bull sports
animal play, 72, 74
    categories, 11, 75
animal world, in China, 170
animal-based food, 187
animals, 171
    creative animals, 46–48
    cultic behaviour, 175–76
    displacement activities, 88
    domestication, 30, 42, 43, 129, 187, 188, 189, 191, 194, 196f13.3
        in China, 176
    movement, and dance, 182
    play behaviours, 10, 11, 17, 18, 32, 229, 313
    play in, 1, 25, 40, 41, 54, 228
    power and identity, 203–04
    ritualization of behaviours in, 24
    used as a medium in gift exchange, 175
anthropomorphisation, 84, 325
anthropomorphism, 174, 313
    critical, 313
apes
    brain development, 79–83
    dental development, 76–79
    life-history stages, 66–67
    play behaviours, 67–69
    pretend play in, 69–71
archaeological record, 14–15
    of assembly and congregation, 15–16
Aristotle, 170
arts, 87, 94
    Aegean. See Aegean Bronze Age art
    and ceremonies, 94
    Epgyptian. See Ancient Egypt
Asia. See also southwest Asia
    dancing with masks in, 162–63
assembly and congregation, 15–16
    evolutionary view of, 18
Athens, 243, 250, 252, 253
athletic contests, 252–53

attributes of ritual, 17
Australia
    aboriginals, 163, 164
    dancing with masks in, 163
australopithecines, 59, 77, 81, 82
    dental development, 76–77
autistic children, pretend play, 59, 60
autobiographical memory, 136
Ayia Triada rhyton, 227, 231

Basta masks, 149, 150
Bateson, Patrick, 3, 40
behavioural plasticity, 10, 45, 322
beliefs, 95, 144, 311, 312, 316–20
    and play, 327
    religious beliefs, 4, 29, 35, 75, 87, 95, 116, 138, 139, 328
    shared system of, 139, 327, 328
    supernatural beliefs, 3, 66, 74–75
    symbolic cognitive system, 94
birds, 35, 42, 47, 174, 197
blocking concept, 304, 306
board games, 14, 17, 216
bodily action/movements, 88, 90, 92, 118, 121, 124, 126, 137, 145, 218, 325, *See also* dance/dancing
bonding hormones, 93
Book of Odes, 180
boxing, 232
    in Aegean, 227
    in Ancient Egypt, 222
    in ancient Mesoamerica, 286–96
Brochtorff Circle, 202
Brochtorff-Xaghra Circle faunal, 190
Broken Flute Cave, 119–20, 125
brown bears, 46
Buġġiba temple, 194
bull fighting, 176
Bull Games of Minoan Crete
    definition of, 237
bull sports, 231, 232
    in Aegean, 226
    in Anatolia and Syria, 244–47
    in Ancient Egypt, 218–22
    as a form of initiation, 232

bull sports (*cont.*)
    and half-rosette symbol, 243–44
    as a human ritual, 247–48
    and palm symbol, 244
bull-grappling, 6, 176, 218, 226, 230, 231, 232
bull-leaping, 6, 226, 231, 232
Burghardt, Gordon, 1, 2, 23

Çatalhöyük (Çatal Hüyük), 139, 191
cats, 42, 43
Çayönü, 134
ceramic Neolithic settlement, 139
ceremonies, 10, 92, 94, 102, 117, 139, 143, 150,
        153, 191, 197, 200, 202, 204, 215, 224, 329
    and arts, 94
    'bring Chahk' rain ceremonies, 101–03
    commemorative ceremonies, 137
    and dance/dancing, 113, 145
    puja ritual, 17
    religious ceremonies, 118, 119, 139, 146,
        147, 150
    sacrificial ceremonies, 270
Chaco Canyon, 121
Chalcatzingo, 269–70
Chalchitan ballcourts, 286
Chalcolithic communities
    Choga Mish mask, 158
    dance, 146
    depictions of masked people from, 155f11.5
    Domuztepe masks, 161
    Khazineh mask, 158
    painted pottery sherds depicting masks,
        159f11.8
    Tall-I Bakun A mask, 161
    Tepe Gawra mask, 161
    Tepe Giyan mask, 159–61
chance games, 4
chariot races, 243
Chichen Itza Great Ballcourt, 297
childhood, 32, 66, 71, 75, 76, 78, 82, 84
    brain development, 80
    dental development, 79
    early, 3, 66, 67, 68, 69, 70, 71, 74, 75, 76, 77,
        80, 83, 84
    middle, 55, 59, 66, 67, 68, 69, 71, 75, 76, 77, 78,
        80, 83, 84
    pretend play. *See* children, pretend play
        development in
    supernatural imagination, 33
children
    Aegean art representations of children, 227
    development, 11
    pretend play development in, 55, 61, 68,
        69, 71, 75
        caring, 71
        cognitive capacities development, 70
        and culture, 71
        decentration, 55
        decontextualization, 55
        and imagination, 73
        imitation, 73
        imitations, 66
        infancy, 69, 70, 74
        integration, 55
        middle childhood, 67

over-imitation, 73, 84
    younger children, 69
chimpanzees, 41, 43, 47, 54, 68, 73, 79, 80
    dental development, 76–77
China, 170, 171, 182–84
    animal domestication, 176
    drumming, 180–81
    horn-butting game, 177, 297
    music and dance, 179–82
    offering of sacrifice, 175
    ritual and ritual propriety, 171–79
Choga Mish mask, 158
Christian cathedrals and churches, 137
circle dance/dancing, 118, 120, 121, 122–23, 125,
        124–26, 312
Classic Bonito period, 121
clay animal figurines, 170
clay masks, 148–53, *See also* masks
    Basta masks, 150
    Er Ram masks, 151
    Hierakonpolis masks, 151–53
    Khirber Duma masks, 150–51
    Nahal Hemar masks, 149–50
    Nevalı Çori mask, 151
    private mask collections, 151
climate and climate change, 35
clowning/clowns, 117
cocaine, 50
cognitive archaeology, 10
cognitive development, 135
cognitive evolution, 130
cognitive stage
    episodic culture, 90
    mimetic culture, 90
    mythic culture, 90
    theoretic culture, 90
Coliseum of Rome, 10
collaborative play, 327
collective identity, 139, 312, 328
collective memory, 117, 136, 137, 139, 328
collective play, 15, 312
colour symbolism, 230
comfort movements, 92
commemorative ceremonies, 137
communal buildings, 118, 119–21, 131–33,
        131f10.1, 136, 137, 139, 188
    circular structure, 120, 131, 133
communal performance, 126
    circle dance, 312
    circle dancing, 124–26
    iconography, 121
    in Pueblo, 116–17
        archaeology, 117–18
communicative abilities, 70, 72
community identity, 102, 117, 135, 136, 328
constitutive dilemma of psyche, 315
construction play, 12, 25, 135
    and pretend play, distinguished, 55
contact sports, 212, 223, 225, 231, 232
converging styles of thoughts, 48, 50
cooperative niche, 138
co-resident communities, 134, 135, 138, 139
Courts of the Minoan Palaces, 15
courtship behaviours, 13, 30, 87
creative animals, 46–48

creative play, 328, *See also* imaginative play;
        pretend play
creativity, 327, 329
    definition of, 48
    and flexibility, 48
    and fluency, 48
    and originality, 48
    playfulness and, 49–50
credibility enhancing displays (CREDs), 138
Crete, 15, *See also* Bull Games of Minoan Crete,
        See also Minoan
critical anthropomorphism, 313
Crónica mexicana, 261n2, 282, 283f17.16, 284,
        285, 292, 295, 301, 330
cross-modal matching, 326
crow family, 47
crystallised activities, 303
cultic rituals, 144, 145
    and dance, 145
    and supernaturalism, 146
cultural conservation, 138
cultural identity, 107, 136, 259
cultural innovations, 26, 134
cultural memory, 136
cultural pheromones, 145
cultural rituals, 23, 24

dance/dancing, 118, 322, 325
    archaeology, 146
    and ceremonies, 113, 145
    in China, 179–82
    Christian point of view, 146
    circle dance/dancing, 118, 120, 121, 122–23,
        125, 124–26, 312
    and cultic rituals, 145
    definition of, 144–45
    early roots, 146
    group therapy, 145
    as a means of social interaction, 145
    multi-sensory experience, 145
    as non-verbal mode of communication, 145
    performances, 17
    and rituals, 144–47
    self-expression, 145
    and trance, 146
    with masks, 162–64
Daoism, 177
decentration, 55
decontextualization, 55
decoupling. *See* metarepresentation
dental development, of chimpanzees and
        australopithecines, 76–77
developmental plasticity, 32
Dhuweila masks, 154–56
disciplined invariance, 12, 18
displacement activities, 31
    of animals, 88
Dissanayake, Ellen, 3–4, 87
diverging styles of thoughts, 48, 50
dogs, 43
dolphins, 42–43, 47, 54
Domuztepe masks, 157, 161
dragonflies, 230
drama, 117, 147, 187, 188, 191, 202, 204, 325, 330,
        331f21.1

drumming, 180–81
ducks, 230

early childhood, 3, 66, 67, 68, 69, 70, 71, 74, 75,
    76, 77, 80, 83, 84
Early Iron Age sites, 256
Egypt, Ancient
    boxing, 222
    bull grappling and bull sports, 218–22
    hunting, 222
    initiation in, 104, 212
    Middle Kingdom tombs, 216, 218, 221,
        222, 231
    New Kingdom, 218, 221, 222–25, 231
    Old Kingdom tombs, 212–16, 218, 220, 221,
        222, 231
    play, ritual and transformation in, 211–18
    ritualized play and royalty, 222–25
    stick-fighting, 222, 223–25
    transformative power of ritualized
        play, 231–33
    wrestling, 222, 223–25
'Ein el Jarba masks, 157
Ek' Balam, 294
El Manatí, 264, 266, 270, 275, 298, 300
El Perú-Waka', sacred play at, 104–06, 112–13
    ballgame at royal palace, 106–07
    royal mortuary assemblage in Burial
        39, 107–12
    signs in surface deposits, 107
El Tajín, 281, 297
elaboration, 92, 94, 324
emulation, 73
endogenous opioids, 93
endorphins, 93
ends-orientated learning, 73
Epi-Palaeolithic community, 130, 135, 138
episodic culture, 90
episodic memory, 136
Er Ram masks, 149, 151
ergot, 50
Estero Rabón, 286
ethology, 87, 88
Europe, 161, 187, 189, 191, 194
    dancing with masks in, 163
evolutionism, 10, 18
exaggeration, 30, 92, 94, 324
existential dilemma, 315
existential uncertainty, 92, See also risk
explicit memory, 90, 91
exploratory play, 89
external rewards, and play, 44
extra-ordinary, 89, 91, 92, 94
    awareness of, 91
    signals by infants, 88

fantasy and reality, distinguishing, 57
fantasy play. See pretend play
feasts, 199–202
feral horses, 46
Feynman, Richard, 49
figurines wearing masks
    Iran, 161
    Sha'ar Hagolan, 161
    Southeast Europe, 161

Fleming, Alexander, 49
foresight, 92
formalism, 10, 12, 18
Freidel, David, 4, 101
friendship, pretend play and, 57–58
funerary masks, 147–48
fur seals, 45

games, 24, 25, 231, 306–07, 323
    as learning mechanisms, 304
    blocking concept, 304
    characteristics, 323
    common traits, 305–06
    crystallised activities, 303
    definition of, 253, 302
    flow of, 306
    intention-in-action, 303
    manifestation of, 323
    mood evocation, 306
    new background, 304–05
    normalism, 317
    repetition, 305
    risk of, 304, 306
    and rituals
        compared, 302–04
    rule governance, 58, 305, 323
    symbolism, 305
Garfinkel, Yosef, 5, 143
Ge Tianshi, 180
Geim, Andre, 49
gender differences, in pretend play, 57
gene-culture co-evolution, 31
Genesis of Animal Play: Testing the Limits,
    The, 1, 11
Ggantija temple, 194, 197
Göbekli Tepe, 16, 132, 134, 136, 137, 138, 139,
    313, 328
goose, 175
gorilla, 54
Gozo, 189, 194, 197
great apes, pretend play, 54, See also apes
Great Kivas, 121
Greece, ancient, 250
    athletic games, 326
    chariot races, 243
    heroization of athletes, 260
    hoplite battles, 255
    institutional athletic contests, 252–53
    javelin, 253–54
    Panhellenic Games, 15, 254
    Phayllos, 258
    theatres and stadia, 10, 14, 15
    Trojan war, 255–56
Greek vase in Copenhagen's National
    Museum, 250–51
group activity, 92
group therapy, 145
Guerrero, 296, 297
    ritual boxing, 324

habituation, 305
Hacilar masks, 156–57
Hagar Qim, 194, 199
Hal Saflieni, 194, 197
half-rosette symbol, in bull games, 243–44

Halley, Claire, 4
Han Wudi, Emperor, 182
Hand Wrestling, 177
helmets, 61, 112f8.13, 225, 253f16.4, 255, 256,
    264, 267, 288, 289f17.20, 292, 293f17.23,
    295, 296
hero-cults, 256, 259, 263
heroization of athletes, 260
Hierakonpolis masks, 151–53, 161
Hochdorf burial, Iron Age, 191
Hohokam ballcourts, 281
Holocene, 129
hominin
    life-history, 82
hominins, 3, 84, 87, 88, 89, 91, 92, 94, 129,
    130, 134
    brain size, 80
    cognitive evolution, 90
        episodic culture, 90
        mimetic culture, 90
        mythic culture, 90
        theoretic culture, 90
    dental development, 76–79
    life-history
        palaeoanthropological evidence, 82–83
        stages in, 75–76
Homo antecessor, dental development, 78
Homo erectus, 83
    brain development, 80–82, 84
    dental development, 77–78
Homo heidelbergensis, 78, 83
Homo ludens, 2, 10, 32, 251
Homo neanderthalensis. See also Neanderthals
    brain development, 82, 84
    dental development, 78–79
Homo sapiens, 1, 59, 83
    dental development, 77, 79
    material signs, 134
    pretend play in, 63
    Upper Palaeolithic, 72
Hopi, 117, 125
hoplite battles, 253, 254, 255, 256, 260
horn-butting game, 177, 297
Huainanzi, 173, 176, 177, 182–83
Huijazoo, 288
humans
    brain development, 79–83
    dental development, 76–79
    evolution of life-history stages in
        hominins, 75–76
    hominin life-history, palaeoanthropological
        evidence, 82–83
    life-history stages, 66–67
    play behaviours, 3, 11, 17, 25, 27, 33, 67–69,
        104, 230, 313, 321, See also play
    pretend play in, 69–71
humour, and play, 50
hump-backed whales, 47–48
hunter-gatherer, 66
hunter-gatherers, 129, 130, 134, 135, 146, 148, 163
hunting, 29, 31, 48, 61, 102, 130, 145, 172f12.2,
    175, 176, 188, 191, 197, 211, 215, 216, 217,
    220, 221, 222, 225, 226, 230, 231, 232
Hyperactive Agency Detection Device
    (HADD), 75

Iliad, 256–57, 302
imaginary companions, in pretend play, 56–57, 62
imaginative play, 68, 70, *See also* creative play; pretend play
imitations, 32, 35, 41, 54, 55, 56, 58, 59, 66, 68, 69, 70, 71, 72, 73, 84, 171, 177, 203, 233, 314, 325, 326, 327, *See also* over-imitation
implicit memory, 90
infancy, 3, 66, 67, 69, 70, 71, 74, 75, 82, 83, 84, 89, 92
innovations, 329
  and creativity, distinguished, 48
  cultural, 26, 134
institutional athletic contests, 252–53
institutional facts, of ritual, 13
institutionalised rituals, 17
integration, 55
intention-in-action, 7, 302, 303
  special, 12, 302, 303, 304, 305
invertebrates, play-like behaviours, 42
Isleta, 125
itzompan skull spring, 282, 284, 297

javelin, 253–54
Jebel Ihroud *Homo sapiens*, dental development, 79
Jerf el Ahmar, 131, 132, 134
John Templeton Foundation, 1
Juniper Cove, 119, 120, 125
juvenile, 55, 59, 66, 67, 69, 71, 75, 76
juvenility, 66, 67, 68, 69, 71, 75, 76, 77, 78, 80, 83, 84

Keres Pueblos, 125
Khazineh mask, 158
Khirbet Duma masks, 149, 150–51
K'iche' Popol Vuh, 103–04
kissing, bonding ritual of, 30
Knossos, 239–41, 313
Kui, 177, 179f12.6, 180
Kyriakidis, Evangelos, 7, 302

La Venta Stela 2, 270, 271, 271f17.4
language ability, 3, 54
large-scale communities, 134, 138, 139
Las Higueras, 297
Late Postclassic Codex Dresden, 269, 275
Lefkandi, 256
Liberia, use of masks in, 148
life-history stages in hominins, 75–76
linguistic expression, in play, 11
locomotor play, 12, 16, 42, 67, 89
Luxuriant Dew of the Spring and Autumn Annals, 174

make-believe play, 8, 61, 140, 316, 319
Malafouris, Lambros, 7, 311
Malone, Caroline, 5, 187
Malta
  animal offerings, 190
  animals and animal parts symbolisim, 190–91
  early, 189
    animals in, 194–97

farming, 189
food and value of animals, 189–91
model-making as play, 204
mortuary sites, 190
play, 202–03
symbolism, 202
Maltese temples, 188, 191
  bone patterns and artworks at, 188
  bones at, 193–94
  environment and feasts, 199–202
  food and feast, 197–200
  Ggantija, 194, 197
  imaginative hybrid characters at, 197
  playing ritual, 203–04
  ritual activity, 188
  symbol and cosmology, 202–03
  Tarxien, 191–94
  temple setting, 188–89
  Zammit's excavation diaries, 188
  Zammit's excavations diaries, 191–94
manipulation of expectations, 92, 94, 324
manoplas, 264, 265, 288, 290, 291f17.22, 291f17.22, 291f17.22, 292, 293, 293f17.23, 294, 294f17.24, 295f17.25, 295f17.25, 295f17.25
Manus, 92
maquetas, 273–75, 274f17.7, 276f17.9
marbles, 47, 101
Marinatos, Nanno, 6, 237
masks, 147, 164, 266, 324
  dancing with, 164
    in Africa, 162
    in Asia, 162–63
    in Australia, 59–60
    in Europe, 60
    in North and Central America, 163
    in Oceania, 59
    in South America, 58
  depicted on painted pottery, 159f11.8
    Choga Mish mask, 158
    Domuztepe mask, 161
    Khazineh mask, 158
    Tall-i Bakun A mask, 161
    Tepe Gawra mask, 161
    Tepe Giyan mask, 159–61
  Domuztepe masks, 157
  funeray masks, 147–48
  helmet masks, 264, 292, 295, 296
  Khazineh mask, 158
  Khirbet Duma masks, 149, 150–51
  performance masks, 147
  pottery masks from Predynastic Egypt, 152f11.3
    Hierakonpolis masks, 151–53
  private collections, 151
  protective masks, 148
  in the proto-historic Near East
    depictions of, 158–61
    depictions of people wearing masks, 153–58
    figurines wearing masks, 161–62
    stone and clay masks, 148–53
  used in tribal communities, 163–64
massively multiplayer online role-playing games (MMO RPGs), 307

material culture, 118, 134, 135, 139, 183, 189, 311, 314–15, 327
Mawangdui, 177
Maya, 101, 268, 297
  ancient, 104
  ballcourts, 278, 280, 285
  ballgame, 7, 102–04, 105, 106–07, 109, 112, 113, 294
  sacred play at El Waka'. *See* El Perú -Waka', sacred play at
  S-shaped motif, 288
  way, 104
memory, 90, 92
  autobiographical memory, 136
  collective memory, 117, 136, 137, 139, 328
  cultural memory, 136
  episodic memory, 136
  explicit memory, 90, 91
  implicit memory, 90
  shared memory, 136, 328
Mencius, 173
mental time travel, 90
mescalin, 50
Mesoamerica, 10, 13, 14, 15, 313
Mesoamerica, ancient
  ballcourts, 272–78
    symbolism of water and rain in, 278–86
  ballgame, 264–65
  boxing, 265
  ritual bloodsport, 265
  ritual boxing, 286–96
Mesoamerican Ballgame, 15, *See also* Maya ballgame
Mesopotamia, 139, 158, 161, 164
metacommunication, 12
metaphors, 170
metarepresentation, 63, 69, 73, 89–91
middle childhood, 55, 59, 66
middle childhood, 67, 68, 69, 71, 75, 76, 77, 78, 80, 83, 84
mimesis, 75, 90, 92, 326, 330
Minoan, 197
  bull games
    Akrotiri, 243
    definition of, 237
    depiction of accidents, 242–43
    divine patronage and symbolism, 243–44
    groups and their function, 237–39
    place of performance, 242–43
    Tell el Dab'a Taureador panel and its Knossian derivation, 239–41
  Courts of the Minoan Palaces, 15
Mnajdra temple, 194
monkeys, 230, 233
mood
  change, in social play, 42
  and creativity, 50
  evocation, 306
Morgan, Lyvia, 6, 211
Morley, Iain, 1, 3, 8, 66, 321
mother–infant interactions, 88–89, 90
  playfulness, 89
motivation to play, 43–44, 51
Mozart, Wolfgang Amadeus, 49
multi-sensory experience, and dance, 145

music, 4, 15, 17, 93, 94, 105, 107, 113, 117, 120,
124, 126, 145, 183, 204, 230, 233, 245,
306, 322
in China, 179–82
Mycenaean graves, 191, 225, 237, 256
mythic culture, 90
myths, 102

Nahal Hemar masks, 149–50, 153, 161, 162
National Science Foundation, 34
Natufian sites, 135
Neanderthals. See also *Homo neanderthalensis*
brain development, 82
dental development, 78–79
neo-cortex ratio and social group size, 134
Neolithic communities, 5, 14, 15, 118, 129, 130,
134, 138, 139, See also Malta Maletese
temples
aceramic, 131, 133, 135, 138, 139
alligator drums, 180
dance in, 146
depiction of masked people from, 155f11.5
public buildings, 118, 137
rituals, 35, 137
stone masks, 161, See also Pre-Pottery
Neolithic B of southern Levant
Nevalı Çori masks, 137, 148, 151, 152f11.2
niche construction theory, 130, 135–36, 330
non-functional behaviours, 9, 10
normalism, 325
North and Central America, dancing with
masks in, 163
Novoselov, Konstantin, 49

Oaxaca, 281, 288, 289, 290
ballcourt, 283f17.15, 284, 287
boxing, 288
manoplas, 291f17.22
object play, 16, 17, 68
Oceania, dancing with masks in, 163
Odyssey, 256
Ojochi, 272
Olmec ballgame, 265, See also Maya ballgame;
Mesoamerican Ballgame
Olmec Rain God, 267, 267f17.1, 267f17.1,
267f17.1, 268, 268f17.2, 268f17.2, 269,
270, 286, 287f17.19, 287f17.19, 287f17.19,
288, 292
Olympia, 252, 256, 260
Olympic stadia, 10
Olympics, ancient, 252
ontogenetic ritualization, 31–33
opium, 50
orbitofrontal cortex (OFC), 93
ordinary, awareness of, 91
organic selection model, 31, 32
Osborne, Robin, 7–8, 316
over-imitation, 73, 83, 84, 326
oxytocin, 93

Paidia, 257
painting, 227, 229
palanganas, 276, 280
palm symbol, and bull sports, 244
Panhellenic Games, 15, 254

parallel play, 25
Paris, a Pre-Pottery Neolithic B mask in, 151
parrot family, 47
participation, ritual as, 91–93
Patolli, 111
peacock, 88
Pengzu, 173
pentagram of performance, 330–31
perceived uncertainty, 92
performance masks, 147
performances, 10, 12, 13, 18, 317, 325, 328
depiction of, 14
pentagram of, 330–31
places for, 14
ritualised, 12
performative power, of ritualized play, 329–30
periaqueductal gray (PAG), 93
Pesseia, 257
pharaonic kingdom of Egypt, 139, See also
Ancient Egypt
Phayllos, 258
pheromones, 144
cultural, 145
Phoenician masks, 148
phylogenies, 33–35, 73
Picasso, Pablo, 49
Piedras Negras ballcourt, 294
pilgrimage and pilgrims, 16
pitz, 294
places, for performances, 14–15
Plato, 253
play, 14, 16–17, 23, 40, 211, 316–17
abnormality, 317
actions, 89, 318
and adulthood, 43
in animals, 1, 25, 40, 41, 54, 228
and belief systems, 327
categories of, 11
and community, 318
as a component of ritual, 326
consequentiality, 318, 323
costs of, 45
criteria for, 25
and cultual attainments of humans, 32
definition of, 11–12, 25–26, 40–44, 311–12
depiction of, 15
deprivation, 46
distinguished, 41
domains of, 11
evolution of, 26–28
features of, 40–41
and fun, 40
function of, 44–46
informality of, 10
literature on, 24–27
manifestation of, 41, 323
and mood state, 322–23
motivation to, 43–44, 51
and novelty, 41
presymbolic play, 55
repetition, 318
ritualization of, 6, 31, 211, 229, 323, 329
and rituals, 319
compared, 316
distinguishing between, 322–23

sexual differences, 45
signals, 8, 26, 53, 54, 317, 318, 324
and social cognition, 326–27
special ontological status of, 323–25
and stress management, 26
and survival, 46
unpleasant aspects, 42
and well-being, 41, 43
and work or serious behaviour, 40
play fighting, 6, 11, 46, 53, 54, 228, 317, 324
play-acting, 204
playful play, 41, 42, 49, 51
playfulness, 3, 23, 41, 42, 48, 49, 50, 51, 53, 188,
314, 322
creativity and, 49–50
mother–infant interactions, 89
play-mothering, 68
plazas of pre-Columbian Peru, 15
Pleistocene, 129
Pleistocene hominins. *See* hominins
Popol Vuh, 281, 282, 297
pottery masks from Predynastic Egypt, 152f11.3
Prayer Rock District of northeastern
Arizona, 120
Pre-Pottery Neolithic B of southern Levant,
149f11.1
Basta masks, 150
Er Ram masks, 151
Khirber Duma masks, 150–51
mask in Paris, 151
masks in private collections, 151
Nahal Hemar masks, 149–50
Nevali Çori mask, 151
presymbolic play, 55
pretence, 25
definition of, 54
features of, 54
pretend play, 11, 16, 33, 41, 53, 63–64, 68, 84, 89,
313–14, 318, 324, 327, 330
in apes, 69–71
and belief system, 327
in children with autism, 60
in children with autism, 59
cognitive capabilities, 74
cognitive foundations, 325–26
and creativity, 61–62, 71–74
cross-cultural universality of, 60
design features of, 60–61
development in children, 55
and early literacy, 62
emotional benefits of, 61
evolution of, 59–60
fantasy and reality, 57
and friendship, 57–58
games with rules, 58
gender differences in, 57
in humans, 69–71
imaginary companions, 56–57, 62
and imagination, 61–62
and imitation, 58
and innovation, 71–74
as a lifespan activity, 59
models of benefits of, 63
and narratives, 62
in non-human species, 53–55

pretend play (*cont.*)
  and ritual, 74–75
  sociodramatic play, 56
  solitary and social, 55–56
  and supernatural belief, 74–75
  and theory of mind, 62–63
  and Theory of Mind, 70
  as a universal human feature, 58
pretend warfare, 214
primates, 3, 24, 26, 29, 31, 34, 34f3.3, 35, 36, 53,
    67, 75, 76, 77, 78, 82, 84, 88, 89, 90, 93,
    134, 179
processual archaeology, 9, 10
prosocial religions, 137–38
prosociality, 139
proto-historic Near East, 162
psilocybin, 50
psycho-active drugs and rituals, 50–51
public dreams, myths as, 102
Puebloan communal performance
    archaeology, 117–18
    contemporary, 116–17
puja ritual, 17
Pythian Games, 258

Qermez Dere, 139

rain ceremonies
  'bring Chahk', 101–03
rats, 45
red-figure drinking-cup, 254, 254f16.5,
    259f16.8 16.9
redirection, 31
religions, 28, 30, 95
  and belief. *See* religious beliefs
  as mechanism of coordination and
      control, 144
  definition of, 143, 144
  evolution of, 137
  invention of, 91–95
  prosocial religions, 137–38
  secret societies, 143
religious beliefs, 4, 29, 35, 75, 87, 95, 116, 138,
    139, 144, 328
  and religious behaviour, distinguished, 94
religious ceremonies, 139, 146, 147, 150
  community unity, 118
religious rituals, 14, 25, 31, 75, 93, 137, 138, 147,
    237, 324, *See also* rituals
Renfrew, Colin, 9
repetition, 92, 94, 324
repetition, in games and rituals, 305
reptiles, 197
rhyton, 225, 227, 231
Rich, Michelle, 4, 101
rites of passage, 13, 202, 211, 212, 232
ritual play, 12, 107, 188, 329–30
ritual propriety, 171–79, 322
ritualization, 30, 87–89, 232
  of behaviours, 4, 24, 173
  definition of, 29
  ethological, 24
  ontogenetic, 31–33
  operations of, 89, 92
  of play, 6, 31, 211, 229, 323, 329

process of, 31, 88
social play and, 30
transformative power of, 231–33
'Ritualization of Behaviour in Animals and
    Man', 31
ritualized play
  performative and transformative power
      of, 329–30
  transformative power of, 231–33
rituals, 17–18, 306–07, 317
  and abnormal stereotypies and compulsive
      behaviour, 29
  abnormality, 317–18
  actions, 312, 318
  in animal world, 29
  atrributes of, 12
  blocking concept, 304
  cognitive foundations, 325–26
  as collections of arts, 94
  common traits, 305–06
  components of, 13, 17
  consequentiality, 318, 323
  criteria for, 29
  crystallised activities, 303
  cultural rituals, 23, 24
  and dance, 144–47
  definition of, 12–13, 27–30, 92, 302
  depiction of, 15
  evolution of, 30–31
  evolutionary view of, 18
  and existential uncertainty, 92
  flow of, 306
  formalism of, 10
  and games, compared, 302–04
  in animal world, 30–31
  intention-in-action, 303
  as learning mechanisms, 304
  literature on, 25
  military training forms, 177
  mood evocation, 306
  and mood state, 322–23
  new background, 304–05
  normalism, 317
  as participation, 91–93
  performative actions of, 13
  periodicity, 13
  and play, 319
    compared, 316
    distinguishing between, 322–23
  and pretend play, 74–75
  psycho-active drugs and, 50–51
  and religions, 137, 138, 143
  repetition, 305, 318, 328
  risk of, 304, 306
  rule governance, 305
  shared system of, 328
  signals, 317, 318, 324
  special ontological status of, 323–25
  as sub-category of play, 326
  as symbolic cognitive belief system, 94
  and symbolism, 303, 305
rock art, in American southwest, 122–24
role play, 58, 324, 327
rook, 47
Roots of Spirituality, The, 1

rule governance, 12, 18
  in rituals and games, 58, 305, 323

sacral symbolism, 12, 17
sacrificial offerings, 190
Santa Rosa, 278, 280
schematic play, 54
sea mammals, 47
secular ritual, 17
sedentism, 130
self-awareness, 3
self-expression, and dance, 145
self-recognition, 54, 70, 72
sense of place and origins, 174
serpents, 35–36
'Seville Statement on Violence', 252
sexual selection, 28, 61, 77
Sha'ar Hagolan mask, 161
Shabik'eshchee Village, 120, 125
shared memory, 136, 328
shortage of food, and play, 43
signals/signalling, 325
  by infants, 88
  play signals, 8, 26, 53, 54, 317, 318
  play signalsi287, 324
  ritual signals, 317, 318, 324
  social signals, 43
simplification, 92, 94, 324
simultaneous ambivalent behaviour, 31
Site 29SJ423, 120, 125
Smith, Peter, 3, 53
snakes, 35–36, 197
social disorder, 176
social heredity, 32
social identities, shared system of, 327
social organisation, and play behaviours, 68
social play, 11, 16, 26, 34f3.3, 42, 43, 67, 68, 328
  cooperative creativity, 49
  and mood change, 42
  neurobiology and functions of, 25
  and ritualization, 30
social pretend play, 55–56
social signals, 43
social structure, 328
social-intellectual play, 61
socially situated symbolic action, 330
sociodramatic play, 56, 58, 61, 62, 328
  and early literacy, 62
  and narrative skills, 62
solemnisation, 14
solitary pretend play, 55–56
South Africa, 164
South America, dancing with masks in, 163
Southeast European masks, 161
southwest Asia, 129, 130, 137
space, 319
Spanish court-games, 242
Sparta, 252
special intention-in-action, 12, 302, 303,
    304, 305
spectators, 13, 14, 15, 240, 244, 296, 323
spiders, 26, 42, 316
spinning, 214
spirituality, 32, 84, 94, 177, 197, 322
Spivey, Nigel, 6, 250

sport
    definition of, 253
    as war 'minus the shooting', 251–52
Spring and Autumn of Mr Lü, 180
S-shaped cloud motifs, 268, 269
stadia and theatres of Ancient Greece and
    Rome, 14, 15
staged combats with wild animals, 176
Star Carr, Mesolithic, 148, 191
Stela A at Tres Zapotes, 271
Sterckx, Roel, 5, 170
stereotypy, 92, 94, 324
stick-fighting, 214, 216, 219, 222, 223–25, 232
stone masks, 148–53, *See also* masks
    Basta masks, 150
    Er Ram masks, 151
    Hierakonpolis masks, 151–53
    Khirber Duma masks, 150–51
    Nahal Hemar masks, 149–50
    Nevalı Çori mask, 151
    private masks collections, 151
Stonehenge, 15–16
supernaturalism, 33, 91, 139, 146
superstition, 93
Surplus Resource Theory (SRT), 26–27, 34,
    34f3.3, 35
symbolic cognitive belief system, 94
symbolic intelligence, 70, 72
symbolism, 135, 200, 202, 305
    in Bull Games of Minoan Crete, 243–44
    colour symbolism, 230
    in games, 305
    material system of representation, 134
    multivalent, 222
    of water and rain in ancient Mesoamerica
        ballcourts, 278–86
    and rituals, 303
    sacral symbolism, 12, 17
Syria, bull games and religious symbols in, 244–47
systematic analysis, 9, 188
    of play, 10, 24
    of ritual and cult, 10

tactical deception, 70, 72
Tall-i Bakun A mask, 157, 161

Tall-i Regi mask, 157
Taos, 125
Tarascos Indians (Mexico), 163
Tarxien, Malta, prehistoric temples of. *See*
    Maltese temples
Tas-Silġ, 190
Taube, Karl, 6–7, 264
team games, 15, 17
Tell 'Abr 3, 132
Tell el Dab'a, 226, 227, 230, 231,
    238, 313
    bull sports, 239–41
Tell el Dab'a Taureador panel,
    239–41, 244
    Knossian derivative, 240–41
Telleriano-Remensis, 281
Temple of Seti I at Abydos, 221
Templo Mayor, 265
Teopantecuanitlan, 297
Tepe Djowi masks, 153–54
Tepe Gawra mask, 161
Tepe Giyan mask, 159–61
theatrical performances, 17
theoretic culture, 90
Theory of Mind, 3, 24, 33, 53, 54, 59,
    75, 327
    and pretend play, 62–63, 70
thoughts and action, distinction
    between, 29
tlachco, 281
tool use, by birds and animals, 47
toys, 314
traditionalism, 12, 18
trance, and dance, 146
transformative power, of ritualized play,
    231–33, 329–30
tribal warfare, 29
Trobrianders, 92
Trois Frères cave in Ariège, 191
Trojan war, 255–56
T-shaped monoliths, 133, 137, 138
Tuleilat el-Ghassul, 161
    masks from, 158–61
typical intensity, 89
tzompantli, 282

Upper Palaeolithic period, 10, 60, 72, 129, 130,
    134, 135
    use of masks in, 148

violence, 176
visual-kinetic matching, 70, 72

Wadi Feynan, 131
Wadi Hammeh 27, 131
Waka'. *See* El Perú -Waka'
warfare, 225, 231
    hoplite battles, 255
    pretend warfare, 214
    and sport, historical relationship
        between, 252
    tribal warfare, 29
    Trojan war, 255–56
Watkins, Trevor, 4–5, 129
Watson, Jim, 49
WF16 (Wadi Feynan 16), 131
what if play, 327
what is play, 327
Whitehouse, Harvey, 137, 328
working memory, 90
worldview, 117
wrestling, 177, 214, 222, 223–25, 232
Wupatki, 281

Xaghra, 197
Xesté 3, Akrotiri, 227, 229–31, 243
Xibalba, 112
Xochicalco, 275, 276
Xolchun ballcourts, 286

Yaxuna, 101, 102
Yucatán, 102

Zammit, Sir Themistocles, 188,
    191–94, 197
Zapotec, 287, 288, 289, 292, 293
Zebbug period community, 203
Zhuji Weng, 173
zoomorphism, 149, 153, 170, 176, 182, 194,
    202, 293
Zuni, 117, 125

Alcohol-induced mood disorder
Alcohol-induced anxiety disorder
Alcohol-induced sexual dysfunction
Alcohol-induced sleep disorder
Alcohol-related disorder NOS

Amphetamine (or Amphetamine-Like)–Related Disorders

Amphetamine Use Disorders
Amphetamine dependence
Amphetamine abuse

Amphetamine-Induced Disorders
Amphetamine intoxication
Amphetamine withdrawal
Amphetamine intoxication delirium
Amphetamine-induced psychotic disorder
 With delusions
 With hallucinations
Amphetamine-induced mood disorder
Amphetamine-induced anxiety disorder
Amphetamine-induced sexual dysfunction
Amphetamine-induced sleep disorder
Amphetamine-related disorder NOS

Caffeine-Related Disorders

Caffeine-Induced Disorders
Caffeine intoxication
Caffeine-induced anxiety disorder
Caffeine-induced sleep disorder
Caffeine-related disorder NOS

Cannabis-Related Disorders

Cannabis Use Disorders
Cannabis dependence
Cannabis abuse

Cannabis-Induced Disorders
Cannabis intoxication
Cannabis intoxication delirium
Cannabis-induced psychotic disorder
 With delusions
 With hallucinations
Cannabis-induced anxiety disorder
Cannabis-related disorder NOS

Cocaine-Related Disorders

Cocaine Use Disorders
Cocaine dependence
Cocaine abuse

Cocaine-Induced Disorders
Cocaine intoxication
Cocaine withdrawal
Cocaine intoxication delirium
Cocaine-induced psychotic disorder
 With delusions
 With hallucinations
Cocaine-induced mood disorder

Cocaine-induced anxiety disorder
Cocaine-induced sexual dysfunction
Cocaine-induced sleep disorder
Cocaine-related disorder NOS

Hallucinogen-Related Disorders

Hallucinogen Use Disorders
Hallucinogen dependence
Hallucinogen abuse

Hallucinogen-Induced Disorders
Hallucinogen intoxication
Hallucinogen persisting perception disorder (flashbacks)
Hallucinogen intoxication delirium
Hallucinogen-induced psychotic disorder
 With delusions
 With hallucinations
Hallucinogen-induced mood disorder
Hallucinogen-induced anxiety disorder
Hallucinogen-related disorder NOS

Inhalant-Related Disorders

Inhalant Use Disorders
Inhalant dependence
Inhalant abuse

Inhalant-Induced Disorders
Inhalant intoxication
Inhalant intoxication delirium
Inhalant-induced persisting dementia
Inhalant-induced psychotic disorder
 With delusions
 With hallucinations
Inhalant-induced mood disorder
Inhalant-induced anxiety disorder
Inhalant-related disorder NOS

Nicotine-Related Disorders

Nicotine Use Disorder
Nicotine dependence

Nicotine-Induced Disorder
Nicotine withdrawal
Nicotine-related disorder NOS

Opioid-Related Disorders

Opioid Use Disorders
Opiod dependence
Opiod abuse

Opioid-Induced Disorders
Opioid intoxication
Opioid withdrawal
Opioid intoxication delirium
Opioid-induced psychotic disorder
 With delusions
 With hallucinations
Opioid-induced mood disorder
Opioid-induced sexual dysfunction

Opioid-induced sleep disorder
Opioid-related disorder NOS

Phencyclidine (or Phencyclidine-Like)–Related Disorders

Phencyclidine Use Disorders
Phencyclidine dependence
Phencyclidine abuse

Phencyclidine-Induced Disorders
Phencyclidine intoxication
Phencyclidine intoxication delirium
Phencyclidine-induced psychotic disorder
 With delusions
 With hallucinations
Phencyclidine-induced mood disorder
Phencyclidine-induced anxiety disorder
Phencyclidine-related disorder NOS

Sedative-, Hypnotic-, or Anxiolytic-Related Disorders

Sedative, Hypnotic, or Anxiolytic Use Disorders
Sedative, hypnotic, or anxiolytic dependence
Sedative, hypnotic, or anxiolytic abuse

Sedative-, Hypnotic-, or Anxiolytic-Induced Disorders
Sedative, hypnotic, or anxiolytic intoxication
Sedative, hypnotic, or anxiolytic withdrawal
Sedative, hypnotic, or anxiolytic intoxication delirium
Sedative, hypnotic, or anxiolytic withdrawal delirium
Sedative-, hypnotic-, or anxiolytic-induced persisting dementia
Sedative-, hypnotic-, or anxiolytic-induced persisting amnestic disorder
Sedative-, hypnotic-, or anxiolytic-induced psychotic disorder
 With delusions
 With hallucinations
Sedative-, hypnotic-, or anxiolytic-induced mood disorder
Sedative-, hypnotic-, or anxiolytic-induced anxiety disorder
Sedative-, hypnotic-, or anxiolytic-induced sexual dysfunction
Sedative-, hypnotic-, or anxiolytic-induced sleep disorder
Sedative-, hypnotic-, or anxiolytic-related disorder NOS

(continued on inside back cover)